To Bunni

With teary wishes

Fondly

Mimi + Eloi

Beyond the Melting Pot

Jewish Life & Learning at the Turn of the Century

DR. ALVIN I. SCHIFF

PUBLISHING
NEW YORK ♦ JERUSALEM ♦ LONDON

Beyond the Melting Pot:
Jewish Life and Learning at the Turn of the Century
Published by Devora Publishing Company
Copyright © 2009 Alvin I. Schiff

The printing of this volume was made possible through the generosity of the Center for the Advancement of Jewish Education, Miami, Florida; Elaine and Al Wolf; Linda and Murray Laulicht Foundation; Esther and Armand Lasky; Pamela and George Rohr; Marilyn and Herbert Smilowitz; The Belz Foundation; and 'an admirer of Professor Alvin I. Schiff.'

COVER DESIGN: David Yaphe
TYPESETTING & BOOK DESIGN: Koren Publishing Services
EDITOR: Chani Hadad
EDITORIAL & PRODUCTION MANAGER: Daniella Barak

All rights reserved. No part of this book may be used or reproduced or transmitted in any form or by any means, electronic or mechanical, including photocopying, recording, or by any information storage and retrieval system, without written permission from the publisher.

Hard Cover ISBN: 978-1-934440-46-9

E-MAIL: sales@devorapublishing.com
WEB SITE: www.devorapublishing.com

Printed in the United States of America

Dedicated to a fourfold journey in Jewish life.

Jewish education is a vital generational concept and life-giving practice insuring the continuity of the Jewish people. As such, it is my great pleasure and privilege to make a fourfold dedication representing the ultimate, unbroken chain of Jewish life.

To my dear wife, Mimi, my best friend and partner with whom I shared all of the lectures in this volume prior to their delivery and each of my writings before publication. Her caring, insightful comments were always helpful, valuable and appreciated.

To the memory of our beloved parents – Jacob and Miriam Mirele Schiff and Harry and Helene Fleschner – who were a constant source of inspiration and encouragement in all my educational and academic endeavors.

To our devoted children – Debbie and Michael Block and Linda and Arthur Poleyeff for their dedicated Jewish Zionist communal involvement and their educational leadership. Debbie is a paradigmatic early-childhood educator; a creative teacher of pre-school children. Linda is a model social worker/educational administrator who named my eleventh book, The Mystique of Hebrew.

To our adored grandchildren – Danielle, David, Marc, Yoni, Tzvika and Daniel – all of whom excel as graduates of or students in intensive Hebraic Day Schools and Yeshivot.

Alvin I. Schiff

CONTENTS

Foreword ix
Acknowledgments xii
Introduction xiv

PART I: INSIGHTS ON JEWISH LIFE

Chapter 1: Challenges for Jewish Living 2
Chapter 2: Values of Jewish Tradition 16
Chapter 3: Transmitting the Jewish Heritage 28
Chapter 4: Eretz Yisrael: Dream and Reality 34
Chapter 5: Visit to Auschwitz 47
Chapter 6: Thoughts About Hebrew Words 51

PART II: THE JEWISH COMMUNITY AND JEWISH EDUCATION

Chapter 1: Changing Priorities in Education 58
Chapter 2: Marketing, Evaluating & Funding Jewish Education . 67
Chapter 3: Toward the Year 2000 – Condition of Jewish Life: Implications for Jewish Education 89
Chapter 4: The Central Agency for Jewish Education 101

Chapter 5: Jewish Continuity Through Whom?............105

Chapter 6: Jewish Life & Jewish Education in
Contemporary Society: Challenge and Response 109

Chapter 7: Creating the Jewish Future:
Insuring Effective Jewish Education.....................121

Chapter 8: A New Blueprint for Community: A Jewish
Renaissance Perspective Assuring Jewish Continuity......137

Chapter 9: Thoughts About Holocaust Research,
Documentation and Jewish Education 146

Chapter 10: Educational Issues in Jewish Identity............156

PART III: ON JEWISH ALL DAY EDUCATION

Chapter 1: The REITS Centennial: An Educational Milestone .176

Chapter 2: The Nonpublic School: Real and Ideal............180

Chapter 3: What Research Says About the Jewish
Day School 184

Chapter 4: What We Know About the Jewish Day School
(in 1990)...201

Chapter 5: The Jewish Day School (in 1987)
Looks to the Next Half-Century 215

Chapter 6: On the Need for Moral Education in the
Jewish Day School 222

Chapter 7: The Jewishness Quotient of Jewish Day School
Graduates: The Effect of Jewish Education on
Adult Behavior....................................231

Chapter 8: The Case of the Jewish Day School (in 1997)
in Light of the Debate on School Choice................243

Chapter 9: Jewish Day School Success:
Jewish Communal Challenge (in 1997) 254

Chapter 10: Post Yeshiva: Jewish Day High School
Programs..259

PART IV: ON JEWISH SUPPLEMENTARY SCHOOLING AND JEWISH FAMILY EDUCATION

Chapter 1: The Synagogue & Jewish Education in
    Historical Perspective 280
Chapter 2: On the Status of the Jewish
    Supplementary School – 1982 287
Chapter 3: Looking Toward the 21st Century: Who Needs
    Hebrew Teachers in Our Supplementary Schools? – 1983 ..293
Chapter 4: The Jewish Supplementary School:
    A System in Need of Change 303
Chapter 5: The Jewish Family and the Jewish School 312
Chapter 6: The Jewish Family in Socio-Educational
    Perspective 318
Chapter 7: Trends and Challenges in Jewish
    Family Education......................................326
Chapter 8: On Initiating a Process for Jewish Family
    Educator Training 338
Chapter 9: Spotlight on Adult Jewish Education
    in the United States 342
Chapter 10: Adult Jewish Education in the
    Modern Orthodox Synagogue......................... 349

PART V: INSTRUCTION & LEADERSHIP

Chapter 1: The *MELAMED* at Mid-Century:
    An Appreciation of the Role of the Hebrew Teacher...... 360
Chapter 2: On the Making of the Jewish
    Teaching Profession...................................373
Chapter 3: The Jewish School Teacher Today and Tomorrow . 380
Chapter 4: Teachers and Principals: The Crucial Link
    to The Bureaus 386
Chapter 5: Imperatives of School Effectiveness 405

Chapter 6: Leadership in Judaic Sources:
A Comparative View 414

Chapter 7: Shared Identity of Jewish Communal Workers:
The Jewish Dimension 426

PART VI: ON ISRAEL, ZIONISM AND JEWISH EDUCATION

Chapter 1: One Hundred Years of Zionism 434

Chapter 2: Zionism and Jewish Statehood:
Challenge to the American Jewish Community 446

Chapter 3: Building Zionist Commitment
Through Education 452

Chapter 4: Towards a Mission Statement
on Jewish Zionist Education 461

Chapter 5: The Tomorrows of Jewish Education 466

PART VII: THE HEBREW LANGUAGE AND THE JEWISH COMMUNITY

Chapter 1: Linguistics and Longevity:
The Interdependence of Language, Heritage
and Nationalism 476

Chapter 2: Hebrew in New York 486

Chapter 3: Twenty-first Century Renaissance
of the Hebrew Language 510

Chapter 4: Ivrit in the Day Schools:
An Endangered Species? 517

Chapter 5: How Critical is Hebrew for Jewish
Continuity and the Effectiveness of Jewish Education? 525

Chapter 6: The Jewish Book News Interview
on the Mystique of Hebrew 533

PART VIII: JEWISH EDUCATION PERSONA, OF BLESSED MEMORY

Samuel Belkin: 1976 543
Zvi Herbert Berger: 2000 544
Yosef Burg: 1999 546
Gershon Churgin: 1978 547
Azriel Eisenberg: 1979 548
Abraham Gannes: 2003 550
Jacob I. Hartstein: 1991 551
Sidney B. Hoenig: 1980 553
Leo Jung: 1988 554
Asher (Arthur) Kahn: 2002 555
Abraham Katsh: 2002 557
Joseph Hyman Lookstein: 1979 558
Israel Miller: 2002 560
S. Maurice Plotnick: 1992 561
Leonard Rosenfeld: 2002 563
Akiva Schiff: 1998 565
Joseph B. Soloveitchik: 1993 567
Nathen F. Winter: 2004 578

References 582
Sources 598
About the Author 603

FOREWORD

How does one begin to write a foreword to a volume which is authored by a foremost Jewish communal leader, distinguished educator and prolific writer who has had a profound impact and transformative influence on the quality and vitality of Jewish education and Jewish communal life?

Dr. Avraham Yitzhak Schiff (my dear teacher, mentor, colleague and friend), presents a brilliant array of meaningful essays, insights, reflections and perspectives regarding the challenges and opportunities currently facing Jewish education against a rich backdrop of historical background and retrospective analyses.

Dr. Schiff's thought-provoking ideas, concepts and practical observations in this volume – from the illuminating analysis of effective Jewish schooling to the critical importance of Jewish educational personnel; and, from the critical analysis of Hebrew language use to the centrality of the State of Israel in Jewish life and Jewish education – will have a profound affect upon the manner in which its readers will conceptualize issues and challenges impacting upon the quality and quantity of Jewish education.

The thematic flow of creative ideas, bold and meaningful

assumptions and practical suggestions found in this seminal work, are a true reflection of Dr. Schiff's vision, passion, and leadership concerning effective Jewish education, educational excellence, the building of community, and the large variety of actualities which comprise the complex mosaic of our Jewish community and Jewish educational enterprise.

As a practitioner, theoretician and researcher, profoundly committed to educational excellence, Dr. Schiff uses the pages of this book to challenge us to think creatively and boldly about the nature and scope of Jewish education, the complexities of alternative learning environments, the personnel condition (read crisis) in Jewish education, and the realities, factors, and core values which influence policy-makers, academicians, educational practitioners, and supporters within the sphere of Jewish life and learning. The point about the influence of leaders involved in Jewish education is clearly demonstrated in the chapter on "Jewish Education Persona" – a section devoted exclusively to Jewish personalities who contributed significantly to the enhancement of Jewish life and learning.

In order to fully appreciate Dr. Schiff's brilliant perspectives and insights into Jewish life and learning, the reader is invited to participate in a fascinating journey through the compilation of well written essays and thoughts relating to the true "values of Jewish tradition"; thoughts about the ability and significance of Hebrew language and its usage; the transmission of Jewish heritage through historical events; and an in-depth understanding and conceptualization of the state of day schools, congregational religious schools and Jewish educational personnel – through the lenses of a veteran expert and scholar.

In the closing paragraph of Dr. Schiff's Editorial "Some Thoughts on the Content of Jewish Education," in the Spring 1986 issue of the *Jewish Education Journal*, which commented on the *Journal*'s "Index" 1975–86, Dr. Schiff writes:

"No summary or analysis of the pages of *Jewish Education* can do them justice. The above comments (in the Editorial about the *Journal* "Index"), merely scratch the surface. Reading the articles is the only way to develop a full understanding of their contribution to the literature of Jewish education."

Similarly, I feel strongly that a careful review and understanding of this volume, is the only way to truly appreciate the profoundly significant contribution this author has made to the field of Jewish education and, will continue to make for many years to come. And for this we owe Avraham Yitzhak Schiff our utmost appreciation and sincere gratitude! Todah Rabbah.

> Dr. Chaim Y. Botwinick, President/CEO,
> Center for the Advancement of Jewish
> Education, Miami, Florida
> Past President, Association of Directors of
> Central Agencies of Jewish Education

ACKNOWLEDGMENTS

Writing, editing and publishing a volume like this is possible only with the support of many people. First, I want to acknowledge the role of my teachers, students, and colleagues, and the many Jewish communal educators, teachers, principals, lay leaders and Jewish communal professionals with whom I have worked in the vineyards of Jewish education during the past sixty years for helping to shape my educational philosophy and for being a valuable resource of information and experience.

Several people have been involved in the production of this work: Sarah Dadusc, my secretary when I served as Executive Vice President of the Board of Jewish Education of Greater New York, for her expert typing; Barbara Kessel, BJE Administrator, who guided the arrangements for publication and oversaw the last minute administrative details prior to printing; Chaim Lauer, former BJE executive for suggesting that I compile a book of selected lectures and writings during the 1980s and 1990s; Dr. Chaim Botwinick, president/CEO of the Center for the Advancement of Jewish Education, Miami, Florida for his constant encouragement and careful review of the original manuscript; and Carolyn Hessel, Director of the Jewish Book Council for her helpfulness during the final stages of publication; and, of course, Mimi for her steadfast counsel and support.

My appreciation is also expressed to the Center for the Advancement of Jewish Education, Miami, Florida; Elaine and Al Wolf; The Linda and Murray Laulicht Foundation; Esther and Armand Lasky; Pamela and George Rohr; Marilyn and Herbert Smilowitz; to the Belz Foundation; and to the anonymous admirer of "ISH" (Professor Alvin I. Schiff), for their generous support of this volume.

May the satisfaction of seeing this compilation in print be a well deserved reward for their input and assistance.

A.I.S.

INTRODUCTION

Trends in education and changes in the goals, format, and methodology of schooling take place in varying time frames. This is true in public education and in the various types of non-public schooling.

The American Jewish community has experienced a variety of changing patterns during its relatively young history. While there were always forces outside their control that influenced Jewish life and Jewish education, American Jews, from the time of their initial settlement on this continent in the mid-seventeenth the century, developed those institutions of Jewish education that *they* perceived as appropriate and adequate to meet their religious, cultural and social needs. Basically, the system of Jewish education is a major dimension of the self-actualization of the Jewish community. In each generation, and in each locale, the pattern of Jewish schooling represented the Jewish and general educational aspirations of the Jewish citizens of this great nation.

Prior to the nineteenth century, Jewish education in the Sephardic settlements in America was sporadic and irregular. Like general education in the eighteenth century, Jewish education was a private enterprise first dispensed by private tutors and then centered in the colonial synagogues where the teacher gave instruction in Jewish studies comprising Hebrew reading, liturgy, selected biblical passages and ritual, and in general studies – essentially English reading, writing and arithmetic. In the mid 1800s, Jews increasingly sent their children to non-Jewish schools and Jewish education became supplemental.

The mid 1800s saw the controversial establishment of Jewish day schools in seven cities. These institutions, however, were very short-lived, existing no longer than twenty years. By 1881, Jews came to regard the tax-supported, nonsectarian universal public school as the absolutely essential preparatory institution for American citizenship. As the day school declined, the Sabbath school and Sunday school, established in Philadelphia in 1838, gained national prominence.

With the massive immigration of East European Jews at the end of the nineteenth century and the beginning of the twentieth century, the Jewish community developed an erratic system of the one-room *heder*, the private tutor, and the *siddur* peddler who went from house to house peddling his wares: *Kiddush, Kaddish*, and *Bar Mitzvah* lessons. The early 1900s saw the establishment of the communal *Talmud Torah*: a five day a week, ten to fifteen hour, supplementary school which became the dominant school of the 1920s and 1930s, thereafter fading rapidly as the synagogue schools multiplied.

The growth of the weekday congregational schools coincided with the rapid spread of the synagogue and temple between 1930 and 1960. The new American synagogue phenomenon accompanied the move of Jews to new Jewish areas of residence in the larger urban communities and to suburbia. After peaking in the early 1960s, the congregation school experienced dramatic decline. But, in the 1990s, serious efforts were made by national and local synagogue and communal agencies to revitalize this form of Jewish education which has been the major vehicle for Jewish schooling from 1930 through the beginning of the twenty-first century.

On another level, the first four decades of the twentieth century saw the gradual emergence of the modern American yeshiva. This was followed by the era of great expansion of Jewish all day education under Orthodox auspices between 1940 and 1970. Thereafter, the Orthodox Jewish day school continued its remarkable growth through the twentieth century and beyond. The first Jewish day schools under Conservative and communal auspices appeared on the American Jewish scene between 1957 and 1970 and continued to grow through the 1980s. In addition, the Reform movement started to encourage the establishment of Reform Jewish day schools in the mid 1980s.

Local Jewish Federations, until the mid 1970s showed little interest in Jewish all day education. However, during the last two decades of the twentieth century, they demonstrated their appreciation of the value of this type of schooling by beginning to support, or by increasing their support, of this fast growing form of Jewish education.

Jewish Family Education and Adult Jewish Education began to occupy a place on the Congregational and Jewish communal agenda in the 1970s and has continued to address the needs of Jewish adults and families, in varying degrees, through the beginning of the twenty-first century.

The role of Zionism and Israel in the Jewish school curriculum was reinforced substantially in both the supplementary school and day school after the Six Day War and continues to be a modest part of Jewish school programs until the present time.

On the other hand, Hebrew language instruction did not fare well during the last four decades of the twentieth century. Immigrant *maskilim* (enlightened Jews) in the early 1900s brought with them the zeal, knowledge and ability to energize small pockets of Hebrew speakers in this country through the establishment of Hebrew cultural schools and institutions patterned after the *heder metukan* (modernized Hebrew school) in Europe in which Hebrew was taught as a living language. They also infused Hebrew language instruction into the Jewish studies programs of the Jewish day school and supplementary school. Their efforts were reinforced between 1925 and 1950 by graduates of Hebrew Teachers Colleges in America trained to be Hebrew language teachers. The role of Hebrew as a living language began to decline in 1960 due to the lack of Hebrew language fluency of teachers hired after 1960. The role of Hebrew, therefore, continued to ebb during the last four decades of the twentieth century.

During the last two decades of the twentieth century a variety of research studies were made about Jewish education. I had the privilege of conducting two major studies – one on the Jewish Supplementary School and one on the Jewish Day School. The results of the Jewish Supplementary School research highlighted an educational system in need of change. It concluded with a set of four recommendations designed to respond to the four overall challenges that derive from the findings: 1) changing the focus and structure of synagogue schooling; 2) increasing the exposure and quality of supplementary education via the integration of formal and informal learning strategies; 3) training professionals for effective performance; and 4) developing appropriate career opportunities for educational personnel.

The Jewish Day School study focused on the Jewishness Quotient of Day School graduates. Among other things, the findings underscored the importance of the extensiveness of Jewish Day School education. The longer Jewish youth study in an all day framework, the greater the probability they will be Jewishly observant adults, intermarry less, and provide their children with intensive Jewish education. Overall, the results demonstrate that Jewish Day School graduates are much superior to adults who studied in Jewish Supplementary School in every area of Jewish commitment and practice.

Since 1950, I have lectured and written extensively about various aspects of Jewish education including the Jewish Day School, the Jewish Supplementary School, Jewish Family Education, Adult Jewish Education, Informal Jewish Education, the role of Israel and the Hebrew language in Jewish schooling, and the relationship between Jewish communal leadership and Jewish education. This volume presents my views and thoughts about these features of the Jewish education enterprise at the end of the twentieth century as reflected in my lectures and writings.

Since I lectured and wrote about similar topics at different times in various settings, cognate salient information and historical data about Jewish Schools and the Jewish Community was provided at each of these lectures. *When compiled into a book, this information would become repetitive if retained in each lecture. The reader, therefore, will find that some of the same information is referred to several times in this volume. I removed many of these repetitions – which communicated my messages to the various audiences at the time they were given – for the benefit of the readers of this compilation.*

The decades at the turn of the century were both a time of consolidation and the development of new initiatives in Jewish education. This period set the tone for Jewish educational endeavor in the twenty-first century in the various areas of Jewish schooling.

The section on *Insights on Jewish Life and Jewish Education* is essentially a collection of brief statements and *divrei Torah* about significant issues of Jewish life and education presented in a variety of Jewish settings during the last decade of the twentieth century.

If this work helps the reader to better understand the trends, changes and challenges of Jewish life and education during the turn of the twentieth century, I will be more than amply rewarded.

I cannot end this brief introduction without expressing deep gratitude to all my colleagues, teachers, and students who played an important role in shaping my professional-academic career. And, to all the educators, rabbis, communal professionals, and lay leaders with whom I share common purpose and aspirations regarding Jewish life and Jewish education, my heart-felt thankfulness. *Rav todot*!

Alvin I. Schiff
July 2007

PART I

INSIGHTS ON JEWISH LIFE

CHAPTER 1

CHALLENGES FOR JEWISH LIVING

TIKUN OLAM

As we read the first *sidrah* of the Torah, we celebrate the creation of the world. Indeed, the physical world is wondrous and awesome, with breathtaking nature, unbelievable potential for development, and extraordinary, incredible opportunity for humankind. Yet, when we look at the world today, we observe a universe filled with greed, destruction, oppression and terrorism. And we ask ourselves: "Couldn't God have created a better world? Couldn't He have perfected creation?" After all, we are informed in the 27th verse of the first chapter of Genesis, *vayivra elokim et ha-adam b'tzalmo*, "God created man in His own image." Shouldn't the image of God be more perfect? Shouldn't God's ultimate creation have been created with perfection?

Our sages thought of this question as well. We are told that the Talmudic sage, Rabbi Yohanan asked, "Why was man created in the image of God?" In response to his own question, he said: "The story of God's creation of man can be likened to a king who ruled over a country. The king decided to build a new city, and he began building it. One day he called together all the inhabitants of the city and in their presence he appointed one of his officers to rule over them. And he said to his officer, 'Until now, I have been dealing with all the needs of the city, with each detail and every facet of city life. From now on, I'm giving all this responsibility to you.'" Said Rabbi Yohanan, "God created man in His own image and gave him the responsibility of making it a better place in which to live." To be sure, God took the first steps in creating a good world. But He didn't complete creation. He left it up to man to perfect the world. Indeed, when we recite *kiddush* each Friday evening, we recognize this fact as we quote from Genesis Chapter 2: "On the seventh day God ceased from all His work which He created, to make…" The verb, *la'asot* – "to make" – seems extraneous here. According to the Ibn Ezra, the word, *la'asot* means that God gave man the power, the ability – *la'asot* – to do, to make, to improve upon His creation, after God ceased creating. Targum Yonatan (Aramaic version of the scriptures) translates *la'asot* as *v'atid mehehvad*, indicating that God rested from His future activity leaving to humankind to complete His initial work. In a similar vein, the Midrash observes that the Torah specifically notes, "God rested from all His work," implying that there is other work yet to be done, but not by Him.

Pursuant to God's incomplete completion of creation, He gave man free will either to follow up and improve upon His creations – to make the world a better place in which to live – or to destroy it by sinful acts. According to Rabbi Nahman of Breslav, there is a dynamic interdependence between individual idealization and the perfection of the world. Without the proper behavior of its individual inhabitants, the world would self-destruct despite episodic accomplishments of man.

This, then, is the challenge to our generation. It is the challenge to the synagogue, to the Jewish school, to our families, to the Jewish community at large, and the challenge to Israel – to work as hard as we can to strive to achieve *tikun olam* – to try to improve the imperfect world that was created by God. We cannot slacken in our efforts to achieve perfection. The *mitzvah* is in the trying. May we have the individual and collective will and strength to bring about *tikun olam*. After all, that is why man was created.

UNITY IN DIVERSITY

According to Rashi, the illustrious eleventh century biblical and Talmudic commentator, Moses convened the Israelites on the day of his death to initiate them into their second covenant with God – a covenant with the Israelites in the desert and with all future generations of Jews. The opening of Moses' discourse has special relevance to contemporary Jewry and Judaism. Said Moses to the Israelites: "You are standing this day, all of you, before the Lord your God: your heads, your tribes, your elders and your officers, all the men of Israel; your little ones (children), your wives, and your stranger that is in the midst of your camp, from the hewer of your wood to the drawer of your water – that you may enter into the covenant of the Lord your God..." (Deuteronomy 29:9–11).

What distinguishes the introduction to Moses' last discourse at the end of forty years of wandering in the desert, prior to the Israelites' entry into the Holy Land, is its emphasis on *Klal Yisrael*, on Jewish peoplehood. Moses was careful to be all-inclusive. He took pains to mention all the Israelites, regardless of status, age, gender or role in the society of wanderers. He did not single out any group of Israelites for special consideration. Moses spoke in the same vein to the leaders and the ordinary folk, to the rich and the poor, to the old and the young, to the men and to the women. They were all equally important in the eyes of God and they all were to enjoy the same rights of covenant and responsibilities.

It is this sense of equality and togetherness that qualified the Israelites to receive the Torah as they stood at the foot of Mount Sinai after they miraculously crossed the Sea of Reeds. When the Israelites reached *Sinai*, the Bible notes, "Israel encamped there at the mountain" (Exodus 19:2). The word "encamped" is written in the singular, indicating that all the children of Israel were united "like one person with one heart." Prior to that moment, the Israelite encampments were characterized by "dissension, quarreling and separate murmurings." As they approached the Sinai experience, the Israelites became one united people worthy of receiving the Torah.

But, lo and behold, they almost forfeited their right to

the Torah. While waiting for Moses to return with the Ten Commandments from the mountaintop where he lingered for forty days and nights, their patience gave out and, desiring spiritual leadership and guidance, they fashioned the Golden Calf – an act that angered the Lord greatly.

Said the Almighty to Moses: "Go down at once, for your people (i.e., nation), whom you brought up out of Egypt has acted corruptly (has self-destructed)" (Exodus 37:7). Actually, God was not angered greatly by the fact that the Israelites made a Golden Calf. What angered Him were the very selfish, contentious attitudes of the tribes. When they saw the Golden Calf, the Israelites exclaimed "These (note the plural pronoun) are your gods, O Israel, that brought you out of the land of Egypt" (Exodus 32:4). According to the sages of the Jerusalem Talmud, the Israelites made thirteen calves; each tribe made its own calf, and together they made one "umbrella" calf for use in times of crisis (*Sanhedrin* 10–5:2). What angered God most and would disqualify the Israelites from receiving the Torah was their disunity coupled with their ability to act in unison, which they would do only in extreme emergency. (The early twentieth century *Torah Temimah* commentary on the Bible notes bitingly that the Israelites were disunited and contentious even when engaging in false worship). That is why God said to Moses, "your people – your nation – has self destructed." Upon seeing the Golden Calf, Moses broke the first set of Ten Commandments. It was not until the tenth of *Tishrei* (*Yom Kippur*), two months later, after the Golden Calf was destroyed, the perpetrators punished, and the Israelites mended their ways that the second set of Tablets was given to them.

The Golden Calf incident was not the first time since they left Egypt that the Israelites almost failed to meet an important challenge because of their disunity. To be sure, they almost didn't make it across the Sea of Reeds due to their infighting and their refusal to act as "one people." As they were approaching the Sea of Reeds, the Israelites saw the Egyptians in hot pursuit (Exodus 14:10). According to the sages of the Jerusalem Talmud, they started quarreling feverishly among themselves. One group of Israelites said, "Let us throw ourselves into the Sea of Reeds." Another group argued, "Let's give up and return to Egypt." A third group exclaimed, "Let's do battle with the Egyptians." And, a fourth group pleaded, "Let's pray and call out to God" (*Ta'anit* 2:5). Because of their infighting they were stymied, frozen in one place. When Moses complained to God about their intransigence and wrangling He said to Moses, "Why do you cry to me? Tell the Israelites to go forward" (Exodus 14:15). Luckily, they did.

Actually, God was saying to Moses, "Tell them to stop their infighting and get on with the business of the Exodus. They have a long future in the Land of Israel about which they should concern themselves. They should follow your lead, Moses, since you have succeeded in uniting them thus far in putting them on the road to freedom." This 3000 year-old refrain – "Stop infighting and get on with the business of Jewish life" – sounds so familiar, so modern. The Almighty is saying the very same thing to the Jewish people as we enter the twenty-first century, "Get your act together. Stop your internecine battling. Get on with the business of achieving the larger purposes of Jewish life – Jewish continuity and enhanced Jewish living as a Jewish people for whom Israel plays a central role."

The *sidrah Nitzavim* is usually read on the Sabbath preceding *Rosh Hashanah*. Interestingly, a major theme of the *Amidah* prayer refers to unity among the peoples of the world and, within that context, to the unity of the Jewish world. "And they all will make one bond to do Thy will with a full heart" (High Holiday *Mahzor*). To be sure, the meaning of the verb used here is not, as generally translated, "They will *make* one bond," but rather, "They will *be made into* one bond," signifying that the peoples of the world, including the Jews, require an outer force to forge their unity.

This is, in essence, the message of the introduction to Moses' discourse. On *Rosh Hashanah* we pray for the needed stimulus to unite us. We do not want to eradicate all the differences between ourselves, tolerant people – *am ehad*.

A major problem, in this regard, in contemporary Jewish life, is the matter of right and left – the political right and left in Israel and the contentious relationship between the religious right and left. The divisiveness, ill will, intolerance, and hatred, which accompany these schisms is more than the Jewish community can bear tolerably. These are not new problems. Time and space are witness to the unfortunate divides in Jewish life. Lack of harmony among Jews has plagued Jewish communities everywhere from time immemorial.

Obadiah Ben Jacob Sforno, sixteenth century Italian physician, Judaic scholar and biblical commentator, poignantly reacted to the Jewish communal divisiveness of his time, characterized by separate, antagonistic native Italian, immigrant Sephardic and German Jewish houses of worship, schools and burial grounds, and dissention regarding the interpretation of Judaic law and religious observance. In his commentary on the Pentateuch, Sforno goes beyond literal exegesis in order to inculcate a love for mankind, in general, and between fellow Jews, in particular. His explanation regarding the *Menorah* seems especially appropriate to our times. Noting the verse in the Bible which describes the seven branches of the candelabrum – the central shaft and the three lamps on either side – Sforno stresses that the language construction of the verse (*Numbers* 8:2) indicates that the *Menorah* will be fully lit only if the candles on the left and right face the center and thus kindle the central lamp. Similarly, he stresses that Jews cannot be a light unto themselves or a light unto the nations unless those on the left, who are concerned essentially with the here and now (material things) – and those on the right – involved in spiritual matters – bend toward the center in a cooperative mode.

What was true for the fifteenth and sixteenth century Jewish communities in Italy is true for the American Jewish community and for world Jewry at the end of the twentieth century. While the more religiously observant among us might hope that all Jews become more traditional in their Jewish behavior in order to guarantee Jewish continuity, they must not, dare not, try to read out any Jews from their covenantal rights. On the other hand, non-observant, liberal and secular Jews must respect the right of traditional Jews to their beliefs even though they disagree with their orthodox views. We are now standing *all of us*, like our ancestors of old, before the Lord. Hopefully we will be able to demonstrate unity in our diversity. Sounds utopian? Why not? What's heaven for, if not to represent our reach?

BALANCING THE TWO SIDES OF THE LUHOT

The uniqueness of the festival of *Shavuot* derives, among others, from the opportunity and challenge it provides to Jews to reflect upon the essence of Judaism in relation to individual and communal behavior. During this past year, unfortunately, there has been a plethora of problems and difficulties to consider from the perspective of Torah, about events in Jewish life, which involved both types of behavior.

The obvious and outstanding question that comes to mind is: What can the Jewish community and individual Jews learn from a *Torah weltanschauung* about the assassination of an Israeli prime minister by a fellow Jew? How can the idea of *Matan Torah* guide the Jewish behavior of both *klal* (community) and *p'rat* (individual) in the future?

Classically, Judaism's precepts are divided into two categories – ritualistic or particularistic (*mitzvot bain adam lamakom*) and humanistic or universal (*mitzvot bain adam lehavero*). Contemporary Jewish history demonstrates a clear imbalance between these two modes of observance by many Jews. Particularly disturbing is the benign neglect by many observant Jews of the universalistic domain of Jewish tradition.

In his eulogy for Yitzhak Rabin, Rabbi Aharon Lichtenstein, *Rosh Yeshivat Har Etzion*, bemoaned the *hilul HaShem* (the profanation of God's name) and asked:

What is wrong with our values? We try to educate people to strive for holiness, to love *Eretz Yisrael, Am Yisrael, and Torat Yisrael.* Shall we then stop adhering to and teaching these values? Shall we abandon the *azarah*? [*Azarah*, the Temple courtyard, here refers to the religious, ritualistic aspects of Jewish tradition.] God forbid! Not the *azarah*, not *ezrat nashim* (the women's gallery), not the *heikhal* (the Temple), surely not the Holy of Holies, nor the *har habayit* (the Temple Mount), not one rung of the ten rungs of holiness in *Eretz Yisrael*! But if we indeed strive for completeness, if we want to adhere to all these values, then we must at all times keep in mind the whole picture, the balance and interplay between these values. Have we done enough to ensure that our approach to each aspect of our sacred values is balanced? Perhaps, even if we have indeed taught the evil of bloodshed – we have exaggerated, as the terrible *gemara* suggests, the value of ritual purity? [This *gemara*, Yoma 239b, describes the cold-blooded, selfish murder of one *kohen* by another priest. The *gemara* relates that the father of the victim, himself a *kohen*, demanded the removal of the sacrificial knife used by the murderer before his son was completely dead in order to prevent its ritual defilement. 'The purity of the knife was more important to him than the murder.'] The *gemara* understands that there is an educational imbalance here and asks: Did they overvalue ritual purity or undervalue the sanctity of life? The conclusion is that it was human life that they failed sufficiently to value, and not that they exaggerated the value of ritual purity. Such acts, as described in the *gemara*, are the height of *hilul HaShem* because 'God is not complete nor is His Name complete if there is bloodshed in Israel.'

It is ironic, as *HaRav Yosef Blau, mashgiah ruhani* of Yeshiva University, has pointed out, that the article of faith on the coming of the Messiah authored by Maimonides and accepted by all Orthodox Jews, inadvertently contributed to the modern *hilul HaShem*. After the Six Day War, the formulation "the beginning of the flowering of our redemption" in the Prayer for the Welfare of the State of Israel was "no longer seen as the start of a long process of unclear duration." For those Jews imbued with Messianic fervor, for whom the time of the coming of the Messiah was rapidly approaching, nothing, including the perceived behavior and actions of a prime minister can stand in the way of his arrival. Rabbi Blau concludes that "active messianism has always proven disastrous to the Jewish people, and thwarted messianism is equally dangerous as it counters the commandment, "Thou shalt not murder."

Zealotry is not tolerated by Jewish tradition. A possible

exception is the murder of *Zimri* and *Kozbi* by *Pinhas haKohen* based upon the principle, "he who has intercourse with an Aramite, zealots will attack him." Fearful that the whole community would be caught up in the plague of harlotry, *Pinhas* killed *Zimri* and his Midianite harlot, Kozbi, in order to stave off Divine wrath. Biblically, this act meets with Divine approval (*Bamidbar* 25:11). However, the *Talmud Yerushalmi* censures *Pinhas* for opposing the will of the sages and claims that he would have been excommunicated were it not for Divine intervention (*Sanhedrin* 9:9, 27b). According to the *Talmud Bavli*, had *Pinhas* sought authorization for his deed, it would have been denied. The only reason for exonerating *Pinhas* is his having caught *Zimri* in the act. Had the result been reversed with *Zimri* slaying *Pinhas*, *Zimri* would have been exculpated on the grounds of self-defense (*Sanhedrin* 82a).

In our day, in order to insure against zealotry (and false messianism), Rabbi Yehudah Amital, *Rosh Yesivat Har Etzion*, stresses the need to foster the ability to discriminate between valid and invalid interpretations of Jewish law. Ibn Ezra's comment on *Matan Torah* is particularly relevant to this point. "The Torah was not given to ministerial angels," to entities without free will. It was given to rational human beings. Therefore, *Ibn Ezra* says, "the *internuncio* – the *shaliah* (the emissary) – between man and God is reason."

The very concept of *Matan Torah* suggests that we use our reasoning powers to develop the balance between both sides of the *luhot* (the Tablets of the Decalogue), between the ritualistic and the humanistic. In this effort, too many Orthodox Jews fall short as we strive to become even more "observant." To be sure, if one analyzes the *humrot* – the restrictive measures – which sectors of the Orthodox community increasingly impose upon themselves, it will be noted that they are exclusively in the realm of the ritualistic and rarely, if ever, concern the universalistic dimension of Judaism. Moreover, consider the absurdity, the ludicrousness of the view of the dean of a yeshiva in *Nablus* who recently stated that the Torah would probably permit the seizing of an innocent, non-Jew passing by for a transplant to save the life of a Jew.

Regarding the last five commandments – the universal *mitzvot* – Rabbi Samson Raphael Hirsch reminds us about the sanctity of life of all members of human society:

> Every one of your fellow men…must be considered equally under His care in every aspect of their destinies, and the eye of God will be upon any action you take against your fellow man. It is by the will of God that each of your fellow men has been placed where he is beside you. It is through God that each man becomes a human being, and, like yourself, endowed with human rights hallowed by God…Therefore, you must not murder him; you must not destroy his marriage; you must not deprive him of his freedom; you must not encroach upon his personal happiness and honor by giving false testimony against him. Indeed, you must not even allow yourself to covet anything that is part of your neighbor's household, and this includes anything he calls his own during his life on earth. (commentary on *Shemot* 20:13)

According to the *Zohar*, when the Torah was given to *Bnai Yisrael*, they were like a mother and her children together in perfect harmony, emphasizing that at the time of *Matan Torah*, their observance of humanistic *mitzvot* was total, complete. Indeed, this attitude and behavior qualified them for the receiving of the Torah. Unfortunately, this mood dissipated when *Moshe* did not come down from Mount Sinai when they expected him to do so. And they had to wait for the second set of *luhot* on the day that corresponds to *Yom Kippur* on our calendar.

The covenantal relationship between God and the Jewish people, initiated with God's promise to Abraham and consummated at Mount Sinai, obligates all Jews to adhere equally to both sides of the *luhot*. The decalogue is formulated in the second person singular, yet the response to the commandments is stated in the first person plural: "*We* shall obey; *we* shall listen" (*Shemot* 24:7). Here the implication is that each individual assumed the obligation not only for himself even as it addresses each Jew individually about his responsibility to observe each of the commandments. The response by the people of Israel was for the members of the Jewish community as well. Hence, "All Jews are responsible for one another" (*Shavuot* 39a). Thus, as an obligation-oriented community composed of obligation-oriented individuals, Jews are responsible to act ethically and responsibly to each other. This is, indeed, the raison d'être of the Jewish people as a community. Any lesser behavior tarnishes our image in the eyes of God and destroys our covenantal relationship with Him.

As an obligation-oriented society, the Rabin assassination has taught us the importance of the counsel of the wisest of men: "The tongue has power over death and life" (*Mishlei* 18:21) and the utter significance of Avtalyon's admonition: "Sages, be cautious with your words, lest you bring exile upon your people" (*Pirkei Avot* 1:11). We learned that rhetoric that demonizes leads to actions that dehumanize. Rabin's death teaches us that one of the greatest dangers facing the Jewish people – throughout our history – has been not our enemies but ourselves. Teaching about the value of human life, the worthwhileness of every human being is clearly a matter of *imitatio dei* (imitating God). A major source of this precept is the Almighty's declaration at the time the Israelites were crossing the Red Sea and the angels wanted to sing a song of victory and praise: "My creatures (referring to the Egyptians) are drowning in the sea and you are singing?" (*Megillah* 10a). God is pained even by the death of a *rasha* (a wicked person).

Our challenge is to teach the practice of *ahavat hinam* – baseless love – as advocated by the saintly, chief rabbi of Israel, Avraham Yitzhak Kook. Just as the second Temple was destroyed because of *sin'at hinam* – baseless hatred – he stressed, so will the third Temple be built because of *ahavat hinam*.

At the end of its mystical elaboration of the meaning of *Matan Torah*, the *Zohar* (94a) notes: "Strength signifies the Torah as it is written, "The Lord will give strength to His people; He will bless His people with peace (*Tehillim* 19:11). In the *zechut* (merit) of our strong, diligent observance of the *mitzvot* of both sides of the *luhot*, may peace come speedily in our times.

JEWISH LEADERSHIP THEN AND NOW

The *sidrah Shoftim*, in a real sense, is the *Parshah* of Jewish leadership. In various ways, it mentions each type of leader in Biblical times: *shofet* (judge), *shotair* (law enforcement official), *kohen* (priest), *levi* (levite), *melekh* (king), *zaken* (elder) and *navi* (prophet). Each leader had a special role to play. Each had his prescribed duties and functions. Each had limitations of authority and power.

The *shoftim* (judges), aided by the *shotrim* (law enforcement officers), had the responsibility to insure that justice was duly administered and maintained in all private and communal affairs in *Eretz Yisrael* in order that the Jewish nation would secure its future in its own land. It was the obligation of the *shoftim* and *shotrim* to ascertain that both the ends and means of law enforcement *zedek zedek,* are just (Rabbi Bunim of *P'sis-hah*). Moreover, the *shotrim* had the essential role in times of war to guarantee that only those unfit or unable to serve in the army were exempt from such service.

The *kohanim* (priests) and *l'vee'im* (levites) were to provide religious guidance to the populace and instruct all the citizens how to conduct their lives according to the precepts of the Torah. This instruction had both a religious goal and an educational purpose (*Maimonides*). The *kohanim*, *l'vee'im* and *shoftim* constituted a supreme court which adjudicated cases that local courts were unable to resolve. (See *Devarim* 17:8–13.) This arrangement was in effect for some time. King Yehoshafat, for example, was known to have appointed *kohanim, l'vee'im* and *shoftim* to such a court (*Divrei HaYamim* II, 9:18). This biblical court was the forerunner of the Sanhedrin whose presiding officer was most often the *Kohen Gadol* (the High Priest).

The *zekanaim*, the elders or the wise people with experience, knowledge (*zaken* – "he who acquires wisdom"), and personal prestige played a special role in the community. In the case of our *Parshah*, the *zekainim* were instrumental in helping clear a community of guilt regarding serious crimes like homicide if, indeed, the community was blameless.

Finally, there was the *navi* (prophet), chosen from among the people. His background would be known to them; yet, he would serve as an instrument of God, communicating God's message to his brethren (commentary, Rabbi Samson Raphael Hirsch).

Here we have, in one *sidrah* reference, the political, judicial, law enforcement, religious, spiritual, and educational leadership of *Bnai Yisrael*. While the positions of the *Kohain* and *Levi* were inherited, the king, prophet, judge and law enforcement official all had to be appointed "from the midst of their brethren," indicating that their appointment must be made from qualified people who adequately fulfilled the criteria for specific aspects of leadership. Regarding the *Kohain*, there were eight levels of *Kehunah* (priesthood) with qualifications and specific functions for each level. The source of the authority for each type of leader and the guidelines for his function was the Torah (*Hirsch*). The fact that there was one source, "according to the Law which they shall teach you" (*Devarim* 17:11) from which the power and regulations of each position derived was, in itself, a force for unity. All the leaders, no matter their disparate roles, served *Bnei Yisrael*, in harmony, as a team (*Da'at Sofrim*) to insure the dignity of each human being in the nation. In this regard, Hirsch notes, that "after the establishment of all the instruments of the state – the judiciary, the monarchy, the priesthood and the prophets – the very first object of the functions of these institutions was a set of regulations that guaranteed the security of human life in a Jewish state."

How pertinent is the discussion in our *sidrah* to the current situation in Israel! In the first instance, we deduce from our *sidrah* that leadership is multi-level and multi-faceted. While is it not possible for Israel to become a theocracy (nor is it desirable), the State of Israel could take a leaf from the text of the *parshah* to guide its response to the numerous internal, political and religious problems it faces. The dissension among the religious Jews of Israel is probably more pronounced now than ever before in our history.

The infighting among the religious parties derives largely from petty, selfish, inflexible leadership. One of the vexatious problems that must be addressed is the flagrant opposition of the Haredi community to service in the Israeli Defense Force despite the fact that it enjoys the protection of the very service it defies.

The dissonance between the various political segments of the population, and even among the members of each party (particularly within the opposition to the present government), also stems from a lack of qualified, committed, and unified leadership. And, as the peace process progresses, the problems of disunity continue to fester and grow. A major contributing factor to the political discordance and religious factionalism in Israel is the absence of a single Judaic source from which the leaders derive their commitment and inspiration. Without such a unified reference and authority, there is an obvious lack of commonality of purpose and function on all fronts – political, religious, legislative, judicial and educational.

"Jerusalem has no leader among all the sons she bore," notes *Isaiah* in our *Haftarah* (*Isaiah* 51:18). According to the prophet, it is up to the people to correct this condition. "Awaken, awaken" (51:17 and 52:1), he calls out to the people of *Zion*. To be sure, according to prophetic Judaism, there are two parts to redemption: God's desire and the readiness of the Jewish nation. Toward this end, the *sidrah* is instructive: "Be wholehearted," (*Devarim* 18:13) it says to the Jews of Israel and the Diaspora, "Make sure (as the *Sforno* explains) that your leaders are endowed with the spirit of the prophets and the commitment of the priests. Your future is at stake. You must act forthrightly. It is only you who can initiate the necessary changes to guarantee the security of human life in the Jewish State. If you will do your part, the Almighty will do His." Redemption, after all, is a partnership.

CHAPTER 2

VALUES OF JEWISH TRADITION

THE HEROINE OF MATAN TORAH

Megillat Ruth is a charming epic idyll of simple village life against the background of stormy conflict and lawlessness portrayed in the Book of Judges. Indeed, this is the reason the Book of Ruth begins with the statement, "And it came to pass in the days when the judges judged, that there was a famine in the land…" (*Ruth 1:1*). According to *hazal* (and stressed by Ibn Ezra), it was the turmoil and waywardness of the Israelites – "a generation that judged its judges" (*Baba Batra 15:2*) – that brought about the famine.

The *Midrash* notes that the famine was caused by the judges themselves "who were wicked and did not judge honestly" (*Tanhumah 8:1*). The famine lasted until the time of Boaz when the land returned to abundant produce and plenty – "God remembered His people and gave them bread" (*Ruth 1:7*). And so, when Naomi and Ruth, Naomi's daughter-in-law, returned to Bethlehem from Moab after the deaths of Elimelech, Mahlon, and Khilion (the husband and sons of Naomi), they came "at the beginning of the barley harvest" (*Ruth 1:22*). This setting is one of the reasons *Megillat Ruth* is read on the holiday of *Shavuot* since it takes place during the harvest period and was the time that *Bikkurim* (first fruits) were brought to the *Bet HaMikdash* (*Sefer Hamanhig*).

About *Megillat Ruth* we are informed: "Said Rabbi Ze'era: This *Megillah* does not refer to matters of purity or impurity, nor to things that are prohibited or permitted. So why was it written? To teach you how great is the reward of those who perform acts of kindness" (*Midrash Rabbah Ruth* 2:14). According to *hazal*, this was the reason the Book of Ruth was canonized. Among Ruth's rewards was unusual longevity. She lived long enough, says the *Midrash*, to observe King Solomon on his throne judging the case of the two harlots (1 Kings 3:16). Rewarding acts of kindness is in good biblical tradition. Ruth's great grandson, King David, dwelt often on this idea in the Book of Psalms. *Hazal* emphasized: "The essence of the Torah, its beginning and its end, is *Gemilut Hassadim* – acts of kindness" (*Sotah* 14a). And *Megillat Ruth* sets the standard for the way people should relate to each other. The heroes of the *Megillah* are *gomlei hassadim* – performers of deeds of kindness. Ruth and Orpah, Naomi's daughters-in-law, acted kindly towards their dead spouses and to Naomi, their mother-in-law. Ruth, we are informed, was better to Naomi than "seven sons." Said Naomi to them, "May God deal kindly with you as you have dealt with the dead and with me." And Ruth dealt kindly with Bo'az, the wealthy leader of the Israelites. In recognition of her kindness, Bo'az emoted: "May you be blessed by God since you have shown more kindness in the end than in the beginning" (*Ruth* 3:1). Bo'az also recognized how Ruth dealt kindly with Naomi: "I have been made aware fully of all that you have done for your mother-in-law after the death of your husband" (*Ruth* 2:11). Subsequently, Bo'az rewarded Ruth for her kindness. In another vein, Naomi recognized God's *hesed* to her after learning that Ruth gleaned in the field of Bo'az (*Ruth* 2:20).

The ultimate *hesed* mentioned in *Megillat Ruth* is the act of redemption – the restoring of the name of the deceased via *yibbum*, the marriage of the deceased's wife to the nearest relative. This is especially significant in the *Megillah* because the marriage of Bo'az to Ruth was beyond the letter of the strict law. According to *halakhah*, Bo'az was not required to marry Ruth. To begin with, she was not born Jewish. Moreover, Bo'az was not the brother of

Mahlon, Ruth's deceased husband. Therefore, the law of *yibbum* did not apply to him. To be sure, the Book of Ruth is very special because the observance of the *mitzvah* of *yibbum* seems to be a natural aspect of the epic story, where, in actuality, there is no *halakhic* requirement for it (Yosef Zvi Karlebach, *Turei Yeshurun* 21).

There are other opinions regarding the writing of *Megillat Ruth* and subsequently, its reading on *Shavuot*. One view holds that the primary reason for the writing of the *Megillah* is "to make known King David's genealogy, that it is like pure, refined silver" (*Zohar Hadash*). Ibn Ezra also attributes the writing of the Book of Ruth to the need for establishing the lineage of King David.

Another opinion has it that Samuel wrote the *Megillah* to demonstrate David's Moabite ancestry – to indicate that it was a Heavenly decision, in order to show that human change – from the lowest rung of society, i.e., being a Moabite, to the highest level of life, is possible (*Binyan Ariel* 248). According to this theory, reading Ruth on *Shavuot* is entirely appropriate since *Matan Torah* makes it possible for all Jews to reach the loftiest heights of *kedushah* (holiness). King David, we are told, died on *Shavuot* (*Haggigah* 82, *Jerusalem Talmud*). Therefore, it is obvious that we should read the story of Ruth on this holiday as a tribute to his memory (*B'chor Shor*). R' Levi Berdichev suggests that we read the Book of Ruth on *Shavuot* – the festival of the giving of the Torah – because the reign of King David was based on the Torah since it is written: "By Me, kings will rule" (*Proverbs 8:15*). *Matan Torah*, therefore, validates David's kingship (*Kedushat Levi*).

Another Judaic source, however, questions whether making known David's ancestry is sufficient reason to have written the Book of Ruth (and subsequently to read it on *Shavuot*). If this were the case, reasons this view, *Megillat Ruth* would have begun with Chapter 2, "And Naomi had a kinsman of her husband's, a man of wealth of the family of Elimelekh, and his name was Bo'az." However, it opens with the sentence, "And it came to pass in the days of Judges" to "underscore Ruth's character and righteousness and the fact that she converted to be closer to the *shekhinah*"

(*Zohar Hadash*). Ruth's conversion, notes this view, is akin to *kabbalat ha Torah* (*the receiving of the Torah*) by *Bnei Yisrael*, hence, the appropriateness of reading this *Megillah* during *z'man Matan toratainu*, "the time of the giving of our Torah."

In this regard, eighteenth century Rabbi Avraham Kalfon of Tripoli notes that the *gematria* (numerical equivalent) of the letters of Ruth's name – 606 – indicates that this was the number of *mitzvot* that Ruth took upon herself in addition to the seven *mitzvot* of *bnai noah* (the *mitzvot* required of gentiles) that she fulfilled as a non-Jew (*Hayye Avraham*). Similarly, this view posits, the Israelites received 606 *mitzvot* at Mount Sinai in addition to the seven *mitzvot* of *bnai Noah* (*Teshuot Hen*).

Another theory has it that the Book of Ruth underscores the principle of "Not study, but practice, is the main thing" (*Ethics of the Fathers 1:17*). At Mount Sinai, upon receiving the Torah, the children of Israel realized the overriding importance of this principle. Therefore, they emoted, "We will do and we will listen." They preceded do with listen (*Sfat Emet*).

One of the earliest sources for the origin of reading the Book of Ruth is *Massekhet Sofrim*, which was edited during the Gaonic period after the completion of the Talmud. This source noted that the Book of Ruth was to be read *motza'ei yom rishon* – during the night of the first day of *Shavuot* – to celebrate David's kingship. However, it became the custom to read it on the second day of *Shavuot* in honor of the marriage of *Ruth* and *Bo'az* which occurred during the time of the barley harvest – the time when *Shavuot* is celebrated.

Another early source notes that we read *Megillat Ruth* on *Shavuot* to stress the fact that "the Torah was given via suffering and poverty." Says the *Midrash* (*Yalkut Shimoni 247*): "The Torah sought to be given to a tribe of poverty, for if the Israelites would be rich, they probably would not engage in Torah study." This same *Midrash* emphasizes yet another reason for reading *Megillat Ruth* on *Shavuot* based upon Rabbi Ze'era's opinion cited earlier: This *Megillah* is all *hesed* (kindness)." Indeed, reference to *Ruth* is made in the *Aishet Hayil* ("woman of valor"), "And the Torah of Kindness is on her tongue" (*Proverbs 31:26*). The author of this statement refers here to his great, great-grandmother who is the exemplar of the Torah's *hesed*.

One of the modern views regarding the value of reading *Megillat Ruth* on *Shavuot* is that of Rabbi Yehudah Leib Fishman (Maimon) who noted, "this *Megillah* is a faithful testimony to the veracity of *Torah She'be'al Peh* (the Oral Law) as it is a true indication of the inadequacy of the Karaitic, literal approach to understanding the Torah. The Torah states, "An *Amonite* or *Moabite* shall not enter the community of the Lord" (*Devarim 23:4*). According to the Oral Law, which elucidates the Scriptures, this prohibition is limited only to the *Ammonite* and *Moabite* males: (*Yevamot 3a*). Otherwise, *Ruth* would have been prohibited from converting and marrying an Israelite (*Hagim U'Moadim*). Ezra imposed an exception to this limitation because of the rampant intermarriage during his time when Jews returned to Israel after their exile in Babylonia.

The aims of *Megillat Ruth* are many and varied. This pithy account of a fascinating segment of Jewish biblical history is replete with ideals and values, each of which is reason enough for its being recorded and canonized. "Together they comprise a beautiful chain of admirable deeds and profound concepts that reflect the beauty of the cultural heritage of the people of Israel" (Hayyim Hamiel, *Ma'ayanei Mikra: Megillat Ruth*).

It is clear that a major message of this sacred book is the primacy of *Mitzvot* between fellow Jews, particularly the performance of acts of *hesed*. Another cardinal teaching of *Megillat Ruth* is the three-fold love of the Jewish people: *Ahavat Hashem* (love of God), *ahavat am yisrael* (love of the Jewish people) and *Ahavat Eretz Yisrael* (love of the Land of Israel).

While these three loves find lofty expression in *Shir Hashirim* (Song of Songs) and are a visible manifestation of *Megillat Esther* via the strong faith of Esther and Mordechai and their selfless devotion to the salvation of their people, they are expressed most poignantly in Ruth's unique pronouncement of faith: "Wherever you will go, I will go; wherever you will lodge, I will lodge" (a reference to *Ahavat Eretz Yisrael*), "Your people shall be my people" (a reference to *Ahavat Am Yisrael*); and "Your God shall be my God" (a reference to *Ahavat Hashem*).

Ruth excels in all these three loves. While Esther concealed her identity because of the particular problems of her exilic setting, Ruth proudly declared her identity – *Ahavat Am Yisrael*. While Esther's external beauty is a paramount feature of *Megillat Esther*, Ruth's inner qualities dominate the Book of Ruth – *Ahavat Hashem* and *Ahavat Am Yisrael*. As King Solomon asserted, Ruth was the paradigmatic *Aishet Hayil*.

Finally, while the fate of Esther and Mordechai was to remain in exile, Ruth made aliyah – demonstrating *Ahavat Eretz Yisrael*. Her every act, her every word were imbued with the love of *Hashem* and the values propagated by the Torah. This alone is ample reason for writing *Megillah Ruth* and for reading it on the day we celebrate *Matan Torah*.

SIMHAH IN JEWISH TRADITION

Osher, gil, gilah, ditzah, hana'ah, hedvah, massos, alizut, alissah, alitzut, oneg, tzahalah, rinah, simhah, sasson, ta'anug. These are the Hebrew synonyms (each with a special connotation) for happiness, gladness, delight, joy, exultation, gaiety and merriment.

According to the Yiddish-Hebrew writer and poet, Morris Vichensky, no other language has so many synonyms for the word *simhah*. This, he claims, is because Jews always had to be happy with their lot. In order for Jews to survive and thrive, the spirit of optimism has been paramount in Judaism.

The ultimate Jewish *simhah* is the joy that *Isaiah* describes regarding the future redemption: "The wilderness and the arid land shall be glad; and the desert shall rejoice and blossom like a tulip. It shall blossom abundantly and rejoice even with joy and singing…" (*Isaiah* 35–1).

In this regard, in similar fashion, King David stresses an oft-quoted assertion that we sing joyously every Friday evening concerning God's final revelation to mankind: "Let the heavens rejoice and let the earth be glad; let the sea roar and the fullness thereof; let the field be joyful and all that is in it: then shall all the trees of wood sing for joy" (*Psalms* 86–11).

The simhah by Isaiah and King David is not physical or material (that is, "this-worldly"). It is, to be sure, as advised by Hose-a, purely spiritual rejoicing. "Rejoice not Yisrael with joy like other nations…." The conclusive, straightforward simhah is, according to the final address of Moses to B'nai Yisrael, the joyousness that takes place before God, "And you shall rejoice before the Lord, your God, you and your sons and your daughters and your manservants and your maidservants and the Levite who is within your gates…" (Deuteronomy 12–12)

Rejoicing **before** *Hashem* actually refers to the *Mishkan* (the Tabernacle) and the *Beit Hamikdash* (the Holy Temple). But, since this was not possible for all Jews, certainly not for Jews in the Diaspora, this kind of celebration meant being happy, expressing gladness and engaging in merriment in ways that would please the Almighty. It emphasizes that gaiety should not be unruly and end up in wild exultation. This is the reason that Jews throughout the ages have not been plagued by drunkenness. *Simhah* before *Hashem* expresses itself in the joys of Jewish observance like *Simhat Torah* and *Purim* when we are allowed to imbibe until we cannot differentiate between "cursed is *Haman*" and "blessed is *Mordechai*." This, according to some, is an exaggerated way of emphasizing the requirement to be happy on Purim.

Our sages relegated *simhah* to an aspect of *kedushah* (holiness) and interpersonal relations. This is known as *simhah shel mitzvah* – happy occasions related to religious observance – such as *brit milah, pidyon haben,* wedding ceremonies, etc. We are informed by our sages: "God's divine presence is found among Jews not in sadness…but in aspects of happiness that relate to good deeds and religious observance" (*B'rakhot* 31).

Simhah in Jewish tradition has special relevance to *Pesah, Shavuot,* and *Sukkot*. For each of these holidays the Torah instructs, "You shall be happy in your holiday seasons." Also, according to *hazal*, we have a special *simhah* relationship to the month of

Adar because of the holiday of *Purim*. "When the month of *Adar* arrives, we increase our joyousness" (*Ta'anit* 29).

Regarding the *shalosh regalim* (the three festivals *Sukkot, Pesah,* and *Shavuot*), *Sukkot* is the only holiday referred to as "the time of our happiness." Did not the Exodus from Egypt, celebrated on *Pesah*, and the giving of the Torah, observed on *Shavuot*, merit the appellation, "the time of our happiness?" Why only on *Sukkot*?

There are a variety of explanations for this reality. The one I feel is most compelling is based upon Rashi's commentary, in *Parshat Re'eh*. "You shall observe the holiday of *Sukkot* for seven days when you have gathered your corn from your threshing floor and your wine from your wine press" (Deuteronomy 16–12). Later on, the Torah notes regarding *Sukkot*, "You shall *only* be joyful" (you shall be, oh, so happy – altogether joyful). Rashi explains this statement as follows: "According to its plain meaning this statement is not made in the imperative form but in the form of a promise." This is the only time that God promised the Jewish people *simhah* without any sadness. Therefore, the holiday of *Sukkot* is described as "the time of our happiness."

Interestingly, the feast of the water drawing for libation, observed in the *Beit Hamikdash* on the second night of *Sukkot*, was celebrated with heightened festivity: with flute playing, enthusiastic singing, dancing while juggling torches and with multi-level brightly lit candelabra which "illuminated all of Jerusalem." The Feast was so festive that *hazal* noted: "Whoever did not see *simhat bet hasho-evah* (the water drawing celebration) never really observed *simhah* in his lifetime" (*Succah* 51).

The day after *Sukkot, Shmini Atzeret* was observed as *Simhat Torah* in Jerusalem and celebrated with great exultation and fervor. And such is the observance down to our own time in our synagogues in the Diaspora on the day after *Shmini Atzeret*, which is the added day of *Simhat Torah* observance for Diaspora Jewry.

The ultimate fulfillment of our aspirations regarding the ingathering of the Jewish people to the land of our forefathers is accomplished via *simhah*: "May it be Your will, *Hashem*...to bring us up to our land in gladness" (The Sabbath *Mussaf* prayer).

The height of personal happiness is expressed in the *sheva brakhot* (seven blessings) under the *huppah*. The various nouns and verbs relating to *simhah* are mentioned 19 times in the last three blessings of *sheva brakhot*.

There are many other ways in which *simhah shel mitzvah* is observed. There are many other times that *simhah* is integrated into the fabric of Jewish living. On the Godly level, it refers to Hashem's "secret way of rewarding those who are God fearing." Also, *simhah* can best be attained via human interpersonal relations, doing *mitzvot* "between man and man."

This dual formula is indeed what is meant by the popular Chasidic song: "A person accomplishes a great *mitzvah* when he is always in the *simhah* mood."

THE PURPOSE OF REMEMBRANCE

We are here today under a bright sun and beautiful blue sky to perpetuate a most patriotic American event. Memorial Day originated to honor American servicemen who died in the Civil War some 135 years ago. Then, it honored those who gave their lives for their country in the Spanish-American War a century ago and, now we are assembled to memorialize those who died in World War I, in World War II, in the Korean War, in the War in Vietnam, and in the Gulf War.

Memorial Day is a day of parades; a day we decorate the graves of the fallen. It is a day of family gatherings, community outings and picnicking. And, in some quarters, it has assumed an air of celebration. But, at its core, May 31 is a day of sacred remembrance.

We remember so that we should not forget. This is the way the Bible treats remembrance and memory. *Zakhor, al tishkah*. "Remember and don't forget!"

In the Bible, the idea of remembering is considered a sacred duty of free men and women everywhere. And today, it is our sacred responsibility to remember why the veterans of our wars died, why these precious Americans gave their lives on the battlefield, why the young beloved servicemen from Oceanside made the ultimate sacrifice.

Let us remember why. *Zakhor, al tishkah.* "Remember and do not forget."

The famed late nineteenth century and early twentieth century poet and storyteller, Rudyard Kipling memorialized his only son who died in World War 1 by emphasizing this biblical concept. He begged the world to remember why our boys died lest we forget that they perished for a higher purpose. They died to keep us free. They died so that we could fervently engage in the struggle for peace. The only good war is the war to make peace.

The best monument to the memory of our servicemen is to fight the war for peace at home with all its religious, racial and ethnic connotations, and to fight the war for peace world over. We are our brothers' keepers.

Harry Truman, the great president and great American, said it best. "It is all too obvious that if we do not abolish war on this earth, then surely, one day, war will abolish us from the earth." Fighting for peace is in the best interest of all mankind. It is the best way to preserve our society and the human race.

Memory is the glue of human history. Today we preserve the memory of our beloved men and women. And, as we keep their memories fresh in our hearts, we must dedicate ourselves to make the United States of America the kind of society of virtue, integrity, brotherly love, and democracy for which they gave their lives.

Until recently we used to say the United States – in the plural. Now, we say the United States – in the singular – implying that true democracy requires a unity of spirit and action for the benefit and betterment of all American citizens.

In Jewish tradition we hallow the memory of the righteous who have departed this world. *Zekher zaddik l'vrakhah.* We say, "May the memory of the righteous be for a blessing."

The servicemen we memorialize today were all righteous souls. May their memories be for a blessing for the residents of Oceanside, for the citizens of our great nation and for all mankind.

POST 9/11 MIRACLE

The attack on the Twin Towers caused an amazing change in the American community. In addition, the destruction brought about an unexpected international change in all the countries of the world. The response to September 11th was beyond our imagination – we would never have believed it.

Who would have thought that in our day there would be such unity throughout the United States? All over we see the display of American flags and hear the singing of the songs of America – "God Bless America," "The Star Spangled Banner," and "America The Beautiful" – before sporting events – basketball, football, baseball, hockey! Who would have imagined that such expressions of patriotism could occur in America? Or the display of signs, "United We Stand" all over the country – in stores, in bus and train stations, in halls, in churches, in synagogues, on taxis, on motor vehicles and in the windows of private houses.

In our wildest imagination, who could have dreamt of the organization of an international coalition to fight malicious terror, evil, violence and tyranny? In our days?

September 11th was the motivation to establish an unbelievable loyalty to America, to achieve a unity thought impossible in the United States and indeed throughout the world. September 11th will be long remembered.

The foundation for world unity, and in particular, the idea of the unity of the people of Israel has deep roots in Jewish tradition. Jewish sources offer an amazing precedent for the concept of "United We Stand." This is illustrated in the *Amidah* prayer recited on *Rosh Hashanah* and *Yom Kippur* during *shaharit, musaf, minhah*, and *maariv*. We recite: "And so, too, O *Hashem*, our God, instill Your awe upon all Your works and Your dread upon all that You have created…that…they will become a single society to do Your will wholeheartedly." What is the real purpose of this unity? The third paragraph of the *Amidah* contains the answer.

"And all wickedness will evaporate like smoke, when You will remove evil's domination from the earth." Unity will come about in order to erase and eradicate terror, evil, violence and malicious intent from the world.

Different English translations of this passage in many High Holiday Prayer Books note its meaning: "They shall form one bond," or "That they may all form a single bond," or "May they blend into one brotherhood to do Thy will with a perfect heart." English translations are incorrect. The author, Rav, wrote this prayer 1,800 years ago. Had he wanted to say, "They shall form one bond" or "May they blend into one brotherhood," he would have written the Hebrew verb *v'ya-assu*, "make" – conjugated in the simple (active) construction. Instead, he wrote *v'yay-assu* in the passive tense meaning, "You will be fashioned into a single society," or "You will be forced to unite in one bond." Why did Rav write the verb in the passive tense? He did this because he understood human nature and the tendency of the peoples of the world to be independent, individualistic, and not cooperative with other peoples. Therefore, Rav wrote *v'yay-assu* to say that a unity will be imposed on all of us: We will be forced to unite.

And, that is what happened in our own time. September 11th was the cause that compelled the citizens of the new reality of "United We Stand." The attack on the Twin Towers and the fear that this wanton destruction could happen anywhere was the motivation for all the peoples of the world to join together with the United States and form a coalition against world terror and against international violence.

When we pray during the High Holidays, especially during the Amidah prayer, we should understand that we are expressing an ancient Judaic concept regarding the American and world unity of our day.

CHAPTER 3

TRANSMITTING THE JEWISH HERITAGE

TEACHING AND LEARNING

Jewish education occupies a unique position in Jewish life. The study of Torah is a cardinal principle of the Jewish faith as underscored in the *Mishnah* (*Peah* 1:1) and in the *Gemara* (*Shabbat* 127a). Knowledge and study are not only a means to religious and ethical behavior, but are in themselves a mode of worship. Indeed, Jewish liturgy reflects the fact that worship finds expression on the intellectual, as well as aesthetic and emotional, planes as it combines the moment of prayer with study. Witness the many sections of *Torah-she'biktav* (written law) and *Torah-she'b'al peh* (oral law) in the *Siddur* and the *Kaddish d'rabbanan* (The Rabbis' Kaddish).

The idea of transmitting Jewish values through learning and practice derives from a variety of sources in the Pentateuch. There are four such indications in the *sidrah Bo* – two at the beginning of the *Parashah* and two at the end.

1. Before the plague of the locusts, *Hashem* hardened *Pharaoh's* heart for two reasons: *l'ma'an shiti ototay aleh b'kirbo* ("in order that I may display my signs among them [the Egyptians]") and *ul'ma'an t'sapper* ("that you [the Jewish people] may recount in the hearing of your sons and of your sons' sons how I made a mockery of the Egyptians"). While the second reason may seem

superfluous, it is entirely appropriate. Memory is an important dimension of Jewish continuity. The only way each new generation can remember its past is by hearing about it, learning about it. In this vein, the *Or HaHayyim* notes that *Hashem* added *ul'ma'an t'sapper* to engrave these miracles permanently in the memories of *B'nai Yisrael* in order to strengthen their belief in God. The *Pnai Maivin* indicates that the term, *ul'ma'an* appears in two contexts in the Torah: "so that you may recount" and "so that you may live long" (*Devarim* 4:40, 6:2 and 11:9). There is a connection between the two contexts. Longevity mentioned in the Bible refers to the results of educating future generations, by continually reinforcing events of Jewish history in the minds and hearts of our children. This is also the view of the *Seforno*.

2. Parental study and knowledge are requisite to parental teaching. It is for this reason that at the end of the statement urging parents to tell their children about God's miracles in Egypt, the Torah clearly posits *vee'da'atem*, "so that you (parents) shall know that 'I am the Lord!'" One would think that parents would instruct their children so that they (the children) should know God's greatness. The reason for *vee'da'atem* is simply that parents must learn first before they impart knowledge to their offspring.

3. Interestingly, the importance of transmitting Jewish values to the young is reinforced by *Moshe's* demand: *bin'oraynu u'vizkaynaynu naylaich* ("with our young and our elders we shall go"). Why did *Moshe* mention the young before the old? According to the *Ketav Sofer*, the young needed to go more urgently to participate in an Israelite experience away from the fleshpots of Egypt, for they were endangered by assimilation. The old were more secure in their tradition and, therefore, their rescue was less urgent. To be sure, experiencing Jewish life is one of the best ways to teach Judaism. Furthermore, it is the best antidote to deculturation. Pedagogic practice that includes consideration of the "affective domain" (emotional or experiential learning) has more impact on students than cognitive learning only.

4. At the end of the *sidrah*, *Moshe* instructs *B'nai Yisrael*, "And you shall tell your child..." From this statement, says Rabbi

Samson Raphael Hirsch, we learn the basic function of Jewish education. We lead our children to faithful observance of God's Law by personal example and by explaining the way we observe *mitzvot* without waiting for them to ask. This is the manner in which the *Mechilta* explains the verse later on in the *sidrah* where the child will question the father *mah zot* (what is this?) about the Passover observance. "Don't wait for your child to ask," advise our sages. That is why the Torah emphasizes, *v'heegad'ta* ("Tell your child") before it mentions that the child might ask the parent, "What is this?" In effect, *hazal* are telling parents, "Take the instructional initiative when it comes to Torah study."

In the *Haggadah*, the question, *mah zot* refers to the *tam*, "the simple son." This suggests that parents and teachers must be attentive to the question and needs of all children, even the naughty child, the simple child and the "special" child – the one that cannot even ask questions.

In sum, this week's Torah reading contains several lessons about *hinukh* (Jewish education): Jewish continuity depends largely on effective Jewish education. To be effective, Jewish education must: 1) involve parents who themselves learn and take the initiative to teach; 2) include appropriate experiential learning; and 3) adapt to the learning needs of all types of children.

THE ESSENCE OF LEADERSHIP

Davar b'eeto mah tov – "a timely word is so good" (*Proverbs* 15:23). This advice of timeliness by the wisest of all men has been viewed over the ages by rabbis, preachers and *d'var Torah* givers as suggesting that the Torah thoughts be connected to the *parshat hashavua* – either the preceding *Shabbat* Torah reading or the succeeding one. Today, I can connect with both simultaneously. *Parshat Naso*, which we read in synagogues in the Diaspora this coming *Shabbat*, was read last week in Israeli synagogues. This is so because in Israel *Shavuot* was observed on Friday. On the following *Shabbat*, June 10, *the sidrah Naso* was read. In the Diaspora, where *Shavuot* is observed for two days, the *Shavuot* Torah reading was read in the synagogues. So, we read *Naso* this coming Shabbat while *B'ha-alotkha* will be read in Israel.

Since my *d'var Torah* is based upon *Naso*, it performs double timeliness, which would make King Solomon quite happy.

Naso is the longest *Parshah* in the Torah. The source for my remarks is Chapter 7 in *Naso*, the longest chapter – 89 sentences – in the Torah. The opening sentence of chapter 7 reads: "On the day that Moses finished setting up the Tabernacle, he anointed it and sanctified it."

This is a puzzling statement. Moses did not construct the Tabernacle. *Bezalel* and *Oholiov* and their helpers, all "men wise of heart" built it. Why then does the Torah attribute the building of the *mishkan* to Moses?

Rashi, the master biblical and Talmudic commentator, asks this question and answers it. Before reviewing Rashi's response, we learn an important lesson in educational psychology from the fact that men, wise of heart, were chosen to build the Tabernacle. Knowledge and wisdom seem to be associated with the mind and not the heart. However, the heart plays a crucial role both in the acquisition of knowledge and in its transmission. The confluence of the cognitive and affective domains is critical to effective learning, teaching and doing. The "wise of heart" were motivated by the proper feelings regarding the construction of the *mishkan*. Rashi notes that the setting up of the Tabernacle was attributed to Moses because Moses devoted himself wholeheartedly to its construction – to see that each item in the Tabernacle was made exactly according to God's instruction to him on Mount Sinai." The key phrase, the operative words in Rashi's answer, are *l'horot l'ovdai hamlakhah* to show, to teach, to guide the workmen."

Rashi emphasizes Moses' conscientious role as guide, supervisor, leader of the construction. The word *l'horot* refers to *moreh* (teacher) and *moreh derekh* (guide), one who shows direction. Moses did not physically engage in the building, but guided it effectively. He guaranteed that the construction would be done properly. He exemplified leadership. He was the paradigm of leadership. Therefore, Scripture attributes the completion of the building of the Tabernacle to him.

Whether it relates to a person, a group of people or an agency entrusted with leadership, the same leadership dynamic applies – leveraging talent, knowledge, experience and position for the accomplishment of a community's goals. The message here to Jewish communal educational agencies is clear.

I retired from the Board of Jewish Education (BJE) at the time that the National Jewish Population Study was being completed. The Jewish community, particularly Federation leadership, was shocked by the findings on intermarriage. Fifty-two percent of all marriages involving Jews between 1985 and 1990 were intermarriages. One benefit of the study was the underscoring of the need for intensive Jewish education for Jewish youth. In the 1980s, the BJE sounded the clarion call for the improvement of the Jewish Supplementary School in our milestone research entitled "Jewish Supplementary Schooling – A System in Need of Change."

During the last decade, several studies have shown the value of Jewish all day education. My own research on "The Jewishness Quotient of Jewish Day School Graduates," published in three volumes in 1994 by Yeshiva University, demonstrated that the intermarriage rate of Jewish day school graduates was 4.5% compared to 52% of the overall Jewish community – and for Jewish day high school graduates it was between 1% and 3%.

BJE's role, while not engaging in the actual teaching and administration of Jewish schools, is to maximize its leadership role in upgrading the Jewish Supplementary School and in providing the necessary support for the continued progress of the Jewish day school. BJE has significant experience in trying to use minimal funding to achieve maximum benefit.

The key is leveraging our collective knowledge, experience, enthusiasm and our communal position to provide the necessary guidance to achieve our goals. The Mosaic leadership model *l'horot* – teaching, guiding, inspiring and supervising the educators engaged in the day-to-day process of Jewish schooling – is the key to our success.

I'm sure that given their commitment, insight, understanding and experience, current BJE leaders with their respective lay and professional leadership qualities, and with the support of the BJE Board and staff, the successful building of the Tabernacle of Jewish education in Greater New York can be reinforced significantly.

More power to you!

AGNON AND ZIONIST EDUCATION

When Shmuel Josef Agnon received the Nobel Prize for literature, he was asked where he was born. In reply he said, "My parents gave birth to me in B'tchach, but I was really born in Jerusalem."

In explaining his answer, Agnon said that his physical birth took place in Galicia, but his spiritual birth was in Jerusalem. "The spirit in my home," he said, "was that of Jerusalem. Otherwise, I would never have mastered Judaic sources. I never would have made aliyah. I never would have become an accomplished Hebrew author, nor would I be here today receiving the Nobel Prize."

The goal of the American Advisory Council of the Joint Authority for Jewish Zionist Education is to establish the Agnon connection. This connection represents the Diaspora reality and the two dimensions of Jerusalem: earthly Jerusalem and heavenly Jerusalem. The former refers to the physical interfacing of Jews with Israel; heavenly Jerusalem symbolizes the spiritual-cultural dimension of Jewish life.

Together these two Jerusalems define the effective Israel Experience. And, in confluence, they describe the goals of Jewish Zionist education in the Diaspora. Overall, the Agnon connection brings diaspora Jews closer to Israel in thought, in feeling and in action. It brings Jews physically to Israel and infuses them with the spirit of heavenly Jerusalem, a deep love for Israel and a deep understanding and love of the Jewish heritage, the source of Israel's centrality to the Jewish people.

CHAPTER 4

ERETZ YISRAEL: DREAM AND REALITY

BEYOND THE PEACE PROCESS

During the last half century, several traumatic, historical events have turned the eyes of the world toward *Eretz Yisrael* – the establishment of the State, the Six Day War, the *Yom Kippur* War, the peace treaty with Egypt, the Intifada and the White House lawn agreement between the government of Israel and the PLO. In this light, it would be well to focus on the Jewish claim to *Eretz Yisrael*, highlighted in this *sidrah* by God's command to *Avram*, "Go forth…to the land I will show you" (Genesis 12:1). Unlike any other people or religion, this command to our forefather, who had unconditionally accepted monotheism as a way of life, forged his descendants into a national religious entity possessing a land and a religion. Both are integral to Judaism. For both reasons – religion and nationhood – *Eretz Yisrael* is a fundamental, pivotal dynamic of Judaism. The land and the Torah are an essential unity and constitute the indispensable source and symbols of Jewish identity.

The *Torah Shebikhtav* (the written Torah) is the basic literary linkage of our people to the land. Rashi's first commentary in *Parashat Breishit* clearly underscores God's intent – the land of Israel for the people of Israel. God reiterated His promise to *Avraham* and his progeny many times in the Bible. And, history has proven that His pledge has been realized. Even the Koran supports the Jewish inheritance of the Land of Israel when Mohammed declared (*Sura* 17:105), "We have instructed the Children of Israel, 'Settle in the land of Israel.'"

However, God's promise regarding *Eretz Yisrael* is not unconditional (see *Vayikra* 26:14–42 and *Devarim* 11:16–17). The Torah-true viewpoint underscores the fact that the Jewish people's ability to thrive in the Land of Israel depends upon its adherence to its Sinaitic covenant with the Almighty. Indeed, the Prophets warned the Jewish people not to deviate from its covenantal commitment. Yet, they also prophesied about the redemption of the Jewish people and its return to its homeland. The *Haftorot* on the Sabbaths of Consolation after *Tisha B'av* are integral to Jewish belief.

And, here we are at the beginning of the year 5754, hopeful about the prospects of peace, yet wary about the many pitfalls that the Rabin-Arafat handshake represents. "Rejoice in trembling" (Psalms 2:11) suggests that Israel look inward toward itself, as well as outward to its Arab neighbors. "And I will make you into a *great* nation" (*Breishit* 12:2), says the Almighty to *Avram*. Our sages, in *Masekhet Sofrim*, expound the word, "great," to mean that *Avram* was able to eat and drink an amount equal to that of 74 people. Commenting on this strange interpretation, the Vilna Gaon cites the text, "Moshe and Aharon and Nadav and Avihu and seventy elders of Israel ascended the mountain…and they beheld God and ate and drank" (Exodus 24:9). The Gaon of Vilna notes that the 74 people beheld God and ate and drank on the mountain; and he explains that *Hazal* were referring to Avraham's prodigious religious insight and extraordinary, God-infatuated commitment. This, after all, was God's purpose in bringing Avram to the Land of Canaan and saying to him, " I will make you into a great nation" – great in adherence to its religious-cultural inheritance.

As much as the peace process is an external challenge to Israel, the vouchsafing of the Jewish way of life, the maintenance of the Judaic moral-ethical-religious belief system is the vital internal challenge of Israeli leadership and society. God bequeathed to the Jewish people via *Avraham Avinu*, a dual treasure – the Land of Israel and the Nation of Israel – a Holy Land and the obligation to be a Holy People in that land. Unfortunately, the rampant, growing secularization of Israel highlights the urgency of the internal challenge.

A way must be found to realize the spirit of the second *Lekh-Lekha* command to Avraham, "Go to the Land of Moriah" (*Breishit* 22:2). This statement, according to Rashi, is a reference to the building of the *Bet HaMikdash* (Holy Temple) in Jerusalem. In our current era, when a national Jewish state exists, this command refers to the need of Avraham's modern seed in Israel to build their *spiritual* life in the land. According to *Hazal*, the word, *Moriah* is a reference to *hora'ah* – Judaic instruction (*Ta'anit* 6a), meaning "from *Zion* the Torah will come forth…" (*Isaiah* 2:3) is the pre-eminent goal for Israel to achieve (see *Torah Temimah* commentary). Indeed, this is as important, even more momentous and consequential for Israel and the Jewish people than peace with Israel's neighbors.

SHEVAT AND ISRAEL'S JUBILEE

Rosh Hodesh Same-ah, Happy New Hebrew month of *Shevat* to all of you. *Shevat* is the 5th month and the 11th month of the Jewish calendar, depending upon whether we count the months of the Jewish year from *Nisan* – the month in which the spring holiday of *Pesah* falls or from *Tishrei* and *Rosh Hashannah.*

In either case, the month of *Shevat* has special meaning for Israel and for the Jewish people every year and especially this year. Interestingly and meaningfully, the symbol of *Shevat* is a bucket or pail, always portrayed drawing water. And the water is the nourishment needed by the trees that are being given special recognition as we celebrate *Tu bishvat* – Jewish Arbor Day – in the middle of the month of *Shevat*. In two weeks, spring officially begins in Israel as the almond tree starts to bloom. The popular Hebrew song informs us, "The almond tree bursts into blossom and the golden sun shines in full splendor."

In Jewish tradition, winter and darkness go together. Springtime and sunlight go hand in hand. The one represents despair and gloom – the other hope and gladness. It is in this light we must observe the Jubilee year of the State of Israel in the month in which spring begins in Israel.

As we celebrate the 50th anniversary year, we realize full well that the young country, that is the Jewish State, has many problems on many fronts – internal and external. Unfortunately, there are those who say there should be no celebrations during this anniversary year. They are wrong. After all, Jews founded the Jewish State, Jews immigrated and made aliyah to Israel and Jews developed its government. And Jews always have many opinions – some very strong and contrary.

Whether we support the current government or not – no matter our political, ideological, religious, secular or social bent – the month of *Shevat* tells us to count our blessings – water and trees are the earmarks of growth and productivity.

Jewish tradition suggests that we count our blessings at this time in our history. According to Jewish tradition, the idea of *yovel* – the biblical Jubilee year in the land of Israel – is relevant to the Diaspora. Commenting on the statement in Leviticus about the observance of the Jubilee year, the sages of the Talmud stress – "Even outside the Land of Israel, the Jubilee should be celebrated." And celebrate we must.

This does not mean that Diaspora Jewry bury its head ostrich-like in the sand of obliviousness. It does not mean that we should not pursue those avenues of endeavor that will insure that Israel is a free-society in accordance with the biblical statement – "And you shall proclaim liberty to all the inhabitants of the land."

But, it does mean that we must not ignore its past accomplishments – not like glassy-eyed novices – but as committed sophisticated long-time supporters of Jewish nationhood and statehood.

After all, the *raison d'être* of the United Israel Appeal and the Jewish Agency for Israel in partnership with UJA-CJF is to foster these social, educational, aliyah, settlement and life-giving programs that are integral to our philosophy of *am ehad*. These are important both to Israel and to the Jewish people who make

Israel central to their lives. This should strengthen our resolve to celebrate our common achievement.

The fact that we may be engaged in trying to solve some social, political and ideological problems should not lessen our responsibility to recognize the remarkable progress that a young 50 year old nation made – with our help – in the face of the greatest dangers and obstacles imaginable – in every aspect of its short life – including progress even in its political structure and national and local governments. Certainly deserving recognition and celebration are the absorption of 2 million refugees and immigrants, the achievement of the Israel Defence Forces, the development of Israel's urban and rural life, its economic development, its health services, medical research, social services, science and technology, education, culture, fine arts, music, theater and media.

And all these can be improved with our support as we celebrate the accomplishments of 50 years of statehood. *Yovel* in Hebrew is literally "a horn" – a *Shofar*. On the 50th it is ours to blow for Israel's achievements.

The first educational challenge to the Jewish community is to transmit the information about Israel's achievements, as well as its problems to the Jewish youth and adult communities. I believe this is our responsibility and obligation. When we celebrate *Yom Ha'atzma-ut* in May it should be meaningful and based upon knowledge. When we observe Balfour Day in November we should know what it is all about.

May we succeed in our mission and may Israel prosper! A happy Jubilee year – to our nation, state and to ourselves.

SOUNDING THE SHOFAR AT THE SALUTE TO ISRAEL PARADE

[Note: At the beginning of each parade from 1963 to 2001, I announced the theme of the Parade, then blew the Shofar.]

Forty-five years ago, when the State of Israel was born on the fifth of *Iyar*, a heavenly voice proclaimed, "Make the desert bloom!

Make the desert bloom!" And, the newly established State set to the task of making arid soil fertile and cultivating barren, dry, treeless land while absorbing hundreds of thousands of tired, ragged, impoverished immigrants from European, Asian and African countries.

The story of Israel's manifold accomplishments since that time is the story of a modern day miracle. Indeed, Israel has made the desert bloom even as it has written human history during the last decade with the absorption of thousands of Soviet and Ethiopian Jews.

Israel's bittersweet experiences – four major wars, subjection to hundreds of acts of terrorism, constant daily threats of obliteration from Muslim fundamentalists and other Arabs – and through it all, a cold unsympathetic, hostile world, have had a sobering effect upon this young nation state. Against this background, Israel's sterling achievements in the human, social, political, cultural, scientific, technological, agricultural and industrial spheres are all the more remarkable! Imagine, Israel is now exporting its expertise to nations on all continents of the globe, even to Muslim countries of the former Soviet Union.

Above all, Israel stands high and alone as a beacon of democracy and freedom in a sea of anarchy, corruption, hatred, and violence.

Unfortunately, Israel's shining accomplishments are shrouded by the media's almost daily preoccupation with Middle East terrorism, political unrest, anti-Israel and anti-American activity, and with the difficulties of the peace process.

Today, we proudly celebrate these achievements as we longingly look forward to the positive results of the peace process so that we will be able to say "Shalom, shalom," and see peace and feel peace. *Am Yisrael Chai!*

There is no better way to usher in Israel's 45th Anniversary year than by blowing the *shofar* accompanied by the traditional biblical reading in the Book of Numbers; "And on your days of celebration…you shall sound the trumpets over your burnt offerings and your peace offerings. They shall serve as a reminder before the Lord Your God. I am the Lord your God." *Tekiah, Shevarim, Teruah, Tekiah Gedolah.*

CENTENNIAL OF ZIONISM

1997 – One hundred years since the first World Zionist Congress in Basel, Switzerland! At that Congress, Theodore Herzl prophesied that within fifty years there would be a Jewish State. And presto! Fifty-one years later the modern State of Israel was born! Miracle of miracles!

With all its internal problems – and they are many; with all its political challenges – and they are manifold; with all the economic difficulties of statehood – and they are plentiful; and with all the threats to its survival and terrorists activities – and they are multifarious – Israel manages to achieve, to thrive, to grow and to make so many headlines with its outstanding miraculous progress in every area of life. Miracle of miracles! For all this we say *yehi hedad* – Long live Israel!

Israel is the ultimate realization of the Zionist dream – a dream which is not merely one hundred years old, nor two hundred years old, nor one thousand years old. Zionism is as old as the Jewish people, beginning with God's promise to Abraham three thousand five hundred years ago.

As we celebrate one hundred years of modern Zionism, we celebrate also the Zionist dream of 3½ millennia. And, it all came about because the Jewish people believed Herzl when he said "*Im tirtzu, ain zu aggaddah.*" If you will it, it will not just be a legend.

And, the Jewish people willed it and worked hard and selflessly for it. And, we are here today to testify to the veracity of Herzl's prophetic statement. In honor of the dream and its fulfillment we dedicate this parade with the traditional blowing of the Shofar, as noted in the Bible: "And on your days of celebration, on your festivals and new moon days you shall sound the trumpet over your burnt offerings and peace offerings. They shall serve as a reminder to you before the Lord, God. I am the Lord your God."

PESAH 5756 AND JERUSALEM 3,000

This year Jews all over the world are celebrating the 3,000th anniversary of the establishment of Jerusalem as the capital of Israel. It therefore seems most appropriate that a *Pesah Dvar Torah* focus on the concluding statement of the *Haggadah* – "Next year in Jerusalem." Indeed, it was this clarion call that served as a beacon of hope for the Jewish people during their two millennia diaspora as they dreamed of and prayed for restoration to *Zion*.

It may be no more than coincidental that two Hebrew statements in the *Pentateuch* – the *gematrias* (the numeric values) of which are 3,000 (an illusion to Jerusalem in 5756 [1996]) – both refer to Exodus from Egypt. The first sentence deals with the beginning of the process of redemption. "So come now, let me send you to *Pharaoh*, that you may bring my people, the Israelites, out of Egypt" (*Shemot* 3:10). The second sentence refers to the results of the ten plagues. "The Egyptians meanwhile were burying all the first-born whom the Lord had struck down: and on their gods, too, the Lord executed judgment" (*Bamidbar* 33:4). This remarkable coincidence may suggest a mystical interpretation for the total redemption this year, at least for the vouchsafing of an undivided Jerusalem in 5756.

As for the 3,000th anniversary of Jerusalem, after ruling in Hebron for seven and one-half years, King David established his kingship in Jerusalem in 996 B.C.E. Prior to making Jerusalem the capital, he captured most of the area (now known as Jerusalem) from the Jebusites and renamed it *Metzudet Zion* (The Fortress of Zion). Subsequently, it was also called *Ir David* (The City of David, *Samuel* II 5:5–9).

Jerusalem is mentioned in the Bible 662 times, 556 of which it is spelled *Y'rushalem* – and not Y'rushalayim – as is the current practice. *Y'rushalem* (*Ir Shalem* – The City of Peace) is a reference to its original name, *Shalem*. According to the *Midrash* (*Breishit Rabbah* 56:10), God called the city *Yireh Shalem* in order to make peace between Abraham and Noah's son, Shem. Abraham called the place where the binding of Isaac took place, *Yireh* (*Bereshit* 22:140). Shem called it *Shalem*, as it is stated in *Breishit* 14:18,

"…and Malki Zedek, the king of *Shalem*." The *Midrash* says that God combined the names to satisfy both of them – a compromise for the sake of *shalom bayit* – peace in the House of Israel.

Remarkably, the commentators are largely silent regarding the concluding statement of the Haggadah. To be sure, the belief that Jerusalem will once again be ruled by the kingdom of David has been embedded in the hearts and minds of Jews for twenty centuries. When they remembered Jerusalem and thought of its future, diaspora Jews were freed from the feelings of their exilic oppression (akin to the Egyptian bondage) and they actually felt like the free men and women described in the *Haggadah*.

According to a Sephardic legend, thinking of Jerusalem made the free men and women feel like the father at the *Seder* comfortably leaning on his pillow as a free man uttering the words, "Next year we will be a free people." The legend notes that Jews in the Diaspora are like the son of a king banished from his homeland. While not being in his parents' palace saddens him exceedingly, when he thinks of his *yihus* – lineage and distinguished birth – his spirits are buoyed up and his strong desire to return to his homeland conquers his feelings of sadness.

The reason "Next year in Jerusalem" is recited at the end of the *Seder* and at the end of the service on *Yom Kippur*, according to Eliyahu Ki Tov, is to fulfill our pledge, "If I will not raise Jerusalem above my greatest joy" (*Psalms* 137:6). These two occasions – the *Seder* and *Ne'elah* – represent the epitome of religious joyousness. At the *Seder*, our joy reaches its zenith because of our happiness about our ancestors' redemption from Egypt. On *Yom Kippur*, at *Ne'elah* time, we rejoice because of our redemption from our sins.

Our joy is greater on the *Seder* night. On *Yom Kippur* we merit forgiveness (redemption) by separating ourselves from all physical needs. On the *Seder* night, however, we eat to our hearts' content, we drink and sing and enjoy the gifts of sustenance with which *HaShem* has blessed us.

The four cups of wine we drink at the *Seder* represent the four languages of redemption noted in the *Pentateuch* (*Shemot* 6:6–7):

"I will take you out from under the burdens of Egypt;" "I will save you from their work;" "I will redeem you with a strong arm and great judgments;" and "I will take you unto Me for a nation."

The fifth cup, the cup of Elijah, represents the term, "I will bring you into the land which I solemnly promised to give to Abraham, to Isaac and to Jacob." It is clear reference to the future – to messianic redemption. It makes us think also of the very relevant *Midrash* on Jerusalem: "The Holy One, Blessed be He, is destined to turn *Tish'ah B'Av* into a day of joy and to rebuild Jerusalem by Himself and to gather all the exiles of Israel into its midst, as it is stated (*Psalms* 147:3), 'God will build Jerusalem; He will gather all the dispersed of Israel.'"

The future of Jerusalem depends upon the ingathering of exiles to Israel, especially to Jerusalem. In this spirit, since the end of the Second Commonwealth and destruction of the second *Beit HaMikdash*, Jewish life in the Diaspora has been Jerusalem-oriented. And this relationship peaks at the end of the *Seder* as we recite with fervor, "Next year in Jerusalem."

The connection between Elijah's cup and the future of Jerusalem, when the Kingdom of David will be restored in it, is strengthened by rabbinic opinion, which indicates that we may drink or should drink the fifth cup of wine. According *to Rav Alfasi's* version of the text in *Pesahim* 118a, *Rav Tarfon* says that we may drink a fifth cup of wine and recite *Hallel HaGadol* (complete *Hallel*) over it. The *Ba'al HaMeor*, on this same text, suggests that *Rav Tarfon* requires us to drink a fifth cup. On the basis of this same *Gemara*, the *Mordechai* notes that if a person is very thirsty at the time of the filling of the fifth cup, he may drink it in honor of the language, "I will bring you to Israel." The Rema (*Orah H'ayyim* 481:1) suggests that Mordechai's interpretation is definite, meaning that Elijah's cup can be viewed as a compromise between the practice of drinking four cups or five cups of wine at the *Seder* (*Tosefot Hayyim, Hayyei Adam*, 130:55).

Homiletically or figuratively, the level of a person's thirst at the end of the *Seder* can be likened to his desire to realize the age-old hope of "Next year in Jerusalem."

Actually, at this time in Jewish history, the end of the twentieth century, this hope can be realized on an individual plane by making aliyah. For *Klal Yisrael*, however, it remains the ultimate dream of redemption.

LONG LIVE JERUSALEM!

Three thousand years ago, King David moved the center of his kingship from *Hebron*, where he ruled for seven years, to Jerusalem. There he established the permanent capital of the land of *Eretz Yisrael*, after purchasing the land from a wealthy landowner.

For 3,000 years, Jerusalem has been the city of Jewish unity, the city of Jewish hope, the city of the dreams of the Jewish people. "Eternity – this is Jerusalem," said our sages. Indeed, it is the eternal capital of the land of Israel and the eternal capital of the Jewish people. Since the time of King David, there has always been a Jewish presence in Jerusalem.

For two millennia of diaspora, Jews prayed for the welfare of Jerusalem. For 2000 years, they have been facing towards Jerusalem in their daily prayers. For two thousand years, they have proclaimed at the end of each Pesah Seder, *L'Shannah ha-ba'ah be-Yerushalayim*, "Next year in Jerusalem."

In 1967, after the Six-Day War, our dreams were answered as Jerusalem was united forever. To the unity of Jerusalem we dedicate today's Salute to Israel Parade on the forty-eighth anniversary of the modern Jewish State. Long live Israel! Long live Jerusalem! To this dual hope we dedicate our *Shofar* blowing today. Long live Israel! Long live Jerusalem!

A SPECIAL *YOVEL* TRIBUTE

Zeh hayom assah Hashem, nageelah v'nism'hah bo. "This is the day the Lord made. Let us rejoice and be happy in it."

During the dark days following the Holocaust, the *Yishuv* in Palestine had the resolve, the vision, the vitality, the courage and the selfless dedication to declare the establishment of a Jewish State. And, we are here today, hundreds of thousands strong, to celebrate the remarkable achievements, the extraordinary accomplishments of a reborn Jewish national home.

Despite all the problems in its short lifetime, despite terrorism and tragedy, despite five life and death wars and despite the overwhelming difficulties in absorbing two million immigrants from all over the globe, Israel has made its mark in the world as an outstanding democratic bastion of freedom.

Its fifty years have been highlighted by so many history-making events. The achievements of the Israel Defense Forces are second to none. The ingathering of exiles and the simultaneous economic growth of Israel border on the miraculous as do its accomplishments in arts and culture, archaeology, modern medicine, and technology, from the reviving of Jewish lives to the revival of the Hebrew language. Israel's growth is one of the great success stories of the twentieth century.

And, today we give a special *yovel* salute to the fulfillment of a Jewish dream. Today we are inspired by thousands of Jewish youth marching in all their pageantry, expressing their pride in their ancestral homeland. Today we enjoy the variety of colorful floats and bands sponsored by Israel's many friends from around the world.

And, today we are privileged to have the presence of Israel's prime-minister, Benyamin Netanyahu. And, today we send our deep love and appreciation from the heart of New York to the heart of *Eretz Yisrael*.

As a founder of the Salute to Israel parade thirty-four years ago, what a feeling of pride it is to celebrate the fiftieth anniversary of the Jewish State on this auspicious occasion.

Am Yisrael chai! Long live the people of Israel! Long live the State of Israel!

YOVEL PLUS ONE

Fifty-one years old! Israel's Jubilee plus one! In Hebrew, 51 is "*nun*" – "*aleph*." "Nun" is 50 and "Aleph" is 1. The *aleph*, the first letter of the alphabet, represents the beginning of a new 50-year cycle for the Jewish State. On balance, despite overwhelming problems and obstacles, the first fifty years were near miraculous: 750% population growth, unbelievable achievements of the Israel Defense Forces, remarkable economic growth and extra-ordinary development of health services, medical research, science, technology, social services, education, culture and the media.

All this, but still no peace. *Aleph* is one and we are one with Israel – one people with one heart. The *Aleph* stands for rejuvenation of efforts to bring about real peace with full security for the State of Israel.

The *Aleph* also means, "champion" – leading the way to harmony and unity among the citizens of Israel and toward mutually beneficial relationships with all Jews the world over.

The *Aleph* means "mastery" – continuing the progress of excellence in all fields of human endeavor. And, the aleph means training, teaching – inspiring our youth to love and support Israel.

Finally, *Aleph* says, "many happy returns" on the fifty-first birthday. May the next fifty years bring about the full realization of the Jewish Zionist dream.

CHAPTER 5

VISIT TO AUSCHWITZ

[Note: From 1988 to 1994, as thousands assembled silently in line according to the countries of the participating youth, I would blow the Shofar to signal the beginning of the March of the Living.]

THE *SHOAH* MESSAGE OF THE *SHOFAR*

The *shofar* today has a three-fold message for the Jewish people and the world at large. The opening blast – the *tekiah* – proclaims that this year's *shofar* blowing in Auschwitz has special significance.

The broken *shevarim* sound represents the broken heart of the Jewish nation as it mourns the victims of the Holocaust. It decries the degradation and dehumanization of our people by the Nazis.

The staccato *t'ru-ah* says to the world: "In the moment of our greatest despair, the Jewish people had the vision, the vitality and the dedication to establish a Jewish State whose fiftieth anniversary we proudly celebrate next week. The State of Israel brought us – 'from deep darkness to great light.'" From the ashes of *Auschwitz-Birkenau*, we go to Israel to celebrate the rebirth of our nation.

With the final *shofar* blast – the *tekiah gedolah* – go our fervent prayers for a real lasting peace with security for the land of Israel and the people of Israel. *Am Yisrael chai.*

MARCH OF SILENCE

Throughout Jewish history, since biblical times, the *Shofar* has heralded crucial events. And today, with the sounding of the *Shofar*, the March of the Living will commence.

We march in total reverent silence – without rhythmic beat, without cadence counting, without talking, without singing, without a sound.

As we march together, we unite with our past – with the souls of our brothers and sisters, of blessed memory. We march on the very same route, in the very same path in which two million Jews marched to their eternity – from *Auschwitz* to *Birkenau* – from their living hell to their violent deaths. And, we walk in the very same steps in which they walked in order to pay homage to their martyrdom, their dignity, their heroism.

We march with heads bowed in sacred memory. As representatives of Jewish youth the world over, we bow our heads to tell them, as they gaze down upon us from their heavenly abode, that we are here on *Yom Hashoah v'hag'vurah*. We bear testimony that *Am Yisrael chai* – the Jewish people lives.

With a thunderous march of silence – the March of the Living – we proclaim: *anachnu poh*. We are here! We are here!

REMEMBERING MUST BE PERSONAL

Zakhor! Gedenk! Remember!

Did you ever stop to think about this motto for Holocaust Day? To whom does it speak?

Zakhor! Gedenk! Remember!

Is it addressed to the vast majority of people who are either too young to know about the *Shoah* or were far removed in other continents of the world and did not experience the Nazi onslaught in Europe?

They have nothing vivid, nothing personal, and nothing real to remember about the Holocaust.

Does it speak to those who were transported to crematoria or were made to live in death camps or in hellish ghettos in outrageously primitive conditions and yet survived the Nazi's final solution? The survivors don't need any reminders to remember. Their bodies and their memories bear the eternal scars of the Hitlerian nightmare. What is more, most of the survivors want to forget that tragic period of their lives.

And yet we persist in repeating *Zakhor! Gedenk!* Remember!

And for good reason: The *Haggadah* at the *Seder* table tells us: "In every generation each person must look at himself as if he himself was saved from the bondage of Egypt." To understand and to appreciate the holiday of *Pesah* each Jew must have a very personal view and feeling of Egyptian slavery.

And, in a similar vein, in our generation each of us must consider himself or herself as *sh-erit hapletah*, a surviving remnant of European Jewry that was wiped off the face of the earth.

Each of us must feel the torture of the Nazi war machine – smell the stench of burning bodies and the piercing odor of the gas rising in our nostrils. Each us of must hear the SS men barking out their orders – "left! right! left! right! – to the showers, to the gas chamber, to the gravesite, to the firing squad." Each of us must feel the butt of the Nazi rifle crushing our skulls and the bayonet piecing the swollen bellies of our babies and young children. Each of us must see our loved ones snatched away, never to be seen or heard from again. Yes, each must feel the unbelievable pain and indescribable suffering of the victims of the Holocaust.

Each, too, must feel the heroism of their lives and deaths; their hope, their dreams, their valiant struggle for life.

Only then can we understand the meaning of the *Shoah*, the most tragic period in Jewish diaspora history, and of modern mankind as a whole. Only then can we know the meaning of the words *Zakhor! Gedenk!!* Remember! And only then can we comprehend the monstrousness of the Nazi atrocities, the vicious terror, and the sadistic, demonic barbarianism that defies description.

Only then will we understand the depth of the agony of *Kristallnacht*, the beatings and rapings, the burning synagogues, the Nazi deception, fraud and massacre, the tragedy of human guinea pigs and human soap, the feeling of crippled half-dead men and women transported from one death camp to another – of victims forced to dig a pit, undress and stand at the edge of the grave as they were mowed down in cold blood. Only then can we remember Treblinka, Auschwitz, Buchenwald, Bergen-Belsen and their masses of wretched humans torn between despair and hope. Only then can we remember the pride of the yellow badge, the heroism of the Warsaw ghetto fighters and the courageous partisanism, the heroic feats of the Resistance movement.

CHAPTER 6

THOUGHTS ABOUT HEBREW WORDS

These ten *divrei meelah* were prepared for session chairmen and moderators of the General Assembly of the Council of Jewish Welfare Funds which took place in Jerusalem in l998. As part of its program to help create closer ties between Israel and the Diaspora and to help build unity among Jews through Hebrew Language and Culture, The National Center for the Hebrew Language distributed brief one-minute *divrei meelah* (*d'var meelah* is a thought about a Hebrew word) for use by session leaders, chairpersons, and moderators at the beginning of their respective sessions. It was hoped that the cumulative effect of these brief statements would help enhance the proceedings of the General Assembly.

Each *d'var meelah* was introduced with the following note: "Attached are ten *divrei meelah* – thoughts about Hebrew words – for you to read to your group. Please choose a *d'var meelah* and feel free to edit it as you deem fit or incorporate it into your remarks."

IVRIT

Here we are in Israel, witness to a linguistic miracle. One hundred years ago, a handful of Jews spoke Hebrew. Fifty years ago, there were several hundred thousand Hebrew speakers. Today, after absorbing immigrants from seventy countries for whom Hebrew was not a spoken language, Israel is the home of five million Jews and one million non-Jews who are conversant with the Jewish national language.

The word "Hebrew" is the translation of the Hebrew term, "*Ivri.*" Abraham, the first Jew, was known as *Avraham Ha-Ivri* – Abraham the Hebrew. There are several explanations for the derivation of the word *Ivri*. The most popular interpretation is that Abraham was descended from *Ever* – the great grandson of Noah. Hebrew – *Ivrit* – was the language *Ever* spoke. Abraham and his descendants have made it their national tongue ever since.

We begin this session with a toast to the oldest, continuous spoken language of mankind.

YERUSHALAYIM

What's in a name? As far as Jerusalem is concerned, there is much ancient history to a name. The *Midrash* notes interestingly that Jerusalem encompasses the spot where the binding of Isaac occurred. Abraham called that place *Yir'eh*. "He will see," meaning, "The Lord *will see to it* that a lamb is available for an offering" (instead of my son Isaac). As noted in Genesis, the ruler of this place before Abraham was "Malki Zedek, the King of Shalem." Shem, the son of Noah, called that place *Shalem*.

The Almighty was confronted with a challenge. What shall he name that place? Said the Lord: "Behold I will name that place *Yir'eh Shalem*, as they both called it. If I call it *Yir'eh*, as did Abraham, Shem will be angered. If I call it *Shalem*, Abraham will be angry. Therefore, I'll call it *Y'ru-shalem* (Jerusalem) to satisfy both of them.

God wanted to make sure that peace prevailed between Shem and Abraham. The combined name *Jerusalem* is a compromise for peace – a lesson for our times.

YOVEL

Here, in the Holy City, we are attending an historic conference celebrating the fiftieth anniversary of the State of Israel. The number

"50" has important biblical antecedents. In the Bible, the fiftieth year is called *Yovel* – jubilee. The Bible notes: "You shall hallow the fiftieth year by proclaiming liberty to all the inhabitants of the land. It shall be a jubilee year for you."

Interestingly, the word *yovel* also means a ram's horn, a *shofar*. At the foot of Mount Sinai, the Israelites were instructed, "when the ram's horn sounds a long blast, may you go up the mountain." Thereafter, in biblical times, the *shofar* was sounded "during days of celebration and over peace offerings." This dual connotation – *yovel* as jubilee, and *yovel* as a ram's horn sounded over peace offerings – has a special message on the fiftieth anniversary of Israel.

GOLAH

Diaspora meets Israel. The West meets the East. *Yehudah Halevi*, 12th century poet and philosopher epitomized the yearning of diaspora Jews to be in the land of their forefathers. *Leebee ba-Mizrach, va-annochee b'sof Ma'arav.* "My heart is in the East, while I am in the far West."

There are several Hebrew terms for the word *diaspora*. *Golah* (or *Galut*) refers to a people in exile. *Hutz La-aretz* means simply "outside of the Land of Israel." *Tfutzot* is a reference to the lands of dispersion where Jews reside.

While each term has a different connotation, they all imply that *Eretz Yisrael* is the Jewish homeland – an important reason for the GA convening here this year.

YISRAEL

The GA takes place in Israel. It might have convened in Judah, or Judea, or in Palestine, or in *Eretz Ha-tzvi*, or in the same place with a different name. But, the founding fathers of the modern Jewish State wisely chose the name *Israel*.

Firstly, the biblical name of the Holy Land is *Eretz Yisrael*, the land of Israel. The Jewish people, in early biblical times, before the destruction of the first Temple, were called *B'nai Yisrael*, the children of Israel.

Yisrael is the name given to our forefather Jacob. "Your name shall no longer be Jacob (a name derived from the word 'heel') but *Yisrael*" – a God-fighter – because "you strove with God and with men and prevailed," said the angel with whom Jacob wrestled on his way to meet Esau his brother.

That encounter between Jacob and Esau turned out to be a meeting of peace between two sibling rivals. And, here we are in *Yisrael*, hoping to see peace in our times between the descendants of Esau and Jacob.

L'SHON KODESH

Here we are meeting in the land of the Jewish national language, Hebrew – *Ivrit* – is known also as *L'shon Kodesh* – the Holy tongue. The sages of the Talmud differentiated between *L'shon Kodesh* and *L'shon Hakhamim* – the language of the wise. *L'shon Kodesh* refers to the language of the Bible and the language of the post biblical Judaic texts. Over the centuries, there were Jews who would use Hebrew only for Torah study and for prayer. Even today, in Israel, there are members of the Jewish faith who believe that Hebrew should be used solely for Jewish learning and liturgy.

L'shon Hakhamim, however, refers to post-biblical Hebrew as a vernacular as a vehicle for secular Hebraic culture as well as the language of the Jewish heritage.

Hebrew, in all its formats – Torah study, prayer, Judaic literacy, medieval, contemporary and modern Hebrew literature, and conversation – has been a major source of Jewish vitality and is largely responsible for Jewish survival in the lands of our dispersion.

And, now, one of our goals is to build unity of the Jewish people through Hebrew.

TZION

Hatikvah, the national anthem of the Jewish people and the State of Israel, refers to the Jewish State as *Eretz Tzion Vee'rushalayim* – the Land of *Zion* and Jerusalem.

The term *Tzion* has rich historic meaning for Jews. At one and the same time, it means Zion, Jerusalem, the Land of Israel and the Jewish people. In the synagogue, as did *Isaiah*, we sing, *Kee Mee-Tzion taytzay Torah* – "From *Zion* shall come forth the Torah," indicating that the Land of Israel is the cradle of our heritage. Over the ages, Jews prayed *U-va L'tzion Go'el* – "May the Redeemer come to *Zion*."

In contemporary times *Hovevei Tzion* – the lovers of *Zion* – at the end of the nineteenth century were the first modern Zionists. Their efforts and the strivings of the Zionist leaders between 1880 and 1948 brought about the establishment of the modern Jewish State. And, now we meet in *Eretz Tzion Vee'rushalayim*.

AHDUT

The underlying theme of this year's GA, indeed, the programmatic context of our conference, is unity in diversity. The Hebrew word for unity is *ahdut* – a term deriving from the three-letter word that spells *ehad* – which means "one."

The popular liturgical poem *yigdal*, often sung at Friday night services, refers to the Almighty as *ehad*. "There is no unity like His oneness." The importance of unity among Jews is highlighted in biblical and post-biblical history. Rashi, the illustrious 11th century biblical commentator, notes that when the Israelites encamped at the foot of Mount Sinai they were united, *k'ish ehad b'lev ehad* – like one man with one heart. These characteristics of solidarity and harmony qualified our ancestors to receive the Torah. This kind of communal posture should be a source of inspiration to Jews everywhere as we cope with the challenges of our diversity.

ZIKAYNIM

The GA is a modern expression of a biblical procedure. As a meeting of leaders, it reminds us of the assemblage of the *zikaynim* – the elders – in biblical times. *Zaken* – literally means "old" or "aged." In Ethics of the Fathers, a sage suggests that *ben sheeshim le-ziknah*. At age 60 one attains old age." But, in the Bible the term *zaken* refers to the "elders of the community, as in *ziknay ha-edah* or as *ziknay ha-ir*, the town elders." The elders were those persons endowed with knowledge, insight and experience who were esteemed by their fellow Israelites because of their leadership ability. That is why another Talmudic sage underscores that *zaken* refers to a person – one who has acquired wisdom, and as a result of his knowledge and experience, is fit to lead.

And, here we are *ziknay ha-edah* – the "elders" of the American Jewish community – in an historic convention preparing to make historic decisions.

KNESSET

Our gathering in Israel this week can rightfully be called a *knesset* – which means "assembly" or "convention." The term *knesset* derives from the verb *kanness* – to convene, to congregate, and to assemble. The word *knesset* has much historical meaning for the Jewish people. In the Talmud, the Hebrew nation is known as *Knesset Yisrael*. During the Second Temple, the Supreme Council of the Jewish people was known as *Knesset Gedolah* – the Great *Knesset*. And, since Talmudic times, the synagogue was called *Bet Knesset*, the House of Assembly.

Given the historic meaning of the term *knesset*, it is no wonder that the Israel parliament was given this name. To be sure, its nomenclature casts upon the **Knesset** vital political leadership – weighty national, communal, cultural responsibility – to consider the needs of the entire Jewish people.

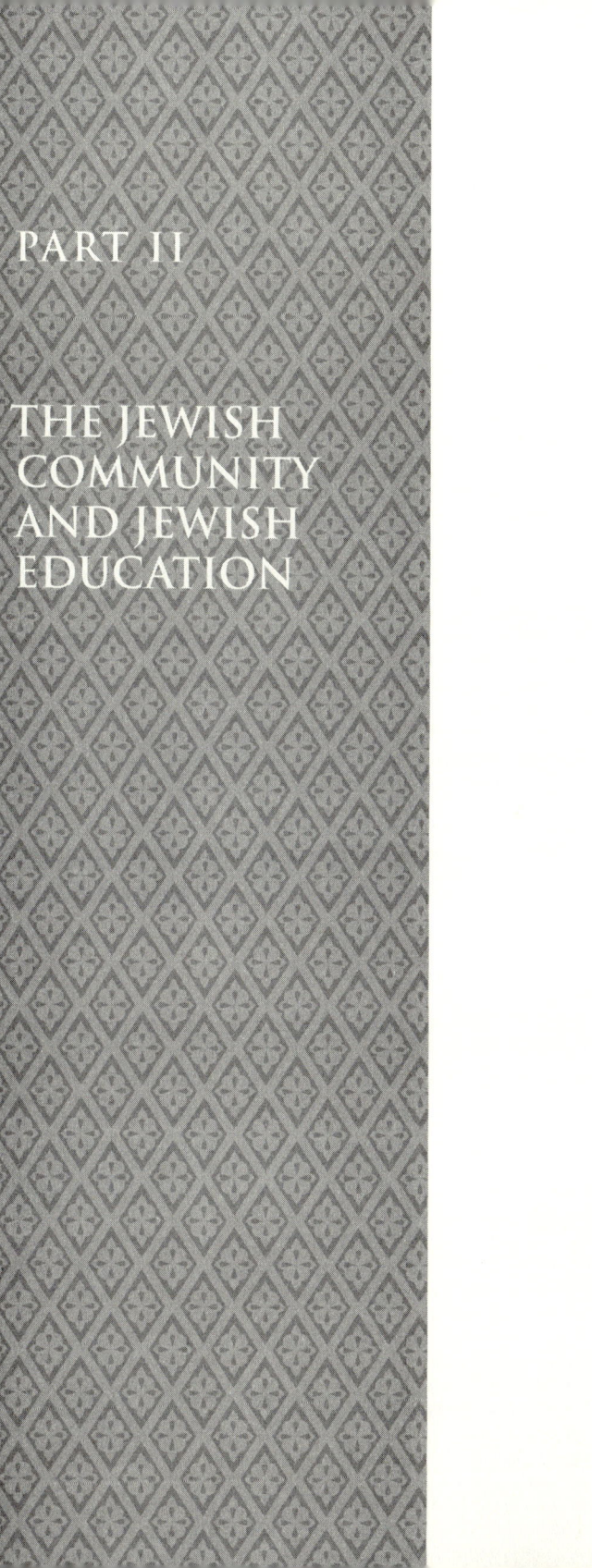

PART II

THE JEWISH COMMUNITY AND JEWISH EDUCATION

CHAPTER 1

CHANGING PRIORITIES IN EDUCATION

It is a special pleasure for me to address this commencement. I've always wanted to participate in graduation exercises of the Hebrew College. I left Boston – my native city – after graduating from the Prozdor – to study in New York. Although I'm proud to be an alumnus of another Hebrew college – The Teachers Institute of Yeshiva University – I always felt I was missing something by not have a degree from Boston Hebrew College. Today, I feel fulfilled in that regard, and am grateful for this opportunity to be an integral part of these commencement exercises.

I want to use this opportunity, as well, to pay tribute to my good friend and colleague, and your esteemed president, Eli Grad. Indeed, the continuous, well-earned reputation of the Hebrew College is due, in no small measure, to his selfless commitment and creative leadership.

I began writing my talk for this occasion on a flight from Washington to Albany last week. The gentleman next to me noticed that I wrote "Changing Priorities in Education" on top of a blank piece of paper.

"Excuse me for being nosey," he said, glancing at my pad of

paper, "Do you really think priorities in education are changing?" He obviously viewed the word "Changing" in the title of my address as an adjective – which suggests that I would speak about priorities that are in the process of transformation.

That may be so. Priorities are changing slowly in Jewish education. In fact, the Hebrew title of my talk, *Shinuyim bim'gammot hahinuch*, indicates that changes are taking place in Jewish educational priorities. However, taking the speaker's prerogative, I will consider the word, "changing" as a dynamic verb – suggesting that we *must* change priorities in Jewish education.

During the last two years, American education has been inundated with studies and reports highlighted by the best-seller, "Nation at Risk." Reacting to the spate of reports, Harold Howe II, former U.S. Commissioner of Education wrote, "Suddenly, corporate barons, presidential candidates, university presidents, governors, and legislative leaders in Congress and in State capitols have mounted a crusade to improve schools. Will the governors, the corporate leaders and the others who are now fanning the fires of educational reform be willing to stay with that important task over time?"

In response, Howe said, "The kinds of changes now being recommended will not come easily or quickly because *they challenge vested interests*. It is essential that the interest of groups outside education be sustained and, particularly that business leadership remain supportive, since one necessity for educational improvement is more *money* to support that improvement."

Howe's blunt analysis and recommendation apply with particular force to Jewish education. There has been a great awakening in the Jewish community – especially among Jewish communal leaders – about the need for quality Jewish education. The changes in communal attitude regarding the importance of the Jewish school can best be illustrated by the Jewish community's position *vis-à-vis* Jewish all day education – the brightest and most promising aspect of Jewish cultural and religious life in America.

It is hard for us now to imagine that as late as the 1960s,

major Jewish leaders – including educators and leaders of ideological movements – opposed the Jewish day school. Still gripped with the *melting pot* ideal of America (which has been replaced so dramatically by the concept of *cultural pluralism*), these men and women of good will fought vigorously against the day school because they believed it was *un-American* and would have an adverse effect upon the Jewish community.

How wrong they were! They themselves are now the first to recognize the fallacy of their thinking. The growth of the Jewish day school has been truly remarkable, especially when we consider that Orthodox Jews developed it against a backdrop of opposition and doubt from the rest of the community.

As the Jewish day school movement continues to develop, the schools increasingly reflect the diversity of the Jewish community. While about 85% of the day school population is enrolled in Orthodox-sponsored schools, there are as many kinds of Jewish all day programs as there are ideological shadings in the spectrum of American Jewry – from Hasidic to Reform and general-secular.

Jewish communal support in the form of local Federation allocations to the day school has grown from $6 million in 1963 to $22 million in 1983. To be sure, during this period, day school enrollment more than doubled. Even taking into account the effect of inflation during this period, we have to recognize the considerable increase in financial aid to the day school by local Federations.

Several communities have been blessed with private business leaders who have facilitated and supported the growth of this vital institution. Your honorees, Maurice H. Saval and Elliot B. Shoolman, are exemplars of this kind of individual patronage. Without their avid backing and outstanding generosity, the Maimonides School and Solomon Schechter Day School simply could not exist.

Without the leadership and needed financial assistance given by the Jewish leaders in other communities, the Jewish Day School movement – now 586 schools and 120,000 pupils strong – could not have made it.

This brings me back to Harold Howe's plea regarding the absolute need for "groups outside education, particularly business leadership," to be supportive of education. Howe probably doesn't know it, but the idea of partnership between business and education, between philanthropy and schooling is as old as the Jewish people. Jewish tradition recognized that if Jewish life is to continue, this partnership must be an absolute priority.

Jewish life in medieval and contemporary times in Europe and North Africa, where the overwhelming majority of Jews lived, was replete with examples of this partnership. Witness the volume of Responsa and *Takanot Kehillot* – the communal regulations – and the minute books of the *Hevrot Talmud Torah* outlining the respective roles of the *gabbaim* and *parnissim* (the communal leaders) and the *melamdim* (the teachers). These kinds of partnerships provide interesting models for making Jewish education a priority communal concern even today.

The greatest challenge to Jewish communal leadership in America is to make this combination a vibrant reality in Jewish life. And, this, as Howe notes for American education, is not easy to accomplish because, to use his words, it *"challenge(s) vested interests."*

The problem on the American Jewish scene is that the "vested interests" are good humanitarian concerns. And who can argue with support for humanitarian causes? Nevertheless, if the American Jewish community is unable to raise substantially more dollars for its variety of local, national and global causes, including Israel, there will be no alternative but to change priorities in Federation allocations. Without dramatically increasing the salaries of teachers, we will have no teachers. Certainly we will not have high-caliber teachers, or quality education, even in our day schools and yeshivot. And, without effective Jewish education there will be no committed Jews to support humanitarian causes.

Just three weeks ago one of the leading day schools in the country interviewed 35 candidates for *one* high school position in Jewish studies and found all of them unqualified. Another leading day school just couldn't find anyone to apply for teaching jobs. Talented young people are simply not choosing to enter a profession that is low paying, offers little or no security, provides few if any benefits, cannot guarantee professional growth opportunities, and offers little in the way of communal appreciation and social status.

Commenting on the same problem in general education, Walter Cronkite recently said: "Imagine any self-respecting doctor working for that kind of money ($22,000, the average annual salary of *full-time* teachers)! You don't have to be a masochist to be a teacher, but it certainly helps." Imagine any self-respecting *Jewish* professional working for $16,000 (the average annual salary of full-time Hebrew teachers)!

The information reported to my office regarding the "mission impossible" of the two day schools I just cited prompted me last week to write an editorial for the next issue of the *Jewish Education* magazine entitled, "Warning, this building may soon be closed!" The possibility of this happening to many Jewish day schools is real – *very real*. The only way to change the situation is to change the priorities of Jewish communal fund allocations and to find more Lavals and Shoolmans. In the words of a hometown Boston boy, John Adams, the second president of the United States, "The whole people must take upon themselves the education of the whole people and must be willing to bear the expense of it."

This brings me to the next priority, which can best be labeled "reach and teach." Unless we *reach* our children, we can't *teach* them!

The truth of the matter is that we have not succeeded in teaching the bulk of our students in our supplementary schools and even many students in our day schools because we have not reached them. In speaking of the failure of public schools, David Seeley, former executive of the New York State Public School Association, underscored the fact that education is virtually an "undeliverable merchandise" for many children because they are not motivated sufficiently to want to learn. The problem, he notes, is that teachers work too hard at teaching, while pupils don't work hard enough at learning. He concludes that you can't teach children. You can only "learn" them. The only way that this can happen is through the encouragement, help, and motivation children receive in their homes. Then, and only then, will good teachers be able to do the rest of the job.

This, then, points the way to the next priority – forging alliances between schools and parents. Our primary emphasis in Jewish schools has been, as logic dictated, on children. However, it is clear now that we must change our emphasis and target our educational efforts at the *families* of our students, particularly at those families whose Jewish commitment and affiliation are marginal. Unless these parents are turned on to Jewish education; unless they associate themselves fully with the goals of the school which their children attend; unless they become knowledgeable partners in the Jewish schooling of their children, Jewish education simply cannot be effective.

To be sure, the Jewish home is a model of support for secular education. When I recently addressed the New York State Board of Regents Bicentennial Convocation, I chose to speak on a Jewish theme: "Education in Early Judaic Sources." At the close of the ceremonies, Henry Steele Commager, one of the honorary degree recipients, was eager to learn more about education in Jewish tradition. I must say I had a wonderful half-hour with this great American historian. He is convinced that the American universities which excel most are those that have high percentages of Jewish students. Commager is right, because most Jews have transposed the traditional intellectual and cultural interest and support for *Jewish* study to the arena of secular learning.

This transposition has made possible the rapid upward professional, academic and economic mobility of immigrant Jews in a free society. But, at the same time, it threatens the quality of Jewish life and Jewish continuity.

Children realize early in their school years that their parents highly value general and professional education. They also readily perceive that their parents feel that Jewish study is of no real consequence other than leading to a perfunctory Bar or Bat Mitzvah ceremony. And so, the Jewish school is saddled with the burden of trying to motivate children to take seriously that which their families dismiss as not particularly vital or relevant to their adult lives.

After the first two years of supplementary school, when the novelty of Jewish schooling wears off, the scenario is clear. By and large, notwithstanding the efforts of their teachers, Jewish children can't wait for their Jewish school experience to be over. After all, there are more important things for them to do with their spare time. Then again, there is not much one can do in 3, 4, 5 hours a week of unmotivated exposure to learning. Benjamin Bloom, leading American educational taxonomer has emphasized that "Time on Task" is needed to master any subject – particularly those requiring an affective, emotion-laden dimension.

There are two ways to resolve this problem – each calling for a dramatic change in educational focus. The first way is to reach parents when they enroll their children in congregational school. This requires an entirely new orientation towards Jewish education, which, for most synagogues, means the reorganization of our synagogue structure. Instead of rabbis, assistant rabbis, cantors, principals and teachers all plying their trade as individuals, they must form professional family educator partnerships, becoming members of family educator teams – planning together and working together to impact the family as a unit – not pupils and adults separately.

This podium is not the place to discuss the methodology of such an approach. Suffice it to say that this new thrust must become a priority concern if supplementary Jewish schooling is to be effective. While the family is the primary shaper of Jewish identity and commitment, peers can exert powerful influence. The second strategy, therefore, calls for developing and nurturing alternative environments in *loco parentis*.

Research in education has amply demonstrated the power of the learning climate. One of the advantages of the day school is its all-embracing (7–9 hours per day) environment. The Jewish day school provides an opportunity for total immersion in a Jewish atmosphere. Appropriately utilized, this significant amount of time in a Jewish environment can create conditions necessary to motivate Jewish learning and practice.

For the supplementary school, alternative environments must be developed additively through weekend retreats and *Shabbatonim* – which have a proven track record of success. In addition, Jewish educational summer camping – like Yavneh – and a summer of yearlong experience in Israel must become a regular part of Jewish schooling.

These recommendations are not new by any means. But enough members of the Jewish community have not taken them seriously. They must become priority concerns.

So important is the "alternative environment" approach that I have suggested substituting – for grades 4 and up of the supplementary school – one weekend in a *Shabbaton* setting for a week of school per month– eliminating three formal school sessions each month. Instead, in this setup, pupils will spend 9 weekends – Friday afternoon through Sunday afternoon – in a Jewish environment, interacting with committed high school and college students who serve as Jewish models for them. They will eat together, sing and dance together, play and pray together and learn together. The total number of hours they will be together in a Jewish atmosphere during one year of such a program will be double the amount of school time in a full year of three-day-a-week sessions in a congregational school.

"Time on Task," an exciting atmosphere, models of Jewish commitment, and Jewish socialization are the earmarks of such an approach. But it costs money. And this brings us back full circle to the first set of priorities for Jewish education.

To sum up – for Jewish education in the 1980s and 1990s to be effective, we need to change our priorities. These include developing real, vibrant partnerships between Issachar and Zebulun on the community-wide level; and meaningful alliances between parents and school and active partnerships between rabbis, teachers and principals on the school level – all in order to create and sustain the necessary conditions which motivate Jewish learning, those that help us *reach* and *teach*.

As far as you graduates are concerned, no matter what your present or future roles in Jewish life in America or in Israel may be, one thing is clear – you must take the lead in helping to assure that Jewish education becomes a priority of Jewish life everywhere. I'm sure that your Hebrew College experience has had a significant impact upon you in this regard.

Famed sociologist F. Stuart Chapin, once noted, "Do not ask if a man has been through college; ask if a college has been through him – if he is a walking university." This is your challenge – to carry forward the banner of Jewish learning as true disciples of Issachar.

Some of you may become prosperous Zebuluns. Hopefully, your partnership with your fellow Issachars will have a significant impact on Jewish life.

Together may you all go from strength to strength!

CHAPTER 2

MARKETING, EVALUATING & FUNDING JEWISH EDUCATION

INTRODUCTION

I was privileged to have my latest book published just several weeks ago. At an earlier meeting today, I gave a copy of it to a lay leader's leader, Barbi Weinberg, and, as you heard, she asked that I explain why I titled this book on contemporary Jewish education *Issachar American Style*.

Barbi believes that my explanation would be an appropriate way to begin my talk.

Issachar was the ninth son of Jacob. When Moses blessed the twelve tribes he coupled the blessing to Issachar with the blessing to Zevulun: *"s'm'ach Zevulun b'tzetecha"* ("be happy Zevulun in your goings out") *"v'Issachar b'o-halecha"* ("and Issachar in your tents"), meaning – "You Zevulun, do well in your commercial ventures; make a lot of money in order that Issachar can continue studying in the tents of learning. In Jewish tradition, we've always coupled Zevulun, the facilitator, with Issachar, the educator.

Indeed, Nachmanides speaks to this combination in his commentary on the Book of Numbers. The Children of Israel left Egypt in 4 groups of 3 tribes each. Leading the march were the tribes positioned in the East – not the oldest three – Reuven,

Shimon and Levi, as we would expect, – but Yehudah, Issachar and Zevulun.

Here Nachmanides makes an interesting observation. In order for the Israelites to make it in the desert, to survive in the wilderness, and then thrive as a nation when they get to the Land of Israel, they needed three kinds of leadership. They needed good leaders who can move people, who can work with them, who can organize them. That's the tribe of Yehudah – *ba'al meluchah*. Then they required educational leadership to give substance to their communal leadership. That's the tribe of Issachar – *ba'al Torah*. But Issachar could not succeed unless he had financial support. He needed adequate funding. He needed the tribe of Zevulun – *ba'al ashirut*.

This threesome King Solomon called "the threefold cord that cannot be rent asunder." *V'ha-hut hameshulash lo bimhayra yinatek*. Good communal leadership, sound education experience, and adequate philanthropic support are the winning combination for Jewish continuity and enhanced Jewish living. In light of this interpretation, it is apparent why my book on contemporary Jewish education is entitled *Issachar American Style*.

The *Talmud* helps me justify *my* reason for being here. *Yoter me'ma sheha-egel rotzeh linok, ha-parah rotzah l'hanik* – "more than the calf wants to suckle milk, the cow wants to give it." And, this cow always wants to give milk. I have been asked to address three topics: marketing Jewish education; evaluating Jewish education; and funding Jewish education *a la* New York's Fund for Jewish Education. Three separate subjects but interrelated.

MARKETING JEWISH EDUCATION

Do you remember Sputnik, 1957? Do you know that Sputnik was one of the most important turning points for education in America? Until 1957, education in America was considered as a consumer good. (It's still considered like a consumer good by many Americans.) After Sputnik, when we realized we had to compete with the Russians and we had to help universities do the kind of research that was necessary to compete effectively with them, Americans began to view education as an investment. We had to invest significantly in education – in higher education and in research – to produce the effects needed to compete with the Russians in the arenas of science, defense and military strategy.

Marketing Jewish education requires Jewish communal leaders to change the concept of Jewish education from that of a consumer good purchased by parents to an activity in which Jewish communal leadership must invest heavily.

Marketing Jewish education speaks to two audiences. First, it speaks to the people that have the means to make it succeed. This audience must find ways to make Jewish education a communal priority. Jewish communal leadership must support it as a priority with the same urgency that African-Americans consider their problems and with the same urgency that Jews for Jesus freaks and missionary groups invest millions of dollars on missionary activities to Jews. Do we invest that kind of Jewish communal money to make Jews out of Jews? If we want to market Jewish education effectively, the providers have to be seized with a feeling of urgency about the need to make the necessary changes in Jewish education and to provide the necessary support to make them possible.

The second audience is composed of the consumers and clients. Some people call this kind of marketing "recruitment". Others refer to it as reaching out to children and parents. I would like to share with you an outreach program developed by the Board of Jewish Education of Greater New York 14 years ago.

RECRUITING STUDENTS

According to our best estimates, 35% of the Jewish school population, 5–18 years of age, would not be exposed to formal Jewish schooling. We decided to use Madison Avenue techniques to reach unaffiliated Jewish families with children. We weren't reaching them through synagogue bulletins, through Center bulletins or through local newspapers. "Let's reach them through the major newspapers, television, and radio," we said. Accordingly, we mounted a media recruitment campaign during the first two weeks of September 1973. You may remember some of our full page ads in the New York Times, "If you're Jewish, chances are, your grandchildren will not be Jewish." "When your child hears the word *shofar* this *Rosh Hashanah*, will he think it's the person who is going to drive his parents to a concert?" We developed some forty messages over a period of 12 years. Between 1973 and 1985, the recruitment campaign brought into the Jewish school system in Greater New York approximately *10,000* Jewish children. Unfortunately, we had to terminate it because it became financially prohibitive. In retrospect, the campaign was able to reach parents who somehow wanted to be reached. The proof is the enrollment in Jewish schools of some *10,000* children who may never have been exposed to formal Jewish schooling without it.

MARKETING BUREAU SERVICES

There is another dimension to marketing Jewish education. Steve Huberman asked, "How do you market the services of the Board of Jewish Education of Greater New York?" First, lay and professional leadership of the bureau must believe fervently that Jewish education is the top Jewish communal priority. Second, the services must be designed to respond to specific needs. When I assumed the professional helmsmanship of the Board of Jewish Education, I proposed that we transform it from an organization that dispenses general services to an agency that provides specialized services. If specialization is good enough for medicine and good enough for law, then it should be good enough for Jewish education. Accordingly, we developed a service approach based almost entirely on the concept of specialization. As a result, we now have eight specialized centers and a variety of other specialized programs. The areas of specialization include, among others, early childhood, family, media, micro-computer, outreach, special education, management assistance, government relations, curriculum materials development, testing, resource development and social planning. Specialized in-service programs for educators are provided through our Principals' Center in conjunction with Harvard, Columbia and the University of Pennsylvania, and through our five Teachers' Centers.

The effect of specialization has been remarkable. In the early 1970s, for example, fifty early childhood teachers and directors would participate in an annual early childhood education conference. In 1988, 1,800 early childhood teachers and directors are regularly involved in workshops, institutes and conferences. During each of the last several years we had to turn away three to four hundred early childhood educators who wanted to pay $35 to participate in the annual all day conference simply because we had no room. There is no synagogue in New York that has enough space for the plenary sessions, exhibits, workshops and seminars. We don't have the money to spend on hotel facilities – nor would we. What is the key to marketing Early Childhood Education services? Heightened specialized quality programming and staffing!

Another example of marketing bureau services. Fifteen years ago there were literally no schools that requested media assistance from BJE. To be sure, most Jewish educators were threatened by the idea of hardware in their classrooms. In the 1987–88 school year, BJE provided 3,700 media consultations and previews. If we had sufficient funds we could have responded to many more requests for media assistance. What is the secret to this marketing success? A highly specialized quality program and quality staff!

In the 1970s, Jewish communal leaders in New York did not think that Jewish special education was an activity that should be funded by Federation. By and large, they believed that children with special needs should be served only through general education and that the Jewish community's responsibility for retarded Jewish youth and learning disabled children does not extend beyond the provision of human services. The marketing challenge here was huge.

Nothing succeeds like success. A highly skilled specialized staff and innovative programming now generate about a million dollars a year in outside grants for Jewish special education in addition to the $100,000 per year budgeted through UJA-Federation funding.

Our Teachers' Centers are another example of creative marketing. In 1976, we established our first Teachers' Center in a 10' × 10' room in Long Island. Presently, we have five teachers' centers, two of which are university-based. In Nassau County, Long Island, a former Jewish Community Center now serves as our Teachers' Center in that area. This past year, 1,600 teachers spent 60,000 hours voluntarily in the Teachers' Centers.

What does all this say about marketing educational services? It says that if you develop appropriate specialized quality responses to real needs you heighten school and community awareness of these needs and actually create a demand for service that responds to them.

I met with your bureau staff earlier this morning. I'm impressed with them as a group and as individual professionals. Los Angeles has the potential and the staffing. The marketing challenge essentially relates to specialized responses to the felt needs in the field. The appropriate responses market themselves.

EVALUATING JEWISH EDUCATION

My next topic deals with evaluation. There are two major dimensions of education. One relates to the cognitive domain, the other to the affective domain. The first suggests that we evaluate knowledge. The second posits that we assess attitudes and involvement. Public education invests heavily in testing pupil knowledge and recording achievement scores. Throughout the various state systems and local districts testing in all grades and all subjects has become a fetish.

To be sure, the testing programs in general education provide useful information about aspects of pupil progress. However, evaluation relating solely to the cognitive domain has its limitations. When we evaluate subject achievement, we do not appraise the child's total progress. We don't examine where he or she is going. We only evaluate what children have been taught, not what they are able to learn; and not their attitudes to learning and to life, for which school should be preparing them.

Besides assessing individual pupil progress, evaluation also means appraising the effectiveness of a school and a school system. Assessing the effectiveness of education is a favorite pastime of the American people. In every generation, new knowledge is added to our battery of information about school evaluation. This past decade and a half is no exception. The 1970s and 1980s are highlighted by Effective Schools Research activity that has added many new, creative ideas to the way we think about educational effectiveness.

EFFECTIVE SCHOOLS RESEARCH AND JEWISH EDUCATION

A quick insight into some of the contributions of Effective Schools Research to our understanding of good educational practice seems in order, particularly since Jewish education does not occur in a vacuum. What are some of the findings of Effective Schools Research that can inform our evaluation of Jewish schools?

To begin with, there is no unanimity about definitions of an effective school in public education. Some findings of Effective Schools Research are well supported; others are more speculative. Therefore, one cannot be totally conclusive about effectiveness. However, the consistency in the research findings across most of the studies suggests that there is general agreement about the key elements of good schooling.

Effective Schools Research demonstrates that a limited number of organizational-programmatic characteristics or correlates are consistently obtained in effective schools and are absent, in whole or in part, in the ineffective ones. While it is uncertain whether they are causal or not, the correlates are helpful to our understanding of school effectiveness. Essentially, they tell us that a good school has:

1. a clear focus and institutional mission, and a clearly defined curriculum;
2. strong administrative and instructional leadership;
3. a positive school climate and orderly atmosphere conducive to learning;

4. high expectations by principal and teachers for pupil growth;
5. sufficient and productive student time on task;
6. careful monitoring of pupil progress; and
7. good home-school relationships.

Now, you may say "let us take these correlates and adapt them to Jewish education. Let us use them as criteria for evaluating Jewish education." Jewish education is a voluntary system with much diversity. We cannot necessarily take one group of correlates and apply them equally to all schools.

THE JEWISH SUPPLEMENTARY SCHOOL STUDY

In New York, as in most other Jewish communities on the North American continent, between two-thirds and three-quarters of all Jewish school-age children, 5–18 years old, will receive some formal Jewish education. For most of these children – 70 percent of them – this means supplementary Jewish schooling, 2 to 6 hours per week, 30 to 35 weeks per year, for five or six years.

There has been a growing awareness over the past decade among Jewish lay leadership that this type of Jewish education needs serious attention. What aspects of Jewish supplementary education must be improved? How can we upgrade this form of schooling? These questions have stymied both lay and professional leadership.

To respond to these challenges, the Board of Jewish Education of Greater New York undertook what Professor Harold Himmelfarb, a foremost researcher on this subject, has called "the most methodologically rigorous and most comprehensive study to date on the topic." The three-year study included intensive lay and professional involvement, guided by a 13-member lay task force and administered competently by an 11-member professional staff study team. The lay-professional process was a crucial feature of the research.

SETTING THE STAGE: THE STAKEHOLDERS

In setting the stage for the Study we realized the need to consider all the stakeholders in the Jewish supplementary school. Essentially there are five categories of stakeholders.

1. **Consumers** – pupils exposed to formal and informal education strategies.
2. **Clients** – parents who determine the kind of Jewish education they will purchase for their children.
3. **Transmitters** – all Jewish education personnel – teachers, principals, rabbis, informal educators, educational consultants and specialists.
4. **Overseers or facilitators** – school committee members who have special roles in assuring that Jewish education is properly maintained, and;
5. **Providers or supporters** – trustees of synagogues and school boards, members and professional staff of federation allocation committees, and board members of central agencies for Jewish education.

We determined that it is absolutely necessary for all these stakeholders to be involved in the study.

THE STUDY SAMPLE

The Study Sample included 40 schools – large, medium and small; urban and suburban; Conservative, Orthodox, Reconstructionist and Reform.

THE STUDY METHODOLOGY

The Study Methodology comprised two research approaches. The first approach was a normative survey method (or a modified ethnographic procedure), which consisted of hundreds of interviews and observations, and included an examination of curricula and administrative forms.

The second approach was a measurement technique, a carefully developed three-part inventory of Jewish knowledge, Jewish involvement and Jewish attitudes-administered after being pilot-tested – to all pupils in all grades of the participating schools. This instrument was based upon the expectations of principals and developed to reflect the minimal levels of Jewish knowledge, Jewish involvement and Jewish attitudes expected of pupils by Bar and Bat Mitzvah age.

NORMATIVE SURVEY FINDINGS

The results of the Normative Survey clearly demonstrated a variety of disturbing realities.

- Jewish education is **not a real** synagogue priority.
- Rabbis are peripherally involved in the supplementary school. Most of them lack the necessary training to help make it effective.
- Principals are serious about their work. But, synagogue school principaling is just a part-time job. The majority of principals lack sufficient Judaic background and adequate knowledge of supervision and curriculum development for Jewish education.
- Teachers are generally committed to their work. But most of them lack *Jewish* pedagogic skills, and do not have sufficient Jewish knowledge. Eleven percent of the 426 teachers in our sample had no formal Jewish education at all. Teachers have no real institutional commitment. They are not in their respective synagogue schools long enough to make a lasting impact. The teachers in our sample spend an average of six hours per week in a given school. Moreover, turnover is great. Two-thirds of them taught in the same school two years or less.
- The overwhelming majority of parents provides little or no home support; nor are they interested. They send their offspring to the synagogue school purely for Bar and Bat Mitzvah.

post-findings consultants said, "their brains fell out during their pre-Bar/Bat Mitzvah **year**."
- The Jewish Knowledge Inventory results revealed a sharp increase in scores in all subjects by pupils who continued school beyond *Bar/Bat Mitzvah* and were in their seventh or eighth year of school.

The results of the *Jewish Involvement* and *Jewish Attitude Inventories* showed that:

- Jewish involvement of pupils is generally passive. It actually decreased from the second to sixth year of school.
- Jewish attitudes of pupils are generally neutral. The Jewish attitudes also decreased from the second to sixth year of school.
- While pupils, on the whole, did not exhibit high Jewish involvement and positive Jewish attitudes, they did not demonstrate negative Jewish involvement or negative Jewish attitudes. All responses regarding Jewish involvement and Jewish attitudes were pareve – passive or neutral – and went from high passive or high neutral to low passive and low neutral, but never to negative levels.

SCHOOL DIFFERENCES

In studying the different school variables, it became clear that school size, ideology, geography, and even number of hours of schooling made no difference in pupils' Jewish knowledge, Jewish attitudes, and Jewish involvement.

CONCLUSIONS

These findings led to our conclusions that the construct of Jewish supplementary schools seems to have a homogenizing, "parevizing" effect upon pupils. The average knowledge score is 49 percent. Jewish involvement is passive. And, Jewish attitudes are neutral.

Schools do a poor job in increasing Jewish knowledge in all subject areas; they show no success in guiding children toward

- And, pupils attend Jewish supplementary school primarily for *Bar/Bat Mitzvah*. While in most instances they seem well behaved, they are not motivated to learn, nor are they really learning.
- The persons involved with the school have no shared vision of curricular goals. Principals and teachers have the highest curricular goals. Rabbis, lay leaders and parents have the lowest expectations.
- There is little or no relationship between the subjects taught and the goals articulated by lay and professional leadership. For example, all the interviewees – principals, teachers, rabbis, lay leaders and parents – felt that the formation of a positive Jewish identity and positive Jewish attitudes is an important goal for the Jewish school. Yet, this aim was far from realized, as we shall see in a few moments.
- The overwhelming majority of schools have no structured curricula. Nor do they regularly follow the curricula prepared by their respective ideological movements.
- The time spent in school is both quantitatively and qualitatively inadequate.

INVENTORY FINDINGS

The Inventory findings are most revealing. The Inventory of Jewish Knowledge shows that:

- Pupil achievement scores were far below expectations. The overall average score was only 49 percent, whereas the expectation was that pupils would know the answers to all, or at least, most questions in the Jewish knowledge inventory.
- The overall increase in Jewish knowledge from the first year of school to the sixth year was only 10 percent. From the second year to the sixth year, Jewish knowledge scores increased by only 4 percent.
- In all subjects, but one, there was actually a drop in pupil scores from the fifth to the sixth year. Twelve- and 12-½-year-olds know less than eleven-and 11-½-year-olds. As one of the

Opportunity" involving some 600,000 people by saying that "Schools bring little influence to bear on a child's achievement that is independent of his background and social contacts."

Several years later, Christopher Jencks and his associates brought evidence that schools do "not make the kinds and magnitudes of difference which most observers had come to expect" and were not the vehicles of progressive social change, which most people had thought. Other studies have supported the Coleman and Jencks thesis that *family background* is the crucial influence on the effectiveness of schooling.

However, Effective Schools Research during the last two decades seems to challenge these conclusions. As I noted earlier in my remarks, this accumulation of research studies suggests that there are a variety of correlates of effective schooling. And, family support is only one of them.

A voluntary system of education, like Jewish supplementary schooling, must consider seriously the conclusions of both of these schools of thought.

Professor Benjamin Bloom, famed Chicago University educational taxonomer, points emphatically to this dual need in a fascinating study on talented people. He found that there are two features common to the backgrounds of all top performers he researched in the arts, sports, academia, and science. The first common factor is home support. "The parents (of the top performers)," he said, "were all genuinely concerned about their children…and willing to devote their time, their resources and their energy to giving each of their children the best conditions they could provide for them. Almost no sacrifice was too great if they thought it would help their children's educational development."

It is clear that to be successful, education must be a synergistic experience. Teacher effectiveness depends upon parents, and parent effectiveness depends upon teachers.

The second characteristic common to top performers is "time on task." Simply put, you can't really succeed in study unless you invest sufficient quality time in it. That means quality teaching and learning.

increased Jewish involvement and demonstrate an inability to influence positive growth in Jewish attitudes. This condition is due to a combination of factors: lack of home involvement and support for Jewish schooling; irrelevant curricular goals; inappropriate school programs; and ineffectual professional personnel, given the needs of pupils and families in the 1980s. Unless Jewish education of the entire family becomes the absolute priority of the synagogue…unless the parents become involved in the Jewish education of their children unless the program is geared to the needs of families…and unless all synagogue personnel are able to relate effectively to pupils and their parents, very little or no improvement can take place.

Let me share with you one disturbing feature of supplementary education relating to this latter point. After the study was completed we spent the better part of a year disseminating the findings. All told, we held twelve different citywide and regional meetings in which principals, rabbis, synagogue presidents, school committee chairpersons and parent leaders participated. Between 8 and 50 persons attended each of the meetings. At each regional meeting I asked the question, "In your respective schools how many times a year do the rabbi, principal, school board chairperson, parent leader, teachers and youth director meet together to plan and review progress of the educational program?" There was unanimity of response. Such meetings never or rarely take place. I suggest you ask the same question in each of the synagogues in the Los Angeles area. How often do all the various stakeholders of each synagogue meet together to develop plans and to review educational progress?

THE FINDINGS IN THE CONTEXT OF GENERAL EDUCATION

While there are major differences between the Jewish supplementary school and the public school, it is instructive to consider these findings and conclusions in light of research in general education.

In 1966, Chicago University Professor James Coleman and associates completed their mammoth study "Equality of Educational

RECOMMENDATIONS

It is precisely because of these two factors – family involvement and quality time on task – that our study makes four recommendations for the improvement of the Jewish supplementary school.

1. Transform the thrust of synagogue schools from supplementary schooling for pupils to Jewish family education (including classroom instruction for pupils);
2. Maximize teaching-learning time through a combination of formal and informal education experiences;
3. Provide all Jewish educational professionals with quality training to become effective Jewish family educators and classroom teachers; and
4. Make it possible for educators to make Jewish education a full-time career. (Every synagogue school should have at least one full-time teacher who is a good classroom instructor, who can work with parents and children in informal settings and who can develop curricula and educational materials. There are about 2000 Jewish supplementary schools in this country. It means we would have a cadre of 2000 full-time teachers in the Jewish community – what a difference they could make!)
5. These recommendations suggest the reorganization of the synagogue and the mobilization of the community to provide the necessary support to make the changes. After having presented the findings and having made recommendations, it is necessary to get all the stakeholders involved in studying the recommendations, refining them, designing strategies for application, developing implementation models, experimenting with these models, validating them, demonstrating how they work, and helping other synagogues replicate them.

Accordingly, BJE initiated the *Supplementary Education Action Plan* (SEAP) process. Upon the completion of the Study Report, we devoted the summer and early fall of 1987 to the development of a detailed set of guidelines for SEAP to help answer the questions: How should the findings be disseminated to achieve the greatest impact? How can we obtain input from all the stakeholders – lay leaders, parents, rabbis, and educators – most efficiently and effectively? What should be their respective roles in SEAP? How can we obtain the necessary support from synagogues for experimentation? How can we obtain communal support for the implementation of the recommendations?

You may ask "Is the New York study applicable to Los Angeles?" Obviously there are differences between communities. However, the answer I will give is the one Professor Harry Passow of Columbia University – one of the country's leading experts in the area of studies in general education – suggested I share with you. In addition to his broad knowledge base in general education, Professor Passow served for many years as chairman of the school board of the largest Conservative synagogue in New Jersey. His advice to communities considering replicating the New York Study is: "Save your money."

I reiterate. "Save your money." The next step for Los Angeles would be to modify the recommendations according to your needs. New York has no ownership on the experimentation process. Here in Los Angeles, Federation, the Bureau and a number of schools might begin experimenting together.

You already have several innovative programs in place: *Havurat Noar*, *Halutz* program, *Dor Hadash*. Why not try to maximize the integration of these programs into the school system and test their impact upon participants? How your community initiates the experimentation is totally up to you. One thing is clear, however. No one can effectively implement a new course of action for the schools. Each school must be fully involved in the planning, development, implementation and evaluation of its own program changes.

I recall learning in my college biology class that when a chick is ready to be born, it breaks its way through the shell. If someone helps crack the shell for the chick, it will die. Like the chick, each school must work at developing the most appropriate response to its own needs.

Some schools might experiment with the *Dor Hadash* concept for 10 to 13 year olds. Many years ago, I proposed that during the last two or three years of supplementary school one week of classes be eliminated each month. In their stead, one weekend retreat each month (from Friday noon through Sunday noon) October through May might be instituted.

TESTING DAY SCHOOL PUPILS' PERFORMANCE

Permit me now to make a brief observation about another kind of evaluation in Jewish education.

In the United States there are no ongoing community-wide testing services. There is, however, one exception. In 1974, the Board of Jewish Education of Greater New York, together with the Yeshiva High Schools Principals' Council (an association of principals of Modern Orthodox high schools), developed a uniform high school admissions exam for the 80 Modern Orthodox elementary feeder day schools in the Metropolitan New York area. (Together these schools represent about one-half of the all day school population in Greater New York.)

At the end of each November or beginning of each December every year, all the eighth grade students take one uniform examination for admission into all the yeshiva high schools. Until the inauguration of this service, admissions procedure to yeshiva high schools was like a wild shopping spree. For example, when my daughters graduated elementary day school, they were unsure which high school they wanted to attend and were interviewed and tested in four different high schools. Each admissions procedure was different. Each required the better part of a day. The different kinds of admissions procedures made it very confusing for an elementary school graduate. Now, all eighth graders take the same examination on the same day for admission into any Jewish day high school of their choice. This testing procedure has had a salutary effect upon elementary day schools. It has helped elevate the standards of elementary school achievement.

FUNDING JEWISH EDUCATION

Now to the third theme assigned to me – Funding Jewish Education. My own personal philosophy is "if you ain't got funding for schooling, you shouldn't be in the business of education." I feel strongly about this principle.

One of the first things I did when I became chief executive officer of the Board of Jewish Education was to seek funding sources for schools. I was fortunate to discover Mr. Joseph Gruss – an unusual person of great wealth and deep, abiding commitment to Jewish continuity and to Jewish education. As a result of his involvement in funding Jewish education, the Board of Jewish Education of Greater New York currently administers $12,000,000 of program support a year to a wide variety of Jewish educational institutions.

The Fund for Jewish Education (FJE) was created out of an urgent need to support and enhance Jewish education as a principal guarantor of Jewish survival. FJE is a tripartite partnership, whereby Joseph Gruss contributes $1.5 million a year matched by $3 million from UJA-Federation of Jewish Philanthropies.

During this past year, FJE distributed $5,000,000 to wide-ranging programs in the Greater New York area. Another $7 million was provided via special Monument Funds established by Mr. Gruss and his late wife.

A lay committee representing Mr. Gruss, UJA-Federation and the Board of Jewish Education sets policy and determines allocations. Drawn from many different professions, reflecting all ideological outlooks, and representing a variety of geographic locations throughout Greater New York, these diverse, committed men and women join together to insure that FJE's funds are expended in the most equitable and cost-effective manner possible.

FJE's goals are to:

- **insure the stability of Jewish schools of all ideologies, including day schools, yeshivot and supplementary schools;**

- provide economic security for career Jewish educators, in order to attract young, talented individuals and retain experienced veteran teachers;
- eliminate health and safety hazards and assure a secure environment conducive to learning;
- support programs for children with special education needs, including learning disabled and developmentally handicapped;
- provide support for new immigrant students from countries which suppress Jewish religious freedom; and
- support outreach programs that touch and teach the minimally affiliated and unaffiliated, and increase the number of children who receive a Jewish education.

SCHOOL GRANTS

FJE's grants are distributed in three separate program categories: School Grants, Educator Benefits and Outreach and Special Projects.

Grants-in-aid are awarded to Jewish schools according to enrollment formula. Special formula variances are given to schools which are crucial to neighborhood preservation or which serve a unique constituency in the community.

Additional grant programs, also based on enrollment formulas, have been developed for schools with large numbers of immigrant students. Grants are also provided to schools with special programs for the learning disabled and developmentally handicapped – recognizing that these costly programs allow the special Jewish child to receive a Jewish education.

EDUCATOR BENEFITS

The Educator Benefits program provides free life insurance coverage in the amount of $75,000 and contributes toward medical and pension benefits of career Jewish educators who teach a minimum of 20 hours per week in day schools and yeshivot, or a minimum of 12 hours per week in supplementary schools. Currently, 4700 Jewish educators receive these benefits.

OUTREACH & SPECIAL PROJECTS

Outreach and Special Projects grants are awarded on a competitive basis for innovative programs proposed by Jewish formal and informal educational institutions. Special priority is given to programs, which seek to reach out to marginally affiliated and unaffiliated Jewish youth. All types of Jewish educational institutions are actively encouraged to submit proposals to the Outreach and Special Projects subcommittee. In general, an institution, which receives these grants from FJE must provide a significant proportion of its program's cost from its own resources.

NEW YORK BENEFACTION

Although heavily dependent upon the bounty of one individual, the role of UJA-Federation is absolutely critical to FJE and to the Gruss Monument Funds – as fiduciary agent, as contributor of $3 million of matching funds each year, and as facilitator of the lay process, which includes organizing the five FJE committees: plenary, executive and program subcommittees.

While the total communal funding is relatively small compared to the need for financial aid and the total expenditure for Jewish education in New York (over $330 million annually for Jewish formal elementary and secondary education alone), it has an extremely important fiscal and psychological impact on Jewish schooling.

Being blessed with a philanthropist the likes of a Joseph Gruss gives a community an unusual advantage. Before the Gruss-UJA-Federation arrangement, New York did not provide direct subsidies to Jewish educational institutions. Living with the towering effect of one individual means accepting his funding ideas and sometimes compromising with communal processes. However, given the size of his annual contribution to Jewish education via UJA-Federation – now over $7 – million who can complain?

If New York had one or two more such benefactors, and if every Jewish community would have such generous supporters, what a difference it could make cumulatively to the national picture of Jewish education. So, I bring you a "gruss" from New York – that is a *yiddish "gruss"* – warm regards. May your Los Angeles community be so blessed.

AFTERWORD

In closing, I have attempted to address three topics as requested of me, relying heavily upon my New York experience. The questions and responses regarding marketing, evaluating, and funding are essential to the well being of the various Jewish educational entities in the community. The relationships between each of these three dimensions of Jewish education are obvious. Their importance derives from their potential cumulative impact upon a voluntary system crucial for Jewish continuity. The communal challenge in each area demands sustained efforts as old needs change and new needs emerge. Essential lay leadership qualities required to succeed in effectuating improvements in each area are abiding commitment to Jewish education as a priority and continued strength of resolve to respond to the needs.

A group of Hassidim once came to study with their *rebbe* and found him weeping. They tried to console him. "Why are you crying?" they asked. "When I was a young man," he said, "I thought I could change the world. So, I set out to try. That's how I learned the world is a very difficult thing to change. Then I turned 30. I decided that it was just as important for me to protect my small corner of the world. So, I invested all my energies in trying to improve my community and my students. That's how I learned that communities and classes of students cannot be made perfect. So, at the age of 40, I set about to change just my family. I spent hours and hours with my wife and children, trying to make my family perfect. But I learned that even families cannot be perfected. When I reached my maturity, at age 60, I realized that there was only one person who would listen to the lessons for which I had been placed in this world to teach. So I set out to perfect myself. But now I know that even that is beyond my powers."

The students were afraid. If the *rebbe* could not perfect himself, what chance have they? Again, they tried to console him. "*Rebbe, rebbe*, you are a great man, a scholar, an ethical exemplar beyond compare. What you do is right and just. You should not cry because you are not perfect. Only God can be perfect."

"You don't understand. I'm not weeping because I am sad," said the *rebbe*. "I'm weeping because of the great blessing that God has granted me," "What blessing?" the students asked. "All through my life I have been faced with great difficulties and challenges," the *rebbe* answered. "And God has given me strength to try and try and try again to respond to them. That's why I'm crying. I cry out of joy."

The challenges of Jewish education are overwhelming. We may not succeed in our initial efforts to respond effectively to them. But God blessed us with the strength to try and try again. The effort is worth it. It will result in the blessings of Jewish life.

More power to you!

CHAPTER 3

TOWARD THE YEAR 2000 – CONDITION OF JEWISH LIFE: IMPLICATIONS FOR JEWISH EDUCATION

Judaism is a unique combination of this worldliness and other worldliness – a religious-national culture encouraging aspirations for the good life in *Olam Hazeh*, and striving for the fulfillment of hopes for *Olam Haba*. As such, it is an amalgam of *Yerushalayim shel mattah* (earthly Jerusalem) and *Yerushalayim shel ma'allah* (celestial Jerusalem) – the former representing socio-national reality, and the latter embracing our dreams for the future of Jewish civilization. Accordingly, Jews consider simultaneously the Psalmist's joy for the present: *Zeh hayom assah Hashem nagilah v'nism'hah vo*, "This is the day which the Lord has made. We will rejoice and be glad in it" – suggesting that which Jews must do now for the moment; and the prophet Zecharia's promise for the future: *v'hayah Hashem l'Melech al kol ha'aretz. Bayom ha-hu yih-yeh Hashem ehad u'shmo ehad*, "And the Lord shall be King over all the earth. In that day shall the Lord be One and His Name One" – the statement of our ultimate hopes and aspirations for the Jewish people and for mankind.

To be sure, we must consider the future of Jewish education in light of the communal realities of today. We cannot plan for Jewish education outside of the context of the Jewish community's Jewish needs. Indeed, the challenges of Jewish education derive largely from the condition of Jewish life.

Oliver Wendell Holmes, a high profile American, traveling on a train one day, could not find his ticket. Watching him search furiously in his pockets, briefcase, and wallet, the compassionate conductor said, "Don't worry, Mr. Justice, when you find your ticket, just mail it to the railroad office." Justice Holmes was not comforted. "I'm not worried about the ticket," he said, "The problem is that I don't know where I'm going."

The first questions we must ask are, "Where is Jewish life going in America? Where is the Jewish community, Jewishly speaking? What is its Jewish life quotient?"

There is a dichotomy among sociologists, demographers, and students of Jewish life about the condition of Jewish life on this continent and the potential for its future. Over the past decade, three schools of thought have emerged. These will serve as the frame of reference for our discussion. In the first place, there are the *integrationists* or the *transformationists*. They see no major threat to Jewish survival. They believe that the integration of Jews into the fabric of American life – the acculturation of the America Jewry – and the transformation of Jewish lifestyles in that process – have no negative effect upon Jewish continuity. On the contrary, the current forms and processes of acculturation are signs of Jewish adaptability and vitality.

Then there are the *survivalists* who are very worried, greatly troubled about deculturation, alienation, assimilation, ignorance of Jewish tradition and intermarriage that abound in the Jewish community. They are deeply concerned about the impact of acculturation on the destiny of American Jewry. Jewish educators have generally been in the latter camp – associating themselves with the position of the *survivalists*.

Between these two schools of thought there is a middle of the road approach, espoused by as number of academicians. In a recent issue of B'nai B'rith's *Jewish Monthly*, Gary Tobin, Director of the Center for Jewish Studies, Brandies University, presents the third point of view, which I term the *"realist position"* to which I subscribe.

"In the next ten years," he writes, "Jews will become increasingly integrated into American society..."

> Today, little distinguishes Jews from other white Americans. Jews marry, divorce and have children at the same rate as non-Jews. Jews are more likely than ever before to live among and marry non-Jews. As a result, distinctive religious, cultural, and political behaviors have diminished. American Jewry will not disappear, but its numbers, strength and vitality can be severely diminished within the cozy confines of American culture.
>
> This could change with one major, galvanizing dose of anti-Semitism. But as long as the negative external forces that bind Jews together are benign, Jewish cohesiveness is more dependent on positive factors and internal strengths.
>
> While the openness of the United States contains the seed of assimilation, it also enables the American Jewish community to shape its own destiny. If Jewish organizations and institutions play a more pro-active role in dealing with the issue of intermarriage, Jewish identity and reinforcing Jewish life, then the heart of the community may remain strong.
>
> Change is inevitable. The direction of that change will be molded by what we do in the next decade.

The *realist* position strongly recommends that the Jewish community learn to compete effectively. Learning to compete with our open society is the underlying challenge for Jewish education as we approach the year 2000 C.E. – 5760.

Learning to compete requires us to face the challenges of Jewish continuity directly and honestly. On the one hand, this means recognizing and abetting our areas of strength and effectiveness. On the other, it means responding effectively to our problems and weaknesses.

WHAT ARE OUR EDUCATIONAL STRENGTHS – OUR EDUCATIONAL ASSETS IN 1990?

1. The first is the Jewish day school option. While there are no definitive studies demonstrating the qualitative impact of Jewish all day education on students, and while not all day schools and yeshivot are equally successful, this form of Jewish schooling clearly offers the best opportunity and the best construct for effective formal Jewish education. To be sure, the Jewish day school provides an alternative Jewish environment and an enriched schedule of Jewish studies, not available in part-time educational enterprises.
2. Our second asset is the Jewish informal education option, particularly the total immersion programs – Jewish educational camping and Israel experiences – and the growing availability of informal Jewish education experiences via synagogues and Jewish Community Centers and youth organizations such as NCSY, USY, NFTY, and the Zionist youth movements.
3. Higher Jewish studies comprise our third educational asset. These options include Talmud study groups in the Orthodox sector and university programs, among others. On the campus there is a growing core, albeit small, of Jewish students who are expressing their Jewishness in *Jewish study* and *Jewish activism*.
4. Our fourth asset is two-pronged – the growing interest of young people in careers in Jewish education and the various creative programs to improve their instructional effectiveness, such as the Conference for the Advancement of Jewish Education, teachers' centers, early childhood centers, media centers, special education centers, principals' centers and computer resource centers.
5. In the setting of the voluntary Jewish community, the central

agency for Jewish education, which provides formal and informal education programs, to teachers and informal Jewish educators, and to principals and program directors that which they *cannot provide* for themselves, thereby enhancing their activity, is a significant asset relating to Jewish continuity.
6. Finally, we take note of the growing awareness of communal leadership concerning the importance of Jewish education and the concomitant increase in Jewish communal support of Jewish education.

WHAT ARE OUR WEAKNESSES – OUR EDUCATIONAL LIABILITIES IN 1990?

As I view the Jewish education scene, we face six main problems (not necessarily in rank order).

1. More young Jews are opting out of Jewish life now than ever before. All one has to do is to look at our campuses or ask our Hillel directors to become convinced of this sad fact. The numbers who opt out far exceeds the small core of Jewishly oriented students.
2. There is more intermarriage than ever before. This means fewer children in Jewish schools. The progeny of intermarried couples – even conversionary marriages – are less likely to enroll in Jewish schools. Moreover, fewer offspring of intermarried couples will make it as committed Jews. And a large percentage of them will intermarry just like their parents did.
3. More Jewish children from Jewish endogamous marriages are not exposed to Jewish education than in the previous generation despite recently publicized figures to the contrary. I estimate that, given the current trends in countrywide school enrollment, about 30 percent of all Jewish children of school age will have no exposure to formal Jewish education. In some communities this figure may be as low as 20 and even 10 percent. However, in arriving at an aggregate

percentage for non-enrollment we must include areas like Suffolk County, New York, with a population of 120,000 Jews, where well over 50 percent of the school age population will grow up without a formal Jewish education. We must also consider the 1989 Report of the Strategic Planning Committee of the Associated Jewish Charities and Welfare Fund of Baltimore, which indicates that, "roughly half of Jewish children in Baltimore receive no Jewish schooling at all."

4. More Jewish school pupils are ill equipped for meaningful Jewish lives than ever before. The BJE of Greater New York study of Jewish supplementary schools adequately confirms this contention both on the affective and cognitive levels, as does the experience of the American Jewish community with this form of Jewish schooling during the last two decades.

5. There is the continuing, gnawing, ever serious personnel problem – primarily, a grave shortage of qualified teachers and no opportunities for full time career teaching in our network of supplementary schools.

6. Despite some instances of significantly enhanced communal support for Jewish schooling and efforts in many communities to increase the level of funding for Jewish education, all forms of Jewish education are under-funded. In general education circles, there is a difference of opinion regarding the relative level of education spending concerning the public sector. Recently, a widely publicized report by the Economic Policy Institute concluded that "The United States – contrary to frequent assertions by Bush Administration officials – lags behind most major industrialized nations in spending on pre-collegiate education." The Hudson Institute, an Indianapolis-based think tank, which claims that America's schools are not under-funded, refuted this conclusion last month. They are just unproductive.

While not denying that lack of productivity is a grave problem in some sectors of Jewish education, we must conclude – based upon sad experience and available information – that Jewish education is seriously shortchanged. It will take more funding to make unproductive schools productive. Introducing new programmatic measures to enhance the effectiveness of Jewish schools requires more money. For this reason, The Baltimore Report, for example, clearly states that, "The Jewish community as whole...must more fully support Jewish education."

As we approach 2000 C.E., we must reinforce our educational assets and build upon our strengths. This means making the day school option more easily accessible to larger segments of the Jewish community. It means intensifying informal Jewish education and reaching larger numbers of youth through this medium. It means reinforcing higher Jewish education programs so that they reach a larger student audience with greater intensity and stronger Jewish focus. And, it means strengthening the efforts of bureaus and other institutions that provide quality in-service programs for Jewish educators. And, it means marketing exemplary programs to the field *á la* National Diffusion Network in general education via a process, which includes program development, validation demonstration, and dissemination.

Simultaneously, we must invest our talent and energy to reduce our educational liabilities and eliminate our weaknesses by responding to three key challenges. Jewish educational leadership must be in the forefront of responding to three critical *global* challenges relating to the family, to personnel, and to the marginally affiliated.

1. We *must intensify efforts to universalize Jewish family education*. Without a supportive home environment and without parental reinforcement, based upon commitment and knowledge, Jewish school impact upon pupils will be negligible.

    The problem today is that the children who are most in need of parental tutelage and reinforcement usually have parents who are least able to help them. This challenge thrusts upon the school, particularly, the Jewish Supplementary School, the task of educating parents to become partners in the day-to-day education of their children – a phenomenon that is now not only acceptable, but desirable in school systems throughout the country. This then becomes the synagogue's new educational role as it changes its thrust from Jewish schooling for children *only* to Jewish education for the entire family, including children and adults alike. The new child-family focus means restructuring synagogue involvement in Jewish education whereby the rabbi, principal, teachers, cantor and youth leaders work as family educator teams. In practice, each of them would become a Jewish family educator, instructing children in classroom settings, leading informal educational groups, working with family members in their homes, and providing individualized tutelage and Jewish family counseling, as needed, to parents and children alike. It means making available full-time career opportunities – at least one in each school – via which a teacher and/or principal would be involved in a variety of interrelated responsibilities: formal instruction, integration of formal and informal educational activities, Jewish family outreach and the development of appropriate programs and curricular materials. It means involving all stakeholders in the planning and development of the various aspects of Jewish family education. And, it means creating partnerships with social workers and Center workers in responding to Jewish family needs.

Initiating Jewish family education programs will not be easy. It will stretch our imagination and pocketbook and try our patience. Planning and implementation will be a long process. It cannot be done at once for all schools. We will need to experiment with a variety of models in order to develop the most effective approaches. In all, it is very challenging. It can be very exciting and extremely rewarding.

2. The second critical challenge that speaks loudly and clearly to Jewish educational leaders is the need for quality full-time

personnel. Jewish educators *must take the lead in developing strategies to attract, recruit, train and retain qualified Jewish educators, particularly teachers.* During the last two years, the Mandel Commission on Jewish Education identified twenty-six possible options for improving the state of American Jewish education. Twenty-four of these were characterized as "programmatic options," – and two as "enabling options" without which none of the other options can be effective. The two enabling options are "community" and "personnel" – meaning the provision of adequate ongoing communal support and the availability of sufficient quality educational personnel for the total system of Jewish education.

More than anybody else, we educators know that without this *Issachar* (educator) and *Zebulun* (philanthropic/communal leader) combination, effective Jewish schooling is doomed.

3. The third challenge relates to outreach to marginally affiliated or under affiliated Jews, to immigrant Jewish populations – Soviet Jews, Iranian Jews, and Israelis, to Jewish teenagers and to intermarried couples.

    It is clear that a key element of the outreach process should be the maximal use of the Holocaust and Israel to induce and strengthen Jewish identity. Those who participated in the March of the Living this year (April 20 though May 2) can give eloquent testimony to the effect of this program on the Jewishness of participants. The juxtaposition of the Holocaust with Israel – observing *Yom Hashoah* in Auschwitz, Poland, and then celebrating *Yom Ha'atzmaut* in Israel – is an unparalleled experience for the formation and reinforcement of Jewish identity.

There is an integral relationship between these three global challenges as Jewish family education relates to the problems of personnel and outreach.

Responding effectively to critical challenges – strengthening our educational assets and eliminating our liabilities – requires a new look at our funding capabilities and procedures. To be sure, more money, much more money, is *needed* to accomplish what is *needed*. As John Kenneth Galbraith once said of this nation's largest municipality, there is nothing wrong with New York that a few billion dollars can't cure.

Who is responsible for funding Jewish education? The answer is: no single resource. There are four levels of funding responsibility.

The first level rests with parents. We must try to insure that those who can afford it bear their share of the school's educational expense. In this effort, we need to be sensitive to parents who cannot afford the cost of educating their children. This is increasingly the case in Jewish day schools. The cost for three students in a day school can be as much as $20,000 per year. Not many families can afford this kind of expenditure.

The second level of funding lies with the sponsoring institution. The boards of synagogues, day schools and Jewish centers must shoulder more responsibility for their respective educational endeavors. This depends upon a willingness on the part of lay leaders to increase their support and their resourcefulness in finding new sources of funding.

The third level of support rests with the Jewish community – essentially the Jewish Federation and Welfare Fund. Given the challenges re Jewish continuity, Federations must examine their current priorities and patterns of funding overseas and local needs in order to guarantee that Jewish education receives its fair share. Currently about one-third of the local Federation dollar is spent on services to the non-Jewish community. Consider how that money, or even half of that amount, can affect positively Jewish education. Jewish educational leaders must never relinquish their advocacy role vis-à-vis Federations' responsibility to fund adequately the Jewish education programs in their respective catchment areas.

The Mandel Commission recognizes the importance of this need. Its efforts to encourage greater communal funding have just begun. As Jewish educators, we must applaud this long-awaited development – a national resource that will help open the faucets of educational support to a thirsty, needy client.

On the fourth level, we must not ignore the potential of governmental support so long as it does not infringe upon the First Amendment. Government funding can flow to the nonpublic sector if properly nurtured. In New York, based upon the child benefit theory, some 40 million dollars annually in cash disbursements, goods and services are made available to yeshivot and Jewish day schools. These include free foodstuffs; free and reduced kosher commodities for breakfast and lunch programs, transportation, textbooks for general studies, guidance, health services and remedial instruction.

Besides the regular channels of state education departments and local school districts, state legislators can be helpful in finding sources of funding for Jewish day schools. The key here is keeping abreast of state legislation. U.S. Office of Education specialist Dr. Charles O'Malley's recommendations regarding this need are right on target. He strongly suggested that central agencies and/or individual schools, depending upon the size of the community, maintain regular contact with their local legislators, as well as local school superintendents, regarding educational legislation. There are numerous examples that demonstrate the practical value of this approach.

While Jewish educational leaders should be involved in maximizing income from each of the four levels, we have special responsibilities in motivating – even in guaranteeing maximal support from the sponsoring institutions and the Jewish community. New strategies for funding might involve the business community qua business community like the public sector is doing in some areas. For example, day schools might invite a local chemical firm to sponsor a science exhibit or a local florist to sponsor sessions on horticulture. Involving the local business community in curriculum areas related to their expertise may generate financial support as well. Schools and central agencies might also consider shared purchasing from the National Association for the Exchange of Industrial Resources – a nonprofit organization.

In dealing with lay leadership, we often hear that nonprofit organizations may be more productive than governmental agencies, but that the profit sector is more cost-effective and productive than the nonprofit. Our challenge in Jewish education is to prove our ability to be more productive than any other form of activity.

With more funds we will be able to accomplish the crucial objective of *learning to compete*. We will be able to make the Jewish education profession more attractive and productive. We will be able to make effective Jewish family education a reality. And, with more money we will be able to increase the use of technology, such as video teaching and learning, computer-based instruction, and distance learning. Without optimal use of new technology, Jewish education cannot be of the 21st century. And, with more money we will be able to invest in much-needed educational research and development, both on the local (bureau) and national levels and to be able to help schools design and implement meaningful assessment programs.

In sum, I make a confession. This paper posits nothing especially new to Jewish educators. Indeed, in this case, "there is nothing new under the sun." What can be new, however, is the urgency with which we consider our respective roles vis-à-vis the future.

If we are able to galvanize the community to respond effectively to the challenges I outlined, we will help bring about the fulfillment of many – if not all – of the wish list items in my 1980 editorial by the time we reach 2000. They relate to advocacy, pupil recruitment, outreach, provision of quality learning opportunities, family education, professional growth, adequate funding and the communal status of Jewish education. Again, the challenges are not new – but a renewed vision and a new spirit of optimism must revitalize our efforts.

Indeed, we have the opportunity and the responsibility to meld *Yerushalayim shel mattah* with *Yerushalayim shel ma-allah*.

CHAPTER 4

THE CENTRAL AGENCY FOR JEWISH EDUCATION

LOOKS IN THE MIRROR

As we enter the last decade of the 20th century, American Jewry takes stock of its resources, looks back at its accomplishments and failures as a community, and prepares to complete the century hoping to chalk up more achievements. On the list of 20th century accomplishments and failures are Jewish communal efforts on behalf of Jewish education. One of the significant communal developments spanning the whole century is the emergence and continued presence of the central agency for Jewish education.

The first such effort was the establishment of the Bureau of Jewish Education of New York in 1910. It was born out of a perceived critical Jewish communal need to upgrade Jewish education: to introduce modern texts and teaching materials, graded curricula, appropriate pedagogic methods, improved preparation and remuneration of teachers and better administration and supervision of schools. Dr. Samson Benderly, founding executive of the Bureau, enumerated the principles that guided the Bureau activity:

- to make Jewish education a community responsibility;

- to make Jewish education, in the sense of the maintenance of schools, a self-supporting undertaking;
- to build up professional Jewish leadership with high standards;
- to create a professional class of Jewish teachers;
- to reckon with the modern world in the selection of the content of Jewish education;
- to evolve methods of instruction that are fully in accord with modern educational theory and practice and to embody the content of Jewish education in books and educational equipment that are on a par with those in the field of general education;
- to so schedule Jewish education that it will reckon with the time available to the child, and not overburden it during the days of its attendance at public school;
- to put the education of the girl on a par with that of the boy;
- to meet the distinctive educational need of the pre-school child;
- to motivate the enterprise of the new Jewish education with the belief in the worthwhileness of a positive Jewish life in America, and in its possibility. It is then, and only then, that we can challenge the overshadowing menace to Jewish education – the unschooled.

The guiding principles and the function of the central agency in New York have been modified significantly over time in response to changing family, school and synagogue needs and the changing nature of the Jewish population.

Since the founding of the New York Bureau, central agencies for Jewish education have been organized in almost all communities with Jewish populations of several thousand or more. Essentially, they were founded in order to marshal communal resources to improve Jewish supplementary educational programs in the respective localities. The latest of the large communal central agencies is the Jewish Education Council established in 1971 in Montreal, the result of a two-year study of Jewish education in this city by this writer. Currently 35 of the 52 extant communal coordinating bodies for Jewish education are autonomous central agencies governed by a broad-based board, operating a range of services to a wide variety of constituents and educational programs.

There are obvious differences between the central agencies in the communities of varying size. While all the bureaus in large cities and some bureaus in the large-intermediate locales operate as "boards" of Jewish education in various ways, the central agencies in the smaller communities are either school associations or communal schools serving the entire Jewish community or a segment of it.

Of the larger Jewish communities, Chicago, Detroit and Pittsburgh have atypical communal arrangements. Chicago has two "central agencies": the Board of Jewish Education (established in 1923), serving the Reform and Conservative population, and the Associated Talmud Torahs (1929), providing service to schools under Orthodox auspices. Detroit's "communal" education agency, United Hebrew Schools (1919), serves only part of the Jewish supplementary school population, and the Hebrew Institute in Pittsburgh (1916) is one of a variety of formal Jewish educational institutions in that city.

Overall, there are 60 functional Federation Jewish education committees operating a range of coordinating services staffed by Federation professionals, 31 of whom have education back-grounds. In several communities, particularly in the smaller locales, the centralized Jewish education operation is wholly a Federation activity staffed by a Federation professional.

Whatever the community, increased attention is being paid by Jewish communal leadership to the challenge of Jewish continuity. Witness the emergence of commissions of Jewish identity and Jewish continuity in many cities. There are currently 14 communities with Jewish education planning committees or commissions whose primary responsibility it is to plan and/or establish policies dealing with Jewish education issues. The growing awareness regarding the importance of programs for Jewish continuity places the spotlight on the central agency for Jewish education. At the same time, flat Federation campaigns and minus levels of grants by Federations for local needs endanger the viability of many bureaus. Moreover, the activity of some of the communal commissions and Jewish continuity (some actually have programmatic functions) has the effect of reducing the role of the bureau to only one of a number of communal players addressing the needs of Jewish education of the community.

Also, the emergence, growth and spread of yeshivot and day schools have challenged the capacity and ability of the central agency to shift gears from dealing solely with the supplementary school to include involvement with Jewish all day educational institutions. For many bureaus, this is not an easy task, given their service orientation and the autonomous development of the day school. In fact, in almost all communities, the day school is perceived as a serious competitor for Federation funding.

In addition, the challenges to the central agency in the 1990s relate to its communal leadership role in planning for Jewish education and culture. On the one hand, this requires the bureau to have skills in planning. On the other hand, the bureau must develop a common language with Federations while it enhances its ability for self-support. But foremost, its leadership role requires it to make the necessary changes in structure and programs to meet the changing conditions of the 1990s.

For these reasons, during the last several years, the Bureau Directors Fellowship – the organization of central agency executives – has been deliberating on the future of the bureaus in continental North America.

CHAPTER 5

JEWISH CONTINUITY THROUGH WHOM?

A MESSAGE TO AMERICAN JEWISH COMMUNAL LEADERSHIP

If the 1990 National Jewish Population Study has served a purpose *vis-à-vis* Jewish education, it has heightened the awareness of Jewish communal leaders about its critical importance. Hillel instructed us in Ethics of the Fathers (2:6), *"Lo am ha-aretz hasid."* Knowledge of Judaism is absolutely essential for intelligent, meaningful participation in Jewish life.

The NJPS conveys the utter significance of the multi-level Jewish educational challenge to the Jewish community. Its findings underscore that Jewish communal leadership has a major responsibility to respond to the acculturation-deculturation syndrome that has affected American Jewry so deeply.

In reflecting on the influence of the French Revolution on European Jews who suddenly found themselves in a Western society, Ahad Ha'am, the nineteenth and early twentieth century Zionist leader and philosopher, posited that in an open society a minority community inevitably must imitate the majority populace. The manner and extent of the imitation will determine how the minority retains its unique identity. For Jews to continue as a singular cultural-religious entity in a sea of western societal influence they must develop means of "competitive imitation." Otherwise, they will assimilate totally as did the families of Moses Mendelssohn in Germany and Adolph Cremieux in France.

There are two ways to achieve "competitive imitation." The first is utilizing the technological development and instrumentalities of western society to reinforce Jewishness. Today, this means maximizing the use of modern computer and media technology and modern pedagogy to edify the ways Jewish values and knowledge are communicated to youth and adults individually and collectively.

The second method Ahad Ha'am recommended for Jews to retain their uniqueness, is to revive their national culture via attachment to their homeland and revival of the Hebrew language as the language of Jewish peoplehood. Thus, he evolved the idea of Cultural Zionism – developing the Holy Land as a center for cultural and linguistic propagation. At its best, cultural Zionism would infuse a Jewish national-cultural spirit and knowledge among Jews and revitalize Hebrew as the *lingua franca* of Jews and as the language of Jewish learning. In our times, this means intensifying our efforts for Jewish Zionist education and maximizing Israel as a source of Hebraic cultural influence. It means also that the Jewish community would spare no effort in guaranteeing that as many Jews as possible learn to read and speak Hebrew – making our ancestral language part and parcel of our daily existence.

Indeed, our sages stressed that our ancestors "were redeemed from Egypt" because, among other reasons, they "did not change their language and continued to speak the Holy Tongue" (*Midrash Rabbah Vayikra* 24:10). In the contemporary setting, Solomon Schechter emphasized that, "The Jews of America cannot live without English, but will not survive without Hebrew." He was referring to Hebrew language usage for liturgy in the synagogue, for Jewish life cycle and calendar events, for home observance, for Judaic textual study and for use as a modern vernacular. It is abundantly clear that these goals cannot be accomplished without intensive formal study. It is towards this end that Jewish communal leadership – locally and nationally, must now exert its influence and maximize its efforts.

To be sure, it is to the credit of the federated communal leadership that plans are being developed and programs are under way to insure Jewish continuity. It is unfortunate that this kind of mobilization of effort is so late in coming. Since it has materialized in the form of Jewish continuity commissions on the national scene and in many local communities, it is essential that the time, energy, and funds invested in Jewish continuity activity be directed to the targets that will best guarantee Jewish continuity.

Given the experience of the continuity commissions to date, both on the national and local levels, it is clearly apparent that we cannot afford to waste precious time and shrinking dollars on ideas and programs that cannot effectuate maximum results.

Toward whom should we target our funding and efforts – the unaffiliated? The marginally affiliated? Or the affiliated? Should we try to respond to the Jewish needs of each population? In what order? Addressing effectively the Jewish educational needs of these groups, each of which is so variegated, requires much talent, knowledge, and financial resources. This writer has for several decades stressed the need to be concerned with each category of youth and adults. However, given the current availability of funding, it is necessary to prioritize the investment of effort and subsidization into the most promising and productive activities. Priority support should be provided to those programs which have the greatest potential for insuring Jewish continuity. This translates, in the first instance, into aid for the Jewish day school, the majority of whose students are recruited from the ranks of the affiliated.

The combination of quality Jewish schooling, a good, positive Jewish home, and sound informal Jewish educational experience is the best guarantee for Jewish continuity. Accordingly, support must be forthcoming for family education programs to marginally affiliated parents of day school pupils and for informal educational programming, particularly Israel experience for Jewish day school teenagers.

Second level priority funding for the marginally affiliated would address the needs of the vast majority of Jewish supplementary school pupils and their parents. This means improving and intensifying the school programs, providing Jewish family education and encouraging informal Jewish educational activities, especially the Israel experience for synagogue school post *Bar/Bat Mitzvah* students.

Third level funding should be targeted for the unaffiliated and made available only after the needs of the affiliated and marginally affiliated are met adequately. Insufficient support to the affiliated and certainly to the marginally affiliated might lead to their joining the growing ranks of the unaffiliated.

The 450,000 day school and supplementary school pupils and their parents are a captive audience and much less expensive to "capture" for Jewish continuity than the unaffiliated.

One clear need that must be given priority consideration in formal education is the matter of instructional quality. The only way to insure competent, effective instruction is through appropriate pre-service and in-service training for teachers and supervisory personnel for all types of schools.

In the long run, Jewish continuity efforts will succeed if they appropriately address the right clients, the right consumers and the right providers of Jewish education with the right Jewish-Hebraic educational programs.

CHAPTER 6

Jewish Life & Jewish Education in Contemporary Society: Challenge and Response

For the purposes of this paper, Jewish identity is viewed as a multi-dimensional phenomenon. For some Jews, it is expressed in religious terms through worship, ritual and the study of religious texts. For others, it is a national Zionist reality expressed through a variety of relationships with Israel, including the use of Hebrew language as a vernacular; considered a cultural phenomenon via involvement with Hebrew and Judaic literature and/or Hebraic arts, and/or involvement with the Yiddish language and literature; and expressed through feelings of Jewish peoplehood and/or all of the above.

Jewish identity and Jewish continuity are interdependent. The Jewish identity of individuals nourishes Jewish group continuity. Conversely, the Jewish group environment and community processes invigorate and energize individual Jewish continuity. Both are also intra-dependent as individuals relate to each other and as sub-groups of the whole Jewish community interface.

Jewish education is viewed as multiple opportunities to

develop, achieve, and strengthen the Jewish identity of individual Jews – young and old – and thus insure Jewish continuity.

THE CHALLENGE: ACCULTURATION – DECULTURATION

As America welcomed immigrants, its underlying melting pot ideology suggested that all newcomers and their descendants would…and should…be unlike their forebears. They would be Americans, with a new identity through the process of assimilation. The process in Canada may have been slower, but nonetheless ever present.

The adaptation and subsequent growth of a new identity explains the challenges and the difficulties of retaining a solely Jewish character in America. The dominant society makes it difficult for members of another ethnic group to retain its traditional culture. The lure of establishing an American identity is grounded in a crippling pluralism for those who wish to preserve conformity to old patterns.

THE JEWISH LANGUAGES AND JEWISH IDENTITY

Jewish identity may be viewed via the prism of a language metaphor. During the latter years of the Second Temple, Jews became multilingual. After the destruction of the Second Temple, as Jews wandered over the globe and settled in various lands for short and extended periods of time, they continued the pattern of multilingual communication. Their identity was expressed generally via trilingualism:

- an internal language (for example, Yiddish or Ladino from the 16th to mid 20th century), the vernacular of their home and street, which they used daily as their means of social communication;
- an external language for their business activity and association with non Jews;
- and a sacred language reserved for prayer and rituals at home and the synagogue and for study of Torah, Talmud and other Judaic sources.

Via internal and sacred language usage, Jewish identity was maintained and nurtured on the personal, family, social, religious and communal levels of the daily living of diaspora Jewry. Enter the acculturation process of American Jewry during the 20th century, especially since the end of World War II. For the overwhelming majority of American Jews, internal and sacred languages no longer play a role in their lives. Consequently, the concomitant social and religious behaviors associated with these languages are no longer exhibited. Besides having no internal language, third and fourth generation American Jews generally feel no need for a sacred language, for synagogue affiliation, or for religious education for their offspring (Horowitz, 1993).

The gradual abandonment of the Hebrew language as an internal and/or sacred language is a cause for concern for many Jewish leaders. Hebrew language has been a significant factor in Jewish continuity and Jewish unity. Ahad Ha'am correctly noted that "more than the Jews have kept the Hebrew language alive, the Hebrew language has kept the Jews alive…" Indeed, Hebrew has been the gateway to Jewish culture. Its use provided Jews everywhere with a sense of belongingness.

THE CHALLENGE OF UNAFFILIATED FAMILIES

The well-publicized findings of the 1990 National Jewish Population Study clearly underscore the extent of the hemorrhaging of the Jewish community. The vast majority of Jews are best described as products of the acculturation-deculturation syndrome as they become integrated comfortably into American society.

This condition has had a three-fold effect upon their Jewish identity and involvement. It has lessened the quantity and quality of Jewishness in their lives. It has diminished the extent and intensity of their synagogue affiliation and Jewish communal activity. And, it has decreased their level of home support for Jewish education (Schiff, 1981). As a result, about one-third of the Jewish child population of school-age does not receive any Jewish education. By and large, parents of children who do not enroll their progeny in a Jewish school do not see a relevance of

Hebrew as a language or the religious oriented training that is currently involved in formal Jewish education…Religion per se is not significant to these individuals…Moreover, the cost of religious education poses a serious problem for many of these parents…Overall, while many of them want to preserve their Jewish heritage, and some are even proud of being Jewish, they are 'more American than their forebears' and 'are not upset by assimilation.' (Perspectives Resources, Inc.)

Involving these parents and their progeny in Jewish education requires new innovative methods of recruitment and marketing. Since for many of them, cultural aspects of Judaism may be relevant, and since the Bar-Bat mitzvah ceremony still has some attraction for some of these parents, new ways of dealing with their interests must be created. Here, the challenge of utilizing Israel creatively looms large.

THE JEWISH EDUCATION RESPONSE: HOME AND SCHOOL AND JEWISH IDENTITY

The Jewish community has related to the challenges of Jewish identity in two ways:

1. Formal Jewish education on the pre-school, primary, elementary, secondary and post high school levels and university settings in the U.S. and in Israeli institutions
2. Informal Jewish education including day and resident camping, synagogue and Zionist youth groups, the Israel Experience, adult Jewish education programs and Hebraic and Judaic Hebrew literacy initiatives.

Needless to say, formal Jewish education is the most pervasive and most important of the various Jewish education settings. Traditionally, the challenge of formal Jewish education in the United States has been addressed by two school formats – the Jewish supplementary school and the all day Jewish educational institution, generally, autonomous yeshivot and Jewish day schools.

All the educational formats, particularly the formal school settings, address Jewish education in two ways – Jewish identity reinforcement and Jewish identity formation. In the first instance, the educational process – whether formal or informal – serves basically as a reinforcer of attitudes, behavior patterns and even skills acquired early in a child's environment. There is significant support for the theory, "that daily contact with family and peer group society is the most crucial influence on educational attainment and eventual adult behavior and job expectations" (Cohen).

In the most comprehensive analysis of American schools ever implemented, James Coleman and his associates conclude that increasing resources of schools had no effect on how much children learned if the home environment was unchanged. They claim that, "…schools bring little influence to bear on a child's achievement that is independent of his background and social context" (Coleman and Campbell).

This finding is all the more significant when it comes to religious schooling. The role of the home in contributing to the success of Catholic education was adequately borne out by the national study on Catholic schools in America (Greeley and Rossi). The researchers in that study found that Catholic education was only able to impact students who came from very religious homes. It had almost no effect on the other children. Similar conclusions were reached in studies on Jewish education (Himmelfarb; Cohen, S.M.).

It is obvious that Jewish education of children in the absence of family involvement cannot be maximally effective in helping develop Jewish ambience in Jewish homes via Jewish communal and organizational involvement and synagogue participation, the quality of the contact and involvement is the crucial factor. Achieving the necessary caliber of outreach and communication is a most serious challenge to our lay, rabbinic, and educational leadership.

FORMAL JEWISH EDUCATION – THE JEWISH SUPPLEMENTARY SCHOOL

Two opposite trends have emerged during the last three decades regarding the institutions of formal Jewish education. On the one hand, we have witnessed a serious decline in Jewish supplementary school enrollment in North America – from 540,000 pupils in 1962, the peak year of Jewish school enrollment, to 285,000 in 1992 (Schiff, 1988; Isaacs). The current enrollment decline is due largely to a decrease in birthrate, intermarriage, and the acculturation pattern of young endogamous Jewish married people who do not feel the need to provide Jewish education to their progeny.

Also, the attitudes of many adults to their own supplementary Jewish educational experiences and family breakup have negatively affected the enrollment of children in Jewish religious schools (Schiff, 1981). In addition, funding and transportation issues impact on the continuation of Jewish education (Barak Fishman and Goldstein).

Moreover, recent studies of Jewish supplementary schooling demonstrate that it has become, by and large, incapable of achieving its goals (Dushkin and Engelman; Himmelfarb; Bock; Hartman; Schiff, 1988). Among the reasons for the current ineffectiveness of Jewish supplementary education are the non-priority status of the school within the synagogue, the lack of home support, and the shortage of adequately trained supervisory and instructional personnel (Himmelfarb; Schiff, 1988; Schoem).

THE JEWISH DAY SCHOOL

In contradistinction to the trend of the Jewish Supplementary School, the Jewish Day School has enjoyed remarkable growth – from 60,000 pupils in 280 schools in North America in 1962 to 182,000 in 660 schools in 1992 (Schiff, 1966, 1983; McMillan and Gerald; Isaacs). Estimates of the 1995 enrollment in Jewish all day educational institutions from preschool through post high school programs reach 200,000.

This dramatic growth is the result of the continued championship, sponsorship and support by Orthodox Jewry (abetted by a considerable Orthodox birthrate) and the advocacy and founding of Solomon Schechter schools by the Conservative movement. The growth was further aided by the recent interest in all day education evinced by Reform Jewish leaders and the financial assistance by federations throughout the North American continent. Contributing significantly to the sustained, increased interest in and support of all day Jewish education is the recognition by its advocates and supporters of the value and need of intensive Jewish education for Jewish continuity and the enhancement of Jewish life.

To be sure, other factors have also contributed to the initial and continuing growth of the day school. Studies of the Jewish day school show conclusively that it has an important effect upon its students insofar as Jewish behavior is concerned. The Barak Fishman and Goldstein and Lipset analyses of the 1990 NJPS data demonstrate that more extensive forms of Jewish education are associated with greater Jewish identification, especially among those under 45 years of age. Mordechai Rimor and Elihu Katz, in a review of the same data, concur (1993). For them, day schools – more than private tutors, part-time schooling, and Sunday schools have a greater bearing on friendship patterns, prevention of intermarriage, attitudes towards intermarriage of progeny, visits to Israel, Shabbat and *kashrut* observance (Jewish dietary laws) and synagogue attendance, among others.

Time spent in school, by most accounts, has a significant influence on Jewish identity formation, even when a variety of factors (including family background) are controlled (Bock; Himmelfarb). Rimor and Katz (1993) claim nine or more years of schooling is critical. Other researchers, including Goldstein and Barak Fishman, suggest a minimum of six years is important. Over time, other studies have demonstrated the positive influence of Jewish all day education (Pollak; Pinsky; Hartman; Ribner; Heimowitz; Friedman).

THE JEWISHNESS QUOTIENT OF DAY SCHOOL GRADUATES

The most recent and most comprehensive and far reaching study of Jewish day school graduates is that made by this writer in collaboration with Mareleyn Schneider. This study of some 3700 Jewish day school graduates, 20–40 years of age, from 26 representative Jewish day elementary and high schools throughout the United States sheds significant light on their adult Jewish behavior, attitudes and involvement.

Overall, Jewish day school graduates are American born, married, college-educated with advanced postgraduate study. The graduates surveyed went to Modern Orthodox, Conservative, and communal (trans-ideological) schools. The study did not include graduates from ultra orthodox or Hasidic yeshivot since the purpose of the survey was to determine the relative effect of Jewish education in light of the graduates' exposure to American societal influences. Reform day schools were not included since they are a recent phenomenon in Jewish education and were not founded early enough to produce graduates 20–40 years of age.

The graduates' Jewish behavior is dramatically different from other 20–40 year old Jews in America. Eighty-one percent keep kosher at home and 80% outside the home. Overall, 70% observe the Sabbath in a variety of ways. Most Jewish elementary day school graduates continue on to Jewish day high schools and most of the high school graduates continue their Jewish studies in one way or another after high school for one or more years.

A major difference between Jewish day school graduates and their non Jewish day school peers relates to their involvement with Israel. Whereas only 15% of American Jewish adults have been to Israel, 89% of Jewish day school graduates have visited Israel on the average four times. Eighty-five percent of Jewish day school graduates attended a Jewish summer camp for an average of four summers.

The most telling difference between Jewish day school graduates and the overall Jewish population is that only 4.5% are intermarried compared to 52% of the marriages of Jews to non-Jews from 1985 to 1990 according to the National Jewish Population Study, and 80% strongly object or object to their progeny intermarrying.

Another significant difference between Jewish day school

graduates and the general Jewish adult population concerns their Jewish communal involvement. About 60% are active in Jewish organizational life.

A major finding of the study demonstrates the influence of continued Jewish education on adult Jewish behavior. Jewish elementary education has a basic effect on adult Jewish observance, attitudes and involvement. Jewish high school has a cumulative effect – a significantly greater impact on the Jewishness of graduates. And, Jewish study beyond high school has a multiplier effect – a decidedly greater influence on adult Jewish behavior, on *kashrut* in and out of the home, on Sabbath observance, visits to Israel, involvement in Jewish community life, intermarriage rates and attitudes.

To be sure, there are variations in the Jewishness of Jewish day school graduates that relate to their parental Judaic orientation, the type of school they attended and the ages and gender of graduates. Graduates with Jewishly observant parents are likely to exhibit higher levels of adult Jewish behavior. However, Jewish day school education impacts the level of adult Jewish behavior of students whose parents were not observant.

In all, the study shows that a Jewish day school education in tandem with a positive Jewish home upbringing and an informal Jewish educational experience has a profound impact upon adult Jewish behavior attitudes and involvement.

ISRAEL EXPERIENCE

Clearly, one of the most effective ways to help form and reinforce Jewish identity is through an Israel Experience. After the NJPS findings became public, the organized, federated Jewish community showed great interest in this kind of "total immersion" program.

During the last several years, the leadership of the organized Jewish community has seriously considered ways of dramatically increasing the number of participants in short term programs. Hopefully, that will occur. However, it must be made crystal clear that an Israel Experience will not be effective if it is planned as a quick fix. To serve the purpose of enhancing Jewish identity, the Israel Experience must be part of an educational continuum, with appropriate pre-trip and post-trip learning components. Moreover, it is obvious that the quality of the programs and their relevance to the participants are crucial.

THE DRIVE FOR JEWISH CONTINUITY

If the 1990 NJPS has served a purpose vis-à-vis Jewish education, it has heightened the awareness of Jewish communal leaders about its critical importance. It is to the credit of the federated communal leadership that plans are being developed and programs are now underway to insure Jewish continuity.

Toward whom should we target our funding and efforts – the unaffiliated? the marginally affiliated? or the affiliated? Should we try to respond to the Jewish needs of each population? Given the current availability of funding, it is necessary to prioritize the investment of effort and subsidization into the most promising and productive activities. Priority support should be provided to those programs which have the greatest potential for insuring Jewish continuity. This translates, in the first instance, into aid for the Jewish day school, the majority of whose students are recruited from the ranks of the affiliated. The problem of the skyrocketing cost of Jewish all day education must be addressed forthrightly by the organized Jewish community.

The combination of quality Jewish schooling, a good, positive Jewish home and sound informal Jewish educational experience is the best guarantee for Jewish continuity. Accordingly, support must be forthcoming for family education programs to marginally affiliated parents of day school pupils and for informal educational programming, particularly Israel experience for Jewish day school teenagers.

Second level priority funding for the marginally affiliated would address the needs of the vast majority of Jewish supplementary school pupils and their parents. This means improving and intensifying the school programs, providing

Jewish family education and encouraging informal Jewish educational activities.

Third level funding should be targeted for the unaffiliated and made available only after the needs of the affiliated and marginally affiliated are met adequately. Insufficient support to the affiliated and certainly to the marginally affiliated might lead to their joining the growing ranks of the unaffiliated.

One clear need that must be given priority consideration in formal education is the matter of instructional quality. The only way to insure competent, effective instruction is through appropriate pre-service and in-service training for teachers and supervisory personnel for all types of schools.

INSTITUTIONAL AND ORGANIZATIONAL RESPONSES

A discussion of Jewish identity and Jewish education in the United States is not complete without reference to post high school Jewish educational institutions and programs including the Hebrew colleges and their educator training programs, the yeshivot, *Metivtot* and *Kollelim*, and Jewish Studies programs in university settings. Those post high school Jewish educational instrumentalities deserve separate attention. Equally important is consideration of both the long-established and newly created Jewish educational agencies involved in enhancing the role of Jewish education. An external study of the effectiveness of these agencies would make a significant contribution to the field of Jewish education.

CONCLUSION

Like lifelong Jewish learning, stimulating, developing, energizing, sustaining and enhancing Jewish identity is a never-ending process. In the first instance, in North America, given the current condition of Jewish life, this process involves an understanding of the nature and scope of the challenge of forming and reinforcing Jewish identity. It requires, too, a basic recognition of the need for quality multiple, multi-level Jewish educational responses.

It is clear that the major educational opportunities for Jewish identity formation and reinforcement are forthcoming from the institutions of formal Jewish learning. This means giving priority to helping maintain and enhance Jewish all day education as the most viable, effective instrumentality of Jewish education. Because of the cumulative effect of post elementary schooling, it means, also, insuring that Jewish day school students continue their Judaic studies, minimally, through high school.

In another vein, it means reconstructing the Jewish supplementary school where the majority of Jewish children exposed to formal Jewish learning receive their Jewish education, transforming it into a viable educational instrumentality via better trained personnel, Jewish family education, curriculum modification – combining cognitive and affective experiences, and continuous Jewish schooling until college years.

On another level, serious attention must be given to the variety of informal Jewish educational opportunities such as Jewish summer camps, synagogue-related youth organizations, JCCs, Hillels on the campus, Zionist Youth groups and short-term and long-term Israel experience programs. In addition, Jewish adult education initiatives merit consideration as significant responses to the challenge of Jewish identity building.

The enhancement of all types of Jewish educational opportunities depends largely upon substantially increased funding from the federated Jewish community, probably best achieved via creative partnerships with family and corporate foundations. This kind of statement, urging more federation dollars for Jewish education, is not new. Neither are the circumstances requiring more financial support entirely new. What is new is the scope and nature of the Jewish identity crisis in North America.

CHAPTER 7

CREATING THE JEWISH FUTURE: INSURING EFFECTIVE JEWISH EDUCATION

The *Midrash* informs us that there are essentially two kinds of future: "There is an immediate future – the day after today; and there is a distant future that holds the many morrows" (*Mekhilta* 22). This suggests that in educating for the future, we must engage in both short-range and long-range planning. For each of these levels, the approach must insure both *individual* Jewish identity and Jewish *group* continuity. The latter term, "Jewish continuity," has been used much too glibly by the Jewish community. "Continuous Jewish group vitality" may be a better way to identify the group need for future survival. Whatever the term, both concepts – individual Jewish identity and Jewish group continuity – are interdependent. When effective, they reinforce each other.

Using a classical Judaic formula to address the theme of this essay, we might say about educating for tomorrow: Educating for the Jewish future depends on successfully addressing five challenges: (1) bringing the goals of family and school into harmony; (2) finding the proper confluence of the affective and cognitive domains; (3) promoting Hebraic cultural literacy; (4) transmitting both universalistic and particularistic Jewish values; and (5) using appropriate instructional technology.

Why these five items? Because they all address the needs of the target populations of Jewish education. These populations can be differentiated by level of Jewish identity and participation. For lack of a better terminology, I refer to them by the descriptive language currently used to label the various levels of Jewish identification – the affiliated, marginally-affiliated and the unaffiliated. The classification *affiliated* refers to committed Jews, generally observant Orthodox, Conservative, Reform, or Reconstructionist. Jews who participate regularly in synagogue and Jewish communal life, visit Israel, and provide their children with an intensive Jewish education. The *marginally affiliated* category includes Jews who belong to a synagogue and/or a Jewish Community Center and/or contribute to Jewish charities, and/or are involved in Jewish communal work, but are not fully involved in any area. Marginally affiliated Jews generally send their children to a Jewish supplementary school through *bar/bat mitzvah*. A small percentage of them have visited Israel. *Unaffiliated* Jews, who constitute the largest segment of the Jewish population, are just what their classification implies. Generally, they do not belong to Jewish organizations and are not involved in Jewish life activity at home or elsewhere. They have not visited Israel, and their children do not receive a Jewish education. Marginally affiliated and even unaffiliated Jews sometimes may experience forms and feelings of Jewishness in their social, vocational and leisure-time settings. These do not, however, represent significant involvements.

Toward whom should we target our funding and efforts, the unaffiliated, the marginally affiliated or the affiliated? Should we try to respond to the needs of each group, and in what order? To do so would require a great deal of talent, knowledge and financial resources, perhaps more than the community can marshal. For several decades I have stressed the need to be concerned with all of these categories of youth and adults. Given the current availability of funding, however, it is necessary to prioritize the investment of effort and funds into the most promising and productive activities.

Priority support should be provided to those programs with the greatest potential for insuring Jewish continuity. This translates, in the first instance, into aid for Jewish day schools, where most of the students are recruited from the ranks of the affiliated.

The combination of quality Jewish schooling, a good, positive Jewish home, and sound informal Jewish educational experiences is the best guarantee for Jewish continuity. Accordingly, more support must be forthcoming for the day schools, including the funding of family education programs for marginally affiliated parents of pupils and of informal educational programming, particularly Israel experiences, for day-school teenagers. Second-level priority funding should address the needs of Jewish supplementary school pupils and their marginally affiliated parents. As with day school families, this means improving and intensifying school programs, providing family education and encouraging informal educational activities, especially the Israel experience for synagogue school post *bar/bat mitzvah* students. Third-level funding should be targeted for the unaffiliated and made available only after the needs of the affiliated and marginally affiliated are met adequately. Insufficient support for the affiliated, and, certainly for the marginally affiliated, might lead to their joining the growing ranks of the unaffiliated. We must build on what already exists.

The 450,000 Jewish day school and supplementary school pupils in North America and their parents are a ready audience; it is much less difficult to insure their Jewish continuity than that of the unaffiliated. Here, the message for the future is: "Galvanize the core as a Jewish communal priority." Addressing the five challenges with which I began this essay will help insure the future of the core and of many other Jews as well.

THE JEWISH FAMILY AND THE JEWISH SCHOOL

A fascinating study of talented people by Professor Benjamin Bloom of the University of Chicago found that there are two features common to the background of top performers in the arts, music, sports, academia, and science fields. The first is *home support*. Bloom notes:

The parents of the talented individuals varied greatly in the level of education they had completed, the type of work they engaged to, their economic level, and their vocational interests and activities. However, they were all genuinely concerned about their children and wanted to do the best for them at all stages of their development. To a large extent, they could be described as child-oriented and willing to devote their time, their resources and their energy to giving each of their children the best conditions they could provide for them. Almost no sacrifice was too great if they thought it would help their children's development. It is clear that to be successful, education must be a synergistic experience. Teacher effectiveness depends upon parents and parent effectiveness depends upon teachers.

This kind of synergy does not exist in our Jewish supplementary schools – certainly not for the vast majority of parents.

Most recently, Dr. James P. Corner, after thirty years of clinical involvement with school children at Yale University's Child Study Center, observed that in successful schools there is home-school social congruence. He stressed that, to be effective, schools must allow for the empowerment and full partnership of parents and staff as true partners in addressing the children's psycho-educational and developmental needs." In the context of Jewish education, home-school congruence and the empowerment and partnership of parents and teachers must be Jewishly based.

The school has become a necessary component of every civilized society and a dominant factor in technological, industrial and cultural progress. This fact, however, does not discharge the home of its basic tutorial obligations in the area of subculture and ethics. Modern research clearly demonstrates the need for the home to act as an educational instrumentality. We cannot deal with students if we disregard their family background, since school is, at best, a reinforcer of attitudes, behavior patterns, and even skills acquired in the home environment.

In research done at Harvard University, Geoffrey Bock shows

that doing well in (the Jewish) school depends on the learning environment, the congruence of school values with home values, with the school culture, and (with) other noncognitive effects of education." Jews have always believed that the influence of the home is paramount in the lives of children. The traditional home is best characterized by the spirit of Jewish practice "from the *mezuzah* on the doorpost to the observance of dietary laws in the kitchen." It is the center of religious activity, the means by which children learn to behave Jewishly. Family practices, such as placing coins in the charity box (*pushka*) before lighting Shabbat candles on Friday eve and feeding the family pets and domestic animals before the family members sit down to eat, serves to transmit the social and humane values of Judaism. Children of all ages acknowledge the pedagogical role of the home by blessing their parents as educators ("my father my teacher," "my mother my teacher") – in the Grace after Meals.

In fact, in Jewish tradition, primary responsibility for Jewish education lies in the home. Parents are responsible for the education of their off-spring. "And you shall teach your children" (Deut. 11:13) is a commandment taken literally. In biblical times, and later in the post-biblical period, elementary level instruction was left in the hands of the parents, particularly the father. In the second century C.E. Rabbi Akiva instructed one of his disciples: "When you teach your son, teach him out of a well-corrected book," suggesting that the father has an awesome responsibility to teach his offspring properly (6:2). When teachers were hired to help parents fulfill this responsibility, they were accorded the same respect due to parents. "He who teaches his friend's son – it is as if he sired him," noted our sages (*Sanhedrin* 19b). Even after the school became a recognized institution in the post-Talmudic era, parents continued to teach their children. The home was the natural place for religious and moral training. Jewish tradition was ahead of its time in ascribing an educational role to parents.

The powerful bond between Jewish parents and children, exemplified by mutual responsibility and mutual respect, made the home a bulwark able to withstand the numerous pressures and stresses from without. If there are reasons for the mysterious ability of Jews to survive against so many odds, they are the family and the school. More than any other people, Jews have recognized their life-sustaining role. Indeed, in calling for Christian-Jewish cooperation in 1960, the Archbishop of York asserted: "We can learn from the Jews about education, about the richness of their home life, and the enormous influence it had upon their people" (qtd. in Schiff, "The Jewish Family and the Jewish School" p. 9).

And now, the Jewish family in America is in crisis. One need only cite the all-too-well-known findings of the 1990 National Jewish Population Survey to confirm this observation (Kosmin, Goldstein, et al). With the exception of a very small percentage of homes – mostly Orthodox – the traditional relationship between education and family has broken down.

This brings us to the critical role of the school. The singular focus of schooling – indulging the Jewish school – has been the education of the child. It is clear, now, that the current challenge of continuity requires that the school broaden its scope to include the whole family. This will change the relationship of the educator to pupils, to parents, and to the community. It will also change the nature of the synagogues that sponsor schools. The last decade has seen some small movements towards change, as creative Jewish educators have developed programming for entire families, but there must be more.

CONFLUENCE OF THE COGNITIVE AND AFFECTIVE DOMAINS

There are basically two aspects to the process of Jewish identification: *identity formation* and *identity reinforcement*. For children, youths, and adults having no or little home involvement with Jewish life, the *formation* of identity is a necessary first level of education. For those having varying degrees of affiliation, knowledge and experience, *reinforcing* their Jewish identity is the appropriate mode.

Learning takes place in various ways. Different things are learned best in different ways. Learning outcomes depend in part upon the nature of the learning processes. Essentially, there are two types of learning process – *cognitive* and *affective*. Cognitive processes pertain to the acquisition of facts and the comprehension of ideas. They help the learner analyze and articulate concepts and communicate information. Cognitive learning has been, and is, the chief – and often the only – ingredient of formal education. For identity formation, however, cognitive learning is not enough. Affective processes, which involve emotions, attitudes, interests, preferences, and values, are needed. The affective domain is indispensable in helping learners develop receptiveness to new ideas and behaviors to assure commitment to particular values. Working in confluence with the cognitive domain, the affective process reinforces the school's work with the family as it helps fashion the Jewish identity of young people.

No matter how successful the school is in its family education programs, for the vast majority of students in the Jewish supplementary school and for a significant percentage of day school pupils as well, the school must serve as an alternative Jewish environment. The most important characteristic of the Jewish day school with its longer day and two sets of teachers is its full-time, all-encompassing Judaic climate. This feature is lacking in the supplementary school where it is most urgently needed. The recommendations of the three-year study of Jewish Supplementary Schools in Greater New York, which I directed in the 1980s, respond to this challenge in a variety of ways (Schiff, *The Jewish Supplementary School*).

The recommendations fall into a pattern of thesis, antithesis, and synthesis. Supported by current research, the thesis contends that the family, more than any other agency is the crucial factor in influencing the eventual outcomes of schooling. The antithesis, deriving from Effective Schools Research activity in the public arena, suggests that, notwithstanding societal or family influences, the school can become the crucial, overriding force transmitting knowledge and values to children and youth. The synthesis incorporates both approaches, as it stresses the importance of the family and the school and recognizes the role of the home and the classroom and the impact of both parents and teachers on pupils.

The New York Supplementary School Study recommends that the synagogue school change its education focus from schooling of the young to education of all members of the family. To enhance the affective quality of synagogue education, it suggests that a new structure be developed in which all professionals, including the rabbi, principal, teachers, youth leaders, and cantor, will become members of a family education team, with the rabbi assuming the role of Judaic content leader. Furthermore, the study recommends that the congregational supplementary school provides pupils with opportunities for increased formal and informal educational exposure. This would mean integrating informal educational activities into every level of the school curriculum emphasizing summer educational camping and week-end fellowship programs (one *shabbaton* or weekend retreat per month for upper grade students in lieu of their weekday and Sunday classes during that week). For high school students, this means integrating an Israel experience with appropriate pre-tour and post-tour educational components.

This new mode of synagogue school operation would require the training or retraining of all synagogue professionals. For some teachers, shifting the focus of the school to families would mean full-time educational career opportunities where none or almost none currently exist in the supplementary school system.

EFFECTIVE HEBRAIC-JUDAIC TEACHING AND LEARNING

The second common characteristic of top performers in the Bloom study is quality time-on-task. In the first instance, this means that you cannot really succeed in study unless you invest sufficient time in it. The time invested, moreover, must be *quality* time.

This dimension – quality time-on-task – imposes upon the Jewish community the awesome responsibility of insuring that Jewish school supervisors and teachers are qualified to achieve quality teaching-learning conditions. Among other things, this challenge means making the Jewish education profession attractive to the most talented persons. It means providing high quality in-service education to the current educational professionals and enforcing high standards of practice. These matters deserve full-length, detailed attention much beyond the scope of this chapter.

Unlike the supplementary school, which is seriously deficient in the amount of time available for learning, the day school generally provides a sufficient number of hours for Jewish Studies. Here the challenge is the quality of learning and the lasting effect of instruction.

It is to the credit of the yeshivot throughout North America that over the years they have increased their emphasis on the study of Judaic sources in the original, especially the Pentateuch, the Talmud, and their respective commentaries. The ideological bent of most yeshivot limits their curricula to these subjects plus the study of *Shulhan Arukh* (Code of Jewish Law). They pay little or no attention to the Hebrew language as a subject, to the Prophets and Writings, to Jewish history, Jewish philosophy, and Israel. Neither the immediate nor the long-range future holds any prospect for change in their curricula.

The emphasis on the study of Talmud is accompanied by increasing stress on ritual practices as viewed from a fundamentalist, sectarian perspective. In this way the ultra-Orthodox, *Haredi* segment of the Jewish community, seems to be successful in reinforcing the narrow, intensive identity of its youth. Thus its continuity seems well assured. Virtually all the *Haredi* students continue their yeshiva studies through high school and beyond.

While the Modern Orthodox day schools and the somewhat less intensive Solomon Schechter (Conservative) schools differ in religious and textual emphases, they all provide balanced Hebraic curricula for their students. The Jewish Studies programs in most communal day schools are not as intensive as in the Orthodox or Conservative schools, and the Judaic programs in day schools under Reform auspices are less intensive still.

My recent research on graduates of Jewish day schools clearly points to the superiority of all day education. It is clear that young adults who studied in a day school are more likely to observe the Sabbath and *kashrut*, to be involved in the community, and to visit Israel than those who did not. They also intermarry with much less frequency (Schiff and Schneider 11–12).

Further, my research shows beyond a doubt, that young adults who graduated from a day *high* school demonstrate significantly higher levels of adult Jewish behavior than those who completed only an elementary day school. And the intermarriage rate of graduates of Jewish day *high* schools is much lower than that of alumni of elementary schools (4). These findings challenge the communal leadership to provide greater support to day schools, particularly high schools, to enable all who wish to complete twelve grades of Jewish education to do so.

We must be concerned with the content of Jewish schooling in its entirety as well as its extensiveness. The content of Jewish schooling relates directly to the language of the texts and the language of instruction of Jewish Studies. The Midrash informs us that the Israelites were redeemed from Egypt because, among other things, they did not change their language (*Midrash Vayikra Rabbah 32:3*). They continued to speak and use Hebrew while in Goshen and during their servitude. The Hebrew language, broadly interpreted to include its use in study, prayer, and daily conversation, is one of the key reasons for the miraculous survival of the Jewish people during the last two millennia against unbelievable odds. There are cases of individual Jews who assimilated and whole communities, which disappeared, because, among other things, they lost contact with the Hebrew language leading to the assimilation of the total community. Alexandria, Egypt, some fifteen hundred years ago is a prime example of the results of this tragic neglect. A working knowledge of Hebrew for the study of texts and for prayer is an imperative for Jewish group survival, since Hebrew is the bearer of Jews' spiritual identity. It is a vehicle of a sacred past, of eternal Jewish values, and, at the same time, a major expression of contemporary Jewish vitality. The mystique of Hebrew underscores the individuality of the Jew, differentiating him from his environment, but not estranging him from it.

Hebraic cultural literacy is one of the most important goals of Hebrew language learning. Even though Hebrew was not a spoken language of the vast majority of Jews during their long diaspora history, the average person used as many as twelve hundred Hebrew words and terms to denote familiar Judaic concepts and practices. These expressions continue to be an essential part of Judaic-Hebraic literacy, and a literate, well-educated Jew should possess this unique linguistic baggage. In educating for the future, Hebrew must become both the vernacular and the sacred language of Jews.

A variety of new instructional efforts including the production of Hebrew language texts and materials and teacher training courses were initiated in the 1980s to improve the teaching of Hebrew language. Hebrew literacy initiatives for adults, moreover have gained momentum in the 1990s. Yet the revival of the Hebrew language in America is still an elusive goal for the overwhelming majority of Jews. We need a comprehensive plan which takes into consideration: (1) the realities of North American Jewish life and education. (2) the various roles of the Hebrew language in the configuration of Jewish continuity patterns; (3) the potential resources that can be utilized in developing effective Hebrew language programs; (4) the variety of approaches to transmitting Jewish values, reinforcing Jewish identity, and strengthening Israel-diaspora ties; and (5) the best possible ways to coordinate, modify, and improve current efforts aimed at improving Hebrew language education.

A Jewish community of active Hebrew language learners and regular users is an attainable goal. The key is to find the ways to teach Hebrew effectively both as a modern language and as the essential link to the Judaic heritage. It may be helpful to examine those foreign language-teaching programs on the university level, which do not begin with instruction in conversation. Similarly, we might pursue the modes and goals of teaching Hebrew reading comprehension as a first step in Jewish elementary schools. The program would continue on to text learning, and then, for a select number of students, to conversation, and finally to writing.

There is strong feeling among many academicians and practitioners that Hebrew "spokenness" is not an attainable goal for the North American Jewish community – that it is certainly not achievable for students in Jewish supplementary schools, and it may even be difficult for many pupils in day schools. This issue must be examined carefully. But the goal of Hebraic cultural literacy for the Jewish community, at large, and Hebrew speaking for an elite segment of the Jewish population may be the best answer to the question of what is the most appropriate role of Hebrew in American Jewish life.

JEWISH VALUES

On the third day of the month of *Tishrei*, Jews observe the Fast of *Gedaliah*, commemorating the assassination of the Jewish governor of Jerusalem appointed by the Babylonians after they destroyed the First Temple in 587 B.C.E. "And who killed him?" asks the Talmud (*Rosh Hashanah* 18b). "Ishmael, the son of Netaniah, killed him." A fast day commemorates each event.

In our time, we have witnessed the murder of an Israeli prime minister. The causes and consequences of this abominable crime thrust upon the educational community in Israel and the Diaspora a major responsibility regarding the moral/ethical education of our youth – an obligation that could change the face and future of Jewish schooling. Rabin's assassination has to change the Jewish education agenda everywhere, for all time. The challenge is to confront irreverent feelings, uncontrolled passion, misdirected energies and inflammatory language wherever they may be found – on the Right or Left, in the hearts and homes of the fervent opponents of the peace process or of its passionate proponents. The educational challenge is to demonstrate that extremism of any kind is dangerous, that the misuse of language can set the stage for unspeakable acts against humanity.

First, we must note the precedents in Jewish history. Our ancestors were not immune to crimes of fratricide. When Avner ben Ner was killed by Yoav (Samuel II 3:27), King David and the Israelites were in shock. "You well know," mourned David, "That a prince and a great man has fallen this day in Israel." Jeremiah was killed by fellow Israelites in Egypt, because they could not bear his unrelenting remonstrations. The Second Temple was destroyed along with Jerusalem and many lives were lost, because relationships among Jews had deteriorated to the point where, our sages inform us, the people of Israel deserved to be destroyed, even though they were meticulous in other Jewish observances. *Sin'at hinam* (baseless hatred), the Talmud suggests, brought about the destruction of the Second Temple.

Rabin's death reminds us that one of the greatest dangers the Jewish people have faced throughout history has been ourselves. There are numerous other lessons we must now teach in all our schools. Foremost is the value of human life, the worthwhileness of every human being. This lesson should be part of a campaign to promote tolerance, understanding, and love of fellow human beings. Jewish education must be in the forefront of reviving the ethical/moral dimension of Jewish life as expressed in the mitzvot *bain adam lahavero* (commandments concerning relationships among people). We must teach our students that one can disagree without being disagreeable, that dissent is a good Jewish tradition. Jews are no strangers to controversy. One needs only to note the sharp differences between Bet Hillel and Bet Shammai, between Abaye and Rava in ancient times. Their disputes, however, were "for the sake of Heaven." They all sought to establish the truth and bring about higher standards of Jewish living. Today we must instruct that dissent in a civil manner is a much needed and valuable social and political instrument in a democratic society.

Schools must place emphasis on the idea of ethical role models. In the introduction of his insightful study, The Prophets, Abraham Heschel stresses that "the significance of Israel's prophets lies not only in what they said, but also in what they were." Heschel's pithy and powerful description of the prophets provides a meaningful message of modeling for our times. He writes: "The prophet is a person who sees the world with the eyes of God...a person who holds God and man in one thought at one time, at all times...who suffers harm done to others...living in dismay, he has the power to transcend dismay."

The adults in the school community – supervisors, teachers, rabbis, cantors, youth leaders and clerical staff – must all be able to serve as models. Parents must be sensitized to the importance of adult members of the home serving as models of Jewish behavior within the framework of Jewish family education. Moreover, Jewish history is replete with "heroes" whose biographies could well serve to inform and inspire. This form of teaching should be highlighted in our schools.

Students must be taught to appreciate and practice *ahavat hinam* (selfless love) as advocated by the saintly, Chief Rabbi of Palestine, Abraham Isaac Kook. If the Second Temple was destroyed because of *sin'at hinam* (gratuitous hatred), he asserted, the Third Temple will be built because of *ahavat hinam*. In each school, curricularizing Judaic ethical teachings is a programmatic imperative on three levels: moral education as a separate subject; integration of ethical lessons into the ongoing subject matter of the school; and the development of a moral climate.

The Jewish educational establishment has a responsibility beyond the classroom walls to help provide moral/ethical instruction in formal and informal settings. Educational leaders everywhere must organize for moral education through conferences, seminars, teacher training, the development of text materials and guidelines, and pilot school programs. In our thrust to highlight Jewish moral/ethical education, we must take care to insure that all points of view – from the political Right to the political Left, from ultra-religious to ultra-secular, from zealous sabras to Jews committed to diaspora living, from ardent Zionists to non-Zionists whose support for Israel is expressed solely in financial terms – are considered with civility, fairness, and honesty.

MODERN EDUCATIONAL TECHNOLOGY

It is impossible in the latter half of the last decade of the twentieth century to speak about "Educating for the Future" without urgent consideration of the implications of the technological revolution for Jewish schooling. The computer has revolutionized modern civilization. It can improve teaching and learning in school and home dramatically. Since the arrival of the cyberspace age, the classroom will never be the same. The computer permits teachers and students to go beyond the classroom walls and become part of a larger, exciting Jewish world. The remarkable information superhighway can benefit education, as it has the corporate and business worlds.

It can make teaching easier and increase student productivity significantly. It can initiate new Jewish learning and reinforce the classroom through the internet, which allows teachers and students to access information from libraries and other online sources with ease. It makes possible desktop video conferencing. In addition, Jewish students see that "the whole world is Jewish." New computer-based multi-media can extend, expand, modify, and strengthen teaching and learning at home and school. Interactive, computer-based instruction can help students discover the internet permits the development and use of new educational tools like e-mail and chat rooms, where students all over the world can talk to each other, and it allows asynchronous learning, which simply means that information can be accessed at any time from any place. Colleges in North America are moving rapidly into this form of learning. Jewish education must do the same. Talking to Jews all over the world would give Jewish students a sense of Jewish connectedness. The global village will help new knowledge; students can pace themselves according to their specific learning needs.

For the young and young-at-heart, using the computer is fun. As of this writing, forty-one million Americans are connected to the internet, and three hundred synagogues in North America have their own websites or e-mail addresses. These numbers are constantly growing. All Jewish youth movements are online. The Council of Jewish Federations, in cooperation with other major Jewish organizations, sponsors the Jewish online network.

A recent study shows that 11- to 14-year-olds are the most frequent individual computer users. The Jewish educational community must insure that Jewish programming is available on the computer for this critical group. It is at their age that Jewish identity is often challenged as their peers replace the influence of their home and as they themselves become increasingly involved in the larger society. The only electronic equipment needed by a school for internet involvement is a computer and a modem.

AFTERWORD

Here I have described five urgent Jewish educational challenges that confront us as we contemplate the future. There are obviously many more education needs that should be addressed both for the *mahar akhshav* and the *mahar l'ahar zman* in the immediate and distant future. Increasingly, in the open North American society, the Jewish school must be able to respond effectively to new societal developments, new communal conditions, new problems, and even new threats. If these five challenges are dealt with adequately the Jewish community will be well on its way to a bright future.

CHAPTER 8

A New Blueprint for Community: A Jewish Renaissance Perspective Assuring Jewish Continuity

Change requires a basic understanding of the conditions requiring change, an objective, open mind to describe the conditions in terms that do not obfuscate reality, and a willingness to do whatever is necessary to bring about the change.

To observe the nature of Jewish life in America is to face a two-pronged truism. On the one hand, Jews have "made it" in the *goldene medina*. The blessings of a free western society have endowed them with economic prosperity, comfortable living and a taste of luxury, which accompany professional growth and unbridled business opportunities.

On the other hand, Jews are "losing it" in America. They are the victims of a fast paced acculturation-deculturation process whereby they are shedding the vestiges of their Jewish heritage. "Making it" as Americans does not necessarily mean "losing it" as Jews. But, if we look at the Jewish community at the end of the 20th Century, we must conclude that this is what has happened to the majority of Jews in North America.

This bi-furcated condition requires an immediate and

effective response (or a variety of appropriate responses) if the Jews are to continue as a vibrant Jewish entity in North America. That response mandates that Jewish education in America become the number one priority of the funding resources of North American Jewry. The emphasis on Jewish education does not imply a negation of the other valuable services provided locally and internationally to Jewish communities. Jewish education must be considered the prime objective of the organized Jewish community in America, even as it responds to other domestic, overseas and Israel needs which it must continue to do effectively. The Jewish Renaissance component of the new vision and blueprint for the North American Jewish community must be primary if Jews are to make it through the 21st Century.

Oftimes, the reallocation of dollars for Jewish communal service in North America is discussed as a domestic vs. Israel problem. However, the challenge of adequate funding for Jewish education must be answered via a reordering of domestic priorities and a redistribution of domestic funding, and not at the expense of allocations to Israel.

THE CONDITION OF JEWISH EDUCATION IN AMERICA

Jewish education has always occupied a unique position in Jewish life. Throughout Jewish history, Jews were expected to be lifelong students of the Torah. Jewish learning in the home, in the school, and in the community was the very plasma of Jewish life. It was the soul of a people and the guarantor of continuity.

In Talmudic times, it was prohibited to live in a city without a Jewish teacher. Nothing save matters of life and death was important enough to postpone the learning of Torah. So crucial was Torah study deemed for the survival of the Jewish people that one of the causes enumerated in the Talmud for the destruction of Jerusalem was the neglect of the education of children. No other people has placed such emphasis on educating its young.

The history of Jewish education in America is marked by many positive and meaningful accomplishments, including: the development of the Jewish day school as a major mode of Jewish schooling; the development of central agencies for Jewish education; the introduction of modern instructional strategies; the establishment of teacher center programs; the creative use of media in instruction; the production of innovative teaching and learning materials; the convening of exciting educational conferences, workshops and seminars; and especially the development of a wide variety of Israel-American programs such as teenage and family tours, summer and year long study in Israeli educational institutions, Israel based teacher education projects and cooperative curriculum activities. American Jewish education has many bright spots. For these we should be proud and thankful.

However, despite all the progress that has taken place in Jewish education, the Jewish community in America may soon lose this instrumentality as an effective method for transmitting Jewish heritage and Jewish values. It may lose the institution most needed for Jewish continuity. Now, as never before, Jewish education holds out much promise for assuring the creative continuity of Jewish life and the Jewish people.

As Jewish education goes, so will go Jewish life. If Jewish education loses its vitality, the very survival of the American Jewish community will be endangered.

TRADITION OF JEWISH EDUCATION ENDANGERED

Jewish education became an important problem in American Jewish life from the moment Jews were transplanted to the North American continent. The task was monumental – relating the Jewish school to the development of American Judaism and to the larger American society. But the resources needed were never equal to the task.

From the start, the open, free, untraditional American setting threatened the development of Jewish education. In the first instance, the increasing diffusion of Jewish intellectuality among the various arts and sciences, and among numerous academic and professional concerns deprived Jewish education of the needed cadre of Jewish educators of quality.

Secondly, the theory and practice of voluntarism in American

Jewish life deprived the Jewish education enterprise of a secure base of ongoing support. Although the American Jewish community generally recognized the value of Jewish schooling, for the most part, local Jewish communities did not assume adequate responsibility for their respective educational programs.

As a result of these two conditions – the transposition of intellectual and cultural interest by a large majority of Jews on the one hand, and the lack of real organized community support on the other – Jewish education was left to the rather meager resources and designs of individual Jews and small groups of concerned leaders.

And so, here we are, in these turbulent, critical times, faced with ever-growing problems in Jewish education – problems which are not really the making of the Jewish educational establishment. Essentially, these fall into two categories: issues relating to Jewish communal responsibility, and problems pertaining to the educational program.

In viewing Jewish life in North America against the backdrop of rapid social change in the larger environment, one is struck by the unresponsiveness of a significant segment of Jewish communal leadership toward adequate support of Jewish schooling. The underlying reason for this condition, in large measure, is that there is no sense of urgency about the failures and problems in this area. The Jewish community does not feel about its Jewishly "disadvantaged" children as many leaders of our general society feel about the need for more effective education for the disadvantaged minorities.

There is a direct relationship between America's prosperity and its education growth. While the United States is a consumer-oriented society, education, since 1957, has been considered not as a consumer product, but as an investment in the future. By contrast, the Jewish community views Jewish education almost entirely as a consumer service. To its credit, Federation leadership is increasingly aware of the need for massive support for Jewish education. Such support, to be sure, means either a major reordering of priorities or the uncovering of large new resources for the funding of Jewish schooling, or both. On another level, the Jewish community lacks in awareness of the state of Jewish education – its strengths and weaknesses – and the factors contributing to whatever successes and failures may be its lot. Clearly, the Jewish day school has proven to be a remarkable success story. On the other hand, the Jewish supplementary school requires much upgrading and improvement as a Jewish educational instrumentality.

The foregoing leads us to two convincing conclusions: The need for greater clarity about the role and status of Jewish schooling is vital. The need for effective Jewish education on all levels – preschool through adult must be fully understood. Secondly, the need for adequate support for all Jewish schooling according to the respective requirements of each type of education must be forthcoming without delay. This means mega dollars to finance existing all day institutions and new Jewish day schools and significant funding to help bring about the necessary changes in congregational schooling.

NEEDED: COALITION OF TOP LEADERSHIP

What we need in the Jewish community is a new alliance – a coalition of top Jewish leaders conjoined by a common purpose – to make all our schools effective (or more effective), and to help insure their continued effectiveness. This alliance must include all leaders of the Jewish community – congregational, communal and educational – who believe in the continuity of the Jewish people. It must be based upon respect for the different needs of individual schools and school groups and upon the desire to meet the requirements of each group appropriately. There cannot be a monolithic approach to meeting Jewish educational challenges.

This alliance must work cooperatively with the various local communal structures and resources, particularly with Jewish day school groups and synagogue organizations. Our common destiny as Jews should unite us even as we endeavor to respond to our individual needs. Our *shared identity* must be ever reinforced as each group strives to strengthen its *unique identity*. The Jewish community's response to crises demonstrates adequately its ability to transcend differences for the common good. Certainly, the present situation regarding Jewish continuity is severe enough, the current Jewish educational challenge crucial enough, and the task before us enormous enough to elicit real partnership in resolving our problems – in turning prospect into promise and in propelling promise into reality.

THE CHALLENGE AND CHANGE

Achieving Jewish renaissance requires a revolution in the basic value system of the organized American Jewish community. It calls for a major transformation in attitude of lay and professional leadership toward Jewish life, a fundamental recognition of the role of the Jewish heritage in the home, in the community and in the work place. This attitudinal change must bring with it:

1. a basic understanding throughout our federated system of the importance of the Hebrew language as a vital force for unity and continuity;
2. a basic understanding of the value and role of Hebraic texts (including biblical, Talmudic, medieval, contemporary and modern Hebrew literature) in the maintenance and enhancement of Jewish life;
3. a basic understanding of the significance of Jewish life cycle events;
4. the realization that the centrality of Israel in Jewish life is essential for Jewish continuity;
5. the clear recognition of the need to provide an effective Jewish education experience to Jewish youth in high school and college;
6. a basic understanding of the importance of providing a confluence of cognitive and affective experience on all and appreciation of the need to nurture and support creative Jewish educators and innovative Jewish education programs.

An essential part of the challenge, indeed, a *conditione sine qua non* for change to happen, is developing strategies for creating attitudinal change. To this effort, the new continental communal leadership must devote significant thought and energy.

It should follow that once the basic attitudinal transformation takes hold, the Jewish community would make Jewish renaissance possible by unconditionally supporting the human resources and educational structures and programs that are absolutely essential for assuring change and bringing about the renaissance.

In the first instance, this means raising substantially the status of the Jewish educator, making the Jewish education profession competitive with other "Jewish" professions such as medicine, law, accounting and business, in order to attract the most talented young people, thus reversing the brain drain, which has affected the potential effectiveness of the Jewish educational enterprise.

Secondly, it means providing the necessary support to the formal Jewish educational institutions which have a captive audience of almost one half million Jewish youth, particularly to Jewish all day education including: scholarship funding to make the Jewish day school accessible and affordable for increasing numbers of Jewish families; the provision of state of the art educational facilities, including modern technology for all schools; increased program support to enhance the development of curricula and curricular materials; the provision of quality in-service programs for all Jewish day school professionals, and the development of family education programs for parents whose home life requires Judaic enhancement.

It means helping the Jewish supplementary school become an effective educational instrument. Among other things, this suggests facilitating the development of quality Jewish family education programs; additional school hours for intensive Hebrew language instruction, and Hebraic text study; and cooperative programming with informal Jewish education, including Jewish summer camping and teen trips to Israel.

Thirdly, it means placing emphasis on teenage Jewish education: assuring that all Jewish elementary day school and supplementary school graduates continue in Jewish high school programs. It means, also, maximizing the number of teenagers who visit Israel for long-term programs; and, if that is not possible, insuring that all Jewish teenagers have the benefit of meaningful short-term experience in Israel. The success of Israel Experience programs depends largely on the quality of pre-trip preparation, particularly in Hebrew language and culture, and upon adequate post-trip follow-up.

In the fourth place, it means providing the necessary support to the various types of informal Jewish education: Jewish educational camping, synagogue youth activities, Zionist youth groups, Jewish community center youth programs, and Israel Experience preparatory and follow-up education.

Finally, it means developing and supporting intensive programs for adult Jewish education – enhancing the Jewishness of Jewish adults – so that they may serve as Jewish models for their children and grandchildren and for the children of their neighbors. This suggests that Jewish communal leaders, synagogue lay leaders and philanthropic leaders should become regular Jewish learners so that they will be paradigms of Jewishness. Such leaders will better understand the Jewish education needs of Jewish youth and adults.

IN A NUTSHELL

Jewish Renaissance means changing the basic value system of the federated Jewish community. While not ignoring the wide variety of local and overseas needs of American Jewry, Israel and world Jewry, the federated Jewish community's new structure must make support of efforts to guarantee Jewish identity and Jewish continuity its priority purpose. This means dramatically increasing funding to Jewish education, particularly the Jewish Day School, and broadening communal support to programs of Hebrew language and culture. It means a significant increase of financial assistance to the Jewish supplementary school, to Israel experience programs for teenagers and young adults, to Jewish educational programs for high school and college youth, to Jewish educational camping and to adult Jewish education.

All this can be accomplished best via active partnership with synagogues and day schools, and with Israel-based organizations; and it should not be at the expense of Jewish communal support to Israel. To be effective, such support must be provided on the local level. The new national-continental communal structure must recognize that the Jewish renaissance of American Jewry can become a reality only if the educational institutions of the local Jewish communities participate actively in the transformational activities and each community becomes a building block of the Jewish future.

In conclusion, to assure the development of a Jewish renaissance movement in America, Jewish communal leadership must recognize that creating a vision for the future of the Jewish community is only the first stage of Jewish renewal. The key to its fulfillment is the actualization of the vision via real ongoing dollar support from the leadership of the community.

CHAPTER 9

Thoughts About Holocaust Research, Documentation and Jewish Education

ON THE THRUST OF THIS PAPER

This paper is wide-ranging. It covers a variety of thrusts in *Shoah* education. To address all the subject mater of this essay would require substantially more funding than is currently available for Research, Documentation and Education. The task of the panel, as I view it, would be to initiate a process of prioritization regarding *Shoah* education needs. A major criterion for the prioritization would be the perception and knowledge (based upon research and evaluation) of what works best in accomplishing the goals of Holocaust education.

The size of allocations relates to the type of programs selected for grants. Mass education recommendations would require large allocations. Grants to individuals and individual institutions would be relatively small. Many such grants could be made.

THE EDUCATIONAL CHALLENGES OF THE CONFERENCE ON JEWISH MATERIAL CLAIMS AGAINST GERMANY

It is clear that securing compensation and restitution for individuals and providing relief and rehabilitation to survivors should remain the top priority of the Claims Conference as long as there are survivors. At the same time, on a communal-wide or country-wide and world-wide level, it is critical to create a climate about the moral responsibility regarding the *Shoah* and a world understanding – both among Jews and non-Jews – about the nature of the Holocaust so that what transpired between 1939 and 1945 will never be forgotten. It will be our way of observing the biblical commandment *lo tish-kah* – "thou shalt not forget."

Achieving this goal is the task of the Research, Education/Documentation dimension of the Claims Conference. In this regard, the funds allocated for Research, Education and Documentation during the last five years for projects in Australia, Europe, the Former Soviet Union, Israel, North America, and South America should be reviewed with an eye towards improving and strengthening such projects. An objective of these grants should be achieving greater world understanding of the *Shoah*.

GOALS RELATING TO HOLOCAUST UNDERSTANDING

The key education challenges of the Claims Conference relate to *Shoah* memory. These challenges include: Keeping alive the memory of the *Shoah* in the minds and hearts of Jews of all ages everywhere; this can be achieved by:

1. motivating study, reading, and viewing about the Holocaust experience;
2. making available appropriate educational materials to Jewish youth and adults;
3. encouraging observance of *Yom Hashoah* in Jewish communities the world over. (In this case, the problem of the two different dates for *Yom Hashoah* observance – January 27 and Nissan 27 – should be resolved.)
4. Keeping alive or creating *Shoah* memory in the minds and hearts of non-Jews everywhere. This can be accomplished by:
   - appropriate communication and use of media;
   - teaching about the *Shoah* in non-Jewish educational settings on high school and university levels;

- making available and promoting the reading and viewing of appropriate educational materials and programs.
- making available appropriate material for public consumption

THE URGENCY OF *SHOAH* EDUCATION

There is an urgency regarding the timing of *Shoah* research, education and documentation. The most valuable and irreplaceable resources for *Shoah* communication and education are the Holocaust survivors. As time moves on, the opportunities decrease for using survivors for documentary research, for audio and video interviews and presentations and for transmitting personally the nature of the Shoah experience to Jews and non-Jews throughout the world.

It is clear that utilizing survivors now should be a priority of the education and documentation programs.

SHOAH EDUCATION AND JEWISH IDENTITY FORMATION

In addition to the knowledge and feeling about the Holocaust acquired via *Shoah* education, the process of Holocaust study and exposure to the appropriate transmission of the meaning of the *Shoah* experience may help increase the Jewish consciousness and involvement of Jewish youth and adults not fully identified with Jewish life. This aspect of *Shoah* education should be explored.

DEFINITION OF *SHOAH* EDUCATION

On the one hand, as noted, the purpose of *Shoah* education is global. It relates to the world-at-large and to world Jewry as a whole. In this case, *Shoah* education is a strategy of reaching the masses. This suggests that the Claims Conference develop effective communication programs and media methodologies for transmitting dramatic messages about the *Shoah*.

On the other hand, *Shoah* education relates to individual Jews and non-Jews. As such, education about the Holocaust can be described via the dichotomy made by Rabbi Joseph B.

Soloveichick between *hinukh* and *limud* – between the process of education (*hinukh*) and the process of learning (*limud*).

According to this dichotomy, education refers to the psychological social and pedagogical preparation for learning. It usually takes place in the early years of a child's life as he develops readiness for learning. The term *limud* – learning – refers to the study process, acquiring knowledge about specific subject matter.

However, the dual aspects – education and learning – are also simultaneous processes thorough the lives of learners. This dualism is best understood as the confluence of the cognitive and affective domains. The cognitive domain refers to the knowledge gained through study and the sharpening of the intellect. The affective domain emphasizes the importance of the emotional dimension of learning. It involves motivation and commitment essential to effective learning results.

The biblical concept of *hokhmat lev* – wisdom of the heart – is an apt description of this confluence. To be sure, the brain is the seat of the intellect. But the Torah recognized that the heart plays a crucial role in the teaching – learning process.

Education relating to the Holocaust must draw heavily upon both the cognitive and affective domains. Without the integrative influence of each component of the instructional or communicative strategies used in transmitting information about the *Shoah*, Holocaust education will not be maximally effective. Shoah teaching must transmit knowledge and feeling together.

TARGET POPULATIONS

There are essentially two approaches to the selection of target audiences – the global or general approach and the focused or specific approach. The global approach is all-inclusive and refers to developing a worldwide understanding of the nature of the *Shoah* and establishing a climate about the moral responsibility regarding the Holocaust era. It would require large expenditures for media strategies.

The focused approach, while more specific is also broad and varied. It refers more directly to traditional methods of education.

While all the target populations to be reached via this approach are important, the various audiences to be addressed must be prioritized according to the availability of funds and the leveraging advantages of reaching each of the specific learner cohorts.

The focused target populations include:

1. All Jewish youth in formal Jewish school settings – Jewish day schools, yeshivot and Jewish supplementary schools, particularly on the junior and senior high school levels.
2. All Jewish youth in informal Jewish educational settings – synagogue youth groups, Jewish community centers, Zionist youth groups and summer camps, especially on pre-teen and teen-age levels. A specialized target population would be March of the Living groups to which the Conference has awarded grants in the past.
3. Non-Jewish youth and selected public and private high school settings.
4. Students in selected universities.
5. Jewish adults in synagogues and Jewish community centers.
6. Selected Jewish communal audiences.

To determine the priority populations as an ongoing procedure, for the duration of the grants programs, a Target Populations task force might be formed to address this challenge.

THE EDUCATIONAL PROCESS

The educational process involves transmitters, programs and program materials.

1. **The Transmitters**

    Without knowledgeable, motivated and properly trained teachers, *Shoah* education, both in terms of content and methodology, cannot succeed. Educator training is a priority. It should be conducted in a way that can leverage the funding.

The educator populations to be considered include Jewish day school and yeshiva principals, Jewish day school and yeshiva teachers, Jewish supplementary school principals, Jewish supplementary schoolteachers, Jewish youth group leaders, Jewish community center staff, and Jewish camping staff.

The choice of educators to be trained is crucial. The place of the training is also important. A priority arrangement for training is obviously with *Yad Vashem*. Scholarships might be made available to teachers and principals to take courses at *Yad Vashem*. Educator training may also be conducted in conjunction with local Holocaust Museums in the Diaspora and with Beit Lohamei Hagetaot, Beit Hatfuzoth, and Central Archives for the history of the Jewish People in Israel. Distance learning via computer technology should be considered seriously. The proper use of this strategy will help to maximize the number of educators being trained.

2. **Programs, Materials and Technology**

Formal and informal Jewish educators need proper tools. Programs (curricula) and program materials are basic elements of the instructional process. The need is for flexible curricula and programs that can be adjusted for different target populations. A variety of programs and program materials should be developed from which educators and educational institutions can choose appropriately for their respective clientele.

A crucial aspect of program development in our modern day and age is the use of technology. The development of a website to facilitate worldwide programming in various languages should be a major component of the *Shoah* educational process.

To guide the development of training programs for *Shoah* educators and the development of curricula programs, program guides and materials and the formation of a functional website, a Program and Training Task Force should be established.

LEADERSHIP TRAINING AND RESEARCH

A significant dimension of educator training is the training of *Shoah* education leaders. This can best be accomplished via grants to schools of higher learning.

1. Chairs in Holocaust Studies might be established at various rabbinical schools (Orthodox, Conservative, Reform, and Reconstructionist) and at the Colleges of Higher Jewish Learning for Jewish Education. These Chairs would be solely for the development of rabbinical and educational leaders who will spearhead the idea and practice of *Shoah* education during the next century.
2. Scholarships and fellowships for masters degrees and doctoral study and research at the schools of Higher Jewish Learning for Jewish Education and at secular universities should be awarded regularly. Funds might be made available to publish and disseminate the research studies.

SUBSIDIZATION OF SURVIVORS' ROLE IN *SHOAH* EDUCATION

A most effective way to transmit information on the *Shoah* experience is via the survivors themselves. While they may not be professionally trained as teachers and presenters, the involvement of survivors who personalize the Holocaust experience can have a powerful cognitive-affective influence on listeners. The survivors can be involved in a number of ways, some of which are currently underway.

1. They can be guided to make presentations in high schools, colleges, youth organizations, Jewish community centers and synagogues, and in public communal settings.
2. They can be helped to write and publish their memoirs for

use in formal and informal Jewish and general education settings.
3. Audiotapes and videotapes should be made of their individual Holocaust experience. These can be edited for use in *Shoah* education.

EDUCATING FOR JEWISH SURVIVAL

The transmission of knowledge of *Tanakh*, Talmud, *Halakhah*, Jewish history, Hebrew language and literature, Jewish liturgy, and Jewish philosophy has been the staple – the traditional medium – of Jewish education throughout the generations. Together, with Jewish family upbringing, Jewish schooling has helped insure Jewish survival. Along with the heinous murder of Jews, the destruction of Jewish life in Europe included the extinction of this vital instrumentality.

Before, during and after the *Shoah*, yeshivot were founded in Palestine/Israel and in numerous Jewish diaspora communities. These institutions are currently being sustained by local and national funding mechanisms. The upkeep of these schools is the responsibility of their respective boards and communities. If there were an unlimited amount of funding, some claims-conference support could be given to these programs that claim they are the legacy of what was destroyed in the *Shoah*. However, given the limited amount of funding available, such support does not seem to be warranted, particularly since these institutions have demonstrated their ability to maintain themselves – albeit, in some cases, with difficulty – over the years. Funding for these institutions would dilute the support available for *Shoah* education, which is the main purpose of the Research, Documentation and Education grants.

Note: On second thought, it is clear that Jewish all day education – Jewish day schools and yeshivot – are the most effective instruments for Jewish education and provide the best insurance for Jewish continuity. There are over 400,000 students enrolled worldwide in Jewish all day institutions and another 250,000 in intensive Judaic study programs in Israel. If some ways could be found to determine the neediest schools and the way Claims Conference could have the greatest impact upon them, then we might consider some method of funding.

ORGANIZING A PLAN FOR FUNDING

A plan for worldwide grants for *Shoah* education should embrace the vision of what needs to be accomplished via Holocaust programming with available funding in order to memorialize the *Shoah* and utilize the Holocaust experiences for the benefit of the Jewish people. The plan should begin with a mission statement, which clearly outlines the general intent of the grants. Following this, the more specific goals and objectives should be developed.

A clearly articulated funding plan will help guide the grant process and eliminate allocation problems in the future. An important aspect of the goals and objectives of the grants is how they may be leveraged to increase the benefits of the support.

To guide the development of a funding plan for *Shoah* education, including the range and size of allocations and the initiation, implementation and evaluation of the grant process, a Grant Task force should be formed.

Together the three task forces – Target Populations, Educator Training and Program Development and Funding Plan – would constitute a worldwide Shoah Education Council with representation from major Jewish communities and in partnership with major Jewish organizations represented on the Board of Directors of Claims Conference with the addition of representatives from several major Jewish educational agencies.

The membership of the Council and its Task Forces would derive from the Board of Directors, as does the membership of the committees of the Conference. Added to the Council and Task Forces would be several leading Jewish educators and academicians from Israel and the Diaspora.

The first function of the Council would be to develop a mission statement. The Council would consider mass education and institutional education; it would prioritize target populations;

articulate the programs for educator training and materials development; and it would develop a funding plan and determine the range and size of allocations. It would develop a review and evaluation procedure to assess the impact of the grants. Finally, it would guide the allocation process of the Claims Conference for Shoah *grants*.

CHAPTER 10

EDUCATIONAL ISSUES IN JEWISH IDENTITY

For the purposes of this paper, Jewish identity is viewed as a multi-dimensional phenomenon. For some Jews, it is expressed in religious terms through worship, ritual, and the study of religious texts. For others, it is a national Zionist reality expressed through a variety of relationships with Israel, including the use of Hebrew language as a vernacular. For still others, Jewish identity is a cultural phenomenon via involvement with Hebrew and Judaic literature and/or Hebraic arts, and/or involvement with the Yiddish language and literature. And, for some, it is expressed through feelings of Jewish peoplehood. For a small number of Jews, Jewish identity is all of the above.

MAKING A DIFFERENCE: JEWISH IDENTITY

Not unlike the Midrashic principle that the whole is dependent upon its parts, Jewish identity and Jewish continuity are interdependent. To be sure, the Jewish identity of individuals nourishes Jewish group continuity. Conversely, the Jewish group environment and community processes invigorate and energize individual Jewish continuity. Both are also intra-dependent as individuals relate to each other and as sub-groups of the whole Jewish community interface.

Jewish education is viewed as multiple opportunities to develop, achieve and strengthen the Jewish identity of individual Jews – young and old – and thus insure Jewish continuity.

THE JEWISH CONDITION:
ACCULTURATION – DECULTURATION

"We live in the best of times and the worst of times." This overused statement most appropriately describes the Jewish condition and Jewish education in the United States. To be sure, Jewish life in the Diaspora communities of the Western Hemisphere has many antecedents which set the stage for the topic of this paper.

According to Jewish tradition, biblical Joseph provided the first example of a "Jew" succeeding in a secular world while retaining his Jewish identity. During the 17 years Jacob lived in Egypt, he was concerned about the "Jewish" continuity of his children and their families. The *Sfat Emet* commentary on the Pentateuch notes that, while Jacob's progeny lived freely in Goshen, their freedom was purely physical. They were enslaved spiritually. The potential for their total assimilation into Egyptian life or secularization of their religious values was real.

When Jacob saw Joseph during the last moments of his life, his fears were assuaged. Rashi's commentary on this last meeting between father and son may be interpreted to mean that Jacob was strengthened as he expired his last breath by the knowledge that Joseph was a "king" among the Egyptians. Yet, he was still Jacob's son – the same Hebrew lad who was taken from Canaan to Egypt. The thought that Joseph retained his own cultural heritage even as he mastered the Egyptian culture enabled Jacob to die in peace. Interestingly, Joseph transmitted this dualism to his children. According to the *Midrash*, Ephraim and Menasheh represented the confluence of Judaic culture and general culture, Jewish scholarship and universal wisdom.

Thousands of years later, as the enlightenment dawned in Europe and spread its beams onto America, society in general no longer sought to interpret the world in two separate ways, to find consonance between secular demands and religious requirements. With notable and flourishing achievements in science, spiritual responses to the mysteries of the unknown were no longer needed, argued the philosophers of the era. In this new atmosphere, the world became human-centered. Religion, if it were to continue, had to be practical and secularized as well as serve social-psychological needs (Schneider).

Moreover, as the French and American Revolutions ushered in an era of freedom, equality, and brotherhood, society recognized choice as a viable option. No longer were people constrained to act in a given, seemingly habitual manner. Traditions could be cast aside.

And, as America welcomed immigrants, its underlying melting pot ideology suggested that all newcomers and their descendants would, and should, be unlike their forebears. They would be Americans, with a new identity through the process of assimilation.

Assimilation in democratic society is characterized as a multi-stage process (Gordon). The first stage is known as acculturation or cultural behavioral assimilation. Newcomers to a society learn the basic values, language, norms, nuances and other cultural characteristics of the host group. At this point, the acculturating foreigners are still considered outsiders. As these immigrants acclimate themselves to their new environment, they became more accepted, enabling them to enter the host society's cliques, clubs, schools and neighborhoods while still remaining closely identified with their original group. This cultural assimilation camouflages the group's inability to enter and fully integrate into the host society's inner sanctum, into their homes, their lives, their churches.

But once this type of assimilation occurs, other types of assimilation can and do often follow: identificational assimilation (a feeling of belonging to and being part of the host society) and receptional imitation (absence of the cognitive dissonance that arises from two conflicting cultures). These types of assimilation typically imply absorption into the host society's culture.

This adaptation and subsequent growth of a new identity explains the challenges and the difficulties of retaining a solely Jewish character in America. The dominant society makes it difficult for members of another ethnic group to retain its traditional culture. The lure of establishing an American identity is grounded in a crippling pluralism for those who wish to preserve conformity to old patterns.

Thus, with the pressures of secularization and assimilation, the Joseph model of confluence for Jacob's descendants has become endangered. The American Jewish community is currently suffering from the acculturation-deculturation syndrome. While patterning itself on the American (secular or Christian) ideal, American Jews are often losing consciousness of their own historical and religious culture.

THE JEWISH LANGUAGES

Jewish identity may be viewed via the prism of a language metaphor. Via internal and sacred language usage, Jewish identity was maintained and nurtured on the personal, family, social, religious and communal levels of the daily living of diaspora Jewry. Enter the acculturation process of American Jewry during the 20th century, especially since the end of World War II. For the overwhelming majority of American Jews, internal and sacred languages no longer play a role in their lives. Consequently the concomitant social and religious behaviors associated with these languages are no longer exhibited.

The linguistic and behavioral changes are clearly generational. Besides having no internal language, third and fourth generation American Jews generally feel no need for a sacred language, for synagogue affiliation, or for religious education for their offspring (Horowitz).

The gradual abandonment of the Hebrew language as an internal and/or sacred language is a cause for concern for many

Jewish leaders. Hebrew language has been a significant factor in Jewish continuity and Jewish unity. Ahad Ha'am correctly noted that "more than the Jews have kept the Hebrew language alive, the Hebrew language has kept the Jews alive." Indeed, Hebrew has been the gateway to Jewish culture. Its use provided Jews everywhere with a sense of belongingness.

The role of Hebrew in Jewish life was portrayed poignantly by Rabbi Yitzhak Nissenbaum (1868–1942), the passionate spokesman for religious Zionism in Europe who was martyred during the Holocaust. Nissenbaum expressed his amazement regarding the dominance of Hebrew in Jewish religious life despite the Talmudic allowance (*Brachot* 13A) to use any language in the performance of *mitzvot*:

> We can imagine what would have happened had the Jews behaved regarding the use of Hebrew only according to *Halakhah* which permits the use of 'any language' in the synagogue and home, and would have used 'any language' for reading the *Shema*, for daily prayer, for reciting grace after meals, for reciting *Hallel*, *Kiddush*, the blessings on the partaking of food and other blessings. If that happened, there would be no trace of Hebrew in our lives, not even in our religious lives. But the people with its national feeling had no desire to use the *Halakhic* permission granted by the scholars of the Jewish religion at a time when the religious feelings of these scholars superseded their national feelings.
>
> The Jewish people took extreme care to recite all these aforementioned things in the Hebrew language. And, thus, the national language of the Jewish people was dominant in the synagogue; and, more significantly, it was the tongue of every Jewish home. The Hebrew mother recited the first prayer *modeh ani* in Hebrew with her children. The sound of Hebrew resounded at the meal table as all the people who ate recited the appropriate blessings before the meal and grace after the meal in Hebrew. It was in Hebrew that every Jew recited his bedtime prayers as he closed his eyes.

It was in Hebrew that he welcomed the Sabbath and festivals with *Kiddush* and bade them farewell with *Havdalah*. It was the sound of Hebrew in every home and synagogue and street that sanctified the secular life of the Jew. This was not possible by the use of 'any language' for religious purposes (Nissenbaum).

As it relates to Jewish identity, the Hebrew language means much more than its use for religious purposes. Hebrew is classical and modern at once. Its role as a force for Jewish identity includes its cultural, national, literary and vernacular dimensions, all of which have ceased to exist for the vast majority of American Jews.

BI-POLARISM

Another way of viewing the condition of Jewish life in the United States is via the bi-polar state of Jewish behavior. American Jewry of the 1990s is a 'more' and 'many more' generation. More Jews pray every day, three times a day; many more do not pray at all. More Jews eat *glatt* kosher; many more do not eat kosher at all. More Jews drink *halav yisrael*; many more drink intoxicating beverages to excess. More adult Jews learn Talmud – *daf yomi* – each day; many more have no contact with Jewish learning at all. The 'many mores' represent the vast majority of Jews, best described as products of the acculturation-deculturation syndrome as they become integrated comfortably into American society.

This condition has had a three-fold effect upon their Jewish identity and involvement. It has lessened the quantity and quality of Jewishness in their lives. It has diminished the extent and intensity of their synagogue affiliation and Jewish communal activity. And, it has decreased their level of home support for Jewish education (Schiff, 1987).

THE NON-SCHOOLED JEWISH CHILD POPULATION

The estimates of the American Jewish child population of school age (4–18 years) who currently does not receive any formal Jewish education vary from fifteen to thirty-five percent. Given the findings of the 1990 National Jewish Population Study (Kosmin et.al.) – particularly the fifty-two percent intermarriage rate between 1985 and 1990 (it is probably higher now in 1996), plus the fact that more than half the Jewish children under age eighteen are being raised outside the Jewish faith – coupled with the low incidence of the children of conversionary intermarriages attending Jewish schools (Schiff, 1979), the higher figure seems to be closer to the reality of non-enrollment in Jewish schools for the total Jewish child population.

The challenge of reaching the non-schooled population goes much beyond the traditional recruitment efforts of the synagogue schools and Jewish day schools. By and large, parents of children who do not enroll their progeny in a Jewish school:

> do not see a relevance of Hebrew as a language or the religious-oriented training that is currently involved in formal Jewish education. They are removed from organized Jewish life in a sense of real alienation from temples, both as a physical structure and as psychological perception. Religion *per se* is not significant to those individuals…Moreover, the cost of religious education poses a serious problem for many of these parents…Overall, while many of them want to preserve their Jewish heritage, and some are even proud of being Jewish, they are 'more American than their forebears' and are not upset by assimilation. (Perspective Resources, Inc.)

Involving these parents and their progeny in Jewish education requires new innovative methods of recruitment and marketing. Since for many of them, cultural aspects of Judaism may be relevant, and since the bar-bat mitzvah ceremony still has some attraction for some of these parents, new ways of dealing with their interests must be created. Here, the challenge of utilizing Israel creatively looms large.

The problem of Jewish identity resonated forcefully at the Reform movement's December 1995 national biennial where intense debate took place about the large number of Reform-affiliated intermarried couples who are bringing up their children in two faiths. The biennial participants narrowly passed a resolution encouraging Reform congregants to bar interfaith couples from enrolling their children in Reform religious schools if these children are being educated in another religion. One Reform leader noted that, in some cases, children with dual religious instruction were coming to their Hebrew classes asking the teachers why they were not praying in the name of Jesus Christ (*The Jewish Week*, 12/8/95).

The 1990 NJPS sent a powerful message to the Jewish federations throughout the country about the unaffiliated Jews and their Jewishly unschooled children. The federations' response was, essentially, to create Jewish continuity commissions. (This development will be dealt with later in this paper.)

THE JEWISH EDUCATION RESPONSE
Home and School and Jewish Identity
The Jewish community has related to the challenges of Jewish identity in two ways:

1. Formal Jewish education on the preschool, primary, elementary, secondary and post-high school levels and university settings in the U.S. and in Israeli Institutions.
2. Informal Jewish education including day and resident camping, synagogue and Zionist youth groups, the *Israel Experience*, adult Jewish education programs sponsored by central agencies for Jewish education and individual schools, and Hebraic and Judaic Hebrew literacy initiatives by outreach organizations and Jewish communal educational and Zionist agencies. Needless to say, formal Jewish education is the most pervasive and most important of the various Jewish education settings.

Traditionally, the challenge of formal Jewish education in the United States has been addressed by two school formats – the Jewish supplementary school (in its early form a communal enterprise but, now, almost solely under synagogue auspices) and the all day Jewish educational institutions generally autonomous yeshivot and Jewish day schools.

All the education formats, particularly the formal school settings, address Jewish education in two ways, Jewish identity reinforcement and Jewish identity formation. In the first instance, the educational process, whether formal or informal, serves basically as a reinforcer of attitudes, behavior patterns, and even skills acquired early in a child's environment. Schooling cannot compensate for the deficit of a culturally deprived home.

Jewish education of children in the absence of family involvement cannot be maximally effective. In helping develop Jewish ambiance in Jewish homes via Jewish communal and organizational involvement and synagogue participation, the quality of the contact and involvement is the crucial factor. Achieving the necessary caliber of outreach and communication is a most serious challenge to our lay, rabbinic and educational leadership.

Formal Jewish Education – The Jewish Supplementary School

Two opposite trends have emerged during the last three decades regarding the institutions of formal Jewish education. On the one hand, we have witnessed a serious decline in Jewish supplementary school enrollment in North America from 540,000 pupils in 1962, the peak year of Jewish school enrollment, to 285,000 in 1992 (Schiff, 1983; Isaacs).

Congregational schooling had grown rapidly in the 1930s and 1940s and flourished for almost two decades after World War II as synagogues thrived and expanded in membership and facilities. The current enrollment decline is due largely to decrease in birthrate, increase in intermarriage, and the acculturation pattern of young endogamous Jewish married people who do not feel the need to provide Jewish education to their progeny.

Also, the attitudes of many adults to their own supplementary Jewish educational experience and family breakup have affected negatively the enrollment of children in Jewish religious schools

(Schiff). In addition, funding and transportation issues impact on the continuation of Jewish education (Fishman and Goldstein).

Moreover, recent studies of Jewish supplementary schooling demonstrate that it has become, by and large, incapable of achieving its goals (Dushkin and Engelman; Himmelfarb; Bock; Hartman; Schiff, 1988; Schoem). Among the reasons for the current ineffectiveness of Jewish supplementary education are the non-priority status of the school within the synagogue, the lack of home support, and the shortage of adequately trained supervisory and instructional personnel (Himmelfarb; Schiff, 1988; Schoem). Current experience of the Conservative and Reform movements regarding the search for qualified Jewish supplementary school personnel underscores the seriousness of this condition.

The Jewish Day School

In contradistinction to the trend of the Jewish supplementary school, the Jewish day school has enjoyed remarkable growth: from 60,000 pupils in 280 schools in North America in 1962 to 182,000 in 660 schools in 1992 (Schiff, 1966, 1983; McMillen and Gerald; Isaacs).

Estimates of the 1995 enrollment in Jewish all day educational institutions from preschool through post-high school programs reach 200,000.

The Jewish day school population represented about 40% of the total North American Jewish school enrollment in 1992 and about twenty percent of the Jewish population of school age children. Increasingly, during the last two decades, larger numbers of Jewish adults have studied in Jewish day schools during their school age years. In 1992, about ten percent of the Jewish population between 20 and 40 years of age attended Jewish day schools through grades 6, 8 or 12. (The 1990 NJPS data reveal that over one quarter of Jewish women under 40 years of age, who received any type of Jewish education, have received 10 or more years of it in a day school.)

Contributing significantly to the sustained increased interest in and support of all day Jewish education is the recognition by its advocates and supporters of the value and need of intensive Jewish education for Jewish continuity and the enhancement of Jewish life.

To be sure, other factors have also contributed to the initial and continuing growth of the day school. These include the impact of the Holocaust and the Middle East, the perception of violence and drug use in public schools, the rise of fundamentalism in America, the attractiveness of the general studies programs of many day schools, and the search for cultural identity (Schiff, 1981).

These two opposing trends – the growth of all day Jewish education, on one hand, and the deterioration of the most populated Jewish educational instrumentality coupled with the erosion of Jewish life, on the other hand – give rise to several queries that beg to be answered, particularly in light of the claims made by the proponents and supporters of Jewish all day education regarding its impact upon the adult Jewish lifestyle of its graduates.

What happens when intensive and extensive Jewish education confronts a world full of secular, intermixing, and challenging modalities? What role does a Jewish day school experience play in Jewish continuity of its exponents? Since the American Jewish community is supportive of Jewish education as a means of insuring Jewish continuity in light of the current trend towards secularization and assimilation among growing numbers of young Jews (as evidenced by limited Jewish observance, lower Jewish communal involvement, decreasing interest in Israel, and increasing rates of intermarriage), what factors in conjunction with education work together to multiply the chances of maintaining and gaining Jewish identity?

Contradictory views have been expressed regarding the impact of Jewish education, including the Jewish day school, upon adult Jewish behavior. One opinion has it that "according to the findings of the 1990 NJPS, the intermarriage rate of those whose education was received in a Jewish day school is eighteen percent in first marriages and twenty-nine percent in second marriages" (Mayer). Another view holds that "the intermarriage rate drops to seven percent for students who complete day school education" (*The Jewish Week*, 11/6/92).

Mayer contends that formal Jewish education cannot stem the tide of assimilation in an open society, that "the type of Jewish education one received has no statistically significant relationship to the outcome of whether one intermarried or not" (Mayer). Fishman and Goldstein (1993) and Seymour Lipset (n.d.) disagree.

According to their understanding of the 1990 NJPS, more extensive forms of Jewish education are "associated with greater Jewish identification," especially among those under forty-five years of age. Mordechai Rimor and Elihu Katz, in a review of the same data, concur (1993). For them, day schools – more than private tutors, part-time schooling and Sunday schools – have a greater bearing on friendship patterns, prevention of intermarriage, attitudes toward intermarriage of progeny, visits to Israel, Shabbat and *kashrut* observance, and synagogue attendance, among others.

Time spent in school, by most accounts, has a significant influence in Jewish identity formation, even when a variety of factors (including family background) are controlled (Bock; Himmelfarb). Rimor and Katz (1993) claim nine or more years of schooling is critical. Other researchers, including Goldstein and Fishman, suggest a minimum of six years is important.

Over time, other studies have demonstrated the positive influence of Jewish all day education (Pollack; Pinksy; Hartman; Ribner; Heimowitz; Friedman).

[NOTE: Elsewhere in this volume is my study on the Jewishness of Jewish day school graduates which demonstrated the strong influence of Jewish all day education.]

JEWISH DAY SCHOOL GRADUATES – SIMILAR BUT DIFFERENT

Day school graduates are like other 20 to 40-year old, white, middle class American Jews regarding country of birth and secular education. They significantly differ, however, in parental background, current Jewish observance, camp experience, visits to Israel, involvement in Jewish organizational life, patterns of intermarriage, and attitudes towards intermarriage.

The home environment of Jewish day school graduates is much more Jewishly oriented than the average American Jewish family, indicating that there is a relationship between parental level of Jewishness and the matter of Jewish education of their progeny.

The level of Jewish behavior (particularly Sabbath and *kashrut* observance) and Jewish organizational involvement of the 20 to 40-year old day school graduates is dramatically higher than that of typical American Jews of this age group.

There is a striking difference between day school alumni and the general Jewish population regarding visits to Israel. Moreover, about eight percent either have made aliyah or were living there at the time of the study. Day school graduates also differ from their American Jewish peers regarding camp experience. Only fifteen percent of day school alumni did not attend a Jewish summer camp. Those who did went to camp for an average of four years.

The most noticeable difference between Jewish day school graduates and other American Jews of their age is in the matter of intermarriage actual experience and attitude toward it.

In examining the graduates' adult Jewish behavior, two propensities emerge: retention and reduction. Jewish day school education helps graduates retain Jewish attitudes and behaviors experienced during their upbringing. It reduces negative attitudes about Jewish behavior, Jewish identity, and Jewish life they may have acquired in the larger environment. In other words Jewish education in conjunction with Jewish home background plus informed Jewish experience (particularly Israel and Jewish summer camp) helps graduates maintain Jewishness, reduce loss of Jewish practice, and acquire positive Jewish values and attitudes.

Israel Experience
Clearly, one of the most effective ways to help form and reinforce

Jewish identity is through an *Israel Experience*. After the NJPS findings became public, the organized federated Jewish community showed great interest in this kind of 'total immersion' program. According to the 1993–1994 CRB Foundation Report, some 7,215 teenagers participated in short term 3-week to two months programs in Israel in 1994 (Geffen and Levenberg). We might add to these an estimated one thousand participants in year-long programs at universities in Israel and about three thousand students in post-high school yeshiva programs.

During the last several years, the leadership of the organized Jewish community has seriously considered ways of dramatically increasing the number of participants in short-term programs. Hopefully, that will occur. However, it must be made crystal clear that an *Israel Experience* will not be effective if it is planned as a quick fix. To serve the purpose of enhancing Jewish identity, the *Israel Experience* must be part of an educational continuum, with appropriate pre-trip and post-trip learning components. Moreover, it is obvious that the quality of the programs and their relevance to the participants are crucial.

Hebrew Literacy Initiatives for Adults

The establishment of the State of Israel in 1948 motivated the organization of Ulpanim for adults throughout the United States, particularly in New York. However, only a minuscule segment of the adult Jewish population has availed itself of this Hebraic study opportunity. During the peak years of Ulpan programming in the 1959s and 1960s, some ten thousand Jewish adults throughout the United States would study Hebrew annually for periods of three months to several years. Between 1957 and 1967, over one thousand Jewish educators participated in an intensive, multi-level six-week (120-hour) summer Ulpan sponsored by Yeshiva University in cooperation with the Department of Education and Culture of the World Zionist Organization and the Jewish Education Committee of New York.

Currently, the major effort in Ulpan teaching takes place at the Ulpan Center in New York and several other cities with large

Jewish populations. Four hundred and fifty adults were enrolled in the New York Ulpan Center in 1994 in the various program levels that range from beginners' Hebrew to advanced level where students learn to read Israeli newspapers and speak Hebrew fluently (Pinchuk).

Sponsored by the Department of Education and Culture of the Joint Authority for Jewish Zionist Education, the Ulpan Center is fraught with problems of recruitment and funding and even may be discontinued because of budgetary difficulties. According to a recent survey of adult programs in Hebrew language, one of the major problems regarding adult study of Hebrew in American Ulpanim is the use of Israeli texts and materials prepared for immigrants in Israel. "In Israel, Hebrew is taught (to newcomers) as a second language in an Ulpan with the entire society reinforcing the lessons of the Ulpan, but in the United States, Hebrew is a foreign language and receives no societal reinforcement" (Wassertzug).

After the establishment of the State of Israel and again after the Six-Day War in 1967, there was a spurt in adult classes in Hebrew language given in synagogues and Jewish centers, many via the Ulpan method. These offerings however, were short-lived after each event.

A variety of noteworthy efforts have been made in the 1980s and 1990s to promote Hebrew literacy, actualize more active involvement with the Hebrew language, and increase participation in Jewish life via the use of Hebrew.

In 1978, Rabbi Noah Golinkin initiated a one-man crusade, "Proclaim Hebrew Literacy throughout the Land," to teach Hebrew to adults. Subsequently, he declared 1991–2000 as "The Decade of Hebrew Literacy." To implement the Hebrew Literacy idea, a text *Al Regel Ahat* (with accompanying teacher guides and follow up material) was developed as a tool for an intensive eight-hour one-day "Hebrew Reading Marathon" geared to prepare students to read Hebrew prayers.

By 1994, according to Golinkin, some 80,000 Jewish adults had been involved in the various levels of the Hebrew Literacy campaign (Golinkin).

Another creative initiative for adults was developed by Rabbi Ehpraim Buchwald, founding director of the National Jewish Outreach Program which mounted the national, "Turn Friday Night into Shabbos" campaign. In 1988, the Hebrew Reading Crash Course initiated "as a hook to get to unaffiliated, marginally unaffiliated and hebraically illiterate Jews involved in Jewish life." According to Buchwald, "Hebrew reading is the lowest common denominator of Jewish identity. Learning to read Hebrew is a cultural non-threatening approach to becoming more Jewish. Without too much investment of time and effort, it can provide a basis for Jewish cultural and religious growth" (Buchwald).

Consisting of five free lessons in Hebrew reading, Jews of all ages can sign up for a crash course four times a year – before Rosh Hashanah, before Hanukkah, before Pesah and during the summer. To recruit participants, creative advertisement has been placed in local Anglo-Jewish newspapers throughout North America announcing the places and times for the courses. The ads are related to the time of their placement as follows: "This Rosh Hashanah Pray in the Original;" "This Hanukkah give yourself a gift of Hebrew;" "This Passover Experience the Exodus From Right to Left;" "How To Read a 5000 Year Old Language in 5 Easy Lessons." At the end of each advertisement readers are told that an 800 telephone, 44-Hebrew, will inform interested people about the dates and places of the courses in their area.

Utilizing the phonic Hebrew textbook *Reishith Binah*, the first five free lessons focus on mechanical reading in preparation for Hebrew prayer reading. To give the courses, about one thousand volunteer instructors have been given guidebooks designed to help them facilitate rapid learning.

Since its beginning in 1988, some sixty thousand adults have taken the five free Hebrew reading crash lessons. Forty percent of these participants signed up for second level courses consisting of a minimum of five sessions in reading comprehension in the Siddur (Rosenbaum).

Growing realization among Hadassah leadership of the need to make Hebrew language education "a key component of every level of Hadassah's organizational structure" led to the launching of *Ivrit La Hadassah* in 1992. During the first year of the program, *Shalav Aleph*, fifty Hebrew circles were in operation. The second year, *Shalav Bet* plus the new *Shalav Aleph* groups, saw the organization of ninety-eight Hebrew study circles with eight hundred participants. In addition, in 1994, *Shalav Gimel* comprised five study circles with twenty students who completed *Shalav Bet* (Drament). The current year has seen a leveling off of participation: one hundred Hebrew study circles with some seven hundred participants.

Questions regarding the long-term effectiveness of the Hebrew literacy initiatives loom large. Are these efforts capable of stemming the tide of Hebraic illiteracy? What is the level of Hebrew ability of the alumni of these programs? What is the practical value of their Hebraic knowledge? Do they use it? What has happened to the thousands of adults who have been exposed to these programs? If valuable, how can they be strengthened to have greater impact? These questions beckon to be answered.

In recognition of the need to intensify the role of the Hebrew language in Jewish education and in the Jewish community, the American Advisory Council of the Joint Authority for Jewish Zionist Education (JAJZE), after two years of deliberation, began in November 1995 to organize a Hebrew Language Center under the auspices of the Department of Education and Culture of JAJZE with the involvement of the Departments of Torah Education and Youth and *Hechalutz*. Initially, the program of the Hebrew Language Center will focus on advocacy networking and resource development.

Finally, when considering efforts regarding Jewish identity building, one must include *Kiruv* (outreach) programs launched over the last two decades by a variety of organizations, essentially Orthodox groups like *Chabad, Aish Hatorah* and *Ohr Somayach*. A study of the effectiveness of these efforts would also shed light on the challenge of and responses to Jewish identity.

CONCLUSION

Like Jewish learning that should be lifelong, stimulating, developing, energizing, sustaining and enhancing, Jewish identity is a never-ending process. In the first instance, in the United States, given the current condition of Jewish life, this process involves and understanding of the nature and scope of the challenge of forming and reinforcing Jewish identity. It requires, too, a basic recognition of the need for quality multiple, multi-level Jewish educational responses.

It is clear that the major educational opportunities for Jewish identity formation and reinforcement are forthcoming from the institutions of formal Jewish learning. This means giving priority to helping maintain and enhance Jewish all day education as the most viable, effective instrumentality of Jewish education. Because of the cumulative effect of post elementary schooling it means also insuring that Jewish day school students continue their Judaic studies, minimally, through high school.

In another vein, it means reconstructing the Jewish supplementary school where the majority of Jewish children exposed to formal Jewish learning receive their Jewish education, transforming it into a viable educational instrumentality via better trained personnel, Jewish family education curriculum modification combining cognitive and affective experiences and continuous Jewish schooling until college years.

On another level, serious attention must be given to the variety of informal Jewish educational opportunities such as Jewish summer camps, synagogue-related youth organizations JCCs, Hillels on the campus Zionist Youth groups and short-term and long-term Israel experience programs. In addition, Jewish adult education initiatives merit consideration as significant responses to the challenge for Jewish identity building.

The enhancement of all types of Jewish educational opportunities depends largely upon substantially increased funding from the federated Jewish community probably best achieved via creative partnerships with family and corporate foundations. This kind of statement, urging more federation dollars for Jewish education, is not new. Neither are the circumstances requiring more financial support entirely new. What is new is the scope and nature of the Jewish identity crisis in the United States.

As the Jewish communal leadership becomes more concerned about the hemorrhaging of the Jewish community and about the need for effective Jewish education, and as the established organizations and newly created initiatives try valiantly to respond to the current challenges of Jewish identity, it becomes urgent that a realistic method of self appraisal be developed to help the funding resources make intelligent decisions about increased financial support. The assessment process should not be used as an excuse to delay heightened support, but should be incorporated creatively into newly expanded funding procedures.

Od Lo Avdah Tikvatenu.

PART III

ON JEWISH ALL DAY EDUCATION

CHAPTER 1

THE REITS CENTENNIAL: AN EDUCATIONAL MILESTONE

The centennial celebration of Rabbi Isaac Elchanan Theological Seminary of Yeshiva University is much more than the anniversary of an institution of higher Jewish learning. It is the celebration of a seminary that for a century has trained rabbinic and educational leaders for the American Jewish community. And it is the birthday of an outstanding Torah citadel that has contributed greatly to the enhancement of Jewish life on the North American continent and beyond.

The birth and growth of the modern American yeshivot were brought about by the East European immigration that began in the 1800s and by the subsequent rebirth of Jewish life on American shores. The underpinnings of this movement derive from the unique position that Jewish education occupies in our tradition.

The study of Torah (the Pentateuch, Prophets, Sacred Writings, Talmud, Rabbinic Commentaries, and other religious writings) is as cardinal principle of Judaism. Knowledge and study are not only the means to religious and ethical behavior, but are, in themselves, a mode of worship. Indeed, Jewish liturgy reflects the fact that worship finds expression on the intellectual as well as the esthetic and emotional planes as it combines the moment of prayer with study. Moreover, in Jewish tradition, Torah learning is an end in itself as it unites the learner with his past and with the sources of his heritage.

In Eastern European Jewish communities a young man trained in a yeshiva was expected to be a lifelong student of the Torah. There were no excuses for not studying the Torah as much as possible. Neither poverty, nor the pursuit of a livelihood, nor the raising of a family could free a Jew from the obligation of *Talmud Torah* (the study of Torah).

Many of the East European immigrants during the last decade of the 19th century and the beginning of the 20th century brought with them the ideal of *Torah Lishmah* (learning for learning's sake) and the zeal for establishing the primacy of Torah study in Jewish life. Yeshiva Eitz Chaim (Tree of Life), the first yeshiva on North American soil, was organized in 1886. It featured a dual program of traditional Jewish learning, augmented by general studies in subjects such as grammar, arithmetic, reading, and spelling. The new educational formula was to pave the way for the integration of the two streams of cultural values that the immigrant Jews in America sought to preserve.

Ten years after the founding of Yeshiva Eitz Chaim, Rabbi Isaac Elchanan Theological Seminary (Yeshivat Rabeinu Yitzchak Elchanan) was established. Named after the illustrious East European rabbinic leader, visionary, and *Halakhic* decisor Rabbi Isaac Elchanan Spektor (who died earlier that year), RIETS incorporated the educational principles espoused by this revered rabbi of Kovno, Russia.

Rabbi Spektor's greatness derived from a remarkable confluence of Talmudic brilliance and encyclopedic knowledge of Judaic sources, with a broad understanding and appreciation of worldly conditions, sincere belief in the restoration of *Eretz Yisrael* as a modern Jewish homeland, and strong communal leadership in his dealings with both Jewish and governmental leaders.

Broad minded and possessed of a peace-loving disposition, Rabbi Spektor was vitally concerned with the welfare of Jews in

Western and Eastern Europe and in North and South America, as well as with his brethren in Israel. In philosophy and in deed, in principle and in practice, he served as a model for Jews throughout the world. Upon his death, it is no wonder that a group of immigrants who revered him, decided to found RIETS to enshrine his memory and to train Jewish leaders who would follow in his footsteps.

In 1915, Dr. Bernard Revel was appointed president and *Rosh Yeshiva* (dean) of RIETS. At that time, Yeshiva Eitz Chaim became part of RIETS. An outstanding *talmid hakham* (scholar), Dr. Revel was a celebrated *ilui* (prodigy) at the European yeshivot he attended. After coming to the United States, he was the first person to earn a PhD from Dropsie College in Philadelphia. Dr. Revel guided the development of RIETS as a center of Torah leadership and was instrumental in its relocation to Washington Heights. The architecturally splendid Main Building has been its home ever since.

After Dr. Revel's death in 1940, Dr. Samuel Belkin, a young, prominent RIETS *Rosh Yeshiva* and noted scholar who taught Greek at Yeshiva College, was named dean of the Seminary; in 1943, he was elected president of the institution then known as "RIETS and Yeshiva College."

Dr. Belkin had studied at the Yeshivot of Radin and Mir, and received a PhD from Brown University. Under his stewardship, even as the Yeshiva became a multi-faceted university beginning in 1946, RIETS experienced great academic expansion. In the area of communal services, for example, the institution extended its scope beyond the education of rabbis on its Washington Heights campus to provide communities throughout the entire United States and worldwide with essential synagogue, youth, and rabbinical in-service training to help Jews withstand the pressures of post-war assimilation.

In 1970, RIETS was restructured with its own Board of Trustees and granted a new charter. Dr. Belkin retired as president in 1975 and served as chancellor until his death the following year.

Dr. Norman Lamm was elected president and *Rosh haYeshiva* of RIETS – the first to be born in America – in 1976. A *musmakh* of RIETS, Dr. Lamm is an alumnus of Yeshiva College and Bernard Revel Graduate School, where he earned his PhD, and holds the Erna and Jakob Michael Chair in Jewish Philosophy at Yeshiva University.

The last quarter of the twentieth century has been marked by several notable accomplishments: the establishment of the Caroline and Joseph S. Gruss Institute in Jerusalem, which provides pre-*semikhah*, *semikhah*, and post-*semikhah* programs; the establishment of the Phil and Sarah Beiz School of Jewish Music; the establishment of the Irving I. Stone Rabbinic Internship Program and Irving I. Stone *Beit Midrash* Program; and the significant expansion of RIETS *kollel* programs, through the establishment of the Marcos and Adina Katz *Kollel* (Institute for Advanced Research in Rabbinics) and Ludwig Jesselson *Kollel Chaverim*, the strengthening of other programs, service scholars of exceptional promise who wish to devote all their academic energies to areas of Talmud and *Halakhah*.

In marking this centennial anniversary, world Jewry takes note of the many achievements of RIETS during its long, distinguished history. Since its chartering by the State of New York in 1897, it has ordained some 2,400 rabbis who have gone on to serve in pulpits, as communal leaders, and as teachers, administrators, and principals in Jewish educational institutions all over the world. Moreover, a significant number have entered the world of academia in universities and schools of higher Jewish learning here and abroad, and have become *roshei* yeshiva and *Halakhic* decisors, In all, a remarkable record of leadership and service to world Jewry, and a true educational milestone.

CHAPTER 2

THE NONPUBLIC SCHOOL: REAL AND IDEAL

I am pleased to participate in what I believe is an historic event – an American Association of School Administrators dialogue between the public and nonpublic sectors. The pleasant memories of my own elementary and secondary public school days in Boston serve as a positive personal backdrop for my current involvement with nonpublic education.

The nonpublic school plays a special role in American society as it derives its right to be from the right of parents to choose the kind of education they desire for their offspring. Harold Dodds, former president of Princeton University, placed the nonpublic school in proper perspective about three decades ago, when he said: "When it is no longer possible for a person to find a school for his child except within a universal state system, it will be too late to worry about freedom."

Beyond the melting pot theory, the existence and growth of the nonpublic school is an eloquent expression of pluralism. And, as a system, the nonpublic school has been on the cutting edge of education since by its very nature it is freer to experiment and to innovate.

Nonpublic schools comprise about 20 percent of all elementary and secondary educational institutions in the United States and about 12 percent of the elementary and secondary school enrollment. Embracing a kaleidoscopic variety of schools under widely diversified, religiously affiliated and nonsectarian auspices, the interschool differences within the nonpublic school system are sometimes greater than those between it and the public school.

The public school/nonpublic school commonalities provide the basis for a common agenda for the improvement of education and the development of a common lobby concernng federal and statewide education legislation. The annual New York Public/Nonpublic School Conference is a creative example of a trailblazing effort to achieve a common platform.

When considered candidly and objectively, the differences between the public and nonpublic sectors encourage mutual understanding of the respective needs and potential of each system. Some of the differences relate to size. The nonpublic school is often a small one-administrator institution, a condition which both benefits it – namely, its ability to personalize education – and disadvantages it because of the programmatic limitations inherent in the smallness of its educational operations.

As we prepare to enter the 21st century what are the challenges faced by the nonpublic school? To begin with, there are fiscal problems from which only an unappreciable number of relatively well-endowed private nonsectarian schools are exempt. How the educational program will be sustained from year to year, month-to-month, week-to-week, and from day-to-day, is a problem of awesome proportions in many nonpublic schools. The fiscal constraints of the nonpublic school underscore the problem of educational personnel in this system, particularly recruiting and retaining instructional staff.

The teacher personnel issue is universal. To be sure, there are a substantial number of highly qualified teachers who choose to teach in the nonpublic school for obvious reasons – schedule and program flexibility, class size, school size and commitment to a special type of education. Yet, the teacher personnel problem is exacerbated in the nonpublic school where salaries are significantly lower and fringe benefit packages significantly smaller than the public school.

Building plant problems – adequate facilities, their maintenance and upkeep – are equally disconcerting. This is compounded by the still troubling incidence of asbestos and other structural and environmental deficiencies. Providing adequate non-instructional services, especially medical examinations, health, transportation and social services, is a particularly serious concern.

Good parenting is essential to good education. To borrow a conclusion from the research of James Coleman, Christopher Jencks and others, nothing is more important in the schools than family support. How to achieve a quality home – school relationship is a major challenge facing many nonpublic schools, particularly in light of the increasing number of single parent families.

On the classroom side of this relationship, we ask teachers to have high expectations for every child. How can all pupils be empowered by schooling? That empowering stretches beyond traditional forms of instructional pedagogy. It goes to the core of the challenge of educating for democracy, of schooling for prejudice reduction, of bringing up a generation of moral, ethical citizens, of helping each child become a productive member of society. This challenge takes on greater significance each year as the cultural diversity of the non-public school population increases.

A school's ability to succeed is best judged by measuring output rather than by a priori specifications for scheduling and by legislated program requirements. This is a weighty problem for the nonpublic school as it addresses itself to regulatory legislation aimed at all schools. Governmental requirements often limit the capacity of the nonpublic school to fulfill its potential. Moreover, measuring achievement in given subjects is not the *only* or most helpful way to evaluate the effectiveness of schooling. How can other values related to the affective domain and achievable through schooling be assessed? This area of the educational program is a vital concern to the nonpublic school.

Exceptionality or marginality of the pupil population is another major challenge. Will the nonpublic school have the sufficient instructional resources to address the needs of special pupils – the emotionally, developmentally, physically and learning disabled? Will it be able to meet adequately and creatively the needs of gifted and talented children? These questions plague the conscience and practice of the nonpublic school.

And finally, how can we maximize the potential effect of technology in our schools? How can the nonpublic school be in the vanguard of the use of technology? How can it harness new technology for the educational benefit – the academic, vocational and moral upbringing of *all* our pupils?

The issues I have just adumbrated serve to underscore some of the commonalities between the public and nonpublic education sectors and the potential for developing a common agenda.

It is clear that two conditions are necessary if the nonpublic school issues are to be addressed effectively. Given the child benefit theory as a guideline, these conditions were most eloquently expressed by John Quincy Adams during the early stages of our democracy: "The whole people," he said, "must take upon themselves the education of the whole people and must be willing to bear the expense of it."

The first condition is adequate support for the secular studies and pupil services components of schooling within proper constitutional limits. The second condition relates to volition and intent. It requires that the public sector be willing to consider the nonpublic school as a full-fledged partner in the most important mission of our generation – the forming and fashioning of the next generation. Communication between both sectors is a *conditione sine qua non* for accomplishing that mission.

A Judaic adage has it that "nothing can stand in the way of the will." If we will it, it will happen.

CHAPTER 3

WHAT RESEARCH SAYS ABOUT THE JEWISH DAY SCHOOL

DOCTORAL DISSERTATIONS 1970–1990

Postgraduate dissertations form a significant segment of research in the social sciences and education. For Jewish education they comprise the lion's share of research done during the last two decades. This is particularly true for Jewish all day education. To learn how research informs us about the current Jewish day school, it is most appropriate to analyze doctoral theses on this subject.

Forty doctoral degrees were awarded in the United States for research relating to the Jewish day school between 1970 and 1990. Ten were awarded in the 1970s and thirty in the 1980s, indicating a significant increase in research interest in this subject area. Forty-five percent of all the dissertations on the day school in the last two decades were completed between 1981 and 1990.

Sixteen of the doctoral degrees were awarded by graduate schools under Jewish auspices, eleven by Yeshiva University, and five by the Jewish Theological Seminary. Twenty-four degrees were awarded by secular institutions, including four by New York University and two each by Harvard, Maryland, Colorado, Fordham, and Loyola (Chicago) Universities. Twenty of the researchers were awarded the degree of Doctor of Philosophy: Sixteen received the Doctor of Education degree: and four, the

Doctor of Hebrew Letters degree. Twenty-six of the doctoral students conducted their research in Orthodox institutions, six in Conservative schools, and two in one or more non-Orthodox settings. Six researchers studied aspects of the day schools without respect to their ideological base. While forty-percent of the day school population in the United States is enrolled in yeshivot under sectarian Orthodox auspices, none of the research was conducted specifically in these settings. These Orthodox institutions were included, however, in the survey-type research treating Jewish all day education as a whole.

Twenty-three theses dealt with the elementary grades, seven researched the high school level and ten addressed all grades or all day education generically. The most popular research topics related to school personnel (12) and curriculum and instruction (9). Other subject areas studied include: school impact (5), reading achievement (5), the development of the day school movement (3), guidance (2), families (2), female role definitions (1), and government relations (1).

DEVELOPMENT OF THE DAY SCHOOL MOVEMENT

The impressive growth of the Jewish day school in America is the result, in large measure, of the foresight and influence of Rabbi Shraga Faivel Mendelowitz, who immigrated from Hungary to the United States in 1913 and who in 1921 became principal of the Yeshiva Torah Vodaath in Brooklyn, one of the five all day schools in the country at that time. In 1928, Mendelowitz founded the Mesivta High School, and in 1944, he organized Torah Umesorah – the National Society for Hebrew Day Schools – whose purpose it was to foster the development of Hebrew day schools throughout the United States. One study demonstrates how his leadership style effectively helped motivate the development of Jewish day schools on the North American continent prior to, during, and immediately following World War II (Parsons). Mendelowitz's goal was "to counteract the deleterious influence of open society on the Jewishness of young Jews and provide intensive Talmudic and rabbinic studies to male students."

The history and impact of Torah Umesorah is the subject of a thesis which traces the phenomenal growth of Jewish schools and their influence on the America Jewish community (Kramer). The study "calls for greater communal efforts in securing needed financial assistance for these schools while maintaining their religious and educational integrity." It notes many "heretofore hostile observers have come to recognize the value and importance of the traditional day school," as broader communal support should be forthcoming for this form of intensified Jewish and general education." The study challenges day school proponents, suggesting that they "need to reorder their priorities" and concentrate on improving the quality of education "with better prepared teachers, better curricular integration and programming and more communal involvement" instead of dwelling on the quantitative growth of the movement.

A 1973 study of trends and issues in Hebrew day school education surveyed 35 representative schools in all parts of the United States, excluding New York City (Freid). According to the respondents to a questionnaire – principals, rabbis and Federation directors – there are five critical issues facing the day school movement:

1. The nature of the supporting constituency of the Hebrew day school movement, which is undergoing change.
2. The "pressure being exerted on the Hebrew day school movement to change the religious philosophy on which it was founded and with which it has operated in the past. This pressure emanates from internal sources – the constituents – as well as from communal sources external to the school." The study notes that in some communities "the shift towards a weakened Orthodox position has already occurred" and that "further shifting in that direction seems likely."
3. Junior high school students' loss of interest in the Hebrew subjects.
4. The perception that Federation, which has major responsibility for providing substantial funding for the schools, will

try to gain control over the program or philosophy of the school.
5. The critical shortage of trained Hebrew teachers "which will remain into the foreseeable future."

CURRICULUM AND INSTRUCTION

Of the nine theses on curriculum, six consider instructional approaches, three present syllabi for classroom use and one analyzes goals.

The three syllabi – *dinim* for elementary grades; rite of passage program for yeshiva high schools; and teaching Samuel in middle grades – all include proposals for both content and methodology. Each dissertation suggests a model for study program in the Orthodox day school. The emphasis on each syllabus is active pupil participation. i.e., the heuristic method for the Book of Samuel (Schwartz), the focus on values education and personality development as part of a senior high school *dinim* course (Deitcher), and the creation of conditions that are necessary for student achievement (Messinger).

Since there has been no systematic and clearly articulated approach to the teaching of *Midrash* based on *midrashic* scholarship and educational research, one thesis presents a rationale and curriculum proposal for the teaching of *Midrash* in the elementary Conservative day school (Kaunfer). The curriculum rationale considers "key issues in the four commonplaces of the curriculum: the subject matter, the child, the milieu and the teacher." The proposed *midrashic* method in embracing both the "method and mode of *midrash*" employs concrete stories, parables, metaphors. dialogues, and word plays and suggests several teaching strategies paralleling *midrashic* techniques, including creative writing, art, drama, and role playing.

A study of commercially produced computer applications in a Rabbinics curriculum demonstrates that they "do not incorporate the latest curricular work being done in a specific field and therefore do not necessarily meet the specific curricular needs of certain schools." Moreover it reveals that "computer applications do not provide innovative educational experiences in the presentation of subject matter" (Smiley). Presuming that an analysis of educational means should be concurrent with the articulation of educational goals the study suggests that the adoption of new means should be concurrent with the improvement of practice.

While curricular integration in Conservative day schools is considered an ideological and practical desideratum, these schools "continue to teach Judaic and general studies as two separate and unique realms mutually coexisting but not correlated" (Solomon). The reason for this is a fundamental philosophical problem – their acceptance of a "structure of disciplines" view of knowledge and curriculum planning. To overcome the bifurcation of the school day into "Jewish" and "English" times, a study of curriculum integration recommends an alternative approach whereby each school helps its students unify their educational experience (Solomon). "Integration can only occur within individuals. Therefore, the specifics of each school program must depend upon the particular talents of the teachers, the concerns of the community and the needs and abilities of the individual students."

What is the most effective method of instruction in Jewish history? One thesis studied two different approaches in teaching Jewish history on the high school level: (1) integrated world and Jewish history courses, and (2) separate Jewish history courses (Bernstein). The findings indicate that the separate approach provided more intensive course work in Jewish history and was more likely to lead to increased involvement in Jewish life. The separate courses were viewed as an effective format for Jewish history instruction by all teachers and principals.

Can especially focused intensive programs influence the attitudes of students? One study examined the effect of an experimental ten-session, theme-centered program designed to change the low Jewish identification level and negative attitudes toward school of high school students (Berdugo). The findings showed slight but gradual impact upon participants who valued the experience as worthwhile and felt that changes occurred. The program enhanced self-awareness, increased openness and offered possibilities to analyze, understand, and explore positions and needs concerning Jewish values and attitudes toward school.

Parent and educator ratings of Modern Orthodox elementary schools demonstrate a disparity in the degree of importance parents and educators in schools outside the New York metropolitan area attribute to stated goals of these institutions (Gans). The response to a survey of the ratings was assigned to one of three categories of goals: preparation for American living, preparation for Jewish cultural living, and preparation for religious living. The educators attribute the greatest importance to goals of religious living and least importance to goals of American living. Parents, on the other hand, indicate that goals of Jewish cultural living are most important and goals of religious living least important. Parent ratings are higher than educator ratings for goals related to secular American and secular-Judaic orientation. Two personal variables – religious education and religious observance – had the highest correlation with goals and parents in contrast with the goals of educators, which did not correlate with these personal attributes.

Reading Instruction

The dual language program of the day school gives rise to various questions about reading. What factors affect reading achievement in Hebrew and English? Is there a relationship between reading ability and achievement in Hebrew and English? Can one predict levels of achievement in reading in the two languages? How can one best learn to read and understand biblical text?

One study investigated the role of visual perception in learning to read Hebrew and English (Kupinsky). The study reached the following conclusions:

1. Visual perceptual ability is significantly correlated with reading achievement in both Hebrew and English.
2. Reading achievement in English is significantly correlated with reading achievement in Hebrew.
3. Students at the kindergarten level are capable of learning to

read two languages with differing alphabets and opposite directionality that are taught concurrently.
4. Visual-perceptual training has a significantly positive effect on the ability to read both Hebrew and English. Visual perceptual training affects higher levels of achievement in both languages.

The study recommends formalized visual-perceptual training in the reading programs of the day school.

A study of factors affecting achievement in Hebrew and in English of third grade students in a Solomon Schechter School determined that "there was significant positive correlation between visual retention and reading achievement in Hebrew and English" (Orlow). But while there was a significant positive correlation between auditory discrimination and reading achievement in Hebrew, this was not the case for English. Moreover, there was no significant relationship between achievement in these subjects and between sex of the learners, selected attitudes of the students, and languages spoken at home, including Hebrew and English. There was, however, a positive relationship between years of attendance and reading achievement in Hebrew and English. Hebrew and English reading achievement were highly predictive of each other.

A longitudinal study of the relationship between reading approaches and achievement in English and in Hebrew demonstrated very significant correlations between reading achievement in English and Hebrew in both first and second grades (Gutman). A test of phoneme analysis administered in kindergarten correctly predicted first and second grade reading achievement in Hebrew and English.

Another study explores the extent to which scores on kindergarten perceptual and language measures predict third grade achievement in Hebrew and English reading comprehension among students in an Orthodox school (Sivan). The findings demonstrate slight prediction value of these tests. The key to better reading achievement in the elementary grades seems to be better reading readiness programs.

A major reason for teaching Hebrew reading is to help pupils read and understand the Bible in the original. One study focuses on the development of reading comprehension strategies for the teaching of the biblical text, in order to change current practices, which tend to teach "about the biblical text (commentaries instead of text) or which translate individual words instead of teaching the main ideas" (Melitz). The thesis proposes metacognitive methods for teaching biblical narrative and suggests specific training programs for teachers in the application of these methods.

SCHOOL IMPACT

Does all day Jewish education have special impact on learners? What is the nature of the influence? A follow-up study of graduates of selected Hebrew day and supplementary schools focused attention on the relative contribution of these institutions in maintaining Jewish identity and continuity (Hartman). Among the findings of this study are that the Hebrew day school graduates (1) perceive themselves and their parents as more religiously observant, (2) perceive their Jewish education as being more effective in enhancing both their own and their parents' religious behavior, and (3) view interdating and intermarriage as more antithetical to their belief system. Hebrew day school graduates interdate much less and intermarry much less.

Graduates of both systems who express a higher degree of satisfaction with Jewish education also perceive themselves and their parents as more religiously observant. Hebrew day school graduates attend secondary or post-secondary schools of Jewish learning significantly longer and select Jewish education and/or Jewish communal work as future vocational choices to a greater degree.

A study on whether or not Jewish schooling affects Jewish identification of pupils in Jewish day and supplementary schools revealed that the number of hours of Jewish schooling does not make a significant independent contribution to total Jewish identification after controlling for the influence of family background, peers, camps, and youth groups (Shapiro). Only family background makes a "large and significant contribution to total Jewish identification." The interaction between the hours of Jewish schooling and parents' residence-friendship patterns make a slight contribution. Other than these, all other interaction variables are not significant. In fact, the peers' variable is negatively related to the total Jewish identification. The most important predictors of total Jewish identification are parents' ritual observance, parents' residence-friendship patterns, parents' parenting behaviors, and the children's Jewish group activity.

Many educators and lay leaders are concerned about the effectiveness of moral education in our schools. Research on the effect of three different types of Orthodox high school education (traditional Orthodox yeshiva for boys, traditional Orthodox school for girls, and a Modern Orthodox co-educational program) on moral reasoning and social interest of students demonstrated that gender, curriculum, and religious conservatism are not factors in influencing moral reasoning (Seymour Friedman). It is suggested that there are certain common fundamental overriding principles of Jewish heritage that have a greater effect on moral reasoning than curriculum and individual differences in religiosity. Social interest, however, is affected by both gender and curriculum but is not affected by religious conservatism. Intensive study of Talmudic texts seems to positively affect the degree of one's social interest. Moral reasoning was found to be unrelated to social interest. It seems that "moral reasoning taps skills in the cognitive domain while social interest is related to attitudes within the affective domain."

Another study attempted to determine whether there are significant differences between moral reasoning stage attainment of Jewish day school students and public school students (Jerome Freidman). It also sought to determine to what degree a cognitive developmental intervention introduced into the curriculum would influence students to advance to a higher stage of moral reasoning. Utilizing Kohlberg's Moral Judgement interviews, the study demonstrated no difference on pretests or posttests between 7th grade day school and public school students. Although all experimental groups increased their moral stage scores as a result of the intervention, mere exposure to moral issues in the standard Jewish day school curriculum – Orthodox, Conservative, and Reform, which vary from 4 to 15 hours per week of Jewish studies – did not result in significant differences among groups. The study recommends that all schools adopt a modified cognitive-developmental approach to Jewish moral education, which would include Kohibergian dilemma-discussions in a non-threatening classroom atmosphere, emphasizing the "why" behind moral reasoning.

A study of the graduates of a Modern Orthodox Hebraic yeshiva high school demonstrates, among other findings, that the "greatest influence on the graduates in transmitting Jewish values were the home and school" (Heimowitz). It also showed that the majority of students identify themselves as Orthodox. Over ninety percent consider the Jewish all day school the most desirable form of Jewish education and send their own children to these schools. And over ninety-percent felt that their yeshiva high school education influenced them positively in identifying with the State of Israel. Moreover, twenty-five percent are considering living in Israel. An analysis of the relationship of instructional and per pupil costs to scholastic achievement in reading and math concluded that "cost quality" relationship is not a significant factor in predicting student achievement (Well). In the area of reading, the most important predictors of success are parental attitudes toward the school, parent professions, parent religious affiliation, and teacher experience. In mathematics, the most important predictor of success is family income. According to these findings, the study recommends that schools should (1) "institute parent education seminars with the specific goal of informing the parents of the program and philosophy of the day school," and (2) "hire teachers based upon their abilities, experience and qualifications and pay such teachers a salary commensurate with their qualifications."

SCHOOL PERSONNEL

Two problem areas have consistently concerned the leadership of Jewish day and supplementary schools: a shortage of qualified teachers entering the Hebrew teaching profession and the high rate of turnover of Hebrew teachers. One research study postulated that the reasons for both of these problems were rooted in the level of job satisfaction (Ravin). While the results of the research conducted in the Washington DC area indicated that both groups of teachers were equally satisfied with their jobs, the findings demonstrated significant differences between the two groups in how individual characteristics (citizenship, marital status, religion, age, longevity of service in one school, weekly teaching hours, teaching experience, income, fringe benefits, and supervisor-teacher relationship) affected job satisfaction.

Jewish day schools generally employ two sets of faculties – one for Jewish studies and another for general studies in the Chicago area. Hebrew teachers in the schools affiliated with the Associated Talmud Torahs (Orthodox) belong to a formally recognized union, while the general studies teachers are not permitted union recognition. Because of this dichotomy, Hebrew teachers participate in collective bargaining for the purpose of contract negotiation and the general studies teachers utilize a meet-and-confer approach. One study analyzed both of these practices (Marks). The findings of the research indicate that general studies teachers believed that the meet-and-confer method is not successful and that a "formally recognized union would be an asset." Hebrew teachers believed their union was "adequate, but not excellent." Moreover, their feeling about the inadequacy of the meet-and-confer approach was much stronger than that of general studies teachers.

Lay-professional relationships are sometimes problematic in the administration of Jewish education. A study of the views of New York City elementary Orthodox Hebrew day school principals' role expectations as perceived by the principals themselves and their lay board chairmen revealed that the principals' views of the scope of their decision-making functions were substantially greater than the board chairmen's views of their decision-making power (Feuerman). This difference was similar in the four areas of schooling examined – religious orientation, curriculum, finance, and personnel. It was greatest in the area of curriculum and the least in the area of religious-orientation. Interestingly, while the lay board chairman's views of the decision-making power of the principal in establishing the religious philosophy of the school almost coincided with the principals', they differed widely in implementation of that philosophy via the curriculum. Generally, the principals and board chairmen agreed that the area of finance is a board function and that religious orientation, curriculum, and personnel are primarily principal functions.

Why do some principals remain in their same posts longer than others? An analysis of factors affecting the mobility of non-Orthodox Jewish day school directors demonstrated that the typical non-Orthodox Jewish day school principal is a married male between the ages of thirty five and thirty-nine, has a Master's degree, works fifty or more hours per week for the school and has a multi-year written job contract (Rosenthal). Directors who are formally evaluated by their boards of education at least once per year showed a greater desire to stay at their present positions than those who were not evaluated. There was no difference between directors with written job descriptions and those without. Overall staying power of non-Orthodox day school principals was much greater at the time of the study (1987) than in earlier years. Average length of tenure is eight years and average number of positions held by present directors is two.

Most day schools have two principals, one for Jewish studies and one for general studies. The relationship of these supervisors is critical to the smooth functioning of the school. One study attempted to determine the relationship between the role expectations and the job satisfactions of the principals of the religious and secular departments (Flatto). Three groups were identified as "significant others" determining the principal's role: board members, teachers, and complementary principals. No significant relationships were found between the secular principal's job satisfaction and congruency of role expectations held by two pairs of reference groups: (1) board members and religious principals, and (2) religious teachers and religious principals. While the study hypothesized that the religious school principal would express more job satisfaction than the secular principal, this was not borne out by the research findings. However, "the results suggested relationships between congruency of role expectations and religious principals' job satisfaction." The relationships between congruency of role expectations and job satisfaction of secular principals were inconclusive.

How do principals perceive potential problems of role conflict? A study of the views of the heads of forty-nine Solomon Schechter Schools regarding principals' interaction with individual teachers, teacher groups, parents, and board members showed no significant relationship between principals' contract status, tenure, job description, educational and religious training, gender, and the potential of role conflict situations (Jordan). However, the study demonstrated a positive correlation between problems of role conflict perception and the age of the principal, the number of years in educational administration, and number of years in current position. The older the school head, the more experienced he/she is and the longer he/she is in the job, the greater the likelihood of problems of role conflict perception. The school heads who had written job descriptions reported more problems of role conflict perception than those who lacked such descriptions. Yet, an overwhelming majority (eighty-eight percent) of total respondents indicated that even in the absence of written job descriptions, they knew what was expected of them. This has interesting implications for board-principal relationships.

Occupational stress is an increasing area of concern in both the private and public sectors. A study on stress and coping techniques utilized by day school administrators indicated that sex, age, and experience of day school administrators are related to the ways they cope with stress (Lasko). School size did not influence the coping techniques used.

Most new teachers are unprepared for the various instructional and guidance challenges that face them in the school and classroom. A case study in staff development in a Jewish day school – the only one ever reported in listings of doctoral dissertations – describes an experiment in the professional growth of teachers (Schachter). Responding to the need for staff development, the year-long project in a Solomon Schechter School was essentially a voluntary effort by faculty members to learn a new teaching strategy called Synectics. The study demonstrates the significance of the conditions of the local school setting and uncovers impediments to staff development. It reveals special problems attending staff development in a day school setting. The key challenge is the "creation of a shared language between the two groups (Hebrew and general studies faculties), each of whom bring to their work different histories of professional preparation and different cultural expectations about schools and learning." Moreover, the study shows that "changes which result from staff development do not always proceed in linear fashion." To be ongoing, staff development requires continuous reflection, evaluation, and experimentation. The challenge to the school is to create the conditions that support these conditions.

A study on teachers' mainstreaming in-service priorities in elementary schools – with learning disabled pupils – concludes that teachers prefer in-service content that (1) will enhance the education of the class as a whole, (2) is skill oriented, and (3) is relevant, practical, and applicable to their perceived needs (Sardy). Teachers prefer content with which they already have a knowledge base and which is congruent with their role expectations as "regular" teachers and congruent with school expectations. Format in-service preferences include those that demonstrate ongoing systemic support, peer feedback, and support, as well as responsiveness to changing needs.

STUDENT GUIDANCE

The Jewish day school, particularly the Jewish day high school, has a special guidance role in addition to its normal functions as a secondary school. It seeks to help the student to solve problems of Jewishness and encourages him/her to develop positive attitudes and commitment to Judaism. According to one study "the guidance function in the Jewish all day senior high school should channel the adolescent's major need of formulating a personal philosophy of life as childhood beliefs change into mature faith (Shudofsky). This will help the adolescent maintain a continuous development and growth of a value system."

The study showed that these theories were not implemented according to accepted guidance processes noted in educational literature, although serious efforts were made to influence students' attitudes in their Jewishness. The study concluded that each school should "give serious consideration to developing a trained Pupil Personnel Services Team of significant variety and depth to help students in their emotional, social, and religious adjustment and help them "utilize the traditional insights of Judaism in coping with needs and problems as they arise."

Helping prepare students for eventual decisions about their careers is a significant challenge to high schools. One study sought to illuminate the need for career education (Grant). The results indicate that the majority of respondents had not decided upon a specific career at the time of their junior or senior year in high school. The great majority planned to attend college but was unsure of what to major in and many were not even sure of their interests.

The study indicates a strong interest in the career education courses which would clarify the opportunities and options that exist. "By so doing, much of the future uncertainty would be alleviated, and hundreds of yeshiva high school students would be guided toward a more sound and secure future."

FEMALE ROLE DEFINITIONS

The feminist movement has had substantial influence on American life. One study (Finkelstein) examined the impact of the woman's movement and outside cultural trends on women's roles and status in an Orthodox Jewish day high school. Traditional Jewish institutions, such as this school, which stress the vital importance of the family and of the woman's role as wife and mother, have found it difficult to incorporate feminist precepts into their value system. The members of this group have a strong sense of pride in their heritage and values. The changing views toward women in the outside society, to which students have open access, frequently conflict with the maintenance of these cultural and religious values and of the social patterns which the group views as preserving them from assimilation into the broader society. The study explored the way in which this coed yeshiva is coping with the problem. The attitudes of administration and teachers were identified and the effects on students were assessed. The qualitative data of the observations and the interviews provided personalized intimate understanding of the social phenomena, and the quantitative tests added objective data. The results of each method, qualitative and quantitative, revealed that boys and girls belong to separate cultures. The qualitative data showed clearly that this is, to some degree, the result of different expectations for girls and boys and differential treatment of the sexes by teachers. The quantitative data showed significant differences existing only between attitudes of the male and female students regarding the roles and status of women. No significant differences were found in the public high school in the same neighborhood.

PARTING THOUGHTS

In reviewing the doctoral studies on Jewish all day education it is apparent that there is an uneven quality in the research and significant differences in the criteria for awarding the various degrees – DHL, EdD, and PhD. To be sure, while all the dissertations involving the Jewish day school refer to this form of education, many of them merely use the setting of the day school to explore facets of teaching and learning. These studies might have taken place in other types of schools.

One thing is clear from the extant doctoral studies. Much more focused research is needed about the nature of instruction and supervision in the schools, the quality of academic achievement, the impact of schooling on students, the relationship of classroom to families, the conditions of teaching and learning, teacher pre-service and in-service education, recruitment and placement, relationship between Jewish and general studies, and demographic religious trends.

CHAPTER 4

WHAT WE KNOW ABOUT THE JEWISH DAY SCHOOL (IN 1990)

At the beginning of the next century, when historians and sociologists will scurry to analyze fully the development of the American Jewish community in the twentieth century, one trend will be clearly outstanding – the phenomenal growth and staying power of Jewish all day education (Schiff, 1966, 1974, 1987; Dubb & DellaPergola; McMillan and Gerald). Given its relative costliness, especially when compared to the free public school – even in tandem with the cost of Jewish supplementary schooling, the flourishing of this institution during the mid 1900s and thereafter is nothing less than remarkable. This is particularly so in view of the decline of the Jewish supplementary school (Schiff, 1983, 1988, 1991).

ENROLLMENT

In 1990, there were about 177,250 pupils (K-12) enrolled in 652 Jewish day schools and yeshivot in North America (158,381 pupils in 604 schools in the United States and 18,870 students in 48 schools in Canada), compared to 62,000 pupils (K-12) in 296 schools in North American in 1962, the peak year of enrollment

(McMillan & Gerald). During the same period, enrollment in Jewish supplementary schools declined from 540,000 to 260,000 (Schiff, 1983; informal estimate 1991; JESNA, 1985).

The 1990 Jewish day school population comprised about 40 percent of the total Jewish school enrollment in the United States and Canada, compared to eleven percent in 1962 (Schiff, 1983, informal estimate 1991). The Greater New York experience sharpens the contrast even more. In 1940, the year marking the beginning of the Era of Great Expansion, the Jewish day school enrollment was about 6% of the total Jewish school enrollment (Schiff, 1966). By 1978, the day school population surpassed supplementary school enrollment; in 1990 it composed sixty percent of the total Jewish school population (Schiff & Kessel). This development appears even more extraordinary when one considers the reaction of Samuel Dinin to the early spurt of day school growth in the 1940s. In 1945, he wrote, "The Jews may get more than 0.8 percent of their children to attend all day schools (the Protestant percentage); they are hardly likely to go above 2 or 3 percent (2 percent being the percentage of private school pupils in this country) for the whole Jewish child population of 800,000."

Variety is a characteristic of this growth which involves virtually all of the ideological groupings in American Jewry – Hasidic, sectarian Orthodox, modern/centrist Orthodox, communal/traditional, Conservative, Reform, Yiddish, Zionist and general secular. The only feature common to all schools is the all day format of Jewish and general studies under one roof.

Developed by Orthodox Jews against a backdrop of opposition and doubt by the rest of the Jewish community (Kramer; Parsons; Schiff, 1966), its degree of acceptance and support by the broad Jewish community is underscored by the fact that 14.3% of Jewish Federation dollars for local needs were allocated in 1989 to Jewish all day education. This represents 56.4% of the total dollar allotment to local Jewish education services and programs (Liebman).

Eighty-three percent of the day school population is enrolled in Orthodox sponsored schools, equally divided between

Hasidic/sectarian and modern/centrist institutions. (The fact that Orthodox Jews comprise less than 10% of the total Jewish population in the United States is powerful evidence of the role of Orthodox Jewry in the development of all day Jewish schooling.) Ten percent of the enrollment is under Conservative auspices, 6% under communal (interdenominational, non-denominational or "other") sponsorship, and 1% in Reform day schools.

Despite the reality that day schools exist in every Jewish community with five thousand or more Jews, the Jewish day school is mainly an urban, large Jewish community phenomenon (Schiff, 1983). For example, of the 80,000 pupils (K-12) in New York area day schools in 1990, only 6,455 were in suburban Long Island and Westchester where approximately 45% of the Jewish population resides (Schiff & Kessel). Ninety percent of the enrollment in North America is in the ten largest urban centers.

Greater New York alone accounts for well over one half of the total day school population. Ninety-five percent of the New York day school enrollment is in Orthodox schools. With rare exception, Orthodox families choose the all day school format of Jewish education for their offspring, at least through high school grades.

Continentally, 29% of the day school enrollment is in early childhood programs (N-K); 58% is in the elementary grades; and 13% is in high school classes. The percentage of students in high school grades is significantly higher in New York (25%) where the vast majority of secondary Jewish day schools are found (Schiff & Kessel).

GROWTH FACTORS

The initial spurt in day school growth in the 1940s and early 1950s was due essentially to three factors: 1) the zealous activity of a small selfless group of Orthodox Day School advocates; 2) the effect of the Holocaust and the establishment of the State of Israel on the Jewish consciousness of American Jews; and 3) the influx of Eastern European Jews after World War II, especially between 1956 and 1958 (Schiff, 1966).

The reasons for day school growth since the 1960s are, interestingly, the opposite of the factors leading to the decline of the supplementary school enrollment. Whereas the birth rate among the general Jewish population has decreased in the last several decades, causing a drop in supplementary school enrollment, the high birth rate among the Orthodox, primarily the right-wing Orthodox, has accounted for dramatic pupil increases in yeshivot and day schools.

The mobility of the Jewish population – particularly the outmigration of Jews from areas of second and third settlement – has often been accompanied by nonaffiliation with a synagogue in the new areas of residence, and, hence, fewer children enrolled in synagogue schools. On the other hand, the immigration of Jews from the Soviet Union, Israel, Iran and other Moslem lands has added children to the classroom registers of the day schools. Heightened Jewish consciousness (and the *baal teshuvah* movement) is another reason for the increase in the number of day school pupils.

In some areas, dissatisfaction with the public school has motivated parents to choose a Jewish day school for their children, while others prefer it because it is a private school (Schiff, 1987). Finally, a growing number of working mothers and single parents favor an all day school environment, especially at the preschool levels.

Will these factors continue to motivate growth in the day school in the decades ahead? The proliferation of day schools has enhanced their viability by creating a positive image in the eyes of the community that the Jewish day school has come of age. The challenge is for day schools to capitalize on this image in their recruitment efforts. Indeed, now may be a good time to convene a continental transideological consultation on day school recruitment and retention.

As for future enrollment, one other question must be posed. Early childhood education is a significant aspect of overall day school growth. How can we ensure that greater numbers of early childhood graduates will continue on to Jewish all day elementary schools? To achieve this all-important objective, Jewish family education, geared to the young parents of these children, must become a regular part of every early childhood day school program.

GOVERNANCE AND FINANCES

The overwhelming majority of Jewish day schools is independently sponsored by local communal groups. About 15% were organized by synagogues, for the most part by Conservative and Reform congregations. Almost all day schools are loosely affiliated with one or more national or local organization. Locally, with the exception of some Orthodox yeshivot, they are associated with and receive services from the communal bureau of Jewish education. In the smaller communities, and even in the intermediate and large communities, the day school often competes with the bureau for Federation funding.

Despite their local and national affiliations, the authority and power for policymaking and program implementation rest solely within each school's board of trustees and its professional administration. Each institution was founded by a local group of interested parents and/or communal leaders (often with professional assistance from Torah Umesorah, United Synagogue, or Yeshiva University) who are desirous of controlling the affairs of the school and of insuring the continuation of its ideological/philosophical orientation. Moreover, they are loath to give up their power since they are saddled with the financial responsibility for the conduct of their respective institutions.

The cost of day school operation is considerable – what with the dual curriculum and dual sets of instructional staffs and administration. Tuition fees have not kept pace with the skyrocketing costs of all day education. Average per-pupil costs rose over nine-fold in three decades, from approximately $500 in 1962 to $4,600 in 1990; they ranged from $3,000 to $12,000 depending upon locale and grade level of school (Pollack & Lang; Schiff & Kessel). High school costs are about 50% higher than the elementary grades.

The largest portion of the school income derives from tuition fees. About 40% of the pupils do not pay full tuition (Pollack & Lang). Moreover, the full fee does not usually cover the complete cost of a child's education.

Day school operation in America is big business. The aggregate cost of yeshiva/day school education in 1990 was approximately $800,000,000. School boards raised approximately one third of this sum. Over the years, Federations have increased their support of all day education via scholarship assistance and subsidies for teacher salaries and special programs. In 1989, Federation allocations to day schools ($40,892,886) represented about 5% of the overall day school expenditure (Liebman).

THE POST HIGH SCHOOL YESHIVA WORLD

An aspect of Jewish all day education that deserves mention is the development and remarkable growth in the Orthodox community of a dual-level system of full-time (as much as 18 hours per day) post-highschool undergraduate and graduate Torah and Talmud study. While there are no exact enrollment figures available for each of these levels of study, it is estimated that in 1990 there were about 6,000 Bais Midrash (undergraduate) students and 2,500 Kollel (graduate) students. In 1950, there were less than 100 students enrolled in these programs (Helmreich). The length of stay in the Bais Midrash is generally two to four years; and in the Kollel, one to twenty years. Most students spend three to five years in the Kollel. Tuition in both of these programs ranges from $3,000 to $6,000 per annum, but really depends solely upon ability to pay. Most students pay little or no tuition. More than that, the Kollel students regularly receive stipends averaging $7,000 per year for room and board so that they can devote full time (morning, afternoon, and evening) to study without having to worry about finances. Married students often receive as much as $10,000 a year, supplemented by their wives' income, usually from teaching in a local yeshiva. The expenditures for this intensive post-highschool system of yeshiva education were estimated to be more than $50,000,000 in 1990 (Joel Beritz, personal communication). The Yeshivot Gedolot – the post-highschool institutions – are organized into the Association of Advanced Rabbinical and Talmudic Schools (AARTS), a group recognized by the Federal government as a national accrediting agency for Pell grants.

PERSONNEL

Two problem areas have consistently concerned the leadership of Jewish day schools – a shortage of qualified Hebrew teachers entering the Hebrew teaching profession and the high rate of turnover of Hebrew teachers. Both problems are rooted in the matter of job satisfaction (Himmelstein; Ravin) largely derived from the level of remuneration and fringe benefits (Himmelstein; Pollack & Lang). To be sure, teacher salaries are significantly less than those paid to public school teachers (JESNA, 1985; Aron & Phillips; Well). Because of this condition, one researcher found that more than half of the teachers in his study sample planned to leave their positions within five years (Lebovitz).

In 1990, in Greater New York, for example, the average salary of male instructors for twenty hours or more of Jewish studies teaching per week was $22,500 and for female teachers $19,120. Salaries for principals averaged $45,000. While the highest teacher salary was $51,000, several principals and administrators earned in excess of $100,000 (Schiff & Kessel).

Despite their personnel problems, the day schools seem to manage from year to year, hoping that next year will be an easier one financially. The personnel problems relating to supervision and administration are similar, yet different from those regarding teachers. There is a shortage of qualified personnel on both levels despite the significantly higher salaries (two to five times as much) for principals, driven up by supply and demand, by the feeling of lay leadership that they can attract highly qualified supervisory personnel if they can out-bid other schools. To be sure, the ability to hire high caliber administrators depends solely on the availability of such personnel and not upon the salaries schools are willing to offer. That availability derives largely from a sufficient pool of qualified teachers who have supervisory potential and are willing to obtain the necessary training in supervision and administration.

The problems are different because of the difference in job requirements. Lay-professional relationships play an important role in the life of a day school principal. A study of the views of New York City elementary Orthodox Hebrew day school principals' role expectations as perceived by the principals themselves and their lay board chairs revealed that the principals' views of the scope of their decision-making functions were substantially greater than the board chairs' views of their decision-making power (Feuerman). This difference was similar in the four areas of schooling examined – religious orientation, curriculum, finance and personnel. It was greatest in the area of curriculum and least in the area of religious orientation. Interestingly, while the lay board chairmen's views of the decision-making power of the principal in establishing the religious philosophy of the school almost coincided with that of the principals, they differed widely in their views about the principal's authority to implement that philosophy via the curriculum. Generally, the principals and board chairs agreed that the area of finance is a board function and that religious orientation, curriculum and personnel area primarily principal functions (Feuerman).

Another study demonstrated that directors who are formally evaluated by their boards of education at least once per year showed a greater desire to stay at their present positions than those who were not evaluated. There was no difference between directors with and without written job descriptions. Overall staying power of non-Orthodox day school principals was much greater at the time of the study (1987) than in earlier years. Average length of tenure is eight years and average number of positions held by present directors is two (Rosenthal).

Most day schools have two principals, one for Jewish studies and one for general studies. The relationship of these supervisors is critical to the smooth functioning of the school. Flatto (1987) showed that there is no relationship between the role expectations and the job satisfaction of the principals of the religious and secular departments.

Another study demonstrated that the older the principal is, the more experienced and the longer in the job, the greater the likelihood of role conflict perception between principals and between principals and boards of directors (Jordan).

CURRICULUM

While the common characteristic of all day schools is the dual program of Jewish and general studies under one roof, the Judaic curricula vary greatly. The general studies curriculum is generally set according to State requirements. In most schools, the morning hours are devoted to Jewish subjects when the students are presumably more alert.

The sectarian Hasidic and non-Hasidic all-boys yeshivot spend well over 60% of their instructional time on Jewish studies and concentrate almost solely on Pentateuch, the prayer service and codes in the early grades (Hebrew reading is taught in the kindergarten and sometimes even earlier) and on Talmud beginning with the fourth grade. These schools devote six days a week – between 30 and 40 hours – to Jewish studies where the language of instruction is often Yiddish. The sectarian girls schools teach Bible, Hebrew language, customs and ceremonies, *Musar* (ethics), *Midrash* and *Shulchan Aruch* in a Judaic studies program ranging from 15 to 20 hours per week. About the same amount of time is scheduled for general studies.

The modern/centrist Orthodox schools divide instructional time equally between Jewish and general studies. The Judaic studies curriculum includes: Hebrew language arts, Pentateuch, Prophets, Siddur, Jewish history, holidays and ceremonies, and *Shulchan Aruch*. Beginning with grade six or seven, the curriculum concentration is on Talmud for boys. During these periods, girls study *Midrash*, *Agaddah*, Hebrew literature, Jewish history and current events. Between fifteen and twenty hours are devoted to the Hebrew studies program.

The Solomon Schechter Schools and communal schools

generally devote about one third of the instructional time (12 to 15 hours per week) to Judaic subjects including Hebrew language and literature, Bible, Jewish history, customs and ceremonies, current events and introduction to Talmud in the upper grades.

In the Reform day schools, Hebrew language and literature are taught as separate subjects. All other Hebraic studies are introduced as part of an interdisciplinary approach to classroom instruction. In all, between 5 and 15 hours are devoted to the Jewish dimensions of the program.

Curricula integration, by and large, is not practiced. In the first instance, Orthodox schools do not advocate it as a matter of principle. However, it is considered an ideological and practical desideratum for Conservative and Reform schools. Nevertheless, as one study demonstrated, these institutions do not integrate Jewish and general subject matter because of a fundamental philosophical problem – their acceptance of a structure of discipline's view of knowledge and curriculum planning (Solomon).

There is a surprising lack of scientific information regarding academic achievement in both Jewish and general studies. There are no standardized tests for achievement in Jewish studies. Yet, from all available evidence it is clear that Jewish day school graduates acquit themselves admirably in high school and university settings. This is due largely to school standards, stringent requirements regarding homework, the general climate of learning in the schools and parent involvement in their children's education. Moreover, the sheer volume of hours and the intensity of exposure to Judaic studies have a notable impact upon students, especially upon those continuing their all day schooling through high school and beyond. In absolute (and certainly in relative) terms, they accumulate a significant body of Judaic knowledge, not unlike the Torah scholarship of yesteryear in Eastern Europe.

FAMILY AND SCHOOL

The role of family in day schools cannot be disregarded. Research in general education adequately confirms the importance of family influence on achievement (Coleman & Campbell; Cohen; Jencks, et al.; Greeley & Rossi). This is so in Jewish schools, particularly with regard to the formation and strengthening of Jewish identity. One study demonstrated that family background "makes a large and significant contribution to total Jewish identification" (Shapiro). It showed that the most important predictors of total Jewish identification are parents' ritual observance, parents' residence-friendship patterns, the children's group activities and parents' parenting behaviors. Clearly, parents with positive Jewish attitudes and family styles prefer to send their offspring to a day school. The synergism between home and school is the key to the successful performance of the children (Heimowitz).

For high performance in every area of life, Benjamin Bloom (1985) has underscored the importance of the combination of a supportive sacrificing home" and quality "time-on-task" in and out of school.

Parental interest, motivation and support differ significantly according to ideological orientation. Sectarian Orthodox parents strongly support school policies. For them, there is no choice but to give their children the most intensive, religious Jewish educational exposure in home and in school. Modern/centrist Orthodox parents generally enroll their children in day schools because of the quality and intensity of the Jewish study program and because of their own Jewish concerns (Nulman; Adams, Frankel & Newbauers; Schiff, 1966); yet, in the modern/centrist schools many parents are not themselves Orthodox or as religious as the school would like them to be. Consequently, they do not necessarily associate themselves with the religious philosophy of the schools. They are interested in having their children "feel Jewish" but not really "act Jewish" (Lasker).

In one study of Modern Orthodox schools, the teachers and principals attributed greatest importance to goals of religious living. Most parents, on the other hand, indicated that goals of Jewish cultural living are most important and goals of religious living least important. Moreover, parents rated the importance of "a secular American orientation" much higher than the Jewish studies personnel (Gans).

In the non-Orthodox day school sector, parents enroll their children primarily because of excellence in general studies and not for "Jewish reasons" (Kapel; Kelman). This fad underscores the relationship between the deterioration of the public school system and greater parental interest in the non-Orthodox Jewish day school (Zeldin).

DAY SCHOOL IMPACT

Overall, the impact of day school education is significant, particularly when compared to Jewish supplementary schooling (Schiff, 1988). A follow-up study of graduates of selected Hebrew day and supplementary schools focused attention on the relative contribution of these institutions in maintaining Jewish identity and continuity (Hartman). The findings of this study demonstrate that: Hebrew day school graduates 1) perceive themselves and their parents as more religiously observant; 2) perceive their Jewish education as being more effective in enhancing both their own and their parents' religious behavior; 3) view interdating and intermarriage as more antithetical to their belief system. Hebrew day school graduates interdate much less and intermarry much less.

Graduates of both systems who express a higher degree of satisfaction with Jewish education also perceive themselves and their parents as more religiously observant. Hebrew day school graduates attend secondary or postsecondary schools of Jewish learning significantly longer and select Jewish education and/or Jewish communal work as future vocational choices to a greater degree (Hartman).

Long-term studies on the impact of Jewish day schooling indicate that it has significant influence on Jewish identity formation, even when a variety of factors including family background are controlled (Bock; Cohen; Himmelfarb). In the final analysis, one of the major reasons for the impact of day schools on attitudes and identification is the full-day Jewish climate in which students are immersed. This, after all, is one of the reasons for the establishment of day schools.

Summing up the day school phenomenon in Jewish life, it seems most appropriate to quote Ludwig Lewisohn, author, novelist and critic, who in his later years became a strong devotee of the day school movement. He wrote in 1950:

> The truest advance in recent Jewish history in the United States, the one altogether hopeful phenomenon, has been the initiation and the slow gradual spread of the day school movement. It arose, necessarily, from classical Jewish sources…Fundamentals must be side by side with the acquisition of an exacting and elegant grasp of English and its literature. The usual (general) subjects of instruction must be augmented by Jewish history, symbol, ceremony, liturgy, with special attention in the grades to the development of the *Yishuv*, the community in *Eretz Yisrael* and the re-established commonwealth. All this can be accomplished in the (elementary) grades where a Jewish (day) high school is not practiced. The public grade schools take from six to seven years to teach so pitifully little that advanced educators see in these half-wasted years the chief symptom of the ills that afflict American education. They point authoritatively to the fact that in Europe boys and girls of seventeen to eighteen are ready for what we call graduate or professional studies. Coming from such [day] schools Jewish children will be reasonably well educated for their age. The possession of one additional language, Hebrew, will make the acquisition of others in high school and college easier. Above all, these children will be, from the beginning, integrated Jews; that is to say, since they are Jews, integrated human beings. As such, as whole human beings, knowing their place in society and in the world, in the realms of man and God, they will be able to meet the non-Jewish world with ease, assurance, and dignity. They will neither defensively overemphasize nor fearfully underemphasize their Jewishness and their Judaism. They and they alone will be equals in temper, poise, directness of

all social approaches of the Catholics and Protestants with whom they will have to mingle and compete in the daily involvement of American life.

THE LARGER CONTEXT

Day school education stands as the one format with the best odds of educating Jewish children so as to produce knowledgeable, literate and committed Jews. But, will the same factors that have led to current parental choices, continue to motivate growth of these schools in the decades ahead? Will the centrist, Modern Orthodox day schools be able to sustain their rapid growth? Will the non-Orthodox forms of Jewish day school education be able to grow? Will the state of and commitment to public education continue to influence the choice of Jewish day schools? These are but a few of the questions raised by this article.

CHAPTER 5

THE JEWISH DAY SCHOOL (IN 1987) LOOKS TO THE NEXT HALF-CENTURY

It is almost fifty years old and growing each year in height and girth, despite early prognostications that it would not survive. While it is shedding some hair, there are no signs of balding or graying, even at the temples. Its appetite increases each year. In the process, it makes more friends. Old friends strengthen their bonds of friendship, and new ones become avid advocates. Some observers, on the other hand, question its ever-growing need for succor, but most often end up supporting it, albeit begrudgingly. Its future depends heavily on its friends. It is the Jewish Day School – the almost rejected younger offspring that has outpaced its siblings and will probably out live them.

The American Jewish all day education experiment of the 1940s has generated a variety of school types and orientations. Several features are common to all of them. These are: autonomous auspices; the provision of general and Jewish education under one roof; an all day environment offering educational opportunities for the confluence of cognitive and affective learning; a shortage of qualified supervisory, administrative and instructional personnel; and growing fiscal problems due to the rapid escalation in the cost of operation.

The Jewish day school has shown remarkable ability to thrive in the face of continued problems and challenges. While its enrollment is still much less than that of the supplementary school, it has overshadowed the one day, Sunday, and midweek congregational schools in a variety of ways, particularly in its ability to transmit more Jewish knowledge to its students. Moreover, it has attracted significantly more communal attention and support over the last two decades. Although the modern Jewish day school can trace its birth to the beginning of the century, its rapid growth began in 1940. Since then, its enrollment has increased each year.

In 1962, the peak enrollment year in Jewish schooling on the North American continent, about 540,000 children were enrolled in Jewish supplementary schools of all types – mid-week, afternoon, one-day-a-week and Sunday schools. In 1986, there are approximately 240,000 pupils in these institutions – a decline of 55%. On the other hand, during the same period, Jewish day school enrollment increased more than two-fold, from 60,000 to 130,000. The day school pupil population now comprises about 30% of the total North American Jewish school enrollment. Moreover, day schools receive a total of $26 million from local Federations, as compared to $5.5 million for the supplementary schools.

Initially solely an Orthodox enterprise and centered in New York City, the Jewish all day school is now ideologically diversified, with 587 school units across the continent. Conservative Judaism, in 1957, via a resolution of the United Synagogue Commission on Education, became seriously involved in supporting and establishing Solomon Schechter schools. Currently, 67 Solomon Schechter schools, 11.4% of the total number of day school units, with about 11,600 pupils, 8.9% of the enrollment, are under Conservative auspices.

The Reform movement, which has traditionally opposed the concept and practice of Jewish all day education, passed a resolution at the 1986 biennial Union of American Hebrew

Congregations conference in support of the development of Reform Jewish day schools. Presently, there are approximately 2,600 children, or 2% of the total Jewish day school pupil population, attending 11 Reform all day schools, which, in turn, are 1.8% of the total number of day schools.

By far, the largest proportion of Jewish day schools (472, or 80.5% of the total) and the overwhelming majority of pupils (104,000, or 80% of the enrollment) are under Orthodox auspices.

The above data clearly demonstrates that the Jewish day school is an ideological institution. However, during recent years, with the encouragement and support of local Federations, particularly in small and intermediate communities that find it difficult, or simply do not want, to support more than one school, communal inter-ideological day schools have been organized. Several of these have been modified from existing ideological institutions. In some cases, it is hard to differentiate between an inter-ideological school and a communal-ideological entity, which is essentially an ideological institution with a communal thrust. There are currently 37 communal all day institutions (6.3% of the total) with about 11,800 pupils, representing 9.1% of the enrollment.

[*For an overview of the growth factors which contributed to the development of Jewish day schools, please refer to the previous chapter.*]

COMMUNAL SUPPORT

Jewish day school education is big business. Annual expenditures reach the almost $400 million mark. What with the continued increases in enrollment (1% to 3% a year) and escalating costs, it could well be a billion dollar enterprise by the year 2000. Currently, Federations account for 6% of the income Jewish day schools receive. What kind of support will local Federations give to all day education in the future? Where will intensive Jewish education rank among Federation priorities? How will support relate to future campaign efforts?

CONTINUATION

To have a lasting effect, Jewish education must be continuous at least through the high school years. This is basic for adolescents in the formation of Jewish identity, attitudes and practices in adult life. The lack of continuation beyond elementary school has a noticeably diminutive effect.

A well-publicized study has shown that an effective afternoon school education through high school can have greater impact upon eventual adult behavior than do 6 or 8 years of day schooling. This study also demonstrates that the best guarantee for a positive school effect is a minimum of 3,000 hours of classroom experience – from kindergarten through grade 12. Currently, with the exception of the yeshivot in the New York area, the rate of continuation of elementary day school graduates is minimal. Only about 22,000 pupils (17% of the total Jewish day school enrollment) are enrolled on the high school level. If all elementary Jewish day school graduates continued on to high school this figure would increase by 40 percent.

Will day schools succeed in influencing students (and their parents) to continue on to day high school programs? Will there be day high schools available in small and intermediate communities to make this a reality? To be sure, even in large Jewish communities, some Jewish day high schools have not succeeded. During the last decade, in New York, one Conservative high school closed its doors. Another was unable to open even after all plans were completed, including the preparation of a facility. The single day high school in the New York area under Conservative auspices is in a precarious situation. Will congregational leadership be able to develop adequate support for Jewish all day secondary education under Conservative sponsorship?

THE SCHOOL PROGRAM

What about the quality of Jewish all day schooling? As the day school movement grows, it reflects increasingly the diversity of the Jewish community. The pluralism is expressed in the intraideological curriculum differences as well as in the interideological program variations.

By and large, the ultra-Orthodox yeshivot – whose enrollment comprises about one third of the total day school population – will continue being sectarian, Talmud-oriented, sex-segregated, and non-Zionist. What will be the nature of the programs of the other Orthodox day schools? Will they continue to be affected by the fundamentalist turn to the right in the Orthodox community? What will happen to the Orthodox coeducational schools, given that an increasingly large number of their faculties – particularly in the upper grades – is drawn from the sectarian *metivtot* and *kollellim*?

If the Solomon Schechter schools succeed in attracting significant numbers of children from marginally affiliated families, will this affect the direction of their educational thrust? While the curricula of the various Conservative schools differ, they now have a strong Judaic base of studies of 12–15 hours per week. Will they continue in this vein? What will be the fate of the integration of Jewish and general studies in these schools? Will the embryonic Reform day school mature into a real bicultural institution with an intensive track of Judaic studies? Will the Reform movement give unqualified support to the development of day schools with strong Jewish Studies components?

What will be the role of Israel in all of the day schools? Will an Israel-based experience become an integral part of the school program?

In considering the responses to these questions, we must be mindful that, as yet, there are no definitive studies on the impact of the modern day school on the adult behavior of graduates. While there are a few research studies like that cited earlier and empirical evidence regarding the post-school Jewish involvement of day school graduates, there is little scientific information available about the quality of the impact of a Jewish all day education on individuals, families, and community. The school effect is largely related to home and peer influences. This phenomenon has to be examined carefully when studying the impact of the day school.

As the students in day schools, excluding the ultra Orthodox, are becoming increasingly affected by current societal trends, will they, like the supplementary school, have to move into value content and family education? Does this point to the need for a redefinition of the goals of the day school as we approach the twenty-first century?

An interesting by-product of the day school movement among the Orthodox, especially the ultra-Orthodox, is the emergence of the *kollel* phenomenon. It is estimated that there are well over 10,000 young men, eighteen years and over, who spend a significant part of their lives, many to age thirty and beyond, wholly devoted to the study of Talmud. What will be the future of this growing corps of highly committed, young, sectarian Jews with intensive rabbinic background and little or no concomitant cultural baggage? What effect will they have on the Jewish community, as they become adults?

THE PERSONNEL PROBLEM

The most serious problem of the day school is the shortage of qualified personnel. It will take yeoman efforts on the part of the schools, parents, and community to make Jewish day school teaching an attractive career to young, talented westernized Jews, but without such a cadre, the future of the day school may be cast in doubt.

In order to attract quality educators, the level of compensation and benefits will have to be raised dramatically. Moreover, professional growth opportunities must be made available within each school. With the current range of remuneration from $8,000 to $15,000 for part-time teaching, and $12,000 to $35,000 (averaging $18,000) for full-time positions, we cannot hope to attract many new talented people. This challenge belongs primarily in the laps of parents (with full knowledge that some cannot afford greater financial burdens) and the sponsoring institutions. Will the local Federations match their efforts and to what extent?

CONCLUSIONS

The future provides unlimited opportunity for Jewish all day education. The fledgling, modern yeshivot in the 1940s and early 1950s flourished despite the unwelcome communal environment and vehement opposition from various quarters of the Jewish community. Now, given the universal acceptance of the Jewish day school idea and an appreciation of its role on the American Jewish scene, the potential for its continued growth should be limitless. This essay has raised a variety of questions (read: challenges) that relate to the realization of this potential. It could be within our grasp if we learn to turn problems into promise and forge promise into reality.

CHAPTER 6

ON THE NEED FOR MORAL EDUCATION IN THE JEWISH DAY SCHOOL

THE JEWISH DAY SCHOOL IS SPECIAL

At the outset, in viewing the title of this paper, one may ask, "why special attention to moral education in the Jewish day school?" Moral education is moral education, is moral education. American children are American children, are American children. Teachers are teachers, are teachers. Can't we treat moral education in the Jewish day school as we would deal with this challenge in other schools?

There is a difference – a uniqueness that characterizes the Jewish day school and makes this educational instrumentality different, special. The Jewish day school is different because most day school children and teachers bring special baggage to their school setting. The day school environment is unique by virtue of its dual purpose, dual objectives, dual curriculum, dual language program, dual sets of teachers and principals, dual role models, and the pervading Jewish atmosphere. These distinguishing sets of characteristics justify special attention to moral education in the Jewish day school.

To be sure, teachers in Jewish day schools share common responsibilities with teachers in other kinds of schools. It is not what teachers know, but what they do; not the content that they have acquired to transmit, but the way they behave in the classroom; not their pedagogical knowledge, but the way they teach that distinguishes all teachers as special influences on the lives of students in their charge. Yet, Jewish day school teachers are different. They may share many goals and objectives with teachers in other schools – public and nonpublic – and may face many of the same problems regarding the realization of these goals. Still, Jewish day school teachers, particularly instructors of Jewish studies, are different because they teach in special settings and have a specialized Judaic-American mission.

REASONS FOR EMPHASIS ON MORAL EDUCATION

A need for teaching morality in Jewish day schools derives from a variety of sources, not the least of which is recent publicity about the unethical behavior of several leading American citizens, some of whom, in their youth, attended Jewish day schools. This is not to say that the Jewish day school bears any responsibility for the immortality of its graduates, or that unethical activity of day school graduates is a more acute problem than that of adults not exposed to a Jewish all day school experience. I think that the opposite is true. However, recent extremely serious incidents of unethical business activity highlight the need for day schools to try to insure, no matter how difficult this may be, that such happenings will not take place in the future.

A letter I received not long ago from a leading litigation lawyer – himself a parent of Jewish day school children – who has become vitally interested in this subject underscores the extent of the challenge:

"In the ―――― leasing case [involving some of our most visible lay leaders] the most gripping point for me was [the defendant's] testimony about his time at the ―――― Bank, how he rose in position in the international division, and how he turned down a post as a leader of a group because it would have required travel on Shabbat. [The defendant] said that he thought that [the bank] was anti-Semitic, and he quit to join his relative, ――――.

"A second series of incidents which comes to mind has to do with the phantom students in the Federal school feeding programs. So-called pious people find it acceptable to misrepresent in order to obtain money from the government. [The prime example of this is the well-publicized summer feeding program in which many institutions of all religious denominations – Jewish and non-Jewish – and many institutions in the public sector were found guilty of fraud relating to phantom campers for whom they collected millions of dollars through the summer feeding program.]

"A third incident is a case which I have handled for a long number of years, ——— vs.———. Here, devout Jews who dress distinctively and probably never miss a prayer were found guilty and convicted of criminal misconduct in connection with a very large-scale commodities fraud. The evidence showed perjured affidavits on the accounts, laundering of money to cheat on taxes, and reneging on a million-dollar debt. This was as if to say that inside the community there's a different set of morals than those which pertain to the outside world.

"A fourth set of incidents has to do with the stealing of Regents examinations in a non-Orthodox day school. The stealing of exams is the result of student proclivity for cheating on tests, which occurs in all schools in the public and private sectors with scant adverse comment."

While the cases cited by this lawyer do not provide evidence that would indicate that Jewish day schools are at fault for that which happened, the schools have a role to play in helping prevent such occurrences from taking place.

The need for special instruction in moral development is interestingly expressed by Arthur Coombs in the delightful little volume *Myths of Education*. "There are many good things about education today. We have beautiful school buildings, good programs, and excellent materials, dedicated teachers and devoted principals. The problem is that the parents send us the wrong children." Like all educational institutions, Jewish day schools have some pupils who are the "wrong" children with real moral dilemmas. Many of them find it very difficult to cope with the society around them. Many of them are the "wrong" children because their families do not associate themselves with the ideological goals of the schools which they attend.

Teachers have to learn to speak the language of the "wrong" children. I'm reminded of an example which might not be far-fetched. When the General Motors car named Nova was exported to Latin American countries, it did not sell because Nova, in Spanish, means, "will not go." General Motors just wasn't able to communicate in the language of the people to whom it was marketing the automobile. Eventually, GM had to change the name of the car. One of our challenges is training teachers to communicate meaningfully with all our children.

Can we teach morality in the Jewish day school without regard to the goals of the Jewish home? Can moral education be wholly effective, independent of an approach involving the homes of the children in the school? James Coleman, Christopher Jencks, and David Cohen, in their trailblazing research in the 1960s, clearly demonstrated the necessity for home support in order to achieve educational effectiveness. This is certainly the case in the area of moral education. Family involvement is vital in making the connection between learning and behaving, between knowing and doing.

Another challenge has to do with the relationship between knowing and doing. An outstanding individual who personified morality and ethical behavior was the first chief rabbi of Israel (then Palestine), Rabbi Abraham Isaac Kook. His commentary on a passage in *Ethics of the Fathers* is instructive in this regard. Commenting on Rabbi Shimon ben Gamliel's statement, "All my days I have grown up among the wise, and have found nothing of better service to myself [literally, nothing better for my own body] *me-sh'teekah* – than silence" (1:17). Rabbi Kook noted that the term *me-sh'teekah* is universally interpreted wrongly. It does not mean "than silence," rather "from silence." Rabbi Shimon's statement should read: "I found nothing good for myself by keeping silent." He was referring to the imperative to speak out about wrongdoing even in the presence of *hakhamim* (leading scholars). We have to bring our youth to the level of articulating moral values and standing up for what is right and just, even if doing so is not very popular. This would be a high stage of moral development.

Mentioning Harav Kook brings to mind the fact that Jewish tradition places much emphasis on teaching by example. And, fortunately, there are numerous models of moral behavior upon which we can readily draw in the course of our teaching. There are many personalities whose ethical lifestyles are paradigmatic, including biblical, Talmudic, Gaonic, and medieval figures, as well as contemporary luminaries such as the Chofetz Chaim and Reb Aryeh Levin. Their lives provide a wellspring of insight as to the meaning of *hesed* (personal consideration of others, lovingkindness). Moreover, each of us can point to numerous examples in our own communal settings of how *hesed* is lived and practiced.

In addition to transmitting knowledge of ethics from Judaic sources and citing examples of moral individuals, it is necessary to develop vehicles for transmitting the concept of ethical behavior in an experiential and visceral way to our children. Schools need to build moral development into the warp and woof of the everyday school environment by providing opportunities for students to practice *hesed*.

This brings us to another reason for emphasizing moral education as a special subject in Jewish day schools – the larger society's relationship to the Jew. To paraphrase Rabbi Yehudah Halevi, one might say that problems which affect the larger society, affect the Jews more. "When the world deals with Jews," Abba Eban once said, "it forgets humanity. When the world deals with humanity, it forgets Jews." How do teachers in Jewish day schools deal with the world's inhumanity to Jews, with the world's indifference to Jews and its baseless antagonism to Israel, with the "Zionism is Racism" resolution of the U.N.? Moreover, how do we react to the revisionist historians of the Holocaust? What do we tell our children? Given these facts, should Jews be only for themselves? How do we interpret "If I am not for myself, who will be for me?" How do these questions relate to the development of moral judgment?

There is a value for considering the subject of moral education in day schools for other reasons. It will help us focus on the great repositories of Jewish tradition and will motivate us to consider the more effective use of Judaic sources that deal with Jewish values and morality. The problem here is that in our daily lives we often compartmentalize Judaic teachings. For many Jews, the commandments or deeds that express man's relationship to God have overshadowed the role of the mitzvot between man and man. In this regard, once again, I come back to the letter from my lawyer friend. He writes:

> The distinction often made between ritual observance and moral conduct is without merit. It has to be done away with. The point should be made that everyone has base tendencies, and wrapping oneself in ritual and prayer is no guarantee that we will be able to resist the temptations of making money improperly. What to do about it is a different problem, and teaching cannot be satisfactory merely to extol appropriate precepts. I think it might be useful to develop a case method approach, with different extracts from the *Mishnah*, *Gemara*, and *Responsa* that bear on the problem, leaving it to the students and their discussions to make appropriate applications. I think it might be useful to take some of the problem areas in the Bible and subject them to moral analyses. Close reading of the texts suggests, in many, if not all situations, that penalties were ultimately paid by those who took advantage of deception to gain ends.

These comments, made by a perceptive, committed Jewish lay leader, underscore some of the challenges at hand.

Prior to describing the building of the sanctuary and the priestly service in the Tabernacle, the Torah begins with God's statement to Moses, "Speak to the children of Israel and tell the Israelite people to bring me gifts and you shall accept gifts for me from *every person whose heart so moves him*." How can we move hearts? How do we create the desire for children to share with others? How do we develop the ability to rise above self, and to help build or contribute to the building of a trust community? In the long run, responding effectively to these questions is the universal *raison d'être* of moral development in all educational settings.

Consideration of moral education also requires educators to focus on the relationship between Torah and *mada* – the confluence between general studies and Jewish studies, between science and religion. Developing moral judgment speaks to the dynamics of this relationship.

FOCUSING RELIGIOUS INSTRUCTION ON MORAL VALUES

The challenge of moral education in the Jewish day school may be considered in light of Kohlbergian thought. How does one resolve moral dilemmas from a religious or halachic point of view? Can one break a Judaic tenet to reach a high moral stage in life? Is this halachically possible? Is there an internal inconsistency between Kohlbergian theory and Judaic thought and tradition?

According to a Belgian Catholic theologian, there are three stages of moral development: the taboo stage, the ethical-moral stage, and the religious-spiritual stage. The third stage integrates and internalizes the ethical-moral stage. It brings people to the understanding that religious-spiritual values elevate a person to the highest possible stage of moral behavior. In Judaism, the ethical-moral and religious-spiritual are integrated willy-nilly. How does this fact square with Kohlbergian ideas? Responding to this question is one of the challenges facing Jewish educators as they develop curricular materials for moral education.

Jacob Lawrence, a black artist, noted perceptively, "Many of us look; few of us see. Many of us see the vast expanse of the lawn; few of us appreciate a blade of grass." This seems to express the real meaning of the Haggadic discourse of Rabbi Yohanan who said, "Every time you find the greatness of God there you find also his humility" (*Megillah* 31a). Reaching this stage of understanding – appreciating the blade of grass – is the goal of moral education.

And now back to the initial dilemma. On the one hand, moral values have been taught directly and indirectly in Jewish schools for centuries. Currently, teaching Jewish ethics is part and parcel of the curriculum of most educational institutions. In fact, many schools provide significant blocks of time for the study of *musar*. Values instruction in the classroom is generally indirect, deriving from Judaic textual study: *Humash, Mishnah, Gemara* and their respective commentaries. What teachers attempt to do is to stress "the light of the Torah" – the particular Jewish values and moral concepts emanating from the text being studied. In addition, many informal educational experiences relating to moral education and the development of ethical personalities are provided in most yeshivot.

If this is the case; if the inculcation of moral values and education for ethical conduct is part and parcel of Jewish day school and yeshiva education, why the need for special attention to this subject? In the first place, in addition to the reasons I have already given, it is clear that there is a need to heighten the focus of Jewish all day schooling on the challenge of improving the methodology and content of moral education. Secondly, we can learn much from what has been going on within Harvard's hallowed halls and elsewhere that can be helpful to the Jewish day school movement. Thirdly, there is much that the Jewish educators can learn from each other. The process of sharing is important for all of us and will help each of us in our respective work settings as we deal with the challenges of moral education.

In this regard, I am reminded of the child who was trying to lift a very heavy box to no avail. He just couldn't lift it. His father, who was watching him, asked: "Son, are you using all your strength?" The son replied, "Yes." The father asked, "Are you sure?" The son said, "I'm sure." The father continued, "Think about it once more. When you tried to lift the box did you use all your strength?" The boy said, "Yes, I'm positive." The father retorted, "No, you're not using all your strength; you didn't ask me." Here at the conference we're asking each other and asking the experts, to help. And we're learning from each other. There are many challenges that day schools face relating to moral education, about which we can learn from one another.

To respond to all the challenges we face in moral education

requires teacher training. This means convincing school leaders that we need greater investment of time, effort, and money for on-the-job in-service education to help teachers succeed in the instruction of moral values.

We know how tight our budgets are, how difficult it is for schools to keep their heads above water. I'm reminded, however, that when a former resident of this city, John Quincy Adams, advocated greater government support for education, he said that "the whole people must take upon themselves the education of the whole people and be willing to bear the expense of it." As Jewish education leaders, we have to communicate this attitude more forcefully to the community at large and to the lay leaders of our schools underscoring that more support has to be provided for moral education programming.

And so, upon reflection, my dilemma was resolved, because it is good moral judgment to learn more about how to improve the methods we use to help our students develop better moral judgment. In this way, we guarantee that they will be more ethical adults, combining the desire to fulfill equally *mitzvot bain adam lamakom*, "mitzvot between man and the Almighty" and *mitzvot bain adam l'havero*, "mitzvot between man and man."

CHAPTER 7

THE JEWISHNESS QUOTIENT OF JEWISH DAY SCHOOL GRADUATES: THE EFFECT OF JEWISH EDUCATION ON ADULT BEHAVIOR

TWO OPPOSITE TRENDS IN JEWISH EDUCATION

During the last several decades, two contrary trends in Jewish education have been evidenced. On the one hand, we have witnessed the remarkable growth of the Jewish Day School. In contradistinction to the positive trend regarding the Jewish day school, we have witnessed a serious decline in Jewish supplementary school. Overshadowing the retrogradation of the supplementary school, and related to it, is the serious defection from Jewish life of growing numbers of Jews. This acculturation – deculturation syndrome has been dramatically demonstrated by the 1990 National Jewish Population Survey findings: a troubling, upsetting 52% intermarriage rate and a similar confounding, disturbing percentage of Jewish children under age 18 being raised outside the Jewish faith; and an estimated 3.5 million "core Jews" out of a total 5.5 million core Jewish population who are not affiliated with synagogues or other Jewish institutions (NJPS).

These two opposing trends – the growth of intensive Jewish education, on the one hand, and the deterioration of the most populated Jewish educational instrumentality coupled with the erosion of Jewish life, on the other – give rise to several queries that beg to be answered, particularly in light of the claims made by proponents and supporters of Jewish all day education regarding its impact upon the adult Jewish lifestyle of its students.

What is the nature of the Jewishness of the Jewish adults who attended Jewish day schools? What key factors are related to the Jewish behavior of day school graduates? How frequently do day school students marry out? Do their non-Jewish spouses convert to Judaism?

Given the trend towards assimilation among growing numbers of young Jews – less Jewish observance, less Jewish communal involvement, less relationship with Israel and a higher rate of intermarriage and mixed marriage – the questions about the Jewishness quotient of Jewish day school graduates assume great significance, particularly since the American Jewish community is supportive of this institution as a means of insuring Jewish continuity.

THE JEWISH DAY SCHOOL AND JEWISH CONTINUITY

During the 1992 General Assembly held in New. York, Torah Umesorah, the National Society for Hebrew Day Schools, published an advertisement in *The Jewish Week*, one of the local Jewish newspapers distributed to the participants. The ad states, "A Jewish day school education will ensure the eternity of our people. The intermarriage rate drops to 7% for students who complete a Jewish Day school education. Educating more young Jews will do more than lowering the intermarriage statistics. It will bring in its path a generation of committed Jews, conscientious and educated Jewish leaders and, above all, the preservation of the Jewish family." (*The Jewish Week*)

In a letter to the editor of *The Jewish Week*, following the appearance of the advertisement, Egon Mayer disputed Torah Umesorah's claim, noting that "according to the findings of the 1990 National Jewish Population Survey, the intermarriage rate of those whose Jewish education was received in a Jewish day school is 18 percent in first marriages and rises to 29 percent in second marriages." Moreover, Mayer notes that using a multiple regression procedure he discovered that "the type of Jewish education one received has no statistically significant relationship to the outcome of whether one intermarried or not."

Viewing the same study, Seymour Lipset concluded, "the NJPS data confirm the assumption that the more exposure to Jewish learning, the more likely the recipients are to be involved in the community and to pass the commitment on to their children. The justified concern for Jewish continuity correctly focuses on Jewish education as the major facility available to the community to stem the hemorrhaging out which is taking place" (Lipset). Putting it another way, Lipset suggests that the "power of education is reflected in the finding that those who have been trained Jewishly are disposed to seek to transmit their heritage through formal education of their children" (Lipset). A clear statement about a value of Jewish education, yet it falls short of demonstrating the full effect of a Jewish day school education.

STUDIES ON THE IMPACT OF THE JEWISH DAY SCHOOL

Regarding the impact of Jewish all day education, a follow-up study of graduates of selected Hebrew day and supplementary schools in the South and Midwest demonstrated that Hebrew day school graduates perceive themselves and their parents as more religiously observant; perceive their Jewish education as being more effective in enhancing both their own and their parents' religious behavior; and view interdating and intermarriages more antithetical to their belief system. Hebrew day school graduates interdate much less and intermarry much less. Moreover, they attend secondary or post-secondary schools of Jewish learning and select Jewish education and/or Jewish communal work as future vocational choices to a greater degree (Hartman).

In separate studies of graduates of Midwestern Jewish day schools under Orthodox auspices and of graduates of a large yeshiva in New York, the authors found a positive significant relationship between Jewish all day education on the high school level and the adult Jewish behavior of graduates (Pollak; Pinsky).

A study of the graduates of a large Modern Orthodox Hebraic day high school in New York demonstrates, among other findings, that the greatest influence on the Jewish identity of its graduates is the combination of home and school factors. Most of the graduates identified themselves as Orthodox. Over ninety percent consider the Jewish day school as the most desirable form of Jewish education and send (or would send) their own children to these schools. And over ninety percent felt that their yeshiva high school education influenced them positively in identifying with the State of Israel. Moreover, twenty-five percent were considering living in Israel at the time of the study (Heimowitz).

Similarly, a study of graduates of three-day schools in Philadelphia demonstrated that "the development of a lifestyle strongly committed to Jewish affairs is primarily the result of an intensive Jewish education and concerned Jewish home" (Ribner).

Another researcher suggests that the day school is effective in developing religious attitudes only if they are already found in the home (Cohen). In the same vein, another study showed that the number of hours of Jewish schooling (differentiating between the Jewish study programs of the day school and supplementary school) does not make a significant contribution to total Jewish identification after controlling for the influence of family background, peers, camps and youth groups (Shapiro). This study found that parents' religious observance, parents' residence, friendship patterns and parenting behaviors made a significant contribution to total Jewish identification.

Yet, several long-term studies on the impact of intensive Jewish day schooling indicate that it has significant influence on Jewish identity formation, even when a variety of factors including family background are controlled (Bock; Himmelfarb). Himmelfarb's findings demonstrate that a minimum of six years and 3000 hours in Jewish schooling are needed for Jewish education to have an impact upon adult Jewish lifestyle (Himmelfarb). Importantly, a study of the graduates of Ramaz – a liberal, modern Orthodox day school whose goal it is "to develop an American Jewish child, and, eventually, an adult who will grow into manhood and womanhood experiencing no clash between being a Jew and an American at one and the same time" (Lookstein, 1978 and 1989) demonstrated that these objectives have largely been realized (Friedman). Ramaz graduates have:

> gone to higher educational attainment, have overwhelmingly entered the professions and the business world, and appear to be doing quite well financially. At the same time, their rates of synagogue membership and attendance, of affiliation with and leadership in Jewish organizations, of identification with the State of Israel are far higher than those found in surveys of the American Jewish population – whether in New York or elsewhere. Further, they have not only continued their own Jewish study, but have overwhelmingly provided a day school education for their children. At the same time, while there has been some religious fall off, the majority continue to observe the laws of Shabbat and *kashrut* and a sizable minority say that they have become more observant over the years.

To be sure, Friedman concludes that Ramaz played a significant role in fashioning the Jewish lifestyle of its graduates. This feeling is underscored by the comment of a 1971 alumna, "I feel certain that I am an observant Jew primarily because I attended Ramaz. My experiences at Ramaz were extremely positive and the fact that, as a teenager, I was able to be part of a strong group of friends who were also observant was very important in helping me form my opinions about Judaism. The example that Ramaz set of how to be an American, as well as an observant and an Israel-oriented Jew has stayed with me" (Friedman). While not examining directly the rate of intermarriage amongst Ramaz graduates, the data clearly suggest that it was not a phenomenon with which the school had to be concerned.

Finally, the NJPS gives us reason to believe in the effect of Jewish day school education. In responding to the question, "How important is being a Jew for you?" 72 percent of former day school students replied "very important" as compared to 56 per cent of the privately tutored, 52 per cent of adults who attended afternoon congregational schools, 37 per cent of those who went to Sunday school, and only 23 per cent of those who had never been exposed to formal Jewish schooling (NJPS).

NEEDED: MORE DEFINITIVE INFORMATION ON GRADUATES OF JEWISH DAY SCHOOL

The problems of Jewish continuity in North America, underscored by the NJPS findings, have awakened unparalleled interest and concern on the part of Jewish communal leadership in the future of Jewish life on this continent. Witness the historic 1992 General Assembly devoted, in the main, to Jewish continuity, hitherto not a major topic at Federation leadership conferences.

The studies cited above shed meaningful light on the role of Jewish all day education as an instrumentality of Jewish identity formation and reinforcement. Notwithstanding these data, the questions raised by Egon Mayer's interpretation of the NJPS findings regarding the impact of a Jewish all day education on adult Jewish behavior of graduates and subsequently on the rate of intermarriage, suggest that we ascertain directly the Jewish profile of Jewish day school graduates. Such a study would answer the questions: What kind of Jewish behavior do adults who attended Jewish day schools in their school age years exhibit in 1992–93? Do those who attended for longer periods of time demonstrate higher levels of Jewish observance and involvement? How does the Jewish behavior of JDS graduates relate to their home backgrounds? to Jewish camp experience? to Israel visitation? to study in Israel? What are the marriage patterns of graduates? What do they feel about intermarriage? How frequently do they intermarry? Do the spouses of day school graduates who marry out convert to Judaism? What kind of Jewish education did (do or would) JDS graduates give their own children? In short, what is the Jewishness quotient of Jewish day school graduates who are at risk of losing their Jewish identity because of the lure of contemporary society?

Assimilation in a democratic society is characterized as a

multi-stage process (Gordon). The first stage is known as acculturation or cultural-behavioral assimilation. Newcomers to a society learn the basic values, language, norms, nuances, and other cultural characteristics of the host group. At this point, the acculturating foreigners are still considered outsiders. As these immigrants acclimate themselves to their new environment, they become more accepted, enabling them to enter the host society's cliques, clubs, schools and neighborhoods while still remaining closely identified with their original group. This structural assimilation camouflages the group's inability to enter and fully integrate into the host society's inner sanctum: their homes, their lives, their churches. But once this type of assimilation occurs, other types of assimilation can and do often follow: identificational assimilation (a feeling of belonging to and being part of the host society), receptional assimilation (freedom from bigotry and intolerance), civic assimilation (absence of the cognitive dissonance that arises from two conflicting cultures), and marital assimilation (large-scale intermarriage between the citizens and the erstwhile strangers). These types of assimilation typically imply absorption of the host society's culture.

This adaptation and subsequent growth of a new identity explains the challenges of the difficulties of retaining a solely Jewish character in America. The dominant society makes it difficult for members of another ethnic group to retain its traditional culture. The lure of establishing an American identity is grounded in crippling pluralism.

What are the mechanisms that the Jewish community might employ in order to insure the continued Jewish identity of American Jewish youth and stop the acculturation-deculturation syndrome from taking full effect?

This writer's extensive experience with the Jewish day school indicates that this intensive form of Jewish education plays a significant role, albeit in tandem with the home and informal Jewish education experience, in fashioning and/or reinforcing the Jewish lifestyle of its graduates. Toward this end, we hypothesize that there is a high correlation between day school study and

Jewishness: Jewish observance, Jewish involvement and marriage patterns.

THE DAY SCHOOL GRADUATE SURVEY

To test this hypothesis, an investigation to determine the Judaic practices and marital status of JDS graduates was proposed. Essentially, the investigation is a descriptive or status study. Its purpose is not to solve any problems of Jewish education but rather to throw light upon existing conditions relating to Jewish education. It will show the correlation between Jewish all day schooling and a variety of adult Jewish behaviors.

METHODOLOGY AND SAMPLING PROCEDURES

To obtain answers to the above questions and others, a questionnaire of 35 items was developed in a Spring 1993 Yeshiva University Azrieli Graduate Institute Seminar in Contemporary Jewish Education whose participants are day school principals and teachers and day school graduates enrolled in post-graduate programs in Jewish education. The questionnaire was refined in consultations with the professional leadership of the Educators Council of America and the Department of Educational Services of the Max Stern Division of Communal Services, Yeshiva University; Torah Umesorah (the National Society for Hebrew Day Schools); the Department of Education of the United Synagogue of Conservative Judaism; the Department of Yeshivot and Day Schools of the Board of Jewish Education of Greater New York; and the Department of Community Consultation and Planning of the Jewish Education Service of North America. It was administered to a purposive stratified sample of 9,000 graduates of 26 Jewish day schools in the United States: 16 institutions under centrist or Modern Orthodox auspices, 5 under Conservative sponsorship, 3 communal schools and 2 right-of-center Orthodox yeshivot. The questionnaire was mailed to 1965–85 graduates from twelve elementary schools and to 1970–90 graduates from fourteen high schools. (About 50,000 individuals, now 20 to 40 years old, graduated from modern/centrist

Orthodox, Conservative and communal elementary day schools in the United States between 1965 and 1985. Approximately fifty percent of these graduates also graduated from modern/centrist Orthodox, Conservative and communal day high schools between 1970 and 1990. The questionnaire was sent to approximately fifteen percent of this population of day school graduates being studied.) Orthodox sectarian *"Litvish"* yeshivot, Beth Jacob Schools and Hasidic institutions (which together comprise about forty percent of the total Jewish all day school enrollment in North America) were not included in the study since their students and graduates, by and large, are not exposed to normative American societal influences. The probability of non-observance or out-marriage by graduates of these schools is either much less likely or remote.

Reform day schools were not included since they are a recent phenomenon and were not founded early enough to produce graduates 20–40 years of age. Moreover, the enrollment in Reform day schools represents less than two percent of the total Jewish day school population.

The age category 20–40 was chosen because, in the first instance, it is an adult population and this survey is investigating adult Jewish behavior. Graduates prior to 1965 from elementary school and prior to 1970 from high school were not included. There are almost no Solomon Schechter Schools and communal day schools founded early enough to produce graduates before 1965 or 1970. The Solomon Schechter movement was established in 1957 and its first schools did not produce graduates until the mid-60s. Moreover, the survey is examining the relationship between contemporary Jewish educational experience and adult Jewish behavior. Graduates before 1965 and 1970, respectively, reflect Jewish education of an earlier period.

STATISTICAL ANALYSIS

Descriptive and inferential statistics about demographic factors, religious observance of respondents and their parents, Jewish summer camp and Israel experience, marital status, adult involvement in Jewish life, intermarriage practices and attitudes were provided in the report of the study.

BIAS CHECK

Several questions might be asked about the responding sample. Do the responses to the questionnaire represent the attitudes and behavior patterns of all the day school graduates to whom questionnaires were sent? What about the non-respondents? Would they more or less be affected by their Jewish educational experiences than those who responded?

To check for external validity, telephone calls were made to two hundred non-respondents to elicit their reactions to key questions in the questionnaire. Their oral responses were compared to the written responses of those who responded in writing to determine the degree of similarity between their responses. Indeed, their responses were almost identical to the written responses that were received.

HIGHLIGHTS OF THE STUDY

Overall, Jewish day school graduates are American born, married, college-educated with advanced post-graduate study. The graduates' Jewish behavior is dramatically different from other 20–40 year old Jews in America. Eighty-one percent keep kosher at home and eighty percent outside the home. Seventy percent observe the Sabbath in a variety of ways: Friday evening candle lighting and synagogue services; *kiddush* at home on Friday night; synagogue attendance and *kiddush* at home on Saturday morning; *kiddush* and refraining from travel on the Sabbath. Moreover, two thirds study Jewish texts on the Sabbath and over one-half attended synagogue services on Saturday afternoon.

A major difference between Jewish day school graduates and their non-day school peers relates to their involvement with Israel. Whereas only 20% of American Jewish adults have been to Israel, 89% of Jewish day school graduates have visited Israel on the average of four times! Moreover, 8% made aliyah or are living currently in the Jewish State. Also, 85% of Jewish day school graduates attended a Jewish summer camp for an average of four summers, compared to 20% of the general Jewish population.

The most telling difference between Jewish day school graduates and the overall Jewish population is that only 4.5% are intermarried compared to 52% of the marriages of Jews to non-Jews from 1985 to 1990 according to the National Jewish Population Study, and 80% strongly object or object to their progeny intermarrying.

Another significant difference between Jewish day school graduates and the general Jewish adult population concerns their Jewish communal involvement. About 60% are active in Jewish organizational life. When one considers that about one-half of the graduates are only 20–29 years old and the other half only 30–39 years, the possibility of larger percentages of Jewish day school graduates involved in Jewish life are real.

A major finding of the study demonstrates the influence of extended Jewish education on adult Jewish behavior. Jewish elementary education has a basic effect on adult Jewish observance, attitudes and involvement. Jewish secondary education has a cumulative effect – a significantly greater impact on the Jewishness of graduates. And Jewish study beyond high school has a multiplier effect – a decidedly greater influence on adult Jewish behavior. For example, whereas somewhat less than half of elementary school graduates keep kosher at home, about 80% of high school graduates observed home *kashrut* and 95% of those who continued their Jewish studies for one or more years beyond high school keep kosher. Similarly, less than 40% elementary school alumni observe the Sabbath compared to 70% of high school graduates and 91% of those who continued their Judaic studies after secondary school.

Moreover, while 76% of elementary school graduates have visited Israel, 87% of high school graduates and 96% of post high school students visited Israel. Forty percent of elementary school graduates are active in Jewish communal life compared to 54% of high school graduates and 72% of post high school graduates.

Finally, whereas 63% of elementary school alumni object to

their children intermarrying, 83% and 95% of high school graduates and post high school students respectively, object to their progeny marrying non-Jews. Eighteen percent of Jewish elementary day school graduates married non-Jews as compared with 5% of high school graduates and 2% of those who continued Judaic Studies beyond high school.

There are variations in the Jewishness of Jewish day school graduates that relate to their parental Judaic orientation, the type of school they attended, the ages and gender of graduates. Graduates with Jewishly observant parents (particularly two Orthodox parents) are likely to exhibit high levels of adult Jewish behavior. However, Jewish day school education impacts the level of adult Jewish behavior of students whose parents were not observant. For example, 43% of Jewish day high school graduates and 75% percent of those who studied beyond high school, whose parents (1% of the total number of parents) were atheist or agnostic when their children were in school, keep kosher in their own homes. And 57% of high school graduates and 63% who continued their Jewish studies beyond high school observe the Sabbath while their parents did not.

In all, the study shows that the impact of a Jewish day school education in tandem with a positive Jewish home upbringing and an informal Jewish educational experience has a profound impact on adult Jewish behavior attitudes and involvement.

CHAPTER 8

THE CASE OF THE JEWISH DAY SCHOOL (IN 1997) IN LIGHT OF THE DEBATE ON SCHOOL CHOICE

EMERGENCE AND GROWTH OF THE DAY SCHOOL

One of the most exciting and meaningful phenomena in the American Jewish community in the twentieth century has been the development and growth of Jewish all day education. In the first half of this century the American Jewish community was wedded to the idea of the public school. The avid support of public education by virtually all Jewish immigrants in the late 1800s and early 1900s derived from their perception of the public school as the gateway to Americanization. They saw in public education the fulfillment of their dreams – being accepted in the larger society and being given the opportunity to advance intellectually, professionally, and economically, as equals, with the gentile population.

Jews desiring to maintain the Jewishness of their public school children organized Jewish educational programs after school hours and on Saturdays and Sundays. These could take the form of private tutelage held in the homes of either the pupils or the teachers; or a small, one room and one teacher school (*heder*); or a Sunday school or community Hebrew school (*Talmud Torah*). Privately tutored pupils and children studying in the *heder* or

Sunday school received one or two hours of Judaic instruction weekly. Students in the *Talmud Torah* generally studied Jewish subjects several afternoons and Sunday mornings for a total of 8 to 10 hours per week.

The private tutor, the *heder*, and the *Talmud Torah* were gradually replaced by the supplementary congregational school, sponsored by Conservative and Orthodox synagogues. By the end of the 1930s the congregational school, where pupils studied from 4–6 hours per week, had become the primary institution of Jewish instruction for children and youth in Conservative and Orthodox synagogues. The curriculum of the synagogue school consisted of Hebrew language (phonics and basic comprehension), *Siddur*, (mechanical prayer book reading in Hebrew), Bible stories in English or in simple Hebrew, Jewish holidays, customs and ceremonies, Jewish history and Jewish current events. The Reform movement adopted the Sunday school idea (two hours a week), stressing Judaic study in the English language. Over the years, many Reform temples added one or two elective weekday afternoons for Hebraic programs.

Congregational schooling, particularly under Conservative and Reform auspices, grew rapidly in the 1930s and 1940s, and flourished for almost two decades after World War II as synagogues thrived and expanded in membership and facilities. By 1962, the peak year of Jewish school enrollment in North America, there were some 540,000 pupils in congregational schools in the United States and Canada. Since then, the congregational school has been on the decline. Thirty-five years later there are only 270,000 pupils enrolled in these schools – a decrease of fifty percent – due largely to a diminishing birthrate, to an increase in intermarriage, and to the acculturation pattern of young endogenously married Jewish couples who do not feel the need to provide Jewish education to their progeny. Family breakup and the adverse attitudes of many Jewish parents to their own Jewish supplementary educational experience have also affected negatively the enrollment in Jewish religious schools. In addition, funding and transportation issues have impacted upon Jewish supplementary education.

Moreover, recent studies of Jewish supplementary schooling demonstrate that this form of Jewish education has become, by and large, incapable of achieving its goals. Among the reasons for the current ineffectiveness of Jewish supplementary education are the low priority status of the school and of life-long learning within the synagogue; the lack of home support; and the shortage of adequately trained supervisory and instructional personnel.

In contrast to the downward trend of the Jewish supplementary school, the Jewish day school has enjoyed remarkable growth – from 60,000 pupils in 280 schools in North American in 1962 to 182,000 in 660 schools in 1992. Estimates of the 1996–1997 enrollment in Jewish all day educational institutions from pre-school through post high school programs reach 200,000. The Jewish day school population represented about 40 percent of the total North American Jewish school enrollment in 1996 and about 20 percent of the total Jewish population of school age. In 1996, about 10 percent of the Jewish population between 20 and 40 years of age had attended Jewish day schools through grades 6, 8 or 12.

Today's Jewish day school has its roots in the European setting of yesterday. The pioneer Jewish day schools in the United States were patterned after the 19th century European yeshiva, the traditional institution of intensive Jewish studies. The chief subjects were *Pentateuch* (written law) in the lower grades, Talmud in the middle and upper grades, along with their traditional rabbinic commentaries. The immigrants who founded the first yeshivot in the United States at the end of the nineteenth and beginning of the twentieth centuries were motivated by the tradition of Torah learning as they had known it in Europe. For them, as for their ancestors, Jewish education occupied a unique position, as a cardinal principle of Jewish faith. The combination of Judaic and secular subjects under one roof also had antecedents in Eastern and Western Europe where several such institutions existed.

The Jewish day schools in America are generally independent, autonomous institutions, founded and supported by autonomous, self-governing lay boards. (That is why we do not refer to them as "parochial schools" since that term implies control by a central church or parish.) Their autonomy is reflected in the variety of the educational programs and in the patterns of program scheduling. The Hasidic and ultra-Orthodox yeshivot and Beth Jacob schools (representing about one third of the total Jewish day school enrollment) are single-sex institutions. In addition to the regular state-required general education program, pupils in the all-boys yeshivot are exposed to Judaic studies twenty to forty hours per week, including a full day of Jewish learning on Sundays – primarily *Pentateuch*, Codes, Talmud and their commentaries – all in the original Hebrew and Aramaic. The curriculum of the girls' schools comprises *Pentateuch* and commentaries, *aggadah* and *Midrash* (legends relating to the Bible), Jewish history, ethics and Hebrew religious literature.

Most of the modern or centrist Orthodox Jewish day schools (comprising about one half of the total day school enrollment) are co-educational institutions. Their programs feature a balance between Judaic and secular subjects. Jewish studies (15–25 hours per week) include Hebrew language and literature, *Siddur*, *Pentateuch*, Prophets, Writings, Talmud and their rabbinic commentaries, Codes, ethics, Jewish history and the Land of Israel and Jewish music.

The Conservative Solomon Schechter schools (with about 10 percent of the enrollment) are all co-educational institutions with balanced Judaic and secular programs. The Hebraic curriculum (12–15 hours per week) is similar to the Modern Orthodox programs, with less emphasis on Talmud and rabbinic commentaries and greater stress on conversational Hebrew.

The Jewish studies curriculum of the communal inter-ideological day schools (with about eight percent of the enrollment) is similar to the Jewish studies program of the Solomon Schechter schools, but with less time devoted to *Pentateuch* and Talmud.

The Jewish day schools under Reform auspices (two percent of the enrollment) provide a combined Judaic and general studies program with five to ten hours of Jewish studies, centering on Hebrew language, Bible, Jewish holidays, Jewish history, Jewish current events and Jewish arts.

The dramatic growth of Jewish all day education began in the 1940s, as Orthodox Jews began establishing day schools despite the indifference, and even opposition from the rest of the Jewish community. Their championship, sponsorship and support of the day school idea, abetted by a considerable Orthodox birthrate, is largely responsible for the flowering of Jewish all day education. The remarkable continued growth of this movement was further aided by the support from leaders of Conservative Judaism and the founding of Conservative Solomon Schechter schools since 1957, by the recent interest of Reform Jewish leaders in Jewish all day education, and by the financial assistance of Jewish communal Federations throughout the North American continent. The recent recognition of the value of intensive Jewish education for Jewish continuity and the enhancement of Jewish life has also intensified the interest in and support for all day Jewish education.

To be sure, other factors have also contributed to the initial and continuing growth of the Jewish day school. These include the impact of the Holocaust, the founding of Israel, the perception of violence and drug use in public schools, the rise of fundamentalism in America, the attractiveness of the general studies programs of many day schools, and the search for cultural identity.

QUESTIONS RAISED BY JEWISH DAY SCHOOL GROWTH

These two opposing trends – the deterioration of the Jewish supplementary school on the one hand, and the growth of all day Jewish education on the other – give rise to several questions that beg for answers, particularly in light of claims made by supporters of day school education about its impact upon the adult Jewish lifestyle of its graduates.

What role does a Jewish day school experience play in the Jewish identity of its exponents? What other factors contribute to the development of the Jewish life style of young Jewish adults? Is the Jewish behavior of Jewish day school graduates related to their home backgrounds? To Jewish camp experience? To Israel visitation? To study in Israel? What kind of Jewish behavior do young adults who attended Jewish day schools exhibit? Do those who attended for longer periods of time demonstrate higher levels of Jewish observance and involvement? What are the marriage patterns of graduates? How do they feel about intermarriage? How frequently do they intermarry? What kind of Jewish education do, or will, Jewish day school graduates give their own children?

Ample research evidence shows a statistically significant relationship between Jewish all day education and adult Jewish behavior. Jewish day schools certainly have an important bearing on friendship patterns, prevention of intermarriage, attitudes towards intermarriage of progeny, visits to Israel, Shabbat, and *kashrut* observance and synagogue attendance.

Time spent in school, by most accounts, has a significant influence on Jewish identity formation, even when a variety of factors (including family background) are controlled. The research of Rimor and Katz (1993) claims that nine or more years of schooling is critical. Others, including Goldstein and Barak Fishman, suggest a minimum of six years is important.

The longer one stays in school, the stronger the relationship between day school attendance and adult Jewish behavior and involvement, regardless of the school's Jewish religious ideology, the background of the parents, or other factors. In other words, adult Jewish behavior and involvement increases with the length of stay in Jewish schools. The level of Jewish behavior increases with the extensiveness of Jewish education. Elementary school has a basic effect; secondary school has a cumulative effect; and post high school, a multiplier effect on adult Jewish behavior (Schiff and Schneider 1994).

Moreover, the combination of intensive formal Jewish education, a positive Jewish home and sound informal Jewish educational experience contributes significantly to the development of positive adult Jewish behavior. But, whatever the combination of factors, extensive Jewish day school education is the most important single contributor to the formation of strong Jewish identities.

The fact that 100 percent of the graduates do not exhibit Jewish behavior, despite long years of schooling, demonstrates that even a Jewish day school education is not a foolproof guarantee of Jewish continuity. Neither schooling alone, however powerful a weapon, nor any of the other factors, taken in isolation (such as family background, camp attendance, Israel visits, religious affiliation in later adulthood, and Jewish organizational involvement) can completely counteract the influences of an open society on young people.

To be sure, some Jewish behavioral gain might not be due to education and/or home. There also seems to be some loss (however small) of Jewish behavior, among some graduates, despite the home and despite the educational grounding. It would be impossible to expect full retention from generation to generation. Some loss from the ranks in more observant sectors is natural, as well as gains in Jewish behavior from non-observant groups. Such loss and gain are normal facts of life, and do not themselves endanger the continuity of the Jewish community.

On the whole, the evidence is strong that Jewish day school education helps graduates retain Jewish attitudes and behaviors experienced during their upbringing, while reducing negative attitudes about Jewish behavior, Jewish identity, and Jewish life that may have been acquired in the larger environment. And, if an extensive Jewish education is bolstered by a positive family environment and other Jewish experiences, it will prevent further erosion and contribute significantly to the continuity of American Jewry.

Because the research data indicates so clearly that extensive Jewish all day education is an indispensable tool for the formation, reinforcement, and continued vitality of Jewish identity, the organized Jewish community is increasingly concerned about all levels of Jewish day school education.

THE AMERICAN SETTING

The Jewish day school is founded on the principle that a synthesis of religious and secular culture is the necessary basis for a Jewish child's adjustment to his larger American environment. While the idea of a synthesis of disciplines was born in Western Europe, the integration of Jewish tradition and American civilization could only flourish on American soil. The significance of the principle of synthesis lies not in its uniqueness or soundness as a theory, but in the framework of its implementation. What makes the idea of synthesis a valuable and workable theory for American Jewry is the fact that the integration of the general and religious disciplines takes place in a Torah environment.

Projected into long-range focus, the principle of synthesis not only serves as the basis for creative Jewish survival, but also plays a significant role in the cultural development of the general American community. In the words of Dr. Joseph H. Lookstein, one of the pioneers of the Jewish day school movement, this institution "is destined to become a major contribution of American Israel to American cultural democracy" (Lookstein).

As the American Jewish community has matured, most of those who were concerned with the Jewish day school's rivalry of the public school gradually shed this feeling. In the first place, the long Jewish romance with the public school has cooled off. Secondly, since Jews constitute less than two percent of the American population, even if all Jewish children attended Jewish day schools, this would hardly make an appreciable difference in the public school population nationally. Locally, too, the absence of all the Jewish children from public schools would not be a cause for concern. Even in Greater New York, where the Jews constitute about fifteen percent of the total adult population, the attendance of the entire Jewish child population in Jewish day schools would not endanger the status of public education.

The leaders of the Jewish day school movement see it as an important force in the American educational scene. This point was clearly underscored during the early growth of the day school in the United States by one of its pioneers, Marvin Fox. In 1953,

Dr. Fox optimistically suggested that the most important single area in which the day school could make a significant contribution to American education is in counteracting the philosophy and practice of "value-free education":

> By reminding America constantly that there are legitimate ways for man to understand himself and his world other than through the insights of scientific naturalism, the day schools can help to avert the dangers of the kind of intellectual totalitarianism which no democratic society can afford. This is the first and most fundamental contribution of the Hebrew day school to the pattern of American education. (Fox)

Fox also believed that the day school would set an example in the matter of discipline, by demonstrating how Judaism reconciles "human equality with reverence for authority," and how "this view expresses itself through acceptance by the young of parental authority and of the authority of the teacher." And in a more general way it should serve as "an important bulwark against the terrible moral confusion of our time. Through the medium of the sacred writings in their broadest scope, the Jewish school tries deliberately to endow its students with moral knowledge and even more, to develop in them moral sensitivity."

Whether or not Dr. Fox's hopes have been realized, the Jewish Day School's intensive dual curriculum has certainly demonstrated, contrary to the opinions of the advocates of "relaxed programming," that pupils do not buckle under a heavy full-day course of study. The yeshiva has shown, beyond a shadow of a doubt, that children can readily master a foreign language, even at a tender, primary school age. The Hebraic program of studies has demonstrated that pupils, adequately oriented, can learn abstract material in the elementary grades that is far more theoretical and more difficult than the subject matter of their parallel general studies classes. For example, the introduction of Talmudic study on the fifth and sixth year level has clearly shown that the elementary school child is capable of abstract and creative thinking far beyond the current educational diet to which he is exposed on the elementary level and even on the secondary level. In this sense, the Jewish day school bears out the long-held contention of some educators and psychologists that, given the right conditions and taught by the proper method, children at any age can be instructed in almost any subject matter ranging from animal husbandry to metaphysics.

The Jewish day school reaffirms the old pedagogical truth that good learning takes place best in an intimate environment. The traditional Judaic concept of personalized instruction is one of the earmarks of the modern Jewish day school. The contrast between this aspect of the teaching-learning situation in the day school and the kind of pupil-teacher relations that generally pervade the large urban public schools is readily observable.

However, it must be noted that whatever influence the day school may have upon the general American scene, that is only secondary and incidental to its major purpose and function. The real vital impact of this institution is upon the Jewish community.

SUPPORT FROM ALL QUARTERS

Because of the value of Jewish all day education to Jewish continuity and to American society as it educates generations of good Americans, good bread winners, and good people, the sponsors of this form of education favor increased support for it from every possible source – the family, the school board, the Jewish community and the public sector (where this support does not do violence to the concept of separation of church and state).

The Jewish community has been and remains steadfast in its championship of the separation of church and state. However, like Catholic and Protestant sponsors of non-public schools, Jewish day school advocates strongly favor all forms of governmental help to their institutions – direct aid, books, materials, facilities, transportation, free and reduced school food programs – based upon the pupil benefit theory. They all agree that school aid or scholarship assistance to the non-public school must be limited to the general, secular education of the recipients of that assistance.

The education laws in every state that recognizes the legitimacy of such schooling and makes provisions for its supervision have adequately underscored this. The Department of Health, Education and Welfare has provided loans to private non-profit schools under the National Defense Education Act. Moreover, the federal government and many states authorize tax exemptions for non-public and non-profit educational purposes.

The American setting encourages each minority group to maintain its own integrity and identity, and to contribute from its own traditions and creative forces to the mainstream of American life. The Jewish day school is one of the ways in which the Jewish community maintains its integrity and encourages its own singular creativity while benefiting American society.

CHAPTER 9

JEWISH DAY SCHOOL SUCCESS: JEWISH COMMUNAL CHALLENGE (IN 1997)

The Jewish community of Australia says it is the best way. The Jewish community of Canada says it is the best way. The Jewish community of England says it is the best way. In the English-speaking world – in fact, all over the world – Jewish communities feel it is the best way to guarantee Jewish continuity. It is the Jewish day school.

Ninety percent of all Jewish children in Jewish schools in South Africa are enrolled in Jewish day schools, as are 90% of Jewish children in Jewish schools in Australia, and 80% in England and Canada. To be sure, world over, 80% of the total Jewish school population is in Jewish day schools.

And, tonight, here in the United States, we celebrate Jewish day school education.

Tonight's dinner is like a homecoming for me. Thirty-seven years ago, in 1960, I was invited by your local Federation to evaluate Jewish all day education in St. Louis. At that time, in your fair city, there was one day school – the pioneering Epstein Academy – with a small enrollment. In that year, in 1960, in North America, there were four Solomon Schechter schools with a total enrollment of much less than 1000 students. Today, your school joins 69 other Solomon Schechter schools in a growing network dedicated to excellence in education, with close to 20,000 pupils. And, in 1960, in North America there were, all told, 30,000 children enrolled in Jewish day schools (5% of the total Jewish school enrollment). Today, on the North American continent, there are more than 200,000 pupils in Jewish all day educational institutions, representing over 40% of the total Jewish school population.

Forty new day schools have been established in the last six years alone! Ten new day high schools have been organized during the last two years. A coalition of major Jewish organizations and philanthropists has recently announced a $36 million effort to fund the founding of 20 more Jewish day schools during the next two years!

And, in two weeks, a major proposal for greatly increased Federation funding for Jewish day schools will be made at the General Assembly – the annual conference of the Council of Jewish Federations – which will be held this year in Indianapolis!

The impact of the growth of the Jewish day school and the importance of this institution in the American Jewish community has been so remarkable that even the left-leaning Anglo-Jewish newspaper – the *Forward* – calls this movement "one of the most significant trends in Jewish life in decades." What the *Forward* didn't say is that this trend has been in effect since 1940 and has gained steam every decade since.

The miracle of the Jewish day school movement is that, it was initiated by a few Orthodox leaders against a backdrop of communal antagonism and indifference. It gradually took hold in North America until every segment of the community – Orthodox, Conservative, Reform, Reconstructionist, secular, Zionist – virtually every Jewish group – supports the idea and value of Jewish all day education. As one Federation leader recently said, "The Jewish community in the United States has finally come to its senses about the most effective way to educate Jewish children and guarantee Jewish continuity."

The vast majority of parents enroll their children in Jewish day schools for the right reason – a superior all around general and Jewish education. Several weeks ago, the Fleet Bank placed a half page ad in the New York Times, which read, "To get children into the top schools, it's the parents who have to be smart." To be sure, parents of Jewish day school students are just smart, very smart!

Let us be clear! Avoiding intermarriage is an explicit goal of the Jewish day school. But, we have a much larger purpose than combating assimilation and intermarriage. To be sure, the Jewish day school is the place where Jewish identity is formed. It is about Jewish living and all the wonderful attributes of a positive Jewish life style. The Jewish day school is the place where Jewish children and youth learn to integrate their Jewish and general outlooks on life, where they learn to become good Jews and good Americans, good bread winners and good people all at the same time. And the research about the effects of a Jewish day school education clearly confirms these facts.

But the research goes much beyond this. The findings of my study and the reality of Jewish all day education challenge the families of Jewish day school students. The findings say to parents: Support your children's education and their future by your own Jewish life style. You have much to gain from such a stance. The research findings demonstrate the importance of a supportive home and a supportive community. The intermarriage rate of graduates whose parents exhibited strong Jewish behavior was much less than those whose parents did not.

Recently, the National Longitudinal Study on Adolescent Health, the largest, most comprehensive study of adolescent behavior – a survey of 90,000 children – showed how crucial is parental support for the elementary and secondary education of their children via their own behavior. It demonstrated how important is the parents' association with the goals of their childrens' schools. The study on adolescent health stresses that the closer-knit the family is, and the closer the ties it maintains with the school, the higher the expectations for the eventual wellbeing of its teen-age children as they grow into adulthood. If this is so in general education, it is all the more significant for the Jewish day school.

My research findings also challenge the Jewish community. They say to the St. Louis community and its Federation: provide the necessary funds to help the Solomon Schechter School and the other day schools in the community attract the best educators, the most effective teachers. The findings also say: provide the necessary funds to help the day schools maintain the highest standards of Jewish and general education.

Given the findings about the superior Jewish and general performance of Jewish day high school graduates, the challenge speaks loudly to the community. It declares: provide the funds to guarantee that all elementary day school graduates will continue through Jewish day high school.

In the Torah portion we read yesterday in the synagogue, Noah's sons, *Shem* and *Yafet*, provide a special message for us tonight. The Bible prophetically states: *Yaf't Elokim l'yefet v'yishkone b'oholei Shem.* "May God extend *Yafet* and may he dwell in the tents of *Shem.*" Our sages in the Talmud (*Megillah* 9b) explain this statement as follows: *Yafet*, representing Greek beauty, Greek culture – meaning world culture and knowledge – should reside in the tents of Torah learning of [the descendents of] *Shem*. In other words, general and Jewish culture should reside together under Jewish auspices.

And, tonight, we – the children of Abraham, the descendents of *Shem* – celebrate the fruition, the realization of this seminal idea: the vibrant, life-giving combination of excellent general and Jewish studies in a single Jewish educational institution.

About two millennia ago, in Athens, a young Jewish bar mitzvah boy made a wish. He wanted to become a Greek oracle. In order to achieve this goal he had to stump the oracle in his immediate community. So he devised a plan. He would catch a very small bird and cup it in his hands and bring it to the oracle. He would ask the oracle what he has in his hands. With his insight, the oracle will say, "a bird". Then the young lad will ask, "is it dead or alive?" If the oracle says "dead", he would open his hands and let the bird fly away. If the oracle says "alive," the young boy planned to crush it to death.

And, so it was. The boy came to the oracle, and asked him what he had in his hands. The oracle, said "a bird". Then the young lad asked excitedly, "is it dead or alive?" The oracle thought for a moment and answered, "Young man, the answer to that question is in your hands."

Friends, the answer to the future of your children's education and to Jewish continuity lies in your hands. God bless your decision to maximize your support to Jewish all day education in St. Louis.

CHAPTER 10

Post Yeshiva: Jewish Day High School Programs

FOR AMERICAN STUDENTS IN ISRAEL

The Development of Israel Study Programs
Full time study in a yeshiva or seminary in Israel for one or two years after graduation from a yeshiva or Jewish day high school is now a commonplace phenomenon in North American, English, French, South African and Australian Modern Orthodox Jewish all day education. The overall impact of the post high school yeshiva and seminary study programs is substantial, particularly regarding religious ritual experience, commitment to continued Torah study and to Zionism, including the desire to make aliyah (Berger). The Israeli Zionist yeshivot for men and seminaries for women inculcate a strong feeling of responsibility for *Klal Yisrael*, a love for the State of Israel, and initiate a continuing relationship with the Jewish State and the *Yishuv*.

In 1957, when I served as pedagogic consultant and supervisor for the Department of Jewish Day Schools and Yeshivot of the Jewish Education Committee of New York (now the Board of Jewish Education of Greater New York) I developed two types of programs for study in Israel. The first type – *Tochnit Yod Bet* (the Twelfth Year Program) – was for seniors in public high school who studied in Conservative and Reform supplementary schools and for seniors in yeshiva and Jewish day high schools. The second type of program – *Tochnit Yod Gimmel* (the Thirteenth Year Program) – was for graduates of public high schools who studied in Reform and Conservative congregational schools and for graduates of yeshiva and Jewish day high schools.

Tochnit Yod Bet, whereby seniors would spend the Spring Term – February through June – and the months of July and August in Judaic study and educational touring, failed to materialize. For public high school seniors, neither the students, the parents, nor the lay and rabbinic leadership showed much interest in the program. While *Tochnit Yod Bet* was acceptable to yeshiva high school seniors and their parents, the respective board of directors of the day schools rejected it because they did not want to lose a semester of tuition.

Tochnit Yod Gimmel involved a post high school year of study either in a university or post secondary yeshiva or seminary in Israel. It failed to attract sufficient number of enrollees from the Jewish supplementary school community. Because of parental, student and synagogue leadership apathy, efforts to send public high school graduates for a years' study in Israel were discontinued in 1959.

However, the post high school year of study idea caught on in the Modern Orthodox Yeshiva and Jewish Day School world. It started slowly in 1958 in Greater New York with 25 graduates. Promotion and recruitment for the program were aided by the World Zionist Organization Torah Education Department in the United States, directed by Rabbi Zvi Tabory. I enlisted the help of Rabbi Simhah Teitelbaum, a yeshiva high school principal who was committed to the idea of study in Israel for yeshiva and Jewish day high school graduates and felt strongly about its potential impact upon them. Together they promoted the program in New York yeshivot and Jewish day high schools. The American office of the Torah Education Department provided technical support.

EARLY GROWTH

Primarily, the first years of the post high school year of study took place in the Yeshiva *Kerem B'Yavneh* and at *Machon Gold*, which initially enrolled men and women.

The program was encouraged and supported wholeheartedly by the Yeshiva High School Principals' Council of the Department of Jewish Day Schools and Yeshivot of the Jewish Education Committee of New York. It grew rapidly and by the mid-1970s it was estimated that over 500 Greater New York Yeshiva High School graduates were going annually to Israel for an intensive Zionist post high school learning experience. In the mid-1960s the program began to attract the attention of yeshiva high school principals throughout the United States and Canada. This further increased diaspora enrollment in Israel Orthodox educational institutions.

The *Minhal Studentim*, the Student Authority of the Ministry of Immigrant Absorption (founded by the *Merkaz Hatefutzot – Israel Foundation for Cultural Relations with World Jewry*) in conjunction with the World Zionist Organization and the Jewish Agency, began keeping records of the diaspora enrollment in the yeshivot and seminaries during the first year it was established in 1968 in the wake of the Six Day War. According to *Minhal Studentim* reports found in the Zionist Archives, there were 2,302 students of various ages in Zionist and *haredi* yeshivot and seminaries in *Mahzor Hahoref* – the winter semester – September 1967 to May 1968. Most of the participants, it seems, were in the *haredi* schools.

According to the "Report on Departmental Activities of the Department for Torah Education and Culture for the Diaspora," published in December 1979, also found in the Zionist Archives, 1,331 students were enrolled in "special study programs" in Israeli Zionist yeshivot for men and 737 students studied in Zionist Torah institutions for women from June 1978 through March 1979, for a total of 2,068 diaspora participants. Most of these students were from the United States.

CONTINUED GROWTH

After 1979, there is no record of the enrollment in post high school study in Orthodox educational institutions in Israel. Records are not available either at the *Minhal Studentim* offices or at the Zionist Archives. Neither does the Torah Education Department have statistical data.

It is obvious, however, that post high school study in Zionist schools and *haredi* institutions continued to grow. It is estimated that by 1990 approximately 1,600 high school graduates were spending a year of study in Orthodox Zionist yeshivot and seminaries in Israel. Currently in 2001–2002, according to figures made available by individual Orthodox Zionists Israeli schools, there are 1208 diaspora high school graduates[1] enrolled in 17 Israeli Orthodox Zionist yeshivot for men and 563 graduates[2] in 16 Orthodox Zionist Seminaries for women for one or more years of intensive Judaic study for a total of 1771 students, In addition, there are several hundred boys and girls in quasi-Zionist Israeli schools.

One of the motivating factors in the increased student participation in Israeli Zionist schools is the arrangement with North American universities to grant credit towards the baccalaureate degree for post high school yeshiva and seminary study in Israel. This type of arrangement was initiated in the Greater New York area with Yeshiva College, Stern College for Women, Touro College, Brooklyn College, Queens College, and Ramapo Community College. Some colleges award as much as a full year's credit for undergraduate study. Students desiring American college credit are required to submit transcripts of study from the Israeli yeshivot and seminaries where they studied. As many as 500 students per year currently transfer credit from Israeli institutions to American universities.

Administrators of the large Modern Orthodox day high schools in Greater New York indicate that about 90% of the graduates of their schools chose to attend the one-year post high school programs in Israel in 1994–1995.

At the request of this researcher, Rabbi Ellis Bloch, director of the Department of Yeshivot and Jewish Day Schools of the Board of Jewish Education of Greater New York, conducted a survey of the Modern Orthodox yeshiva and Jewish day high schools in the Greater New York area during the Spring of 2002 to ascertain the level of participation of the June 2001 graduates in the 2001–2002 *Tochnit Yod Gimmel*. Twenty-two schools responded to this inquiry. The findings indicate that the enrollment of the male graduates of individual high schools in post high school yeshiva study in Israel ranges from 28% to 97% of the graduating classes and averages 65%. The participation of female graduates of individual schools in *Tochnit Yod Gimmel* ranges from 20% to 91% and averages 45% of the total number of graduates. Eighty-two percent of the ten leading Zionist Jewish day and yeshiva high schools were enrolled in post high school study in Israel in 2001–2002.

All told, based upon the information received from responding schools, 900 graduates of Modern Orthodox Zionist high schools in metropolitan New York are currently enrolled in 2001–2002 post high school programs of study in Israel.

Tochnit Yod Gimmel is enthusiastically supported and encouraged by yeshiva teachers and administrators (Blau and Goldmintz). The "year in Israel programs are viewed as an essential part of the yeshiva experience for university bound adolescents" (Kupchick). Recognizing the central place that post high school Israel study has for graduates, many yeshiva high schools now sponsor Israel guidance departments that rival their college guidance departments in stature, assistance to seniors in choosing the right program, assistance with the application process, arranging for financial aid and the transfer of credits to American universities (Berger). "Schools, parents and students in modern yeshiva high schools in North America expect that as a matter of course, the majority of graduates will spend the year after graduation in a yeshiva program in Israel" (Bernstein).

A recent survey of Yeshiva University students found that 73% have studied in Israel, most immediately prior to beginning college. Almost a third of these students were not planning to attend Yeshiva University before their year of study in Israel and decided to do so in order to continue their Judaic studies (Martila and Kiley).

As *Tochnit Yod Gimmel* developed and students enjoyed their year of study in Israel, many decided to spend a second year – *Shannah Bet* – in Israeli yeshivot and seminaries. The desire to continue for a second year often created tension between students and their parents who wanted them to return home and begin their university study. It seems that parents are now more receptive to the idea of a second year of study in Israel. Currently, according to the heads of several leading Israeli Zionist institutions as many as 75 percent of their students remain for *Shannah Bet*.

The annual cost of the study programs in Israel varies between $10,000 and $13,000, significantly less than the cost of university study in North America. The annual fee includes room and board, but not always does it include medical insurance and books. Academic scholarships and financial aid are available at most of the Israeli Zionist yeshivot for men and seminaries for women. It is estimated that tuition fees cover about 80 percent of the cost of the budgets for diaspora students studying in the Israeli yeshivot and seminaries.

The increase in the number of North American participants in the 1960s and 1970s prompted the establishment of many new yeshiva programs in Israel, ranging from Modern Orthodox, Zionist *Hesder* yeshivot, Haredi yeshivot, and women's Beth Jacob schools. Many of these institutions were founded by American *olim*. Most of the newly organized women's seminaries are solely for diaspora high school graduates and do not enroll Israeli students. According to Rabbi Moshe Sosevsky, dean of Yeshivat Or Yerushalayim and one of the pioneer American educators in overseas Zionist study programs for post-high school Orthodox boys, "Today, for the Modern Orthodox, study in Israel has become almost an extension of Yeshiva high school. Whereas once only the most serious post high school students came to Israel to study now more than 70 percent of American Yeshiva high school graduates come for one year." The Zionist post high school programs for women according to Sosevsky evolved similarly.

The institutions established by American Orthodox educators provide a more structured schedule than the Israeli Yeshivot and seminaries. They also maintain more formal guidance programs for participants. They are highly sensitive to the needs of American high school graduates who are away from home for an extended period for the first time.

The Orthodox Zionist programs available to North American high school graduates differ widely. The differences are primarily the institutional commitment to Zionism and to the State of Israel, the acceptance of the validity and importance of secular education, attitudes towards the non-religious Jewish community and the study of subjects other than *Torah She-Be'al Peh* (Oral Law – Talmud) and *Halakhah*, particularly Jewish history including Zionism, *Tanakh*, Jewish Thought, modern Israel and conversational Hebrew and the sponsorship of educational tours of Israel.

PHILOSOPHY OF ISRAELI ORTHODOX ZIONIST EDUCATIONAL INSTITUTIONS

The criteria for determining which institutions qualify as Zionist schools include a variety of religious-national, academic, political and linguistic characteristics. It is interesting to note that as early as 1942, Rabbi Maimon Fishman, world leader of religious Zionism, member of the Jewish Agency Executive, and the first Minister of Religion in Israel, suggested that in order to qualify for Jewish Agency and World Zionist support, the language of instruction in yeshivot be Hebrew and not Yiddish.[3] Currently, the language of instruction for Israeli students in all *Hesder* Yeshivot is Hebrew. For diaspora students in programs sponsored by Yeshivot *Hesder*, teaching takes place via a mixture of Hebrew and English. In a Zionist institution catering to diaspora students, Hebrew language is an essential subject, whether or not all the instruction takes place in Hebrew. Moreover, a broad Judaic curriculum, educational tours of Israel, lectures on Zionism, and current Israeli issues are important indicators of Zionist policy. Recognition of the significance of secular learning is another important Zionist value.

A Zionist institution promotes the idea of aliyah among its students and celebrates Israel Independence Day and *Yom Yerushalayim*. It also observes *Yom Hazikaron* (Remembrance Day) and *Yom Hashoah Vehag'vurah*. Celebrating *Yom Ha'atzma'ut* and *Yom Yerushalayim* means the recitation of *Hallel* during the morning *Tefillah*, the arrangement of festive activities and wearing holiday clothes.

The quasi Zionist institutions observe *Yom Hazikaron* and *Yom Ha'atzma'ut* in a variety of ways. For example, in *Michlallah* on Remembrance Day in 2002, one of the Judaic Studies teachers spoke to the student body on the meaning of *Yom Hazikaron*. Then, the students watched a video of a mother speaking about her son (an American *Oleh*) who was killed in 1982 by *Hizballah*. After the video, the girls walked (35 minutes) to Mount Herzl where they participated in a brief ceremony honoring the memory of fallen Israeli soldiers.

On *Yom Ha'atzma'ut, the Michlallah* students visited *Kastel* and *Givat Hatakhmoshet* (Ammunition Hill). Upon their return to the campus, they "had a big barbecue on the lawn, played cards and Frisbee." The students all thought it was "a very nice day" and a good way to celebrate Israeli Independence Day.

Orthodox Zionism requires that the educational institutions support the State of Israel and promote service in the Israeli Defense Forces for Israeli students as well as the religious ideals of *Eretz Yisrael* and *Shivat Zion*. This means displaying the Israeli flag in the school building and incorporating the prayer for the State of Israel in Sabbath and holiday services when the Torah is read. And, finally, Orthodox Zionism means doing acts of *hesed*, as volunteers in areas of communal and educational need.

ISRAELI SUPPORT OF *TOCHNIT YOD GIMMEL*

As noted earlier, the *Tochnit Yod Gimmel* post high school program was developed with the support and guidance of the Torah Education Department of the WZO. The Department helped recruit the participants, made available applications for admission to the various yeshivot and seminaries, processed the applications, helped with the collection of tuition payments, and organized the flight arrangements. More, the Torah Department supplied specifically prepared applications to the "partner" yeshivot and seminaries – *Kerem B'Yavneh, Bet Midrash Le Torah, Machon* Gold, *Har Etzion, Sha'alavim, Yeshivat Hakotel,* and several more. In 1995, the arrangement or "contract" between the Torah Department and the Israeli institutions was terminated because the Israeli schools opened their own offices in North America for recruiting students, processing applications, conducting interviews, collecting tuition and arranging flights to Israel.

A major source of Israeli support to *Tochnit Yod Gimmel* from 1968 to 1990 was the *Minhal Studentim*, the Student Authority of the Ministry of Immigrant Absorption in conjunction with the WZO, headed by Haim Zohar. The *Minhal Studentim* consisted of two divisions – the university division and the religious institutions division which awarded per capita scholarships and building grants for dormitories to Yeshivot, Orthodox women's seminaries, the Hebrew Union College in Jerusalem, *Neve* Schechter of the Jewish Theological Seminary, and later to Pardes when it was founded. In addition to providing scholarship aid and grants, the *Minhal Studentim*, in cooperation with the Torah Education Department of the World Zionist Organization, conducted a variety of activities for diaspora participants, including tours of Israel. The religious institutions division also provided personal advisement to the participants in the Israeli programs in the offices of *Minhal Studentim* and in all the Israeli schools, which were visited regularly by the *Minhal Studentim* staff.

ORTHODOX ZIONIST YESHIVOT FOR MEN

The study programs of the Zionist Yeshivot for men take place five days per week – Sunday through Thursday. Some Yeshivot offer programs on Friday as well. The school day begins at 7 or 7:30 A.M. with *Shaharit* services and continues with formal classes (and breaks for lunch, *Minhah*, supper and a short afternoon recess) through the evening often until 10 or 11 P.M., and ends with *Ma'ariv* services. Most of the day is spent, not in formal class sessions and lectures, but in *havrutot* – study groups. Most often, American and Israeli students participate together in *havrutot*. Most of the institutions schedule monthly or bi-monthly Shabbatonim, which feature *"Ruah"* (spiritual programs of song, dance and storytelling), lectures and discussion groups led by faculty and students. They also sponsor intensive *tiyulim* – field trips and educational tours to the Negev, the Galil and the Golan Heights, as well as to Jerusalem. A full week program at an army base is arranged with *Tzahal* (IDF) in several of the Zionist Yeshivot. Weekend *mifgashim* with Israeli families are also scheduled in many yeshivot.

Orthodox Israeli boys with positive Zionist orientation and outlook usually attend *Hesder* yeshivot after completing the twelfth grade. The Yeshivat *Hesder* is a traditional yeshiva with curricular emphasis on Talmud. However, it differs substantially from its haredi counterparts regarding Zionism and the State of Israel and attitude to secular studies and non-religious Jews. The *Hesder* yeshivot provide a five-year course of study including two 6 to 9 month stints in the Israeli army during their stay in the Yeshiva.

Several *Hesder* yeshivot host *Tochnit Yod Gimmel* programs under separate auspices for graduates of diaspora yeshiva high schools. When recruiting American students, the *Hesder* Yeshivot emphasize strict adherence to Talmud study and "responsibility for one's fellowman, the unity of the Jewish people and the centrality of *Eretz Yisrael*" (brochure of Yeshivat Sha'alavim). They stress the importance of developing "a deep love of Israel, together with an insight into the social problems of the nation of our forefathers" (brochure of Yeshiva Kerem B'Yavneh, 1991).

While the large part of the study day is spent in study groups – usually 3 or 4 students per group – *Tochnit Yod Gimmel* participants are exposed to intensive formal instruction in Talmud, Bible and Commentaries, Jewish Philosophy, Jewish history, including Zionism and Israel. The *Hesder* yeshivot encourage students to engaged in *hesed* activities – volunteer work with needy Israeli families and communities. Many *Hesder* programs are located in and around Jerusalem.

As noted, the language of instruction in the programs for Americans is Hebrew and English. The level of Jewish studies, particularly Talmud instruction, varies among the various yeshivot and is usually adjusted to the background needs of the American students. Some yeshivot "specialize" in advanced learning programs. The *Hesder* yeshivot stress Modern Orthodox Zionist values and celebrate Israeli holidays – *Yom Ha'atzmaut* and *Yom Yerushalayim* in a variety of ways and observe *Yom Hashoah* and *Yom Hazikaron* for Israeli soldiers. The *Yom Ha'atzmaut* programs often feature IDF officers. In one yeshiva, the guest speaker last year was the IDF Chair of Staff, Shaul Mofaz.

While most of the yeshivot catering to Israeli populations that sponsor programs for Diaspora youth keep these programs separate, they attempt to integrate American and Israeli students, especially in *Bet Midrash havrutot* study, in extra curricula activities, *Shabbatonim*, and volunteer service. Diaspora Yeshiva high school graduates who choose to attend these schools directly enroll in the regular Israeli programs. A very small number of the American students choose this route.

ORTHODOX ZIONIST SEMINARIES FOR WOMEN

The programs of the Israeli seminaries for women also vary in their educational philosophy, approach to Judaic study, levels of instruction and attitudes toward Zionism and the Jewish State. The Zionist schools offer intensive 5-day-a-week programs and generally stress Hebrew language, *Tanakh*, *Parashat Hashavua* with commentaries, and Jewish history including Zionism and Israel. Some provide intensive programs in *Halakah*. Several schools provide opportunities for Talmud study. Like their male counterpart, all the Zionist Seminaries sponsor intensive educational tours to the Negev, Galil, and Golan Heights, and schedule *Shabbatonim*. Most of the institutions sponsor a *Hesed* day (volunteer aid program) each week in which students help destitute families, make food packages for the poor, work as volunteer aides in hospitals, nursing homes, centers for the aged and programs for children with special needs. They visit elderly people in their homes, help tutor Russian and Ethiopian immigrants and participate as big sisters in "big sister-little-sister" programs. All the Zionist seminaries celebrate Israeli Holidays and observe *Yom Hashoah Vehag'vurah* and *Yom Hazikaron*.

In addition to extracurricular activities, educational touring, and *Shabbatonim*, some of the seminaries (and yeshivot) provide time for sports and athletic programs.

PROGRAM SUCCESS

The Modern Orthodox Zionist yeshivot and seminaries enjoy an excellent reputation in the Modern Orthodox community in North America and elsewhere. They are considered highly successful. According to American high school principals, many of whom regularly visit the Israeli institutions in which their graduates study, instruction is generally effective, and often superior. Students and parents are generally happy. When asked about the post high school program in Israel, one parent, a travel agent who knows Israel well and whose daughter participated in *Tochnit Yod Gimmel* in 2000–2001 responded, "It is the best thing that Israel can do for diaspora teenagers and for diaspora Jewry." Given the very positive impact of the yearlong study in Israel on the Jewish Zionist values of our youth, it is the best possible program for the benefit of Jewish education and the Jewish people. 'Graduates' of these programs usually recommend the schools in which they studied to their younger classmates and siblings. The spread of the *Tochnit Yod Gimmel* is, indeed, due in large measure, to the quality of the programs.

However, the Israeli institutions are not problem-free. Problems that emerge during the year of study include inability of parents to complete payments, overzealous involvement of some students in non-academic pursuits, and non-adjustment of some students to the new school environments and academic requirements.

While some problems do exist, they affect a very small percentage of the student population and have virtually no impact upon the overall programs of the schools in which they may exist. The problems are usually handled effectively and rarely is there a need to expel a student. For students who have difficulty in adjusting and may cause problems to the institutions where they are enrolled, several new men's and women's programs have been established. Instead of merely expelling these students, the schools encourage them, after contacting their parents, to enroll in these special institutes.

The success of *Tochnit Yod Gimmel*, it must be emphasized, is due to five factors:

1. The nature of the student body: The students who enroll either come committed or become committed to serious Judaic study.
2. Parents of students take a deep interest in their welfare and in their progress.
3. The admission process, including personal interviews of students and parents, is intensive and thorough and helps insure proper selection and placement of students.
4. The instructors, *maggidei-shiur, rashei yeshiva* and program directors take a personal interest in their students. They consider it their personal-professional mission to help.
5. The unique Jewish-Israeli spiritual-cultural environment of the yeshivot and seminaries.

A recent study of *Tochnit Yod Gimmel* parent-student relationships shows that "all students (interviewed) became more religious by the end of the year, and a considerable number of students reported being more observant than their parents" (Tobin).

It is interesting to note that current literature regarding students – Jewish and non-Jewish – who study abroad in various countries indicates that they "often undergo changes in lifestyle and values as they adapt and learn from their new culture"(Tobin). In the case of study in Orthodox Zionist institutions in Israel, the strengthening of religiosity was generally supported by parents since the culture of the Orthodox Zionist experience in Israel is essentially the same as that experienced by students in their homes and yeshivot in America. Parents usually expect that their children are going to change religiously. And, they continue to send their sons and daughters to Israel for a post-high school year of study.

However, some parents of alumni interviewed by this researcher were not fully pleased with the increased level of their children's religious observance. And several parents were unhappy. To be sure, the fear of "fruming out" is justified, in some cases, because of the influence of certain instructors and guidance counselors (Tobin). Some parents felt that their children were "brainwashed." Others were accepting of the influence of the post-high school program, but would have preferred a more open, broader Israeli experience for their offspring.

In considering the influence of *Tochnit Yod Gimmel*, one must bear in mind that certain behavioral manifestations, which are associated with late adolescence, are normative for *Tochnit Yod Gimmel* participants. Parents of alumni indicated that all their children matured as young adults as they searched for their own identities and as they moved away from dependence upon their parents. All parents felt that this aspect of their children's Israel experience was very positive.

There is a direct relationship between the success of *Tochnit Yod Gimmel* – its impact upon participants – and their prior educational background. Ideals and concerns central to the Diaspora educational process are reinforced by the atmosphere of the Israeli programs. Other matters, such as national-religious beliefs and "American" Jewish values not specifically emphasized in the context of the Israeli yeshiva programs do not demonstrate the same level of strengthening (Berger). When examining the effect of Zionist yeshiva study upon 315 young participants a full year after the conclusion of a year's study in Israel, there was a very slight "drop off" in areas of commitment to Torah study and plans to move to Israel. On the whole, however, the spiritual-cultural changes that occurred during the year of study in Israel remained

(Berger). This explains the relatively large percentage of *olim* from among the American *Tochnit Yod Gimmel* participants.

The 2001–2002 year of study in Israel clearly demonstrates that the success of the post-high school yeshiva program derives, in large measure from the commitment and attitude of yeshiva high school graduates and their parents to Torah study and Israel. While the *Intifada* caused very serious declines in the number of Jewish youth participants and adult Jewish visitation from the United States to Israel for short term and long term programs in 2001, and while some organizations hesitated to promote Israel-based programs and a major American Jewish movement even cancelled youth trips to Israel, the post-high school yeshiva program continues unabated despite a tiny number of dropouts in some schools. Interestingly, many of the students who did not come to Israel in September, decided to enroll in the spring semester, 2002.

During an interview on January 22 that I arranged with twenty-four American female students in Orthodox Zionist seminaries in a restaurant where they were the guests of the parents of one of the students, they were asked if they knew of any girls "back home in Greater New York" who decided not to come to Israel in September 2001 because of the *Intifada*. The students burst out in laughter when they heard this question and pointed to the end of the long table around which they were seated. Sitting at the end of the table were three Jewish day high school graduates who did not come in September, but "just came three days ago for the spring semester."

Most of the Zionist yeshivot and seminaries reported an increase in enrollment in 2001–2002. During the winter and spring months of 2001, yeshiva high school seniors and their parents seriously considered the problems related to attending school in Israel in the 2001–2002 school year – the safety of the participants, the unrest in many parts of the country, and the need to curtail some educational trips. Yet, they decided *en masse* to enroll in the programs of their choice. In order to ensure the safety of their students, yeshivot and seminaries took special measures to guarantee their well-being such as restricting travel, providing extra security in the schools, and even requiring students to have cell phones – all this to make sure that the programs would continue without problems.

As part of the research for this report, this writer interviewed individual students and groups of students studying in Orthodox Zionist yeshivot and seminaries. One of the questions asked in the interviews was, "What are the reasons you came even during the time of unrest in Israel?" The answers included: "Every Jewish boy and girl should study in Israel;" "As observant Jews, it is incumbent upon us to visit and study in Israel as often as we can as long as we can, if we do not live in Israel;" "It is a *mitzvah*;" "This is what we were taught to do at home and in school;" "It's the thing to do;" "Every graduate – almost every graduate of American yeshiva high schools – does it."

Parents and grandparents (this writer among them), for their part, continue to visit their children and grandchildren regularly thus providing an important source of adult visitation to the Jewish state. Parental and grandparental visits are a regular feature of the Orthodox Israel study program.

An example of the commitment of Orthodox Zionist parents and their teenage daughters and sons to study in Israel is underscored by the fact that hundreds of students returned to the United States for the *Pesah* holiday and despite the rampant terror and escalation of violence virtually all often returned to Israel after Passover. On April 19, 2002, a Jewish Press headline read, "Tourism Is Down But American Orthodox Students Are Returning To Israel Yeshivas In Droves." The article that followed described the discussions that took place in hundreds of homes about the situation in Israel. (This writer's family experienced such deliberations regarding his granddaughter's study in Israel.) The article highlighted the nervousness of parents and grandparents who finally agreed that their children return to Israel for the remainder of the semester. For many or most of the first year students it meant returning for a second year beyond the end of the spring term.

Many families "talked it over with their rabbis" who

encouraged their return to Israel. In interviews with returnees at the airport, a reporter summarized the feelings of many students with the remark of several boys and girls. One young man from Riverdale, New York noted, "You have to have a certain degree of trust in *Hashem*." Another said, "Israel is where all the *Kedushah* is. That's our homeland." And a third opined, "That's the place for us to be now."

In a similar vein, the April 3 issue of the Jerusalem Post featured a magazine article entitled, "Remaining Faithful, Thousands of Orthodox Youths From North America Defy Terror Warnings To Study In Israel."

And, it must be underscored that the principals and teachers in the Jewish day high schools in the U.S. and Canada continue to promote *Tochnit Yod Gimmel* via meetings with groups of students and parents and individual students and parents. Each of the American Zionist yeshiva high schools in Greater New York sponsor annual Israel nights for parents and students in which representatives of selected seminaries and yeshivot are invited to come and speak. These evening programs are coordinated in the New York area by the Board of Jewish Education of Greater New York.

Another measure of the success of *Tochnit Yod Gimmel* is the aliyah of former students. A survey made by the *Minhal Studentim* in 1990 of the Israel study participants in 1970–71 showed that 33 percent had made aliyah. A meeting of *Hesder* Yeshiva leaders in January 2002 with this writer came to the conclusion that about 45 percent of all former *Hesder* Yeshiva students have made aliyah. According to Rabbi Meir Brayer, 452 *Yod Gimmel* participants in Yeshivot *Har Etzion* – about one third of all the former students – have made aliyah since the *Har Etzion* program began in 1971.

BEYOND 2002

As for the future, there is every indication that the program will continue to grow as the yeshiva and Jewish day high school populations in North America increase and as new schools join the list of yeshivot that maximize the number of graduates participating in long-term Zionist study in Israel. According to Rabbi Ellis Bloch of the Board of Jewish Education of Greater New York, there may be a slight drop in the number of participants in 2002–2003, not because of the *Intifada* but because of the economic situation in the United States. In his conversations with the principals of yeshiva and Jewish day high schools in Greater New York, many have noted that substantial numbers of parents are out of work and cannot afford the expenditure for Israeli study programs. In order to grow, the Israeli institutions will have to be able to provide larger and better facilities, including up-to-date classrooms, dormitory residences and lunchroom facilities and offer a wide range of extracurricular activities. Also the schools need to learn the art of fund raising, and to provide for financial aid for students.

Moreover, the majority of students in Zionist Orthodox yeshivot and seminaries spend two years in intensive Judaic study at Israeli institutions and then return to the Diaspora. This would be helpful in relieving the teacher shortage in Jewish all day and supplementary schools in the respective communities of the students who completed the pedagogic program. In this regard it should be noted, that it is estimated that each year about twenty percent of the participants in Israeli haredi women's seminaries enroll in special teacher-training programs available at their schools under the supervision of the Ministry of Education. Most of these students receive special pedagogic certificates approved by the Ministry of Education for teaching specific subjects such as *Humash*, *Tanakh* and *Halakah*.

In sum, when viewing the history, development, status and impact of *Tochnit Yod Gimmel* upon participants in Israeli Orthodox Zionist yeshivot and seminaries, the success of the program is impressive and its value significant. Yet, there are a variety of challenges that face the Jewish Zionist education. These challenges speak also to American and Israeli support groups. The challenges suggest important agenda items for discussion and action.

NOTES:

1. This figure compares favorably with the number 995 provided by Rabbi Abraham Brun, director of the *Iggud* Yeshivot *Hesder*.
2. This figure provided by Rabbi Brun compares favorably with the number 525 provided by the *Iggud Hamidrashot* – the organization of Zionist Women's Seminaries.
3. Internal memorandum from Haim Zohar, JAFI, *Criterionim shel Hatzionnut*, 18, 1986.

PART IV

ON JEWISH SUPPLEMENTARY SCHOOLING AND JEWISH FAMILY EDUCATION

CHAPTER 1

THE SYNAGOGUE & JEWISH EDUCATION IN HISTORICAL PERSPECTIVE

Supplementary Jewish education is essentially congregation-based, and, as such, its well-being speaks to the viability, potential and future of the synagogue as well. Therefore, a brief introduction describing the historical relationship between the synagogue and Jewish schooling is in order.

FROM EARLY TIMES TO THE TWENTIETH CENTURY

Throughout the ages, the synagogue has played an important – albeit changing – role in Jewish education. From its inception in Babylonian captivity, and later in Palestine, the synagogue served as a house of instruction for adults.

During the synagogue's formative stages, synagogue liturgy developed around the instruction of the Pentateuch and the Prophets. Indeed, "the scriptural readings supplied the content and form of the instruction" of the adult (Morris 85). An example of this is the early synagogue practice in *Eretz Yisrael* of weekly readings in which the Torah was first completed in seven years, then in three years, and later still, in Babylon, in an annual cycle.

And, ever since, the synagogue has, in a variety of ways, served as an institution for adult Jewish education – a kind of popular university.

During its early years, the Jewish school for youth was a private all day establishment unattached to the synagogue. The first schools for children and youth – those organized by Simon Ben Shetah for sixteen and seventeen-year-olds in the first century B.C.E. and the elementary schools initiated by Joshua ben Gamla about 125 years later – were private institutions set up by individual teachers. Beginning with the time of Bar Kochba, in the second century of the Common Era, Jewish schooling for the young became identified with the synagogue.

In addition to physically housing the Jewish school, the synagogue of the Babylonian, pre-Gaonic and Gaonic periods had a direct relationship to the organization and curriculum of the Jewish school. Indirectly, through the participation of children in worship-related activities, the synagogue also had significant impact upon their education. The chief aim of Jewish elementary schooling in the Middle Ages was to prepare young boys for participation in synagogue service. It is noteworthy that several gaonic responsa use the term *tinokot shel bet haknesset* (children of the synagogue) interchangeably with *tinokot shel bet rabban* (children of the school).

The pattern of school-synagogue relationship that prevailed in Babylon was evident also in the west Mediterranean countries (Spain, Southern France and Italy) in the eighth and ninth centuries. In subsequent generations through the 1400s, the introduction of Hebrew language and grammar and the study of the Prophets and Writings enriched the traditional liturgy and Torah curriculum. Advanced study included *Mishnah*, Talmud and such codifiers as Alfasi and Maimonides. In Spain, secular instruction was added to the Judaic program.

In northern France and Germany, during the same period of time, the synagogue was the locus of formal Jewish schooling. Here, during the thirteenth century, the term *heder* came into use. In the Franco-German *heder* (a special room in the synagogue) the curriculum, which included the scriptures and the Talmud, was punctuated by tutelage for the strict observance of the Commandments.

While the communities of Eastern Europe – particularly Poland and Lithuania – were fashioned according to the German-Jewish life-style of the refugees who fled there, changes were made in the educational approaches of the schools in these communities. The synagogue continued to be the central institution for the education of adults during the fifteenth, sixteenth, seventeenth and eighteenth centuries in Eastern Europe. However, it was no longer the setting for elementary Jewish schooling. Beginning with the sixteenth century, Jewish education for the young was provided in a private *heder*, a *yeshiva*, or a community *Talmud Torah* developed and maintained especially for the children of the poor.

While the curriculum in both the *heder* and *Talmud Torah* concentrated on the Pentateuch and liturgy, the organization, instruction and supervision of the *Talmud Torah* were infinitely better than those of the *heder*. An innovation in the East European school was the use of Yiddish as the language of instruction. On the advanced level, the yeshivot focused heavily on the Talmud and its commentaries. The *heder* and the *Talmud Torah* also became the normative forms of Jewish schooling in the Jewish communities of Italy, North Africa, Turkey and the Balkans, where sizable Jewish populations existed.

During the modern post-emancipation period in Europe, a wide variety of school types developed, generally not connected with the synagogue. These included the *heder metukan* (modern school), the *Mizrachi* (religious Zionist) school, the *Tarbut* (cultural) school, the Yiddish-secular school, and the Beth Jacob girls' school.

JEWISH SCHOOLING AND THE SYNAGOGUE IN AMERICA

In America, the first Jewish schools established in the eighteenth and early nineteenth centuries by the Spanish and German immigrants were housed in and conducted by the various synagogues. The East European immigration in the 1880s, however, brought with it the *heder* and *Talmud Torah*, by and large, unrelated to the synagogues. These became the dominant forms of Jewish schooling in the latter part of the nineteenth century and beginning of the twentieth century. The poor, scanty instruction by ill-prepared, unqualified *"lo-mutzlah:"* teachers in the private *hadarim* left a permanent scar on Jewish education in America. In contrast, the community *Talmud Torah* patterned after the *heder metukan* in Russia, engaged professional teachers and was professionally administered. Its curriculum included Hebrew language and literature history, Bible, customs and ceremonies, prayers, and occasionally, Jewish arts (music and arts and crafts).

Against this backdrop, the synagogue school developed gradually in modern American Jewish life. As synagogues were founded in the early 1900s many of them organized supplementary school programs. By 1940, about 80% of the total Jewish school enrollment was under synagogue auspices. The 1940s and 1950s saw the growth of large one-day-a-week and three-day-a-week congregational schools. Concomitant with this development was the almost total eclipse of the communal *Talmud Torah*, which, with rare exception, ceased to exist by the mid-1960s. Demographic changes hastened the disintegration of the *Talmud Torah* as the suburban congregational school grew by leaps and bounds.

The main difference between the communal *Talmud Torah* and its synagogue counterpart was, in addition to its sponsorship, the schedule of instruction. Whereas the students in the *Talmud Torah* studied five days a week, two hours each day, for forty-eight weeks per year, the synagogues conducted either three-day-a-week schools, one-and-a-half to two hours each session for thirty-two weeks (Reform).

The rapid growth of the synagogue school necessitated the hiring of large numbers of teaching and supervisory personnel. This led to the establishment of the ideological association of educators as counterparts to the respective rabbinic groups.

With the growth of the schools, the synagogues themselves grew, and the interdependence between school enrollment and synagogue membership became a reality. Their quantitative growth lulled many synagogues into a sense of complacency. As the enrollments grew, so grew the building plants and the education budgets. And so, too, grew the desire of many synagogues to conduct their educational programs independent of other community means for developing and maintaining their own educational systems. Full-time principalships and even full-time teaching positions became the norm in the large synagogue schools.

By the end of the 1940s a significant number of relatively well-trained practitioners who had achieved both higher Jewish learning and general education were teaching and supervising congregational schools. Even though the financial rewards of employment in synagogue schools were far from satisfactory, there were more opportunities for full-time and part-time teaching and full-time principalships than ever existed before in the country.

Encouraged by increasing enrollments and growing professional resources, the congregational school looked forward to years of continued development and improvement as it became the heir of the fast disappearing communal *Talmud Torah*. Moreover, the synagogue school was motivated also by the new standards for intensive Jewish education being set by the rapidly growing Jewish day schools.

Needed were the upgrading and intensification of the two to four-hour one-day-a-week school, and the four to six-hour three-day-a-week congregational program. Toward this end, each ideological grouping, buoyed up by the growth of its congregational schools, turned inward to develop coordinated ideological programming among its respective schools. For almost three decades, beginning with World War II, there was a strong feeling of self-sufficiency among the synagogue groups regarding their educational enterprises.

Despite the rapid growth of the congregational schools, the educational programs of the synagogues frequently did not receive adequate lay attention, support or leadership. As one educator put it, the school has been the "stepchild of the synagogue." This is amply demonstrated by the relatively low status of the lay educational committee members and the professional educators in the synagogue hierarchy. The results of this condition were often reflected in the operation and effectiveness of the school program.

Where enrollments warranted full-time principals, rabbis gladly left the supervision of the school in the hands of the principal. In the smaller, less affluent synagogue schools, many rabbis grudgingly accepted the administrative responsibility for the conduct of the school, usually with the aid of a head teacher. With some notable exceptions, the attitude of the rabbi to the school and its personnel and his role in the educational program have been a source of irritation and frustration to synagogue educators.

DURING THE SECOND HALF OF THE 20TH CENTURY

In 1963, supplementary school enrollment started declining rapidly. At its onset, despite forecasts about the potential severity of the decline, the synagogue community demonstrated little anxiety. However, when disaffection of Jewish youth from Judaism reached alarming proportions in the late sixties, much concern was voiced about the effectiveness of Jewish schools – a concern which eventually led to a rash of community surveys of Jewish education and to serious introspection regarding supplementary Jewish schooling.

Studies of the congregational school program demonstrate that this form of Jewish education leaves much to be desired. They challenge the present form, content, and approaches of supplementary education. One study on the curriculum of the three-day-a-week school highlighted the low level of achievement in Hebrew reading, Hebrew conversation, Bible and Jewish history as it bemoaned the "cynical pretentiousness" of the one-day-a-week school.

The awareness of the shortcomings of the school program has led each of the ideological movements to examine its school curricula and to develop serious projects for curriculum reform. Each of the movements is in the final stages of publishing new curriculum guidelines. Since there is no binding power regarding the curriculum practices of the autonomous schools, the fate of these recommended programs of education remains to be seen. Moreover it will take several years of experimentation and careful evaluation to assess the effectiveness and potential impact of the new curricula.

One fact emerged boldly and clearly from all the surveys and self-searching. Without the support and partnership of the home as well as a supportive climate in the Jewish community, the synagogue school will never be truly effective. To this end, greater interest and activity has been evidenced in parent education and family education programs – so far, too little and too late to counter the vanishing Jewish generation, but, nevertheless a thrust in the right direction.

Despite findings of the various studies, which point to the ineffectiveness of congregational education, a variety of worthwhile instructional activities have been taking placed in many synagogue schools. The meaningful learning experiences in these institutions prompted one widely quoted researcher to state, "in many ways, it is unfortunate, however, that Jewish students spend so little time in Jewish schools because, unlike the schools that their parents attended, there are some exciting things" (Asaf vol. 1, p. 4).

To be sure, the relatively few hours of synagogue school attendance – no matter how exciting – cannot sufficiently counteract or compensate for the influence of an unsupportive home and environment. Needed are additional hours for confluent education – the combination of formal learning and Jewish life experiences during the week, on weekends, and during extended vacation periods.

CHAPTER 2

ON THE STATUS OF THE JEWISH SUPPLEMENTARY SCHOOL – 1982

The Jewish supplementary school – what will it be like one decade hence? This is one of the most difficult and painful questions one may ask about the Jewish community in America. Difficult – because the response is dependent on so many variables not within the control of the supplementary school itself. Painful – because Jewish supplementary education has been in critical decline over the past two decades. Peaking at 540,000 pupils in 1962, the current enrollment is about 230,000 – a 58 percent decrease in twenty years, due to low birthrate, intermarriage, broken homes, outmigration, and apathy to Jewish schooling.

Supplementary Jewish education began in late 1800s and early 1900s as either private *hedarim* or communal *Talmud Torahs*, largely unrelated to the synagogue. During the 1920s and 1930s, the communal *Talmud Torah* (which was initially developed as a communal response to educating the children of the poor) was the dominant form of Jewish education. With the move of Jews to suburbia and the development of synagogues, which sponsored their own schools, the communal *Talmud Torah* all but disappeared by 1960, leaving the supplementary school – with some notable exceptions – a congregational institution.

By and large, the Jewish supplementary school is a Conservative and Reform institution. Orthodox parents almost always enroll their children in day schools or yeshivot.

There are 1835 Jewish supplementary schools in North America – 760 schools under Reform auspices (largely one-day-a-week schools); 785 schools under Conservative auspices (generally weekday afternoon schools); 250 Orthodox weekday congregational schools; and 40 communal afternoon schools. Forty-three percent of the pupils are enrolled in Conservative schools and 37 percent in Reform congregational programs. Eleven percent are in inter-ideological, communal or "independent" schools and 9 percent in programs under Orthodox auspices.

In 1982, 70 percent of those enrolled in any Jewish educational program were in supplementary schools. In their heyday, most supplementary schools were of the one-day-a-week variety. Currently the overwhelming majority are two and three-day-a-week programs.

More and more, the supplementary school is being compared to its younger sibling – the Jewish day school – which continues to grow, albeit more slowly than heretofore, despite its own variety of communal, ideological and fiscal problems.

The crucial questions about the supplementary school understandably focus upon its viability and potential for survival. The decline has brought about several new conditions in Jewish supplementary education.

The trend is clearly towards the small school and small-small congregational school. In many communities the small school is now the norm. In the Greater New York area, for example, 211 schools – 57 percent of the total number of supplementary schools – enroll fewer than 100 pupils, and about half of these have enrollments of fewer than 50 pupils. The average school size in the 1982/83 academic school year is 130 compared to 260 one decade ago – a 50 percent change.

Consolidating small schools under intra-ideological or inter-ideological, communal auspices is a serious concern to most communities. Inter-ideological and intra-ideological consolidation is a threat to many declining congregations who feel dependent upon their afternoon and one-day-a-week schools – no matter how small they may be – for new memberships, hence for their continued viability. This is a sad commentary on the status of these synagogues. For many congregations, the problem of the small school and the challenge of the communal interest in school mergers is exacerbated by the growing interest of many Jewish community centers in Jewish education – both informal and formal.

Demography plays a crucial role in the attempts to consolidate schools. The physical distance between potential merging institutions makes consolidation an unachievable goal in many locales. Parents object to the extra travel time it may impose upon their children. Moreover, bus transportation is an expensive addition to an already unbearable educational budget. In light of the fact that mergers will not be a common reality within the near future, many educational leaders are seeking ways to maximize the effectiveness of the small school and utilize the intimate environment to greatest educational advantage.

The waning fiscal capacity of congregations to support their respective schools as a result of their diminishing memberships and income is a common phenomenon. Many synagogues that heretofore would not relate directly to their local Federations have appealed for Federation aid. As a result, support to congregational schools is a key item on many communal agendas. Crucial to the continued existence of the congregational school – not to speak of its future growth – is the quality of the relationship between the synagogue and the sources of communal funding. But even more important than this relationship is the ability of synagogue lay leaders to assume greater financial responsibility for the operation of their respective educational programs. In 1981, only 5 percent of the total Federation subsidies allocated to Jewish schools was awarded to congregational schools, compared with 16 percent to community schools and 79 percent to day schools.

Questions about the quality of instruction and supervision

loom large in light of the part-time nature of supplementary school educational positions and the qualifications of the personnel to fill them. According to the Department of Research, JESNA, there are approximately 19,000 supplementary schoolteachers. Only 600 of these are full-time personnel. Most are employed for 4–12 hours per week.

The Judaic qualifications of supplementary school instructional personnel range from no knowledge of Hebrew (in one small community there are no persons who know how to read Hebrew available to teach in its congregational school) to intensive Judaic and Hebraic scholarship. The range of professional qualifications varies from no formal pedagogic training or experience to outstanding educational credentials.

Most teachers are unlicensed by the National Board of License or its six affiliated boards (New York, Chicago, Philadelphia, Los Angeles, Miami, Baltimore) which certify teachers for Conservative, Orthodox and communal supplementary schools, or by the certification program of the Union of American Hebrew Congregations for teachers in Reform congregational schools.

Teaching in a supplementary school does not provide a living wage. Teacher salaries range from $1,000 to $25,000, depending upon educational background, teaching load and years of experience. The hourly rate ranges from $5 to $26 and averages about $10. On the average, full-time teachers earn approximately $16,000–$18,000.

Administration and supervision of supplementary schools is rapidly changing. To be sure, full-time supplementary school principalship is a fast disappearing occupation. Only about 540 persons heading supplementary school programs in 1982 (approximately 25 percent of the total number of administrative personnel) were full-time. The part-time school heads essentially include moonlighting public school teachers and principals, full-time rabbis, head teachers with a variety of administrative responsibilities, and lay persons with some educational experience.

Most principals lack adequate training in supervision. Only a fraction are licensed by the National Board of License or its affiliate local Board of License. Excluding rabbis who administer their respective congregational schools as part of their rabbinic duties, annual salaries range from $4,000 to $40,000, depending upon educational background, hours of employment and length of service.

Given the limited hours of instruction, the scope and objectives of the curriculum are receiving serious reconsideration by school boards, educator organizations, synagogues and bureaus. As congregational lay leadership and rabbis place greater stress on the acquisition of synagogue skills, Hebrew language instruction recedes in importance. (The problem of sufficient time for Hebrew language instruction is compounded by the lack of qualified instructors.)

Not unrelated to the matter of inadequate time for instruction is a gnawing problem confronting supplementary education since its earliest times in America, namely: the host of attractions and activities competing for the child's time. These form the all-too-well-known list of reasons for nonattendance and absenteeism: piano and dance lessons, Little League and doctor appointments, and family vacation schedules.

Continuation is another serious problem confronting supplementary education. Without the cumulative effect of elementary and high school exposure (with sufficient instructional hours), the Jewish supplementary school cannot hope to be effective. Yet, only a small percentage of the elementary school graduates enroll in secondary school programs and most of these only one or two years.

The problems of conflicting interests and noncontinuation are directly related to the insignificant role of the home in the area of Jewish education. Simply put, Jewish education is not a priority to most supplementary school parents.

Moreover, an essential dimension of the effectiveness of a school program is the environment of the pupil. The inadequacy of the Jewish home environment of most pupils poses a grave challenge to all those interested in the welfare of the supplementary school. This reality is responsible for the trend towards parent education, family education and experiential learning, and the stress on compensatory modes of Jewish education as part of the school program.

The breakdown of the nuclear family and the rise of the single parent family pose a real challenge to Jewish education. In one school in New York, for example, 75 percent of the students are children who live with single parents. This problem is further aggravated by two other characteristics of the pupil population: the growing autonomy of children (and their role in determining their own attendance in Jewish school) and the increasing diversity of needs of pupils resulting from intermarriage, growing variety of learning abilities, and behavior of children.

All these problems and challenges, and many more, are the deep concern of Jewish education, professional and lay leadership alike. Not all Jewish educators agree about its current status and prospects for its future. But, there is strong consensus that much has to be done quickly and on many fronts, if this American Jewish institution is to survive and thrive.

The golden age of the supplementary school is now over. Will it return again as gold or even silver? This is one of the most serious questions facing the Jewish community in the 1980s. Jewish communal leadership cannot afford not to meet this challenge without utter commitment and creativity.

CHAPTER 3

Looking Toward the 21st Century: Who Needs Hebrew Teachers in Our Supplementary Schools? – 1983

Over the past several years this writer has written rather extensively about two aspects of Jewish education – pupil enrollment and the role of family in Jewish schooling. When we consider the data for these two dimensions in tandem, and project them forward to the year 2000, it seems quite clear that by that date, Hebrew teachers – as we know them today – will not be needed in Jewish supplementary schools.

Let's look at the facts. In 1962, the peak year of Jewish school enrollment in the North American continent, there were an estimated 540,000 children enrolled in Jewish supplementary schools. Currently, in 1983, there are approximately 220,000 supplementary school pupils, a decline of 60 percent.

The reasons are fairly obvious. The major cause is the decline in birthrate, which is now at an all-time low of 1.4 to 1.6 per family. Jews are simply marrying less and marrying later than the rest of the population. Compare 8–10 births per thousand among Jews to 15 births per thousand in the non-Jewish white population.

Another reason for the decrease is intermarriage. According to recent studies, only a small percentage of children of intermarrieds are enrolled in Jewish schools. Sociologist Egon Mayer notes that most children of intermarrieds are not socialized as Jews. Only 3 percent of the children of mixed marriages and 38 percent of conversionary marriages are affiliated in any way with a synagogue. Moreover, Professors O.U. Schmelz and Sergio Della Pergola, Hebrew University demographers, in a report in the 1983 American Jewish Yearbook, indicate that only 25 percent of all children of out-marriages contracted since 1965 are reported as being Jewish by their parents.

A third factor is the growing incidence of broken homes and single parent children. The problems of scheduling parent visitation rights and the logistics of transportation make it difficult for single parent children to attend school regularly or at all.

Another reason is out-migration. Whereas, in the past, young Jewish couples moving to suburbia and exurbia sought to belong to a synagogue, many of them now feel comfortable without affiliation with a congregation. The result is no Jewish schooling for their progeny. In one suburban county in Greater New York, for example, out of 41,000 Jewish children of school age, only 9,000, or 22 percent, are enrolled in Jewish schools of all types. The increased mobility of the Jewish population underscores the seriousness of the out-migration factor.

A final reason for non-enrollment is the negative attitude of many young parents to religion and to Jewish schooling. Several studies have shown that a significant number of young parents "don't like the synagogue" and don't feel that they can afford or want to spend their hard-earned money on membership dues or tuition fees. The reluctance to enroll children in Jewish schools is heightened by negative feelings about their own Jewish school experiences, coupled with the growing autonomy they give their children, endowing them with decision-making powers regarding their attendance at a Jewish school.

All these factors have caused the continuous enrollment drop, which has averaged about 3 percent per year since 1962. If the decline continues at the same rate for the next 17 years, there will be 51 percent fewer children in Jewish supplementary schools in 2000 than there are in 1983 – an enrollment decrease from 220,000 to 108,000 pupils. Compare with 540,000 pupils in 1962!

Such a dramatic decline is not far-fetched. Professor Schmelz and Della Pergola estimate there will be 25 percent to 35 percent fewer Jewish children of school age in year 2000. This projection is substantiated by the findings of the recent New York Jewish population study which estimates that there are some 100,000 Jewish children in the 10–14 and 15–19 age cohorts, respectively, only 66,000 Jewish children in the 0–4 age cohort. This latter population cohort represents the potential New York Jewish school enrollment from 1988 to 2000 – 33 percent fewer Jewish children of school age than during the last decade. Moreover, the figure of 66,000 includes a larger proportion of children of Orthodox families who will be enrolled in yeshivot and day schools than represented in the population of the 10–14 and 15–19 age cohorts. When we add the other factors (in addition to birth rate) to both these child population projections, an enrollment drop of 51 percent is not unrealistic.

There has been sufficient alarm within the Jewish community to prompt a variety of responses to the problems discussed above. The minus-zero Jewish population growth and low fertility have been on the agenda of several major national and local organizations during the past few years. Similarly, the dangers posed by intermarriage and single-parenthood are being addressed seriously in some quarters. The problems of Jewish mobility, non-membership in synagogues and non-enrollment in Jewish schools are also receiving increased attention.

The Jewish community, as a whole must actively confront these continuing conditions, if we are to reverse the undesirable social and familial trends that threaten the continuity of the Jewish community. Unless the tide is stemmed, the effects of the projected pupil population decline will be dramatic.

There will be a severe reduction in the number of schools. Many large schools will become medium-sized; many medium-sized schools will become small or cease to exist; most small schools will close their doors. The changing school-size phenomenon will encourage much merger talk and some merger activity. It will stimulate much more consideration, if not actual planning and development, of communal schools and alternative schools. Above all, fewer school personnel will be needed.

But the problem is not mainly one of demographic decline. Our greatest challenge is essentially qualitative. How can we provide the kind of education that will have a lasting influence on Jewish attitudes and behavior?

Research studies demonstrate that the more committed Jewish parents choose to send their children to a Jewish day school. Many parents of supplementary school pupils, by contrast, are either marginally Jewish or do not fully associate themselves with the philosophy and purposes of their respective synagogues. Nor do they fully appreciate the instructional aims of the school or understand sufficiently the content of the instruction to which their children are exposed. This leaves their children insufficiently motivated for effective learning, and lessens the possibility that the Jewish school can have a lasting influence.

The sociological characteristics of the modern Jewish family also work against the education process. Many pupils are single-parent children or children being brought up by one parent who has remarried, or children exposed to severe family problems with not-yet-divorced parents. A significant number of children are the products of intermarriage where one parent has converted to Judaism. And in families with two Jewish parents, the level of Jewish knowledge and practice is often no different, or only slightly higher, than among families that don't enroll children in Jewish schools at all.

While it may be true that under certain conditions the Jewish school has an effect, which might be independent of familial background and other socializing influences, it seems clear that without significant home involvement in the process of Jewish education, the conditions for maximizing the effectiveness of Jewish schooling cannot be fulfilled. And when schooling has an effect independent of the family, it often creates a serious problem at home – the disruption of *shalom bayit*. The very success of the school frequently alienates children from parents who are touched by the influence of the school.

There is not a plethora of research data delineating the specific impact of the home on the effectiveness of *Jewish* schooling per se. There is, however, sufficient empirical evidence and experience in the field, as well as well-documented research findings in general and private education, to underscore the relaionship between the home and school.

Doing well in school, as Geoffrey Bock recently put it, "depends on the learning environment, the congruence of school values with home values, the school culture and other non-cognitive effects of education." The title of David Seeley's recent book, *Education Through Partnership*, and the title of the volume, *Families and Communities as Educators*, recently published by Teachers College, Columbia University, both highlight the importance being accorded by educational leaders to the establishment of productive relationships between school and home.

Taken together, the enrollment data and family factors (the small number of supplementary school pupils, on the one hand, and their special familial, educational, cultural and psychosocial needs, on the other hand), suggest that the current pattern of 2–6-hour-a-week supplementary school instruction and part-time personnel cannot possibly provide the necessary combination of positive home-school experiences necessary for effective Jewish education. Given the present nature of home-school relationships, it seems amply clear that part-time Hebrew schoolteachers are not what the doctor prescribes for 21st-century Jewish supplementary school children.

To succeed with children the school must succeed with parents, making them partners in the process of child education.

Until we deal with the needs of Jewish families as intergenerational units comprising people of differing ages and varying educational needs, the Jewish education of the young members of those families will not be effective. The only way to do this is to develop teaching learning strategies that involve the whole family. What synagogues need – indeed, what the Jewish community requires – therefore, in order to provide effective Jewish schooling for children, are full-time Jewish family educators to replace the part-time congregational supplementary schoolteachers. Indeed, supplementary Jewish education must be transformed into a Jewish family education program.

This means reorienting the task of the rabbi and cantor. Similarly, the roles of teachers and principals in synagogue settings must be modified. Each of them – rabbi, cantor, teacher and principal – would become a full-time Jewish family educator instructing children in classroom settings, leading informal educational groups, working with family members in their homes, and providing individualized tutelage, Jewish family counseling and referrals as needed to parents and children alike.

The Jewish family educators would work in teams – plan and organize their work and establish their goals at the beginning of each semester, trimester or bimonthly or monthly period, as required. To be sure, this approach requires the restructuring of the synagogue, the congregational school and the curriculum of instruction as well as the retraining and training of personnel. (Parenthetically, the need to make maximum use of the available energies and skills of all key personnel becomes more evident and ever more pressing in those synagogues undergoing membership and enrollment declines.)

It will not be easy to induce the necessary modifications into the synagogue structure. Nor will the individual rabbis, rabbinic groups or lay leaders take easily to what amounts to a structural and programmatic revolution in the synagogue. But, given the prognosis developed in the foregoing pages, there may be no other viable alternative for the synagogue, particularly for the small congregation that cannot merge with another synagogue.

A large proportion of Jewish families is not part of the synagogue world. Many of these are, however, affiliated with Jewish community centers. As the leadership of the JCC's becomes more aware of the importance of Jewish education for their members and considers ways to provide them with Jewish educational experiences, it behooves the synagogues to seek ways to cooperate with the JCC's.

One key aspect of cooperation, which should be initiated post haste, is the area of early childhood education. The major growth area in the last decade in Jewish education has been on the nursery school and kindergarten levels. Brought about largely by the changing family structure and socio-economic conditions, especially single parents and working parents, this condition will probably continue for another decade or more.

Synagogues should find ways to coordinate efforts with JCC's in organizing staffing, programming and maintaining community early childhood education classes. Jewish family educators would be involved in both the classroom and the parenting phases of the program.

In developing and implementing the Jewish family education idea, the bureau of Jewish education has a key role to play as advocate, planner, mediator and educator-trainer. In the small communities, the bureaus might indeed operate or participate in the daily operation of the Jewish family education program.

The Jewish content to which children are exposed must be synthesized with overall family needs. To accomplish this requires the retraining of teachers and principals and the special preparation of future teachers, the retraining of rabbis and cantors, and the special preparation of future rabbis and cantors. This training should lead to the acquisition of knowledge and skills necessary for effective teaching in the 21st century school and home, in individualized small group and large class settings.

This kind of preparation has serious implications for the pre-service training programs of the various rabbinic seminaries, Hebrew colleges and Jewish professional schools. It suggests closer cooperation between the central agencies for Jewish education and these schools for instituting family education components in their respective curricula.

The training of Jewish family educators should enable them to a) identify needs of marginally or minimally affiliated Jews; b) demonstrate ways in which Jewish tradition can meet these needs; and c) utilize modern technology in each of the teaching-learning settings in which they will be involved.

In addition to special preparation, being a Jewish family educator will require commitment to the mission of Jewish family education and special professional lifestyle. Although there will be regularly scheduled hours of instruction, this lifestyle, like that of the rabbi, will not be tied down to specific hours each week. It will necessitate mediating synagogue and education structures and negotiating the best ways to involve families in Jewish life activities. It will require time for guiding individuals and family units in holiday and Sabbath observance. It will involve the family of the Jewish family educator in interactive ways with families they teach and touch. In a word, the Jewish family educator will be a total Jewish educator.

In essence, the Jewish family educators will be assigned to work with families instead of classroom programs only. Scheduled classroom instruction of children and parents will take place in accordance with needs of family learners.

One of the major challenges of the Jewish family educator team will be to provide alternative home environments for children and for families during weekends, vacation periods, and summer time – best accomplished via retreats, Shabbatonim, camp programs, and supervised tours of Israel. These can make available the "set of Jewish experiences" as Leonard Fein refers to them, necessary for influencing the future Jewish behavior patterns of Jewish school pupils – and their families.

The Jewish family educator idea is not beyond the fiscal reach of the Jewish community. It requires the resolve of our lay and professional leadership and cooperation between the synagogue, Jewish center, local bureau and Federation. Once implemented, the Jewish family educator plan – *whose details have yet to be spelled out* – will help solve other personnel and financial problems of synagogues, especially those with dwindling membership. It will help solve the perennial problem of the part-time and part-part-time teacher.

What will make the family educator plan financially feasible is that far fewer personnel will be needed for formal classroom instruction. Moreover, family educator team members can be drawn from personnel already on full-time payrolls of the synagogue and community – rabbis, principals, cantors and family workers – in addition to changing the part-time status of a select number of teachers into full-time family educators. The shifting of professional responsibilities within the synagogue, redeployment and training are the major challenges that will need to be addressed in regard to Jewish family educator recruitment.

It will be necessary for local federations to assume greater fiscal responsibility than they currently have for congregational education (even as they continue to increase allocations for Jewish all day education) in order to be able to attract full-time educators. It goes without saying that the compensation of the Jewish family educator should be commensurate with his/her training and responsibilities. Unquestionably, the Jewish family educator should be among the highest salaried Jewish communal and synagogue professionals.

Federation involvement in helping to staff the Jewish family educator programs has another dimension. Together with the bureau, it must address the challenge of making available family workers and family life educators (with appropriate orientation and training) from family service agencies to work as Jewish family educators in synagogue and Jewish center settings. If appropriate personnel cannot be made available or redeployed from other agencies, then budget lines might be allocated via the bureaus for the Jewish family education program.

Another challenge related to staffing and training is the matter of licensure. Currently, a very small percentage of teachers and principals in supplementary schools are licensed by the National Board of License or its local affiliates. To be sure, the resolution of this unfortunate condition is not in sight. The Jewish family educator plan will require the development of a set of realistic standards which, with the support of communal and synagogue leadership, could be universally implemented.

On the national level, it would be appropriate for JESNA and the Council of Jewish Federations to draw up guidelines for the support of Jewish family educators programs, not unlike those recently completed by JESNA for Federation support of the supplementary school.

One of the major reasons that many of the reforms attempted in general education during the past several decades have been doomed to failure is that they did not involve the potential implementers of the respective plans for change. Crucial to the success of the Jewish family educator idea is the planning process, which must include adequate representation by all interested parties, particularly the future Jewish family educators.

At first reading, the Jewish family educator idea may sound drastic and overly ambitious. It may even evoke strong opposition and raise serious questions from various quarters of the Jewish community that have legitimate interests and concerns, particularly national and local rabbinic groups, principals councils and cantorial associations. The Jewish family educator proposal *is* drastic and ambitious. It does challenge established organizations in the community. As presented in the foregoing pages, it will obviously need refinement and elaboration. However, it is a necessary response to a condition that has been worsening over the years with no cure in sight. The Jewish family educator is a dramatic way to achieve a breakthrough in Jewish supplementary education. If not on a large scale, let's try a pilot program now. *Mitzvah ha-ba-ah y'yadcha, al tachmitzenah.* "When an opportunity knocks on your door, don't lose it."

CHAPTER 4

THE JEWISH SUPPLEMENTARY SCHOOL: A SYSTEM IN NEED OF CHANGE

THE BIPOLAR STATE OF JEWISH BEHAVIOR

The majority of American Jews are best described as products of the acculturation-deculturation syndrome as they became integrated comfortably into American society. This condition has had a threefold effect upon their Jewish identity and involvement. It has lessened the quantity and quality of Jewishness in their daily lives; it has diminished the extent and intensity of their synagogue affiliation and Jewish communal activity; and it has decreased their level of home support for Jewish education.

There has been a growing awareness over the past decade among Jewish lay leadership that this trend must be counteracted, particularly that Jewish education of the majority of Jews must be upgraded. Between two-thirds and three-quarters of all Jewish school-age children, 5 to 18 years old, will receive some formal Jewish education. For most of these – 70 percent of them – this means supplementary Jewish schooling, 2 to 6 hours per week, 30 to 35 weeks per year, for five or six years.

What aspects of Jewish supplementary education must be improved? How can we upgrade this form of schooling? These are questions that have stymied both lay and professional leadership.

THE STUDY

To respond to these challenges, the Board of Jewish Education of Greater New York undertook what Professor Harold Himmelfarb, a foremost researcher on this subject, has called, "the most methodologically rigorous and most comprehensive study to date on the topic." The three-year study process included intensive lay and professional involvement guided by a 13-member lay task force and administered competently by an 11-member professional staff study team.

SETTING THE STAGE: STAKEHOLDERS

In setting the stage for the Study we realized the need to consider all the *stakeholders* in the Jewish supplementary school. Essentially there are five categories of *spokesmen* or *stakeholders*.

1. *Consumers* – pupils exposed to formal and informal education strategies.
2. *Clients* – parents who determine the kind of Jewish education they will purchase for their children.
3. *Transmitters* – all Jewish education personnel – teachers, principals, rabbis, informal educators, educational consultants and specialists.
4. *Overseers* or facilitators – school committee members who have special roles in assuring that Jewish education is properly maintained.
5. *Providers* or supporters – trustees of synagogues and school boards, members and professional staff of federation allocation committees, and board members of central agencies for Jewish education.

We determined that it is absolutely necesary for all these stakeholders to be involved in the study.

THE STUDY SAMPLE

The Study Sample included 40 schools – large, medium and small;

urban and suburban; Conservative, Orthodox, Reconstructionist, and Reform.

THE STUDY METHODOLOGY

The Study Methodology comprised two research approaches. The first approach was a *Normative Survey Method* (or a modified ethnographic procedure), which consisted of hundreds of interviews and observations, and included an examination of curricula and administrative forms. The second approach was a *Measurement Technique*, a carefully developed three-part Inventory of Jewish Knowledge, Jewish Involvement and Jewish Attitudes – administered after being pilot-tested – to *all* pupils in *all* grades of the participating schools. This instrument (with an exceptionally high reliability of .91) was based upon the expectations of principals and developed to reflect the minimal levels of Jewish knowledge, Jewish involvement and Jewish attitudes expected of pupils by Bar and Bat Mitzvah age.

FINDINGS

By and large, the Study findings confirmed our assumptions. But in some cases our hypotheses were not borne out.

NORMATIVE SURVEY FINDINGS

The results of the *Normative Survey* clearly demonstrated a variety of realities.

- Jewish education is *not* a *real* synagogue priority.
- *Rabbis* are peripherally involved in the supplementary school. Most of them lack the necessary training to help make it effective.
- *Principals* are serious about their work. But, synagogue school principaling is just a part-time job. The majority of principals lack sufficient Judaic background, and adequate knowledge of supervision and curriculum development for Jewish education.

- *Teachers* are generally committed to their work. But most of them lack *Jewish* pedagogic skills, and do not have sufficient Jewish knowledge. Eleven percent of the 426 teachers in our sample had no formal Jewish education at all. Teachers have no real institutional commitment; they are not in their respective synagogue schools long enough to make a lasting impact. The teachers in our sample spend an average of six hours per week in a given school. Moreover, turnover is great. Two-thirds of them taught in the same school two years or less.
- The overwhelming majority of *parents* provide little or *no* home support programs, nor are they interested. They send their off-spring to the synagogue school purely for Bar and Bat Mitzvah.
- Pupils attend Jewish supplementary school *primarily* for Bar/Bat Mitzvah. While in most instances they seem well behaved, they are not motivated to learn, nor are they really learning.
- The persons involved with the school have no shared vision of curricular goals. *Principals and teachers have the highest curricular goals.* Rabbis, lay leaders and parents have the lowest expectations.

There is little or no relationship between the subjects taught and the goals articulated by lay and professional leadership. For example, all the interviewees – principals, teachers, rabbis, lay leaders and parents – felt that the formation of a positive Jewish identity and positive Jewish attitudes is an important goal for the Jewish school. Yet, this aim was far from realized, as we shall see in a few moments.

- The overwhelming majority of schools have no structured curricula. Nor do they regularly follow the curricula prepared by their respective ideological movements.
- The time spent in school is both quantitatively and qualitatively inadequate.

INVENTORY FINDINGS

The Inventory findings are most revealing. The *Inventory of Jewish Knowledge* shows that

- Pupil achievement scores were far below expectations. The overall average score was only 49 percent, whereas the expectation was that pupils would know the answers to all, or at least, most questions in the Jewish knowledge inventory.
- The overall increase in Jewish knowledge from the first year of school to the sixth year was only 10 percent. From the second year to the sixth year, Jewish knowledge scores increased by only 4 percent.

In all subjects but one there was actually a *drop* in pupil scores from the fifth to the sixth year. Twelve- and 12-½-year-olds know less than eleven- and 11-½-year-olds. As one of the post-finding consultants said, "Their brains fell out during their pre-Bar/Bat Mitzvah year."

- The Jewish Knowledge Inventory results revealed a sharp increase in scores in all subjects by pupils who continued school beyond Bar/Bat Mitzvah and were in their seventh or eighth year of school.

The results of the *Jewish Involvement and Jewish Attitude Inventories* showed that:

- Jewish involvement of pupils is generally passive. It actually decreased from the second to sixth year of school. Jewish attitudes of pupils are generally neutral. The Jewish attitudes also decreased from the second to sixth year of school.
- While pupils, on the whole, did not exhibit high Jewish involvement and positive Jewish attitudes, they did *not* demonstrate *negative Jewish involvement and negative Jewish attitudes*. All responses regarding Jewish involvement and Jewish attitudes were pareve – passive or neutral – and went from

high passive or high neutral to low passive and low neutral, but never to negative levels.

SCHOOL DIFFERENCES

In studying the different school variables, it became clear that school size, ideology, geography and even number of hours of schooling made no difference in pupils' Jewish knowledge, Jewish attitudes and Jewish involvement.

CONCLUSIONS

These findings led to our conclusions that the construct of Jewish supplementary schools seems to have a homogenizing, parevizing effect upon pupils. The average knowledge score is 49 percent!

Jewish involvement is passive! And, Jewish attitudes are neutral!

Schools do a poor job in increasing Jewish knowledge in all subject areas; they show no success in guiding children toward increased Jewish involvement and demonstrate an inability to influence positive growth in Jewish attitudes.

This condition is due to a combination of factors: lack of home involvement and support to Jewish schooling; irrelevant curricular goals; inappropriate school programs; and ineffectual professional personnel, given the needs of pupils *and families* in the 1980s.

Unless Jewish education of the entire family becomes the absolute priority of the synagogue...unless the parents become involved in the Jewish education of their children...unless the program is geared to the needs of families...and unless *all* synagogue personnel are able to relate effectively to pupils *and* their parents, very little or no improvement can take place.

THE FINDINGS IN THE CONTEXT OF GENERAL EDUCATION

While there are major differences between the Jewish supplementary school and the public school, it is instructive to consider these findings and conclusions in light of research in general education.

In 1966, Chicago University Professor James Coleman and associates completed their mammoth study *Equality of Educational Opportunity*, involving some 600,000 people by saying that "schools bring little influence to bear on a child's achievement that is independent of his background and social contacts."

Several years later Christopher Jencks and his associates brought evidence that schools do "not make the kinds and magnitudes of difference which most observers had come to expect" and were not the vehicles of progressive social change, which most people had thought. Other studies have supported the Coleman and Jencks thesis that family background is *the* crucial influence on the effectiveness of schooling.

However, *effective schools research* during the last two decades seems to challenge these conclusions. This accumulation of research studies suggests that there are a variety of correlates of effective schooling. And, family support is only one of them.

A voluntary system of education, like the Jewish supplementary school, must consider for the improvement of the Jewish supplementary school.

1. Transform the thrust of synagogue schools from supplementary schooling for pupils to Jewish family education (including classroom instruction for pupils);
2. Maximize teaching – learning time through a combination of formal and informal education experiences;
3. Provide all Jewish educational professionals with quality training to become effective Jewish family educators and classroom teachers; and
4. Make it possible for educators to make Jewish education a full-time career.

These recommendations suggest the reorganization of the synagogue and the mobilization of the community to provide the necessary support to make the changes possible.

After having presented the findings it is necessary to get all the stakeholders involved in studying the recommendations, refining them, designing strategies for application, developing implementation models, experimenting with these models, validating them, demonstrating how they work, and helping other synagogues replicate them.

Accordingly, BJE initiated the Supplementary Education Action Plan (SEAP) process. Upon the completion of the Study Report and Executive Summary, we devoted this past summer and early fall to the development of a detailed set of guidelines for SEAP to help answer the questions: How should the findings be disseminated to achieve the greatest impact? How can we obtain input from all the stakeholders – lay leaders, parents, rabbis, and educators – most efficiently and effectively? What should be their respective roles in SEAP? How do we select pilot schools? How can we obtain the necessary support from synagogues for experimentation? How can we obtain communal support for the implementation of the recommendations?

The process of disseminating the findings and obtaining input from all stakeholders began in July.

By mid-December, some 30 meetings and consultations – two to four hours each – will have been held with UJA-Federation lay and professional leadership, lay and professional leaders of the regional Conservative, Orthodox and Reform synagogual bodies, synagogue presidents, school board chairpersons, rabbis and principals of almost all Jewish supplementary schools in Greater New York. These meetings will be followed up by further consultations in order to respond to specific questions and suggestions arising from the earlier meetings.

The rest of the process includes the completion of a design for experimentation to involve up to twelve pilot schools during the 1988–89 school year.

During the 1988–89 school year each of the pilot schools will develop its own model family education program under BJE's guidance.

Simultaneous with this development BJE will plan strategies for training and retraining Jewish educational professionals with the rabbinical seminaries (Hebrew Union College-Jewish Institute of Religion, Jewish Theological Seminary and Yeshiva University), with UJA-Federation, and with the ideological groups. And, we will work with UJA-Federation and individual synagogues to enhance career opportunities for Jewish educators.

In September 1989, the following year, the experimental models will be operative. Formative and summative evaluations will be made during the 1989–1990 school year and during the following two years.

By 1991, we hope that we will be able to demonstrate the new family education models and be able to observe the effects of the professional training programs on the new family focus of synagogue education.

Will the synagogue school be able to respond effectively to the Jewish educational needs of our children and families in the 1990s and beyond? The answer to this question lies in our collective hands.

CHAPTER 5

THE JEWISH FAMILY AND THE JEWISH SCHOOL

The Jewish family and the Jewish school have much in common. Both are primary institutions of Jewish life, both are crucial to the perpetuation of Judaism and the continuity of the Jewish people, and both have been endowed with sanctity. The Jewish family has a special place within the structure of Jewish law, which defines familial relationships from birth to death. The study of Torah – a cardinal principle of the Jewish faith – is not only a means to religious and ethical behavior, but is in itself a mode of worship.

If there are reasons for the mysterious ability of Jews to survive against so many odds, they are the Jewish family and the Jewish school. More than any other people, Jews have always valued the life-sustaining roles of the family and the school. Indeed, the Archbishop of York, in calling for Christian-Jewish cooperation recently stated, "We can learn from the Jews about education, about the richness of their home life and the enormous influence it had upon their people." Now both the Jewish family and Jewish school are in crisis, besieged by problems that endanger their very existence.

There is an indispensable relationship between the Jewish family and the Jewish school. In Jewish tradition, the primary responsibility for Jewish education lies in the home. Parents are responsible for the education of their offspring; *"v'sheenantam Livanecha"* ("And you shall teach your children") is a literal commandment.

In biblical times, and later in the post-biblical period, elementary level instruction was in the hands of the parents, particularly the father. In the second century C.E., Rabbi Akiva counseled one of his disciples: "When you teach your son, teach him out of a well-corrected book," (*Pesahim 112a*), suggesting that the father has the awesome responsibility to teach his offspring properly. When teachers were hired to help parents acquit themselves of this responsibility, the teachers were considered as parents. "He who teaches his friend's son – it is as if he gave birth to him" (*Kiddushin 29a*). Even after the school became a recognized institution in the post-Talmudic era, parents continued to teach their children. The home was the natural place for religious and moral training.

Jewish tradition was ahead of its time in ascribing an educational role to parents. To be sure, the school has become a necessary component of every civilized society and a dominant factor in the technological, industrial, and cultural progress of the modern world. However, this fact does not discharge the home of its basic tutorial obligations in the area of subculture and ethics.

In Colonial America, the Commonwealth of Massachusetts (the standard-bearer for all levels of general education in the United States) ordered families to "teach their children – so much learning as may enable them to speak the English tongue and have knowledge of the Capital law." Home instruction was mandated in order to prepare children properly for the formal school experience. This 17th century, western hemisphere, communal requirement echoes a Judaic tenet: "When a child begins to speak, his father is expected to speak to him in the holy tongue and teach him Torah" (*Midrash Sifre, Parshat Ekev, 46*). Before a child was exposed to formal schooling, his father was required to initiate his son into the world of Jewish learning and worship.

Modern research clearly demonstrates the need for the home as an educational instrumentality. Indeed, we cannot deal with students without due regard to their family background since school is, at best, a reinforcer of attitudes, behavior patterns, and even skills acquired in the home environment. In the most comprehensive analysis of American schools ever implemented, James Coleman and his associates concluded (in 1966) that unless unfavorable home environments were changed across the United States, nothing the school could do would have any effect on how much the children learned.

Similarly, in analyzing data relating to the elements that lead to an effective educational experience in school, David Cohen of Harvard University emphasizes, "Daily contact with family and peer group society is the most crucial influence on educational attainment and eventual adult behavior..." Schooling alone cannot compensate for the deficit of a culturally deprived home. This is demonstrated by the fact that "None of the billions spent on compensatory education seems to have improved achievement beyond what would have occurred in any event."

These findings are all the more significant for religious schooling. The role of the home in contributing to the success of Catholic education, for example, was underscored by the findings of the national study of Catholic schools in America about a decade and a half ago. The researchers in that study found that Catholic education was only able to impact students who came from very religious homes. Catholic schools by themselves had almost no telling effect on the other children.

For children who do not have the benefit of a Jewish family background, it is absolutely necessary to develop alternative environments. Indeed, the major advantage of a day school over a supplementary school, particularly for these children, is its whole day format. The day school provides the opportunity for children to spend significant amounts of time in an alternative environment each day, totally immersed in a Jewish setting. Jewish residence camping has a similar advantage. A recent study indicates that a Jewish camp experience has significant influence upon the eventual Jewish lifestyle of Jewish children because it provides a total Jewish environment for extended periods of time.

It behooves Jewish educational leaders to develop extensive formal and informal settings in which one could concentrate on the affective domain when dealing with pupils from marginally Jewish or non-committed Jewish backgrounds.

Simultaneous with the attempt to create alternative environments within the framework of the Jewish school – during school time and leisure time – it is absolutely necessary to impact the homes of the children. In general education there was a period of time when educators recommended that parents keep a distance from the school. "The latest secret weapon in the fight against school failure," the former education editor of the New York Times recently wrote, "is called parents. After years of being told to stay out of the teacher's way, mother and father are being invited, urged, even begged to come back in." While there are questions about just how parents should be incorporated in the school program, there is wide agreement that it is absolutely necessary for parents to play a more vital role in helping reinforce that which children learn in school. What is true for general education is even more so for the Jewish school.

In Jewish education, the problem is that the children who need the most reinforcing have parents, who are least able to help them. This thrusts upon the schools the task of educating parents to become partners in the day-to-day instruction in our schools. Without the home as helper and parents as partners, the chances for long-range effect of Jewish schooling are very, very minimal. To be sure, the reinforcing combination of a good Jewish home and a good school experience is the single most effective guarantor of Jewish continuity.

Over the years, individual schools and ideological groups have made serious attempts to reach and teach parents, the results of these programs have been extremely modest. Needed is a new array of strategies through which the synagogue and school can implement Jewish home education for all parents as a primary objective.

Implementing parent education programs requires great resourcefulness, great patience, and much time. To this task the lay, educational, and rabbinic leaders of our synagogues and schools must commit themselves if we are to reverse the trend of disaffection and alienation of young Jews. But first, teachers, principals, and rabbis will have to be trained to assume these vital instructional roles.

An essential aspect of home environment is the commitment of both parents to Jewish living and Jewish education. If one of the parents is not Jewishly oriented, the possibilities for creating the necessary family climate and support for Jewish schooling are practically nil. This underscores the critical need for developing strategies to reach the disinterested parent whose influence on the prospective effectiveness of Jewish education is bound to be deleterious. Without special attention to the total home environment, our school efforts toward achieving Jewish continuity are doomed to failure.

In developing ways of impacting the home, the *havurah* model should be seriously considered. Retreats and study groups led by parents themselves might parallel the school experience. Family retreats should be considered for their potential influence upon the total family unit. The single parent family must also not be overlooked in the process.

In sum, it is abundantly clear that the modern Jewish family needs the Jewish school for its own perpetuation. And the Jewish school needs the Jewish family in order to be able to fulfill its lofty purpose. This interdependence has been a pillar of the Jewish past. It is now a *sine qua non* for the Jewish future.

RETURN TO THE FAMILY ROOTS

The role of the family in Jewish schooling can be enhanced by involving the family in the educational process through a cooperative, inter-generational program of discovering roots. The tracing of roots is in good Jewish tradition. The Bible often notes the parentage of the personalities of the biblical period. The purity of lineage was of utmost importance to our forebears.

Tracing roots can play an equally important role in our own times, especially through the Jewish school. It can be most useful in helping our children achieve knowledge of and pride in their ancestry.

Tracing geneology can be a valuable instructional strategy.

1. It personalizes the Jewish educational experience as it strengthens the family relationship of the learner with his Jewish studies.
2. It involves a variety of people from the child's immediate family in meaningful and interesting activity.
3. It gives the learner a sense of history as it bridges the generations and uncovers more and more generations of family members.
4. It helps pupils understand the geographic relationship between themselves and the countries of origin of their parents, grandparents, or great grandparents.
5. It develops a feeling of peoplehood as it broadens and deepens the sense of family.

CHAPTER 6

THE JEWISH FAMILY IN SOCIO-EDUCATIONAL PERSPECTIVE

Getting to this point in the history of the Board of Jewish Education of Greater New York, an academic conference on Jewish family education is like giving birth after a 10- or 11-month pregnancy. It's long overdue, particularly from the vantage point of those who toil daily in the vineyards of Jewish supplementary schooling.

This conference is especially significant in light of findings and conclusions of our three-year-long comprehensive study of the Jewish supplementary school. The Study findings underscore the appropriateness of the title of our conference "Integrating Home, School and Congregation." It is therefore, meaningful to initiate our proceedings by viewing the Jewish family from a socio-educational perspective.

To set the stage for our deliberations, my presentation is based upon the premise of the potential reversibility of a cause and effect phenomenon. This assumption posits that, currently, the Jewish family significantly impacts the quality of Jewish schooling. Conversely, the Jewish school can have a significant impact upon the Jewish home.

In considering the Jewish family from a socio-educational perspective – more particularly from a *Jewish* socio-educational viewpoint – we must focus on two interrelated challenges.

On the one hand, we worry about the viability of the Jewish family and agonize over the factors that contribute to its ability to endure and to thrive. On the other hand, we are concerned about the relationship of the Jewish family to Jewish continuity. How can we guarantee that the Jewish family will contribute to the survival of the Jewish people and to the enhancement of Jewish life?

Jewish education has a vital role regarding both of these challenges. In the Jewish world, as in the larger society, the term "education" is a code word that signifies a process of schooling, which involves children and youth. In bringing up our children Jewishly, there is one essential dimension of their training, which goes beyond the four walls of the school and classroom that is necessary to insure their eventual Jewish behavior. Simply stated, this dimension – *a conditione sine qua non* – without which Jewish education cannot be effective is: children need (children must have) imitable adult models – particularly in their immediate environment.

The environmental impact upon children – upon their identity formation, their childhood behavior patterns, their learning styles and their eventual adult behavior – comes from three sources: the family, the school and society.

When the influences from all three sources are in congruence, children grow up according to the confluence or combination of these influences. When they are in conflict – when the influences contradict each other – then children will behave according to the stronger impact upon them. It is obvious that *family* and *society* are generally more powerful influences on children than the school. Moreover, it is abundantly clear that the influences of our current society are not helpful in achieving *Jewish* behavioral objectives. Therefore, the more the goals of the home and school are similar, the more likely their combined influence will prevail over the counter-influence of society on their Jewish attitudes and behavior.

In today's American culture, family life is much different than it was in the early 1900s, much different than it was in the mid-1900s and even in the 1960s and 1970s. Modern urban industrial life has taken its toll on the traditional family eroding its moral and economic centrality. Family pathology statistics have soared, initiated by stressful marital relations and shallow family lives.

The impact of society upon the average Jewish family is not much different than its influence upon the non-Jewish home. We have more single parents than ever before, more "latch-key" children, more unwed mothers, more teenage mothers, more grandparents bringing up children, more blended families (by-products of divorce and remarriage), more intermarried spouses and more homes with two working parents.

Children of the 1980s have more freedom and are exposed to less adult authority figures in the home than ever before. Once upon a time, adults were adults and children were children, and parents said "no."

It has now come to the point where one hears, as did the 1,100 nursery and kindergarten teachers and directors at the annual New York BJE Early Childhood Conference several weeks ago, about the mother who said to her teen-age daughter as she was going out with friends to an ice cream parlour, "Have a good time." The daughter snapped back, "Don't tell me what to do." Indeed, times have changed regarding parent-child relationships.

And, we are all beginning to see the results of the impact of our technological age. Sadie Hofstein, executive director of the Nassau Mental Health Association, who told us this story about the teenager, recounted that recently a group of children was asked to draw pictures of fish. Some of them drew rectangular boxes because the only kind of fish they ever saw was frozen fish.

Just think of the other ways that our technological age has affected our childrens' perception of reality. Consider the influence of TV. Upon graduation from high school, the average American teenager will have spent many more hours in front of the tube than in school.

Add up all the influences of our modern, value-free, open,

technologically sophisticated society upon our children – and American Jews, like all other Americans, are faced with a challenge of huge proportions. But, the most critical challenge we face as a Jewish community results from the changes in Jewish living styles, best described by the descriptive: we are a "many more generation."

- Today – more Jews are eating *glatt* kosher; many more are not eating kosher at all.
- More Jews drink *halav yisrael*; many more imbibe other kinds of beverages to excess.
- More Jews pray every day – three times a day; many more do not pray at all.
- More Jews make *kiddush* on Friday night; many more do not observe Sabbath at all.
- More Jews study Talmud – *Daf yomi* – every day; many more have no relationship to Jewish learning at all – never read a Jewish book.

The "many-more" phenomenon is the reason that the Jewish family is the object of much concern and deliberation in the Jewish community. Demographers call this phenomenon "sociological death," affected by the growing rates of intermarriage, apostasy and assimilation.

The effect of this phenomenon upon our children is very substantial. It constitutes a major reason for the failure of the Jewish supplementary school to transmit effectively Jewish knowledge and values to our children. Missing is the linkage of parents to our schools and schools to parents. Lacking is the Jewish home environment, which nurtures an appreciation for Jewish schooling and reinforces the values taught in school. When the family, which, according to Eric Erickson is the "primary nurturer" of children's *weltanshauung*, is not supportive of their schooling, that schooling is in deep trouble.

We are well aware that research in general education, particularly the studies of James Coleman, Christopher Jencks and

David Cohen in the 1960s, clearly underscore the role of the family in influencing the educational achievement potential of pupils. In their national study of Catholic education, Andrew Greeley and Peter Rossi have amply demonstrated that Catholic schools only impact on those students who come from Catholic observant homes.

The thesis emanating from these findings is that the home is the overriding factor in assuring quality Jewish education for our pupils – in both cognitive and affective terms. Thus, it seems that since identity formation essentially takes place in the home – the school, at best, is a reinforcer of attitudes and values acquired in the family setting.

Countering this thesis, Effective Schools Research, conducted mainly in the 1970s and early 1980s, gives only token recognition to the role of home-school relations. This body of research suggests that, notwithstanding lack of support from the home, a variety of school-based factors can guarantee successful school outcomes. These factors include a clear focus and a clearly defined curriculum, strong administrative and instructional leadership, a positive school climate, high expectations for pupil growth by principal and teachers, sufficient student time-on-task and careful monitoring of pupil progress. This antithesis thus posits that despite the extent or lack of home support, education in the classroom can be effective.

This thesis-antithesis juxtaposition presents a dilemma regarding the parental role in schooling. Benjamin Bloom, in his 1985 research on outstanding achievers, resolves the dilemma by providing the synthesis. He found that two features were common to highly successful performers. The first is strong, unqualified parental support to the point of personal sacrifice for the education of children. The second is quality time-on-task in and out of school.

The implication of this synthesis for Jewish schools is self-evident. To succeed, Jewish education must be a synergistic experience. Teacher effectiveness depends upon parental support, and parental effectiveness depends upon teacher ability and skill. This mutuality finds resonance in Benjamin Bloom's research.

In a voluntary setting, like Jewish education, this synergistic relationship between home and school is absolutely critical. BJE's recent study of Jewish supplementary schools in Greater New York, which I was privileged to direct, demonstrates the absolute need of Jewish family background and support for Jewish schooling, if that education is to be effective. Moreover, the findings of this study also show how vital is the instructional setting.

A major challenge in Jewish education is reaching and teaching parents who do not fully associate themselves with the goals of their children's schools. In one sense, these parents are a captive audience. Yet, they are hard to reach and even more difficult to teach. For the children of such families, the Talmudic interpretation of the teacher role in terms of *ke'ilu y'lado* – whereby the teachers are considered like parents – is not sufficient.

However, the teacher in *loco parentis* simply cannot guarantee that the school influence will have a lasting effect unless parents are able to reinforce this influence. In Jewish education, this requires that parents have Jewish knowledge, be living examples of Jewish values and be strongly supportive of their childrens' Jewish schooling. That is what (in tractate *Kiddushin*) requires parents to be life-long learners of Torah. The Bible, Talmudic and rabbinic writings are replete with exhortations about the obligation of parents to teach their children, including statements such as, "and you shall tell your son about the exodus," "and you shall teach God's Commandments to your children." Only if parents are unable to discharge this primary responsibility may it be delegated, in part, to others. However, parents are never freed entirely from this obligation.

Parenthetically, it is interesting to note that the most recent evidence from Effective Schools Research and evaluations of Head Start and other early childhood programs clearly indicate that intensive parental involvement with their children's school work is highly correlated to student success.

The problem today is that the children who are most in need of parental tutelage and reinforcement usually have parents who are least able to help them. This challenge thrusts upon the school the task of educating parents to become partners in the day-to-day education of their children – a phenomenon that is now not only acceptable but desirable in school systems throughout the country. This then becomes the synagogue's new educational role as it changes its thrust from Jewish schooling for children *only* to Jewish education for the entire family, including children and adults alike.

The new child-family focus means restructuring synagogue involvement in Jewish education whereby the rabbi, principal, teachers, cantor, and youth leaders work as family educator teams. In practice, each of them would become a Jewish family educator, instructing children in classroom settings, leading informal educational groups, working with family members in their homes and providing individualized tutelage and Jewish family counseling, as needed, to parents and children alike. It means making available full-time career opportunities – at least one in each school – via which a teacher or principal would be involved in a variety of interrelated responsibilities: formal instruction, integration of formal and informal educational activities, Jewish family outreach and the development of appropriate programs and curricular materials.

It means creating partnerships with social workers and Center workers in responding to Jewish family needs.

Initiating Jewish family education programs will not be easy. It will stretch our imagination and pocketbook and try our patience. Planning and implementation will be a long process. It cannot be done at once for all schools. We will need to experiment with a variety of models in order to develop the most effective approaches. In all, it is very challenging. It can be very exciting and extremely rewarding.

According to Jewish tradition, the school is an agent of the parents. For many schools this translates into the challenge of teaching a growing number of parents what the substance and goals of this "agent" are. But what it really means is Jewish parent empowerment that can lead to pupil empowerment and enduring Jewish education and enhanced Jewish living for Jewish families.

CHAPTER 7

TRENDS AND CHALLENGES IN JEWISH FAMILY EDUCATION

A TRADITIONAL CONCEPT

Jewish education involving parents and adult family members is an idea as old as the Jewish people. In Judaic tradition, life-long learning – Torah study, as broadly defined – has been a critical dimension of Jewish life, particularly for men (Talmud, *Peah* 12; *Yoma* 35a; *Rosh Hashannah* 18a; Maimonides, *Mishneh Torah* 1:10). Moreover, the role of the home in education is paramount (*Pirkei Avot*, 1:4). An adult man engrossed in the study of Talmud during an evening or Shabbat afternoon in his home was a common scene in the Eastern European *shtetl*, as was the practice of fathers reviewing the weekly Torah portion with their sons. Mothers and daughters were involved in Jewish family education through the home rituals and activities in which they engaged.

Judaic learning was considered so important that it was elevated to the level of prayer by the sages of the Talmud. Indeed, the prayer book contains numerous sections from the Bible and Talmud for which the reader merits the mitzvah of study as well as prayer when reciting them. The *Kaddish d'Rabbanan* was formulated specifically to follow a study portion of the prayers (Maimonides, *Nusah Ha-Kaddish*). A prime example of the interlacing of study with prayer is the inclusion of *Pirkei Avot* (Ethics of the Fathers) in the traditional prayer book. Incorporated into the liturgy in the 9th century, *Pirkei Avot* achieved a prominent place in the prayer book of Amram Gaon. Group Torah study in the Synagogue, after daily morning and Shabbat *minhah* services, is still a common practice in almost all traditional synagogues. Moreover, daily learning, particularly the *Daf Yomi* – the study of a page of the Talmud each day, instituted in Lublin, Poland by Rabbi Meir Shapiro in 1923 – is a regular occurrence in many segments of the Orthodox community.

When speaking about Jewish family education two decades ago, even to Jewish educators, my words, by and large, fell on deaf ears. Only a few educators and fewer lay leaders considered this subject worthy of serious deliberation. Now, Jewish family education is generating a great deal of excitement and interest. What has led to this avalanche of interest by the Jewish community? The answer to this question requires a retrospective look. In reality, involving Jewish parents in Jewish life and Jewish school activities and offering parent education programs are not entirely new subjects on the Jewish educational agenda. What is new is the universality of interest and the urgency and intensity with which Jewish family education is now being considered.

AMERICAN HISTORICAL PERSPECTIVE

On a formal community-wide level in the United States, the earliest Jewish family education effort was sponsored by the Bureau of Jewish Education of New York in the early 1900s (Winter). At that time, the goal of family education was a combination of Jewish acculturation and Americanization. In 1927, Samson Benderly, director of the Bureau, inaugurated the Jewish Home Institute, a correspondence course for mothers of young children. Lacking sufficient funds, this creative project was abandoned soon after its initiation (Winter).

Since then, parental involvement in Jewish education has taken many different forms. For example, from the 1930s to the 1950s, emulating practices of the public school (which until recently, with the exception of isolated individual and group efforts, discouraged parental involvement), participation of parents in Jewish schooling was often in the nature of PTA activity. Parent involvement was expressed not by actual learning, but through service to the school, such as serving refreshments to children, providing financial support to schools by purchasing needed equipment and providing scholarship aid.

After World War II, following the lead of American education, many Jewish early childhood educators began working with parents as part of their educational activity. As a rule, Jewish early child educators consider parent education a significant part of their instructional work.

As the modern synagogue grew in membership, adult education programs were organized by individual synagogues. These generally included courses in Hebrew reading, Hebrew language, Jewish history, Bible and prayer, as well as lecture series by prominent leaders and scholars. In both these courses and lecture series, only the highly motivated synagogue members participated with regularity. Both types of programs continue to be sponsored by synagogues and synagogue schools.

Each major ideological movement has developed its own form of parent education. The Union of American Hebrew Congregations of the Reform movement has had a longstanding interest in adult Jewish education, which has been expressed over the years in a wide variety of policy statements on the importance of lifelong learning and through the publishing of books on the Bible and Jewish history (Segal; Manuel Gold, personal communication, 1990).

In 1970, the United Synagogue Commission on Jewish Education initiated the Parent Education Program (PEP), a program for parents of students in the first grade of afternoon Conservative schools. It had three basic elements: subject matter correlative with the religious school curriculum, with special emphasis on issues relating to parent-child relationships; the uniqueness and direction of parenthood as understood in Jewish tradition; and general Jewish knowledge and skills. An ambitious endeavor, PEP required parents to study a minimum of 2-½ hours each school week. Soon after the beginning of PEP, the United Synagogue launched the Family *Kallot* program. Each *Kallah* was designed to provide intensive Jewish living experiences for parents *and* children as family units over a period of 5 days at Camp Ramah in Pennsylvania.

By the fall of 1978, three different study programs had been developed – PEP I for parents of elementary schoolchildren on formal subject matter, PEP II for parents of adolescents on societal problems involving teenaged youth, and PEP III for pre-nursery and nursery school parents offering guidance on Jewish family living. In 1985, the PEP program was reconstituted as the Family Education Program. Although it has shown positive results in the participating synagogues, PEP never achieved wide popularity (Hyman Campeas, personal communication, 1990).

In 1949, the Community Services Division of Yeshiva University launched YUDAE, a program aimed at bringing Jewish learning to adults through their Orthodox synagogues. A unique feature of the program was its credit-bearing coursework that led to a university certificate upon completion. At its peak in the 1960s, several thousand adults in the United States and Canada were enrolled in YUDAE.

In another vein, Yeshiva University organized Torah Tours in 1962. The purpose of this program has been to reach out to the more isolated communities and to strengthen the synagogue through family *Shabbatonim* for adults and children, separately and together. At these retreats participants use creative group techniques to plan and develop the activities themselves.

Staffed by Yeshiva University students, Torah Tours reaches some 30 communities throughout the United States (Mordechai Schnaidman, personal communication, 1990).

In the area of all day Jewish education, Torah Umesorah, The National Society for Hebrew Day Schools, launched an ambitious parent education program in Metropolitan New York in the 1950s involving hundreds of parents each week in serious coursework in Judaic studies. Currently, it is co-sponsored by the National Council of Young Israel as an adult education lecture series. For over two decades, beginning in 1950, Torah Umesorah's National Association of Hebrew Day School PTAS published *The Jewish Parent*, a magazine for families of yeshiva students. This publication served to inform its readership about various aspects of the Jewish day school and to strengthen ties to the day school movement (Joshua Fishman, personal communication, 1990).

In the late 1970s there developed a new interest in Jewish education for adults and families. In many communities, pre-breakfast and lunch-and-learn sessions were organized in professional offices and communal agencies. Among other indicators of the growing interest in this area was the mini-conference on Jewish family education sponsored in 1980 by the Conference of Alternatives in Jewish Education. At that conference, which convened several of the pioneers in the field, six categories of Jewish family education were delineated: celebration and observance, workshops, *sedarim*, joint learning, ongoing learning experiences, and extended time programs.

During the 1970s and 1980s, a variety of creative education efforts for children and the Jewish family were launched in communities throughout the United States. In Baltimore, for example, the *Home Start/Behrman House* project by Dr. Hyman Chanover; in Cambridge, Massachusetts, the Harvard-Hillel School by Sherry Kohler Fox; in Detroit, the hands-on Jewish Experiences for Families and other activities; in New York, the Parent and Children for Education synagogue-based program by Joan Kaye, and the *Mishpacha* program by the Early Childhood Education and Outreach departments of the Board of Jewish Education; in Los Angeles, the creative holiday materials, research and advocacy activities by Dr. Ronald Wolfson; and in Washington, the Jewish Discovery Room for hands-on activity by the Board of Jewish Education. By the end of the 1980s, most Jewish communities could point to some Jewish family education activity in their locales.

REASONS FOR UPSURGE OF INTEREST IN FAMILY EDUCATION

Two factors fuel the current interest in and development of Jewish family education programs. First is the increasing awareness of the growing bipolar state of Jewish behavior. A minority of the Jewish community is involved intensively in Jewish schooling, whereas increasingly larger numbers of Jews demonstrate little or no interest in Jewish life for themselves or for their children. This latter group – comprising, by far, the vast majority of American Jewry – is the product of the acculturation/deculturation syndrome of Jewish life as Jews became integrated comfortably into American society.

Jewish communal leadership now feels the urgent need to find ways to address the Jewish needs of alienated and marginally affiliated Jews and to involve them in the Jewish community. One way of doing this is through Jewish family education.

The second reason for the upsurge of interest in Jewish family education is the BJE of Greater New York's 1988 landmark study of the Jewish supplementary school, *Jewish Supplementary Schooling: An Educational System in Need of Change*. The findings and conclusions of this comprehensive 3-year effort, which used both normative survey and scientific measurement techniques, confirmed the worst fears of lay and professional leaders in Jewish education. Supplementary school is, with very few exceptions, not an effective instrumentality for the transmission of Jewish knowledge and values. The fact that 70% of the Jewish school enrollment is found in congregational schools makes attention to these findings all the more urgent.

A major reason for the non-effectiveness of the Jewish supplementary school is the lack of Jewish home environment and family support for Jewish schooling. The overwhelming majority of parents of Jewish supplementary school pupils have very little knowledge of Judaism and are very marginally affiliated with organized Jewish life. They enroll their children in the synagogue school solely for Bar/Bat Mitzvah preparation. They are unsure of what they want or should expect from the school and provide little or no support, encouragement, or reinforcement at home. Moreover, most parents feel that they have neither the time nor the desire to become involved in the school or the synagogue.

These findings remind us of George Bernard Shaw's biting comment, "There might be some doubt as to who are the best people to have charge of children; but there can be no doubt that parents are the worst." Just ponder this statement vis-a-vis Jewish upbringing.

The BJE study concludes that, unless Jewish education of the entire family becomes the absolute priority of the synagogue, unless the parents become more involved in the Jewish education of their children, unless the school program is geared to the needs of families, and unless all synagogue personnel are able to relate effectively to pupils and their parents, very little or no improvement in Jewish supplementary education can take place.

The wide dissemination of the BJE study findings, conclusions, and recommendations has had a major impact on the Jewish educational community: the hiring by growing numbers of synagogues and communities of Jewish family educators, the intensification of extant Jewish family education programs, the launching of major communal and regional conferences on Jewish family education, the initial efforts by some synagogues to reorganize their program thrust and retool for Jewish family education, and the strengthening of the role and influence of the handful of Jewish educators who have been laboring with dedication in the vineyards of Jewish family education.

Over the past few years, a variety of national, regional, and local conferences on Jewish family education have taken place. The 2-day conference sponsored by the Principals Service/Resource Center of BJE of Greater New York at Columbia University in 1989 might serve as a model for bureau-based Jewish family education meetings (Schiff, 1989). A key element of this conference was the composition of the participants. It included all the stakeholders in Jewish family education – rabbis, principals, teachers, youth leaders, parents, and synagogue and communal lay leaders.

EVERYONE IS DOING JEWISH FAMILY EDUCATION

The universality of Jewish family education (JFE) is a trend in itself. The list of sponsors of JFE programs in North America reads like an encyclopedia of Jewish organizations. It includes central agencies for Jewish education, family service agencies, synagogues, congregational schools, Jewish day schools, independent early childhood programs, Jewish community centers, federations, Jewish community relations councils, Jewish museums, schools of higher Jewish learning, national Jewish organizations and their local chapters, fraternal groups, ideological commissions of education, human relations agencies, and Zionist organizations. In addition, there are many instances of interagency collaboration and co-sponsorship of Jewish family education programs.

Among the variety of sponsoring groups, it is clear that the synagogue is the primary agency for Jewish family education. The case for congregationally based Jewish family education can easily be made because synagogues most readily possess the combination of factors needed for Jewish family education to succeed. Synagogues can reach the largest number of families. They were established, in the first instance, to serve families. The three Hebrew terms used interchangeably for the word "synagogue" clearly convey this point: *bet knesset* (house of assembly), *bet tefillah* (house of prayer), and *bet midrash* (house of study). As a multifunctional agency, the basic synagogue structure lends itself to providing Jewish family education services for its members. Moreover, it has the staff for effective Jewish family education. Accordingly, the recommendations of the BJE of Greater New York Study emphasize the importance of the team approach to Jewish family education involving all synagogue professionals – the rabbi, assistant rabbi, school principal, cantor, teachers, youth leaders, and parent and lay volunteers.

TYPES OF JEWISH FAMILY EDUCATION

Not all the activities promoted as Jewish family education by the various organizations are really Jewish family education. Some programs are planned carefully to include children and parents.

Others are hip-pocket efforts. Some are developed out of the conviction of the absolute need for and value of Jewish family education; others are sponsored because "it's the thing to do" at this time. Some are programs involving the whole family; others are purely adult education activities. Some place great stress on the Jewish aspects of home life: others are family life education programs with little or no attention to the Jewish component of Jewish family living.

An analysis of over 100 projects publicized as Jewish family education demonstrates that there are essentially eight types of programs.

1. *parallel education programs* in which parents meet regularly, or occasionally, to study the same subjects and texts that their children are studying in school
2. *shared experiences* for parents and children in an institutional setting, generally centering around Shabbat and holidays, that lend themselves to hands-on activities
3. *family learning experiences* through actual celebration or observance of Shabbat, holidays, or special events
4. *projects and/or materials* about the Jewish family for home study or work by parents and children
5. *education for parents*: seminars, lectures, workshops, or discussion groups about Jewish themes
6. *guidance* concerning family life to individual parents and to couples
7. *community-wide events* for families, including Shabbat and festival meals, sedarim, and special events, such as Yom Ha'atzmaut and Yom Hashoah
8. *retreats and weekend Shabbatonim* or week-long camp experiences for families

The most popular of these activities are education for parents, (particularly formal lectures), individual parental guidance, and shared experiences in institutional settings, usually hands-on activity about Jewish holidays and the Jewish life cycle. Do-it-yourself projects at home and museum activities are being promoted with more regularity. Gaining in popularity are retreats and camp programs for families. Retreats are expensive and depend upon the availability of significant funding. In this regard, it must be noted that Israel experiences for families are not yet a serious consideration for most organizations because of their expense and time-consuming nature.

In view of the current variety of programs, the question emerges: which of these programs are the best or most effective? The answer, of course, must be "all of them," if they respond effectively to particular needs. Although some may be effective in producing specific results, the programs' effectiveness must be evaluated in terms of how they enhance the Jewish living of the families involved. Again, the answer depends on the participants' needs and the nature of their communities.

It is abundantly clear that much more well-planned experimentation with Jewish family education must take place before considering which approaches should be disseminated or emulated as most effective.

JFE NEEDS AND CHALLENGES

Any discussion on Jewish family education is incomplete without attention to the needs and challenges facing it. Five needs require immediate responses:

1. The need to plan programs for single parents, a growing segment of our community.
2. The need to address two critical target populations more aggressively
    a. young parents and their preschool children, as done by *Mishpacha* programs successfully piloted by the BJE of Greater New York and sponsored also by several other agencies.
    b. pre-Bar/Bat Mitzvah youth and their parents via organized study experiences and self-study materials. An example of appropriate materials *is Coming of Age as A*

Jew (Glatzer), the two-volume Bar/Bat Mitzvah manual and workbook for parents and children recently published by the Board of Jewish Education of Greater New York.
3. The need to harness modern technology – the videotape and computer – for family home study and activity by making available extant software, new software, arranging the materials in sequential order for home use, and developing guidelines for families.
4. The need to develop training programs for Jewish family educators, such as the colloquium, "Educating the Jewish Family Educator," presented by the BJE of Greater New York in 1990, which included these components:
   - understanding the Jewish needs of marginal Jewish families
   - ways of conceptualizing change in Jewish family life
   - establishing the basic knowledge needs of Jewish family educators regarding Judaism and educational practice
   - exploring models of professional training
   - learning how teams of specialists can work together most effectively
   - learning how to develop JFE materials
   - developing evaluation techniques for Jewish family education
5. The need, given the plethora of Jewish family education efforts currently taking place, to define the elements of effective Jewish family education (Jewish family education means so many different things to different people), establish criteria for determining effectiveness, develop procedures for evaluation, and evaluate the effectiveness of current program prototypes.

The final need stated above will help guide the future development of JFE efforts. As such, it takes precedence over all others.

Jewish family education faces a number of administrative and institutional challenges. The first is restructuring synagogues so that the emphasis of the congregational school is on education of the entire family – including the child – instead of schooling for the child only. This requires that all synagogue personnel be organized into JFE teams.

The second challenge is integrating formal and informal education programs, creating the necessary confluence of the cognitive and affective domains. The artificial division between formal and informal instructional activities reduces the potential effectiveness of the education process.

Defining, empowering, and supporting the role of Jewish family educators are crucial to the success of any JFE enterprise. Support presupposes the provision of full-time career opportunities for at least one Jewish family educator in each synagogue.

Developing strategies to empower parents to teach, guide, and provide support to their children is a critical dimension of each family education effort if that effort is to take permanent root in the home life of the family members and is to help the children succeed in the synagogue and school. Parents must become involved in planning these strategies and all programs involving families. In doing so, they become vested in the programs and in Jewish life activities.

Finally, a major challenge is the development in each community of the means to sponsor Israel experiences. Well-planned total immersion programs in the Jewish State have had a remarkable influence upon Jews of all ages. As such, we must exploit Israel as an educational resource for families.

In sum, the Jewish community, spearheaded by the pioneering programs developed by forward-looking Jewish educators, has entered a new era of Jewish education. Since this phase of Jewish schooling emphasizes the education of the whole family it augurs well, both for the future of the Jewish education enterprise and for the Jewish community.

CHAPTER 8

ON INITIATING A PROCESS FOR JEWISH FAMILY EDUCATOR TRAINING

"There are three partners in (the creation of) a person – the Holy One blessed be He, and his father and his mother" (*Niddah*, 31a).

The threefold partnership mentioned in this Talmudic statement does not only refer to the birth of a baby. The term *ba'adam* literally, "in a person," suggests that the partnership goes much beyond the instance of birth. Indeed, the Hebrew word for parent, *horeh*, is derived from the same root as teacher, *moreh*. Parent and teacher are one and the same in the home. Thus, Jewish tradition long ago recognized the overriding influence of parents on the maturation of their children from infant to "person" – *adam*. According to the sages of the Talmud, the partnership between God and the parent relates directly to the spirit and content of that maturation.

About two decades ago, we were informed by research in general education that school, at best, is a reinforcer of attitudes, behavior patterns and even skills acquired earlier in the home.

This condition brings us together today. Adding significance to our meeting is the two-page *New York Times* article whose subtitle is, "The Home's Link to School Success – A Special Report."

The essence of the report is contained in the opening sentence of the front-page article, dated June 13, New Haven, the home of Yale University: "For more than 20 years in this city of scholars and elms, school children and their parents have been studying a basic axiom: students in troubled schools learn better when families and educators work together." The essay notes that when concern about academic performance and a child's social and psychological growth are entwined, "the child feels better about himself and learns more." The Yale research process turns on a seemingly simple insight: "that a child's home life affects his performance in school, and that, if schools pay attention to all the influences on a child, most problems can be solved before they get out of control" – shades of the James Coleman, Christopher Jencks and David Cohen studies in the 1960s.

While the Yale University school population is generally underprivileged, as were the populations of the Coleman, Jencks and Cohen research, the study has important implications for Jewish supplementary education, where the population is, by and large, Jewishly disadvantaged. I believe we can easily make the leap from economically underprivileged, i.e., the urban poor, to Jewish underprivileged, i.e., the suburban marginally affiliated or under-affiliated Jewish families. The landmark three-year study conducted by the Board of Jewish Education of Greater New York, from 1984 to 1987, recommends exactly what Dr. James P. Corner of Yale suggests as a result of his research: Teach the whole child as part of his family and, in the process, relate to all the family members, particularly, the parents. The BJE study stresses the importance of developing a synergism between home and school, not unlike Dr. Corner's prescription for effective public education.

To create this synergism, we have to have Jewish family education. And for Jewish family education to be effective, the appropriate Jewish family educators must be in place. Since Jewish family education as a discrete, formal profession, is a relatively new undertaking in the Jewish community, one of our first tasks is to train a cadre of Jewish family educators.

For that purpose we are convened today to help guide the

development of a Jewish family educator training process. I am, therefore, pleased and privileged to welcome you to this colloquium, which honors the memory of Ida and Israel Berman, who, in their lifetimes, were major benefactors of Jewish education. The interdisciplinary nature of the colloquium participant is, in and of itself, an important occurrence in the process of Jewish educator training.

Here we are, heads of departments of graduate education of the Hebrew Union College-Jewish Institute of Religion, Jewish Theological Seminary and Yeshiva University; psychologists, family therapists and family life educators from the Jewish Board of Family and Children's Services and the Ackerman Institute of Family Therapy, Mount Sinai Hospital; social workers, group workers, rabbis and several outstanding Jewish family educators. As we join BJE staff members in this trailblazing effort, I bid you "*Shalom* and *Hatzlahah.*"

I see our combined challenge today as a three-step process.

1. The first step is exploring and defining the Jewish needs of Jewish families in relation to their social and psychological needs as parents in the 1990s. This will lead to the process of conceptualizing change and growth in Jewish family life;
2. The second step is developing the guidelines for strategies – individual, synagogal and communal – to meet these needs. This includes the development of instructional techniques, program methods and materials as well as evaluation processes.
3. And, finally, the third step is developing the procedures for creating a cadre of specialists to implement the strategies. This involves exploring models of professional training and giving serious attention to organizational and systems analysis of the network of synagogue, communal agencies and family structures needed to sustain Jewish family education and Jewish family educators.

As we engage in this effort, we must recognize that we are not working in a vacuum. Jewish family education is taking place all over the continent. Some of its most prominent practitioners are here today. We must learn from their experience, which is essentially programmatic. Moreover, we must take a good look at programs that work and why they work, and try to find out what makes a Jewish family educator competent and effective. These facts are basic to our challenge – to participate in a scientific effort to guarantee the effectiveness of Jewish family education via careful study, research, training and evaluation.

The thoughtful papers, which were pre-circulated last week will serve as a springboard for our deliberations and help focus our attention on the objectives of the colloquium. We are at the beginning of an historic effort, which, when concluded, can have a profound effect upon:

1. the Jewish school – it will make it more effective;
2. the Jewish educators – it will increase their effectiveness and provide many more career opportunities in Jewish education;
3. Jewish families – it will give them more purposeful activity and make family life more meaningful;
4. synagogues – it will give them a new lease on life;
5. rabbis – it will provide them with more meaningful roles vis-à-vis their congregants and make them more effective practitioners; and
6. the Jewish community – it will enhance the quality of Jewish life and help insure Jewish continuity.

What a promise for the future of Jewish education! We're here to join in that promise by giving it our best shot as we combine theory and practice in Jewish family education.

Hatzlahah rabbah.

CHAPTER 9

Spotlight on Adult Jewish Education in the United States

LIFE-LONG LEARNING IN AMERICAN SOCIETY

American society is moving away from the conviction that formal education for most Americans ends at age seventeen or eighteen. There are a variety of reasons for this basic change in a belief that was rooted in the American psyche for well over two centuries.

In the first instance, formal learning beyond high school is needed for increasingly larger numbers of professions and job opportunities. Secondly, formal learning is a necessity in our fast changing technological society just to keep abreast of new developments. And, due to the increase in life expectancy, more and more people live longer, many years after their formal education has ended. This means growing numbers of retirees with free time to spend as they please.

Since formal education is needed or desired by more persons during adulthood, our society provides many ways to acquire knowledge beyond high school and college years. These include proprietary courses, industry-based workshops and seminars, lectures and course-offerings in public libraries and public schools in evenings, weekends and vacation periods, and university-based degree and non-degree programs specifically geared to adult learners.

Despite the growth in life-long learning opportunities, adult education as an academic discipline has not been extensively studied or researched. A study of Jewish adult education in specialized settings would make an important contribution to the knowledge base of general adult education as well as to Jewish life-long learning.

JEWISH LIFE-LONG LEARNING

Adult Jewish education is actually as old as the Jewish people. Rashi, the great biblical and Talmudic commentator, tells us that Abraham and Sarah taught adults about monotheism (Genesis 12:5). In essence, they were the first adult Jewish educators. The prophets were teachers as were the Levites. The Talmudic sages were adult educators par excellence. *Mishnah Avot* (Ethics of the Fathers) is a prime example of their ethical teaching. Rabbinical tradition encourages Jewish adult self-study. The various *Targumim* (translations of the *Pentateuch*) were created to foster individual and group Torah learning. The Talmud (*Brachot* 8) suggests that every adult review each weekly Torah reading *sh'nayim mikra v'ehad targum* – twice in the original Hebrew and once in translation.

In Babylon, before and after the onset of the Common Era, the Talmudic sages established special periods for adult Torah study during the month preceding the holiday of *Pesah* and the month prior to *Rosh Hashanah*, when there was lull in agricultural activity immediately before the fall harvest and immediately before the spring planting season. During these months, known as *yarchei kallah* or simply *kallah*, scholars and others, particularly farmers who were free from their labor, engaged in serious text study and heard lectures by *roshei yeshiva*. The *kallah* periods have been described, fittingly, as the first "Jewish people's university."

To be sure, since that time adult Jewish learning became second nature to adult Jews in Israel and the Diaspora, both in Sephardic and Ashkenazic communities. In the middle ages and early contemporary times, most Jewish communities sponsored a *hevrah Shas* – a group of adult students who learned *Shas*, the six orders of the *Mishnah* and Talmud. A more modern example of this kind of group Torah learning is the Lehrhaus – a non-denominational *beth Midrash* (house of study) – established by Franz Rosensweig shortly after World War 1.

In our own time, there are numerous examples of serious adult text learning in Israel and the Diaspora. Of particular note is the spread of the study of *daf yomi*, a daily leaf of Talmud in the Orthodox community throughout the world.

ADULT JEWISH EDUCATION AS INFORMAL EDUCATION

Informal education is thousands of years old, dating back to pre-literate times when it was the only kind of education practiced – in incidental ways. In America, one of many forms of informal education is adult education. In addition to the incidental learning that typically exemplified informal learning over the ages, adult education can be intentional and can involve deliberate planning, organization and even curriculum development and evaluation.

Although informal education, including adult education in American society, has not received due recognition, it is an important means of imparting information and teaching people of all ages about their national and religious heritages and their relationship to the society in which they live. In Jewish life, informal Jewish education, encompassing summer camps, youth organizations and adult education programs in synagogues, Jewish community centers, Zionist organizations and other social groupings, offers an effective way for teaching about Jewish culture, ritual and ethical behavior, Israel and the Hebrew language. Indeed, "Jewish Continuity-Jewish Renaissance," which has been targeted by the Jewish Federations in the United States as an important Jewish communal purpose in light of the growing assimilation and rate of intermarriage is being implemented and/or planned for implementation via informal as well as formal Jewish education programs.

The American Jewish community, including all forms of organized Jewish life, particularly the synagogue movements, is giving increasingly greater attention to the value of informal Jewish education. In this context, adult Jewish education is emerging as a widely recognized vehicle for transmitting Jewish knowledge and for strengthening Jewish identity and loyalty. Worldwide, this development is underscored by the sponsorship of the first International Conference on Jewish Adult Education by the Joint Authority for Jewish Zionist Education of the Jewish Agency for Israel and the World Zionist Organization, the Division for Adult Education and the Israel Unit for Relations with the Diaspora of the Ministry of Education and Culture in Israel, and the Israel Association for Adult Education at *Ma'aleh Hahamisha* in December 1997.

To be sure, adult Jewish education is becoming a serious agenda for Jewish institutions throughout America. Over the past decade there has been a marked increase in both the number of programs and number of participants in adult Jewish learning. For example, several communities are engaging in the two-year Wexner-Heritage Program for adult Jewish leadership. The Florence Melton Adult Mini-School has been opening new community classes, which maintain classes in participating communities; the National Jewish Outreach Program continues to expand to new adult audiences and the National Hebrew Literacy Campaign is finding new participants as well. In the Orthodox community, Agudath Israel is promoting, ever more vigorously the study of *daf yomi*, the daily leaf of Talmud, and the Chafetz Chaim Heritage Foundation is increasing its educational programming for ethical Jewish living.

In 1997, the Alliance for Adult Jewish Education was organized to encourage Jewish educators involved in this relatively new area of Jewish education to share their experience and to explore a number of critical issues concerning the field of adult Jewish learning in order to arrive at a unified definition of adult Jewish education. An increasing number of national and local organizations are offering opportunities for their members to study and are encouraging them to engage in regular Jewish learning.

ADULT JEWISH EDUCATIN AND JEWISH SCHOOLING OF THE YOUNG

In Judaism, life-long learning – the study of Torah from the time one is old enough to read until death – is a hallowed tradition. From the earliest times, Jews have performed this *mitzvah* at home, in school settings, in the synagogue and even when traveling. They took, literally, the biblical commandment, "And you shall speak of them (the words of the Torah) when you sit at home, when you go on the way, and when you lie down and when you rise up." Learning took place individually, in small groups – *havrutot* – and in larger groups in the classroom or lecture hall.

As the Jewish people became westernized and acculturated into the various societies in which they resided, less and less Judaic learning occurred in the home. Also, the amount of time provided for the formal Jewish schooling of the young decreased. This has had important ramifications for adult Jewish education since Jewish schooling of children and youth relates directly to adult Jewish learning. The level and content of adult Jewish education depends largely on the Jewish educational background of the adult learners.

In the United States, in the first decades of the twentieth century, Jewish children generally received minimal Judaic tutelage in *hadarim* (private one room classrooms) or via private tutors. In the 1920s and 1930s most Jewish children who received a Jewish education were enrolled in communal *Talmud Torahs* where they studied Jewish subjects for as many as ten to twelve hours per week, forty to forty-five weeks per year. In the 1940s, congregational schools began to supplant the *Talmud Torah*. Since then, the vast majority of Jewish youth exposed to formal Jewish education have been schooled in congregational schools in which pupils study from two and six hours a week. Moreover, the academic year in the congregational schools is much shorter than it was in the *Talmud Torah*. Also, almost all the students in congregational schools end their Jewish education at Bar/Bat Mitzvah. Enrollment in the congregational school has declined by some fifty percent since its peak year 38 years ago – from 540,000 in 1962 to 270,000 in 2000. This demographic phenomenon, brought about essentially by low birth rate, by the results of intermarriage and by lack of commitment to Jewish youth education, means that there are less Jewish adults with even a minimal Jewish supplementary education background in most American synagogues today.

It must be noted that approximately twenty percent of Jewish school age children are not exposed to any formal Jewish education. Moreover, viewing the total Jewish youth population, who receive an elementary Jewish education, we must realize that only fifteen percent are involved in Jewish study of any kind during their teenage and college years. Since Judaic learning is such a basic aspect of Jewish life, the challenge of adult Jewish education, particularly for Jewish adults with minimal or no Jewish backgrounds, assumes paramount importance in the Jewish community. *Lo am ha-aretz hasid* – "a Jewishly ignorant person cannot be a pious Jew," Hillel counseled. More than that, Judaic knowledge is important for its own sake and is key to Jewish practice. When asked, "what is more important – learning or practice?" the sages of the *Midrash* answered unequivocally *Talmud gadol, she hatalmud mavee leey'day ma'asseh*. "Study is greater (more important) because study brings about practice." For adult Jews without a Jewish study background, adult Jewish education assumes very practical significance.

In contrast, to Jewish supplementary (congregational) education, the Jewish Day School in the United States has grown significantly – from 60,000 pupils in 1962 to 200,000 in 2000. About one quarter of the Jewish child population is currently enrolled in Jewish all day institutions – eighty percent of which are under Orthodox auspices. Pupils in these schools receive between 15 and 30 hours per week of Judaic instruction. Most of these students spend 12 years in a Jewish all day school setting. As adults, they bring with them a strong background of Jewish knowledge. For them it seems adult Jewish education is a natural extension of their pre-adult years of Judaic study.

ADULT JEWISH EDUCATION AND THE SYNAGOGUE

Traditionally, the synagogue was always a place of Jewish learning. Currently, in the United States, the synagogue has become the institution generally regarded as the setting where adult Jewish learning occurs. In Hebrew, there are three terms often used for "synagogue" – *beit knesset* (a house of assembly), *bet tefillah* (a house of worship) and *bet midrash* (a house of study).

Adult Jewish education relates to the third dimension of the synagogue. All the synagogue movements – the Conservative movement, the United Synagogue of Conservative Judaism; the Orthodox movement including the Modern Orthodox National Council of Young Israel and the Union of Orthodox Jewish Congregations, and the ultra Orthodox Agudath Israel of America and the various other ultra Orthodox and Hasidic groups; the Reconstructionist movement, the Jewish Reconstructionist Federation; and the Reform movement, the Union of American Hebrew Congregations – have significantly increased their adult Jewish education activity during the last decade. The most intensive attention to adult Jewish learning has been in the Orthodox synagogues.

The effectiveness of adult Jewish education activity in the American synagogue depends largely on two factors – the role and ability of the rabbi, as teacher and organizer, and the support of the lay administration. Across the board, both the rabbinic and lay leadership of the congregations have shown greater interest in adult learning, which augurs well for the future.

CHAPTER 10

ADULT JEWISH EDUCATION IN THE MODERN ORTHODOX SYNAGOGUE

INTRODUCTION

In 1992 when the results of the 1990 National Jewish Population Study were released, the leadership of the American Jewish community was shocked by its now well-publicized and reiterated findings. Jews were opting out of Jewish life and marrying out of the faith in increasing numbers. Half of the Jewish adults were not bringing up their offspring as Jews. This frightening reality made Jewish communal and synagogue leaders scramble to find ways to insure Jewish continuity. Among the measures they decided to take was the development of informal Jewish educational strategies including adult Jewish education (AJE).

Least affected by the hemorrhaging of the Jewish community are the Orthodox Jews – Modern-Centrist Orthodox, the sectarian Ultra-Orthodox, and the Hasidim. Given the philosophy and life style of Modern Orthodox Jews, who integrate both the traditional and secular worlds in their daily living, they form a unique bastion of Jewish life in America. Even though Modern Orthodox Jews represent but eight percent of American Jewry, their educational programs, which contribute significantly to Jewish continuity, merit investigation.

THE SURVEY OF AJE IN THE MODERN ORTHODOX SYNAGOGUE

My research focuses on the Modern Orthodox synagogue in the United States. It is based upon a purposive, stratified sampling of Modern Orthodox congregations. Forty-one synagogues with membership ranging from 90 to 1300 family units, representing a total of 17,500 families were surveyed.

The extent and level of AJE in the synagogues was measured, essentially, by: the annual budget allocated to adult Jewish education; the percentage of congregants involved in regular, daily and weekly Jewish learning in the synagogue and home; the extent of volunteer-led study groups; and the content and type of Jewish learning.

On the average, a rather modest sum – 14 percent of the aggregate annual budget – is allocated for adult Jewish study. (The real expenditures for AJE are significantly higher if one includes the proportionate amount of the salaries of the rabbis in the respective adult education budgets.)

The moderate expenditures are balanced by the extent of volunteer-led classes – a rapidly growing phenomenon in Orthodox synagogues. Given the intensive Jewish education background of most of the members, relatively large numbers of congregants are Jewishly learned, able to study original sources on their own, and capable of conducting classes in Judaic study. There are a total of 277 volunteer-led classes – an average of seven per synagogue – in the congregations studied. This characteristic, unique to the Orthodox synagogue, underscores the relationship between youth education and the extent, level and content of adult study.

The overwhelming majority of the adult population in the Modern Orthodox synagogue was educated in yeshivot and Jewish day schools through the secondary level. Moreover, a significant number of adults have acquired advanced post-high school Judaic knowledge. It is not uncommon in the Modern Orthodox synagogue to observe intensive Jewish study of original sources led by physicians, lawyers, businessmen and academics.

The survey demonstrates that eight percent of the total

membership, sixteen percent of the male population, study daily in synagogue sponsored programs. (In addition, there are many daily *havrutot* that take place in the Modern Orthodox community not under synagogue auspices.) Twenty-eight percent of the total membership is involved in weekly text study. (In addition to these learners, another forty percent of the membership hear weekly *divrei Torah* or discussion of *Halakhah* in connection with Sabbath morning and afternoon service. All told, some eighty percent of the membership is involved in adult Jewish study.) The percentage of daily and weekly learners is growing as young yeshiva trained adults join the congregations. Because of the intensive Jewish educational background of the majority of members, text study, in the original Hebrew and Aramaic, especially for men – *Mishnah, Gemara, Mishnah Brurah*, Pentateuch and commentaries – are the most popular subjects. The majority of the synagogues sponsor *daf yomi* (daily Talmud study), a phenomenon that was non-existent a generation ago.

The type of AJE programs varies with the age of the congregants. The older members are less involved in regular Talmudic study due to their less intensive Judaic backgrounds.

Divrei Torah by the Rabbi – brief discussions of *Halakhah* or biblical exegesis – before and after daily morning and afternoon worship – are a staple of all the synagogues. Annually *Tikun Lail Shavuot* study from 11 P.M. to 5:00 A.M. involves more and more congregants and their children. The two hundred family congregation (a participating synagogue in this survey) to which I belong, is a good example of the increasing popularity of this form of Jewish learning. In the 1960s and 70's, only a handful of men – often not even a *minyan* – engaged in the all-night *Shavuot* study. In 1997, over 200 adults – men and women – including a number of guests for the holiday and well over one hundred youth, ages 8–18, studied Judaic texts under the guidance of the rabbi and a dozen volunteer leaders in various settings throughout the night.

Increasingly, women participate in co-ed classes and in women's study groups. The *Bet Midrash* format whereby *havrutot* – small groups of 2–6 adults engaging in Jewish learning simultaneously – is also gaining in popularity. One of the growing dimensions of AJE in the Modern Orthodox synagogue is *Kiruv* – outreach programs for the community. This aspect of AJE derives from the strong desire of the rabbinic and lay congregational leadership to bring more Jews into the Modern Orthodox community. *Kiruv* includes beginners' services, a variety of introductory courses on Judaism cosponsored by national and local Jewish outreach organizations, and Hebrew language programs.

The *Seudah Shlishit shiur* on Shabbat is a major Jewish educational movement in which as many as thirty percent of the adult population participates in scholar-in-residence programs on the weekends is another well-practiced form of AJE.

Demography plays a role in the extent of AJE in the Modern Orthodox synagogue. The congregations in the Greater New York area allocate significantly more funds per family for AJE and their membership is more actively involved in adult study. This finding obviously relates to the Judaic background of congregants. There are many more opportunities for secondary level day school education in the Greater New York area. Indeed, a much larger percentage of Greater New York elementary day school graduates continue on to high school, and most of the secondary school graduates avail themselves of the opportunities for post high school Jewish education in Israeli and New York area yeshivot. Moreover, the Orthodox environment is more pervasive in metropolitan New York. This is critical since the extent and intensity of AJE depends, in good measure, on the Jewish commitment, level of observance, and level of Jewish education of congregants.

In sum, the Modern Orthodox synagogues in this survey are seriously committed to the idea of AJE. The congregations use AJE as a vehicle to strengthen Modern Orthodoxy and to raise the level of Judaic knowledge of their congregants. Adult Jewish study for the majority of the Orthodox participants is a life-long practice and not merely a leisure-time activity. As new members who have similar and even more enriched Judaic backgrounds, join the synagogues, this tendency will grow and intensify. Also, there will probably be more and more serious learners on a regular weekly and daily basis. And, many synagogues will probably expand their outreach programs to the broader community, since both the rabbinic and lay leadership consider this an important challenge.

ENHANCING AJE IN THE MODERN ORTHODOX SYNAGOGUE AND THE JEWISH COMMUNITY

It is clear that the synagogue is – and should be – the major player in AJE in the United States. In the first place, about half of all American Jews are members of synagogues. The potential extensiveness and intensity of AJE in the synagogue is demonstrated by the adult Jewish learning that takes place in the Modern Orthodox congregation. AJE participation can be enhanced significantly and intensified in this setting via greater attention to the whole family, by special consideration to the educational needs and interests of the various age cohorts in the adult community, from newly weds and single unmarried young adults to recent retirees and octogenarians, and by more effort in attracting larger numbers of women to study.

WOMEN AND JUDAIC STUDY

Involving more women in Jewish study requires increased learning opportunities for co-ed and women's learning groups. Modern Orthodoxy must learn to deal with the challenge of the heightened spiritual and educational aspirations of Modern Orthodox women. Women's study is slowly becoming a regular characteristic of Modern Orthodox life. (It has even penetrated the Ultra Orthodox community. Twenty percent of the 70,000 participants in the *Siyum haShas* on September 28 were women. In the main, their participation represented identification with daily Jewish learning and support of Torah study, and not necessarily learning itself.)

CONFERENCE ON AJE

In order to embellish and enrich AJE under Modern Orthodox auspices it would be useful if a conference regarding AJE would be convened. Initially, since the rabbi is generally the key functionary as leader and teacher in AJE it seems natural that the Rabbinical Council of America, together with the Max Stern Division of Communal Services of Yeshiva University would organize such a conference. Lay leaders should obviously be involved via the Union of Orthodox Jewish Congregations of America in the planning and implementation of the conference, which would deal with the purpose, content and methods of AJE, and ways of increasing regular daily and weekly study, family involvement and women's study.

LONG RANGE PLANNING: YOUTH EDUCATION

Enhancing AJE in the Modern Orthodox synagogue calls for long range and short range planning. Long range preparation involves the maximizing of synagogue efforts to ensure that all Jewish children of synagogue families receive an intensive Jewish education. This means the avid promotion of day school education through high school and beyond for the progeny of the synagogue membership.

In suggesting this kind of long-range planning, we might refer to a relevant insight of the Rav, Rabbi Joseph Dov Soloveitchick, the spiritual and intellectual mentor of Modern Orthodoxy in the second half of the twentieth century. In a seminal lecture comparing a Jew to a *sefer Torah*, the Rav noted that the *mitzvah* of writing a *sefer Torah* which is incumbent upon adult Jews is the *ketivah* – the actual writing. But, this *mitzvah* cannot be performed without a preparatory stage involving the careful, exacting preparation of the parchment as the receptacle for the writing.

Similarly, he noted the *mitzvah* of Jewish education involves two stages, which he calls *hinukh* and *limud*. During the first stage – *hinukh* – the child is prepared attitudinally and didactically via cognitive and affective means for the second stage, which is the actual *limud* – the learning – which cannot succeed without proper *hinukh*. So, too, intensive adult Jewish education, the kind that involves regular daily and weekly study of Judaic texts, requires preparatory stages during childhood and youth.

SHORT RANGE PROGRAMMING: PARENT AND FAMILY EDUCATION

There is a special role for AJE vis-à-vis those adults who have not had the benefit of sound Jewish schooling during their youth. In order for these Jewish adults to be able to function as involved Jews, they require special study for which the synagogue must be prepared adequately to provide. This means short range planning – based upon the need for immediacy to increase the number of Jewish adults who live Jewishly and are able to contribute to Jewish continuity.

Short range planning involves the provision of educational programs to meet the needs and interests of the members of the synagogue as individuals and as family members. It means increasing the opportunities for Jewish learning for parents and children. The father-son and mother-daughter study groups sponsored by some synagogues should be emulated throughout the Jewish community. For the Conservative and Reform synagogues, this means enhancing the opportunities for Jewish study for parents of children in the congregational school and creatively promoting this idea. This kind of activity would not involve the Orthodox congregations since they generally do not sponsor supplementary schools. Almost all Orthodox children attend Jewish Day Schools.

Some Modern Orthodox Jewish day schools sponsor weekly Judaic study for parents of students, generally utilizing the same teachers and focusing on the same subject matter studied in school. Properly guided, such a program provides a remarkable opportunity for home discussion and family involvement in Jewish learning. This kind of activity might be replicated in all the Jewish day schools under Modern Orthodox, Conservative, Reform and communal auspices.

There is a mutual benefit in maximizing the educational opportunities for parents. Their very learning creates an ambience for the children. Parent learning models will, among other things, affect the motivation of children regarding their own Jewish schooling since they can share Jewish knowledge and experience with their learning parents. This is one of the characteristics of Jewish education in the Modern Orthodox synagogue and home – a phenomenon that makes AJE under Modern Orthodox auspices unique.

MAKING JEWISH STUDY A PRIORITY

A positive feature of AJE in the Modern Orthodox synagogue is the way the adult learners generally relish their learning and make Torah study an absolute priority in their daily and weekly schedules. For those who study *daf yomi*, this daily routine assumes first place among their daily activities, next to their work schedule, whether it be early morning study before or after services, at lunchtime or in the evening after dinner.

On the evening after the *Siyum haShas* on September 28, 1990, the synagogue to which I belong instituted the daily *daf yomi*. In a congregation of two hundred member families, ten men decided to make this an absolute priority. Their serious attitude towards *Torah lishmah* – learning for learning's sake – and the enjoyment they derive from it are personal characteristics that should be emulated by the members of all synagogues. To be sure, their attitude towards Jewish learning derives from a combination of their Jewish commitment, their Jewish observance and their Jewish educational background.

LEARNING AS A UNIFYING FACTOR

As demonstrated by the worldwide *Siyum haShas* in the Orthodox community, Torah study can have a strong unifying influence on learners. Taking a leaf from the idea of *daf yomi*, the synagogues and Jewish community centers and other organizations in a given community might develop common Jewish study programs for their respective memberships. The same texts might be studied in the original or in translation and the same topics explored in the individual institutions on a variety of levels. At the beginning of the program year, and once or twice during the year, and at the end of the year a joint communal session might be held on the common content. Such a program, which requires careful planning and coordination, could have a coalescent influence on the community and contribute to a feeling of Jewish peoplehood.

COMMUNITY-WIDE PROGRAMMING

On a more integrated community-wide level of activity, the various institutions in the community might co-sponsor community-wide learning projects.

1. Hebrew Language Study
2. A Hebrew language program with various levels of instruction in reading, conversation and literature seems like a natural way to involve the whole community in Jewish study.
3. The Community *Kollel*
4. Several Orthodox Jewish communities sponsor *Kollelim*. This practice, whereby the community and/or one or more synagogues support several *Kollel* (post-rabbinic) fellows and their families enables members of the community to study with the fellows during various times of the day. The *Kollel* program, sponsored by Yeshiva University and *Mishmeret Hatzeirah* in Israel, in cooperation with the *Hesder* Yeshivot, places young Israeli scholars for two to three year periods in American Jewish communities (for example, in Boca Raton, Chicago, Cleveland and Kansas City) to lead study sessions which emphasize *Torah Umada* and religious Zionism. The *Kollel* idea merits consideration by the Jewish community at large.
5. Partners-in-Learning
6. The Partners-in-Learning outreach program developed by several synagogues might be extended to more synagogues and communities. This practice involves one-to-one mentoring to help adults with minimal or no Jewish background to gain basic knowledge about Judaism.
7. *Rosh Hodesh* Learnathon
8. Also, communities might institute *Rosh Hodesh* learnathons for individual adults, families and especially for women. In Jewish tradition, *Rosh Hodesh* – the New Moon – was a

semi-holiday. Women in particular would not engage in any work. The learnathon, once a month, could be a festive occasion combining study with refreshments and music.
9. Community "Jewish University"
10. In another vein, the community might sponsor (via representatives of all communal institutions) a community "Jewish University" in which each of the synagogues and other Jewish organizations develop their own programs which are included in a community-wide catalogue made available to all Jews in the community. The "Jewish University" would publicize all the adult Jewish educational programs and thus create a community-wide ambience regarding adult Jewish learning.

JEWISH STUDY – A FAMILY AFFAIR

Finally, taking a leaf from the role of learning amongst Modern/Centrist Orthodox Jews, adult Jewish study in the Jewish community should become a permanent feature of the Jewish home, whereby adults are encouraged to study on their own and with their children. At least one Sabbath meal should feature *divrei Torah* given by various members of the family.

In conclusion, I briefly summarized my study of adult Jewish education and offered a variety of possibilities for the future of AJE in Modern Orthodox congregations and in the Jewish community. The purpose of this study is to motivate the realization of the hallowed Judaic tradition of life-long Torah learning as an operative concept in American Jewish life with the hope that it will be a continuity-insuring process.

PART V

INSTRUCTION & LEADERSHIP

CHAPTER 1

THE *MELAMED* AT MID-CENTURY: AN APPRECIATION OF THE ROLE OF THE HEBREW TEACHER

Jewish education, as the major instrument for Jewish unity and continuity, is the indispensable means for Jewish survival. The teacher is the living force, the dynamics of Jewish education. He is the activator and often the energy of the continuous, conscious adjustment to Jewish ideals and Jewish values. Tradition recognized this when it proclaimed: "It is prohibited to live in a city that does not have a teacher of children."

The story of the development of Jewish education in America, from its earliest beginnings in the Spanish Portuguese community to the East European *heder* in the late 1800s, to the *Talmud Torah* of the 1920s and 1930s, and finally to the congregational school and the yeshiva of today, is actually the story of the growth of the Hebrew teaching profession. It is the story of Jewish communal development as affected by the Hebrew teacher. The increase of Jewish school enrollment in the past few decades is the result, in large measure, of the devotion and selfless dedication of the Hebrew teacher. The kind of Jewish life that is to be ours in the coming years lies in the pulsating hearts of the Jewish teachers. As Rudyard Kipling depicted:

> "No printed word nor spoken plea,
> Can teach young hearts what man should be,
> Nor all the books on all the shelves,
> But what the teachers are themselves."

It is to the Hebrew teacher we salute and offer this modest tribute.

THE EARLY BEGINNINGS

The first teachers of the 20th century were immigrants who came with the waves of immigration from Eastern Europe during the first decade of the century. Prominent among them was the *siddur* peddler. With *siddur* under arm, from early morn to late at night, he would pass it from street to street, house to house, door to door, up many dingy flights of stairs, even to the sixth, seventh, and eighth floors to peddle his wares: *Ivrit*, *Kiddush*, *Kaddish*, and *Maftir*. His private lessons were 10, 15, or 20 minutes long depending upon the remuneration he received. His gross income from *siddur* peddling would range from 20 to 50 cents weekly. The number of *siddur* peddlers diminished quickly with the advent of skilled teachers and as schools were gradually established.

Side by side with the *siddur* peddler was the *heder melamed*, who maintained his private school in a converted stable, a cellar, a saloon, or in some other rent-free firetrap. The *heder melamed* was a jack-of-all-trades. At one and the same time, he was a Hebrew teacher, Bar Mitzvah tutor, babysitter, translator of letters, and writer of letters to European countries, *mohel*, marriage performer, healer, cantor, and soothsayer. Many of these functions he would perform while fulfilling his classroom chores. The sign on one typical private *heder* establishment brings this into full view. It announced that they were "famous pedagogues" and that their "prices are very cheap." The listing of subjects in the announcement contained errors in the Hebrew spelling of four subjects: *Tanakh*, *Ivrit*, *Gemara* and *dikduk* (grammar).

The teachers of the first two decades in the 20th century were a colorful mixture of the *lo yutslah*, the *talmid hakham*, the *maskil*, the Hebraic scholar, the young salesman in quest for a part-time position, and the college student preparing for another profession. There were the old experienced instructors and also the young serious teachers. The institution of education did not keep abreast of the growth of the Jewish community in America. This was reflected in the teaching force of the period.

RECRUITMENT IN EARLY TIMES

Gradually, communal schools took their place in the arena of organized Jewish life on this continent. How did these schools recruit their instructors in the absence of a community licensing authority or organized placement service? The problems of recruitment were often solved by the teachers themselves, who went door-to-door shopping. Recruitment was also accomplished by ads in the paper. For example, one ad might read: "In the Second Avenue *Talmud Torah*, there is now an opening for a Hebrew teacher. All applicants will appear before the principal on Tuesday, at 8:30 P.M. sharp." Often there would be a line of 20 to 30 applicants for one position. Candidates were usually interviewed by the principal and members of the Board. Criteria for selection were subjective and dictated frequently by influence. In one recorded case, the candidates were standing in line, waiting anxiously to be interviewed. A Board member entered late, passed amongst the candidates, and signaled one of them to a corner. He said to him, "I am sure you will make a good impression upon the rest of the Board and also upon the principal. If you guarantee me 2% of your salary, I will guarantee you a position." The Board selected the candidate. The 2% was divided equally between the Board member and the principal. In another similar instance, a candidate, in order to secure a job, had to guarantee to pay a portion of his weekly salary to the principal and to regularly send him "*mishloah-manot*."

DEPRESSION YEARS

The depression years were unfortunate and dark years for all America. The Hebrew teacher did not emerge from this period unscathed. To some of us, a statement made to the late A.H. Friedland in 1934 may not sound wholly unfamiliar: "Schools owe new mortgages on their buildings." During this period, teachers were discharged in the middle of the year and no compensation made to them. Salaries were cut retroactively. "Salary cuts," states Friendland, "are affected 2 or 3 times during the same year, and even the reduced salary is not being paid. Experienced teachers are replaced by inexperienced teachers who do not command high salaries. Janitors are the only privileged personnel in the school system because their salary is not withheld. Classes are combined and recombined irrespective of numbers of children or differences in level of achievement."

During these difficult years, one principal ceased calling teachers' meetings because, under the circumstances, he did not feel like imposing upon the teachers the expenditure of carfare. This was the time of the depression when the older teachers were overcome by the realization that bad as the present is; a still gloomier future is in store for them. They, in turn, transmitted this mood of despair to their younger colleagues.

But the depression years passed and, as in other professions, the teacher's position also improved.

SOME ADVANCES IN TEACHER WELFARE

Even today, the economic status of teachers leaves much to be desired. However, now we can cite happenings, such as the following: A teacher who had been serving in a congregational school for ten years suddenly took ill. The parents and lay leadership appreciated the work of this teacher. They not only paid every cent of her salary during the six months of her absence, but in addition to this, the PTA paid all expenses for a two-week vacation in Florida.

Numerous cases of leniency regarding sick leave benefits, which were unheard of 30 years ago, have been reported during the last decade. There are even a number of teachers who have been granted modified sabbaticals-with-pay to visit Israel, for study, etc. The trend, though gradual, is there. The fact that welfare agencies everywhere are supporting Jewish education is a good sign for Hebrew teachers. In New York City, there is evidence of increasing interest on the part of Federation in Jewish education. Many communal leaders, once apathetic and even antagonistic to the cause of Jewish education, are beginning to show their interest in Jewish educational activities. These too, are good signs for the Jewish educator.

Communal realization of the importance of Jewish education leads inevitably to wider recognition of the role of the teacher in the Jewish community and to more substantive action for teacher welfare.

There is an increasing interest in creating fuller teacher benefits – tenure, leaves, pension and unemployment insurance, to mention a few.

Jewish teaching is now beginning to assume the status of a profession. Despite many setbacks, the emergence and growth of new educational institutions have aided the teaching profession. Various landmarks highlight the development of the Hebrew teaching profession In New York City. These are: The Hebrew Teachers Union, founded in 1923; the Board of License, established in 1928; the Board of Review, organized in 1929; the Jewish Education Association Code of Practice, issued in 1933 and reformulated by the Board of Review in 1944; the Group Insurance Plan, initiated in 1934; the Jewish Teachers Retirement Association, founded in 1946; and the SAAD plan, initiated in 1947. All told, the Hebrew teacher has come a long way. A challenge, however, still remains for teachers to help their own cause.

THE TEACHER'S JOB

What of the Hebrew teacher's job today? What do pupils, parents and colleagues expect of the teacher? What does society expect of him? What does the school administration expect of him?

The teacher is all things to everybody. He is group leader, group worker, communal leader, follower and co-worker. He is doctor, friend, helper, psychologist and adviser. Often he is sergeant-at-arms, patrolman, mimeograph specialist, clerk and even mechanic, painter and cleaner.

"Society," says a well-known American educator, "expects a teacher to be a well adjusted, perfectly integrated personality, a kind of supreme personality attuned to his profession and the total environment. A teacher must have all the proper social and religious attitudes, superior intelligence and personality endowment." And, the Hebrew teacher often fulfills such stringent expectations. No wonder he as been compared to an angel and to a star in heaven.

In a composition written by a member of the graduating class of one of our day schools, a child wrote: "I like my Hebrew teacher because he is above all personal problems and he has so many of them."

The problem of dealing with a classroom full of children is not always appreciated. A teacher's patience is often tried in many ways, some of which are reflected in the following anecdotes:

A teacher asked a good pupil, "Jackie, how do you spell *akhshav* ("now") in Hebrew?" Jackie answered wrongly. The teacher then politely retorted: "The dictionary spells it differently." "But," argued Jackie, "you asked how I spelled it."

Another teacher, after drilling the numerical value of the alphabet for a number of days, asked one of his pupils: "The letter *Aleph* is one; the letter *Gimmel* is three; the letter *Yud* is ten. What does the letter *Nun* equal? And what is the letter *Kof* in numbers?" The pupil retorted – "That ain't fair. You answered the easy ones yourself and leave the hard ones for me."

And there are some unexpected moments, such as the time when a precocious pupil approached his teacher and asked: "*Morah*, can anyone be punished for something he didn't do?" "Why no, of course not." He said, "Well, I haven't done my homework." "You bad boy. I wish I was your mother for about 24 hours." "All right, teacher," the pupil retorted, "I'll speak to Dad and maybe I can fix it up."

TEACHER PROFILE: A COMPARISON

1929: How do you compare with your counterpart of 30 years ago? In 1929, chances that you were a man were 2 to 1. If you were a married male, you were about 27 years old. If you were a woman, you were probably only 23 years of age. In all likelihood you were single. Seventy-five percent of all Hebrew teachers in 1929 were unmarried. If you were a *Talmud Torah* teacher, you were most likely foreign born. Only ⅓ of *Talmud Torah* instructors in America were native Americans. If you taught in a yeshiva, however, there wasn't one chance in a thousand that you were U.S. born. Thirty years ago, no yeshiva teacher was a native of this country. It was safe to assume that you had completed or were attending college. Eighty-three percent of teachers were college graduates or pursuing college courses. You probably earned about $1500 a year, at an average of $1.70 an hour, and to achieve this – if you were a *Talmud Torah* teacher – you taught 4 hours daily, about 20 hours per week. You were probably not licensed, the Board of License being only one year old at that time.

1959: What about the typical teacher of today? You are probably a male. Fifty-eight percent of the Hebrew teachers in New York City are males. Almost all Nursery and Kindergarten teachers are females. If you are a female teacher, you are probably 30 years of age.

The average size of your classes is 25 pupils. If you teach in a day school, the overwhelming odds are that you teach one class. Odds have it too, that you teach two afternoon classes. Talking about odds, if we bet on your teaching load per week, we would be sure of winning if we wagered that you teach less than 20 hours per week. However, the possibilities are fair that you have 2 positions: mornings in a yeshiva, afternoons in a *Talmud Torah* or a congregational school. You are probably licensed. About 62% of full time teachers are licensed and a goodly portion of the others have permits from the Board of License of New York City. You have held your present position (or one of your present positions) for less than 10 years, and there is a 50–50 probability that you have been at your present position for only 1 or 2 years. Yeshiva teachers usually stay longer in their positions, while congregational schools show the greatest turnover of staff.

TEACHER'S INFLUENCE

Henry Brooks Adams said: "A teacher affects eternity. He can never tell where his influence stops." We can cite many incidents, which demonstrate the influence of Hebrew teachers upon their students. We will limit ourselves to a few: A former student of a West Bronx Hebrew School, now a president of a synagogue in the far West, instituted a no-tuition policy in his congregational school. It had been his burning desire for a long time to achieve such a goal for a Jewish school. Recently when in New York, he visited his old favorite schoolteacher. The reason for his visit became evident when he enthusiastically stated to his old teacher friend: "Do you know I have instituted a no-tuition fee educational system in the congregational school, whose president I am?" The teacher asked him why he was so enthusiastic in making such a statement to him, whereupon the synagogue president replied: "It was you who inspired me to do this. I remember once in a class you stated. 'Someday the time shall come when Jewish education will not be dependent upon tuition fees of parents, and that those who can pay will not be favored over those who cannot pay.' I remember clearly hearing you state this very fact. Since that time, it has been one of my uncompromising goals to achieve that purpose. I want to thank you for your inspiration in helping me carry this out."

A number of years ago, a rather talented young boy attended a local *Talmud Torah*. His teachers, realizing his ability, tried to cultivate in him a deep interest in Jewish learning. How successful they were they did not realize until very recently. This student graduated from *Talmud Torah* with honors. His teachers took personal interest in his work and prevailed upon him to continue his Hebrew studies. After his graduation he attended Hebrew High School classes and managed to keep up with pupils who had previously graduated from a yeshiva elementary school. While attending high school, a JEC consultant (who knew this young lad from his visits to the *Talmud Torah*) met him in a trolley car. At parting time, the boy said to the consultant in Hebrew: "If I will forget Hebrew, let my right hand whither." Several years later, the mother called the consultant and said that she was entirely satisfied with the interest the teachers took in the child and with his dedication to Jewish learning. She was happy about the influence they had over her child. However, she now had a problem. The boy had enrolled as a full time student in a *Yeshiva Gedola* and, to the exclusion of all other interests, was studying Talmud and Bible. What should she do? The happy ending of this story is that the boy will be ordained this year. He will also graduate from Brooklyn College (where he is majoring in Hebrew) at which time he hopes to pursue graduate work in Jewish education and embark upon a teaching career.

There are many Jewish leaders today, including rabbis and teachers, who came to Hebrew school from an indifferent home environment. The spark of their love for Jewish values was kindled by their Hebrew teachers. The devotion, the *"iber gebenhiet,"* the friendship of many teachers, won for them adherents. In a way, they are the *Abrahams* of our time.

In this sense, they are actually creators. Teachers create Jewish life. They breathe Jewish spirit into their students. To wit: The statement by the *Ba'ale Tosafot*: "Whoever brings one soul into Jewish living, it is said about him that it is as if he created that person and brought him into this world."

The quantity, as well as quality of a teacher's influence is often not appreciated, even by the teacher himself. During 20 years of service, at an average of 50 children annually, the teacher touches the lives of 1,000 children and 2,000 parents.

RECOGNITION AND GRATITUDE

Though the teacher influences many people, personal or public recognition of his influence and deeds are infrequent in his lifetime. Rare is the parent who goes to the teacher to tell him the right things he has done for the child. Even more unusual is the former student who goes back to tell the teacher what contribution he made to his life. The highly intuitive teacher may sense what he has done and realize his own reward, but he is only human and prizes the return of those who can put gratitude into words.

The experience of one teacher illustrates how much these rare rewards mean. A young physician, walked into a high school office, "Is Mr. S. still teaching here?" he asked. When given an affirmative answer, he said, "I must see him, because if it had not been for him, I would not be here today. One day after class I told him that my parents needed me and that I was going to leave school. I could never become a doctor. My dream would never be fulfilled. 'Come in and see me after lunch,' he said with his usual smile. I did that noon – 12 years ago – and from that moment on, I have never lost my direction. It was all because he said, 'You are intelligent, you are healthy, you have a deep understanding of people, you are religious, you have ambition, and you are industrious. Of course you can be a physician, and you can be a learned Jew, too. You can be a tribute to your parents and your people alike. We need young people like you. Let nothing stop you.' And somehow I never doubted his word."

What the teacher did quietly and without fanfare vis-à-vis the parents is a story, in itself, that remains untold. The teacher who had provided this encouraging experience vividly recalled the incident when the physician mentioned it to him, but he had no idea how much it had meant to the boy, nor had he known that he had spoken to him at the most crucial period in his life.

Not long ago, a young soldier came home on furlough and visited his Hebrew teacher. He felt compelled to visit him and thank him for his tutelage while he, the soldier, was a child. "The fact that I could pray at the battlefront gave me enough stamina to escape enemy capture, whereas 90% of my buddies failed. I think now how little I wanted to study then, and, how, by your example and motivation, you inspired me to learn to pray. My thanks can never be too great to you." His whole-hearted, warm, firm handshake at that moment was worth countless dollars and immeasurable rewards.

Even though not often expressed, gratitude for a teacher's guidance is generally deeply felt. Once a teacher befriended an orphan student. On many occasions he invited the boy to his home. The boy's mother would frequently consult the teacher about problems of rearing her child. The boy graduated from school with honors. Years rolled by. He attained his law degree and then a PhD in political science at Yale, and received a responsible governmental position in California. The teacher never forgot his orphan student. He thought that the boy bore a grudge against him, since he had not heard from him in years. However, one day the telephone rang. It was the mother of his former pupil. She read a letter she had just received from her son. At the end were special regards for his teacher and a note that he would write a letter to his former teacher. The letter did come in a few days. It was full of Jewish spirit, warmth and gratitude to his old mentor. In fact, it had a lengthy postscript in simple faultless Hebrew. Of this, the teacher once wrote: "If anyone offered me a thousand dollars for the regards I received from this pupil I would answer him, 'You take the thousand dollars and let me keep the regards.'"

"No bubble is so iridescent or floats longer," said Sir William Ogler, "than that blown by the successful teacher." The influence of the teacher has often reached to the second and third generation. Do we not constantly hear of parents who enroll their children in school and ask that their children be given the opportunity to study with the same teacher that they had while attending the same school? In one such case, a mother came from an outlying area to register her child on condition that he be placed in the class of her former teacher.

A number of years ago, in a large well-organized Jewish school, staffed with good teachers, one teacher was particularly effective with his students. His outstanding performance was generally recognized by faculty and parents. After many years of teaching, he decided to settle in Israel. A few weeks after his departure two of his pupils were returned to port. They were caught as stow-aways. Their simple explanation for their action was: "We wanted to be with our teacher and since he was going to Israel, we went with him."

AND, IN CONCLUSION

Dr. Abraham Heschel once said, "In our teachings there is no higher distinction than that of being a teacher. This has been so throughout our history. We do not celebrate kings and heroes. We celebrate teachers. The teacher is an essential pillar of Jewish living, past, present and future. Judaism is teacher-centered, and according to its tradition God himself teaches." The author was no doubt referring to the well-known *Midrashic* statement that "during special times each day, God sits and teaches young children." Teaching is indeed a Godly profession.

An anonymous dedication puts the teacher in proper perspective. In it the author says:

> I sing the praise of the unknown teacher. Great generals win campaigns, but it is the unknown soldier who wins the war. Famous educators plan new systems of pedagogy, but it is the unknown teacher who delivers and guides the young. He lives in obscurity and contends with hardship. For him no trumpets blare, no chariots wait, no golden decorations are decreed. He keeps the watch along the borders of darkness and makes the attack on the trenches of ignorance and folly. Patient in his daily duty, he strives to conquer the evil powers which are the enemies of youth. He awakens sleeping spirits. He quickens the indolent, encourages the eager, and steadies the unstable. He communicates his own joy in learning and shares with boys and girls the best treasures of his mind. He lights many candles, which, in later years, will shine back to cheer him. This is his reward. Knowledge may be gained from books; but the love of knowledge is transmitted only

by personal contact. No one has deserved better of the republic than the unknown teacher. No one is more worthy to be enrolled in a democratic aristocracy, 'king of himself and servant of mankind.'

We salute the teacher, who in the words of Plato, "holds the torch and passes it on to others." To him who lights the tapers of the child's heart, to him who lights the way of the Jewish future in America, to the teacher – guardian of the Torah, we pay noble tribute.

CHAPTER 2

ON THE MAKING OF THE JEWISH TEACHING PROFESSION

PROLOGUE

The challenge of improving the Jewish teaching profession has many faces. While the basic variations between the two "systems" of Jewish schooling may suggest different approaches to the teacher personnel challenge, the underlying philosophy of response is common to both day schools and supplementary schools. Vitally needed for both arenas is the making of a profession.

Some of the problems of Jewish school teaching are universal – common to teaching as a whole. Strange as it may seem, the practice of teaching generally is not considered a profession. It simply lacks the basic features that characterize most modern professions. Moreover, there are problems of Jewish teaching that are endemic to the Jewish school.

To begin with, the making of a Jewish teaching profession means having in place quality career-teacher preparation programs. Building a Jewish teaching profession means also making it attractive to talented young people, developing the capacity to retain good teachers, providing working conditions conducive to effective performance, and conducting staff development programs that encourage professional growth.

These characteristics strongly point to much-needed

restructuring (read professionalization) of the Jewish teaching occupation. Essentially, the professionalization process will aim towards the promotion and support of competence in teaching and *sippuk nefesh* (satisfaction) from teaching. Highly qualified teachers are usually the ones most dissatisfied with working conditions and the ones most likely to leave the profession. Making teaching a satisfying career is basic to retaining good teachers.

In restructuring the Jewish teaching occupation, the reasons other professions have succeeded must be considered with great seriousness. What are the features that characterize most modern professions and help insure competent performance? To be sure, they are rigorous entry requirements, careful adherence to licensing procedures, supervised induction, autonomous performance, peer-defined standards of practice, and increased responsibility (career growth) with increased competence.

How does the Jewish teaching profession measure up against this basic list of features? The answer to this question is obvious. The road to achieving these characteristics will be long and arduous. Restructuring the Jewish teaching occupation will entail substantial costs, not easily achieved in light of the current Jewish communal perception of teaching in Jewish schools.

When considering ways to accomplish this restructuring, it is imperative to increase significantly the entry salaries of new teachers and the base salaries of all current teaching personnel in order to make Jewish teaching a competitive profession. Providing substantial salary increments was considered the most important challenge of the Jewish community by a representative group of more than 1,000 lay and professional leaders in a recent study by this writer on the relevance of the major national studies on education to Jewish schooling.

In contrast to this finding, but not in opposition to it, are the findings of a recent Rand Report on the crisis in the general teaching profession. The Rand Report stresses that the non-pecuniary aspects of teaching are at least as important as salaries in attracting and retaining good teachers. One way to assure better salaries is to upgrade the other aspects of the teaching profession.

Historically, until basic changes were made in the structure of the legal and medical professions at the turn of the century (note that teaching is a century behind these professions), they were characterized, according to the Rand Report, "by low wages, easy access, poor training, no real standards of practice and a poor public image" – features not uncommon to the Jewish teaching profession today.

Both approaches – making the teaching profession financially rewarding and competitive, and motivating fundamental reform in the Jewish school systems – must take place simultaneously.

In order for each of these approaches to work, i.e., for increased remuneration and professionalization to become realities, Jewish teaching, in the first instance, must become a full-time occupation. In good measure, this has been achieved (or is more readily achievable) in Jewish all day education. In the Jewish supplementary schools, achieving full-time teacher status remains a serious problem, which can be resolved in good measure by making necessary changes in the concept and construct of synagogue education.

Secondly, the teacher's work environment must be altered. This means providing teachers with greater opportunities to observe each other, work in teams, make choices, plan their own work, and help beginning teachers adjust to their teaching loads.

Thirdly, we need to review the procedures of licensure. Despite valiant efforts by several communities and by the National Board of License, teacher certification makes little or no impact upon the profession. At best, it makes little difference in the quality of Jewish schooling.

Fourthly, while we go about professionalizing Jewish teaching, we must promote a more positive image of the Jewish teaching occupation. The problem of the image of teaching is that all adults have gone to school and everyone knows something about teaching, about the classroom, about the school. This universal familiarity with teaching somehow affects people's view of it as a profession. Since Jewish teaching is so crucial to Jewish continuity, its importance and specialized professional dimensions (i.e., teaching a sub-cultural lifestyle in both formal and informal settings within a voluntary environment is so very different from public school teaching) must be communicated forcefully to the Jewish community.

Finally, to insure an adequate pool of future teachers, the Jewish community must offer recruitment incentives such as scholarships and forgivable loans to academically talented youth. This kind of approach for juniors and seniors in high school and for college students has been a productive means of attracting young people to other professions. Committed Jewish youth might find the idea of Jewish teaching attractive if training scholarships were offered. This presumes the availability of training programs – in itself a vital objective – and the professionalization of Jewish teaching.

For the long haul, this writer feels that professionalization should include the development of career ladders. The value and possible realization of career ladders (like merit pay) has been debated seriously over the last several decades in general education. While there are, admittedly, difficulties with the implementation of this idea – particularly regarding evaluation of teacher performance – the benefits can outweigh significantly the disadvantages of career laddering. This approach deserves serious exploration and experimentation in Jewish education.

While the concept of the career ladder should be considered by all Jewish schools, its application will vary with local conditions. The need to adjust teacher improvement plans to specific local needs is borne out by experience in the public sector. The voluntary nature of the Jewish community and Jewish education results in the independence and autonomy of each educational unit. Developing and implementing new teacher career programs provides a unique opportunity for interschool cooperation in each locale.

Having said all this, we must continuously search for ways to upgrade the Jewish teaching profession. The following is one such effort – a career ladder of sorts. Originally formulated in 1983 as a proposal to the Fund for Jewish Education in Greater New York, as yet, it has not been funded. Nevertheless, this writer would like to share it with the Jewish education community and obtain reactions to it.

Fundamentally, this career ladder idea is a strategy for Jewish day schools. But it can be adapted for the Jewish supplementary school. It is based upon the premise that professional growth potential is basic to motivating performance, creating positive work environments and retaining good teachers.

This strategy might best be called an instructional ranking model. Similar strategies have been attempted with varying records of success across the country in public school districts. If adopted by the Jewish educational community, this plan would upgrade the instructional status of a select number of teachers in each school, with commensurate increases in their salary levels.

The objective of this proposal is to develop an experimental instructional ranking system for Judaic and general studies elementary and secondary day school teachers which is modeled after the university pattern of instructional ranking, where teaching personnel are classified as lecturer, instructor, assistant professor, associate professor, professor and distinguished professor.

Judaic and general studies teachers might be categorized as teacher, senior teacher, master teacher, and distinguished teacher. (In public education other titles for the rankings have been used or suggested, such as: associate teacher, staff teacher, senior teacher, and master teacher; or associate teacher, professional teacher, and teacher specialist; or instructor, professional teacher and career professional.)

The selection criteria for the various teaching ranks would be based on quality of instruction and longevity of service. The quality of instruction criteria might include recommendations by recent school alumni, peers, and supervisors relating to the various aspects of instruction, classroom management and climate, lesson preparation, use of educational materials, preparation of subject matter, teacher/pupil relationships, teacher/family relationships, use of feedback and evaluation, participation in interstaff responsibilities, and participation in professional growth and development activities.

Longevity of service criteria might be as follows: senior teachers – minimum of 5 years; master teachers – minimum of 10 years, and distinguished teachers – minimum of 15 years. The longevity criteria might serve as an added incentive for teachers to remain in their respective schools.

The numbers of teachers per school to be recognized as senior teacher, master teacher and distinguished teacher will vary with the size of the school faculty. Each of the ranks will carry with it a differential salary adjustment. In order to achieve this objective, it is recommended that the school pay one-half of the differential salary increase to be matched by a communal Federation/BJE grant.

In the first two levels – teacher and senior teacher – teachers would be full-time classroom instructors. In the third and fourth levels – master and distinguished teachers – they would take on special responsibilities, which would reduce their teaching loads. These responsibilities might include curriculum development activity and work with beginning teachers.

The instructional ranking program would be accompanied by a variety of advocacy and promotional activities which would give special recognition to "ranking" teachers as well as focus attention on the importance of the Jewish teaching profession.

After two or more years of experimentation, assessment of the impact and value of the project should take place through interviews with teachers, principals, school alumni, parents and lay leaders, and meetings with ranking teachers. Other ways to evaluate the impact and value of teacher ranking should also be sought. Based upon the evaluation, the model will be refined and disseminated.

Implementing career ladder procedures, and other non-pecuniary aspects of Jewish teacher professionalization, cannot take the place of providing greater economic security and social status to teachers. One must stress, over and over again, that raising salaries and providing fringe benefits (like the program sponsored by the Fund for Jewish Education and administered by the Board of Jewish Education in Greater New York, which provides life insurance, health and pension benefits to all full-time Jewish educators), and giving proper respect to teachers are *sine qua non* conditions of the professionalization process.

EPILOGUE

Reaching lofty goals is not an easy task in any realm of life. Attaining them fully is not always possible. But, to paraphrase the *Mishnaic* dictum, we are not free from striving to achieve them. The first necessary step in this direction is setting the goals. And set them – identify them, define them, examine them, describe them, refine them – we must.

In Robert Browning's immortal words, "Our reach should exceed our grasp. Otherwise, what's heaven for?" Who knows? We may even be surprised by the extent of our reach.

Let us dedicate ourselves to raising the level of teaching to heights never yet attained – for the sake of Jewish continuity, for the betterment of Jewish education, for the honor of the Jewish teacher, and for the glory of the Jewish community.

CHAPTER 3

THE JEWISH SCHOOL TEACHER TODAY AND TOMORROW

Not unlike larger society, the Jewish community has been agonizing, for the last several decades, about the problem of educational personnel-unfilled positions and the shortage of qualified personnel. There are obvious differences about the nature and extent of the problem in these disparate settings, especially between the full-day public or private school and the voluntary, part-time Jewish supplementary school.

One thing is clear, however. *Ve es khristelt zich, azoy yiddelt zich* – what happens in general education regarding the question of human resources has a significant impact on Jewish education. Therefore, a recent study, "Profile of Teachers in the United States", completed by the National Center for Education Information (NCEI) in Washington, DC, should be of more than passing interest to the Jewish educational community.

It has been widely purported that the key reasons for the inability of the school to attract talented young people into educational careers are low salary, poor working conditions and low social status. In the Jewish community, we might add two more reasons: the part-time nature of teaching in most Jewish schools and the lack of professional growth opportunities.

The NCEI report punctures a large hole in the main argument concerning the school's ability to attract and keep the best teachers. C. Emily Feistritzer, author of the report, and Director of NCEI, says it simply: "Teachers complain they don't get paid enough for the work they do. Yet, when their salaries are compared with earnings of full-time, year-round workers with comparable levels of education, they seem to fare pretty well."

The NCEI study found that teachers with four years of college make $7 more a day than other people with a four-year college education. The average salary for these teachers, according to NCEI, is $24,559 for a 180-day contract year, or $136 per workday. By comparison, the study notes, the average four-year college graduate makes $32,216 for a 250-day year, or $129 per workday. On the basis of this report, the American School Board Journal, published by the National School Boards Association, titles its October editorial "Teacher's Pay Isn't So Awful After All."

The NCEI survey involved 1,144 public school teachers and 488 private school teachers. Almost half of the public school respondents indicated that they would continue teaching, even if they were able to make $5,000 more per year in another occupation. Most preferred their current ten-month teaching job to teaching a full year with more pay. Moreover, according to the teachers, having a chance to use their intellectual abilities and to work with children and youth (which, to them, are the major advantages to teaching) is more important than "a good salary." Despite these feelings, 85 percent of the male teachers and 88 percent of the female instructors complained that they aren't paid enough.

The two national teachers' unions – the National Education Association (NEA) and the American Federation of Teachers (AFT) – take strong exception to the NCEI conclusion that the American teacher is well paid, particularly when compared with other occupations. The per diem salary figure cited in the survey,

NEA claims, blatantly overlooks several factors, including the fact that "many teachers work as many as 75 hours a week" during the school year.

Polls taken by the NEA show that teachers would be willing to work a longer year if compensated accordingly. NEA claims that parents are the ones who object to a longer school year. An NEA spokesperson concludes that, "teachers are significantly underpaid relative to their academic preparation and job responsibilities."

The AFT also takes strong issue with the report's "inane conclusions." It claims that the NCEI survey does not accurately represent teachers in big cities. The study assumes that teachers work a 35-hour week while other surveys indicate that they work an average of 41 hours a week. The AFT opines that "teacher salaries probably are artificially high right now" because of the relatively long-timers still in the profession. Finally, both unions charge that the conclusion of the report that teachers are paid adequately flies in the face of every major study of education reform during the past decade.

For her part, Emily Feistritzer claims that the NCEI study is "a straightforward look at the situation." She takes "violent exception to criticism that the survey is tainted or misleading." She concludes that it is not surprising that the unions would attack her study. "They're in the business of driving salaries up for teachers."

In contrast to the NCEI study, the recent report of the prestigious Task Force on Teaching as a Profession of the Carnegie Forum on Education and the Economy, entitled "A Nation Prepared: Teachers for the 21st Century," contends that teaching is an unattractive, high turnover, early exit occupation because "teacher salaries are extraordinarily compressed when compared to other occupations demanding a college degree. They start low and remain low. Most teachers approach the top of the scale 10 to 12 years after entering the work force."

The Carnegie Report further claims that "the conditions under which teachers work are increasingly intolerable to people who qualify for jobs in the upper tiers of the American work force, the people who must be attracted to teaching."

What do these conflicting points of view regarding the classroom teacher in general education mean for Jewish schools where compensation for full-time teaching is considerably less and where, with the exception of one community, there are no teachers' unions? The best estimates indicate that the range of teachers' salaries in Jewish day schools in the United States is $12,000 to $35,000 per year, averaging $18,500 for "full-time" employment, 20 to 35 hours per week, 180 to 220 days per year, depending on whether the yeshiva or day school employing the teachers is in session on Sunday.

The status of supplementary schoolteachers is much different, given that almost all teachers in the supplementary schools are part-time, and teach from two to 12 hours per week. The average annual wage of "full-time," 12 hour-a-week supplementary schoolteachers is $9,000 to $11,000.

What is the impact of this financial data on the Jewish teaching profession? What role does salary play in the decision of many committed Jews not to become teachers in Jewish schools? In New York, many Orthodox Jews, with intensive Jewish educational backgrounds, have opted for teaching in public schools instead of Jewish day schools and yeshivot. The Association of Orthodox Jewish (public school) Teachers has 5,000 members. What will attract the best teachers among them to the day school or yeshiva?

Given our knowledge of the vocational interests of young American Jews, what would it take to attract and keep bright young Jews in the Jewish teaching profession? What level salary? What other job characteristics must teaching in the Jewish school have to make it attractive to talented young people? What about merit pay, career ladders, professional growth opportunities and other career incentives?

The part-time nature and salary for supplementary school teaching makes it virtually impossible as a career option. What new approaches can be developed to restructure supplementary school teaching into full-time employment? Providing full-time employment via a combination of teaching in supplementary schools and working in informal education and adult education settings has been proposed by many Jewish educational leaders during the last two decades. As yet, such full-time employment opportunities are not readily available. This writer feels that synagogues must be reorganized so that teachers will become full-time family educators, working in teams with rabbis, cantors, principals and youth leaders, dealing creatively with the Jewish intergenerational needs of families.

In addition to creating full-time positions, what alternative strategies would be useful for recruiting and retaining supplementary schoolteachers? Is the recruitment and training of lay teachers a viable alternative for the supplementary school? How can this be accomplished without posing a threat to the professional teachers?

Despite all that has been written about young people not entering the Jewish teaching profession, there are some young committed Jews who are becoming career teachers. Will they stay? What will keep them? How important are factors such as fringe benefits, working conditions, length of school year, professional growth opportunities and social status?

The Carnegie Report stresses that, in addition to making teachers' salaries and career opportunities competitive with those in other professions, giving teachers a greater voice in the decisions that affect schools will make teaching more attractive to good teachers who are already in our schools as well as people considering teaching as a career. The imposition of bureaucratic authority in elementary and secondary schools is universally deplored in the plethora of school reform studies and reports (issued during the last half decade) which all emphasize the need to increase professional autonomy.

According to the Carnegie Report, effective teaching requires persons of "substantial intellectual accomplishment…who can communicate what they know to others, stimulate students to strive towards the same levels of accomplishment and create environments in which young people not only get a taste for the learning but build a base upon which they will continue to learn and apply what they know to the lives they go on to lead." The Report notes that schools have been succeeding less and less in attracting such teachers. In order to achieve this goal, it recommends far-reaching changes in the ways teachers are trained, certified, recruited, motivated and involved in the educational process. The Report suggests:

- The creation of a National Board for Professional Teaching Standards.
- The restructuring of schools to provide a more professional environment.
- The introduction of a new category of Lead Teachers to provide active leadership in schools.
- The requiring of a Bachelor's degree in Arts and Sciences as a prerequisite in the professional study of teaching.
- The development of new professional training programs leading to a Masters degree in Teaching.
- Relating incentives for teachers to school-wide student performance.
- Providing teachers with the staff support essential to teacher productivity.

Are these recommendations applicable to Jewish education? Can or should the Jewish community attempt to implement similar ideas for the Jewish teaching profession?

How the Jewish community responds to the challenges of school personnel will affect not only the future of Jewish education, but the viability and vitality of the Jewish community.

CHAPTER 4

TEACHERS AND PRINCIPALS: THE CRUCIAL LINK TO THE BUREAUS

SOME ASSUMPTIONS

- The current condition of teachers and principals in Jewish schools is not the making of Jewish educators.
- While very critical, this condition is improvable.
- Teachers and principals in Jewish schools are, by and large, devoted, dedicated and committed Jewish communal personnel, anxious to be effective and to succeed – to contribute to Jewish continuity and to enhance the quality of Jewish life.
- Many Jewish educators continuously search for ways to be more effective and to grow professionally.
- Jewish educators need and deserve much more support from the Jewish community than they presently receive.

CHALLENGE AND RESPONSE

The following is essentially a set of challenges and potential responses to the critical condition of Jewish school personnel. Based largely on my own experience in New York, as per the suggestion of Dr. Emanuel Goldman, chairman of this annual meeting, they are framed as a conversation – a presentation in the making – to be completed after serious deliberation by bureau directors.

THE CHALLENGES

The formal Jewish education vocation has evolved into disparate types of jobs or work styles varying in nature, scope, and time commitment. These are: day school teaching, day school principalship, day school administration, supplementary school teaching, supplementary school principalship, early childhood teaching and early childhood directorship. There are some commonalities and generalizations that apply in full, or in part, to each of these employment arrangements. The common or vocational characteristics can be summarized in one overarching statement.

Essentially there are eight criteria that characterize a true profession. They are:

1. Rigorous preparation
2. Rigorous entry requirements
3. Supervised induction
4. Carefully developed certification procedures
5. Peer defined standards of practice
6. Autonomous performance
7. Rigorous evaluation, and
8. Assignment of greater responsibility to practitioners with increased competence. (Darling-Hammond)

Let us apply these guideposts to teaching and principaling in Jewish schools.

1. Rigorous Preparation

Excluding the one and two-year pre-service programs in the right-wing Orthodox teacher training schools for women in New York, there are no large-scale pre-service programs for teachers in Jewish schools in North America.

To be sure, currently, in 1988, there are only 45 bachelor level students enrolled in all the Hebrew colleges on this continent. Most of the 101 master degree students in the colleges are already teaching in Jewish schools. A large number of these are Israelis not particularly interested in full-time careers in Jewish education.

Moreover, there are hardly any young people preparing for careers in Jewish education in American universities.

Compare this reality with Hebrew college enrollment two decades ago. In 1966, there were 1,800 bachelor level students in the 14 accredited Hebrew teachers colleges. All of these institutions have since dropped the word "Teachers" from their official names (Schiff, "Career Choice").

In the three postgraduate programs of the rabbinic seminaries (Hebrew Union College – Jewish Institute of Religion, Jewish Theological Seminary and Rabbi Isaac Elchanan Theological Seminary, Yeshiva University), only a very few students are being prepared for supervisory and administrative roles.

2. Rigorous Entry Requirements

Given the shortage of personnel, Jewish schools generally settle for almost anyone interested in becoming a teacher or principal. Most teachers begin their careers with minimal Judaic backgrounds. A recent study of Jewish education in Cleveland showed that 53 percent of all teachers had no Jewish education beyond high school.

The Jewish Supplementary School Study in Greater New York demonstrated that over 80 percent of the teachers had only elementary or high school Jewish education. Eleven percent had no formal Jewish education at all (Schiff, *Jewish Supplementary Schooling*). Moreover, most teachers lack adequate knowledge of Jewish pedagogy and most principals do not have sufficient knowledge of supervision of instruction in Jewish studies and Hebrew language programs.

There are, of course, exceptions to settling for unqualified teachers. One example of this is the principal of a yeshiva high school in New York who interviewed 35 applicants for a *Tanakh* teaching position. Not finding a suitable candidate, he finally went to Israel to recruit a teacher.

3. Supervised Induction

Induction procedures vary greatly from school to school. In some schools, careful step-by-step orientation is provided by principals and/or senior faculty and/or bureau staff. In the vast majority of our educational institutions, induction procedures are inadequate or non-existent.

4. Carefully Developed Certification Procedures

To begin with, there are a very small number of certified teachers and principals in our schools. Moreover, there is no standardization of certification procedures. The current national, regional and ideological certification practices are entirely inadequate or irrelevant to the vast majority of Jewish schools. To its credit, the national Board of License of Jewish Schools is currently initiating a self-study to remedy this situation.

While much different in scope and nature than that of the public schools, the problem of certification in Jewish schools can be informed by the current certification dilemma in general education. In the public school arena, education leaders ask, "Should we tighten certification requirements which are needed, or should we loosen them to counteract the teacher shortage?" Jewish education's response to this dilemma has been to relax them altogether.

In public schools the greatest shortage is in the districts that serve the most disadvantaged. In Jewish education, using the term "Jewishly disadvantaged," we might make the same observation.

5. Peer-defined Standards of Practice

This is nonexistent in Jewish education.

6. Autonomous Performance

This is nonexistent in Jewish education. Moreover, there is little or no teacher empowerment in our schools.

7. Evaluation Process

Carefully planned and implemented personnel evaluation is the exception and not the rule. By and large, there are no regularized, effective evaluation procedures for teacher or principal performance.

It is no consolation that the conditions regarding peer-defined standards of practice, autonomous performance, teacher empowerment and evaluation are not much better in general education. In the public schools, teachers are not generally involved in defining standards of instructional practices, teacher evaluation and staff development. As a rule, they "lack power and input in all the important decisions" about their schools. To be sure, teachers in the public schools are frustrated "about their powerlessness in teaching" (Boyer).

8. Assignment of Greater Responsibility to Practitioners with Increased Competence.

One of the earmarks of Jewish education is the *lack of growth opportunities* for teaching personnel.

How do bureau directors view these eight criteria of professionalism? How important is their fulfillment for the advancement of Jewish educators and for the enhancement of Jewish schooling? How do central agencies currently relate to each of the criteria? What differential roles might bureaus play regarding the application of each criterion to school-based procedures? To communitywide practices? To continental activity?

Developing responses to these questions is a necessary step in ameliorating the condition of Jewish school personnel. It is a major challenge to Jewish educational leadership and should be one of the immediate tasks of The Bureau Directors Fellowship. To underscore the need to place this challenge on future agendas of BDF, let us briefly highlight the professional characteristics of the persons employed in instructional and supervisory positions in Jewish schools on this continent.

CHARACTERISTICS OF THE JEWISH EDUCATION NON-PROFESSION

1. Teaching and principaling in most Jewish schools is, at best, a part-time vocation. The vast majority of Jewish educators teach 12 hours or less per week. The New York Jewish Supplementary School Study found that there are no full-time teachers in these

schools. Only one-third of the principals are full-time and this percentage is declining.

The only full-time career educators are in the day schools and the bureaus.

2. Teacher salaries are absolutely and relatively low – averaging $21,000 to $23,000 for 30 hours of teaching in day schools and $9,000 for 12 hours of supplementary school instruction. There is a wide gap between teachers' and principals' salaries, particularly in the day school, where principals earn, on the average, between $55,000 and $65,000 annually. In some day schools, administrators earn as much as $80,000 and more.

Fast-tracking to principalship and even to bureau positions is a growing vocational phenomenon. On the one hand, the reasons for this are the lack of qualified, experienced candidates for senior positions and inadequate career ladder opportunities. On the other hand, ambitious teachers are not satisfied with their income potential if they remain teachers. The logical step within the Jewish education enterprise is to aspire to an administrative post even if they lack the necessary qualifications.

Neither teachers nor principals enjoy the kind of social status or communal recognition they deserve. This generally results in low self-image and low self-esteem.

Jewish schoolteachers work under great stress. The sources of the stress are essentially the principal, parent and school board member. In the supplementary school it is the rabbi as well.

Turnover is very high. The recent Cleveland study found a 20 percent turnover annually in Jewish schools. In Greater New York, 62 percent of Jewish supplementary school teachers have been in their respective schools two years or less and 83 percent four years or less.

Jewish education does not attract new young talented persons. However, interestingly, some young committed Jews do choose to become Jewish schoolteachers. Witness the young people at the conferences of the Coalition for the Advancement of Jewish Education.

3. There are some good and some excellent teachers and some

good and effective principals in both the day schools and supplementary schools. I have an ambivalent feeling when generalizing about teachers and principals in Jewish schools because of this minority population. I must admit that when I attend teachers' and principals' meetings and conferences, I often get a good feeling. Many of the participants are truly committed and dedicated. Many are enthusiastic about their work. But, in reality, the vast majority of teachers and principals need significant improvement and upgrading.

The challenges here are: How do we upgrade current Jewish school personnel as quickly and effectively as possible? How do we attract new, vital talent into our field?

THE RESPONSES

Looking at the development and progress of the medical profession since the Flexner Report in 1904, the advantages of professionalization stare at us boldly. The question is: Can Jewish education ever become so professionalized? Should it make attempts at such professionalization?

On the other hand, perhaps *laissez faire* is the best approach in the voluntary setting in which Jewish education operates. Perchance, we have the best situation that can exist. Some Jewish educators will pull themselves up by the bootstraps without imposition of professional criteria upon our vocation. The vast majority of Jewish educators will never be fully professionalized, particularly since Jewish education will remain a part-time profession for most Jewish school personnel.

If we feel, however, that Jewish education must be professionalized, what course of action should we take?

The following is a set of potential responses by the bureaus to this challenge. The responses are presented as opportunities and possible strategies leading to professionalization.

1. ADVOCACY

The first response mode is making active advocacy a central agency priority on both lay and professional levels 1) to improve the image of Jewish educators, 2) to increase significantly their earning capacity, and 3) to improve their working conditions. Basic to this priority program is an understanding of the cultural and social contexts within which schools function. A fundamental contradiction inheres in the American societal context. On the one hand, the American people place a high value on education. They feel strongly about the need for an educated citizenry; they appreciate the importance of education as a factor for national strength. On the other hand, Americans consider teaching, in the words of a former U.S. Commissioner of Education, "a profession entirely appropriate for persons of second and third rate ability, and therefore have all too commonly proceeded to provide them with second or third rate educations and pay them third or fourth rate salaries (McMurrin).

The perennial question of teacher compensation is more than a dollars and cents issue. According to the New York State Association of Independent Schools it is "not fundamentally managerial or economic or political." This prestigious organization of elite private schools where teacher salaries, like those in other school systems, are low claims that teachers' compensation is basically a moral issue. "When heads and trustees finally decide on next year's teacher salaries let them ask themselves without obfuscation and without rationalization: Are we doing the *best* we can?" (Calder)

The question Jewish communal leaders should ask is "Are we doing the *best* we must do in order to insure quality Jewish education and Jewish continuity?"

The advocacy mode on the local and national levels suggests: 1) launching think tanks comprised of top community lay leaders; 2) utilizing top public relations firms to develop specialized communications techniques; 3) organizing communal task forces; and 4) sponsoring Town Hall type meetings.

The targets of the advocacy program are synagogue and day school lay leaders, rabbis and Federation lay and professional leadership. Jewish school personnel and potential Jewish educators – high school and college students – should also be targets of the advocacy program. In the 1966 study of 1800 students in the Hebrew teachers colleges only 15 percent finally chose to enter Jewish education. For the vast majority of potential Jewish educators, Jewish education lacks adequate salary inducements, sufficient communal recognition and satisfactory working conditions (Schiff, "Career Choice").

The study findings demonstrate that four conditions are necessary to convince Jewish youth with intensive Judaic backgrounds to make Jewish school career choices:

1. A competitive salary structure, including competitive entry level salaries, good fringe benefits and long term annual salary increments;
2. Social status at least equal to that of rabbis and top Jewish communal professionals;
3. Good working conditions and potential for job satisfactionat Professional growth opportunities.

A recent study of young professionals in Jewish communal service concludes that these are the very same characteristics that will attract and keep young Jewish professionals in Jewish communal service. (Reisman)

In this regard, the efforts of the Conference of Jewish Educator Organizations during the last two years are noteworthy. The "Year of the Jewish Educator" plan should be wholeheartedly supported by bureau directors and their staff. Unfortunately, this is not the case.

In addition to the above goals for the advocacy program, one other purpose is self-evident: making Jewish education a full-time career for a significantly larger number of educators. This requires providing full-time career opportunities to many supplementary school personnel by expanding the job description of an increasing number of Jewish schoolteachers and principals to include Jewish education activities and curriculum development. This is one of the recommendations of the Greater New York study of Jewish Supplementary Schools (Schiff, *Jewish Supplementary Schooling*).

It is obvious that even after significant efforts are made to provide full-time career opportunities to increasingly larger number of Jewish school personnel, for the foreseeable future, most teachers in Jewish supplementary schools will be part-time personnel. Special attention must be given to the needs of these educators, particularly since so many of them have such minimal Judaic backgrounds. How the bureau can effectuate the necessary upgrading of their basic Judaic knowledge is a question that may be beyond the challenge of professionalization. Nevertheless, it requires an immediate response.

2. INNOVATIVE RECRUITMENT PROGRAMS

Closely associated with advocacy plans are active efforts to recruit new talent. This means developing creative strategies for reaching high school and college students, utilizing young, effective teachers and administrators to communicate the positive message of a Jewish education career and the potential the future holds for Jewish educators.

This challenge is underscored by the nature of the recent award winners of the Wexner Foundation Graduate Fellowship Program. Forty-nine percent of all applicants and 71 percent of the award recipients were candidates for rabbinical schools. Of the 14 fellowships, 10 were awarded to rabbinical aspirants and two each to aspiring Jewish communal workers and educators (Reisman).

3. PRE-SERVICE, EARLY SERVICE AND IN-SERVICE TRAINING

Needed are pre-service programs for potential educators and early in-service education for newly appointed teachers requiring additional preparation in content and methodology to guarantee their effectiveness and success in teaching.

Several creative programs sponsored by the BJE of Greater New York Early Childhood Education Center might well inform the rest of the Jewish education enterprise. About a decade ago, realizing the ongoing need for early childhood teachers with both Judaic and general education backgrounds, the Early Childhood Education Center of BJE established a teachers' training program at Stern College, Yeshiva University. Currently, in the 1988–89 School Year, 27 students are enrolled in this program. BJE staff gives some of the course offerings, make all the student-teaching placements and supervise the student teachers. As incentives, BJE arranges for stipends paid by the host school, where appropriate, especially to those student teachers, who work as assistants. As an added incentive, the Jewish Early Childhood Association (the organization of Jewish early childhood educators) provides grants to assistant teachers and head teachers – who do not have sufficient background to be certified – to encourage them to return to college and begin or continue their studies toward certification. As far as in-service education is concerned, the Center offers basic skills courses to teachers in need. The Directors' Support Network sponsored by the Center enables new directors to acquire or reinforce supervisory and administrative skills.

The two-year old Holmes group of 100 universities working in five regional groupings may be an instructive model for central agencies. Noting the serious problems in teacher preparation and teacher readiness in general education, the Holmes group is "looking for a new vision of teaching" and "is seeking a new alliance to make that vision come true." A crucial element of the Holmes group effort is "schooling at the grass roots" with genuine school-university collaboration.

To achieve this purpose, a number of universities in the Holmes group are forming partnerships with public school systems to create "professional development centers" that function like teaching hospitals (Lanier and Featherstone). In effect, this is a unique way of uniting theory and practice in education.

In Jewish education, lacking strong university teacher education settings, we might ask: Is creating such centers a desirable or realistic goal? If it is, how should we go about achieving it? The New York Supplementary Education Action Plan proposal for a

BJE Teacher Center Institute, in cooperation with local universities and the three New York based rabbinical seminary educator training programs, might serve as the model for Jewish education.

Another strategy that might be emulated by bureaus is New York BJE's Interschool Visitation Program (IVN) for Day School teachers, sponsored with the Yeshiva Elementary and High School Principals Councils.

IVN's program objectives are:

1. to reduce the burnout rate among novice teachers in day schools
2. to designate veteran "master" teachers as mentors to new teachers and to create a rubric wherein they can share their knowledge and experience with others
3. to raise the level of knowledge and skill among novice teachers, specifically in the areas of teaching methodology

IVN's Major Program Activities include:

1. annual identification of about 50 new teachers and 15 veteran "master" teachers
2. five full-day programs of school visits, consisting of model lessons in the classroom by master teachers, followed by post-lesson analysis and discussion
3. a series of ten evening seminars and hands-on workshops on teaching methodology in Bible, Prophets and Hebrew language
4. a full day's visit to BJE's Teacher's Center, including a hands-on workshop on curriculum materials development

Incentives are provided to new teachers and master teachers participating in the program. Veteran teachers are compensated for their efforts and novice teachers given stipends for the purchase of books, materials and for transportation costs.

Since its inception in 1980–81, the program has served 200

new teachers and cultivated 26 master teachers. According to teacher-participants and their principals, IVN has generated a renewed sense of excitement, professionalism and challenge about the teaching of Judaic Studies. The most eloquent testimony to IVN's success is the fact that of all participants since 1980, only one has left the field of Jewish education.

Already, some of the program's graduates have assumed leadership positions. One master teacher is now a principal and two others are assistant principals of major day schools. Others are the "star" teachers in their respective schools and motivate their peers to attend continuing education programs.

Another approach to pre-service and early in-service training in Jewish schools might be patterned after the Alternative Teacher Certification Programs of the State of California. Originated as the Teacher Trainee Program and renamed the District Intern Program, it embraces four basic elements of training for novice teachers:

1. Teaching and learning processes (classroom management and student diagnosis)
2. Curriculum development and instructional techniques
3. Planning the classroom environment
4. Working with parents (McKibbin)

The California program features the pairing of mentors with novice teachers over a one-to two-year period. This strategy has proven to be very effective in early childhood programs in New York. During the past five years, New York BJE's Early Childhood Center has been operating a "one-on-one" program in which selected experienced teachers meet individually on a regular basis with new instructors, exchange classroom visitations and meet as a group to share ideas and experiences. The one-on-one program, under the guidance of a BJE early childhood specialist, has had a salutary effect upon both the novice teachers and the mentors, the latter group being groomed for directorship positions.

Developing in-service strategies for principals also requires the immediate attention of bureau directors. In this regard, the

Principals' Center concept innovated at Harvard University's School of Education in 1980 might serve as a model for Jewish schools as it has in general education.

The value of this concept is confirmed by our experience in New York. Our Principals' Center, developed with Harvard University, is a self-motivated, self-directed program of professional growth by and for principals of Jewish schools. Over the years, it has developed programmatically in two directions – as a resource center for a variety of support services and as an information center. The year-round regional sharing programs include in-depth exploration of relevant topics. The highlight of the Principals' Center activity is the annual university-based two-and-a-half-day conference at end of the school year utilizing university faculty. To date the conferences have been held twice with Harvard and once each at University of Pennsylvania and Columbia University.

4. AUTONOMOUS PERFORMANCE AND TEACHER EMPOWERMENT

Providing opportunities for teacher autonomy and the enabling of teacher empowerment will give a new face to the teaching experience in Jewish schools. With the exception of Detroit, teachers' unions present no problem in effectuating new status for teachers in Jewish schools.

Autonomous performance is a hallmark of the professions in the American free enterprise system. Medicine, law, accounting, and engineering thrive on it. Similarly, industry and corporate life encourage it. Professional empowerment goes hand-in-hand with autonomous performance.

In facilitating both of these aspects of professionalism for teachers, new roles for principals might also be developed. Principals can serve as facilitators and real change agents by providing opportunities for teachers to observe each other, work in teams, make choices, plan their own work and help beginning teachers adjust to their teaching loads.

Moreover, teachers can become involved in selecting teachers and administrators in their schools and be invited to participate in such crucial matters as teacher evaluation, staff development, school budgets and student promotion, procedures. Also, teachers can have a voice in what they are expected to teach and can regularly participate in textbook and curriculum decisions. Providing teachers with significant roles in shaping school policies would be the best expression of empowerment.

Teacher autonomy and empowerment are based on the assumption that teachers are professionals who are accountable for what goes on in their classrooms. Working on this assumption, the Rochester (New York) School District is creating a revolution in teacher professionalism in the public sector. It substantially raises salaries, guaranteeing that by 1990, teachers will earn an average of $45,000. Lead teachers will be able to earn up to $70,000 by that time.

In the new Rochester contract with teachers, traditional guarantees associated with seniority and tenure are eliminated. Instead there is a career ladder that bases advancement on performance rather than years of service and education credits. The accountability agreement requires teachers to put in five additional days for in-service training. Lead teachers must work as mentors with beginning teachers and with those who need improvement. Part of the contract is a home-based guidance system.

The Rochester experiment can well serve as a model to bureaus for what might be accomplished in Jewish education.

5. STRATEGIES FOR TEACHER AND PRINCIPAL EVALUATION

A recent survey of 42 public school systems in Pennsylvania found that the vast majority of teachers earned top ratings in the teacher evaluations concluded in these districts. "Was this the birth of a new (and long awaited) excellence in teaching or were there other ways of interpreting the data?" was the question asked by the surveyors (Langlois and Colarusso 32, 33).

Their conclusion was that the teacher ratings are the sign of a problem, not a solution. Moreover, the surveyors felt that "school executives don't know how to evaluate" and that "supervision and evaluation have become empty, time-stealing rituals."

Jewish education doesn't have the problem of a poor rating system. We simply don't rate teachers. But we do have a problem of teacher evaluation. Our challenge is to help principals learn to be real supervisors and teacher evaluators.

The Pennsylvania surveyors recommended three strategies to improve teacher evaluation:

1. Institute a team approach to evaluation;
2. Put teacher supervision and evaluation at the top of the principals many tasks;
3. Free up time for evaluation by cutting down on other administrative activities.

Given the value of these recommendions have become empty, time-stealing rituals."

1. Institute a team approach to evaluation
2. Put teacher supervision and evaluation at the top of the principals many tasks.
3. This, then, forms the substance of another critical challenge – principal evaluation. It is especially significant in a voluntary system like Jewish education where school-based management is a general practice. Developing methods of assessing the effectiveness of principals without compromising their supervisory roles is a matter of extreme importance. Given the small size of Jewish schools and the overall administrative responsibilities of the principals, their position and potential as change agents are critical to the well-being and effective operation of their respective institutions. One of the ways to make principal evaluation a non-threatening procedure is to help principals become involved in self-evaluation. In developing methods for initiating educator evaluation, the possibility of peer evaluation strategies should be explored thoroughly.

6. PROFESSIONAL GROWTH OPPORTUNITIES

Two approaches may be used in responding to the need to provide professional growth opportunities for teachers. The first is developing an instructional ranking model à la university teaching, as this writer has recommended on numerous occasions: teacher, senior teacher, master teacher and distinguished teacher; or associate teacher, staff teacher, senior teacher or master teacher (Schiff, "On the Making of the Jewish Teaching Profession").

Teacher ranking might use the medical profession's terminology as did the city of Rochester, New York: intern teacher, resident teacher, professional teacher and lead teacher – the latter term taking a leaf from the Carnegie Report on teaching (*A Nation Prepared*).

Creating the category of lead teachers is an excellent way of rewarding outstanding service and competence. Given their pedagogic experience and effectiveness, lead teachers can provide educational leadership in a variety of ways including teacher training, curriculum development and teacher evaluation.

Another approach to providing teacher growth opportunities has been recommended by Lee Shulman who notes that the teachers he respects most are uncomfortable with the ladder idea. "They want opportunities to differentiate their functions during the course of the careers, but not necessarily in a one way fashion. We probably need a new metaphor: a ladder may be misleading because ladders go up, suggesting something else is down. We need a model like the one in medicine, where getting better and more respected as a physician does not mean that you've stopped caring for patients. The chief of medicine at a good hospital takes on leadership responsibilities, but continues to be fully involved in practice" (Brandt 44).

Using the lead teacher idea as a lateral concept with differentiated pay for added pedagogic curriculum and administrative responsibilities is one way of implementing this non-ladder approach to growth.

Regarding principals, professional growth and empowerment might be achieved via principals' councils established and staffed by the bureau. A cost-effective way of involving principals, in their own self-development, the council acts as a support group, a sharing mechanism and a learning environment. Within the council setting, principals can work on common projects, develop self-growth activities in a non-threatening climate and initiate program proposals for implementation in individual schools.

AFTERWORD

If one applies the criteria of a profession to Jewish education, we find, indeed, that it is wanting in all the attributes that characterize a true profession.

Given the current level of awareness by Jewish communal leadership of the importance of Jewish education for Jewish continuity and for the enhancement of the quality of Jewish life, there is reason to believe that support will be forthcoming to help professionalize the Jewish education vocation.

The key to upgrading the career of Jewish educators lies, in great measure, in the hands of the respective bureaus of Jewish education. Individually and collectively, it is both a challenge and an opportunity.

NOTES:

Working as an instructor or director in a Jewish early childhood program may be an exception to this generalization. According to the director and staff of the Jewish Early Childhood Center of BJE of Greater New York, early childhood teaching and directorship qualify to be called professions when measured against the criteria in this presentation. In terms of rigorous preparation, all early childhood directors in New York, with rare exception, and most head teachers working in JCC's synagogue programs, Modern Orthodox, and Conservative day schools have a Master's degree in education – a requirement for New York State Certification. Entry requirements for early childhood teaching are explicit. In the large majority of schools, where there are early childhood directors, supervised induction does occur. Professional growth opportunities are available on the early childhood level. Advancement is possible from assistant teacher to head teacher to assistant director to director – the steps of the early childhood education ladder.

2. Bais Yaacov Academy, Bais Yaacov Seminary of Boro Park, Sara Schenirer Teachers' Seminary, Beth Rivkah Teachers' Seminary, Bnos Leah Seminary of Prospect Park, and Rika Breuer's Teacher's Seminary. These seminaries have a total enrollment of approximately 500 students.

CHAPTER 5

IMPERATIVES OF SCHOOL EFFECTIVENESS

Today's assembly of the whole professional family of the Hebrew Academy of Nassau County, bringing together two hundred and sixty administrators, early childhood, elementary, middle school Jewish studies, and general studies teachers, specialists, general and Jewish studies high school instructors – male and female faculty members – is an important school activity.

In *A Place Called School*, John Goodlad, one of the educational giants of the twentieth century, stresses the importance of all school personnel (including non-educational staff) being part of and feeling part of the same team. In some way, each individual staff member must share in the grand vision for the school. "There can be no real continuous progress unless everyone embraces the same school philosophy," emphasizes Goodlad. On its part, the school's first responsibility is to the social order of the institution, what he called the "nation-state," referring to the duality – the school (educational society) on one hand, and the individuals (teachers and administrators) on the other hand working together as one unit.

HINUKH IN JEWISH TRADITION

It may be like bringing coals to Newcastle for the Jewish Studies faculty, but there are some basic Judaic tenets vis-à-vis Jewish education that, I believe, must be shared with Jewish studies and general studies teachers when speaking to the totality of the instructional staff. Historically, Jewish schooling played a unique role in Jewish life – more than in any other culture or nationality. Biblical and post-biblical literature is replete with statements about the uniqueness and importance of *Hinukh* – the special role of Jewish schooling.

The Jewish people were the first to introduce the idea of compulsory education. Some 2,000 years ago, Shimon ben Shetach initiated the concept of required schooling for high school aged youth – 15 and 16 years old. Some years later, Joshua ben Gamla formulated the principles and practices for the Jewish education of children six and seven years and older. According to the Talmudic sages, it is forbidden to live in a city without a *melamed tinokot* – a teacher of young children. This was a revolutionary concept two millennia ago. Schooling, we are told, was not to be interrupted even for the building of the Temple in Jerusalem. Nothing, save matters of life and death, was important enough to postpone the study of Torah. No other people has placed such emphasis on education for its young.

The role of the teacher was considered holy. Teaching is a Godly profession. Our sages inform us, "God, himself during each day spends time in instructing young children." The influence of teaching – the impact of the instructional process – was keenly recognized by Jewish tradition. "Whoever teaches the offspring of friends, it is considered as if he (she) gave birth to that child" declared our Talmudic sages.

While teachers were never compensated adequately for their work, their role in enhancing Jewish life was always acknowledged in Judaic literature and in communal documents. Since we teach the whole child and prepare our students for life's journey, both Jewish and general studies faculty are vitally important for their future. The inherent value of the combination or synthesis of Torah and *Mada* – of Jewish and general culture – is why we attach so much significance to the Jewish Day School idea and practice.

CHALLENGES TO THE JEWISH DAY SCHOOL

The current challenge to the Jewish Day School in America is crystal clear. The 1990 National Jewish Population Study demonstrated that there was a 52% intermarriage rate among American Jews. Whether the intermarriage rate is 52% or 47%, as the 2000 National Population Study shows, the Jewish community must take the necessary steps to combat this disease. The only way to win the war against such assimilation is through Jewish education – specifically, Jewish all day schooling.

My 1994 study of 8,000 Jewish Day School graduates, entitled, "The Jewishness Quotient of Day School Graduates," showed that the overall intermarriage rate of former Jewish Day School students is 4.5% and only 1% for those who completed a Jewish Day School high school. My findings put to rest the contention of several secular Jewish academics that Jewish education makes no difference when it comes to intermarriage. Moreover, the study motivated greater Federation support of Jewish all day education and it encouraged the founding of some thirty Jewish Day School high schools during the last decade.

ELEMENTS OF SCHOOL EFFECTIVENESS

We must ask ourselves what are the concomitants of educational success in the Jewish Day School? In answering this question, I'd like to share several thoughts with you:

Benjamin Bloom, famed educational taxonomer at the University of Chicago, in a fascinating study entitled, *Developing Talent in Young People*, found that there are two features common to the background of all top performers he researched in the arts, sports, academia and science.

The first common factor is home support. In summarizing his research, Bloom notes that "the parents of talented individuals… are genuinely concerned about their children and want to do the best for them at all stages of their development. To a large extent, they could be described as child-oriented and willing to devote their time, their resources and their energy to giving each of their children the best conditions they could provide for them. Almost no sacrifice was too great if they thought it would help their children's development." It is clear that to be successful, education must be a synergistic experience. Teacher effectiveness depends upon parents and parent effectiveness depends upon teachers.

The second characteristic common to top performers in the Bloom study is quality "time on task." One cannot really succeed in study unless he/she invests sufficient time in it under the tutelage of excellent instructors in school, in the classroom. Quality "time on task" refers also to time spent outside the classroom, particularly in the home.

EFFECTIVE SCHOOLS RESEARCH

The second thought I'd like to share with you is about the Effective Schools Research movement led by Ronald Edwards in the 1970s and 1980s. The findings of this research still hold true today. After many exhaustive studies, Effective Schools Research developed a variety of correlates of educational effectiveness. I'll share several of these with you now.

The first correlate is "a clearly defined curriculum" in which all stakeholders in the school participate in developing.

The second correlate is "strong instructional leadership." There are some bad schools with good principals, but there are no good schools with bad principals. This is a challenge to every school – public and private.

The third correlate emphasizes how basic is "a positive school climate and orderly atmosphere" conducive to learning. Faculty collegiality is a crucial element of a good educational program. In a good school, teachers and principals work together. In an effective school, neophyte teachers observe veterans who demonstrate skill.

A good school is a place where teachers create warm, social-emotional relationships with students and help them get ready to learn. The importance of readiness for learning cannot be overemphasized. In the early 1900s, William Chandler Bagley called this kind of student baggage "ripeness" – the ultimate readiness for learning.

The fourth correlate is "high expectations by principals and teachers for pupil growth," a vital concomitant of educational success. "Teachers set high standards for learning and let students know they are expected to meet them." Parents must share in the high expectations. They are told about student successes and requested to help their children to keep working towards excellence. Research shows that even in the best of schools, higher expectations yield high results as they affect pupil and parent perceptions.

CONFLUENCE OF THE COGNITIVE AND AFFECTIVE DOMAINS

After visiting Jewish Day Schools throughout the world – in Australia, South Africa, Turkey, Belgium, France, England, Canada, Israel and in fifty communities in the United States – I've come away with a strong feeling for the importance of the confluence of the cognitive and affective domains in the educational process. The Torah provides us with a remarkable example of this kind of confluence.

Bezalel, the architect of the Tabernacle in the Wilderness, was known as wise of heart. Here the question is why was Bezalel not called wise of mind? Is not the seat of a person's wisdom and intellectual powers – the mind, the brain? The answer is obvious. The *lev* – the heart – is the key to the effectiveness of study and performance. A person's emotional feelings about learning are basic to its efficaciousness and permanence. Pupils motivated to learn in class and outside of the classroom are the very ones to succeed in school and in their life's work.

Research tells us that motivating quality time to do homework has a powerful impact on the effect of learning. The superior achievement of Japanese students, for example, is attributable to a combination of quality study time in school and extraordinary effort outside the school. This kind of example supports the findings of Benjamin Bloom's research on top performers.

MODELING

Another educational concept that deserves more attention is the idea of "modeling." Research done at the Annenberg Institute of Psychology and Communication at the University of Pennsylvania in the 1950s shows that the greatest impact of the instructional process is through modeling. A teacher's personality, behavior, attitude and relationships to students are most crucial. I'm convinced that these traits are key aspects of the hidden curriculum. Abraham Heschel, in his learned study *The Prophets*, emphasized that the major contribution of the biblical prophets, their effect upon people, was essentially the result of "who they were", more than what they said and what they did.

Modeling in a school is a multileveled phenomenon. It has a cascading effect upon the human resources of the institution. In the first place, administrative leaders are the models for teachers. In a good school, they serve as inspirational paradigms. Secondly, teachers are models for students and their parents. And, thirdly, experienced instructors are models for new teachers.

INSTRUCTIONAL PROFESSIONALISM

Principals and teachers – together with the lay leadership of the school – play critical roles in establishing school-wide and classroom standards of study both in Jewish and general studies. Whereas in the past, piety, knowledge, and devotion were the qualities most often required of prospective Jewish Day School Judaic Studies teachers, the times in which we live demonstrates the need for pedagogical and motivational skills for both Judaic and general studies faculties.

In the many conversations I have had with the Rav, Rabbi Joseph Ber Soloveitchik, *z'l*, about the training of Jewish educators, he stressed the absolute crucialness of professionalism. Not only was he the giant of Jewish law and lore, but, in practice, the founder of the first elementary Jewish Day School outside the confines of Greater New York – The Maimonides School in Brookline, Massachusetts – which he visited for a full day every Friday. He took special pains to see that teachers, in his words, "were on the right pedagogical wavelength."

ISRAEL AND THE SCHOOL PROGRAM

There is a major challenge that Jewish day schools face at the beginning of the 21st century. In the topsy-turvy world in which we live, particularly, with all the unrest in Israel and the continuing terrorism, Jewish day schools must provide special knowledge about the Jewish State via programs in both Jewish and general studies. Whether or not there is violence in the Middle East, Israel and Zionism should be regular subjects in the yeshiva curriculum. This is one area in which both Jewish and general studies departments can cooperate on each class level, particularly in social studies relating to the history, geography, government and culture of *Medinat Yisrael*. It is not easy, nor always desirable, to integrate Jewish and general studies, even in *Torah U'mada* institutions, but, this is one subject area where investing time and energy and working hard together are well worth the effort.

SCHIFF GAP THEORY

One final challenge, common to all schools, all grades and all subjects, relates to the curriculum. Over the years, as a result of my meetings with principals and teachers in schools throughout the world, I've developed what I call the Schiff gap theory. I've used it in my classes in Curriculum Development and Curriculum Design and I'd like to share it briefly with you today.

When we approach the task of creating curricula for the various grade levels and for the variety of subjects we teach, initially we develop mental ideas about what we want to accomplish and what we think students should know upon the completion of the particular subject area we are planning. This first stage of curriculum development, which represents our conceptualization of the instructional components of the school or class program is called the **ideal curriculum**.

Then, we begin the implementation process and start to concretize the vision of what should be taught in a written document, which we call the **formal curriculum**. Between the ideal curriculum and the practical formulation of the programmatic vision there is a gap. Not everything we envision is always encapsulated in writing.

After the formal curriculum is completed – by whoever prepares it – the curriculum becomes the property and responsibility of the teachers who judge its relevance in light of their classroom conditions. They view the practicality of the curriculum through the eyes of their pupils. This stage of curriculum design is called the **perceived curriculum**.

Between the perceived curriculum and the formal curriculum there is another gap. Teachers feel obligated to adjust the formal curriculum to their class needs. Then, they begin to implement the perceived curriculum. The implementation stage, which begins with lesson planning, is called the **operational curriculum**. It is the actualization of the ideal, formal, and perceived stages of curriculum design. What the teachers actually teach – including the hidden curriculum, the spontaneous, unintended learning that takes place during the instructional process – and how they teach the subjects at hand create the operational curriculum. And, there is a gap between the operational and **perceived curriculum**.

And we are not finished yet. There is one obvious final stage in curriculum design. This stage relates to the teaching-learning process. According to David Seeley, the former Executive Vice President of the New York State Public School Association, the learning part of the teaching–learning process, is what makes a teacher effective. No matter how hard the teacher works on instruction, if real learning does not take place, the subject he/she is teaching is, in essence, "undeliverable merchandise."

Seeley stresses that the problem of ineffective teaching is that teachers "teach 'em too much." They don't "learn 'em enough." Learning, the real outcome of teaching is the final stage of curriculum design. This stage is called the *experiential curriculum*. And, there is a gap between the experiential curriculum and the operational curriculum. Not everything teachers plan to teach and actually teach in the classroom is absorbed by pupils, certainly not by all pupils.

And so, we have five stages of curriculum design and four gaps:

>from **ideal** to **formal**,
>from **formal** to **perceived**,
>from **perceived** to **operational**
>and from **operational** to **experiential**.

The key to successful curriculum planning is narrowing the gaps between the five curriculum design stages. This can happen only if teachers and principals plan together and periodically adjust the curricula to the teaching-learning conditions.

And, this brings us back to the school environment that encourages cooperative activity amongst teachers and between teachers and administrators. Since the Hebrew Academy, traditionally, has had a propensity for faculty collegiality and for administrative-teacher cooperation and tries to excel in the one team-one family feeling, I'm sure that the new school year including the various levels of curriculum implementation will give all of you a great sense of satisfaction and achievement at the end of the year.

CHAPTER 6

LEADERSHIP IN JUDAIC SOURCES: A COMPARATIVE VIEW

Contemporary research literature abounds with studies, articles and reports regarding leadership skills and characteristics. Industry has produced many volumes on the subject. Sociological literature is replete with discussions on traits and skills of leaders. Similarly, in general education, there are many studies and reports on the attributes and abilities needed for effective school leadership.

In light of the profusion of research and essays about leadership, what does Jewish tradition say about this subject? What can we learn about the qualities of desirable leadership behavior from the Bible, the Talmud, and medieval Jewish sources? It would be interesting to compare the insights of the Judaic tradition to our conventional ways of thinking about leadership.

Alvin Toffler, author of the celebrated works, *Future Shock* and *The Third Wave*, feels that our uncertain times create a demand and "intensifying cry" for strong and even authoritarian leadership in every walk of life, particularly, again, on the political scene. As an example, he notes that in Great Britain, "Margaret Thatcher is elected because she offers at least the illusion of being the Iron Lady." Witness, also the reelection of President Reagan by people who didn't agree with his political, social, educational and economic outlook, let alone benefit from his policies and practices.

The need for strong professional leadership, according to Toffler, is felt in every form of organization. Historically, in the First Wave, during the agricultural revolution, which corresponds roughly to biblical times, leaders needed only to be shrewd. "Literacy and broad powers of abstract thought," Toffler says, "were not necessary at all. The leader during this period was typically free to exercise sweeping personal authority in the most capricious, even whimsical fashion, unchecked by constitution, legislature, or public opinion. If approval was needed, it was only from a small coterie of other secondary leaders."

Toffler notes that the Second Wave leader, during the 18th and 19th century industrial revolution, by contrast, felt an impersonal and increasingly abstract power. He had many decisions to make on a far wider variety of matters…his decisions had to be implemented through a chain of organized activities whose complex relationships to one another had to be understood and orchestrated. He had to be literate and capable of abstract reasoning.

Now, in the beginning of the Third Wave of human existence, there are a variety of current leadership theories we might consider. During the last several decades, "studyafter study indicates that the effective leader is one *who has a clear vision of what should be done*, but, more importantly, knows how to get high performance out of all types of people in all kinds of circumstances." (Brewer "Essentials")

We are informed that in the corporate world, "leadership over human beings is exercised when persons with certain motives and purposes mobilize in competition or conflict with others, institutional, political, psychological, and other resources so as to arouse, engage and satisfy the motives of followers." (Burns 13) While they may share common characteristics, not all effective leaders have the same style of leadership. According to

James H. Brewer, author of the Kelwyn Leadership Personality Compatibility Inventory, "Successful leaders come in all shapes and sizes and from all kinds of backgrounds. Leadership training that prescribes one way to lead is doomed. People bring their identities and personalities with them to training and we are unlikely to change trainees fundamentally. We can help them understand their own qualities and how to use them to manage effectively." (Brewer "Leadership Training")

The necessary attributes of leadership in current management literature may be summarized as follows:

The leader must be intelligent, knowledgeable, understanding, flexible, able to make difficult decisions, able to motivate staff to achieve maximum potential, confident in his own ability, able to learn from others, and not be threatened by differences.

Furthermore, these essential traits and skills can be consolidated into three ability groupings:

1. Ability to communicate professional goals to staff;
2. Ability to organize staff intellect and energies into an effective and efficient team, the members of which feel comfortable and confident about their respective roles;
3. Ability to influence others and direct their energies toward achieving the leader's personal and professional goals. (Brewer, lecture)

A prominent researcher in administration notes that leaders must be able to "grow a healthy ego; communicate well; develop people power; set clear priorities; show integrity; be visible; become well-rounded; hire talented people; manage effectively; be politically savvy; and be decisive." (Heller)

In a recent study, the Board of Examiners of the New York City Board of Education asked a variety of teachers, principals, parents and communal leaders: "If you were selecting a principal for your school, what five *personal* characteristics would you consider most important?" According to the 1,500 respondents to this question, the most important *personal* characteristics, in rank order, are: good human relations, innovativeness, integrity, fair-mindedness, and good humor.

In response to the question, "If you were selecting a principal for your school, what five *professional* characteristics would you consider most important?" Their response, in rank order, was: administrative and supervisory skill, relates well to parents and community, dedication, personal character, and skill in evaluation. (Teitelbaum and James)

Here we note that the respondents listed three *personal* traits – "relates well to parents," "dedication" and "personal character" – as *professional* characteristics. Obviously, many people have difficulty differentiating between personal qualities of leadership and professional skills. Unquestionably, they are integrally related.

In exploring Judaic sources concerning leadership, two principles inform our discussion. The first is *imitatio Dei*. According to the Talmud, Jews are obliged to imitate the Almighty. The second tenet is that leaders and heroes, like ordinary people, are human, not superhuman. The Bible portrays biblical heroes with all their human frailties.

Having said this, we begin our brief exploration of Judaic sources with a profile of Abraham, the patriarch, as a prototypical example of leadership, based upon biblical, Talmudic, and post-Talmudic literature. The biblical narrative impressively conveys that Abraham had a sense of *personal mission*. He knew exactly what he wanted to accomplish. According to the Talmud, Abraham was a man of *unusual vision and rare personal conviction*. We are told that he observed all the commandments, even though they had not yet been revealed (*Yoma* 28b).

Abraham waged a strenuous battle in the cause of spreading the *idea of monotheism* and won over many converts. When he left Haran to journey to Canaan, the Bible tells that, in addition to taking with him all the wealth he and his wife, Sarah, had amassed, they took "the persons they had acquired in Haran" – literally, the "souls they had made." Rashi, the great medieval Bible commentator, quoting the Midrash, tells us that this phrase refers to the many converts to monotheism that they had made. "Abraham proselytized the men and Sarah proselytized the women." (Genesis 12:5) According to tradition, Abraham set up an inn and provided free meals to everyone who came by. When people finished eating and thanked him, he would say, "Don't thank me, thank God, the real provider of our food." (*Breishit Rabbah* 54)

Abraham was a great *humanitarian*. His tent had open doors on all four sides to encourage strangers to visit and dine (84). Even though he had many servants, being a rich man, he himself waited on his guests. He was a doer (*Baba Metzia* 87a). He wanted to perform the mitzvah of *hakhnassat orhim* (hospitality to strangers) himself. In this way, Abraham combined humanitarianism (the qualities of the prophet) with spiritual leadership (the qualities of the priest) as he taught his guests to say Grace after Meals.

Abraham's humanitarianism reached its pinnacle in his dramatic appeal to save the people of Sodom. We recall how he argued with God. The Midrash compares his arguments with those of Job. The Talmud states that "Abraham, our father, was punished and his descendants enslaved in Egypt" because he pressed scholars into military service to save his nephew Lot (*Nedarim* 31a). Parenthetically, the story of the saving of Lot vividly demonstrates that Abraham was courageous and decisive.

In *Kabbalah*, Abraham is the personification of *hesed* – loving kindness and gentleness. (*Zohar*) So great was Abraham's *hesed* that the sages of the Talmud declared: "A person who shows mercy to other people is clearly of the seed of Abraham." (*Baitzah* 32b)

The Bible informs us that Abraham was a very successful businessman. "And Abraham was very rich in cattle, in silver and in gold." (Genesis 13:3) It is obvious that Abraham was an outstanding communicator. Witness his many encounters with neighbors, kings, landowners, and relatives.

Abraham was a *man of the world*. In Apocryphal literature, Abraham is described as the *founder of two cities* – Hebron in Canaan and Tzoan in Egypt – and as a *community legislator* – two principal functions of a great leader, according to a Hellenistic concept. His broad knowledge is described in extravagant terms. We are told that he even instructed farmers in the art of improved plowing in order to hide the seeds from the ravens. (*Book of Jubilees*)

Abraham personified *individuality and independence*. According to Philo of Alexandria, the famed first century philosopher, Abraham was the archetype of a "truly free man," being a "friend of God," emancipated from "vain opinion" and from the whims of time, not dependent upon the views and desires of other people.

Dr. Joseph Hertz, former chief rabbi of the British Empire, in his commentary on the Pentateuch, concludes that, "Abraham's fine sense of independence would not permit him to benefit in the slightest degree by the rescue of his kinsman." We recall how Abraham told the King of Sodom: "I will not take a thread nor a shoelace nor anything that is yours so that you should not say "I have made Abraham rich." (Genesis 14:23)

Faith and perseverance were Abraham's trademarks. We are informed in the *Mishnah* that he "was tried with ten trials and stood firm on all of them, to make known how great was the love of Abraham towards God." (*Ethics of the Fathers* 5:4)

Samson Raphael Hirsch, the German Jewish nineteenth century scholar, suggests that the repeated trials should be taken as evidence in themselves of the high regard in which God held Abraham. As the *Midrash* has it: "The potter will strike only those pots that are good and whole to test them, because he knows that they will withstand even repeated blows." (*Breishit Rabbah* 32:4)

Maimonides, in his *Guide to the Perplexed*, maintains that "the purpose of a trial by Heaven is to give posterity a sublime illustration of an important leader trait – perfect faith in God. Hence, the tests of Abraham and Job are recorded in scripture for all eternity..." (*Guide* 3:24). And, therefore, the *Midrash* compares a *nisayon* (a trial) to a *nes* (a banner) since both words share a common Hebraic root. (*Breishit Rabbah* 32:4)

According to Maimonides, Abraham attained the highest level of prophecy, next to Moses; and he was the near-perfect leader (*Guide* 2:45). As such, it seems appropriate to study several passages dealing with the attributes of prophets and leaders in Maimonides' *Mishneh Torah*, the fourteen-volume compendium of the Written and Oral Law, popularly know as the *Yad Hahazakah* (The Strong Hand).

It is appropriate to study a Maimonidean text for another reason. We recently celebrated the 850th anniversary of Maimonides, who himself was a unique model of leadership, being, at one and the same time, a brilliant philosopher, an outstanding Talmudic scholar, a renowned physician and a distinguished communal leader.

But first, we listen to Abraham Joshua Heschel, who places the prophet into proper perspective: "The significance of Israel's prophets," he writes, "lies not only in what they said, but also in what they were." (*Prophets* XII)

"The prophet is a person, not a microphone. He is endowed with a *mission*, with the power of a word, not his own, that accounts for his greatness, but also the *temperament, concern, character and individuality*." (XIV)

"The prophet's task is to convey a divine view, yet as a person he *is* a point of view." (XIV)

"The prophet is not only a prophet. He is also a poet, preacher, patriot, statesman, social critic, and moralist." (XIV)

And, so we see, the prophet is a multifaceted personality, representing the many sides of a leader.

In introducing his ideas on prophetic leadership, Maimonides posits that the people interacting with the prophet must believe in his potential for leadership. As such, Maimonides teaches:

> It is a basic principle of the Torah to know that God endows people with prophecy. [And, he notes] prophecy does not devolve except upon a person who is very, very wise, strong in his ethical qualities so that his evil inclination does not overcome him, but his mind overpowers it always; and he possesses a wide range of accurate knowledge…a person so imbued with these characteristics…will be elevated to holiness, retreating from the ways of common people who go along in the darkness of their time. He will constantly motivate

himself and teach himself not to have any extraneous, capricious thoughts, but his mind will be turned toward the heavenly throne…and then the holy spirit will devolve upon him immediately…and when this spirit rests on him, he should will reach angelic heights…and he will change into another person altogether…(a prophet, a leader). (*Mada* 7:1)

Commenting on Maimonides' statement that prophecy comes only to a person who, among others things, is *wise* and *strong* in ethical qualities, Joseph Caro, famed 16th century Halachist notes:

The Talmud states that the Holy-One-Blessed-Be-He rests his prophecy on one who is *wise*, *strong* and *rich* (*Nedarim* 38a). Our rabbi (Maimonides) does not interpret the words "strong" and "rich" literally but explains them according to *the Ethics of the Fathers*, where it is written, "Who is *strong*? He who subdues his passions (evil inclination)…Who is rich? He who is happy with his lot" (4:1).

Maimonides insists on the literal meaning of the word *wise* as a requisite for prophecy. But, he does not consider physical strength and wealth *per se* as basic requirements for prophetic leadership (*Mada* 7:1).

In another vein, Maimonides feels strongly that a prophet's disposition is crucial for effective leadership. "Prophecy," he says, "does not come through sadness, nor through laziness, but through happiness" (7:4).

After the biblical period, prophecy ceased. The role of prophet was taken over by the wise communal leader or the *dayan*, the religious judge.

Regarding the traits of the *dayan*, Maimonides teaches:

Only those are eligible to serve as members of the Sanhedrin (the Court)…who are wise men and understanding, that is, who are experts in the Torah and versed in many other

> branches of learning; who possess some knowledge of the general sciences such as medicine, mathematics, (the calculation of) cycles and constellations; and somewhat acquainted with astrology, the arts of diviners, soothsayers, sorcerers, the superstitious practices of idolaters, and similar matters, so that they be competent to deal with cases requiring such knowledge. (*Hilchot Sanhedrim, Judges* 2:1)

Here we see how Maimonides stresses the need for the communal leader to know his community and the nature of the people for whom he provides leadership and be prepared to deal with them according to their respective needs. Maimonides is very clear about other personal requisites of leadership. He writes:

> Every conceivable effort should be made to the end that all the members of that tribunal (the Sanhedrin) be of mature age, imposing stature, good appearance, that they be able to express their views in clear and well-chosen words, and be conversant with most of the spoken languages, in order that the Sanhedrin may dispense with the services of an interpreter. (*Sanhedrin, Judges* 2:6)
>
> In the case of members of a small city court, all the above-mentioned requirements are not insisted upon. Nevertheless, it is essential that every one of its members posses the following seven qualifications: *wisdom, humility, fear of God, disdain of financial gain, love of truth, love of fellow men, and a good reputation.* (2:3)

Maimonides excludes several kinds of people from leadership. He writes, "Neither a very aged man nor a eunuch is appointed to any Sanhedrin, since these are apt to be wanting in tenderness; nor is one who is childless be appointed because a member of the Sanhedrin must be a person who is sympathetic" (2:3).

For Maimonides, the way a leader deals with people is of paramount importance:

It is forbidden to lead the community in a domineering and arrogant manner. One should exercise one's authority in a spirit of humility and reverence. The man at the head of the community who arouses excessive fear in the hearts of the members thereof, for any but a religious purpose will be punished. (25:1)

He is also forbidden to treat the people with disrespect, though they be ignorant. He should not force his way through a group of people to get to his seat, for though they be uninformed and lowly, they are the children of Abraham, Isaac and Jacob, the children of God, brought out of Egypt with great power and with a mighty hand. (25:2)

The leader "should patiently bear the burden of the community, as did Moses in the wilderness."

Maimonides is careful to instruct leaders how they should behave in every aspect of their personal lives. He generally refers to the leader as a *talmid hacham* – a wise man. Maimonides writes:

> Just as the wise man is noted for his wisdom and his moral traits, by which he is distinguished from the rest of the people, so he ought to be noted for his proper behavior, for his food and drink – for the manner of his speaking, walking, dressing, and the management of his affairs and transactions. All these actions should be decent and altogether proper (*Mada* 5:1).

He encourages the wise man to teach by example, "talk gently to people, love peace and strive for it, not be haughty or arrogant, not be a glutton, dress neatly, and manage his personal affairs judiciously" (5:7, 9, and 10).

Moreover, stresses Maimonides, "a wise man is honest in all his transactions. When he says "no" he means no, and when he says "yes" he means yes – he does not encroach on another man's occupation, and never mistreats anyone. In short, he prefers rather to be among the offended than among the offenders" (5:13).

From the above discussion, it is crystal clear that Maimonides, reflecting the spirit of the Talmud, considered the subject of leadership qualities to be exceedingly important for the welfare of the Jewish community.

In conclusion, it seems instructive to compare our conventional thinking and research on leadership to that offered by our Judaic sources. Current literature abounds with lists of traits of good leaders. These generally indicate that "good leaders are almost supermen who display qualities such as high intelligence, superior scholarship, enthusiasm, friendliness, affection for people, an abundance of vitality and nervous energy, and a good sense of humor" (Spain). Although effective leaders may [possess] many, if not most, of these qualities initially, they generally began humbly and built upon the strength which they possessed.

Paralleling the advice of our Judaic sources, one current text on leadership development counsels:

> Persons who find themselves in positions of leadership should be interested in utilizing more effectively the equalities they already possess. They should also strive, over a period of years, to develop additional strengths. Most of the qualities which effective leaders possess result from interest in the world and the people who inhabit it. These qualities are, in essence, the marks of a mature person. Certainly, leaders should establish for themselves patterns of living, which will continually support basic human values and lead to sound emotional growth and intellectual vitality. (Spain)

In short, there is a striking resemblance between Judaic sources and current thinking on the subject of leadership qualities. To some professionals in the 1980s this may come as a surprise. Yet, the similarities should not be unexpected. To be sure, due to amazing advances in technology during the last century, the quality of human life and the availability of cosmic knowledge have changed beyond description. However, twentieth century homo sapiens are endowed with basically the same human traits and propensities as their predecessors during the last three millennia.

Effective leadership in every age has required an understanding of human characteristics and needs as they apply to the particular circumstances of the times and places in which people live. Towards this end, both Judaic sources and modern literature on leadership underscore the significance of the personal traits of the leader. Both emphasize the importance of a strong sense of purpose and clear vision and the ability to communicate the leader's mission by personal example as well as by direction.

Both Jewish tradition and current experience stress the need for a leader to possess a strong positive self-image, to believe in his own ability and to have and demonstrate genuine concern for the people under his leadership. Finally both consider knowledge and maturity to be vital assets of leadership.

In all, the similarities between the Judaic sources and current thinking on leadership suggest, to use a Solomonic phrase, "There is nothing new under the sun."

CHAPTER 7

SHARED IDENTITY OF JEWISH COMMUNAL WORKERS: THE JEWISH DIMENSION

I am honored and most pleased to join a distinguished group of scholar-practitioners who have served as Sidney Vincent scholars-in-residence at the annual Conference of Jewish Communal Service. This forum honors the memory of a Jewish communal worker who, in his professional and personal life, served as a model of knowledgeable, creative, compassionate and forward looking Jewish communal leadership.

The scholar-in-residence practice is in good Jewish tradition. That tradition informs us that wisdom, at best, is the accumulation of experience. Indeed, one interpretation of the Hebrew word *ziknah* (which literally means "old age" attained at age 60) is "the one who has acquired wisdom." This interpretation, I believe, is the justification for my role this year at our annual conference.

Accordingly, based upon my own experience, I would like to share some thoughts with you about a major challenge for Jewish communal workers. Each CJCS scholar-in-residence had a special reservoir of experience upon which he drew for his remarks.

My particular background suggests that my comment should be introduced by a *dvar Torah*.

But, first, I was asked to tell about what motivated me to become a Jewish communal educator, given that there were other more lucrative and professionally satisfying opportunities available to me. The answer is twofold. On the one hand, I was brought up in a very positive Jewish home that nurtured a love for Judaic learning and an uncompromising love for Israel and the Jewish people. On the other hand, as a pre-collegiate teenager growing up in Boston during World War II, I was exposed to and suffered, with other members of my family, the consequences of anti-Semitism.

The combination of these factors fired me with the desire to do something to enhance Jewish life. As such, I chose Yeshiva University over other colleges and Jewish education over medicine. I've never regretted this choice.

This coming Sabbath, in the Torah reading, *B'ha'alotcha*, Moses was instructed to tell Aaron, his brother the High Priest, "When you kindle the lights, the seven lights should shine towards the front of the Menorah."

According to Obadiah ben Yaakov Seforno, 16th Century Italian physician and biblical exegete whose commentaries were usually aimed at inculcating a love for mankind, the peculiar sentence construction of this statement has special meaning. Seforno noted that the language of the Torah instructs Aaron to kindle the lights in such a way that the three lamps on the left of the center light and the three lamps on the right would both face the center. The center light – the most important of the lamps – was kindled only when the other lights faced it.

Seforno extrapolated from the Menorah arrangement a message for the Italian Jewish community of his time. The three candles on the left, he said, represented the left-wing Jews or those involved in "this-worldly" aspects of life. Those on the right, expressed the philosophy of right-wing Jews or those with a tendency for "other worldly" involvement. Unless the "leftists" and the "rightists" work together, the middle candle representing Jewish vitality and continuity, cannot be duly kindled or continue to shine once lit. Seforno emphasized that continuity and vibrancy of Jewish life is endangered by the lack of mutual respect and cooperation between all elements of the Jewish community.

What was true for the 16th Century Jewish community in Italy is valid for 20th Century American Jewry and for worldwide Jewry as well. Seforno's message has particular application for the Conference of Jewish Communal Service in the 1990s.

To be sure, every individual, like each light of the Menorah, has a *unique identity* and a *shared identity*. A person's unique identity is essentially his own self with its constellation of personality traits. It is a composite of individual needs and personal responses to those needs. For example, an artistically talented person will seek ways to express his/her giftedness via personal and/or professional artistic involvement. A person endowed with attributes of physical strength and agility will capitalize on these characteristics professionally or avocationally. A handicapped individual will try to address his/her needs through specialized forms of self-help.

While each of these people has a unique identity, together they share a common need for clean air, healthful food and good technology for effective communication. If they live in the same community they have similar communal goals for a safe, secure neighborhood and good, efficient local government. Their shared identities might also be expressed via common patterns of dress and similar religious outlooks.

Groups of people, societies and organizations also have unique identities and shared identities. Their unique identities are the result of the common group purposes they espouse and the common activity in which they engage. Oncologists acquire ideals and work habits unique to their profession. Faculty members of a given university have their unique academic needs and patterns of activity. Sanitation workers express their uniqueness through their common efforts to improve their work conditions and through their union activities to improve their economic security.

Besides being members of a special subset and having particular group needs and involvement, all of these people belong to larger societies. Oncologists are part of a medical profession and express their shared identity in many ways with all doctors. The faculty of Harvard University are members of a larger academic family. Sanitation workers are part of a larger governmental force of employees. Members of all three subgroups share in the common purposes and concerns of their overall vocational groupings.

The unique identity/shared identity concept is especially significant to the Jewish communal profession. It speaks to us in very special ways. All of us, whether we are group workers, vocational counselors, Jewish educators, Federation executives, community relations personnel or caseworkers, have our particular organizational/agency needs, which we express together with our co-workers via a unique identity. This is important for the strengthening of our respective professions and eventual contribution to the Jewish community and to the American society.

Over and above our immediate professional involvement, we all share common goals and concerns as Jewish communal workers and participate in common activities. The CJCS is a prime expression of our shared identity. However, there is one overriding commonality that unites us as we enter the last decade of the 20th Century with its host of challenges to American Jewry. This is our shared Jewish ideological preference or commitment. As Jewish communal workers, we have a shared responsibility for Jewish continuity and the enhancement of Jewish life.

To be sure, until the 1970s this aspect of Jewish communal work, with the obvious exception of Jewish education, was not a major concern of Jewish communal service as it subordinated the Jewish dimension of our respective functions to the larger human service endeavor. Increasingly, over the last several decades, the Jewish nature of our work has surfaced as a significant component of our professional involvement. Indeed, Jewish communal workers, by and large, appreciate the particularistic concerns of

Judaism as they continue to value the universal Jewish dimensions of human services.

The Association of Jewish Community Organization Personnel membership application, for example, expresses this dual feeling when it states:

> We are men and women engaged in community organization work locally, regionally, and nationally, within and on behalf of the Jewish community. We are dedicated to the development, enhancement, and strengthening of the professional practice of Jewish community service. We seek to improve the standards, practices, scope, and public understanding of the professional practice of Jewish community organization. We recognize the importance of supporting these efforts toward creative Jewish survival.

Working towards creative Jewish survival is our shared identity, our common purpose.

Vouchsafing creative Jewish survival while providing our respective professional services has a variety of ramifications. There are 800 Jewish communities ranging from a few families to 1,800,000 people in North America. With almost no exception, every one of these communities provides human services to respond to the needs of its members. No other nation or people takes care of its own like Jews. This dimension of Jewish communal life in America, which has its roots in the *hevrot kehillot kodesh* of earlier generations in European and North African Jewish communities, is the most profound expression of the universal values of Judaism.

More specifically, helping insure creative Jewish survival has personal connotations for Jewish communal workers. These include Judaic study to increase our knowledge of Judaism. To be effective in transmitting Jewish values to others requires knowledge of, and commitment to these values.

Our shared identity will also involve each of us in activities on behalf of the State of Israel and in support of Operation Exodus and of Soviet Jewish acculturation in our respective communities. It will motivate us to support programs that combat anti-Semitism on the one hand, and reduce assimilation, on the other. And, it will encourage us to more intensive personal Jewish behavior and practice. And, as we become more involved in the processes of our shared identity, we will appreciate the need to socialize our common Jewish interests.

In the long run, our involvement as Jewish communal professionals depends upon the continuity and vitality of the Jewish community. By strengthening our shared identity we help enhance the vitality of Jewish life and subsequently increase the opportunities for continued growth of our respective professional endeavors. This mutuality of purpose is what Jewish communal work is all about in the last decade of the 20th Century.

As Seforno implies, the light of the Menorah – the sum total of the individual candles shining together – is actually greater than the combination of the light derived from the individual candles. As Jewish communal workers, our impact on the Jewish community is all the more profound when we act in concert for the enhancement of Jewish life.

PART VI

ON ISRAEL, ZIONISM AND JEWISH EDUCATION

CHAPTER 1

ONE HUNDRED YEARS OF ZIONISM

VISION AND REALITY – REALITY AND VISION

Two guiding principles serve as the frame of reference for this article: (1) the vision and the reality of Zionism must be viewed as an historic continuum, and (2) there always has been and continues to be a mutual intrinsic relationship between Jews in the Diaspora and Jews in *Eretz Yisrael* concerning the vision of Zionism and its fulfillment.

The term "Zionism" was first used in 1892 by Nathan Birnbaum at a meeting in Vienna (Laquer). Yet, the concept of Zionism is another matter. The idea of Zionism is thirty-eight times older than the anniversary of the first Zionist Congress in Basel, Switzerland. It is as old as the Jewish people – and even older. According to the first Rashi commentary on the Pentateuch, the Zionist vision was fashioned by the Almighty at the time of the creation of the world when He declared that the land to be conquered by the Israelites rightfully belongs to them because the Creator of all the land bequeathed *Eretz Israel* to the children of Israel (Genesis 1:1).

Jews throughout the ages have prayed for the day that they would occupy this land as a nation. Jews exiled to Babylonia first expressed the hope of returning to their ancestral homeland 2,500 years ago. And, since that time, Jews, young and old, would recite before Grace after their weekday meals, "By the waters of Babylon, there we sat and cried when we remembered Zion" (*Psalms* 137:1).

THE VISION OF ZIONISM AND MESSIANISM

The vision of Zionism, expressed as the coming of the Messiah, suffuses the entire Judaic tradition. It was this fervent belief that lightened the yoke of exile for generations. So strong was the messianic belief that no less a rabbinic luminary than the Hatam Sofer at the beginning of the nineteenth century required his students to study the legal portions of the Talmud applicable only in *Eretz Yisrael*, such as the *halakhot* relating to *yovel* and *shmitah* and the regulations concerning *korbanot* that would become operative with the rebuilding of the Temple once the Messiah arrived.

While Jews lived physically in the Diaspora for two thousand years, emotionally and spiritually they resided in *Eretz Yisrael*. Twelfth-century Judah Halevi's poetic outcry captures the profound vision of the Zionist tradition of two millennia when he proclaimed, "My heart is in the East, but I am in the far end of the West." And, as a good Zionist, Halevi made it to the Holy Land.

To be sure, messianic fervor and biblical belief in the Promised Land do not make a Zionist. What is needed is the combination of personal desire and actual involvement to make *Shivat Zion* a reality. The many exilic examples of belief coupled with willingness and personal participation in the redemption process "prove that [modern] Zionism had an impressive genealogy in Jewish history and that it was but the awakening of an ever imminent national spirit acknowledged by Jews and Gentiles alike" (Sokolow).

According to a recent study of Zionist ideology, the common denominator of modern Zionist visions comprises four major propositions: (Shimon).

1. Jews are a distinctive entity possessing attributes associated with the *modern* concept of nation, as well as attributes associated with religion;

2. The situation of the Jewish entity under conditions of dispersion is critically defective;
3. The solution ranges from the ingathering and settlement of Jews in *Eretz Yisrael* under conditions of religious and cultural autonomy to the more radical aspiration for a sovereign Jewish state and the gathering therein of a major part of the Jewish people;
4. The fulfillment of the visions involve Jewish self-help, the renewal of national self-respect, morale, and culture, settlement in *Eretz Yisrael*, and diplomatic activity to facilitate such settlement.

If we examine these criteria for defining *modern* Zionism we must conclude that Zionist activity has taken place over the centuries. Although the main strands of modern Zionism are essentially secular, its historical antecedent was religiously rooted and messianically motivated.

Whether moved by religious fervor, concerned primarily with the alleviation of distress, or driven by feelings of national pride, the efforts to settle in *Eretz Yisrael* or to make it a homeland for Jews are Zionist activities. In Ben Gurion's words, the Jewish right to *Eretz Yisrael* "emanates from the unbroken connection of the Hebrew nation with its historic homeland" (quoted in Shimon). That unbroken connection is the historic Zionist link.

A dramatic story about Shmuel Yosef Agnon expressed the power of the Zionist vision. During the ceremony when he was awarded the Nobel Prize for literature, Agnon was asked where he was born. His response startled his listeners. "My parents gave birth to me in P'chach, Galicia" he said, "but like all Jews, I was born in Jerusalem." After the King of Sweden, who asked him the question, expressed his amazement at his answer, Agnon explained: "Physically I was born in Galicia, but my spiritual birth was in Israel. Were it not for the spirit of Jerusalem (*Yirushalayim shel ma'allah*) that pervaded my home, I never would have studied Judaica. I never would have mastered Hebrew. I never would have become a Hebrew writer, I never would have made aliyah and I would not be here to receive the Nobel Prize." Agnon's response was the epitome of the fulfillment of a Zionist dream.

The dual aspiration of Zionism is expressed poignantly in the daily *Amidah* by (1) the prayers for the rebuilding of Jerusalem and the speedy renewal of "the Kingdom of David," a clear reference to the Davidic Messiah, and (2) the prayer for freedom from exilic oppression and persecution. For the Jewish masses throughout the ages, the national purpose of the Jewish religion was reinforced by the reality of Jew-hatred and persecution.

MODERN ZIONIST PROPHECY AND REALITY

After being elected as the first President of the World Zionist Organization, at the first Zionist Congress, Theodore Herzl, the modern prophet of Zionism, wrote in his diary, "If I were to sum up the Congress in a word, it would be this. At Basel, I founded the Jewish State. If I said this aloud today, I would be greeted by universal laughter. In five years, perhaps and certainly in fifty, everyone will see it" (quoted in Parzen).

Fifty-one years later, the prophecy is a reality. But the father of the modern Jewish state did not guarantee its welfare or its Jewish character. The establishment of a modern Jewish state by no means suggested the fulfillment of all Zionist aspirations. The fledgling state had to be safeguarded against Arab terrorism and warfare. It had to be supported economically. It had to be made a viable homeland for hundreds of thousands of Jewish immigrants. It had to develop a distinct Jewish character and continue the Jewish people's national, cultural and Hebraic renaissance. Finally, it had to develop the ability to disseminate Jewish culture and Jewish consciousness and reinforce the idea of Jewish peoplehood.

Preceding Herzl in the nineteenth century were the ideological precursors of modern Zionism. Their visions varied significantly, but their solutions to the problems of Jewish exilic existence had one element in common: a physical space over which Jews ruled. Chief among the precursors were two rabbis – a Balkan Sephardic Jew, Zvi Yehudah Alkalai, and an East European

Talmudic scholar Zvi Hirsch Kalischer, each of whom developed plans and advocated for the physical, cultural, and linguistic restoration of the Jewish people to its homeland.

All Jews did not accept the Jewish national vision at the time modern Zionism was being fashioned. Reform Judaism in the nineteenth century rejected the vision of Jewish nationalism as antithetical to its belief system which held that Jews were members of the Mosaic faith whose allegiance centered only on the synagogue (Shimon). The extreme ultra-Orthodox Jews, while strong in their belief in the Jews' eventual return to *Eretz Yisrael*, repudiated modern Zionism since they felt it involved the violation of sacred Judaic principles and practices. And then there were the assimilationists who retained a superficial identification with the Jews but rejected the practices of Judaism. Their vision of individual and group emancipation, unlike that of the Zionists, was total integration into their respective European societies.

FROM ASSIMILATION TO ZIONISM

For Moses Hess, the Marxist Socialist ideologue who advocated assimilation and later realized that "even conversion itself does not relieve the Jews from the enormous pressure of German Jew-hatred," increasing anti-Semitism resulted in a turn to a Zionist solution for the Jewish problem (Shimon).

Another example of an assimilationist-turned-Zionist was Leon Pinsker, a devout leader of a failed movement to russify Russian Jews. In his biting pamphlet, *Auto Emancipation*, which appeared in 1882, he emphasized that *Jews* must emancipate themselves from *galut* by becoming a nation like other nations, and by attaining a territory – not necessarily *Eretz Yisrael* – to achieve nationhood.

Herzl was an assimilationist who literally was shocked into becoming a Zionist. Were it not for his assignment to cover the Dreyfus trail, who knows whether there would be a Jewish state today. It could very well be that the Jewish people would have had to continue to exist in the post-Holocaust era as a nation in exile.

ZIONISM AND HASKALLAH

The vision of modern Zionism embraced the thinking of the *maskilim*, the intelligentsia who revolted against the ghetto and, at the same time rejected Jewish religion and abandoned the synagogue. The *maskilim* laid the foundation for secular Zionism and were responsible for the rebirth of the Hebrew language. The flowering of Hebrew literature and Hebraic journalism in Eastern Europe during the last two decades of the nineteenth century went hand-in-hand with the renaissance of Jewish nationalism.

MODERN THEORIES: POLITICAL, PRACTICAL, AND CULTURAL ZIONISM

It is no accident that, since both Pinsker and Herzl became Zionists out of existential necessity, their goals and visions, were political and social. Early in Herzl's efforts, he was ready to settle for Argentina and later for Uganda. Both times he was persuaded by Zionists motivated by historical and cultural purposes to consider only Palestine as the land of the Jewish people. Under his leadership, the vision of political Zionism dominated the first Zionist Congress when the World Zionist Organization was established. The official program of Zionism simply read, "The aim of Zionism is to create a publicly recognized and legally secured home for the Jewish people in Palestine." The operative clauses to obtain this objective were essentially political, economic, and social. They included the promotion of the settlement of Palestine by Jewish farmers, laborers, and artisans, the organization of world Jewry into local and general bodies in conformity with the laws of their respective countries; the strengthening of Jewish sentiment and national consciousness, and the initiation of steps to attain such government assistance as may be necessary for achieving the aims of Zionism (Parzen).

One of the stalwart Zionists who joined hands with Pinsker in the formation of small Zionist groups was Ahad Ha'am, whose vision of Zionism differed radically from Herzl. Ahad Ha'am viewed assimilation and not persecution as the greatest threat facing modern Jewry. To him, the Zionist vision was needed to regenerate the spiritual life of the Jews and help them face the challenges that modern societies posed to Jewish survival. In his pointed essay, *Lo zeh Haderekh*, which he wrote after visiting the new colonies, he bitterly criticized the lack of cultural purpose in the colonization effort of the new immigrants in Palestine. Colonization, he posited, requires a spiritual-cultural dimension and a Hebraic linguistic emphasis. Consequently, he promoted the idea of Jewish national education as a prerequisite for aliyah. Otherwise, he felt that the Jewish people could not build in Palestine the Jewish national cultural center it needed to survive as a nation on its own land.

During the first two decades of modern Zionism, the political purposes clearly overshadowed the vision of the cultural and religious Zionists and even the goals of the practical Zionists. The Zionist vision of the practicalists, who challenged Herzl and confronted him with an ultimatum to abandon his designs regarding Uganda, was to reclaim *Eretz Yisrael* by settlement and practical work.

Over time, the vision of the practicalists triumphed in securing and building a homeland for the Jewish people. In large part, this was insured by the Second Aliyah brought about by the failure of the October Revolution in Russia in 1905 and the resultant pogroms. The Second Aliyah *olim* were dedicated to implementing *Torat Ha'avodah*, the work vision of Aharon David Gordon. The natural outcome of a labor philosophy was the founding of the *Histadrut*, whose dominant leader was David Ben Gurion.

They included the promotion of the settlement of Palestine by Jewish farmers, laborers and artisans: the organization of world Jewry into local and general bodies in conformity with the laws of their respective countries: the strengthening of Jewish sentiment and national consciousness; and the initiation of steps to attain such government assistance as may be necessary for achieving the aims of Zionism.

The Zionist vision of the practicalists, who challenged Herzl and confronted him with an ultimatum to abandon his designs regarding Uganda, was to reclaim *Eretz Yisrael* by settlement and practical work. Among others, the Jewish National Fund was the vehicle through which practical Zionists, led by Menahem Ushishkin chose to operate for the restoration of the land through colonization and Jewish labor.

ZIONISM AND OUR HEBREW LANGUAGE

To Ben-Gurion and his colleagues, the revival of the Hebrew language was an integral part of the Zionist vision. The battle for Hebrew as the language of instruction at the newly-founded Haifa Technion, in which Eliezer Ben Yehuda and his associates engaged between 1912 and 1914, is an aggressive expression of this aspect of the Zionist vision. It involved Jewish leadership the world over, including American Zionists headed by Rabbi Stephen Wise and Professor Richard Gottheil who avidly promoted the study and use of the Hebrew language in every area of life in Palestine. To them, Hebrew was basic to the Zionist vision.

In his study, *Halashon Ha'Ivrit be Yisrael U-v'a-Amin*, Dr. Simon Federbush (1967) writes eloquently of the fulfillment of this vision.

"The revival of our Hebrew language, which accompanied the beginning of our national redemption, is one of the world's miraculous phenomena. The amazement of the nations of the earth regarding this happening for which there is no parallel in any country or language was expressed by one of the world's righteous people. If the survival of the Jewish nation is a miracle, then the revival of the Hebrew language is the miracle of miracles."

AMERICAN ROLE IN MODERN ZIONISM

The contribution of American Zionists is underscored by the fact that no less than 78 settlements in Israel bear the names of American Jews. American Zionism is actually a success story. When it began, it did not generate much popular support and enthusiasm. Indeed, it had its share of opponents and detractors. According to Jewish Theological Seminary Professor Jack Wertheimer, the problem now is that "since the triumph of Zionism seems so all-encompassing (there are virtually no anti-Zionist or even non-Zionist organizations in America), it no longer represents a fighting cause that inspires American Jews" (Wertheimer).

A THREE-PART PROGRAM FOR ISRAEL AND THE DIASPORA

In contemplating the future of Zionism in America and Israel we begin with the fact that most likely, during the next decade the vision of the ingathering of exiles – with the last immigration from the former Soviet Union and Ethiopia – will have been fully realized (Carmen). And as the national liberation feature of Zionism comes to a close, we must turn to the historic Judaic vision of Zionism. The restoration of Eretz Yisrael to a prominent place in Jewish life does not ease the search and struggle for Jewish identity whether in Israel or in the Diaspora.

Historically, Zionism is based upon three Judaic components: language, religion, and territory. Heinrich Graetz, the prolific nineteenth-century historian, emphasizes that "The Torah, the nation of Israel and the Holy Land stand…in a mystical relationship to each other. They are inseparably united by a mystical bond" (quoted in Shimon). And according to historian Jacob Katz (1986), Jewish nationalism "is the transforming of ethnic facts into ultimate values." This transformation posits a major challenge to Israel and to Zionism as both the State and the operative concept that brought about the struggle for ultimate meaning. To achieve the ultimate values of Zionism in the post-Zionist period, each of the components – language, religion, and territory – must become operative principles of Jewish life

HEBREW LANGUAGE

The Hebrew language must become, once again, a functional unifying factor of world Jewry, and ever-ready presence of Jewish peoplehood. What a challenge this poses to Jewish Zionist leadership and to Jewish educators. Sadly, the Israel Ministry of Education's 1994 Shenhar Report, which addressed the "ongoing decline of the status of Jewish Studies at all levels of the educational system," noted "a paradoxical change in the status of the Hebrew language: the more it has become the dominant language and culture, the more it has become distant from the language of the Bible and religious writings. Once the key to general and Jewish education, it has now become a separate subject, isolated from other (Judaic) disciplines" (Shenhar Report, 1991). Israeli writer and thinker, Yosef Dan (1994), in a lengthy article in *Ha'Aretz*, bemoans the absolute secularization of the Hebrew language, which is contrary to the Jewish continuity needs of the Jewish people. "So much literary creativity in Israel," he underscores, "does not draw an iota from the Bible, *Mishnah, Gemara,* Jewish philosophy, *Kabbalah, Hasidut* or even from the classical literary works of modern Hebrew literature." This condition requires a Zionist response. It challenges the Israeli education system to develop a comprehensive, integrative approach to the Hebrew language, restoring to it its traditional cultural sources.

It is precisely because Hebrew is so crucial to Jewish continuity and so basic to meaningful Jewish existence and to Jewish unity that the American Advisory Council of the Joint Authority for Jewish Zionist Education, with support of the Department of Education and Culture in the Diaspora (of the Jewish Agency – World Zionist Organization) has helped to establish a National Hebrew Language Center. The level of the Center's effectiveness will be a measure of the success of both American Zionist and Jewish educational leadership and activity. The challenge of Hebrew language in all its formats – biblical, liturgical, rabbinic, literary, and conversational – is what motivated me to write my book, *The Mystique of Hebrew* (Schiff, 1996) and to establish the National Hebrew Language Center.

THE JEWISH RELIGIOUS TRADITION

The second component of Zionism is the Judaic religious tradition, which can be broadly interpreted to include the ideas and experiences associated with spirituality, ritual observance, human values, and cultural and national involvement. The concept of Judaic religious tradition being at the heart of Zionism may be anathema to many secular Zionists today, as it was to many *maskilim* in Europe. Yet, the current challenge of religion to post-Zionism and to Israel is to enhance the Jewish character of the Jewish communities in the Diaspora and in Israel.

Ahad Ha'am, the secularist, shared with religious Zionism the definition of the Zionist challenge as not so much a response to the "problem of the Jews' as an answer to the "problem of Judaism." The search for a resolution to this problem must be at the heart of Zionist endeavor in the post-Zionist era. Secularism has exacerbated the dilemma of whether Israel can be both democratic and Jewish at the same time. This dilemma has given rise to the statement of the new president of Israel's Supreme Court to the effect that "if he had to choose between an Israel that is Jewish but not democratic and an Israel that is democratic but not Jewish, he would prefer an Israel that is democratic and not Jewish." In this case, Jacob Chinitz (1996) notes, "We have an open acknowledgement by a major leader of Israeli society, that the Jewishness of Israel is secondary, not primary, and can no longer serve as the *raison d'être* of the State."

Zionism today must embrace Judaism and Jewishness, as well as Jewish nationalism, as its goal for the Jewish future in the Diaspora and in Israel. In this sense, we are not truly in an era of post-Zionism. If Zionism is rooted in the Jewish past and continues to be invigorated by Jewish tradition, it becomes an eternal philosophy guiding the destiny of the Jewish State and the future of the Jewish people. As Hebrew University Professor Michael Rosenak (1992) notes, "The significance of *Eretz Yisrael* was intrinsically bound up with the significance of biblical and Talmudic Judaism." And, so it must be now, even as we differ in our interpretation and application of biblical and Talmudic Judaism to our modern times.

The poet Bialik expressed this intrinsic link poignantly in his memorable poem, *Im yesh et naf-shekha la-da'at*, describing the study of Judaic sources as the fountain from which the Jewish people drew strength and courage in their bitter exile. Indeed, Torah study, broadly defined, is a cardinal principle of the Jewish faith, the importance of which must be incorporated in the Zionist vision and reality of the Jewish future in the Diaspora and in Israel.

CENTRALITY OF ISRAEL

Territory, the third leg of the Zionist idea, means much more than a physical space to house the Jewish people. It means that *Eretz Yisrael*, the homeland, is the home of Judaism in which its Jewish inhabitants feel at home with Jewishness. It means, that after its founding, Israel becomes a major cultural center, a major cultural force for Jewish life everywhere. "From Zion shall go forth the Torah" can be a realistic vision for the Jewish future.

The vast majority of Israelis believe in the exclusive centrality of Israel. For most Israeli Zionists, aliyah is the necessary condition of Zionism. In contrast, most American Jews tend to view the Jewish world as having at least two centers, Israel and America. For most Diaspora Jews, even for religious Jews, *galut* does not exist as they live in a variety of free, blessed settings.

This divergence of views poses a challenge to Zionism of the future to help both communities better understand each other. The center and the periphery have much to teach each other, if only, as Professor Arnold Eisen (1992) notes, "they would learn to speak in a way which the other is prepared to hear." In responding appropriately, Zionism can become a unifying factor in creating a sense of Jewish peoplehood with a common heritage and a common destiny, which is, after all, the concept of *Am Yisrael* true to the covenental idea of Jewish life.

Jewish togetherness is expressed in the very first act of modern Jewish nationhood. The Declaration of Israel's Independence underscores that the Jews of Palestine and the Jews of the Diaspora "met together in solemn assembly to declare the establishment of the Jewish State." That togetherness must be at the core of the Zionist vision today and tomorrow.

CHAPTER 2

ZIONISM AND JEWISH STATEHOOD: CHALLENGE TO THE AMERICAN JEWISH COMMUNITY

CELEBRATING THE ESTABLISHMENT OF ISRAEL

In the fall of 1997, the Knesset allocated 300 million shekel – $86 million – to the Knesset Fiftieth Anniversary Committee for year-long celebratory events in honor of Israel's jubilee. This caused an uproar in Israel and an explosion of feeling and opinion about 50th anniversary celebrations.

"Not this year, dear. We have a heartache," read the headline of the January 2nd Jerusalem Post. "Is anyone really in the mood for a party?" asked the author of the ensuing article.

In the first place, there is the question of cost. President Weizman asked if it was "right to shell out millions of shekels on celebrations." It is also a matter of duration. Should the 50th anniversary observance be year-long? Or rather only a week or a few selected days?

It is also a matter of celebratory mood during hard times. The director of *Habimah* Theater, Ya'acov Agnon, who directed the events of Israel's 40th anniversary year, and his counterpart at the Cameri Theater, Noam Semal, suggested that terms such as "commemoration" – instead of "celebration" – be used in our hard times.

Hard times, they stressed, mean the level of unemployment. Hard times mean the problem of terrorism and lack of peace. Hard times mean serious budget cuts. But, then there is the view of Yitzhak Modai, former finance minister and former Chairman of the Knesset Jubilee Committee, and many others like him, who are "in total disagreement with the negative views about celebration." After paring down the anniversary budget, which he thought was too high, Modai stressed that, "in Jewish tradition, a fiftieth anniversary is not something to be taken lightly. It is an important occasion for starting things afresh." Secondly, "from a modern point of view," he emphasized, "a country is looking for the opportunity to show the world who the people of Israel are and what they are all about; and this is such an opportunity."

"And, finally," Modai highlighted, "we *do* have something to celebrate. The State of Israel is a unique phenomenon. There is no other country, which has created what we have created in just fifty years. We should do what we can to show ourselves to the world, and even more, to show ourselves. Many of our own people aren't even aware of our accomplishments as a nation."

"And, you know what?" he said, "Maybe because these are very difficult times, from any point of view, a smile won't hurt anybody."

The debate between the opponents and supporters of year-long celebrations, to which I just referred, was hot and furious. To be sure, it is still not over.

The irony of this debate is that, since the appointment of the *Knesset* Anniversary Committee last fall, there have been 4 chairmen, 3 changes in chairmanship in the months of January and February alone. Hopefully, the *Knesset* will be able to overcome political and personality problems and focus on the best means to observe the *Yovel* in the Jewish state with its current national budget of 120 million *shekels* or 34 million dollars. The first official government 50th anniversary activity took place in *Kiryat Gat* on *Tu B'Shvat*. And, this modest celebration caused an uproar among those who felt that the opening celebratory event should have been in Jerusalem – Israel's capital city. Another problem relates to the elaborate celebration scheduled to take place on April 12th in *Hebron*, including festive prayers in the Cave of Machpelah. The battle over this event is really a struggle between the political Left and Right in Israel. On the other hand, there is strong consensus in Israel between Likud and Labor to utilize the 50th anniversary year to encourage the 500 thousand Israelis living abroad to return by strengthening the ties between them and the Jewish state and by offering them special benefits to make their return more appealing. This debate is about activity in Israel for Israelis. What about North America? What about the Jewish community in the United States? In Baltimore? What should be our stance regarding the celebration of Israel's *Yovel*?

As I noted in a *D'var Torah* I offered at the recent Winter Board meeting of the United Israel Appeal, chaired so ably by your own – Shoshana Cardin, the Golda Meir of Diaspora Jewry, the leadership of the American Jewish community has an obligation in regard to Israel's *Yovel*.

As we celebrate the fiftieth anniversary year, we realize full well that the young country that is the Jewish State has many problems on many fronts – internal and external. After all, Jews founded the Jewish State. Jews immigrated and made aliyah to Palestine and Israel. Jews developed its form of government, and Jews set the policies and practices of Israeli life. And Jews always have many opinions – some very strong, and some contrary to their own good.

Whether or not we support the current government – no matter our political, ideological, religious, secular, or social bent – Jewish tradition suggests that we count our blessings at this time in our history. According to Jewish tradition, the idea of *Yovel* – the biblical jubilee year in *Eretz Yisrael* is relevant to the Diaspora. Commenting on the statement in Leviticus about the observance of the Jubilee year, the Sages of the Talmud stress that "even outside the Land of Israel the Jubilee should be celebrated." And celebrate we must!

This does not mean that Diaspora Jewry bury its head ostrich-like in the sand of obliviousness. It does *not* mean that we should not pursue those avenues of endeavor that will insure that Israel is a free society in accordance with the biblical injunction, "And you shall proclaim liberty in the Land to *all* its inhabitants."

But, it *does* mean that we must not ignore Israel's past accomplishments – not like glassy-eyed novices, but as committed, sophisticated, long-time supporters of Jewish nationhood and statehood. After all, the *raison d'être* of American Jewish efforts on behalf of Israel, locally via Federations and communal organizations, and, nationally, via the United Israel Appeal in partnership with UJA and CJF, is to foster those social, educational, aliyah, settlement and life-giving programs in the Jewish State; programs that are important both to Israel and to Diaspora Jews who make Israel central to their lives. This kind of commitment should strengthen our resolve to celebrate our common achievements.

The fact that we may be engaged in trying to solve some knotty social, political, and ideological problems should not lessen our responsibility to recognize the remarkable progress that a young fifty-year-old nation has made – with our help – in the face of the greatest dangers and obstacles imaginable in every aspect of its young life.

Certainly deserving recognition and celebration is the absorption of two million refugees and immigrants into Palestine and Israel since the 1930s – under the most difficult conditions. On May 14, 1948, when the British Mandate came to an end, the Jewish population in the land numbered some 650,000. Now there are 5 million Jews in the country. The latest ingathering of exiles from Ethiopia, via Operation Moses and Operation Solomon, and the former Soviet Union borders on the miraculous. And during this entire time, Israel has had to confront threats of war, *Intifada* and terrorism.

The achievements of the Israel Defense Forces are second to none – beginning with the remarkably successful fifteen-month defense of Israel's armies of Egypt, Jordan, Syria, Lebanon, and Iraq. Then, there was the tense, yet victorious Sinai campaign in 1956 after the blockade of the Straits of Tiran and the prevention of

Israeli ships passing through the Suez Canal, and the concomitant conversion of the Sinai peninsula into a huge Egyptian military base as Egypt, Jordan, and Syria signed a tripartite military alliance aimed at wiping Israel off the Mid-East map.

Then came the Six-Day-War in 1967 with its lightning swift triumph, followed by the unfortunate but victorious Yom Kippur War in 1973; and the 1982 Operation Peace for Galilee. No rest for the war-weary Israelis and their overused Israel Defense Forces. The 50th Anniversary is, indeed, a time to recognize the IDF and to show gratitude for the super efforts of Israel's military forces on behalf of its security and sheer existence.

Then, there is the economic growth of Israel – the unbelievable multiplying of exports, the development of a second deep-water port at *Ashdod*, the continuing annual GNP increase and the accelerated growth of so many industries and the manufacturing of machinery, electronics, medical instruments, and chemicals.

And, at the same time, Israel has seen the remarkable development of health services, medical research, social services, science and technology, education, culture, music, fine arts, and the media.

Moshe Katzav, Deputy Prime Minister and Minister of Tourism, poignantly summarized the story of Israel's growth. "Israel", he said, "is one of the great 20th century success stories. Our economy is booming, our industry is high-tech, our education is envied, our agricultural products fill the stores of Europe and America, and we help underdeveloped nations make their deserts bloom."

In addition, the fifty-year period of statehood has been highlighted by so many history-making events in Israel. Think back to the Eichman Trial in 1961–62. Consider the completion in 1964 of the national water carrier bringing water from Lake Kinneret in the north to the semi-arid south. Note, also, that in 1975, Israel became an associate member of the European Common Market.

Relish the visit of President Anwar Sadat to Jerusalem and the ensuing peace treaty between Israel and Egypt in 1979.

Think of the destruction by the Israeli Air Force of the Iraqi nuclear reactor in 1981, just before it became operative. Imagine what might have happened had Saddam Hussein had that nuclear power now or in 1991. Thank God for Israel.

In 1985, Israel signed a trade agreement with the United States – a not insignificant event.

We saw, in horror, how Israel was attacked by Iraqi Scud missiles in 1991 during the Gulf War and emerged miraculously with almost no fatalities. We witnessed unbelievable unity as the *Yishuv* braced for the attacks and prepared for any eventuality including retaliation, if necessary.

In the 1990s, Israel established diplomatic relations with China and India, Morocco and Tunisia, and full diplomatic relations with the Holy See; and trade relations with Oman and Qatar, and with many East European and African countries. And, in 1996, the world witnessed the signing of the Israel-Jordan Peace Treaty.

All these events and accomplishments, and more, deserve to be recognized and celebrated.

The first educational challenge to the Jewish community, therefore, is to transmit information about Israel's achievements, as well as its problems and challenges, to the Jewish youth and Jewish adults. When we observe Israel Independence Day this year, just two months from now, the celebration should be a meaningful expression of genuine appreciation based upon knowledge of Israel's accomplishments. More than that, the *Yovel* on Independence Day should initiate a round of educational activity, culminating in the observance of Balfour Day on November 2nd, and the observance of the U.N. General Assembly vote for the Partition Plan on November 29th.

The educational challenge has a philanthropic component as it underscores the need for the American Jewish community to continue to provide increased support for the Jewish State.

Im nirtzeh, ain zu aggaddah – If we will it, it will happen.

CHAPTER 3

BUILDING ZIONIST COMMITMENT THROUGH EDUCATION

Shalom haverim! Boker Tov! Mazal tov on becoming a Movement. Movement, action, vitality is what Zionism in America needs. My personal warmest wishes to AZM in its new program and structure.

To be sure, Jewish Zionist education is one of your priority challenges. I am pleased to share in this historic occasion. Indeed, it is an historic opportunity for American Zionists to actualize the fourth aim of the Jerusalem Program adopted at the twenty-seventh Zionist Congress in Jerusalem in 1969: "The preservation of the identity of the Jewish people through the fostering of Jewish and Hebrew education and of Jewish spiritual and cultural values." More power to you as you assume this responsibility!

I have been asked to speak about three things:

1. The Joint Authority for Jewish/Zionist Education;
2. The American Advisory Council to the Joint Authority; and
3. some of my views on Jewish Zionist education.

Regarding the theme of our Congress: *He-atid mathil akhshav* "The Future Begins Now." Our Sages instruct us in the *Midrash* that there are two kinds of tomorrows – *yesh mahar akhshav v'yesh mahar l'ahar zeman*. There is a *mahar akhshav*, an immediate tomorrow – a tomorrow that begins NOW; and a *mahar l'ahar zeman* – a tomorrow that is a long way off.

Given the condition of American Jewish life as underscored by the terrifying findings of the 1990 National Jewish Population study, we are faced with the urgency of acting quickly and effectively. The urgency is NOW. Tomorrow is here NOW. Towards this end, the Zionist Movement must immediately be on the cutting edge of Jewish education activity – both formal and informal.

Just like the American government viewed education after Sputnik, we must urgently consider Jewish education, not as a consumer good, but as a necessary investment in our future. To put this urgency in proper Zionist context, we might take a leaf from Ahad Ha'am, the leading Zionist theorist and advocate for cultural Zionism at the turn of the century. While we may not agree with his anti-Herzlian Zionist philosophy, some of his ideas merit serious consideration today.

One of Ahad Ha'am's many seminal essays is entitled *hikui v'hitbol'lut*, "Imitation and Assimilation." He stressed that beginning with the French Revolution, ushering in an era of Liberté, Egalité, and Fraternité, "freedom, equality and brotherhood," Jews in Western, open society faced critical challenges of survival.

Ahad Ha'am noted that a minority population in Western, open society has to be impacted by the majority culture. There are, he said, two kinds of imitation; *hikui shel hitbatlut* – absorptive, assimilative imitation – the kind of imitation that Ahad Ha'am observed in Germany, in France, and in Prussia.

Interestingly, an historian of American Jewry, Hyman Grinstein, noted that the American Jews of the 18th century all but disappeared by the beginning of the 20th century. This is the kind of imitation we are currently observing today with a 52% intermarriage rate and 46% of all Jewish youth under the age of

18 being brought up outside of our faith, or without any religion, without any Jewish affiliation. The result of this kind of imitation is what a major social scientist calls "hemorrhaging out."

The other kind of imitation *hikui shel hit-harut* – competitive imitation, imitation using the tools of Western Society, Western knowledge and know-how, Western educational methodology and technology – to ensure the creative survival of Jewry, especially via the centrality of Israel (which he called "cultural Zionism") in Jewish life.

This, indeed, is a major Zionist challenge today – guaranteeing creative Jewish continuity via effective Jewish education, in our case, Jewish Zionist education.

In the first place, to respond appropriately to this challenge, the Zionist movement must be in the forefront of support of and involvement in intensive all day Jewish education, the most effective form of Jewish schooling. To be sure, the largest percentage of American *olim* and the overwhelming majority of students who spend a year of study in Israel are day school products. It is abundantly clear that these young people are less likely to intermarry. In the 1940s, Zionists were among the first to advocate the establishment of Jewish Day Schools. In my book *The Jewish Day School in America*, I cite resolutions by *Mizrahi, Hapoel – Mizrahi* and the Labor Zionist Organization of America as examples of this support.

Moreover, the American Zionist movement must support efforts to improve and transform the Jewish supplementary school into an effective educational instrumentality. Sixty percent of all Jewish children enrolled in Jewish schools study in supplementary schools. Integrating Israel trips and Israel-based study into the current supplementary school program will go a long way to help improve its effectiveness.

Thirdly, we must *Zionize* all Jewish education efforts by integrating study of Israel and Israel experience into all Jewish educational curricula and into all informal Jewish educational programs. The Joint Authority for Jewish Zionist Education addresses this critical challenge.

Zionist education does not deal with the totality of the Jewish educational experience of Jewish children of school age and beyond, nor with the overall Jewish life experience of Jewish adults. But, it can have a significant impact upon the quality and direction of Jewish education and Jewish life in the United States.

Not everyone was happy with the idea of a Joint Jewish Agency – World Zionist Organization Jewish Zionist Educational Authority. For many Zionists, the merger of JAFI and WZO educational programs meant the loss of control of the WZO education departments. But, the realization of the need for more coordination, greater cooperation and increased cost effectiveness in Jewish Zionist education programming led to the creation of the Joint Authority.

In essence, the Authority was established to intensify, maximize, coordinate and integrate (where appropriate) the efforts of the Departments of Education and Culture and Torah Education and the Youth and *Hechalutz* Department (in the U.S. the American Zionist Youth Foundation) and the various JAFI funded programs.

The plan for the implementation in the United States of the work of the Jewish/Zionist Joint WZO/JAFI education authority seeks "to create a fully integrated and coordinated system which will create simple and effective means to make available the full range of Zionist educational programs, services and activities offered by the Joint Authority and the Jewish community" to American Jewry.

The Authority is governed by 36 commissioners from all parts of the Jewish world – 18 commissioners representing WZO and 18 delegates of the Jewish Agency. Eight of the Commissioners are from the U.S. – four of them representing the American Zionists.

In the United States, the Authority was approved by the American Zionist Federation Executive Board and the United Israel Appeal Board in October, 1990 and passed by the Commission of the Jewish Zionist Education Authority in June 1991.

The Joint Authority was mandated to establish regional

advisory councils in countries with significant Jewish populations. In the U.S., the American Advisory Council (AAC) was founded "to assist in the planning and implementation of the Authority's programs in the U.S. by providing input on program planning, monitoring program implementation and evaluation of program effectiveness."

The 43 AAC members were appointed by a nominating committee representing WZO and JAFI. The Council includes prominent educational professional and lay leaders representing all aspects of Jewish Zionist formal and informal education. Si Schwartz, a key member of the Council has been a bulwark of strength and support to the chair and the council as have been Bernice Tannenbaum and Rabbi Israel Miller.

In the autumn of 1991, the AAC began its work to serve as a bridge between JAJZE and the Jewish educational system in America. It is the Council's responsibility to advise the Authority on its work in the United States, and to assist the Authority in the dissemination of its message and program. The Council hopes to ensure that available dollars are used most effectively and efficiently.

As Chair of the AAC, I view the role of the AAC as a threefold responsibility and opportunity:

1. to create strong linkages between the Zionist and non-Zionist communities. (We have an opportunity to *Zionize* the American non-Zionist Jewish leadership regarding Jewish Zionist education and to develop mutual support systems for Zionist educational activities);

2. to guarantee the relevance of Joint Authority programs to the American Jewish community. (This means ensuring that the monies invested in programs prepared in Jerusalem for the U.S. are spent wisely and with maximum effectiveness);

3. to help maximize the cooperation between the WZO departments and programs in the U.S. and help increase their effectiveness.

Regarding the first challenge, AAC has demonstrated a real sense of mutual understanding and cooperation between the JAFI and WZO appointees. In fact, one cannot discern any difference in attitude between the Zionist and non-Zionist members.

The second challenge – guaranteeing the relevance of Jerusalem-based programming via American input in planning – still remains a challenge. To be sure, we have not yet succeeded in creating the necessary mutual relationship with the Joint Authority leadership in Jerusalem. But, we are hopeful even as we realize the difficulties and hurdles the Authority has to overcome in its early stages of development. It is not an easy task to develop the right kind of partnership between the Diaspora and Jerusalem, but we are confident it will happen. *Yi-h'yeh tov, vih'yeh tov!* in the words of the Israeli hit song.

Addressing the third challenge, relating to the WZO departments of education and the AZYF, has given us a feeling of real *havershaft*. The warm relationship between the program and department heads augurs well for future cooperative efforts and for maximizing the effectiveness of their activities.

Operationally, the AAC has three full-day meetings a year. A working committee of twelve members meets monthly to prepare the agenda of the Council meetings and to serve as the operating mechanism of the Council.

The council is staffed by Karen Rubinstein, who serves as coordinator, and Rabbi Danny Allen, Assistant Executive Chairman, United Israel Appeal. To be sure, the Council should have full time staffing. The work of the Council is being carried out by eight subcommittees:

1. The **Senior *Shlihim* Committee** has prepared guidelines for the appointment of Senior *Shlihim*. These were utilized in the selection of Dr. Rafi Sheniak as the new director of the Department of Education & Culture.

2. The **Budget and Finance Committee** is currently collecting budget information and rationalizing it in order to make recommendations regarding budgeting. To date, the committee has helped AZYF make its budget presentation more comprehensible.

3. An **Inventory Committee** is now developing a map of youth

Zionist education programs in the U.S. It will also prepare a Zionist education needs analysis. Si Schwartz will chair this effort.

4. **Mission Statement Committee** will develop an historic document on the aims of Jewish Zionist education.

5. One of the major problems of WZO's Zionist education involvement is the lack of knowledge that the broader American Jewish community has of the multi activities of the WZO Education departments. *Aseeta v'lo pir-sam-ta, lo aseeta* goes the Israeli saying. The **Communications Committee** will address this need.

6. **The Hebrew Language Education Committee** will help develop plans and programs to try to vitalize Hebrew language instruction.

7. **The Jerusalem 3000 Anniversary Committee** will work with Jerusalem headquarters in developing Diaspora programs for the 3000th anniversary observance in 1996.

8. And finally, a *Shlihut* **Committee** has been established to address the challenge of *Shlihut*. Yesterday we heard how effective *Shlihim* are important and necessary to the Zionist movement and to the cause of Israel.

In the meetings of the AAC, we attempt to address those topics that will be on the agenda of the triennial meetings of the Commission of the Joint Authority in Jerusalem. Towards this end, we schedule the AAC meetings about 6 weeks prior to the Commission meetings. To date, AAC has provided input regarding Joint Authority procedures, the Israel program experience, the appointment of senior *Shlihim*, Hebrew language education, Jerusalem 3000, and the Joint Authority plans for a centralized publishing house.

After all is said and done, the goal of Jewish Zionist Education is to help make Israel central to the lives of American Jews and, by so doing, contribute to the creative continuity of the Jewish people. This means promoting and supporting effective ways of imparting Jewish knowledge and knowledge about Israel, and successful methods of creating positive attitudes towards Israel.

It means sensitizing Jewish youth to the geo-political status of Israel. It means sponsoring *more* trips and more effective educational programs in Israel for increasing numbers of youth and adults. It means involving more and more youth in year-long study programs in Israel. It means developing ways to make Hebrew language instruction effective – not an easy job by any standard. It means developing more effective methods of increasing aliyah from the U.S.

It means intensifying Zionist activity on the college campus with an eye towards developing the next generation of Zionist leadership (so eloquently expressed by our young panelists yesterday). It means giving youth the opportunity for, and encouraging them to become involved in, planning Zionist activity. It means working with all age groups in all possible settings. It means support to the various synagogue efforts to enrich Jewish life through Jewish tradition. And, it means removing the barriers between formal and informal Jewish educational approaches. Needed is a confluence of the affective and cognitive dimensions of learning. Informal Jewish education must stress more formal Zionist instruction and formal education must include more Zionist experience.

Major sociological studies have shown how important is the home influence on the effectiveness of education. My own research in Jewish education, particularly the three-year study of the Jewish Supplementary school I directed from 1984 to 1987, bears out the *conditione sine qua non* importance of family to the effectiveness of Jewish education. To be maximally successful with children we must reach the home and treat with the whole family. In so doing, we reach and teach, touch and teach both the adults and the youth together.

The Torah reading this past Shabbat gives us an important biblical insight into providing inspirational, educational experiences to the whole family. When Pharaoh wanted to allow only the adults to leave Egypt for a short while to worship God – Moses said emphatically *bin'arainu u-vizkainainu nailekh* – "we will go with our young and old together." What a wonderful motto for the Zionist movement – *bin'arainu u-vizkainairiu* – involving whole whole families in Zionist experiences and activities.

In closing, our Zionist educational challenge is bold and clear. In our open society, our acculturation in America must be in the nature of *hikui shel hitharut*, "competitive imitation". It is a challenge to which we Zionists must commit ourselves and our means fully and wholeheartedly.

If we do, who knows, we might even hasten the arrival of the Messiah in our times. *Hatzlahah rabbah!*

CHAPTER 4

TOWARDS A MISSION STATEMENT ON JEWISH ZIONIST EDUCATION

RATIONALE FOR JEWISH ZIONIST EDUCATION

Israel is central to the purpose of Jewish education. As such, a true Jewish education is Jewish *Zionist* education. Judaic texts and Jewish history inform the goals of Jewish Zionist education and are the resources for its expression. Jewish peoplehood is its essential construct, its necessary framework.

Studying Judaic texts, imbibing Jewish values through learning and through contact with inspiration models, experiencing the rich variety of Jewish tradition, visiting Israel via guided tours and spending an extended time in study there are the methods of Jewish Zionist education. An all-encompassing process, Jewish Zionist education speaks to Jews of all ages, of all political, religious, social and ideological groupings and in all demographic settings. It takes place in the classroom, in the home, in the Jewish community center, in the synagogue, on the college campus, in the summer camp, in the community-at-large and in Israel. It aims to foster Jewish identity, transmit Jewish heritage, perpetuate Jewish values, enhance Jewish living patterns, strengthen the relationship between Israel and American Jewry, and make Israel central to meaningful Jewish Diaspora experience.

To achieve this goal means educating generations of Jewish youth who recognize the importance of Israel in Jewish life; who understand the need and the value of aliyah, both for Israel and for the Jewish People; who love and support Israel, even though they may, from time to time, be critical of some of its political processes, its elected leaders and its way of solving internal and external problems. They know and appreciate that the State of Israel is the realization of an age-old Jewish dream, the fulfillment of a biblical promise and a biblical prophecy, a symbol of Jewish peoplehood, a prime locus of Jewish creativity, a place of refuge for Jews from lands of oppression, the instrument of Jewish national normalcy, and a political/national/social reality with all the problems of new statehood in an era and area of virulent anti-Jewish and anti-Zionist feeling and activity. Inculcating these attitudes, behavior patterns and knowledge is the task of Jewish Zionist education.

GOALS OF JEWISH ZIONIST EDUCATION

The adult product of an effective Jewish Zionist education is a person who has a multi-dimensional relationship with the Jewish past, present and future. He/she has a basic knowledge of Judaic sources, Jewish history, contemporary Jewish affairs and the modern Jewish State; a working knowledge of the Hebrew language and an understanding of the effect of the Holocaust upon the Jewish people.

He/she believes in the centrality of Israel in Jewish life, in the special role of Jerusalem and in the importance of aliyah. He/she is imbued with the feeling of *Klal Yisrael* and expresses this belief in Jewish peoplehood via his/her involvement in Jewish communal life. He/she has visited Israel as a youth more than once, visits Israel as an adult at least once every five years and actively supports Israel financially and personally. He/she maintains a Jewish home, gives his/her children a sound Jewish Zionist education and devotes some time each week to Jewish study.

IMPLEMENTING JEWISH ZIONIST EDUCATION

Jewish Zionist Education in the United States in the 1990s must have realistic goals. To be sure, Jewish Zionist education addresses a variety of age cohorts and populations, particularly Jewish school pupils, participants in Jewish informal education programs, members of Zionist youth groups and students on college campuses. It speaks to adults and families affiliated with synagogues, Jewish community centers, Jewish Zionist organizations and Jewish communal agencies.

To be effective for each of these populations, Jewish Zionist education must include both cognitive and affective components. The cognitive and experiential proportions of the Jewish Zionist education program will depend upon the setting. Formal education will be largely cognitive. Informal education will be mostly experiential.

Currently, the focus of Jewish Zionist education efforts should be limited, in the main, to the *Zionization* of the Jewish education or Jewish cultural programs of each group or institution. It should be aimed at enhancing the role of Israel and Hebrew language in the respective school curricula and informal education programs. This can be accomplished most effectively through a multi-dimensional approach.

On the formal educational level it means:

1. integrating Israel into the study of Bible, Jewish history, Liturgy and Jewish holidays;
2. highlighting Israel in the study of Jewish contemporary events;
3. including instructional units on Israel in the curriculum of each grade;
4. emphasizing Israel experiences within the school program – *especially Yom Ha-atzmaut* and *Yom Yerushalayim* celebrations;
5. singing *Hatikvah* at school assemblies and special programs;

6. sponsoring extracurricular activities about Israel – participating in Salute to Israel Parade, Israel Fairs, pen pals, etc;
7. promoting Israel support programs – United Jewish Appeal, Jewish National Fund, Operation Exodus;
8. developing home activity programs about Israel;
9. sponsoring Bar/Bat Mitzvah pilgrimages and high school tour programs to Israel;
10. introducing specialized Hebrew language programs in preparation for visits to Israel;
11. sponsoring year-long high school and post-high school study programs;
12. sponsoring regular, ongoing Israel-based pre-service programs as part of the training of teachers and principals;
13. sponsoring regular, ongoing Israel-based in-service programs for teachers and principals during the summer months;
14. sponsoring lay leader education tours to Israel.

On the informal educational level, focusing on Israel and Hebrew language means:

1. sponsoring short-term and long-term educational trips to Israel for all Jewish youth of high school and college age;
2. providing appropriate follow-up experiences in the home communities and on the college campus;
3. sponsoring guided family trips to Israel;
4. introducing formal and informal learning about Israel in the synagogue, Jewish Community Center, summer camp, and on the college campus;
5. sponsoring Hebrew language programs geared to providing a working language base for conversational Hebrew;
6. assisting Jewish youth organizations to reinforce the Israel components of their programs.

In summary, a major task of the Jewish Community in the United States is enhancing the role of Israel and Zionism in the formal curriculum and in informal Jewish educational programs.

Accomplishing this presupposes an understanding of the importance and centrality of Israel in Jewish life, a willingness to devote significant resources to this challenge and the ability to provide the appropriate educational activities for the variety of Jewish populations.

CHAPTER 5

THE TOMORROWS OF JEWISH EDUCATION

Our Sages instruct us in the *Midrash* that there are two kinds of tomorrows: a *mahar akhshav*, an immediate tomorrow, and a *mahar l'ahar z'man*, a tomorrow that is a long way off. In modern terminology, they were referring to short-range and long-range planning and implementation.

My comments relate to both tomorrows, but mostly to the future that is around the corner, the tomorrow that we have to deal with today. They will deal with several questions.

1. What are the Jewish education needs in the Diaspora to which Israel can make effective responses?
2. What is *unique* about that which Israel can provide to the Diaspora to insure and enhance the future of Jewish education in the Diaspora?
3. How can that uniqueness best be translated into cost-effective activity?
4. What can we learn from past experience upon which to build future responses and programs?

I relate first to the last of these questions: the Jewish Agency does not have to build on *niyyar hadash*, on a *tabula rasa*. Its Jewish Education Committee has broken new ground in Israel-Diaspora Jewish education relations by planning and taking several new bold initiatives:

1. It has involved communal lay leadership in the Jewish education process in ways never before attempted and thus has established new links between the Diaspora and Israeli educational resources.
2. It has made Jewish education a priority on the Jewish communal agenda.
3. It has approached old and new challenges and problems with a refreshing openness and objectivity.
4. It has introduced research procedures to explore Jewish education needs and conditions as a basis for making recommendations for change and has developed experimental projects to test their validity.

My first vision for the future, both for the *mahar akhshav* and for the *mabar l'ahar z'man* is building upon the committee's accomplishments in the realms of Israel experiences and senior personnel.

I will treat collectively the other three questions, without proposing to deal with the political, structural or technical strategies of implementation – either through the Jewish Agency or the World Zionist Organization – separately, jointly or under an integrated authority. Nor will I address ways of eliminating duplication of effort and unnecessary competition regarding the provision of services to the Diaspora, however important and urgent these challenges may be.

My response to the questions speaks essentially to programmatic challenges in the Diaspora. Though my comments derive from my own American experience, I submit that the frame of reference for all Israel-based and Israel-involved programs must be responsiveness to differential regional, ideological and ethnic needs.

What is not needed by the Diaspora is that Israel be "used" to solve, or that Israel try to solve, all Diaspora education problems. Israel cannot and must not try to remove the burden of responsibility from Diaspora communities for their own Jewish education enterprises. The primary responsibility for the support of Jewish education rests with parents, educational institutions and communities, in that order. Israel's contribution must be unique to its special place in Jewish life.

There are three possible approaches to utilizing the uniqueness of Israel in meeting Jewish education needs in the Diaspora:

1. The first approach suggests that Israel initiate programs to meet Diaspora needs as *it* views them and that Israel provide services to the various Diaspora communities as *it* sees fit.
2. The second method views Israel as a multi-dimensional resource at the beck and call of the Diaspora. It posits that the various communities make their own individual contacts either through a centralized Israel-based authority or directly with those educational institutions and agencies from which they want assistance. Subsequently, the Diaspora communities make their own arrangements for service and programs
3. The third approach emphasizes that in those areas where Israel can be helpful, Israel and the Diaspora jointly study Diaspora needs and plan responses cooperatively. In this mode of operation, Israel and the Diaspora are partners. The *Golah* is not just a recipient or user of service. In fact, the benefits of cooperation can go both ways.

The most effective manner of utilizing Israeli resources for the benefit of Diaspora education is obviously the third approach, the *collaborative* model.

Via this approach, Israel and the involved Diaspora community examine their respective needs and strengths in relationship to each other. In developing this method of operation, we should seriously consider the model of the International Center for University Teaching of Jewish Civilization, chaired by Prof. Moshe Davis, which has received major support from the Joint Program for Jewish Education (with its tripartite sponsorship by the Ministry of Education, the Jewish Agency for Israel and the World Zionist Organization).

This model is uncomplicated. Simply described, academics from universities in the Diaspora are convened with Israeli counterparts to analyze, debate and provide input regarding a specific university challenge in the Diaspora.

These meetings, which take place in Jerusalem, (the city described by our Talmudic sages as *ir she-m'haberet yisrael zeh laze* – a city which has literally become a cultural ingathering of exiles) have resulted in valuable syllabi for university teaching of Jewish civilization. It is the *process* utilized by the International Center for University Teaching that I strongly recommend as a paradigm for working with other levels of Jewish education in the Diaspora. This process says, "bring early childhood, elementary school and high school personnel and informal Jewish educators to Israel to work with appropriate counterparts in Israel under proper guidance." The rich academic and pedagogic resources in Israel can best be challenged and harvested when their task is to help respond to specific problems and needs, jointly identified and considered by Israel and the Diaspora.

This approach would render obsolete certain practices, such as sending Israeli early childhood experts to the United States to guide nursery and kindergarten programs for *all* the Jewish communities throughout the country. Not only is this kind of activity financially costly, it is practically an impossible task for the most experienced American educator to accomplish, let alone an Israeli working independently three to four days per week, without any previous American educational experience. This approach would eliminate other Israeli initiatives, doomed to failure, because of lack of planning and involvement with Diaspora educationists.

And now, to the current Jewish education needs as I see them, to be addressed by a consortium approach:

1. The first *mahar akhshav* challenge (tomorrow's need that must be fulfilled today) relates to the impact upon pupils of the media's treatment of Israel, particularly the Lebanon war, the *Intifada* and some of Israel's more controversial policies and practices regarding the peace process. Needed is a massive educational campaign developed cooperatively by the best minds of Israel and the Diaspora to neutralize or counteract the influence of the media on our pupils.

In dealing with the attitudes of our Diaspora youth to Israel we must understand that today's children are different from their predecessors of a generation ago. For example, young Jews in open, Western society hardly sing *Hatikvah* anymore. This is not necessarily a sign of a negative attitude to Israel, but rather an outgrowth of a liberal mentality. After all, American youngsters do not automatically recite the pledge of allegiance in school, as pupils were wont to do a generation ago.

To reach modern Jewish youth and teach them about Israel, we have to integrate formal and informal educational methodologies as we strive for a confluent affective and cognitive impact – achieving behavioral change while knowledge is being accumulated.

2. The impact of the media is not unrelated to the phenomenon of the new young teacher who has not lived through the Holocaust or the establishment of the State of Israel. In this regard, I quote from a memo I received just prior to this writing from Rabbi Manuel Gold, BJE's pedagogic specialist for Reform religious schools in Greater New York. He writes:

A number of principals, of both Conservative and Reform Supplementary Schools, have recently reported the development of an alarming phenomenon. Teachers of their high school-age students, who are themselves graduate and post-graduate students, in response to recent events, are taking anti-Israel and pro-Arab positions. The principals are dismayed and disturbed by this development.

It is difficult for those of us who are strongly committed to the State of Israel to understand the causes and development of this position. It is frightening to project the kind of leadership these young teachers will provide the Jewish community in the future, especially vis-à-vis Israel. Have we failed in some way to transmit a strong and loving attitude about the State of Israel? Have we become negligent in our failure to emphasize the unity of Zionism and the State of Israel? Have we fostered an attitude of separation between *an* "ideal" Zionism and *an* "imperfect" State of Israel? Are these young teachers experiencing a return to the ghetto/*galut* mentality that makes them so embarrassed by the inevitable human errors that mere mortals are bound to commit, that they have withdrawn their support for the State of Israel at the first signs of trouble? Or are these young teachers victims of the 'peace at any cost' syndrome?

Whatever the causes, we must acknowledge that we who were their teachers have, in some way, failed to imbue them with the kind of spirit that led to the creation of the State of Israel, and that flourished in the early years of its existence. These young teachers did not have that pioneering experience, and we did not find a way to replace it with another experience. We hoped our enthusiasm somehow would rub off on them. It didn't.

Is this, in some way, the American/*Galut* counterpart to the problem now becoming apparent in Israel, in which the recent generation lacks the spirit and zeal toward Zionism – Israel expressed so strongly by the earlier generations who struggled to create the State?

It is for us now to evolve methods and strategies to reverse this trend. We must not be reticent in expressing our strongest feelings of support for, and commitment to, Zionism-Israel. We must create vehicles by which young people can experience for themselves the meaning of that commitment in their lives.

The distortions of the principles of openness and fairness may have caused some educators to forget that openness and fairness do not require us to abandon our beliefs and principles. As Jews, we will always be fair and open to our adversaries, but we must teach our youngsters never to abandon their hopes, their dreams and their beliefs.

3. Can teachers, children and their families really learn about and experience Israel and be influenced by Israel, from a distance?

The need here is to utilize the information gathered for the Education Subcommittee on the Israeli Experience about increasing the impact of Israel on those who *do* come to study and to tour.

It is crystal clear to me that the flow of traffic should be from West to East. The emphasis of all the efforts of the Jewish Agency, the WZO and the State of Israel should be on bringing Jews *to* Israel. Only where *Shlihim* are absolutely necessary to respond to specific local Diaspora needs, should the traffic be from East to West. And that should involve only a select group of Israeli educators properly prepared for their respective missions.

I'm reminded, here, about the Australian journalist who took a course in beginner's French when he was assigned to the Paris desk of his newspaper. The problem was that no one spoke beginner's French. The problem with many (or most) *Shlihim* is that they are assigned responsibilities in Diaspora communities yet do not speak the actual or metaphorical "language" of the people they came to help. Over and above the linguistic hurdle, they are often culturally and spiritually not attuned to the needs of the communities and schools they came to serve.

Increasing the flow from West to East means maximizing the use of Israel's universities and yeshivot for Diaspora Jewish educators. It means tailor-making programs for *senior* personnel, particularly school administrators and informal Jewish education program directors; teachers and group workers; and lay leaders in Jewish education. It means continuing to develop and provide programs like *amitai yerushalayim* – the Jerusalem Fellows – and the Melton Center Senior Educators Program, in various cost-effective ways, for the young professional elite. It means encouraging, continuing and enhancing programs that work. Again, here the subcommittee's research findings and recommendations can be extremely helpful. It is necessary to develop the capacity to continually assess, modify and prioritize ongoing activities.

All the above possibilities carry a mandate to create ongoing follow-up programs and materials that will enhance the "Israel experience" and maintain the level of enthusiasm that being in Israel initially engendered.

If year-round programs are more effective than short-term three to six week tours, then recruitment efforts should concentrate on bringing high school and college youth to Israel for a full year. Every care must be taken to assure that these programs are appropriate to the participants' needs.

If a "March of the Living" program – the combination of an educational tour to Poland and Israel – is effective, support for this type of program should be forthcoming.

Early Childhood programs desperately need materials to help make Israel real to nursery and kindergarten children. This means facilitating cooperative Diaspora-Israel activity. An example of a successful joint effort on the early childhood level is the *Aleh* Hebrew language program developed cooperatively by the Board of Jewish Education of Greater New York and the WZO.

The recent BJE Study of Supplementary Schools (the most comprehensive and most methodologically rigorous study on this subject to date) underscores how great is the need for family education. Here, working with the proper agencies in the Diaspora, Israel can serve as a vital, life-giving resource to the Diaspora Jewish communities. The idea of bringing families to Israel is not at all new, but its implementation is needed *now* more than ever. Jewish supplementary education simply cannot be effective without the involvement and full support of the Jewish home, something it seriously lacks at the present time.

Israel can play a crucial role in the resuscitation of the congregational afternoon school if Israel-based family education programs become a significant reality. According to the "Israel Experience" report, this *can* happen since many people, it notes, are willing to spend time and money on intensive tours and family experiences in Israel.

Several other questions must be addressed sooner or later. How do Israel and the Diaspora deal with the Jewish education of the children of *yordim*, a ticklish, sensitive issue, but one with which we must honestly grapple. *Yeridah* is an unexpected phenomenon with which we, as a people, are not yet prepared to deal with psychologically and structurally. Using a select number of *yordim* with the proper pedagogic training or training the *yordim* who already populate the staffs of many Diaspora schools is a challenge we all have to face together. Their numbers are too large to overlook.

Israel is not the result of the Holocaust, but a response to it. How can we better get this message across to our students? Programmatically, this means preparing proper materials and methods of instruction. Israel must become an integral component of all Jewish school and Jewish Center programs and *not an option*. Israel must become *central* to the Jewish school curriculum and informal Jewish education activities. How we effect this critical change as soon as possible is a question we must deal with in the immediate tomorrow.

Finally, we have to face the problem of teaching the Hebrew language – *conversational* Hebrew – as realists. Except in the Jewish day school, there is simply not enough time spent in the Jewish school to produce Hebrew speakers, unless summer Hebrew camping becomes an integral part of the Jewish education process, and, of course, an Israel experience during high school years.

PART VII

THE HEBREW LANGUAGE AND THE JEWISH COMMUNITY

CHAPTER 1

Linguistics and Longevity: The Interdependence of Language, Heritage and Nationalism

[Note: This essay is the presentation I prepared to give to the Conference of UNESCO in Lyons, France, in 1997, at the request of a member of the planning Committee of the Conference who read *The Mystique of Hebrew*, published in 1996. I never gave the paper because it was boycotted by Arab delegates who were supported by the French representative to UNESCO. Subsequently, I was disinvited because of "scheduling problems".]

According to Douglas H. Whalen, Senior Scientist at Haskens Laboratories, Yale University, there are some 6,000 languages spoken today. Half of them are expected to vanish within the next century because of the influence of more common languages such as English, Chinese, and Spanish. In Australia, only ten people can speak Jingulu, an aboriginal language. In Alaska, there are only three households in which the native tongue Kuskokwim still prevails. Worldwide, Whalen noted, some 100 languages have just one native speaker (*New York Times Magazine*).

In addition, some modern languages bear little resemblance to the ancient languages from which they developed. For example, modern Greek speakers cannot understand Homer's *Iliad* or *Odyssey* unless they have special training in classical Greek. Hindustani is hardy similar to Sanskrit, its progenitor. And modern Chinese speakers cannot read Confucius with understanding unless they have special schooling in the subject.

Therefore, the continuity of Hebrew, one of mankind's oldest languages and the oldest continuous language raises the question: In the face of 2,000 years of dispersion, how did Hebrew, in modern times, emerge as an *altneusprache* (an old-new language) that is currently the vernacular of some 5,000,000 Jews and 1,000,000 non-Jews in Israel, the spoken language of another million Jews in the Diaspora, and the language of prayer and learning of another 4,000,000 Jews world-wide?

The miracle of the continuity and revival of Hebrew as a living language has impressed people speaking endangered "minor" languages such as Basque, Irish, and Welsh. Linguistic delegations from Spain, Ireland, and Scotland have visited Israel to learn about the various methods of language instruction, particularly the Ulpan, the study institute for adults that stresses oral comprehension, conversation, and daily terminology and the *Ivrit b'ivrit* approach – the method of teaching other subjects in the Hebrew language. Both of these instructional techniques helped bring about the renaissance of Hebrew.

Hebrew was never a dead language in the accepted sense of the term. Yet, it was revived. It never ceased to be a medium of religious expression for the Jewish people. Yet, it was reborn. This is its mystique. This is the bipolar power of the Hebrew language, the vehicle of a sacred past, of eternal Jewish values. At the same time, it is a major expression of contemporary Jewish vitality.

Even though it was not used or was rarely used as a vernacular in the lands of Jewish dispersion since the destruction of the Second Temple in Jerusalem almost 2,000 years ago, it was employed regularly during the last two millennia by the vast majority of Jews wherever they resided as a language of prayer, study, and ritual observance. And, although it did not die, it was revived during the last century as a common, everyday spoken language. This revival in Palestine/Israel bordered on the miraculous, since the immigrants who came to Israel from dozens of countries throughout the world and comprised the vast majority of the Jewish population brought with them such a large variety of linguistic baggage.

Hebrew, as an ancient language, is well over 3,500 years old. Although there are Canaanite, Akkadian, Amorite, and Egyptian linguistic antecedents that are considered by some as pre-biblical forms of the language we now know as Hebrew, the Bible is the first corpus of texts written in this medium. It was a fully-fashioned literary vehicle.

In biblical times, Hebrew was the common language of the various peoples living in the Mideast area called Cana'an, such as the Moabites, the Amorites, and the Edomites. It is for this reason that Hebrew was known in the Bible as *Sefat Cana'an* – the language of Cana'an (*Isaiah* 19:18).

Abraham, the father of the Jewish nation, according to Jewish rabbinic tradition, spoke in the language of the Bible. This notion is reinforced in the *Midrash* (a collection of commentaries and interpretations on the Bible), that notes that Abraham was descended from *Ever*, the great-grandson of Noah, who spoke *Ivrit* or Hebrew, the language of *Ever* (*Midrash Rabba Genesis* 18:14). To be sure, the root letters of *Ivrit* and *Ever* are the same. In medieval and contemporary times, Hebrew was regarded by some scholars, including leading Christian scholars in Europe, to be Adam's original tongue, the *prima lingua*, the prime or first language of the human race (Goldman; Simpson).

Hebrew continued to be the language of Abraham's descendants, the Israelites, when they were enslaved in Egypt for 210 years. The *Midrash* observes that the Israelites were redeemed from Egypt as a Hebrew nation because, among other things, "they did not change their language". (*Midrash Leviticus* 32:5) They stubbornly retained their linguistic identity. Hebrew was the common everyday language of the Israelite masses from the time they conquered the Land of Cana'an, until the end of the First Commonwealth with the destruction of the First Temple in Jerusalem in 586 B.C.E.

When the Jews returned to their homeland from Babylonia some 100 years later, Hebrew was revived, but not without difficulty. Nehemiah, the leader of the returnees, had to employ strong measures to guarantee the continued use of Hebrew for Bible study, for public reading of the Bible, and for daily conversation. He notes, "Half of the children (of the returning exiles), spoke *Ashdodit* (the language of *Ashdod*) and did not know how to speak *Yehudit* (Hebrew)" (Nehemiah 13:24). Nehemiah "waged the first war in Jewish history against the detractors of the Hebrew language" because he realized that Hebrew was a *conditione sine qua non* for the survival of the Jewish people, for its spiritual continuity, and for the re-establishment of the Jewish nation in the Land of Israel (Federbush).

Similar challenges regarding the use of Hebrew by the Jewish people were faced in subsequent periods of Jewish history. During the days of Yehudah Ha-nasi (Judah the Prince, patriarch of Judea and redactor of the *Mishnah*, the first part of the Talmud – the body of early Jewish civil and religious law), Hebrew was in danger of disappearing as a national language and being replaced by Aramaic, both as a vernacular and as a means of literary expression. Rabbi Judah warned the Jewish people about the neglect of Hebrew. He meticulously spoke Hebrew at home. The Talmud relates that even his maidservant had such a command of Hebrew that his students learned from her Hebrew words and terms that they had either forgotten or had never known (*Rosh Hashana* 26; *Megillah* 18).

Rabbi Meir, a leading scholar of the second century, who made major contributions to the development of the Oral Law, also tried to stem the tide of the Aramaic language. He ruled, "When a child begins to speak, his father should speak Hebrew to him and teach him Torah (in the original Hebrew text); and if the father fails to speak to him in the Holy Tongue and does not teach him Torah, it is as if he buries him" (*Sifrei*, Deut. 11:19).

During the eleventh and twelfth centuries in North Africa and in the Spanish peninsula, Arabic took root in a large segment of the Jewish population as the language of literary and philosophical writing while Aramaic, used in Babylonia for almost a millennium, continued to serve as the language of Talmudic study and discourse. Twelfth-century Maimonides, the most illustrious figure in the post-Talmudic era, an outstanding rabbinic authority, rationalist, philosopher, and royal physician, wrote many of his works in Arabic to accommodate the Jewish masses, many of whom did not know Hebrew. However, Maimonides became convinced that Judaic literature should be written and studied solely in Hebrew. Toward this end, he refused to translate his fourteen-volume *magnum opus* – *Mishneh Torah*, the massive codification of Jewish law – from Hebrew into Arabic. And, it seems, he later regretted having done most of his writing in Arabic. Moreover, he stressed that the study of Hebrew was a religious obligation of the highest order (Haramati).

Following in Maimonides' footsteps were many religious leaders who vigorously combated efforts to de-Hebraize Jewish life, to develop a Judaism in translation, to use the languages of the lands of Jewish residence as the vehicles of Bible study and communion with the Almighty. These leaders helped transform Hebrew into a religious-national value of Jewish life in exile. As such, Hebrew became the ethnic-national ingredient ingrained in the consciousness of the Jewish people – a sustaining feature of a landless nation.

In viewing Jewish history over the last two millennia, one observes a unique linguistic phenomenon among the Jewish people. The Talmud notes that the Jews were trilingual (*Baba Kama* 83). They had an internal language, an external language, and a sacred language toward the end of the Second Commonwealth; in the first century B.C.E. their internal language was an Aramaic-Syrian dialect, which served as their vernacular. Greek was their external language, which they used in their relations with gentiles. Hebrew was their sacred language for religious and national purposes. In the Middle Ages and contemporary times, for example, the internal language of Jews in the Spanish peninsula was *Judesmo*, a Spanish-Jewish dialect. Italian or Spanish was their external language and Hebrew, the language of their religious study, prayer, and ritual observance. In Eastern Europe, *Yiddish*, a German-Jewish language, was their internal language and, depending upon where they resided, either Polish, Russian or Hungarian, and the like, was their external language. Hebrew was their sacred tongue. Using Hebrew as their sacred language meant that they communicated in the holy tongue thrice daily with their Maker. This is why an historian of the Hebrew language observed, "The Hebrew people never spoke any language as a religious nation other than Hebrew" (Federbush).

Contributing significantly to the survival of Hebrew as a living language was the use of written Hebrew as a means of communication. A prime use of Hebrew during the medieval and contemporary periods was in the *Responsa*, lengthy answers by rabbinic authorities about matters of Jewish life. Hebrew was used to inform and guide the Jewish community regarding Jewish religious and ethical practices. An example of this kind of writing is the nineteenth-century bestseller, *Kitzur Shulhan Arukh*, a concise summary of the authoritative Ashkenazic code of Judaic law and custom (Ganzfried).

Communication between the leaders of the various Jewish communities was almost always in Hebrew. In 1903, the leaders of the Jewish community of Safi, Morocco, wrote in Hebrew to Theodore Herzl, after receiving from him informational materials on Zionism in the German language. In their letter to Herzl, the Jews of Safi requested that the "honorable prince" communicate with them about Zionism in Hebrew. They also asked that he send them the Hebrew translation of *Judenstaat*, his treatise on the establishment of a Jewish State, and make available the Hebrew rendition of other books and materials relevant to the Zionist idea.

Letter writing between ordinary Jews was often done via the Holy Tongue, and Jewish communal records were always kept in Hebrew. Communal regulations and announcements were promulgated primarily in Hebrew. Business documents between Jews were often written in Hebrew, and merchants frequently kept their private business records in Hebrew. Invitations to weddings and other family events were issued in Hebrew, and wills were written in the Holy Tongue, as were inscriptions on gravestones. This wide variety of Hebrew language usage helped guarantee Hebrew's survival.

The development of Hebrew as a modern vernacular corresponds, in a practical way, to the development of the modern Jewish State. Ahad Ha'am, the brilliant Hebraist, secular Jewish philosopher, and Zionist leader, saw the natural indispensable linkage between these two developments He stressed the vital integrative relationships between the revival of Hebrew, its continuance as the Jewish ethnic language, and the renaissance of Jewish nationhood in Palestine. This relationship was at the heart of his theory of the Jewish State as the *merkaz ruhani*, the spiritual cultural center for Jewish life everywhere.

To be a national language, Ahad Ha'am insisted, its usage as a mother tongue or vernacular is not sufficient. The national language must incorporate the spiritual and cultural wealth of the nation and its national ideals. As such, the combination of Jewish religion, literature, and language has been the Jewish people's portable property after exile began with the destruction of the Temple in 70 C.E. And, Ahad Ha'am opined, when the Holy Land would once again become the physical center the the Jewish people, the Hebrew language would be the bridge between the Land and the Diaspora.

Although the initial steps toward the revival of Hebrew in modern times took place in Europe, its full-blown development occurred in the Jewish homeland. The revival of Hebrew as a modern spoken language began in Palestine in the later decades of the nineteenth century with the arrival from Eastern Europe of Zionist pioneers, chief among them Eliezer Ben-Yehuda.

The pioneers were determined to revive ancient Hebrew and make it the common language of the new State about which they dreamt and for which they devoted their lives. According to most accounts, Ben Yehuda largely was responsible for the near-miracle – making Hebrew the national language of Palestine (now Israel) spoken by the masses (St. John). He believed fervently that a Jewish rebirth in Palestine was not possible without the revival of Hebrew. For him, spoken Hebrew, as the soul of a living people, was the essence of Jewish Renaissance. Without a language capable of expressing all the nuances of life, both ancient and modern, the rebirth of the Jewish people in its land would be meaningless.

Ben Yehuda insisted on using Hebrew in home and raising his children speaking the language. While his neighbors conversed in the language of their former countries of residence or in Yiddish or Ladino, Ben Yehuda did not allow any language other than Hebrew to be spoken in his home. Thus began the process of nativization and normalization of Hebrew in modern times. Modern Hebrew was born in Palestine as Ben Yehuda removed the fear of linguistic innovation from the hearts of many religious Jews (the bulk of religious Jews in Jerusalem continued to restrict the use of Hebrew to sacred activities), and provided for secular Zionists a channel for their ethnic feelings and expression. Moreover, he created many new words based on the Bible and Talmud and even developed some new words with Arabic roots. To propagate the use of these new words he disseminated them in the newspaper he published. Other lovers of Hebrew helped ensure that the ancient tongue of the Prophets would once again become the vernacular.

Thus, the revival of Hebrew was part of a complex historical, social, psychological, and linguistic process. In effect, the revitalization took place in the new Zionist settlements through people who were inspired by the idea of ethnic and cultural Jewish rebirth, particularly through the arduous efforts of enthusiastic persistent teachers. And the pupils then became the Hebrew instructors of their parents (Glinert).

Ben Yehuda and his associates and followers engaged in *milhemet ha-safah*, a language war, between 1912 and 1914, fighting for a place for Hebrew in Palestine along with other languages and particularly for Hebrew as the language of instruction in the newly founded Technion in Haifa. They established an educational system in which Hebrew, with almost no exceptions, became the only language used. To accomplish this in the *yishuv* meant transforming a language used only for special purposes – prayer and study – to a single vernacular for all the communication needs of this varied population (Harshav). And, during the era of the British Mandate (1918–1948), Hebrew was recognized as an official language of Palestine, along with English and Arabic.

In retrospect, the mystique of Hebrew is its constancy – its uniformity. As Jews resided in countries all over the globe, their ancestral language was influenced in different times and places by Aramaic, Greek, Latin, Arabic, Spanish, French, German, Polish, and Russian languages. This led to regional differences in Hebrew language usage (Haramati).

Nevertheless, Hebrew maintained uniformity throughout: it retained its ancient structure and character (Spiegel). The essential uniformity of the Hebrew language in its various stages of development prompted the author of the essay on Hebrew in the *Encyclopedia Judaica* to make the bold claim that twentieth-century intelligent Hebrew speakers with a high school background are able to read and understand literature written in Hebrew from the earliest times to the most modern (Orman). And conversely, according to Charles Berlitz (1982), the prominent American language educator, "If the prophets who compiled the books of the Old Testament could return to present-day Israel, they would still be able to read the Israeli daily press." Both these claims might be somewhat exaggerated. However, they underscore the fact that the changes that took place over time in vocabulary, morphology, syntax, and pronunciation did not transform the fundamental nature of Hebrew.

Currently, different people use Hebrew in different ways for different purposes. Many secularists see Hebrew primarily as a vehicle of modern communication and modern literature. In contrast, most ultra-Orthodox Jews, a small minority in Israel, consider Hebrew to be a holy tongue to be used solely for Judaic learning and prayer.

From an historical, sociolinguistic perspective, the Hebrew language is a multifaceted linguistic vehicle of Jewish life from earliest times until the present. Hebrew, in all its usages, has contributed significantly to Jewish survival throughout the ages. Therefore, one cannot appreciate the value of Hebrew via any single dimension of the language. Hebrew must be considered in all its forms and variety of usages, including biblical Hebrew, *Mishnaic* Hebrew, rabbinic Hebrew, liturgical Hebrew, modern Hebrew, and Hebrew terminology associated with Judaic literacy and used in the Jewish internal languages such as Ladino and Yiddish. This means considering the use of Hebrew in the synagogue, educational settings, the home, business, the arts, culture, professions, and the street. Hebrew's multi-dimensionalism is its distinctiveness as a survival mechanism. Indeed, it demonstrates clearly that the survival of Hebrew as a Holy Tongue, the survival of the Jewish people in its homeland and in the Diaspora, and the continuity of Jewish nationalism are interdependent.

CHAPTER 2

HEBREW IN NEW YORK

[*For an overview of the origins and development of the Hebrew language, please refer to the previous chapter.*]

The development of Hebrew as a modern vernacular corresponds, in a practical way, to the development of the modern Jewish State. The revival of Hebrew as a modern language required overcoming a variety of linguistic problems concerning pronunciation, spelling, vocabulary and grammar. The Sephardic Oriental variant was established as the standard pronunciation (as opposed to Ashkenazic Hebrew deriving from Western and Eastern Europe).

The most outstanding achievement of the modern revival period is the transformation of a "dead" language to a language of everyday use. In truth, the Hebrew language never "died," as it remained an active medium of religious expression wherever Jews wandered and settled. Its revival utilized words from the vast liturgical, rabbinical and literary works in *Mishnaic*, medieval, and contemporary times, many of which dealt with matters of science, medicine and even mathematics and astronomy. The four thousand words invented by Ben Yehuda and the thousands of new words introduced into modern Hebrew during the last century were derived largely from these sources.

Hebrew, then, is both classical and modern at once, not to be compared to the difference between classical and modern Greek. Unlike Sanskrit, Hebrew did not give way to a modern counterpart (in the case of Sanskrit – Hindustani), hardly similar to its progenitor. Unlike Latin, Hebrew was not confined at any time to church ritual, but was considered an appropriate language of communion between the Jew and his Maker (Schiff 1981: 2).

Hebrew in modern times has emerged as an *altneuschprache* (an old-new language) which is the vernacular of some five million Jews and non-Jews in Israel. It is this *altneuschprache* as used in the United States, particularly in New York City, that is the focus of this essay.

NEW WORLD HISTORICAL PERSPECTIVE

The Early Period 1654–1880

The Jewish immigrants who came to the United States in the seventeenth and eighteenth centuries were largely of Sephardic origin (descendants of Jews who lived in Spain or Portugal before their expulsion in 1492). Their essential relationship with the Hebrew language was their reading knowledge of prayers. While there were in each generation several Jews who were known to be Hebraists (Marcus 426), Jewish scholarship and Hebrew speaking Jews were virtually unknown (Grinstein 24).

In his address at the consecration of the Mill Street Synagogue in 1818, Major Mordechai Manuel Noah, the preeminent Jewish communal leader of his time, spoke of the necessity of teaching Hebrew, "for with the loss of Hebrew language may be added the downfall of the House of Israel" (Grinstein 255). By and large, his plea fell on deaf ears. The use of Hebrew continued to be limited to rote prayer recitation, writing inscriptions on tombstones, recording birth dates, marriages and deaths, liturgical readings at wedding and circumcision ceremonies, memorial prayers and the "sale" of *aliyot* (the custom of auctioning the honors of reciting a blessing over the Torah) during synagogue services.

There are indications that some people had more than passing familiarity with the Hebrew language. Occasionally, Hebrew advertisements appeared in the Jewish press. In 1826, a Hebrew circular appealing for funds for which to purchase a synagogue building was sent by Congregation Bnai Jeshurun in New York to various synagogues in the United States. Hebrew was the language used for *kashrut* seals ascertaining that foods were kosher. In 1835, a Hebrew grammar and the first volume of a Hebrew concordance were published by a printer who established a Hebrew printing shop in 1820 (Grinstein 350).

From 1840 until 1880, when masses of Jews began coming from Eastern Europe, the Jewish immigrants were mostly from Germany and Western Europe. They established liberal Reform synagogues and used German as well as Hebrew in their prayer services. Over time, English became the main medium of worship in the Reform congregations.

Hebrew pronunciation varied with the immigrant's origin. By and large, the early settlers in the seventeenth and eighteenth centuries used the Sephardic pronunciation while the immigrants from Western and Eastern Europe employed the Ashkenazic pronunciation.

Whatever the level and extent of Hebrew language usage in America prior to 1880, the number of Jews in the United States, as a whole, and in each of the cities where Jews resided was "too small to provide the atmosphere for Hebraic cultural activity" (Halkin 125).

The East European Period 1880–1960
With the great East European migrations from 1880 to 1920, new influences were introduced in the use of Hebrew as the Jewish population in the United States soared. In 1880, there were approximately 100,000 Jews in New York City. By 1960, there were well over 500,000. Twenty years later, this number had tripled.

The main influence on the use of Hebrew as a modern language was the development of Zionism (the worldwide Jewish movement begun at the end of the nineteenth century for the establishment in Palestine of a national homeland for the Jews in response to growing anti-Semitism and continued oppression of Jews) and the *Haskalah* (the eighteenth and nineteenth century enlightenment movement of German, Central and East European Jews to modernize Judaism and make it cosmopolitan by promoting secular knowledge and culture, and encouraging the adoption of the dress, customs and language of the general population). Proponents of the *Haskalah* and Zionism wanted to modernize the Hebrew language and make it a common everyday medium of expression.

Among the masses that came to America during this period were dedicated Zionists and followers of Ahad Ha'am, the Hebraist thinker and Zionist leader who pioneered the use of Hebrew for Jewish cultural and national communication, and Ben Yehuda, who helped develop Hebrew into a spoken language (Mintz 42). They brought with them the zeal, knowledge and ability to energize small pockets of Hebrew devotees at the turn of the century. In 1882, a *Hovevi Zion*, 'Lovers of Zion' society was founded in New York (Urofsky 82). Its members, along with other Zionists, devoted themselves zealously to Palestinian colonization and to the rebirth of Hebrew. Also in New York, the first Hebrew speaking society *Mephitze Sephat Ever Vesiphrutah*, 'The Promoters of the Language of Ever and its Literature' was founded in 1902:

> Each of its weekly meetings on Sunday evenings offered a well-prepared lecture, which was followed by discussion from the floor, all in Hebrew. It became a lasting sensation. Its sessions drew 150–300 participants through the season. Out-of-town visitors came to see the miracle of spoken Hebrew, and upon returning home, spread the news that Hebrew is becoming again a living tongue (*The Jewish Communal Register* 567).

In 1909, *Achieber*, another Hebrew language society, was organized to promote Hebrew aggressively. It arranged Hebrew lectures throughout the city and encouraged Hebrew writers to ply their trade. In 1913, it founded *Hatoren*, first a monthly and then a weekly Hebrew journal. By 1918, there were ten Hebrew-speaking organizations with a total membership of 500 in New York City (*The Jewish Communal Register* 568). One of the groups, *Agudah Ivrith* of the College of the City of New York, made its goal the creation of a Hebrew stage, which lasted several years.

Outside of New York there were twenty Hebrew-speaking clubs. One of their most prominent activities was sponsoring evening courses in Hebrew for adults. In addition, there were Hebrew-speaking clubs in many Hebrew schools. In 1917, there were "several thousand whose language of conversation is Hebrew either steadily or intermittently." At least ten public lectures were given in Hebrew each week during World War I (*The Jewish Communal Register* 569).

In 1914, Henrietta Szold, as president of *Hadassah* (the Women's Zionist organization in the United States), organized adult Hebrew study groups and youth camps to spread the use of Hebrew (Urofsky 143). In 1918, the Zionist Congress in Pittsburgh issued six guiding principles, the sixth of which was "Hebrew, the national language of the Jewish people shall be the medium of public instruction" (Urofsky 256).

Zionist pronouncements and efforts had effect only on small groups of committed followers. Among these was a select group of outstanding Hebrew scholars, writers, poets and teachers in the 1920s, 30s and 40s who, as a direct expression of Ahad Ha'am's ideology, set a high standard for America Hebraism. Their influence on the general Jewish population was hardly noticeable as they spawned a short-lived Hebraic movement for the elite. Yet, almost all Jews during those years, even non-Zionists, with the exception of the ultra-Orthodox and most of the secular *Yiddishists*, recognized the promotion of Hebrew as a positive Jewish value (Patai 132). And, although only a limited number of Jews were Hebrew scholars and/or Hebrew speakers, most Jewish males had a basic familiarity with the language (Mintz 44). A significant aspect of Hebrew language usage was the introduction of Hebrew Zionist songs into the Jewish community in the 1920s. Thousands of Jewish youth in schools, camps and Zionist youth groups would sing these songs in the 1930s, 1940s and 1950s. Hundreds of Hebrew songsters were published during this time.

One of the moderately successful results of Hebraic Zionist influence was the founding of Hebrew camps. The first camp, *Achvah* (1926–1940), for Hebrew-speaking teenagers in New York City, was followed by the establishment of *Massad* in 1943. At *Massad*'s peak in 1968, there were three camps with over 1200 campers and counselors all speaking Hebrew for eight weeks during the summer months. *Massad* closed in 1982.

Other Hebrew camps include Camp *Yavneh* (founded in 1944 by the Hebrew College of Brookline, Massachusetts) and the *Ramah* camps (established in 1946 by the Conservative movement). During the 1950s some 3,000 campers were immersed during the summer months in Hebrew-speaking programs. Currently, their stress is on Judaica rather than Hebrew.

HEBREW LANGUAGE USAGE IN EDUCATIONAL SETTINGS

The Early Period 1654–1880
From the time Jews set foot on the soil of America in 1654, the immigrants provided their children with a Jewish education according to the traditions of the country from which they originated. In most instances, this included some form of Hebrew language instruction generally limited to "mechanical reading, liturgy, a smattering of the *Pentateuch* in the original, elementary Hebrew grammar, preparation of boys for *Bar Mitzvah* (special synagogue service at age thirteen) and laws and ceremonies of the Jewish religion" (Fromer 16).

Where Bible was studied in the original, in the traditional synagogue day schools and in private classes, it was taught by the translation method into the vernacular since Hebrew was considered to be a "dead" language on a par with Latin or Greek. As such, Hebrew was variously translated into German by the German immigrants, into Yiddish by the East European Jews and into English by the American born (Grinstein 29). Some teachers introduced Hebrew grammar as they translated the Bible from the Hebrew, explaining the root of each verb, its tense and gender.

The traditional program of Hebrew studies in the day school began with the Hebrew alphabet, then moved on to syllables and words in the *Siddur* (the daily and Sabbath prayer book), and then to *Pentateuch* translation. Occasionally, Hebrew writing was added. One or two hours each day were usually devoted to Hebrew.

In the one day Sunday or Sabbath schools, first organized in 1838 in Philadelphia, little or no attention was paid to Hebrew language. However, in the traditional synagogue afternoon schools, Hebrew language – reading, *Siddur*, grammar and Bible translation – was incorporated into the program much the same way it was studied in the day schools.

Several efforts to establish Hebrew high schools met with little success, as did attempts to establish schools of higher Jewish learning.

From 1880 Until the Present Time

With the arrival of East European immigrants, the tenor of Jewish education changed. The immigrant Zionists and *Maskilim* (enlightened liberal Jews who advocated and supported *Haskalah*) brought with them the desire and oftentimes the know-how to infuse Hebrew language instruction into the Jewish education programs. They even developed the beginnings of *Ivrit b'Ivrit*, the method of using Hebrew as a medium of instruction for all Judaic subjects. However, the attempts to teach Hebrew as a spoken language was limited to a few afternoon schools where knowledgeable and enthusiastic secular and religious Zionist educators were able to influence the direction of Jewish schooling (Wolowelsky).

Ivrit b'Ivrit schools opened in New York as well as in Boston, Philadelphia Chicago, Detroit, Indianapolis, Pittsburgh and San Francisco. These schools, enrolling in total during the peak 1930s and 1940s some 15,000 students each year, were the exception and not the rule. The vast majority of schools established by East European immigrants were patterned after the *Hadarim* in Europe where Bible and Talmud were taught via translation into Yiddish. In the United States the Bible and Talmud were translated into English. The translation method involved the recitation by the teacher of the Hebraic text followed by line-by-line or phrase-by-phrase translation. The students were then required to repeat the text and translation, first in unison and then individually.

A more pervasive influence of *Haskalah* on Hebrew language in the United States was the founding of eleven Hebrew Teachers Colleges between 1910 and 1929 – in New York (five colleges) and in Philadelphia, Boston, Chicago, Cleveland, Baltimore and Pittsburgh. All instruction in these institutions was in Hebrew. Hebrew language, grammar and literature represented the major area of concentration of most of the colleges (Dushkin 65–73). Students were trained to teach Jewish subjects and Hebrew language using Hebrew as a medium of instruction.

The enrollment in the Hebrew Teachers Colleges peaked in the 1950s at about 3,000 students. By 1966, it declined to 1,800 students, as secular colleges introduced Judaic studies and Hebrew language programs, and as Jewish youths lost interest in these types of programs (Schiff 83). Over time, it became more difficult for the Hebrew Teachers Colleges (which all became Colleges of Jewish Studies by 1975) to conduct class work entirely in Hebrew, since the Jewish feeder schools were no longer Hebraic (Schiff 1988). In 1994, about one thousand students attended these schools where the language of instruction was largely English.

The influence of Zionism and *Haskalah* on Hebrew language usage in Jewish schools was short lived as synagogue afternoon schools began in the 1930s to replace the communal Hebraic Talmud Torah schools, known generally as "Hebrew Schools," which provided supplemental Jewish religious education to Jewish students after public school hours. Congregational Jewish education emphasized the study of prayer, Jewish laws and customs, Jewish holidays, Jewish history and preparation for *Bar/Bat Mitzvah*. This was accompanied by a reduction of the number of weekly hours of instruction from 10–12 hours for 48 weeks to 4–5 hours for 36 weeks. Together, these developments reduced the role of Hebrew language in the schools (Schiff 1988) in which 270,000 pupils (60% of the total 1993 American Jewish School population of 450,000) are enrolled.

The growth of the *Modern Jewish Day School* (the all day educational institution in which students study both general and Jewish subjects) since 1940 has added a major dimension to the use of Hebrew language in the United States, especially in New York City. The Judaic studies programs in these schools are intensive, averaging about 20 hours per week. There is much variation among the day schools regarding emphasis on Hebrew language, ranging from minimal attention in the Reform day schools (comprising about 2% of the pupil population), to intensive study of biblical and post-biblical texts, Talmud, and commentaries, mostly translating them into Yiddish in the *Hasidic* and ultra-Orthodox *yeshivot* (comprising about 40% of the enrollment), and to a balanced curriculum of Hebraic studies with a variety of emphases on Hebrew language in Modern Orthodox schools (44%), in community day schools (5%), and in Conservative Solomon Schechter schools (9%). About 25% of all day school students are exposed to *Ivrit b'Ivrit* instruction.

Hebrew language was introduced into the New York public school system in 1929. By 1942 there were three thousand students in sixteen junior, senior and evening high schools in the city. With the elimination of language requirements in the high schools and the movement of Jews to the suburbs, Hebrew language instruction in New York City public schools all but disappeared by 1970, after it peaked to over 7,000 students in twenty-four public junior and senior high schools in the 1950s.

Hebrew language and Hebrew text study was basic to many early America colleges. Ten universities established before the American Revolution included Hebrew among the "learned languages" of the curriculum. Among these schools were Harvard, Yale, and Dartmouth, which made the study of Hebrew obligatory. In Harvard, whose first two presidents were Hebrew scholars, all freshmen were required to study Hebrew for one full year (Goldman).

The study of Hebrew in colleges declined during the eighteenth century and all but disappeared by the nineteenth century. However, the custom of giving valedictory addresses in Hebrew, as well as in Greek and in Latin, continued in several universities until the onset of the twentieth century.

During contemporary times, the growth in Hebrew language and Jewish studies programs in U.S. universities began in the 1930s. By 1966, there were sixty-four institutions offering Hebrew courses of which twenty-five had an undergraduate Hebrew major (Band 258). By 1989, the National Association of Professors of Hebrew identified ninety-three Modern Hebrew programs in U.S. colleges and universities with an enrollment of 5,115 students. Only about half of the modern Hebrew programs extended beyond the second level.

The dropout rate after the first year course was due to the fact that "most of the students have no real interest in Hebrew" (Morahg 22).

There is a strong relationship between Israel and enrollment in Hebrew language courses, particularly for those who continued on to second, third or fourth levels of Hebrew language. A 1993 University of Wisconsin survey of 322 undergraduates enrolled in modern Hebrew programs demonstrated that the most powerful factors motivating the study of Hebrew were "travel to Israel" (88%), "interest in Israel" (85%), and "ability to talk to Israelis" (82%).

The establishment of the State of Israel in 1948 motivated the organization of Ulpanim (study institutes in modern Hebrew language according to new Israeli methods of language teaching which stress oral comprehension, conversation and daily terminology) for adults throughout the United States and particularly in New York. However, only a miniscule segment of the adult Jewish population has availed itself of this Hebraic study opportunity. During the peak years of Ulpan programming in the 1950s and 1960s, some ten thousand Jewish adults throughout the United

States would study Hebrew annually for periods of three months to several years.

Currently, the major effort in Ulpan teaching takes place at the Ulpan Center in New York and several other cities with large Jewish populations sponsored by the World Zionist Organization. Four hundred and fifty adults were enrolled in the New York Ulpan Center in 1993 in the various program levels, which range from beginner's Hebrew to advanced level where students learn to read Israeli newspapers and speak Hebrew fluently. Classes meet for two to six hours per week for nine to fourteen weeks. Students can progress from one level to another over a period of one or two years (Pinchuk). According to a survey of adult programs in Hebrew language, one of the major problems regarding adult study of Hebrew in America *Ulpanim* is the use of Israeli texts and materials prepared for immigrants in Israel.

In Israel, Hebrew is taught (to newcomers) as a second language in an Ulpan with the entire society reinforcing the lessons of the Ulpan, but in the United States, Hebrew is a foreign language and receives no societal reinforcement (Wassertzug).

CURRENT HEBREW USAGE IN THE UNITED STATES

Jews came to the shores of America in several waves. Each group of immigrants brought with it a linguistic lineage that included, among others, the language of the country from which they migrated (Spanish, Portuguese, German, Dutch, Russian, Polish, Hungarian, etc.), Hebrew (their ancestral language of prayer and Judaic study), and often a Jewish language peculiar to their residential setting – essentially *Ladino* by Sephardim immigrants from Spanish speaking lands, and *Yiddish* by those coming from Eastern European countries.

As a result of the acculturation-deculturation syndrome that has affected American Jewry, and the accompanying transposition of intellectual and cultural interest away from Judaism by a majority of Jews once they arrived in the United States from European lands, the active users of Hebrew, even if mostly only in prayer and Judaic study, are relatively few, probably not more than twenty percent of the *five million core* Jews in the United States and not more than forty percent of the Jewish population of *one million* in New York City.

According to the 1991 New York Jewish Population Study, of the one million Jews residing in New York City (over two-thirds of them in Brooklyn and Manhattan) and 400,000 in the suburban counties (Nassau, Suffolk and Westchester), slightly more than one quarter claim to speak Hebrew and 16% claim they can read a Hebrew newspaper (Horowitz 51).

More males (30%) than females (23%) speak Hebrew. More young adults speak Hebrew than older adults. Generational differences are also apparent. Forty-one percent of first generation Jews (this figure includes many Israeli immigrants) claims to speak Hebrew, compared to 24% and 21% of second and third/fourth generation adults. There is obviously a relationship between those who have Israeli ties and use of Hebrew language. Seventy-seven percent of first generation American Jews, 47% second generation and 33% third/fourth generation Jews have close friends or family in Israel. Sixty-six percent of first generation, 48% and 31% respectively of second and third/fourth generation adults have visited Israel (Horowitz 52).

There are other generational differences regarding the use of Hebrew. Thirty percent of first generation Jews attend synagogue weekly, compared to 17% of second generation and 10% of third/fourth generation Jews. Seventy-three percent of first generation Jews, compared to 65% of second generation and 54% of third/fourth generation adults, attend synagogue on High Holidays where they are exposed to Hebrew in the prayer service. In other activities where Hebrew terms and/or Hebrew blessings are used – Israeli Independence Day celebration, Holocaust commemoration, Purim celebration and lighting Sabbath and Hanukkah candles – first generation Jews are much more involved than second, third and fourth generation adults (Horowitz 63).

The variety of contemporary Hebrew language users in New York City may be divided into several categories: the *daveners* (daily worshippers), occasional worshippers, lifetime "learners," occasional learners, student speakers and readers. Moreover, there is an ideological base to the use of Hebrew. Hasidic and Ultra Orthodox, centrist or Modern Orthodox, Conservative, Reconstructionist and Reform, and secular Jews all relate to Hebrew language usage in distinct ways.

The *Hasidic* and *Ultra Orthodox* (about 110,000 or 11% of the City's Jewish population) use Hebrew essentially in the same manner, as did their predecessors in Eastern Europe. The Jewish culture of their communities in New York is not much different from the *shtetl* way of life of their ancestors in Eastern Europe in the 18th and 19th centuries. For the Hasidic and Ultra Orthodox Jews, Hebrew is *leshon hakodesh*, a Holy Tongue referred to as *loshn koydesh* in their Yiddish usage, employed solely for prayer and Torah study. It is not to be used for any other purpose. Even in Israel, they prefer to use Yiddish as their daily vernacular rather than the language of the country.

The Ultra Orthodox and Hasidic Jews, largely concentrated in Brooklyn and Rockland County, about 30 miles north of New York City, are the daily *daveners* and daily learners. Adult males spend as much as two hours a day in Hebrew prayers. Many young males, up to the age of thirty and more, spend most of their waking hours studying Judaic texts. Many working males devote as much time as possible to learning Torah – *Pentateuch*, Talmud and Commentaries and Hasidic lore. But these are orally translated and discussed in Yiddish. Most Hasidic and Ultra Orthodox Jews are trilingual: Yiddish is their Jewish language, the vernacular of their home; English is the language of their business activity and association with non-Jews and Jews who do not speak Yiddish; and Hebrew is their internal language, their sacred language of study and prayer. Their communities in Borough Park and Williamsburg, Brooklyn, and in Monsey, New York are essentially Yiddish speaking islands. Their daily Yiddish conversation with family and friends is punctuated with Hebraic religious terminology. Since Hasidim are forbidden by and large, to watch TV, listen to secular radio programs and read English newspapers in their homes, contact with English is limited to external associations.

This trilingual attribute is two millennia old. As Spolsky and Cooper have said, "multilingualism clearly predates the destruction of the Second Temple in 70 C.E. By the first century, a pattern had developed whereby Jews knew and used Hebrew for religious and literary purposes, spoke a Jewish vernacular (Aramaic), and also as members of a minority group, knew and used non-Jewish language."

Like the Ultra Orthodox and Hasidic Jews, Centrist or Modern Orthodox Jews, (population about 120,000 or 12% of the city's Jewish residents) pray solely in Hebrew and study biblical, post-biblical and rabbinical literature in the original Hebrew. As they differ in their relationship to Western society, Modern Orthodox differ also in their relationship to modern Hebrew. While giving the Hebrew language the respect it deserves as a Holy Tongue, Modern Orthodox Jews believe in its use as a living form of expression – as a vernacular, although Hebrew rarely reaches that level without extensive Israeli exposure.

Conservative, Reconstructionist and Reform Jews live largely in the suburban counties of Greater New York – Nassau, Suffolk and Westchester – and the suburbs of all the cities where Jews reside. Conservative Jews (population 290,000 or 29% of Jews in New York City) pray in Hebrew. While the Hebraic content of their prayer books is similar to the Modern Orthodox, their Hebrew prayer service is interspersed with English prayers.

While the Reconstructionist prayer book is essentially in Hebrew, the Hebraic liturgy of Reconstructionist Jews (15,000 or 1.5% of Jews in New York City) is generously interspersed with English prayers. The prayer book used by *Reform* Jews (300,000 or 30% of the Jewish population in New York City) is basically a Hebrew-English liturgical text. Whereas prayer books used by Reform synagogues in the mid-nineteenth century with the introduction of Reform in the United States were entirely in Hebrew (Grinstein 356, 362), Hebrew as a language of worship and study was eliminated essentially within the Reform wing of Judaism as it developed in the United States in the nineteenth century. Currently, there appears to be a revival of interest by

Reform Jewish leaders in increasing the use of Hebrew in worship (*Union Prayer Book 1922; Gates of Prayer, The New Union Prayer Book* 1975).

One of the ways in which the ideological groups differ in the extent of the use of Hebrew prayers is in the amount of time worshippers spend in prayer. The active Reform worshippers (about twenty percent of the total Reform population) attend one service a week – usually on a Friday evening for one-and-a-half to two-and-a-half hours including the sermon. The active Reconstructionist worshippers (about twenty percent of the total Reconstructionist population) attend Friday evening and Saturday morning services for one-and-a-half to two-and-a-half hours including a sermon and/or discussion period. The active Conservative worshippers (about 20 percent of the total Conservative population in New York City) attend synagogue on Friday evening for one-and-a-half to two-and-a-half hours and on Saturday morning for two to two-and-a-half hours. Some Conservative Jews worship daily. The active Orthodox worshippers (about 80 percent of the total Orthodox population) attend morning, afternoon and evening services in synagogues during the weekdays or pray at home twenty-five minutes to one-and-a-half hours each day, on Friday evening for one hour, and Saturday morning for three hours.

The use of Hebrew liturgy is not limited to the synagogue. The devout Jew – particularly the male – recites Hebrew blessings upon rising, after taking care of his personal needs, before partaking of food, after eating (a lengthy grace after each meal), before retiring at night, upon hearing thunder, seeing lightening, seeing a rainbow in the sky, or an ocean, upon smelling fragrances, upon seeing an outstanding Torah or secular scholar or head of state, upon baking *hallah* (Sabbath or festival bread) and upon hearing good or bad tidings.

At the Sabbath and Festival table, *zemirot* (Hebrew liturgical poems) are sung. At life cycle events – *brit milah* (circumcision ceremony), naming the baby boys and girls, pidyon *haben* (redemption of the first born male child at 30 days), *Bar/Bat Mitzvah* and weddings – special ceremonies are conducted in Hebrew. When he travels, the devout Jew recites *tefillat haderekh* (the wayfarer's prayer). At every religious occasion he hears a *d'rashah* (a homily) in *Yiddish* or English containing numerous Hebraic religious terms and biblical quotations.

While the vast majority of American Jews are of Ashkenazic origin, a small yet significant part of the American Jewish population has Sephardic roots, estimated at 200,000 to 250,000 (Alcosser; Lieberman; Levy). The most identifiable segment of this population is the Syrian Jews – thirty-five thousand in New York and fifteen thousand elsewhere in the United States. They usually congregate in their own communities and, as a group, have a special relationship to Hebrew. According to Dr. Zevulun Lieberman, Mayhem Professor of Sephardic Studies at Yeshiva University and Syrian Jewish Community *Hakham* (rabbinic scholar), eighty to ninety percent of Syrian Jews in New York spend about thirty minutes each day in Hebrew prayer; sixty percent can speak Hebrew although they do not engage regularly in Hebrew conversation; twenty to thirty percent of the adults participate in Judaic-Hebraic classes weekly. Almost all Syrian Jewish children attend Hebraic *Ivrit b'Ivrit* day schools patterned after the Syrian Jewish custom in Allepo, Syria, whereby all instruction in Jewish Studies beginning with the third grade takes place in Hebrew (Lieberman). In the New York day schools, they are exposed to three to four hours of Hebraic learning daily.

The rest of the Sephardic Jewish population in the United States is not as conversant in Hebrew as the Syrian Jews, but uses Hebrew more regularly than other non-Orthodox American Jews. According to Edward Alcosser, the executive vice president of American Sephardi Federation, more than one third of Sephardim (excluding the Israelis) pray daily in Hebrew, fifteen to twenty minutes each day; about one-half attend Sabbath and holiday services fairly regularly and recite and listen to Hebrew prayers and readings from the Bible for about two hours at each service. Almost all can read Hebrew phonetically. About forty percent understand written and spoken Hebrew. Moreover, Hebrew is interlaced in the everyday vernacular of first generation Sephardim who speak Ladino, Farsi, or Arabic. Ninety percent of Sephardic children receive some kind of Jewish education in which they learn to read Hebrew prayers as well as other Judaic subjects.

About forty thousand Sephardim in the United States are recent immigrants from Iran. Most of them reside in New York. They speak Farsi at home and have a good reading knowledge of Hebrew (Alcosser).

In order to promote the use of Hebrew as a modern vehicle of communication, particularly as a medium of Hebraic cultural expression, the *Histadruth Ivrith* (the Hebrew Language and Culture Association) of America was founded in 1920. In 1930, it organized the *Hanoar Haivri* (the Hebrew Youth Organization), which existed for some twenty years and, at its zenith, had several thousand Hebrew speaking members.

The major activity of *Histadruth Ivrith* has been the sponsorship of Hebrew language periodicals – the *Hadoar*, a weekly for adults with advanced Hebrew knowledge, and *Lamishpahah* for those with intermediate understanding of Hebrew. In the 1940s the *Hadoar Lanoar*, a simplified juvenile Hebrew monthly, and *Musaf Lakorai Hatzair*, an intermediate monthly youth magazine, were carried as supplements to the *Hadoar*.

THE HEBREW READERS

During both medieval and contemporary times, the publishing of religious Hebraic literature was second nature to the Jew. In Europe, during the late nineteenth century, the *Haskalah* and Hebrew language revival movements saw the publication of a variety of journals, dailies, weeklies and occasional books in modern Hebrew on secular, cultural, non-rabbinic topics, and especially on contemporary Judaism and Palestine. In Eastern Europe, writers and poets like Chaim Nachman Bialik, Shaul Tchernichowsky, and Ahad Ha'am created a modern genre of Hebrew literature read by a core of Hebraic devotees schooled in Jewish religious tradition who opted for a secular-cultural-national approach to Jewish life.

This literature significantly influenced the development of Modern Hebrew, particularly the style of written communication.

In early America, until the end of the nineteenth century, there was little publishing of any sort. The Hebrew texts – essentially Bibles, prayer books and related Hebraic materials – used by Jewish immigrants in the U.S. were brought with them from their countries of origin or sent to them once they arrived.

From the time of the arrival of East European Jews, prodigious efforts were made to publish in Hebrew. Since 1881, when *ha Massef ba-Arez heHadashah* (The Journal in the New Land) appeared only once as the literary organ of the New York-based *Society of Lovers of Hebrew in the United States*, at least seventy different Hebrew periodicals were published. With the exception of two pedagogic magazines issued in Chicago, all the periodicals were published in New York City.

The bulk of the publications were cultural, literary efforts – mostly monthly magazines and annuals – appearing during the last decade of the nineteenth century and the first three decades of the twentieth century. Readership of these periodicals varied from a handful – twenty subscribers in the case of the *Hashiloah* (1900–1902) to several hundred (The Jewish Communal Register 568).

One Modern Hebrew periodical currently being published had its beginnings in the early part of the twentieth century. *Hadoar* first appeared as a daily in 1921 and became a weekly in 1923. Its peak readership was about 15,000 in the early 1940s (Halkin). As of 1993, it became a bi-weekly with a circulation of 4,000 and estimated readership of 10,000 (Galanter). Most of the subscribers and readers of modern Hebrew periodicals during the first half of the twentieth century were Jewish educators (Learsi 97).

From 1903 to 1972, a dozen periodicals were published on rabbinical issues and Judaica. These were relatively long-lived. Four of the journals – *haPardes* (1913), *Bitzaron* (1939), *Or Hamizrach* (1954) and *Hadorom* (1957) – are still being issued. Since 1972, many additional occasional periodicals and books on rabbinical issues, Jewish studies, *halakhah* (laws) and biblical and Talmudic exegesis authored by Orthodox rabbis and scholars have been published in Hebrew, although the current trend in the Orthodox community is to publish some of this literature in English.

The early 1900s saw the appearance, for one-year periods, of a Hebrew monthly. *Hed heHinukh* (1915) for teachers, and a monthly, *Kuntros haModiyin* (1916) for principals (*The Jewish Communal Register* 567). Thereafter, between 1919 and 1954, seven education quarterlies, each lasting for two years, were published. The quarterly *Shevilei Hahinukh*, sponsored by the National Council for Jewish Education, appeared from 1940 through 1985. Reaching a peak readership of about 1,500 in the 1960s, *Shevilei Hahinukh* ceased publication for lack of subscribers, since U.S. born Jewish schoolteachers found it difficult to read, while Israeli teachers in Jewish schools preferred Israeli educational publications.

Seven weekly Hebrew newspapers and one daily saw the light of day for short periods of time between 1889 and 1921. The first Hebrew newspaper in the United States – *haZofeh baArez haHadashah* (The Spectator in the New Land) – appeared weekly in New York before the onset of mass immigration from Eastern Europe, from 1871 through 1876.

In the early 1900s, there were several abortive attempts to publish juvenile Hebrew periodicals. These were followed by a more successful effort, *Hadoar Lanoar* (1930–1960) read by some 10,000 Jewish youth in New York during its peak subscription years in the 1940s, and *Musaf LaKorai HaZair* (1940–1950). After they ceased publication they were replaced by *Olam Hadash* (1961-) with a current circulation of 6,000 in North America and an estimated readership of 15,000 (Bloch).

LaMishpahah, a family-oriented monthly in simplified Hebrew, has about 6,500 subscribers in North America, the bulk of them in Greater New York, and an estimated readership of 25,000 (Galanter). There are two Ultra-Orthodox weeklies in Hebrew – *Hamahaneh HaHaredi* and *Panim Hadashot* – read by

Ultra-Orthodox Jews who lived in Israel and sold in storefronts in Brooklyn, with an estimated combined readership of 6,000.

Challenging the current role of Hebrew reading and study of Hebrew texts in the United States is the increased number of English translations of Hebraic sources. During the last two decades much effort has been invested in translating classical Jewish texts into English. A veritable Judaic English language library of hundreds of books for children and adults has been developed. On the college campus, most Judaic studies courses utilize anthologies of texts translated into English. One can now study the Bible, the Talmud, most of their traditional commentaries, almost all the major post-biblical medieval through contemporary Judaic sources, without needing to know one word of Hebrew (Mintz).

THE IMPACT OF ISRAELIS ON HEBREW USAGE

Israelis in the United States may be classified into two general groupings: *yordim*, permanent residents who are in the United States for four or more years and plan to remain; and temporary residents including Israeli emissaries, students, business people and long-term visitors. The demographic profile of the Israeli migrant population in New York and the rest of the country is a matter of much variability. Estimates vary from 20,000 to 300,000 in New York and from 89,000 to 500,000 nationally (Harel; Ritterband; Rosen; Herman). American born children of Israelis in the U.S. would make the total number of Israelis in the United States considerably larger.

In metropolitan New York, Israelis generally live in close proximity to each other, establishing their own sub-communities in several sections of the City – Riverdale, Rego Park, Forest Hills and Flatbush – where Hebrew is fluently heard in apartment houses, on street corners, in stores and restaurants. Their language is laced with terminology derived from the English language, for example: *svedder* for sweater; *televiziah* for television; *integratziah* for integration; and *correlatziah* for correlation. The latter terms and their like are used generally by Israeli academics who find them more convenient than Hebrew words to convey the same meaning.

Israeli adults, by and large, speak Hebrew among themselves and in their homes and are avid readers of the Israeli press and publications. While exact figures are not available, the number of weekend editions of *Ma'ariv* and *Yediot*, two of Israeli's most popular dailies sold in North America is about 22,000 with a readership of approximately 90,000 (Lazarov). About one third of the circulation and readership is in New York. In addition, Hebrew booksellers in New York import thousands of fiction and non-fiction books each month from Israel (Harel). The most often read publication by Israelis, especially by *yordim* who have been in the United States for several years, is the Brooklyn-based weekly *Yisrael Shelanu* (Our Israel), founded in 1979 (Prawer). Currently, 70,000 copies are sold each week in the Tri-State area, largely in New York City (Yisrael Shelanu). In some communities, Israelis have established their own local Hebrew publications.

Among other kinds of Hebrew reading material available to Israelis in the United States, and to other Americans in areas populated by Israelis, are storefront posters, menus in eateries, and organizational and commercial mailings to Israeli homes. In 1991, *Yisrael Shelanu* published *haMadrich Shelanu* (Our Guide), a Hebrew telephone directory featuring lists of businesses and advertisements about New York and the United States to recently arrived Israelis. In addition, one hundred and fifty thousand copies of Israel Yellow Pages are distributed annually throughout the United States, seventy percent of which go to the New York area (Israel Yellow Pages). Other ways Israelis maintain their Hebrew connection are: Hebrew radio and television programs, a 900 telephone number that provides Hebrew language news bulletins from the Middle East, and frequent lengthy telephone conversations with friends and relatives in Israel. For some, regular flights to Israel are part of their way of life (Rosen).

The Israelis in America are not a dominant force regarding the spread of Hebrew since they use Hebrew solely as their private language of communication among themselves (Caspi). There is ample reason to believe that Israeli youths in New York and elsewhere in the United States are assimilating rapidly and do not constitute a major core of regular Hebrew speakers. Israeli children generally attend public schools and do not enroll in synagogue supplementary Hebrew studies programs since the overwhelming majority of *yordim* are secular. Only a small percentage of Israeli children attend Jewish day schools because these schools are almost always under religious auspices and Israelis are not accustomed to paying for Jewish and general education (Sheniak). In New York there are less than 2,000 Israeli children of school age enrolled in Jewish day schools where they study Hebraic texts and speak Hebrew in their Judaic studies classes (Sheniak; Prawer).

Israelis in New York have organized several supplementary Hebrew studies programs – in Great Neck 1978, Forest Hills 1984, Canarsie 1985, Mid Island 1986, Woodmere 1990 – in which about 400 children were enrolled in 1993 for four to six hours per week (Silberstein).

A branch of the Israeli scout movement was established in the 1980s in order to help Israeli youths retain their national identity and their Hebrew language proficiency and maintain Israeli cultural contact. In 1993 there were some three hundred Israeli youths in New York and a similar number in the rest of the United States in Israeli scout programs. Recent experience with the various Israeli scout groups in New York demonstrates that Israeli children of *yordim* do not speak Hebrew regularly. In several scout troops it has been difficult to conduct meetings in Hebrew (Sheniak). United States born progeny, particularly second and third children, tend to speak to their parents in English even when their parents address them in Hebrew, a situation not unlike the preceding Yiddish speaking immigrant generations. To address this problem, the *Noar Vehalutz* Department of the Joint Authority for Jewish Zionist Education in Jerusalem and its counterpart in New York, the American Zionist Youth Foundation, established, in 1992, the *Het Vakeshet* (Bow and Arrow) program which arranges Israel summer visits for 16–17 year old children of Israelis. About one hundred children of *yordim* in the New

York area have participated in this program each summer since its founding (Prawer; Silberstein).

Many Jewish schools engage resident Israelis as teachers. However, their impact on Hebrew language instruction is minimal since the emphasis in the curricula is not on Hebrew language per se, but rather on Judaic subjects in the day school, and on synagogue skills in the supplementary congregational school. In addition to the resident Israeli teachers, there are some one hundred Israeli *Shlihim* (emissaries) to schools, youth organizations and communal institutions. While not a major factor in motivating greater use of Hebrew among Americans, the presence of the *Shlihim* in Jewish communal institutions, youth organizations and schools has raised Jewish consciousness about Hebrew language and Hebraic culture. The Israeli Cultural Affairs officers in the larger Jewish communities do not directly attempt to impact the level of Hebrew language usage. Their main thrust is providing Israeli cultural enrichment through art, music, theater, film and special events (Tarbut).

Despite the relationship between the American Jewish community and Israel, the Jewish State has not been able to contribute significantly to enhancing the role of Hebrew in the United States. To the contrary, it has been witness to the eclipse of Hebrew by English as the national – and the international – language of the Jewish people. The language of oral and written communication between Israeli officials, political leaders and academics and the American Jewish community is solely English. Meetings and conferences involving Israelis and American Jews are always conducted in English. At best, the overwhelming majority of American Jews can manage only a few Hebrew terms. The current Israeli use of English makes it unnecessary for Jews in New York to learn to communicate in Hebrew (Mintz).

HEBREW IN NEW YORK: A SUMMARY

When viewed in demographic perspective, there are significant differences between Hebrew language use in New York and the rest of the United States. Hebrew usage in New York is more widespread, more habitual, and more varied than elsewhere in the country. This is attributable to three conditions: the size of the Jewish population, the type of Jewish residents (their ideological and ethnic backgrounds), and the Jewish educational institutions in the community.

While the number of Jews in New York City – and even in the surrounding suburban counties – has declined annually since the onset of the 1970s because of low birth rates and population shifts to the Sunbelt and the West Coast, 1.8 million Jews, one third of the total United States Jewish population, resided in metropolitan New York in 1994. More significantly, about seventy-five percent of American Orthodox Jewry, approximately ninety percent of all Ultra Orthodox and Hasidic Jews, and the vast majority of Israeli immigrants and Sephardic Jews in the United States live in Greater New York. In addition, over one half of all American Jewish day school pupils and over three-quarters of all students in schools of higher Jewish learning are in Jewish educational institutions in New York.

Translated into Hebrew language usage, these demographic factors mean that in New York, many more Jews pray in Hebrew and devote much more time to Hebrew prayer. Also in New York, considerable more time is spent in Hebrew language learning and in Hebraic text study. Finally, Hebrew is spoken regularly by more adults in the New York area than elsewhere.

CHAPTER 3

TWENTY-FIRST CENTURY RENAISSANCE OF THE HEBREW LANGUAGE

WHY THE CURRENT FOCUS ON THE HEBREW LANGUAGE?

The importance of Hebrew language as the link to the Jewish past and to Israel, and as a unifying force in Jewish life has been underscored by Jewish leaders and scholars in every generation of Jewish history.

Jews are accustomed to tightrope existence. In every age our forebears developed group dynamics appropriate for creative survival in their particular environments. Currently, the tightrope requires the maintaining of varying kinds of equilibrium. It means bi-polar adjustment – "keeping the constants," preserving the transcendental value of Jewish tradition, on the one hand, and "keeping up with the times," developing new adaptive mechanisms, on the other.

The Hebrew language might be viewed from this dual perspective. The language of the Bible, the *Mishnah*, rabbinic literature, and liturgy, *Hebrew is a constant.* As the language of modern Hebrew literature, the newspaper, the theater, the convention hall, the bus stops, *Hebrew in flux* meets a current need. It is the vernacular of a people reborn in its land of rebirth – the language of the businessman, the scientist, the *yeshiva bohur*, the farmer, the housewife, and the university professor alike.

Hebrew, the constant, is essential for Jewish group survival since it is a major channel for the Jew's spiritual identity. While not a sufficient cause for the continuity of Jewish cultural-religious life, it is a necessary one. Without the classical Hebraic sources, our people lack the wellspring from which its lifeblood is nourished. Without its bedrock of classical literature in the original, our heritage is stripped of its meaning, purpose and re-creative powers. For valid continuity of Jewish group life, therefore, a working knowledge of Hebrew to enable textual study of original Hebraic sources is a *conditione sine qua non*.

The circumstances of our times, highlighted by the realities of a Jewish state, add both a new dimension and a new challenge to contemporary Jewish life. The dimension is the newfound vitality of the Hebrew language, and the challenge – greater and more effective utilization of its life-giving powers. Modern Hebrew vernacular is a measure of the miracle of Jewish durability. It is the vehicle of a sacred past of eternal Jewish values. At the same time, it is a major expression of contemporary Jewish vitality.

Jewish history has demonstrated that communities ignoring Hebrew or neglecting the use of Hebrew have disappeared. Throughout our history, in every land of our dispersion under the most difficult conditions, Jews survived primarily because of their attachment to the Hebrew language. They studied the Bible and *Mishnah* in Hebrew. They prayed in Hebrew. They used Hebrew during life cycle ceremonies. They inscribed their tombstones in Hebrew. Often, they wrote business contracts with their fellow Jews in Hebrew, and, in some communities they conversed in Hebrew among themselves. Hebrew was the common cord that united them with fellow Jews in other lands. And, the Hebrew language unified *kibbutz galuyot* – the ingathering of exiles – into a single nation in the State of Israel.

Miraculously, because of the utter commitment of several cultural leaders at the end of the nineteenth century and the beginning of the twentieth century – especially Eliezer Ben Yehudah and Ahad Ha'am – and because of the Hebraic knowledge base of the Jewish immigrants to Palestine, Hebrew became the national language of the Jewish State. Now, the connection between Diaspora Jewry and Israel can be strengthened by the ability to communicate in our ancestral tongue.

Indeed, the knowledge and use of Hebrew everywhere can enhance Jewish life significantly. The visits of Diaspora Jews to Israel will be enriched via their ability to communicate in Hebrew with Israelis, to read signs and posters and Israeli newspapers, to listen to Israeli radio and television, and to enjoy Israeli theater. At the same time, those studying Hebrew in the Diaspora will be motivated to visit the Jewish State where Hebrew is spoken.

WHAT NEEDS TO BE DONE TO REVIVE AND ENHANCE HEBREW LANGUAGE?

The renaissance of the Hebrew language that took root one hundred years ago was led and facilitated by the enormous investment of human power to create the necessary drive for Hebrew language study and usage. Needed today is the galvanization of eminent Hebraists and leading Hebrew educators – not unlike the cadre of committed Hebrew teachers and Hebraists in Palestine who fought relentlessly in the early nineteen hundreds against the strong influence of those who wanted German, French or English to become the *lingua franca* of Palestine.

Needed, also, is the development of an advocacy program for Hebrew whereby use will be promoted vigorously throughout the Diaspora. This will require the effective use of media – TV, radio and newspapers – and active contact with Jewish communal, educational, synagogual, rabbinical and social services, and Jewish center organizations.

There are a variety of settings in the Diaspora – schools, synagogues, universities, central agencies for Jewish education, Ulpanim, and Hebrew publishing ventures – where successful Hebrew language programs have been developed. But those are isolated instances and require substantial reinforcement and coordination. Therefore, concerted worldwide networking must take place.

An important dimension of networking will be a centralized effort to learn and develop the most effective system for revitalizing Hebrew in the twenty-first century. One thing is certain: without committed knowledgeable transmitters of the Hebrew language, a Hebraic renaissance cannot take place. Hence, it will be crucial to train teachers in the most successful methods of Hebraic instruction on all levels – from early childhood to adult.

Part of the centralized efforts at networking will be the evaluation of the current programs that appear to be successful in order to help determine what are the most effective methodologies.

Developing educational resources that can drive and inform the efforts to Hebraize world Jewry is essential. Based upon the knowledge of what works best in the various settings, it will be necessary to utilize technology to the fullest. Communication via website, email, facsimile, tape and CD-ROM is fundamental to modern language education.

The preparation of fluent Hebrew speakers will best be accomplished via face-to-face contact. Over the years, the Ulpan process has demonstrated success in Israel and in the Diaspora. This mode of instruction will need to be reviewed and assessed in order to determine how it can best serve the needs of the twenty-first century.

HOW SHOULD HEBREW LANGUAGE PROGRAMMING AND ACTIVITY BE INITIATED?

To be effective, a worldwide Hebrew language program must be a carefully coordinated effort between Israel and the Diaspora. It goes without saying that Israel should be at the epicenter of this effort. However, without the active participation and leadership of Diaspora Jewry, the spread of Hebrew language cannot become a reality.

To begin with, the National Center for the Hebrew Language in the United States is a natural partner for Israel. Three years old, the Center has developed several small-scale activities and a website which has attracted some 100,000 hits from about 50 countries each month in the Fall and Winter of 2000 and 2001.

Structurally, for the global effort, a small directorate of absolutely committed volunteers should be formed. The directorate (or board of directors) should strategize the first steps to be taken. This includes a development of a clear mission statement based upon the vision of the future role of the Hebrew language in the world Jewish community. Next, would be an elaboration of the aims, goals, and objectives of the new worldwide effort from the most general aims to the most specific objectives. These should be divided between long-range and short-range desiderata.

After the evaluation process mentioned above is completed, it is vital to determine, as carefully as possible, what kinds of endeavors have the best chance of succeeding in the various Jewish communal and educational settings. One way of accomplishing this is via a think tank of Hebrew language specialists, sociolinguists, formal and informal Jewish educators, psychologists, sociologists and communal educational and synagogue lay leaders. This think tank might be organized by an ad hoc task force of the directorate whose function it would be to explore the possibilities for the development of an international program. The job of the task force is akin to a committee of a corporation charged with the responsibility of doing a feasibility study. Absent a directorate, the task force could serve as the initial organizing leadership group for the worldwide Hebrew language venture.

HOW SHOULD THE HEBREW LANGUAGE EFFORTS BE SUSTAINED?

The Mishnaic aphorism *Im ein kemah, ein Torah* means that Torah study cannot take place without substantial material support. In modern terms, it requires us to make available sufficient funding for a massive, worldwide Hebrew language renaissance endeavor. Beginning with an initial donor or set of donors, this effort would need to attract the generous support of philanthropists and funding mechanisms throughout the Jewish world.

Nahmanides, the 13th century Spanish scholar, biblical and

Talmudic exegete and Zionist, who made aliyah toward the end of life, emphasized the critical importance of a three-fold arrangement for Jewish education to succeed. This triumvirate includes superior educational leadership, as represented by the scholarly tribe of Issachar, in combination with outstanding communal leadership, as portrayed by the regal tribe of Judah, and general philanthropic support, as represented by the wealthy tribe of Zevulun. This kind of triplet is absolutely essential for the twenty-first century. Without superior Jewish educators, excellent instructional activity and programming cannot take place. Without outstanding communal leadership, the necessary planning and execution of the plans cannot be launched. And, without the generous support of committed philanthropists, neither the plans nor the programs nor actual instructional activity can become a reality.

The Hebraic renaissance program would reach out to Jews of all ages all over the globe. It would develop a membership campaign to enroll Jews everywhere. It would also recruit local, national and international groups in support of its activities. While the individual and group fees would be minimal, it is hoped that, collectively, they would provide an important source of funding.

PROPOSAL: THE ESTABLISHMENT OF THE BEN YEHUDAH CENTER

In light of the foregoing, it is proposed to establish the Ben Yehuda Center in honor of the major human force who was instrumental in developing the Hebrew language as the national language of the Jewish homeland. The Center will operate as an independent entity in partnership with the Ministry of Education, Culture and Sport in Israel, the Jewish Agency for Israel, the World Zionist Organization and its affiliate groups, *Keren Hayesod* and its federated affiliates, key national and local Jewish communal organizations in Europe, South America, Australia and South Africa, the American United Jewish Communities and the local American Jewish federations, the World Jewish Congress, the synagogue movements, the Conference of Presidents of Major Jewish

Organizations in the United States and its constituent members, especially the American Jewish Committee, the Anti-Defamation League and the American Jewish Congress, the Jewish Council for Public Affairs and its national and local Jewish community relations agencies, Jewish Education Services of North America and the local central agencies for Jewish education, the World Student Union, Hillel and the Jewish Center movement, especially the Jewish Communities Association of America.

The nature of the partnership with each group will evolve after the establishment of the Center. The Center, located in Jerusalem, will have a direct relationship with the National Center for the Hebrew Language in the United States.

The Ben Yehuda Center will be funded by a core group of philanthropists and philanthropic organizations. All the partners will be expected to contribute proportionate amounts of support according to their annual budgets.

The Center will be led by a lay board – the Directorate – and be professionally administered by a CEO and COO, and staffed according to the needs of the programmatic activities as they develop. The advocacy dimension of the program will be guided by a Communications Department; and the funding activity will be implemented by a Development Department. Built into the structure of the Center will be R and D – research and development capability – and a regular self-evaluation mechanism.

Once approved by the directorate, the mission statement will be reviewed periodically to insure that the Center is responsive to Hebrew language needs and developments throughout the Jewish world.

CHAPTER 4

IVRIT IN THE DAY SCHOOLS: AN ENDANGERED SPECIES?

I t is a pleasure to present my views about the Hebrew language at the 2003 Annual Conference of *Edah*. As I noted in my introductory *D'var Torah*, if the Modern Orthodox community wants to succeed in making Hebrew a living language, particularly in our day schools and yeshivot, and utilize the advantages of Hebrew as a spoken language to the benefit of our Hebraic-Judaic studies programs, we could achieve this goal despite the problems we currently face. The key to a successful Hebraic effort is realizing the concept "with one heart as one person" – being united in the desire to activate Hebrew language programs in our educational institutions and in our community. *Ain davar ha-omed bifnay haratzon*. Nothing can stand in the way of a strong desire to reach a given goal, to accomplish a special task, if the necessary climate and skills are in place.

To begin with, we have to overcome an American illness. Recently a linguistics professor was seen jogging in Riverside Park wearing a shirt that declared, "Monolingualism Can Be Cured." People staring at the writing on the shirt were puzzled about what kind of disease "monolingualism" is. "An American disease," cried out one onlooker. "We can't speak more than one language." To be sure, American Jews suffer from this very same illness that has plagued several generations of American citizens.

For Jews, however, Hebrew is much more than a second language, much more than just curing monolingualism. The importance of Hebrew Language, as the link to the Jewish past and to Israel, and as a unifying force in Jewish life, has been underscored by Jewish leaders and scholars in every generation of Jewish history.

The Jerusalem Talmud underscores the value of spoken Hebrew for individuals: The good news, say Hazal, is that whoever speaks in the sacred tongue has a place in the World to Come.

During the Middle Ages, there was a tendency (not unlike our modern times) to teach Judaic subjects in the vernacular of the country where Jews resided. Rabbinic scholars promoted the use of spoken Hebrew and warned against the consequences of Judaic instruction in a foreign language. Rabbi Moshe Isserles (the *Rema*), the sixteenth century *Halakhic* authority who authored the *Mappah*, the Ashkenazic version of the *Shulhan Arukh*, declared, "In the Hebrew language itself there is holiness." The *Rema* believed that Hebrew derived its holiness from its dual function in Judaism as the language of the sacred texts – the language of study and prayer – and the language of daily conversation (*Shekalim* 3).

Another sixteenth century rabbinic leader, Rabbi Judah Loew (The *Maharal* of Prague), in a letter of support to the author of a book on Hebrew grammar, *Em Ha-Yeled*, noted, "It is a matter of truth and faith and a great *mitzvah* for a parent to accustom his child to learn to speak Hebrew and to learn Hebrew grammar as our forefathers did." The *Maharal* stressed that "every nation has a special nature or essence and a special form. Its essence is its intellectual content, and its form is its language – the practical national expression of its essence and spirit. Without its language, a nation has no form." Without spoken Hebrew, the Jewish people are not a compete nation (Federbush).

According to Hebrew linguistics authority, Prof. Shlomo

Haramati, as a result of the initiatives and advocacy of rabbinic leaders and scholars during the Middle Ages, the language of instruction in many yeshivot was Hebrew (Federbush).

In later times, particularly in Western society, Hebrew was not used by many Jews because they felt it necessary to speak solely in the language of their host countries in order to gain equal rights. Leading the battle for the survival of spoken Hebrew in the eighteenth and nineteenth centuries were such rabbinic luminaries and scholars as Jacob Emden (1697–1776), Yehezkel Landau (the *Noda Bi-Yehudah* 1713–1793) of Prague, Moshe Sofer (the *Hatam Sofer* 1763–1839) of Pressburg, and Zvi Hirsh Horowitz (mid 1700s–1817) Chief Rabbi of Frankfurt, all of whom emphasized that the use of Hebrew as a language of conversation as well as a language of study and prayer, is a religious duty.

Rabbi Emden stressed the need to help children acquire Hebrew language proficiency prior to the study of *Humash* and other Judaic subjects. He claimed that Sephardic Jews in Italy, Turkey, Holland and North Africa in the eighteenth century were more effective in their schools than Ashkenazim in Germany, Northern France and Eastern Europe. Unlike the Sephardim, the children in Ashkenazic schools began learning Torah before they acquired conversational Hebrew language skills (Haramati).

Rabbi Landau emphasized that the "only correct way to teach a child about his heritage and its sources is through spoken Hebrew, which is after all, the language of Torah and *mitzvot*, the language in which God spoke to the Jewish people at Sinai." "It is essential," he stressed "to teach every sentence in the Torah via explanations in Hebrew" (chap. 18).

Rabbi Sofer reasoned that the Bible and Talmud, must be taught in Hebrew because the oral law is based on the analysis and exegesis of the Hebrew text (Federbush). In 1816, Rabbi Zvi Horowitz authored a poignant repudiation of those who taught Judaic subjects via the translation method. He wrote: "One of our greatest sins at this time…is the fact that there are children who study Bible with teachers who instruct them in a foreign tongue to the point where they do not know how to speak Hebrew at all (Horowitz).

At the beginning of the twentieth century, Baruch Epstein (1860–1914), Russian Talmudic scholar and author of *Torah Temimah*, provided enthusiastic support for Hebrew language instruction and usage. He wrote:

> Whoever has a hand and heart of faith, whose spirit and soul are faithful to his people, his religion and language, and wants to build a loyal household in Israel, should try hard to insure that his sons and daughters, from the time that they are being nursed by their mothers, hear spoken Hebrew and are encouraged to emote in Hebrew. After that, the parent will be able to implant in their heart feelings of pure faith… In all their daily activities including their play, from the time they wake up until they go to sleep, children should speak Hebrew with their parents and among themselves. And their sacred language will become their mother tongue.

Given this scholarly, historical-theological background, we now ask: what about the Hebrew language and the Jewish Day School and the Hebrew language and the Modern Orthodox community in twenty-first century America?

Many of the yeshivot and day schools founded in America in the early 1900s were *Ivrit b'Ivrit* institutions, for example, Eitz Chaim in Boro Park, the Hebrew track of the Rabbi Jacob Joseph School in Manhattan, Flatbush Yeshiva, Crown Heights Yeshiva, the Salanter Yeshiva in the Bronx, and Shulamith School for Girls. Later in the mid 20th century, other *Ivrit b'Ivrit* schools were founded including Ramaz, the Hebrew Institute of Long Island, The Yeshiva of Central Queens, the Manhattan Day School, the Maimonides School, established in Boston by Rabbi Joseph B. Soleveitchik and the Herzliah schools in Montreal. These schools demonstrated that *Ivrit b'Ivrit* can become the universal norm for Modern Orthodox Day Schools – that Hebrew can be a living language in our classrooms and in our community.

With the right approach, *Ivrit b'Ivrit* can become the universal norm for Modern Orthodox Day Schools. And, Hebrew can be a living language in our classrooms and in our community. Our challenge is a dual one – teaching Hebrew language properly and instituting Hebrew as the language of instruction in the Jewish studies programs.

We are all aware of the problems: non-Hebraic school focus and philosophy; non-Hebraic school professional leadership; teachers unable or unwilling to instruct in Hebrew; and the feeling of some lay leaders and educators that *Ivrit b'Ivrit* does not provide a religious enough climate and that Talmud cannot be taught in Hebrew.

These problems will not be easy to solve, but they can be overcome. Between 1957 and 1961, several hundred principals and teachers received Hebrew language training via a very intensive summer ulpan program co-sponsored by the Board of Jewish Education of New York, Yeshiva University and the Education and Culture Department of the World Zionist Organization. Many of the participants in the program were engaged to lead or teach in Hebraic yeshivot. This kind of program can be activated once more either in the United States or in Israel. Given the sound Judaic background of Jewish day school teachers, they can learn to speak Hebrew without too much difficulty. The key is the will to do so.

A leading authority on Hebrew language instruction, Dr. Jonathan Paradise of the University of Minnesota, suggests that for the American Jewish community, we must create a "need" for the Hebrew language. He notes that Hebrew is not currently perceived as a necessary "commodity" of American Jewish life. "This fact, more than any other," he stresses, "is at the root of the unhappy situation regarding Hebrew language education in America." Dr. Paradise makes a long list of suggestions for making Hebrew one of the "identity badges" of American Jews. These include Hebraic signs in synagogues and Jewish community buildings, bilingual printing of Jewish programs, Hebrew songs at Jewish events, special awards and certificate programs for Hebrew achievement, ulpanim for the adult population, and many more Hebraic activities.

To be sure, the "need" for Hebrew already exists in the Jewish day school. We don't need all the gimmickry to develop the need. The problem is that we don't perceive Hebrew language as a "necessary commodity" in Jewish day school education. Changing this perception should become the role of the rabbinical, lay and educational leadership of the Modern Orthodox community – indeed, a task for *Edah* – to help make Hebrew a "necessary commodity" of Modern Orthodox schooling. The National Center for the Hebrew Language stands ready to partner with *Edah* to achieve this goal.

Taking a leaf from the *Sifri* and the Rambam regarding the age at which we should begin to teach children to speak Hebrew, we should start, in earnest, with our early childhood programs. Language acquisition, research demonstrates, is particularly easy for 3, 4, and 5-year-olds. According to a leading developmental psychologist, Professor S. Curtis, the ability to learn a language is so great in young children, that they can learn as many spoken languages as one can allow them to hear systematically and regularly at the same time.

Besides the Jewish identity value of learning Hebrew, the benefits of becoming bilingual are numerous. Learning a second language at an early age has a positive effect on intellectual growth. It enriches and enhances a child's mental development, and provides students with more flexibility in thinking, greater sensitivity to languages and a better ear for listening. And, it improves a child's understanding of his/her native language.

Learning to speak Hebrew deepens a child's Jewish identity. It makes him/her feel good about speaking the Jewish national language. It creates stronger ties to Israel, facilitates his/her full entrée to classical and modern Jewish texts, and makes visits to Israel more personal and meaningful.

There are several ways that Modern Orthodox Jews can support Hebrew language programming in our day schools and in our respective communities. Among others, we can promote the idea of making Shabbat in our homes Hebrew language days, including Hebrew conversation at the dinner table. Children who give *divrei Torah* at the Shabbat meal can be encouraged to give them in Hebrew. This would involve their teachers in preparing the *divrei Torah*. Observing Shabbat via *Loshon Kodesh* will make Shabbat a *Shabbat Kodesh*. "Make your Shabbat *Kodesh via Loshon Kodesh*" would be a meaningful motto for Modern Orthodoxy.

Families can make the Hebrew language the spoken vernacular at home on special days and evenings, particularly at mealtime. Speaking Hebrew on *Rosh Hodesh*, on birthdays and anniversaries adds meaning to celebration. There are many interesting games that can be played with the Hebrew language. Hebrew stories can be read. Hebrew language tapes can be listened to by the whole family as well as Hebrew programs on Israel TV. Videotapes and Internet can be family projects. The National Center for the Hebrew Language can help *Edah* in providing the necessary program material for these projects.

Referring back to the *Sifri* and to the Rambam, if parents are to speak Hebrew to their children when they are old enough to talk, their fathers and mothers must be able to speak Hebrew. And, if we initiate intensive Hebrew language programs in the nursery and kindergarten grades of our day schools, children learning to understand and to speak Hebrew should have the active support of their parents. This then, holds out a challenge to the Modern Orthodox community – to *Edah* – to teach Hebrew to the parents of young children. The National Center for Hebrew Language would be most happy to arrange ulpanim for this purpose. This can be best achieved via the co-sponsorship of the day schools and synagogues in each community.

While parents are learning conversational Hebrew, and certainly, once they can communicate in Hebrew fluently, they will be supportive of *Ivrit b'Ivrit* programs in their respective schools. This is a tall order! A very tall order! These recommendations may not sound very realistic. Neither did Ben Yehudah's and Ahad Ha'am's proposals to turn Palestine (Israel) into a Hebrew speaking country in the early 1900s against all odds sound very realistic.

And, look what happened to a Jewish population in Palestine that initially did not speak Hebrew at all.

This kind of activity may be far-fetched. It is! But with solid leadership – lay, rabbinic and educational – and a strong desire, Hebrew can become the living language of Modern Orthodox Jews in America.

After several years of earnest effort on our part, can you imagine a Modern Orthodox community speaking Hebrew fluently? What a remarkable achievement! What a Jewish identity boost! What an important link to Israel!

And if we accomplish this, our sons and daughters studying in Israel in post-high school programs will not come back without being able to speak Hebrew (after spending a year or two in Israel) because their studies in Israel were conducted in Hebrew. Instead they will go to Israel ready to participate in yeshiva and seminary learning via the language of Israel.

Moses would say, in the language of the Bible, "It is not too mysterious, too miraculous or remote for you. It is not up in the heaven; neither is it beyond the sea. No, it is something very near to you in your mouth and in your heart and you have only to carry it out" (Deut. 30:11–13)

Moses' strong statement "in your mouth" for us means "with spoken Hebrew." "In your heart," refers to our strong desire and motivation to make the revival of Hebrew happen.

With our mouths and our hearts – it can be realized in our days.

CHAPTER 5

HOW CRITICAL IS HEBREW FOR JEWISH CONTINUITY AND THE EFFECTIVENESS OF JEWISH EDUCATION?

Bibi Netanyahu, like Golda Meir and Yitzhak Rabin before him, has stated emphatically that the most critical problem facing the Jewish people is not the security of Israel or even the achievement of peace, however crucial these matters are to the Jewish State and to Jewish existence. *What is most critical is the question of Jewish continuity – the Jewish character, the Jewishness* of the Jewish people.

This challenge serves as the frame of reference for my plenary presentations. To be sure, Jews can no longer take for granted our continuous survival *anywhere in the world.*

My assumptions, remarks and conclusions are based largely on my American experience. I suggest that you compare these with the conditions and problems of Jewish education in Australasia. The similarities and differences will serve as an interesting basis for discussion.

An estranged son wanted to find favor with his aging mother who prayed in Hebrew every day. So he sent her a Hebrew-speaking parrot. After several weeks he phoned her. "Mom, do you like the parrot?" "Did I like the parrot?" she replied. "I loved it" she exclaimed. "It was absolutely delicious."

Actually, we're here to speak about not killing the Hebrew language. This is the reason I wrote my book *The Mystique of Hebrew*, from which I'll be quoting.

I begin my presentation with five scenarios.

SCENARIO I

The Israelites were redeemed from Egypt for *four* reasons, the first two of which were that they did not change their names and did not change their language. They continued to use Hebrew and speak in Hebrew.

Not changing their names is a subset of not changing their language. Keeping their Hebrew names and continuing to speak Hebrew referred to the religio-national-cultural dimension of their lives. Language was the critical cultural quality of their existence in Egypt. The fact that the Israelites did not change their language was key to their survival and eventual redemption.

As an aside, it is interesting to note that Rashi, the great biblical and Talmudic commentator, implies that not all Israelites were redeemed. Most of them assimilated, i.e., did not use or speak Hebrew. Consequently they died spiritually in Egypt.

SCENARIO II

About one thousand years later, Alexandria, Egypt became a vibrant center of Jewish life – an autonomous Jewish community 600,000 strong – with many wealthy Jews and many, many synagogues. Its central synagogue famous for its size and splendor is mentioned in the Talmud (*Succah* 51b).

The basis for the Alexandrian Jewish culture was the *Septuagint* – the Greek translation of the Bible.

The *Septuagint* translation was a miracle since seventy Judaic scholars in seventy separate rooms came up with one single translation of the Bible. Some say that this was really not a miracle.

Had they been in one room together and agreed on one single translation, that would have been a miracle.

The Jews of Alexandria studied the Bible and other Judaic sources in Greek translation. Philo, the leading Jewish philosopher of the *first* century C.E. in Alexandria studied and wrote in Greek. It is doubtful whether he had any knowledge of Hebrew. "If gold rusts, what shall iron do," writes the English poet William Blake.

Our Talmudic sages ask, "If a cedar tree is felled by fire what can the hyssop do in the face of flame?" If the leaders of Alexandria did not know Hebrew, it is clear that the ordinary Jews of Alexandria did not know or use the Hebrew language.

And what happened to this outstanding Jewish community? The decline of the Alexandrian Jewish community began with the process of Hellinization when the Jewish Community lost contact with the Hebrew language. Several centuries later, the Jewish remnants of Alexandria were absorbed into Islamic culture.

SCENARIO III

In the Talmud in two places – *Berakhot* 13 and *Sotah* 32 – there is an interesting disputation regarding the recitation of the *Shema* between Judah the Prince and the Sages of the Talmud.

Judah held that the *Shema must* be recited in *Hebrew* only. The Sages opined that it could be recited in any language, if the person praying does not understand Hebrew. Most Jews did not understand Hebrew in Judah's time.

The *Halakhah* was decided according to the opinion of the Sages – that the *Shema* can be recited in any language.

This brings us to Scenario IV.

SCENARIO IV

Scenario IV is an intriguing socio-historical-religious reality of Diaspora Jewish life during the last two millennia, eloquently described by Rabbi Yitzhak Nissenbaum, the passionate spokesman for religious Zionism in Europe who was martyred during the Holocaust. Nissenbaum (1926) expressed his amazement regarding the dominance of Hebrew in Jewish religious life despite the Talmudic allowance to use *any* language in the performance of *mitzvot*. "We can imagine," he wrote (and I translate from his original Hebrew source):

> what would have happened had the Jews behaved regarding the use of Hebrew only according to the *Halakhah* which permits the use of 'any language' in the synagogue and home, and would have used 'any language' for reading the *Shema*, for daily prayer in the synagogue, for reciting the prayers for the sanctification of the Sabbath and Festivals, the blessings on the partaking of food and other blessings. If that happened, there would be no trace of Hebrew in our lives, not even in our religious lives.
>
> But the people, with its national feeling, had no desire to use the *halakhic* permission granted by the scholars of the Jewish religion at a time when the religious feelings of these scholars superseded their national feelings.
>
> The Jewish people took extreme care to recite all these aforementioned things in the Hebrew language. And, thus, the national language of the Jewish people was dominant in the synagogue; and, more significantly, it was the tongue of every Jewish home. The Hebrew mother recited the first morning prayer, *modeh ani*, in Hebrew with her children. The sound of Hebrew resounded at the meal table as all the people who ate recited the appropriate blessings before the meal and grace after the meal in Hebrew. It was in Hebrew that every Jew recited his bedtime prayers as he closed his eyes. It was in Hebrew that he welcomed the Sabbath and festivals with *Kiddush* and bade them farewell with *havdallah*, the special ceremony marking the end of the Sabbath. It was the sound of Hebrew in every home and synagogue and street that sanctified the secular life of the Jew. This was not possible by the use of 'any language' for religious purposes.

What a powerful statement about the will of a people entrenched in their heritage, who took care that all life-cycle events were conducted in Hebrew!

And finally, to Scenario v in the late 1900s and early 20th century.

SCENARIO V

Ahad Ha'am, the brilliant secular Jewish Philosopher, Zionist leader and Hebraist, in his seminal essay, "*Imitation and Assimilation*, posits that a minority culture in Western Society must willy-nilly emulate the majority culture. The French Revolution that brought about liberté, egalité, fraternité provided a major challenge to Jews who had lived sheltered lives. There are two kinds of imitation, writes Ahad Ha'am – *absorptive imitation* and *competitive imitation*.

Absorptive imitation leads to assimilation.

The family of Moses Mendelssohn, a founder of the *Haskalah* and the Reform movement fell prey to absorptive assimilation. Four of his six sons intermarried as did the children of his other sons and the family of *Adolph Cremieux*, founder of the Alliance Israelite Universelle, disappeared as well through assimilation.

Ahad Ha'am stressed that imitation leads to total assimilation unless the minority learns to compete with the majority. According to a seminal study by socio-linguist, Bernard Spolsky, the daily use of Hebrew served as a barrier to assimilation. The sacred literacy of the Jews "seemed to balance the pull towards the majority language." Moses Mendelssohn gave up on Hebrew as the sacred language of the Jewish masses in Germany.

Ahad Ha'am viewed the role of Hebrew both as a unique expression of the Judaic heritage and as a key instrument of the creative survival of the Jewish people. Every nation, he noted, participates in the world scene in a special way via its national language. The Jewish people's "national stock" lies in the Hebrew language, which, in addition to being connected to a land, is the link between the dispersed Jewish communities of the Diaspora, and the link between generations of Jews. To be a national language, Ahad Ha'am insisted, its usage as a 'mother tongue' or vernacular is not sufficient. The national language must incorporate the spiritual and cultural wealth of the nation and its national ideals. As such, the combination of Jewish religion, literature, and *language* has been the Jewish people's portable property after the exile began with the destruction of the Temple in 70 C.E. And, when the Holy Land becomes once again the physical center of the Jewish people, Ahad Ha'am opined, the Hebrew language would be the bridge between the Land and the people in the Diaspora.

What is the Hebrew language to which Ahad Ha'am was referring? It is summed up pithily by Hayyim Greenberg, leader of the Jewish Agency for Israel and the World Zionist Organization in the mid-twentieth century. He said simply, "Hebraism is much more than a language."

By this simple statement, Greenberg means that *Hebrew is an alphabet.*

It is liturgy.
It is Bible.
It is Talmud.
It is medieval Hebrew literature – the writings of Ibn Gabirol, Yehudah Halevi, Joseph Karo, and Maimonides.

It is modern Hebrew literature – the prose and poetry of Hayyim Nahman Bialik, Shaul Tchernichovsky, Shmuel Yoseph Agnon, Amos Oz, and Yehuda Amichai.

Hebrew language is Hebraic culture literacy. During our long Diaspora history until modern times, the average Jewish lay person incorporated as many as 1,200 Hebrew words and terms in the non-Hebraic vernacular which he spoke to denote Judaic concepts and practices which could not be understood fully in the vernacular. Finally, Hebrew is conversation at the bus stop, in the grocery store, on the playground, in the library and on the basketball court, and it is Hebrew slang.

THE MYSTIQUE OF HEBREW

The multi-faceted nature of the Hebrew language contributed significantly to the mystery of its revival. Its mystique is that it was never a "dead" language (in the accepted sense of the term), yet, it was revived.

The mystique of Hebrew is captured beautifully in a statement by Dr. Simon Federbush. He writes: "The revival of our Hebrew language, which accompanied the beginning of our national redemption, is one of the world's miraculous phenomena. The amazement of the nations of the earth regarding this happening, for which there is no parallel in any country or language, was expressed by one of the world's righteous people, 'If the survival of the Jewish nation is a miracle, then the revival of the Hebrew language is the miracle of miracles'" (Federbush).

From an historical socio-linguistic perspective, Hebrew language is viewed as a multi-faceted linguistic continuum of Jewish life from earliest times until the present. To be sure, Hebrew, in all its usages, has contributed significantly to Jewish survival throughout the ages. Therefore, we cannot appreciate the value of Hebrew via any *single* dimension of the language. We must consider Hebrew in all its forms and variety of usages including biblical Hebrew, rabbinic Hebrew, liturgical Hebrew, modern Hebrew, and Hebrew terminology associated with Judaic literacy. This means dealing with Hebrew in the synagogue, in educational settings, in the home, in business, and in the street. Hebrew's multi-dimensionalism is its distinctiveness as a survival mechanism.

The mystique of Hebrew is that it underscores the individuality of the Jew. In a very positive sense, Hebrew differentiates the Jew from his environment while not estranging him from it.

Hebrew in modern times has emerged as an *altneuschprache* (an old-new language) which is the vernacular of some five million Jews and non-Jews in Israel. The miracle of the revival of Hebrew as a living language has impressed peoples speaking endangered "minor" languages like Basque, Irish and Welsh. Delegations from linguistic entities in Spain, Ireland and Scotland have visited Israel to learn about the various methods, particularly the Ulpan and the *Ivrit B'Ivrit* approach in education, which helped bring about the renaissance of Hebrew.

And what about the challenge of the Hebrew language today?

A recent essay in the Jewish Week – an Anglo-Jewish newspaper in New York – about Hebrew points to its importance in Jewish life:

> If you want to taste the real thing, Hebrew is it. No Jew who has read the Torah in Hebrew will call it the Old Testament again. If you want to fall in love with where you come from, Hebrew is it. This is the language your ancestors dreamed in and died for. If you want your children to feel passionately about being Jews, give them the key. If they don't learn to use it when they're young, not only won't they know Hebrew, they'll be translating Jewish values, too and diluting them in the process. For a language and its values are not separable. A *brit* is more than a covenant; *tzedakah* is more than charity; a *brachah* is more than a blessing. And if you do send your kids to a Jewish day school, jump up and down not only for great SAT's but for outstanding Hebrew grades as well. Don't subscribe to the hidden agenda of many schools – that Hebrew is all very well but English is what counts. SAT's will get your children into University, but Hebrew will get them into life.

It seems appropriate for residents of a member nation of the British Commonwealth to end with a statement by Joseph Hertz, former Chief Rabbi of the British Empire about the absolute importance of the Hebrew language for the Jewish people. He said, "A *Hebrewless* Jewry (a Jewry without Hebrew) has no future, because it cannot fairly be said to have a present."

And, the present and future of Jewish life is largely up to you!

[*For a comprehensive analysis of the "mystique" of Hebrew, please refer to Chapter Three of this section: "Twenty-first Century Renaissance of the Hebrew Language."*]

CHAPTER 6

THE JEWISH BOOK NEWS INTERVIEW ON THE MYSTIQUE OF HEBREW

JBN: *Do you think that Hebrew is in a different class from every other language in the world? Is it "the" holy tongue or "our" holy tongue?*

Schiff: Hebrew is different from every other language in the world for a variety of reasons. First, it is the oldest continuous language with essentially the same fundamental nature and, in many ways, its original uniformity. To be sure, there are modern languages with ancient roots. However, they bear little resemblance to the ancient languages from which they developed. For example, modern Greek speakers cannot understand Homer's *Iliad* or *Odyssey* unless they have special training in classical Greek. Hindustani is hardly similar to Sanskrit, its progenitor. And, modern Chinese speakers cannot read Confucius with understanding unless they have special schooling in the subject.

Secondly, the Hebrew language was landless for two millennia; yet it survived the vicissitudes of changing times, changing demography, and the constant oppression of its users. Thirdly, it is the holy tongue in which the Bible was written. Maimonides and other Judaic and rabbinic scholars, such as Rabbi Moshe Isserles, sixteenth-century author of the *Mappah* the authoritative *Shulhan Arukh* of Ashkenazi Jews, and Rabbi Yehezhel Landau, eighteenth-century rabbinic luminary in Prague, attributed special holiness to the Hebrew language because it is the language of the Bible. Rabbi Landau stressed that Hebrew "is the language of Torah and *mitzvot*, the language in which God spoke to the Jewish people at Sinai."

Hebrew tradition is replete with allusions to the age and sanctity of Hebrew. According to the Talmud (*Sanhedrin* 38), Hebrew is the first language – the *prima lingua* – that Adam spoke. The rabbis note that Hebrew was the "one language" spoken by all the inhabitants of the universe before the generation of the Tower of Babel (Genesis: 11:1). Rabbi Yehudah Halevi, in the *Kuzari*, suggests that Hebrew was the first and, therefore, the most important language because God himself spoke to Adam in Hebrew. The *Midrash* deduces from the names that God gave Adam and Eve (Genesis 2:33) that He spoke Hebrew at the time of creation.

Jews were not alone in their belief in the age and sanctity of the Hebrew language. In medieval times, several Christian scholars regarded Hebrew to be Adam's original tongue, the first language of the human race and the language of God.

Hebrew has been especially sacred to the Jews who continued to use it for worship and for study during the Talmudic, gaonic, medieval, rabbinic, and contemporary periods.

Over the centuries, the Jews were tri-lingual, having an internal, or Jewish language of Judeo-Greek, Yiddish, or Judezmo, Ladino, etc., for personal communication; an external, or gentile language (the language of their host countries) for contact with the gentile world, and a sacred language (Hebrew, or Hebrew-Aramaic) – *Loshon Kodesh* for study and prayer. Their internal language was peppered with Hebraic terms, creating a level of Hebraic literacy. And, during the long Diaspora, there were always some Jews somewhere, who spoke Hebrew.

The Jewish Book News Interview on the Mystique of Hebrew · 535

JBN: *What do you think of those who claim that all languages stem from Hebrew?*

Schiff: To be sure, Hebrew has a long, interesting relationship to other languages. The *Kuzari* posits that when the world was divided into separate languages, each borrowed terminology from Hebrew. Indeed, Hebrew has contributed significantly to other cultures and languages. For example, the Hebraic contribution to the English language is clearly evident in the Hebrew words adapted by English, such as, alphabet, camel, cherub, manna, jubilee, sabbatical, shibboleth, etc.

There is some scholarly support for monogenesis of language, the thesis that all human languages are derived from a single mother tongue. In his book, *The Word*, Isaac Mozeson makes a strong case for Hebrew being that language, a thesis not yet accepted by most linguistic scholars. According to Mozeson, more English words can be linked clearly to biblical Hebrew than to Greek, Latin, and French. His extensive research reveals the Hebrew source of some three thousand English words and terms. It shows that:

1. "Borrowings" from Hebrew by the English language are far more extensive than now conceded in etymological texts;
2. The number of sound-alike, mean-alike terms in Indo-European and Semitic languages far exceed the allowable number of borrowings or "coincidences;"
3. Hebrew is a uniquely profound system of languages that resembles the organicism of natural science rather than the product of human development;
4. If there is an original language, it is the language of the Hebrew Bible.

Yet, there are reasons to believe that there were other languages as old as or older than Hebrew. Even though spoken language developed many years prior to human's ability to write, the earliest records of language usage are in writing. Sumerian cuneiform and Egyptian hieroglyphics from about 3000 B.C.E. are the earliest known written records. The oldest Sanskrit and Chinese writings date back to 2000 B.C.E. making them as old as Hebrew, while Greek and Latin records go back to 1400 and 500 B.C.E., respectively.

JBN: *Rabbi Adin Steinsaltz is reported to have visited U.S. synagogue schools and offered a critique recommending that a much greater emphasis be placed on teaching Hebrew. What do you think of this prescription? Also, it seems that American synagogues have failed miserably to teach Hebrew to the students. What do you think?*

Schiff: Synagogue Jewish schooling has been on the decline since mid-century. In the second, third and fourth decades of the twentieth century, serious Hebraic learning took place in the communal *Talmud Torah*, which was the normative organized format for after public school Jewish education. The congregationalization of Jewish supplementary education brought with it a steep reduction of days and hours of schooling – from a five-day, 10–12 hours per week, 44 weeks per year format to a one to three day, 2–6 hours per week, 32–36 weeks per year schedule of classes. Moreover, attendance in the *Talmud Torah* was regular and punctual whereas absenteeism in the congregational school is rampant.

Furthermore, over time, the level of teaching has declined as the Hebraically-oriented, European-born and American Hebrew Teachers College trained teachers retired and were replaced by less knowledgeable personnel. The decline in the quality of teaching was further exacerbated by the Bar/Bat Mitzvah syndrome, whereby hardly any student continued their Jewish education beyond Bar/Bat Mitzvah.

The reduction of the number of hours of exposure to Hebrew study and the poorer quality of instruction were joined by the growing disinterest of parents in the Hebraic education of their progeny. And, as the rabbinic and lay leadership of the synagogues stressed increasingly the importance of the Bar/Bat Mitzvah performance of pupils and preparation for the synagogue service, often to the exclusion of other purposes of Jewish education, Hebrew language and textual learning in Hebrew became secondary, at best, and expendable at worst. In fact, after the first or second year of synagogue school, when students learn to read the Siddur, Hebrew, as a language, is either offered only as an elective or not taught at all in many congregational schools. The recent study of Jewish supplementary schooling, which I directed, clearly shows that parents enroll their children for the sole purpose of Bar/Bat Mitzvah preparation. Without adequate parental support, there can be little achievement in the content areas of the Jewish school curriculum. Since the main concern of most rabbis has been preparation for synagogue or temple service, an active knowledge of Hebrew, other than reciting the *Maftir* and *Haftarah* in Hebrew and following the Hebraic segments of the synagogue service, is not considered a needed outcome of Jewish schooling. The findings of the study on synagogue schools also demonstrated that less than half of the rabbis felt that the Hebrew language should be a curricular goal of their school.

Given the above conditions of learning, the possibility of improving Hebrew language instruction in the synagogue school is remote. Needed, first, is the uncompromising acknowledgement by lay, rabbinic and educational leaders of the absolute importance of the Hebrew language as a significant dimension of Jewish vitality and as a unifying factor in Jewish life. One of the reasons the National Center for the Hebrew Language was founded was for the purpose of advocacy. Synagogue leadership is a prime target for the center's promotional activity. To succeed in Hebrew language education, the synagogue would have to make Hebrew language instruction a priority and requirement for all students.

It is necessary to develop a cooperative network of Jewish educational institutions and central agencies for Jewish education to:

1. Prioritize the role of Hebrew language in our schools,
2. Improve the effectiveness of Hebrew language instruction by

state of the art knowledge of applied linguistics and second language pedagogy. No single approach to all schools would be possible. A variety of methods, including total immersion activities should be guided by a central resource. Networking is the second reason the National Center for the Hebrew Language was established;
3. Increase significantly the hours of exposure to Hebrew study;
4. Gain parental support, including the provision of Hebrew classes for parents;
5. Employ well-trained, knowledgeable Hebrew teachers (helping guide the preparation of skilled Hebrew language instructors is another role of the Hebrew Center);
6. Insure that pupils have added opportunity to learn and use Hebrew in informed education settings, particularly in Jewish summer camps.

Achieving success in Hebrew language instruction in the synagogue school is a tall order, indeed. But, Jews have always adjusted to the miraculous or near miraculous. The dream of a Jewish state was deemed unrealizable by most Jews, one century ago. Moreover, the revival of Hebrew was considered impossible at the turn of this century by all Jews with the exception of a handful of diehards like Ben Yehuda. So be it with Hebrew today in the Diaspora.

JBN: *When was the last time that Hebrew was the common language of the Jewish people?*

Schiff: Hebrew was always the common language of the Jewish people in a very unique way. This is its mystique. Hebrew had and continues to have bi-polar power. It is the vehicle of a sacred past, of eternal Jewish values. At the same time, it is a major expression of contemporary Jewish vitality.

The importance of the Hebrew language as a link to the Jewish past and to Israel, and as a unifying force in Jewish life has been underscored by Jewish leaders and scholars in every generation of Jewish history. Jews are accustomed to tightrope existence. In every age, our forebears developed group dynamics appropriate for creative survival in their particular environments. Currently, the tightrope requires the maintaining of varying kinds of equilibrium. It means bi-polar adjustment – keeping the constants, or preserving the transcendental values of Jewish tradition, on the one hand, and keeping up with the times, or developing new adaptive mechanisms, on the other.

The Hebrew language might be viewed from this dual perspective. As the language of the Bible, the *Mishnah*, rabbinic literature, and liturgy, Hebrew is a constant. As the language of modern Hebrew literature, the newspaper, the theater, the convention hall, the bus stops, Hebrew in flux meets a current need. It is the vernacular of a people reborn in its land of rebirth – the language of the businessman, the scientist, the yeshiva *bohur*, the farmer, the housewife, and the university professor alike.

Hebrew, the constant, is essential for Jewish group survival since it is a major channel for the Jew's spiritual identity. While not sufficient cause for the continuity of Jewish cultural-religious life, it is a necessary one. Without the classical Hebraic sources, our people lack the wellspring from which its lifeblood is nourished. Without its bedrock of classical literature in the original our heritage is stripped of its meaning, purpose, and recreative powers. For valid continuity of Jewish group life, therefore, a working knowledge of Hebrew, to enable textual study of original Hebraic sources, is a *conditione sine qua non*.

In every age, this was a common characteristic of Jews – sometimes a minority of Jews and, at times, a great majority of Jews. Currently, this aspect of commonality is endangered in the Diaspora.

The circumstances of our times, highlighted by the realities of a Jewish state, add both a new dimension and a new challenge to contemporary Jewish life. This dimension is the newfound vitality of the Hebrew language, and the challenge – greater and more effective utilization of its life-giving powers. Modern Hebrew vernacular is a measure of the miracle of Jewish durability. It is part of the mystery of the Jewish people's stubborn existence. This aspect of Jewish survival and vitality is also endangered in the Diaspora. Its revival in the Diaspora would help provide a life-giving link with Israel to Diaspora Jewry and would also serve to unify Jews everywhere.

PART VIII

Jewish Education Persona, of Blessed Memory

This section is a personal tribute to Jewish personalities who contributed significantly to the enhancement of Jewish life. It contains essays presented in alphabetical order on Jewish educational leaders with whom I had a close relationship and who influenced my career. They are in the form of eulogies or remarks of appreciation on their lifetimes. One of the essays is a special dedication to the memory of a giant, Rabbi Joseph B. Soloveitchik.

Samuel Belkin, 1976
Zvi Herbert Berger, 2000
Yosef Burg, 1999
Gershon Churgin, 1978
Azriel Eisenberg, 1979
Abraham Gannes, 2003
Jacob I. Hartstein, 1991
Sidney B. Hoenig, 1980
Leo Jung, 1988
Asher (Arthur) Kahn, 2002
Abraham Katsh, 2002

Joseph Hyman Lookstein, 1979
Israel Miller, 2002
S. Maurice Plotnick, 1992
Leonard Rosenfeld, 2002
Akiva Schiff, 1998
Joseph B. Soloveitchik, 1993
Nathen F. Winter, 2004

SAMUEL BELKIN

With the passing of Dr. Samuel Belkin, American Jewry has lost a towering personality whose life represented a dynamic period of development in the Jewish community and American society.

If scholarship, teaching ability, creativity and personal leadership are desired qualities in an educator, Dr. Belkin was the *mehanekh par excellence*. His entire career is synonymous with educational genius. From his earliest years as a *yeshiva bohur* in Mir and Radin in the mid-1930s until his investiture as Chancellor of Yeshiva University in 1975, Dr. Belkin's life was one brilliant academic-educational episode: *smichah* from the Chofetz Chaim at age 17; honors student at Harvard College at 19; election to Phi Beta Kappa and a PhD degree in Greek literature from Brown University at age 23 – only four years after arriving in the United States; Rosh Yeshiva at 25 at the Rabbi Isaac Elchanan Theological Seminary, a position he held simultaneously with a professorship in Greek; dean of the Seminary, at 29, and President of Yeshiva University at 32.

Unassuming, concerned, determined and indefatigable, Dr. Belkin built a small school of higher learning into a full-fledged university – America's largest academic institution under Jewish auspices with an enrollment of some 8,000 students in four high schools, six undergraduate schools (including three programs for the training of Hebrew teachers), and eight graduate schools, including the Rabbi Isaac Elchanan Theological Seminary, Bernard Revel Graduate School for Judaic Studies, Albert Einstein College of Medicine, Ferkauf Graduate School of Humanities and Social Sciences, Wurzweiler School of Social Work, Sue Golding School of Medical Sciences, Belfer School of Science, and the Cardozo School of Law.

Filled with a passion for creative Jewish continuity, fortified by a broad philosophy which saw a place in Judaism for the world of knowledge and science, enriched by a profound grasp of Judaic sources and Western ideas, endowed with unusual insight and enormous perseverance, and moved by great optimism, he dreamed of developing a unique role for Jewish life in America. As leader of this country's foremost Orthodox institution, he strove to establish a strong symbiotic relationship between Torah education and secular learning.

Toward the realization of his dream, to which he literally gave his life even as he embodied it (he was a living symbol of synthesis to a generation of students), Dr. Belkin dedicated with unparalleled selflessness his genius, energies and days without seeking or expecting personal reward.

When the history of the twentieth century will be chronicled, Samuel Belkin, the teacher-educator will emerge as one of its leading figures and great architects who enriched Jewish life during his lifetime and helped shape its future for generations to come.

ZVI HERBERT BERGER

It's hard to believe that Zvi is no longer among the living – that he has gone the way of all flesh. I knew Zvi for 57 years – as a dear friend, ardent fellow Zionist, trusted colleague and loyal co-worker. My earliest memories of Zvi go back to the *Hashomer Hadati* – the forerunner of the Bnai Akiva movement. He was such an avid Zionist. As a teenager, Zvi was at his best giving *Sihot* – leading discussions on the history of Zionism, the role of religious Zionism, the Jewish claim to *Eretz Yisrael*, the geography of *Eretz Yisrael* and the Zionist heroes of Europe and Palestine.

Zvi was an honors student at Yeshiva University. He loved biology and science. But, his special love was for his studies in the Teachers Institute for Men where he excelled and graduated at the top of his class, becoming an accomplished Hebraist and Hebrew teacher.

I remember Zvi at Massad Hebrew Camps where we served as counselors. Zvi was the nature counselor. How he relished working on the nature section of the Massad Hebrew dictionary! Like everything else he did, he edited this section quietly, carefully and conscientiously. After graduating from Yeshiva University, he went on *Shlihut* for the *Hashomer Hadati* to Boston where he taught in the Maimonides School, founded by Rabbi Joseph Soloveitchik. At the same time, he studied at Harvard University where he received a Master's degree in science with honors. After his *Shlihut* was over he made aliyah with his wife Miriam. In Israel, he was so happy teaching science and Judaic studies in the Bnai Akiva High School in Kfar Haro'eh. However, as fate would have it, he had to return to the United States because of Miriam's illness.

Zvi was a walking encyclopedia of Judaic knowledge; he wore his mantle of scholarship with such humility – Zvi was a bibliophile *par excellence*. He devoured books on every aspect of Jewish life. You name the book; Zvi read it, had it or intended to purchase it. His greatest pleasure wherever he went in North America, Europe or Israel was to go to a Jewish bookstore, browse and buy.

Above all, Zvi was a *gutte neshomoh*, so caring, so concerned about the welfare of Jews everywhere. Nothing was beneath his dignity. When he served with distinction as executive director of the Bureau of Jewish Education in Miami he would help busy secretaries with their work. Later, in Denver, where he also served as executive director of the bureau, he thought nothing of doing mimeographing because he felt his secretary was working too hard. At the Board of Jewish Education of Greater New York, where he was associate executive director, Zvi was known to always roll up his sleeves to help his fellow colleagues. When something had to be done Zvi pitched in to do it without fanfare – and often without getting credit for what he accomplished. How the staff members loved him for his personal traits and for his helpfulness!

He leaves his family, friends and colleagues a rich heritage of love, caring and Jewish educational experience.

YOSEF BURG

Excerpts from a letter to his son,
Avrum Burg, Knesset Chairman
October 26, 1999

I am deeply saddened by the passing of your father. Not only was Yosef Burg a *talmid hakham*, a highly cultured, intellectual and a charismatic, indefatigable leader of the Jewish State, before, during, and after its formation, but he was a model of *menschlichkeit* and sound judgment throughout his lifetime.

Among others, I recall two experiences that demonstrated his many unique qualities and his ability to communicate his ideas to a wide variety of people. After the Yom Kippur war, the Board of Jewish Education of Greater New York, which I headed, organized a pro-Israel demonstration in front of the United Nations in which some 50,000 Jewish school students participated. The highlight of the demonstration was the presentation of a Torah scroll to *Tzahal* to replace the one captured during the war by the Egyptians. Your father represented Israel and received the Torah on its behalf. In his remarks he was brilliant and inspirational.

More than that, in his several meetings with students, teachers and principals after the demonstration, he showed his uniqueness via his broad knowledge, insights and humor, and the way he was able to establish such warm rapport with audiences of all ages and stripes. He succeeded admirably in instilling in the participants good feelings regarding their concern for and support of Israel. The question and answer periods after each of his brief addresses were paradigms of personal interaction and exchange of views. During the meetings, he demonstrated his remarkable ability to bridge the gap between the various religious trends and between religious and secular Jews.

The second experience was the world leadership summit consultation of Modern Orthodox Zionist Jewry sponsored by the Torah Education Department of JAFI-WZO. Held in London in January 1986, the two-day meeting, which I chaired, was convened to help determine the way Modern Orthodox Jews should relate to Israel and to JAFI-WZO via Jewish Zionist education. Some fifteen rabbinic, lay, and educational Diaspora leaders were invited to the sessions conducted in Hebrew. Your father represented the Modern Orthodox Zionist community in Israel. His participation was scintillating. On occasion, he kept us in stitches with his apt humorous remarks. Overall, his comments highlighted our meetings, particularly when we discussed the relationship of Orthodox Jews to the modern Jewish State with a large non-Orthodox majority and the ways Orthodox schools should identify meaningfully with Israel.

I often saw him when I visited Israel and will miss him. His passing leaves a huge void in Israel, in world Jewry and particularly in Modern Orthodoxy and in the National Religious Party where he was the voice of reason.

GERSHON CHURGIN

Scholarly, studious, erudite, unassuming, modest, generous, open-minded and supportive. These adjectives best describe the personal traits of the gentle academic who spent most of his professional life on the faculty of Yeshiva University as professor of Hebrew Literature, Philosophy and Education at the Teachers' Institute for Men, Yeshiva College, Bernard Revel Graduate School and the Harry Fischel Summer Institute.

I met Dr. Churgin when I was his student in Pedagogy at the Teachers' Institute. He had a quiet, charming, non-directive manner of teaching – allowing for maximum expression of student ideas. Via his vast knowledge he was able to respond to every kind of question posed in class. I personally benefited from his open-minded, supportive approach to students. He gave me my first opportunity to teach on the college level as a 21-year old college graduate. It was his encouragement and warm guidance when I served as his associate instructor of pedagogy that guaranteed that I would stay in the field of Jewish education.

Born in Pinsk, Russia, he spent his childhood in Palestine and graduated from the Teachers' Institute in Jerusalem. Armed with his teacher's diploma, upon immigrating to the United States, he began his teaching career and enrolled in Columbia University from which he received his bachelors and masters degrees with honors. Shortly thereafter, while teaching in Baltimore, he earned his PhD in philosophy at Johns Hopkins University.

Dr. Churgin was an eminent Judaic scholar – philosophical and pragmatic at one and the same time. When observing his informal way of teaching it was obvious that he loved the subject matter he taught and was very fond of his students. An exemplar of the synthesis of the religious and secular domains, his unique style of teaching influenced many students regarding their involvement with Judaic and Hebraic studies. His deep knowledge and exceptional command of the Hebrew language added to the effectiveness of his instruction.

Dr. Churgin was widely known through his writings, with many articles appearing in the scholarly Hebrew publication *Bitzaron*, which he co-edited. His writings dealt with the philosophies of David Newmark, Ahad Ha'am, Morris Raphael Cohen, Saadia Gaon and Nahum Krochmal. He was the author of two highly regarded books: *Ofkei Mahshavah* (Horizons of Thought: Students in Jewish and General Philosophy), published by Yeshiva University's Department of Special Publications, and *Currents in Modern Philosophy*.

Professor Churgin made a major contribution to the field of Jewish education in New York as a long-time member of the Board of Examiners of the New York Board of Licensure for Hebrew teachers, which interviewed all applicants for certification. While his questions on Judaica and education were penetrating, he was known to be compassionate in his consideration regarding an applicant's eligibility for licensure.

With his passing, the Jewish community lost a master educator with remarkable knowledge and a keen ability to transmit it to generations of students.

AZRIEL EISENBERG

Dedicated, diligent, dynamic, optimistic, industrious, persevering. These are adjectives that best describe one of the great Jewish educational leaders of the twentieth century. Born in Europe, he arrived as a young boy before the outbreak of WWI and like all Jewish children at that time, he went to public school, high school and college; and by 1935 he received his PhD from Teachers College, Columbia University. While in college he attended the Teachers Institute of the Jewish Theological Seminary and there he was inspired to become a Jewish educator.

His career was a continuum of successive leadership positions as principal, director of the bureaus of Jewish Education of Cincinnati and Cleveland, director of the Philadelphia Council of Jewish Education and acting dean of Graetz College. In 1949, he was elected to the post of executive vice president of the Jewish Education Committee of New York (now the Board of Jewish Education of Greater New York). Upon retirement, he was persuaded to accept the directorship of the World Bureau of Jewish Education, a position he held for two years.

While I met him as a student representative to the JEC Assembly in 1949 and in several other JEC meetings during the early 1950s, I worked closely with him after being invited to serve as pedagogic consultant and supervisor of the Department of Yeshivot and Day Schools of JEC in 1956.

Azriel Eisenberg was a wonderful boss – friendly, helpful and challenging. He loved his work as administrator of the world's largest central agency for Jewish Education. At JEC, he innovated many programs. As a lover and promoter of Hebrew, he initiated the *Lador* series of Hebrew booklets for elementary schools, which grew into a comprehensive library of eighty booklets. He also developed the widely read children's periodical *World Over*.

Ahead of his time, he organized departments of music, art, drama and dance. Dr. Eisenberg loved young people and via his enthusiastic encouragement and influence he was responsible for the recruitment of many promising Jewish educators. And, Azriel loved young children. Regularly, he would give gifts of books to my daughters and signed them "*ha-dod* (uncle) Azriel."

He loved working and was a prolific author with more than fifty hardcover books to his credit. At times, he would escape from the world of educational politics to the quietude of research and writing, but never at the expense of his administrative work.

He was a man of rectitude and integrity, firm yet flexible, who eschewed intrigue, political maneuvering and pretense, and shunned those in whom he detected such characteristics. With his sense of humor, good common sense and robust feelings he was able to overcome communal difficulties, which were inherent in the activity of a central agency for Jewish education in the mid-twentieth century. And, with his warm personality and loyalty to friends and colleagues, he was able to turn problems into promise and promise into accomplishment.

ABRAHAM GANNES

Honesty, integrity, commitment and dedication mark the life and career of Abraham Gannes, trusted colleague, dear friend, model Jewish educator and ardent Zionist leader. I met him at first when I was a graduate student at Teachers College, Columbia University, through an article he penned for the *Jewish Education* quarterly in 1949 on informal Jewish education. I met him again through his other writings, particularly via his pioneering doctoral dissertation at Dropsie on Central Agencies for Jewish Education. In his research and writings, he clearly captured the essence of Jewish education in America and he astutely portrayed his philosophy, the challenges it faces and the promise it holds for the enrichment of Jewish life.

Abe's paradigmatic personality, his utter devotion to his work and his common sense in teaching and administration contributed greatly to his success in all of his professional undertakings – as teacher-educator in Philadelphia, as bureau head in Miami, as director of Camp Cejwin, and as director of the American Department of Education and Culture of the World Zionist Organization.

Abe was unique, functioning as an equal in a world of older Jewish educational leaders, who, for the most part, received their Jewish educational background in Europe. He was totally a product of the American Jewish school system, which he later helped enhance via his talent, Hebraic knowledge, and effective performance.

A model Jewish educator, he was one of the early proponents of the value of the confluence of the cognitive and affective aspects of teaching and learning. In theory and practice, he excelled in developing the combination of formal and experiential Jewish Zionist education. This thrust was highlighted in all phases of his professional endeavors, especially in Camp Cejwin and at the WZO Department of Education and Culture.

I was closely related to his work at the WZO and admired him for his utter dedication, outstanding ability and concern for fellow Jewish educators as he developed and promoted programs in Jewish Zionist education. During his tenure as director, the Department of Education and Culture reached its pinnacle of success. He was respected by his colleagues both in Israel and in the United States and succeeded in forging a strong bond between Israel and the American Jewish community in matters relating to Jewish education.

On a personal level, Mimi and I always enjoyed our meetings with Abe and Miriam in the United States and in Israel. They were an inspiring couple, devoted to each other, to the Jewish people and to Eretz Yisrael.

JACOB I. HARTSTEIN

With the passing of Jacob Hartstein, the Jewish community is bereft of a remarkable human synthesis: eminent Jewish educator, esteemed communal lay leader, and distinguished general educator. In each capacity, he excelled and made major contributions. In each, I was privileged to observe him at work and benefit from his knowledge and experience.

Upon graduating from Yeshiva College's first class in 1932, he began his career as a teacher in Talmudical Academy (Yeshiva's high school). Later, he served as instructor of Jewish education, registrar and administrator of the Teachers' Institute for Men while teaching general education and psychology at Yeshiva College and simultaneously earning Master's degrees from City

College and Columbia University and then a doctorate from New York University. In his positions at Teachers' Institute and Yeshiva College, he guided hundreds of young aspiring Jewish educators. At the same time, he pioneered the development of relationships between yeshivot in New York City and the New York State Education Department.

On the national scene, among others, he was an active member of the National Board of License for Personnel in Jewish Schools. As a lay volunteer, Dr. Hartstein served in a variety of lay leadership roles in synagogue and Jewish communal life, in Jewish education and in Zionist and Israel-oriented activity. For three decades, he was a respected board member of the Board of Jewish Education of Greater New York, actively participated in committee work and co-chaired BJE's trailblazing self-study in 1970–72.

As a secular educator, Professor Hartstein was a major force in the Jewish and general communities as he helped establish and lead several institutions of higher learning. He was founding dean of Yeshiva University's first graduate school, which later branched out into several specialized schools – Ferkhauf Graduate School of Psychology, Wurzweiler School of Social Work, Azrieli Graduate Institute of Jewish Education and Administration and the Bernard Revel Graduate School. In addition, he was architect of Yeshiva's transition to University status in 1945 and was instrumental in the founding of its Albert Einstein College of Medicine.

In the larger society, Dr. Hartstein held a variety of academic posts including professor and chairman of the Department of Psychology, professor and chairman of the Department of Education, and founding dean of the School of Education of Long Island University. At the City University of New York he was, among others, founding president of Kingsboro Community College. Endowed with creative insight, genuine humanitarianism and exceptional administrative skill, Dr. Hartstein's leadership roles were punctuated by his deep commitment to Jewish continuity and the enhancement of Jewish life, by his ever-pressing concern for teacher welfare and academic freedom, and by his intense desire to help schools respond the individual needs of students.

Above all, Jacob Hartstein was a *mensch* – a quiet, diligent, unassuming, caring human being with a deep love for Jewish tradition and Jewish learning and for *Klal Yisrael*.

SIDNEY B. HOENIG

Scholar, rabbi, teacher, researcher, author and educational administrator, Professor Sidney B. Hoenig wore ever so gracefully the mantles of Torah and good deeds. Ordained at the Rabbi Isaac Elchanan Theological Seminary of Yeshiva University in 1931, he was awarded the PhD degree from Dropsie University several years later, and in 1975 he received an honorary Doctorate in Hebrew Letters from Yeshiva University.

At the time of his passing he was president of the Jewish Book Council of the National Jewish Welfare Board. Dr. Hoenig was a prolific writer and authored hundreds of articles and books on a wide variety of subjects, particularly on the Bible, Dead Sea Scrolls, the Great Sanhedrin, the Second Commonwealth, the lunar calendar, Jewish religious observance, and Jewish family education.

Dr. Hoenig spent most of his adult life as a teacher at Yeshiva University. During his 40 year association with YU he taught in almost every one of its schools: the Talmudical Academy High School, Yeshiva College, Teachers Institute for Men, Teachers Institute for Women and the Barnard Revel Graduate School where he occupied the Pinhas Churgin Chair of Jewish History. For several years prior to his retirement, he served as Dean of the latter institution.

Unlike most scholars and academicians, he was not an ivory tower personality. His communal activities included a variety of administrative positions and involvements. He directed the Young Israel Central School for Adult Education in the 1940s, served as Chaplain of the Brooklyn Navy Yard during World War II, organized and directed the Department of Adult Education of the Community Services Division of Yeshiva University, was an active member of the Cultural Committee of the American Joint Distribution Committee, and helped guide the programs of many other religious, cultural and educational organizations.

Dr. Hoenig was a deeply religious man. His piety led him early in his professional career to write his pioneering works on Jewish ritual. In his personality, he combined the religious passion and boundless faith of the *Hasid* and the insatiable, intellectual curiosity of the *Litai*. These qualities helped sustain him during times of personal tragedy.

He was mentor and friend to many Jewish educators, contributed to the *Journal of Jewish Education* and participated as panelist and speaker at many conferences on Jewish education.

Indeed, he was a unique educator model for so many of us who labor in the vineyards of Jewish communal service. We will miss his candor, faith, optimism, pleasantness, concern and guidance.

LEO JUNG

From the time I was his student in a course on Jewish Philosophy, in 1945, in Yeshiva College, I admired Dr. Jung as the exemplar of the good Jew and became a close disciple. Born in 1892 in Moravia, he studied in the great yeshivot of Hungary and was ordained at the Rabbinic Seminary of Berlin. He then continued his education at Cambridge University and received his PhD from London University. He lived to the ripe old age of 96.

Dr. Jung's personal, social, communal and religious demeanor earned for him the appellation "the twentieth century teacher of Jewish ethics". As professor, rabbi, preacher, lecturer and prolific author, he epitomized in word and deed the man of ethics, the model of the ethical personality. Dr. Jung was a genuine scholar and creative author who, in his writings and lectures, skillfully brought together relevant biblical, Talmudic, rabbinic and secular sources that firmly buttressed his lofty ideas.

By his unique personal example, and by his inspiring teaching, he influenced the lives of thousands of students, congregants, friends and colleagues. In every role he served, whether as distinguished spiritual leader in Manhattan's Jewish Center for over fifty years, as professor at Yeshiva University, as President of the Jewish Academy of Arts and Sciences and of the Rabbinical Council of the Union of Orthodox Jewish Congregations of America, or as chairman for forty years of the Cultural-Religious Committee of the Joint Distribution Committee, he displayed his unique traits of leadership and humanity. As his associate chairman, I saw a master at work as he selflessly enhanced Jewish life in Israel and in the Diaspora. Moreover, it was my privilege to witness how he was personally involved on a daily basis with tzedakah – saving and improving the lives of Jews all over the world and in keeping alive important Torah institutions everywhere.

I experienced his singular humanitarianism on many occasions, particularly when I helped him, at age 95, edit his timely volume "Business Ethics and Jewish Law". On a bitterly cold, rainy, winter afternoon, when at age 94, he called me to share something with me, I begged him not to come to my office in such inclement weather and offered to visit him. He said that this would be impossible since he was in Riverdale, Bronx. And, an hour later, with raincoat over his winter coat, plastic covering over his hat, and galoshes, he appeared at my office to tell me of his soul-lifting meeting with Dr. Mordecai Kaplan, 10 years his senior, who was founder of the Reconstructionist Movement and rabbi of the leading Reconstructionist synagogue several blocks from the Manhattan Jewish Center. Rabbi Jung had had no contact with Rabbi Kaplan for 60 years.

Dr. Jung came to tell me that he felt it was time to visit with Dr. Kaplan, who lived in a nursing home where he had short periods of lucidity each day. Dr Jung visited with him until Dr. Kaplan showed signs of lucidity at which time they had a "wonderful heart to heart" discussion about what unites Jews rather than what divides them.

This was Dr. Jung, the man.

ASHER (ARTHUR) KAHN

What can one say when a dear, dear friend, a soul mate for 64 years, passes on to his heavenly abode? Rabbi Yohanan ben Zakkai characterized his famous student Yehoshua ben Hannania as the Solomonic "three-fold thread" – with profound knowledge of all branches of Torah lore, an encyclopedic grasp of worldly culture, and intense piety expressed via love and respect of fellow man.

Asher Kahn's exemplary life excelled in each of these qualities. He was conversant in every aspect of Judaic culture – Biblical, Talmudic, Medieval and modern Hebrew literature, the Hebrew language, Jewish history and philosophy. And, he wore the mantle of *Talmid hakham* with grace and humility. Asher also excelled in every branch of general studies from English literature to math and physics; from ancient history to political science in contemporary times. And, he was deeply religious – carefully observing the ritual *mitzvot* and the human values of Judaism. Asher was an avid Zionist who played a major role in the support of the State of Israel. He was the prototype of the Jewish reverential, ethical personality.

As a student at Yeshiva University, he set an unparalleled record of scholarship, never receiving less than 100% in every test he took. In addition, to his studiousness, I recall as his roommate during the World War II years, that he would rise at 1:30 A.M. each morning, after 1-½ hours of sleep and go to a nearby local hospital to serve as an aide between 2:00 and 5:00 A.M. because of the severe shortage of nurses, particularly during the wee hours of the morning. He would then return for 2 more hours of sleep after which he assumed his role as dorm counselor during his junior and senior years of college, waking students up for the minyan and supervising the *shaharit* service. In the dormitory he also served as a student health service volunteer in the infirmary during his free hours. Asher was the amazing combination of scholar, ethicist, community volunteer and student leader.

Upon his ordination in 1948, Yeshiva University asked him to serve as rabbi in Tulsa from where the family of Dr. Bernard Revel, founding president of Yeshiva University hailed. And he stayed in the same congregation for fifty years until his retirement. As rabbi, he had a powerful influence on the Jewish community and the community-at-large. As one of his congregants reflected on his life, "he was the most effective speaker in Tulsa. The combination of his rich scholarly content, his strong personal belief in the veracity of his ideas, his impassioned delivery, eloquence and resonant voice made a deep lasting impression on everyone who heard him. He was able to sway the most unsympathetic listener." Asher's genuine altruistic idealism and selfless commitment to the welfare of all his parishioners and all the residents of his larger community made him "a towering force for good in Tulsa." At the community dinner in honor of his 20th anniversary as rabbi, some 2,000 people came to pay tribute to him. Among the participants and speakers were, the governor of Oklahoma, the mayor of Tulsa, Oklahoman senators and congressmen, university presidents, clergymen of every stripe, local communal leaders in addition to Jewish communal and religious leaders from Oklahoma and all over the United States. It was their way of expressing their admiration for a model rabbi and paradigmatic *mensch*.

ABRAHAM KATSH

When I was asked to write a brief "In Memoriam" for Dr. Abraham Katsh, *z"l*, a flood of memories rushed through my head. They related to his learned family background and upbringing, his devotion to scholarship, his initiative and assertiveness, and his charm and infectious smile that influenced friends and disarmed would-be critics.

Our paths often crossed in academic, educational, and communal settings. Each time we met, I came away with a greater understanding of why he was a man of memorable achievement. He came from an erudite family: His father was the chief rabbi of Petach Tikva and a brilliant Talmudic scholar, as are his siblings. Professor Katsh was quick to apply his inquiring mind, nonchalant demeanor, boundless energy, natural persistence and not insignificant political skills to every task he undertook.

The remarkable combination of his personal, academic and professional traits enabled him to 1) be the first Jew to gain access to the valuable Judaic Archives of the Leningrad Library for research and filming of documents; 2) found the Institute of Hebrew Culture and Education at New York University and the Auxiliary Jewish Culture Foundation for informal Judaic programs for college youth and faculty; 3) establish a chair in Jewish Studies in NYU's School of Education; and 4) keep Dropsie University afloat, as its president, during its waning years of life.

Dr. Katsh was an ardent Zionist, an avid supporter of *Eretz Yisrael* and a devotee of the Jewish national language. That is why against great odds, he was able to introduce modern Hebrew as a serious subject of study in a university where, as a matter of principle, only biblical Hebrew had been taught.

His interests and activity were not limited to academic research and the modern Hebrew language. During mid-century, for example, while at NYU, he used his administrative talents to chair the National Board of License for Jewish schools. In Israel he was largely responsible for establishing the Newman Award for outstanding literary contributions to the Jewish people. He was also an active board member of the American Association for Jewish Education and a prime mover in the National Association of Professors of Hebrew in American Universities. Professor Katsh's interest in recognizing scholarship and Judaic achievement led to his leadership role in the Jewish Academy of Arts and Sciences, which bestowed fellowships on deserving Jewish leaders in academia, education and communal work.

Given his intellectual acumen and his erudite background, it seems that Abraham Katsh was destined for outstanding Judaic accomplishment. And that is what happened.

JOSEPH HYMAN LOOKSTEIN

With Joseph H. Lookstein's passing, the American Jewish community has lost one of its most influential leaders; Jewish education is bereft of one of its most eloquent spokesmen and creative practitioners; the Jewish people is without one of its most notable and colorful personalities.

A rabbi, by training and profession, he achieved renown for his rabbinical and communal activity as spiritual leader of Manhattan's Kehillath Jeshurun for 55 years, and as president of several major Jewish organizations, particularly the Rabbinical Council of America, the Synagogue Council of America, the New

York Board of Rabbis, and the Commission on Jewish Chaplaincy of the National Jewish Welfare Board. A silver-tongued orator, Rabbi Lookstein was ordained at the Rabbi Isaac Elchanan Theological Seminary of Yeshiva University where he served with great distinction for over four decades as University Professor of Homiletics and Practical Rabbinics.

Highlighting his long, productive career in Jewish communal service, were his pioneering efforts and distinguished leadership in the field of Jewish education. As a young man of 25, he founded the Hebrew Teachers Training School for Girls (later incorporated into Yeshiva University as the Teachers' Institute for Women), where he served as principal for ten years. In 1961, he became Chancellor of Bar Ilan University and commuted regularly between New York and Ramat Gan. Under his guidance, the University grew from a small college with several hundred students to a full-fledged university. On the international scene, he served as Chairman of the World Council for Jewish Education from 1964 to 1969.

Rabbi Lookstein's crowning educational achievement was the founding, in 1937, of the Ramaz School, which he headed as principal for more than three decades. His special contribution in this influential enterprise, which became the prototype of the modern Jewish day school, was his considerable attention to the integration of the beauty of *yefet* with the tents of *Shem*. He championed the cause of excellence in general studies side by side with high standards in Jewish learning.

In all of his involvement in Jewish life, Joseph H. Lookstein, the Orthodox Jew, was the staunch advocate and avid implementer of the concept of *Klal Yisrael*. He saw the vital need to work closely with Jews of all persuasions for the betterment of the total Jewish community even as he diligently applied his not insignificant talents to the development of his own Orthodox institutions.

His unusual productivity and remarkable record of achievements were made possible by an extraordinary constellation of personal traits and professional competencies. He was driven by a unique sense of purpose, an abiding faith in the Jewish people and genuine love for his calling. He had a keen sense of judgment and a rare capacity for leadership. These characteristics were amply fortified by an uncommon combination of personal dynamism, eloquence, humor, and indefatigableness. His human qualities and his enormous contribution to the enhancement of Jewish life in America, in Israel, and the world over will be his everlasting monuments.

ISRAEL MILLER

"The life story of righteous people is good deeds," our Talmudic Sages inform us. This statement fully applies to Rabbi Israel Miller, of blessed memory, who was lovingly known as "Izzy" to his friends and admirers. A gentle, soft-spoken, scholarly human being, he was one of Jewry's most outstanding communal leaders who championed Jewish causes and advocated Jewish human rights at home and around the globe.

Professionally, Rabbi Miller began his career, after ordination in 1941 at Yeshiva University's Rabbi Isaac Elchanan Theological Seminary, as a rabbi in the Bronx and later served until 1994 as senior vice president of Yeshiva University.

Rabbi Miller's illustrious career is filled with great personal accomplishment and remarkable service to the Jewish people, including the presidency of almost every major Jewish communal organization. He served as chairman of the prestigious Conference of Presidents of Major American Jewish Organizations and, also, since 1982, as president of the Conference of Jewish Material Claims Against Germany. His keen insight and tireless energies led to the landmark compensation agreement for the criminal theft and loss of life resulting from Nazi barbarity.

Rabbi Miller played a singular role in modern Jewish life, as he was received by the last six U.S. presidents. Because of his unique communal status, as well as his broad knowledge and experience, three presidents consulted with him about a variety of international matters. He was especially respected for his negotiations with foreign governments on behalf of world Jewry with his trademark gentility and grace. As a young rabbi, he served as a chaplain in the United States Army and later was president of the Association of Chaplains of the Armed Forces and chairman of the National Jewish Welfare Board Commission on Jewish Chaplaincy.

Among other groups, he led the American Jewish Conference on Soviet Jewry. And, as leader of a delegation of the Rabbinical Council of America to the Soviet Union in 1965, he was accorded the privilege of speaking from the pulpit in Moscow. This resulted in a front-page story in The New York Times as "Man in the News," with an extensive biographical sketch headlined, "Down-to-Earth Rabbi."

Rabbi Miller's support of the State of Israel knew no bounds. He was founding president of the American Zionist Federation, vice president of AIPAC, a member of the Board of Governors of the Jewish Agency for Israel, and the executive of the World Zionist Organization. Rabbi Miller was a leader of Jewish Zionist education; he was chairman of the National Yediot Israel Committee of the World Zionist Organization and convener of many conferences and activities on behalf of Zionist education. His interest in informal Jewish education led to the vice-presidency of the National Jewish Community Centers Association.

Above all, Rabbi Miller, the prominent figure and eloquent spokesman for American and world Jewry, was "Izzy," the down-to-earth, modest, warm, friendly, and engaging human being.

S. MAURICE PLOTNICK

A unique Jewish personality, a unique pioneering Jewish educator, a human paradigm of the synthesis of worldly knowledge and Jewish scholarship, of general culture and Jewish tradition has left us. I met S. Maurice Plotnick for the first time 50 years ago. I remember, as a teenager in Boston, being so impressed with the young principal of the Maimonides School founded in 1937. His engaging British accent, his gentlemanly demeanor, his utter enthusiasm about his work and his ability to communicate lofty thoughts and difficult concepts in a most facile manner won him a whole community of admirers. Maimonides was the first

Jewish Day School in the United States organized outside of the Metropolitan New York area. In 1942, young Maurice, then in his twenties, was invited to Boston by Rabbi Joseph B. Soloveitchik, the school's founder, to provide leadership to the fledgling yeshiva. And, he succeeded in helping establish it as an outstanding institution of general and Jewish learning.

Maurice was a remarkable amalgam of high intellect and practical insight, of other-worldliness and this-worldliness. He possessed the combination of personal and professional qualities that Moses was advised, in this week's *sidrah*, *Yitro*, to seek when appointing leaders for the Israelites. French philosopher, Henri Bergson, would say that Maurice "thought like a man of action, and acted like a man of thought." He was a man of broad intellectual interests and deep, abiding commitment to Jewish values. He had exceedingly high academic standards. Yet, he was sensitive to the needs of every child. I vividly recall on one of my regular visits as consultant to the Westchester Day School, finding him in his office with a gifted kindergarten pupil on his lap. Maurice was teaching him algebra. "It is a pity," he said, "to waste such brain power."

When it came to school administration, Mr. Plotnick, the executive, was able to apply the personal traits of a *yekke* with his penchant for *punctlichkeit* together with his mathematical genius for organization. Before the advent of computers, one could observe this human computer using a pegboard and other homemade devices to develop intricate program schedules. Pedagogically, Headmaster Plotnick was in the forefront of educational innovation – regularly introducing and experimenting with new educational methodologies. In his life-long work, Maurice demonstrated that modern, all day Jewish schooling under traditional Jewish auspices, could gain adherents from a wide variety of Jewish backgrounds. He showed that one need not compromise excellence in Jewish studies to achieve excellence in general studies; and conversely, a demanding schedule of Jewish studies need not be at the expense of a high caliber general studies program.

S. Maurice Plotnick was, above all, a *mensch* – a warm,

engaging, caring personality. To see the twinkle in his eyes and broad smile envelop his face when sharing a deep thought, a pleasant experience or a glad tiding with a child, a parent, a teacher, a board member or a colleague was to observe a genuine human being with deep feelings and love for all of God's creations. I will always remember his "menschlichkeit," his integrity and his boyish exuberance. I will always remember S. Maurice Plotnick as a wholesome human being – combining the traits of *talmid hacham* and *maskil*, British scholar and perspicacious pedagogue, Jewish thinker and skilled executive – all packaged in the person of a sensitive, caring, concerned Jew whose life was devoted to the enhancement of Jewish life and Jewish continuity.

RABBI LEONARD ROSENFELD

Rabbi Leonard Rosenfeld was different in a very positive way. The paradigm of idealism regarding Judaism, Zionism, Israel, *Torah Lishmah*, Jewish education and family, he took a firm no-nonsense stand in each of these areas of interest and concern. "Lennie," as I knew him for some fifty years, was a brilliant student in Judaic and general studies at Yeshiva University, deeply respected by fellow students and teachers alike. After ordination, he entered the rabbinate, guiding the development of a newly organized synagogue in Kew Gardens, Queens, New York. At that time he also taught at Yeshiva University.

Enhancing Jewish education was one of Leonard Rosenfeld's avid desires. Consequently, he became involved, in the early 1950s, in the founding of the Department of Yeshivot and Jewish Day Schools of the Jewish Education Committee of New York (JEC) – later known as the Board of Jewish Education of Greater New York. His tenure as director of the Department of Yeshivot and Jewish Day Schools is highlighted by many pioneer achievements as he brought the Jewish Day School world in Metropolitan New York – from liberal Hebraic schools to right wing Talmudic yeshivot – under the umbrella of JEC, which, until then, had no real relationship with Jewish all day education. His indefatigable efforts on behalf of yeshivot and day schools insured that they would receive federal support via the New York State Education Department without violating church-state law. The federal, state and city aid that he helped secure took the form of lunch grants, surplus Department of Agriculture kosher food, milk subsidies, school bus transportation, and other kinds of assistance such as audiological and optometric testing of students and special aid for children with special needs. He also developed a loan program for yeshivot and Jewish day schools.

My friendship with Lennie began in 1952 when I was principal of the elementary school of the Hebrew Institute of Long Island (HILI) in Far Rockaway, New York, where he served as chairman of the Board of Education. He was an active, creative participant in Jewish studies faculty meetings, conducted in Hebrew. He was respectful of all the teachers, but could not tolerate the relaxation of standards of teaching and learning. After three years as principal of HILI, I was invited to join him at the JEC as pedagogic consultant and educational supervisor of the Department of Yeshivot and Jewish Day Schools.

Collaborating closely with him for ten years, I was able to observe an unusually creative mind at work for the benefit of *Klal Yisrael*. As administrator of the Department he had a pervasive influence on the direction and program of JEC. In 1967, upon Dr. Eisenberg's retirement, Rabbi Rosenfeld was appointed JEC Executive Vice President, a position he held for only three years because he was intent on fulfilling his dream of making aliyah while he was young enough to appreciate this move. And, so, in the summer of 1970 with his wife, Rosalie, and his grown children, Tirzah and Ezra, and his mother, he made aliyah to Israel, first living in Jerusalem, then settling in Alon Shevut in the Gush Etzion region. In Israel, as in the States, his deep sense of humanitarianism expressed itself in his concern for the welfare of friends and colleagues and in his everyday helpfulness to them. If there ever was a Jewish educator who was motivated by idealism and practiced what he believed in, it was Rabbi Leonard Rosenfeld.

AKIVA SCHIFF

The fourth in a family of six children, Mr. Schiff was born shortly before the turn of the century in Brestovitz, a little Polish town known as "the station between Volkovisk and Oradock." Most of the inhabitants of Brestovitz (population – 350 families) were Jewish merchants who depended upon the peasant farmers of the area for their modest livelihood. Akiva Schiff's parents supported their family with the meager income from their grocery store. His father, a learned and respected member of the community, spent most of his day in Torah study while his mother tended the store.

Like all boys in Eastern Europe at the beginning of the 20th century, Mr. Schiff studied in a *Heder*. He excelled in his studies, and at age 13, together with several other advanced students, he was sent to learn in the famous Bialostok Yeshiva, where he earned the title of the *Bialostoker Masmid* because of his diligence in Talmudic studies. Learning in European yeshivot concentrated exclusively on the Talmud and its commentaries. In addition to his acknowledged excellence as a *Gemara* student, Akiva Schiff acquired, through diligent self-study, thorough mastery of the Hebrew language, Hebrew literature and Bible.

Life for the yeshiva *bahur* in Europe was not easy, particularly during the World War 1 period. When Poland was overrun by the Germans, many Jewish youth were made to do slave labor. In order to escape this fate, which he and two of his brothers tasted for a short time, they devised a scheme in which he feigned serious illness while his oldest brother and youngest sibling were disguised as doctor and nurse's aid, respectively. They did this because the Germans were known to fear sickness. Needless to say, their scheme worked. When the German soldiers entered the modest Schiff home and saw a "doctor" and "medical attendant" administering to a bandaged groaning "patient," they left in a hurry.

After seven years of Torah study at Bialostok Yeshiva, Akiva Schiff returned to Brestovitz and began his teaching career. However, after a short while, together with his mother and two of his brothers, he left Brestovitz to join his father and other brothers who had earlier immigrated to the United States. After a hectic journey during which many obstacles had to be overcome, and the Schiff family lost whatever funds it managed to take along, they finally arrived in New York weary, hungry and penniless. From New York they traveled to Boston where his father and brothers had settled.

Immediately upon settling in the United States, Akiva Schiff – the autodidact and *masmid* – began studying English, classics, languages, math and science. After several years of intensive study, he passed entrance examinations to Harvard University Medical School. However, after he started medical school, Akiva Schiff, the idealistic Jew, had a change of heart because he realized that the Jewish *neshamah* needed more treatment and healing than the Jewish body. So, he went to New York where he decided to dedicate his talents and energies to teaching and inspiring Jewish youth. He was among the first three Hebrew teachers to receive a Hebrew teachers' license from the newly established Board of License for Jewish Schools in New York.

Akiva taught in the well-known Tifereth Hagro Talmud Torah in Brownsville where, in his own very passionate and devoted way, he instructed a generation of Jewish children in Torah lore. His *Talmud Torah* students invariably had the unique distinction of being able to qualify, upon graduation, for admission to Yeshiva high schools, many of them to advanced classes. In 1958, he joined the faculty of the Hebrew Academy of Nassau County as master teacher where he taught Bible and Talmud and guided Hebrew teachers and *rebbeim* in their instructional activity.

He acquired profound knowledge in all fields of Hebraica and Judaica. He was super-conscientious and utterly devoted to his work, to his pupils and colleagues, and he was modest, humble and unassuming. Most of Akiva Schiff's waking hours outside school were spent in diligently planning lessons and preparing class work, carefully evaluating and correcting compositions, tests and homework and thinking about his teaching. In the loftiest sense, he epitomized the teacher to whom teaching was not only a profession – but a calling.

One side of Akiva Schiff's persona that was little known to his colleagues and students was his versatility. He was an accomplished chess player (winning a variety of tournaments), an excellent handball player, a long distance swimmer of unusual ability and endurance, and a versatile musician with special skill in the mandolin and guitar. At age 80, Akiva Schiff took up the violin, which together with learning Talmud became his favorite pastime for the last 20 years of his life.

In addition to all these qualities, Akiva Schiff was a qualified draftsman – a skill he acquired autodidactically in order to help the United States war effort during World War II. Too old to join the military during the war, he served as master draftsman in the Brooklyn navy yard from 1941 to 1946. He returned to Jewish education after the war, even though he could have earned much more as a draftsman.

He was an avid reader with particular interest in, and keen insight into, national and international politics. An ardent lifelong Zionist, Israel always played a central role in his life. Shortly after coming to New York, he joined *Ahuzah*, a small Orthodox Zionist group whose idealistic members invested regularly in *Eretz Yisrael*. For fifty years, Akiva Schiff contributed one half of all his earnings to the physical and spiritual growth of the country – initially by purchasing land from Arabs in the 1920s and 1930s, by helping develop it and maintain it and by supporting the development and maintenance of Yeshiva education.

Since the founding of *Ahuzah*, Akiva Schiff served as its treasurer and then as its president. He was zealous in his love of *Eretz Yisrael* and *medinat Yisrael* and in his devotion to the enhancement of Torah learning for all youth in the Jewish homeland.

JOSEPH B. SOLOVEITCHIK

Rabbi Joseph Ber Soloveitchik, *zt"l*, was a towering intellect with unparalleled mastery of Judaic sources (particularly Talmud and Jewish philosophy), encyclopedic knowledge of secular subjects and general culture, and, in addition to Hebrew, Aramaic, Yiddish, and English, intimated comprehension of Greek, Latin, German, Russian, and Scandinavian languages and literature. He was a brilliant, exciting teacher, and an inspiring, captivating, fearless public orator and charismatic communicator.

The Rav, as he was lovingly known, was aptly referred to as a *gadol*. Indeed, he was a *gadol hador*, the scion of *gedolei hador* (see *Brachot* 63a). More than that, he was a *gadol olam*, as were his forebears. To be sure, he was a titan among giants whose persona embraced much more than the public qualities that made him a legend in his lifetime. He called himself a *melamed*, yet he was beyond a shadow of a doubt the outstanding Rosh Yeshiva of our times. The Rav was a *Gaon* who possessed an array of personal attributes – some well known, others less discernable. These qualities and notions will now be made public, as people who knew him will begin to ascribe to him those unique characteristics and concepts with which they were familiar. In this light, it is my privilege to respond to the request of the editors of the *Observer*, a not insignificant challenge, to share some of my personal remembrances of the Rav.

I first saw Rabbi Soloveitchik when he came to Boston as Rav in 1932, and, as a child of six, I remember the excitement associated with his arrival. I remember his visit two years later to the Beth El Hebrew School, the *Talmud Torah* of the Beth El Synagogue, one of the large congregations in which he served as Rav. There were no Jewish day schools in Boston at that time. The Beth El Hebrew School was an intensive, high-standard supplementary Jewish educational institution where students studied for a minimum of ten hours per week, exclusive of mandated junior congregation on Shabbat and special programs throughout the year. As an eight year old, I vividly recall his visit to my class, when an excited teacher accompanied by the principal, Mr. Tumaroff, introduced him to the students, after which the Rav engaged us in conversation for a very long time. I remember coming home that evening and telling my parents about the "big" rabbi who visited our class and made us feel so very good about *limudei kodesh*.

Moreover, he spoke to the pupils in clear, understandable English, unlike the older *rabbanim* in the community. In addition to visiting classes, one of the reasons the Rav would come to our school was to encourage the children in the graduating class to continue their Jewish education after they completed elementary school. Towards this end, the Rav organized a Hebrew High School at Beth El, which was eventually incorporated into the Prozdor of the Hebrew Teachers College in Roxbury. Years later, I learned from Mr. Sidney Hillson, principal in the late 1930s, that Rabbi Soloveitchik would visit Beth El in order to discuss ways of enhancing the curriculum.

Despite the scope and intensity of the Beth El Hebrew School program, the Rav realized the need for an all day Jewish school environment and an even more intensive Judaic Studies program for Jewish children in the Boston area. And, after overcoming the apathy and opposition of communal leaders and parents (the antagonism and resistance were severe), the Rav succeeded in 1937, as a young man of 34, five years after coming to Boston, to establish the co-ed Maimonides School in Roxbury. With the exception of the Hebrew Parochial School founded in Baltimore in 1917 (renamed Yeshiva Hafetz Hayim in 1933 in memory of the famed scholar Rabbi Israel Meir Kahohen of Radin, Lithuania, and now popularly know by the name Talmudic Academy), the Maimonides School was the first modern yeshiva in the United States established outside of New York City. It took no small amount of perspicacity, courage, leadership, perseverance, and the investment of much time and energy to launch Maimonides, now a major Jewish day elementary and high school.

The Rav took special interest in his new educational institution, which he visited regularly during the first three decades of its existence. The board of education of Maimonides was chaired diligently by his wife Tanya, until her untimely demise in 1967, and, since that time, by his daughter Atarah Twersky. The Rav's visits to Maimonides were moments he cherished. He was very proud of the school. Yet, he realized that its achievements were due largely to the efforts of the principal and teachers. He once told Rabbi Moses Cohn, long-time principal, "I get all the credit for all the work you do."

In founding Maimonides, the Rav made it crystal clear that girls would be given equal education opportunity. This decision was based upon his strongly held opinion that the *akeret habayit* was ever so crucial in raising the Jewish child, particularly in Western society. As such, every Jewish girl had to have a solid Judaic background. His feeling about the influential role of the mother (spouse) regarding the educational progress of children is supported by a variety of contemporary research studies in education.

The Rav felt deeply about developing an intelligent, educated Jewish laity, both male and female. He believed that women were no less endowed intellectually than men. Consequently, it behooved the Jewish community to provide girls with as excellent a Jewish education as possible.

Moreover, the Rav stressed that Jewish education for women was halachically appropriate and desirable. For these reasons he enthusiastically supported the founding of Stern College for Women and its Beit Midrash program and gave the opening *shiur* in the Beit Midrash in 1977.

Rabbi Soloveitchik's charismatic, oratorical artistry was beyond compare. He was able, via his vast command of Judaic-Hebraic literature, coupled with his incredible grasp of philosophy, mathematics, and other secular subjects, his penetrating insight into contemporary affairs and his perspicuity – to reach all levels of his audiences. As Rav in Boston, his base of operation was divided among a variety of synagogues: Roxbury, Dorchester, and Mattapan – contiguous communities populated by some 80,000 Jews. As a child, I often heard this area referred to as *Yerushalayim d'*America.

One of Rabbi Soloveitchik's main functions was giving *shiurim* before *minhah* on special Sabbaths, alternating among the various synagogues. Several friends and I in the *Hashomer Hadati* (now known as Bnei Akiva), would religiously follow him from shul to shul sitting attentively for two and three hours at a time.

We did not understand all that the Rav was saying (even though we were conversant in Yiddish) and, more often than not, understood very little, yet we were mesmerized by his *koach hahasbarah* – his remarkable ability to communicate, to elucidate and interpret – and we relished the fact that we were in the presence of a *gadol*.

The synagogues were all large – some with seating capacities for as many as 2,000 people. Many hundreds walked distances to attend the Rav's shiurim. He was able, without a microphone, to keep their rapt attention for the length of his lectures. On the podium, at each of his discourses, was a large stack of seforim to which he often referred. For the opening of one of his shiurim, which he always prepared diligently, he had copies of the New York Times and several local newspapers. To us, it seemed like a special happening. We were to be treated to an analysis of current events. To be sure, the Rav used this opportunity, in 1940, to address the United States government about the Nazi intentions and activity in Europe. His fiery words made such an incredible impression upon us. For months on end, during our weekly Hashomer Hadati sichot, we discussed anti-Semitism and the need for a Jewish homeland. Moreover, we organized a letter-writing campaign to the White House, which like other Jewish efforts, was to no avail at that time.

The Rav was committed to kashrut in the Jewish community of Boston. He was the *rav hamachshir* for Morrison and Schiff, the delicatessen factory founded by my grandfather. From my uncle and cousin, who headed Morrison and Schiff, I heard many stories of the Rav's strict application of kashrut laws.

When the Rav was invited to be the Rav of the Boston Jewish community, the *Va'ad Ha'ir* requested Morrison and Schiff to engage him as *rav hamachshir* to supplement his salary. As long as my grandfather was alive, Morrison and Schiff did not need a *mashgiah*. After he died in a tragic accident, the *Va'ad Ha'ir* and Morrison and Schiff decided that kashrut supervision would be in order. This happened at the time the Rav arrived in Boston.

Many years later, during the Rav's long tenure, from 1932 to

1980, as *rav hamachshir*, some of his friends thought he should give up the *hasgahah* at Morrison and Schiff since, they said, it was beneath his dignity. He refused because he didn't want people to think that there was something wrong with the kashrut of Morrison and Schiff. Moreover, he was grateful to Morrison and Schiff for hiring him when he needed the supplemental income and he enjoyed his relationship with the company.

In addition to the Rav, Morrison and Schiff engaged a *mashgiah temidi* to oversee the *sh'hitah* and the manufacture of the delicatessen. The Rav spoke regularly to the *mashgiah* who appreciated his guidance and prompt responses to questions he had.

Once a month, my cousin Joseph, who was an officer of Morrison and Schiff, and later its president, would drive the Rav to a Manchester, New Hampshire slaughterhouse where bull meat was prepared. During the one and one half hour trips, the Rav knowingly discussed an unusually wide variety of topics – mostly in Yiddish – with my cousin.

Generally, when Joseph came to pick up the Rav for the drive to Manchester, he would wait for the Rav to finish his daily fast reading of four or five newspapers. My cousin told me that very often there were "urgent" phone calls from all over the world, particularly from Israel and England and from rabbis in North America.

One morning, the Rav entered my cousin's car and said excitedly: "vos zogst due vegen di Red Sox" noting that he was amazed at the Red Sox performance that week.

One story, above all others, that my cousin related to me demonstrates the Rav's deep knowledge of the secular world and science and his amazing ability to grasp new scientific information.

The Rav knew that before joining Morrison and Schiff in executive capacity, Joseph served as chemical engineer in Oakridge, Tennessee, where research and experimentation with atomic energy took place in preparation for the atomic bomb. About seven years after World War II, during one of their trips to Manchester, the Rav asked Joseph to tell him about the procedure of creating atomic energy. Joseph was amazed at the Rav's knowledge and ability to grasp new scientific concepts. The Rav seemed most interested in the processing of new uranium 234–235, which was the only fissionable uranium, and readily engaged in conversation about the two processes of obtaining atomic energy – the electromagnetic method and the gaseous diffusion method. According to Joseph, the Rav demonstrated great eagerness to learn more about the production of atomic energy.

One morning in 1978, when my cousin came to pick up the Rav for their visit to Manchester, he noticed a limousine with diplomatic flags parked near the Rav's home in Brookline, Massachusetts and several police cars surrounding the limousine. The police on guard refused to let my cousin come near the Rav's house. After a fifteen-minute wait, from the distance, he saw an elderly gentleman and three younger men leave and enter the limousine. En route that day to Manchester, the Rav told Joseph that Menachem Begin had come to see him and asked him to become chief rabbi of Israel. The Rav was not eager to discuss the reasons for his refusal, but mentioned that he had many challenges to address in the United States.

Another story about the Rav reveals the depth of his concern and compassion for people particularly for former students. One day Joseph received an urgent telephone call from the Rav who was in New York for his weekly *shiurim* at the Rabbi Isaac Elchanan Theological Seminary. "Mr. Schiff, I understand that Morrison and Schiff used milk powder last month in the manufacture of cocktail frankfurters," he said rather heatedly in English. The Rav's information came from a former student, who, it appears, wanted "to score points" with the Rav. This former student worked at the Department of Agriculture and made a chemical analysis of Morrison and Schiff's delicatessen products. It turned out that his analysis was faulty and he was promptly fired by the Department of Agriculture for making a serious erroneous judgment and for communicating his findings to the public, which was against Department of Agriculture's policy. After hearing about the former student's termination, the Rav called my cousin and, in

Yiddish, asked him to do the Rav a favor. Could Joseph help the former student to regain his job at the Department of Agriculture? After all, the Rav said, he meant well and should be forgiven his unfortunate error. "I have *rahamanut* for him. This will destroy his professional status and earning power," the Rav explained.

One final observation about my cousin's intimate view of the Rav. The Rav was always immaculately dressed and groomed at a time when most *rabbanim* my cousin knew did not pay much attention to their attire and appearance.

I recall two incidents when I was a young child in the late 1930s involving the Rav in kashrut matters. I remember the Rav talking animatedly with my father, who supervised *hashgahah* for the Va'ad Ha'ir, about the fee levied on the kosher butcher shops for kashrut supervision. The Rav was complaining about the increasing difficulty to collect the annual fee from the thirty or so kosher establishments in Greater Boston. He wanted fervently to guarantee the continuation of kashrut supervision in Boston and wanted my father's help in this matter.

I remember, too, the Rav leading a demonstration against a butcher shop in the Grove Hall section of Roxbury, a densely populated Jewish area. I recall the Rav standing on a truck speaking out against the shop that claimed to be kosher but would not submit to kashrut supervision. The Rav told my father that he was personally involved because he wanted to insure that no other butcher shops would think of dropping communal *hashgahah*.

My brother recently told me a story about the Rav that speaks volumes about his sensitivity towards his wife Tanya. It involved a cousin of my brother's daughter-in-law who served for some time as the Rav's helper.

When the Rav grew older, during the days he would give *shiurim* in the Rabbi Elchanan Theological Seminary and stayed overnight in the YU dormitory, a yeshiva student would usually room with him as a helper. One evening, the Rav noticed that his helper got all dressed up. When the Rav inquired as to the reason, the yeshiva student told him that he was going out on a date. While they talked, the Rav noticed that the socks of the helper, who was seated during their conversation, were torn. The Rav suggested that he go to the Rav's dresser and use a pair of the Rav's socks. The helper did as the Rav recommended, returned to the Rav and told him that all the socks were white. The Rav smiled, acknowledged the fact that all his socks were white and told the yeshiva student that his wife had difficulty with colors and found it hard to pair his socks. In order to spare her the problem of sorting and pairing his socks he decided to wear white socks only.

When I was director of Graduate Jewish education and coordinator of undergraduate education programs at Yeshiva University in the 1960s, I would often discuss matters relating to Jewish educator training with the Rav. One thing stands out in my mind regarding these conversations. He emphasized the need for "excellent pedagogic preparation" for yeshiva and day school teachers on the primary, elementary and secondary school levels. He was equally emphatic about the importance of training qualified supervisors for Jewish schools. The Rav frequently said, given the sophisticated Western society in which Jewish schooling takes place and the kind of professional preparation teachers and principals in secular education receive, it is imperative for teachers and principals in Jewish schools to be trained according to the best principles and practices of education. He strongly advocated for the professionalization of Jewish educators.

In one of my long discussions with the Rav in 1976, at the request of Dr. Norman Lamm at the beginning of his presidency, about the Rav's feelings regarding proposals made by the President's commission appointed by Dr. Lamm, regarding the future of Yeshiva University, the Rav made many comments that revealed how avidly he felt about the Modern Orthodox Zionist way of life. The Rav was always much more at ease in his home. The first of our two discussions took place in Brookline. At the end of our meeting, the Rav said pointedly, "You didn't ask me what gave me the most *agmat nefesh*." I then asked this question. In his response, he spoke emotionally about the dissonance sometimes created by the post-high school Yeshiva experience of YU students in Israel. The Rav was very disheartened by the tension created by some of the children of his former students who, after returning from a year or two of study in Israel, rejected their family's religious views and practices. After all, he noted, these former students, Modern Orthodox Zionist *musmachim* were observant Jews and did not deserve such treatment from their progeny. He felt a kind of personal responsibility to his former students.

Besides being the epitome of Issachar (the Biblical-Talmudic personification of Torah learning and teaching), the Rav experienced the vantage point of Zevulun (the personal depiction of the support of Torah learning). He was a member of the initial Professional Advisory Committee of The Program Development Fund for Jewish Education (PDF), a cooperative enterprise sponsored by Joseph Gruss, and The Federation of Jewish Philanthropies of New York, which I was privileged to chair. Other members of the committee included Dr. Gerson Cohen. President of the Jewish Theological Seminary; Dr. Eugene Borowitz, professor of Jewish philosophy, Hebrew Union College-Jewish Institute of Religion; Dr. Isadore Twersky (the Rav's son-in-law), Nathan Littauer, professor of Hebrew Literature and Philosophy, Harvard University; Dr. Emanuel Rackman, Rabbi of the Fifth Avenue Synagogue and co-chair of The Program Development Fund; Mr. Sanford Solender, executive vice president, Federation of Jewish Philanthropies; Sol Litt, PDF chair; and Joseph Gruss, PDF benefactor. The committee met every six weeks in my office at the Board of Jewish Education of Greater New York for five years, 1973–78.

The Rav came punctually to the meetings, participated actively in our deliberations and helped guide the development of the Fund for Jewish Education in New York. His input was crucial in establishing allocation guidelines, which eventually led to the distribution of 90% of the funds to yeshivot and day schools in Greater New York. This was no mean accomplishment. The PDF and its successor organization, The Fund for Jewish Education (FJE) have distributed well over $200 million in support of Jewish education in Greater New York. (By 2001 over 400 million dollars had been distributed to schools in Greater New

York.) Overwhelmingly, the money was contributed by Mr. Gruss (via the Carolyn and Joseph Gruss Monument Fund), whose admiration for the Rav knew no bounds.

Two years prior to the official founding of PDF in 1973, Joseph Gruss challenged Federation to match a $100,000 contribution towards building repairs for yeshivot. After a group of Federation lay leaders responded to the challenge, which I presented to them on behalf of Mr. Gruss, the question arose, "How can we best allocate $200,000, a relatively small sum, to so many yeshivot crying for the support?" The Rav, Dr. Emanuel Rackman, and I met several times to develop criteria of eligibility and guidelines for the distribution of the funds. The success of the building repair program led to the establishment of PDF, and later the FJE.

During one of our visits with the Rav in Boston, Dr. Rackman and I were witness to his genius. The Rav realized that if the PDF program succeeded, there would be more support forthcoming to yeshivot from the same funding source. How right he was! A judgment he rendered was vital in determining how the funds would be spent. Only a mind and heart such as his could make such a recommendation. In discussing the physical facility needs of yeshivot, we determined that, in order of priority, grants should be awarded for removing hazardous conditions and Fire Department violations. In the first category, the Rav suggested that buses for the yeshivot in Brooklyn be included since they could be considered a *deerah ara-it, a temporary residence not unlike a succah*, and, therefore, qualify for a building grant. Traveling through unsafe streets in a rickety bus is a hazardous condition. The Rav knew full well that the beneficiaries of this recommendation would be Hasidic and right wing yeshivot whose leadership and rank and file did not support him and publicly opposed his views of Jewish life, especially his ardent support of Zionism and the State of Israel. Nevertheless, the Rav ruled that busses are a priority condition for building repair funding. Since that decision, made in 1971, millions of dollars have been expended on new busses for yeshivot.

Concerning the Rav's Zionist orientation, like the Netziv, his great grandfather who supported *Hibat Zion* from the beginning (in the last two decades of the 19th Century) and was a member of its executive, and like his great uncle Rabbi Meir Bar Ilan, a forceful leader of Mizrachi during the first half of the 20th Century, the Rav was personally involved in religious Zionism and served, since 1946, as honorary president of the Religious Zionists of America, and, since 1968, as honorary president of Mizrachi-Hapoel Mizrachi World Organization. As an ardent supporter of the State of Israel, he demonstrated his sympathies for, and strong support of, the State by receiving Israeli Prime Ministers, Presidents, and Chief Rabbis who paid their homage to him in Boston. Among other things, he observed *Yom Ha'atzmaut* by reciting Hallel.

On a personal level, I vividly recall the Rav's visits for *nihum aveilim* to my brother's home in Brookline, Massachusetts, where we sat *shiva* for our parents. Each time the Rav would visit, he would enter silently, take a seat near us and sit in absolute silence for a long period of time, epitomizing *va'yidom Aharon*, the silence of Aharon after the deaths of his sons, *Nadav* and *Abihu*. During each *shiva* visit, which he made in late afternoon, the Rav would sit silently and stare into space until it was time for the *Minhah* service in which he participated intensively.

One final observation about the Rav is in order. In my discussions with him about Yeshiva University's role in the American Jewish education scene, it was so apparent that he was fiercely loyal to YU, particularly since it embodied his philosophy of Judaism and was the only school of higher Jewish learning that guaranteed the implementation of his ideas regarding *Torah U'Mada*.

Rabbi Joseph ben Soloveitchik, *zt"l*, was the master artist and YU was his canvas. He was the master architect and YU was his blueprint.

NATHAN H. WINTER

It is a privilege to have been asked to pen an appreciation of a dear devoted colleague, Nat Winter.

Nat was a very special person combining the worlds of academia, practical education, and community service with great personal commitment, dignity, and professionalism. He was a true *Marbitz Torah*, always teaching, as he interacted with adults, lay leaders, rabbis, teachers, and youth.

Dr. Winter enterprisingly shepherded the Graduate Jewish Study and Jewish Education programs at New York University via a professorial chair as director of the Institute for Hebraic and Judaic Studies and as chairman of the Department of Hebrew Culture and Education. When I lectured for many summers in the Training Program for Community Education at NYU, sponsored jointly by the Council of Jewish Federations and Welfare Funds and the American Association for Jewish Education – which he skillfully directed – I observed Nat's unique administrative and instructional talents and his abiding commitment to Jewish education.

The Solomon Schechter movement in New Jersey owes its development and growth to Nat's idealism, energy, drive, and persistence. Similarly he was the driving force for the creation and support of the JTS Prozdor Hebrew High School programs in New Jersey.

Nat was a great motivator for developing new programs to meet emerging needs in the community as he guided lay leaders, rabbis, and educators. In our many meetings to discuss Jewish communal challenges, he demonstrated penetrating insight into problems and extraordinary ingenuity regarding responses to Jewish educational needs.

During a Jewish educational career that spanned fifty years, Nat spread his intellectual and practical educational wealth throughout the Jewish community via his inspirational leadership as synagogue educator, congregational school principal, educational consultant to the United Synagogue of Conservative Judaism, organizer of Jewish day schools, academic innovator, Jewish summer camp leader, and author.

Two generations of teachers and principals owe Nat their unqualified gratitude for educating them and inspiring them when they were his students and for guiding them in their professional careers.

And, two generations of lay leaders succeeded in their lay responsibility and lay roles because of Nat's enduring, paradigmatic professional leadership.

Nat was intolerably stubborn about doing the right thing in the right way for the sake of the Jewish community through quality Jewish education. He could not tolerate mediocrity. He was a man of enduring faith, exceedingly good judgment of people and ardent love of *K'lal Yisrael*. These personal qualities made it possible for him to succeed eminently on so many communal and educational fronts and contribute notably to the enhancement of Jewish life.

REFERENCES

REFERENCES

PART II – THE JEWISH COMMUNITY AND JEWISH EDUCATION

6. Jewish Life and Jewish Education in Contemporary Society: Challenge and Response.

Bock, G.E. "The Jewish Schooling of American Jews: A Study of Non-Cognitive Educational Effects," Diss. Harvard University, 1976.

Cohen, David. "Why Curriculum Doesn't Matter," *The New Leader*, Nov. 15, 1971.

Cohen, S.M. "The Impact of Jewish Education on Religious Identification and Practice," *Jewish Social Studies*, July-October, 1974.

Coleman, James S. and Campbell, Ernest o. *Equality of Educational Opportunity*. The U.S. Government Printing Office, Washington, DC, 1966.

Dushkin, A.M. and U.Z. Engelman. *Jewish Education in the United States*. New York: American Association for Jewish Education, 1959.

Fishman, Barak S. and Goldstein, A. *When They Are Grown They Will Not Depart: Jewish Education and the Jewish Behavior of American Adults*. Cohen Center for Modern Jewish Studies, Brandeis University, Waltham, MA, 1993.

Friedman, N. "The Graduates of Ramaz: Fifty Years of Jewish Day School Education." in Gurock, Jeffrey S. (ed.), *Ramaz: School, Community, Scholarship and Orthodoxy*, Ktav Publishing House, Hoboken, New Jersey, 1989.

Goldstein, A. and Fishman, S. Barak. *Teach Your Children When They Are Young: Contemporary Jewish Education in the United States*. Cohen Center for Modern Jewish Studies, Brandeis University, Waltham, MA, 1993.

Greeley, Andrew M. and Rossi, Peter H. *The Education of Catholic Americans*. Aldine Publishing Co., Chicago, 1966.

Hartman, E. "A Follow-up Study of Graduates of Selected Hebrew Elementary Schools." Diss. Memphis State University, 1976.

Heimowitz, J. "A Study of the Graduates of Yeshiva of Flatbush High School." Diss. Yeshiva University, 1979.

Himmelfarb, H. "The Non-Linear Impact of Schooling Comparing Different Types and Amounts of Jewish Education." *Sociology of Education*, Vol. 50, April 1977.

Horowitz, B. "The 1991 New York Jewish Population Study." United Jewish Appeal-Federation of Jewish Philanthropies of New York, 1993.

Isaacs, L. (ed.). "Trends: Report on Developments in Jewish Education for Community Leadership." Jewish Education Service of North America, 1992.

JCCA, COMJEE II: *Task Force on Reinforcing the Effectiveness of Jewish Education in JCCs.* Commission on Maximizing Jewish Educational Effectiveness of JCCs, New York, 1995.

Kosmin, B., S. Goldstein, J. Waksberg, N. Larer, A. Keysar and J. Scheckner. "Highlights of the CJF 1990 National Jewish Population Survey." Council of Jewish Federations, New York, 1991.

Laufer, Nathan. Conversation with the President of the Wexner Heritage Foundation Lay Leadership Program, Dec. 24, 1995.

Lipset, S. "Education Findings from The Jewish Population Study." Council of Initiatives in Jewish Education, n.d.

Mayer, E. "Letter to the Editor." *Jewish Week*, November 13–19, 1992.

McMillan, M.M. and E. Gerald. "Characteristics of Private Schools." E.D. Tabs., National Center for Educational Statistics, Washington, DC, April 1990.

Nissenbaum, Yitzchak. "Imrei Drush." in Simon Federbush, *Halashon Ha'Ivrit B'Yisrael U'Va-amim*, Mosad Harav Kook, Jerusalem, 1967.

Perspectives Resources Inc. *An Exploratory Study of Attitudes Toward Formal Jewish Education.* UJA Federation, New York, 1979.

Pinchuk, Miri. Interview with Director, Ulpan Center, New York, May 1994.

Pinsky, I. "A Follow-up Study of Graduates of One of the Oldest Existing American Jewish Day Schools: The Rabbi Jacob Joseph School." Diss. Yeshiva University, 1961.

Pollak, G. "The Graduates of the Jewish Day Schools, a Follow-up Study." Diss. Case Western University, 1961.

Ribner, S. "Study of the Effects of Intensive Jewish Secondary Education on Adult Lifestyles." American Association for Jewish Education, 1977.

Rimor M. and E. Katz. "Jewish Involvement of the Baby Boom Generation." Louis Guttman Israel Institute of Applied Social Research, Jerusalem, November 1993.

Schiff, A.I. *The Jewish Day School in America.* Jewish Education Committee Press, New York, 1966.

Schiff, A.I. "Jewish Education: Problems, Prospects and the Challenge." *Jewish Education*, vol. 45, No. 4, 1981.

Schiff, A.I. "Jewish Supplementary Schooling: A System in Need of Change." BJE of Greater New York, 1988.

Schiff, A.I. "Jewish Continuity through Whom? A Message to American Jewish Communal Leadership," in *Journal of Jewish Education*, Spring 1994.

Schiff, A. I. and Mareleyn Schneider. *Jewishness Quotient of Day School Graduates.* Yeshiva University, New York, April 1994.

Schiff, A.I. *Far-Reaching Effects of Extensive Jewish Day School Attendance.* Yeshiva University, New York, July 1994.

Schiff, A.I. *Fortifying and Restoring Jewish Behavior: The Interaction of Home and School.* Yeshiva University, New York, October 1994.

Schoem, D. "Ethnic Survival in America: Ethnography of a Jewish Afternoon School." Diss. University of California, Berkeley, 1979.

Shapiro, Z. "From Generation to Generation: Does Jewish Schooling Affect Identification." Diss. New York University, 1988.

7. Creating the Jewish Future: Insuring Effective Jewish Education.

Bloom, Benjamin. *Developing Talent in Young People.* New York: Ballantine Books, 1985.

Bock, Geoffrey. "The Jewish Schooling of America Jews: A Study of Non-Cognitive Educational Effects." Dissertation, Harvard University, 1976.

Cohen, David. "Why Curriculum Doesn't Matter." *The New Leader* 54:22, November 15, 1971.

Coleman, James. *Equality of Educational Opportunity.* Washington, DC: Office of Education, 1966.

Comer, J.P., N.M. Haynes, E.T. Joyner, and M. Ben-Avie, eds. *Rallying the Whole Village.* New York: Teachers College, Columbia University, 1996.

Greeley, Andrew M. and Peter H. Rossi. *The Education of Catholic Americans.* Chicago: Aldine, 1966, p. 145.

Heschel, Abraham. *The Prophets.* Philadelphia: Jewish Publication Society, 1962.

Kosmin, Barry, Sidney Goldstein, et. al. "Highlights of the CJF National Jewish Population Survey." Council of Jewish Federations, New York, 1991.

Schiff, Alvin. "The Jewish Family and the Jewish School." *Amit Woman* 59:3, Jan. / Feb., 1987.

———. *The Jewish Supplementary School – A System in Need of Change.* The Board of Jewish Education of Greater New York, 1988.

———. *The Mystique of Hebrew.* New York: Shengold Publishers, 1996.

Schiff, Alvin I. and Mareleyne Schneider. "The Jewishness Quotient of Jewish Day School Graduates: Fortifying and Restoring Jewish Behavior: The Interaction of Home and School." Research Report 3, Yeshiva University, New York, 1994.

10. Educational Issues in Jewish Identity.

Bock, G.E. "The Jewish Schooling of American Jews: A Study of Non-Cognitive Educational Effects." Diss. Harvard University, 1976.

Buchwald, E. Interview with Director of National Jewish Outreach Program, CIJE (1995) Current Activities. Council for Initiatives in Jewish Education, May, 1994.

Cohen, S.M. "The Impact of Jewish Education on Religious Identification and Practice." *Jewish Social Studies*, July-October, 1974.

Coleman, J.S. & Campbell. E.Q. *Equality of Educational Opportunity.* Washington, DC: The US Government Printing Office, 1966.

Diament, C. Communication from Office of the National Jewish Education Director. Hadassah, June, 1994.

Duskin, A.M. & Engelman. U.Z. *Jewish Education in the United States.* New York: American Association for Jewish Education, 1959.

Fishman, B.S. & Goldstein, A. "When They Are Grown They Will Not Depart: Jewish Education and the Jewish Behavior of American Adults." Cohen Center for Modern Jewish Studies, Brandeis University, Waltham, MA, 1991.

Friedman, N. "The Graduates of Ramaz: Fifty Years of Jewish Day School Education."

Jeffrey S. Gurock, editor. *Ramaz: School, Community, Scholarship and Orthodoxy.* Ktav Publishing House, Hoboken, New Jersey, 1989.

Geffen, P.A. & Levenberg. J.A. *Israel Experience Youth Programs*. The CRB Foundation, Hoboken, New Jersey, ND.

Goldstein, A. & Fishman, S.B. *Teach Your Children When They Are Young: Contemporary Jewish Education in the United States*. Cohen Center for Modern Jewish Studies, Brandeis University, Waltham, MA, 1989.

Golinkin, N. Communication from Director of Hebrew Library Publications, Inc., 1964.

Gordon, M. *Assimilation in American Life*. New York: Oxford University Press, 1964.

Greeley, A.M. & Rossi, P.H. *The Education of Catholic Americans*. Chicago: Aldine Publishing Co., 1966.

Hartman, E. "A Follow-up Study of Graduates of Selected Hebrew Elementary Schools." Diss. Memphis State University, 1976.

Heimowitz, J. "A Study of the Graduates of Flatbush Yeshiva High School." Diss. Yeshiva University.

Himmelfarb, H. "The Non-Linear Impact of Schooling Comparing Different Types and Amounts of Jewish Education." *Sociology of Education*. April 1977, Vol. 50.

Horowitz B. *The 1991 New York Jewish Population Study*. United Jewish Appeal Federation of Jewish Philanthropies of New York, 1993.

Isaacs, I., (ed.). *Trends: Report on Developments in Jewish Education or Community Leadership*. Jewish Education Service of North America, 1992.

JCCA, COMJEE II, "Task Force on Reinforcing the Effectiveness of Jewish Education in JCCS." Commission on Maximizing Jewish Educational Effectiveness of JCCS, New York, 1995.

Kosmin, B., Goldstein, S., Waksberg, J., Lerer, N., Keysar, A. & Scheckner, J. "Highlights of the CJE 1990 National Jewish Population Survey." Council for Jewish Federations, New York, 1991.

Laufer, N. Conversation with the President of the Wexner Heritage Foundation Lay Leadership Program, December 1995.

Lipseet, S. Education Findings From the Jewish Population Study, Council of Initiatives in Jewish Education, ND.

Mayer, E. Letter to the Editor, *Jewish Week*, November 13–19, 1992.

McMillan, M.M., & Gerald, E. "Characteristics of Private Schools." E.D. Tabs, National Center for Educational Statistics, Washington, DC, 1990.

Nissenbaum, Y. "Imrei Drush." in Simon Federbush, *Halashon Ha'Ivrit B'Yisrael U'vaamim*, Mosad Harav Kook, Jerusalem, 1967.

Perspectives Resources Inc. "An Exploratory Study of Attitudes Toward Formal Jewish Education." UJA Federation, New York, 1979.

Pinchuk, M. Interview with Director, Ulpan Center, New York, May 1994.

Pinsky, I. "A Follow-up Study of Graduates of One of the Oldest Existing American Jewish Day Schools, The Rabbi Jacob Joseph School." Diss. Yeshiva University, New York, 1961.

Pollack, G. "The Graduates of the Jewish Day Schools: A Follow-up Study." Diss. Case Western University, 1961.

Ribner, S. *Study of the Effects of Intensive Jewish Secondary Education on Adult Lifestyles*. American Association for Jewish Education, New York, 1977.

Rimor, M. and E. Katz. *Jewish Involvement of the Baby Boom Generation*. The Louis Guttman Israel Institute of Applied Social Research, Jerusalem, 1993.

Rosenbaum, Y. Communication from Program Director, National Jewish Outreach Program, 1994.
Schiff, A.I. *The Jewish Day School in America*. New York: Jewish Education Committee Press, 1966.
Schiff, A.I. "Jewish Education: Problems, Prospects and the Challenge." *Jewish Education*, Vol. 45, No. 4, 1981.
Schiff, A.I. "Jewish Supplementary Schooling: A System in Need of Change." BJE of Greater New York, 1988.
Schiff, A.I. "Jewish Continuity Through Whom? A Message to American Jewish Communal Leadership." *Journal of Jewish Education*, 1994.
Schiff, A.I. and M. Schneider. *Jewishness Quotient of Day School Graduates*. New York: Yeshiva University, 1994.
Schiff, A.I. *Far Reaching Effects of Extensive Jewish Day School Attendance*. New York: Yeshiva University, 1994.
Schiff, A.I. "Fortifying and Restoring Jewish Behavior: The Interaction of Home and School." Yeshiva University, October 1994.
Schneider, M. *History of a Jewish Burial Society: An Examination of Secularization*. San Francisco: Mellen Research University Press, 1991.
Schoem, D. "Ethnic Survival in America: Ethnography of a Jewish Afternoon School." Diss. University of California, Berkeley, 1979.
Shapiro, Z. "From Generation to Generation: Does Jewish Schooling Affect Jewish Identification." Diss. New York University, 1988.
Spack, E. Written Communication from Executive Director of the Conference for the Advancement of Jewish Education, 1995.
The Jewish Week, Advertisement, "1,000,000 Jews Can Now Be Rescued Right Here in North America." November 6–12, 1992.
Wassertzug, M. *The Teaching of Hebrew at the Jewish Community Center*. The JC of Greater Washington, Washington DC, 1993.

PART III – ON JEWISH ALL DAY EDUCATION
3. What Research Says About the Jewish Day School – Doctoral Dissertations 1970–1990.

Aronowitz, Michael Weinronk. "Adjustment of Immigrant Children (ages 6–15) in School as a Function of Parental Attitudes Toward Social Change and New Experience: A Study of Soviet Jewish Families in San Francisco." Diss. University of California, 1985.
Berdugo, Yehuda. "The Design, Implementation and Evaluation of a Theme-Centered Interaction Program for Adolescents in a Jewish Day School." Diss. University of Pittsburgh, 1979.
Bernstein, David. "Two Approaches to the Teaching of Jewish History in Orthodox Yeshiva High Schools." Diss. New York University, 1986.
Deitcher, Howard. "Rites of Passage: An Instructional Guide for High School Teachers." Diss. Yeshiva University, 1985.
Elimelech, Haim. "Causal Factors for the Termination of Day School Principals." Diss. Yeshiva University, 1988.
Feuerman, Chaim. "A Study of the Views of Principal Role in Elementary Orthodox

Hebrew Day Schools in the New York City Area: Expectations Held by Principals and Their Lay Board Chairmen." Diss. St. John's University, 1977.

Finkelstein, Eleanor. "A Study of Female Role Definitions in a Yeshiva High School." Diss. New York University, 1980.

Flatto, Zehava. "Role Congruency and Job Satisfaction of Principals in Jewish Day Schools." Diss. Yeshiva University, 1978.

Freid, Irving. "Trends and Issues in Hebrew Day Schools." Diss. Ohio State University, 1973.

Freidman, Jerome. "A Comparison of Moral Reasoning Stages Among Jewish Day School and Public School Students." Diss. Harvard University, 1987.

Freidman, Seymour. "The Effect of Jewish Religious Education on the Moral Reasoning and Social Interest of Yeshiva High School Students." Diss. Fordham University, 1983.

Gans, Murray Z. "Parent and Educator Ratings of Goals of Jewish Day Schools." Diss. University of Colorado, 1986.

Gladstein, Sally Sara. "Teachers' Mainstreaming In-service Priorities in Jewish Elementary Day Schools." Diss. Yeshiva University, 1986.

Grant, Arnold. "The Perceptions of High School Students Toward Career Education Needs." Diss. Yeshiva University, 1983.

Gutman, Renee H. "Longitudinal Study of Hebrew and English Reading Abilities in 5–7 Year Old Hebrew Day School Students." Diss. City University of New York, 1990.

Hartman, Eliyahu. "A Follow-up Study of Selected Hebrew Elementary Education Institutions." Diss. Memphis State University, 1976.

Heimowitz, Joseph. "A Study of the Graduates of the Yeshiva of Flatbush High School." Diss. Yeshiva University, 1979.

Jordan, Cecile Blank. "Perception of Role Conflict Problems Reported by Heads of Selected Private Schools: The Solomon Schechter Schools in North America." Diss. University of Houston, 1983.

Kaunfer, Alvan H. "Teaching Midrash in the Conservative Day School: A Rationale and Curriculum Proposal." Diss. Jewish Theological Seminary, 1989.

Kramer, Daniel. "History and Impact of Torah Umesorah and Hebrew Day Schools in America." Diss. Yeshiva University, 1977.

Kupinsky, Bonnie. "The Relationship of Visual Perception to Beginning Bilingual Reading Instruction in English and Hebrew." Diss. Wayne State University, 1981.

Langsam, Naftali. "Principal Personality Style and Organizational Goal Achievement in the Hebrew Day School." Diss. Fordham University, 1980.

Lasko, Samuel. "A Study of the Relationship of Demographic Variables of Jewish Day School Administrators and Coping Techniques Utilized with Different Stressors." Diss. University of Maryland, 1986.

Marks, Linda. "Analysis of Meet-and-Confer and Collective Bargaining as a Practice in Chicago Area Hebrew Day Schools." Diss. Loyola University of Chicago, 1990.

Melitz, Amram. "Metacognition Reading Theories and Learning Strategies in Torah Study." Diss. Jewish Theological Seminary, 1990.

Messinger, Howard. "A Dinim Curriculum: Content and Methodology." Diss. Yeshiva University, 1981.

Orlow, Eva. "The Factors in Reading Achievement in Hebrew and English of Third Grade Students." Diss. Temple University, 1977.

Parsons, Sanford. "The Role of Faivel Mendelowitz in the Founding and Development of Hebrew Day Schools in the United States." Diss. New York University, 1983.

Ravin, Noach. "The Effects of Individuals and Job Characteristics on Job Satisfaction of Supplementary and Hebrew Day School Teachers." Diss. American University, 1981.

Rosenthal, Stephen. "An Analysis of Factors Affecting the Mobility of Private Non-Orthodox Jewish Day School Directors." Diss., University of San Francisco, 1987.

Schacter, Lifsa. "The Professional Growth of Teachers: A Case Study in Staff Development in a Jewish Day School." Diss. Jewish Theological Seminary, 1986.

Schwartz, Sheldon. "The Teaching of a Hebrew Samuel I Curriculum." Diss. Yeshiva University, 1968.

Segall, Bernard. "Language and Self-Identity Among a Sample of Jewish Families of Day School Students." Diss. University of Colorado, 1989.

Shapiro, Zvi. "From Generation to Generation: Does Jewish Schooling Affect Jewish Identification?" Diss. New York University, 1988.

Shudofsky, Noam. "The Nature and Role of Guidance in Jewish All day Senior High Schools." Diss. Yeshiva University, 1977.

Sivan, Tamar. "Kindergarten Language Perceptual Factors as Predictors of Third Grade Hebrew and English Reading Comprehension Among Jewish Day School Students." Diss. Jewish Theological Seminary, 1984.

Skoff, Benson. "Tax Funds for Jewish Education: Presentation and Analysis of Varying Jewish Views 1947–74." Diss. Washington University, 1975.

Smiley, Mark S. "Adopting New Means In Education: A Case Study of Computer Applications in a Rabbinic Curriculum in a Jewish Day School." Diss. Jewish Theological Seminary, 1988.

Solomon, Bennet, "Curricular Integration in the Jewish All day School in the United States." Diss. Harvard University, 1979.

Well, Harvey, "Finances and the Jewish Day School: An Analysis of the Relationship of Teacher, Instructional and Per-Pupil Cost to Scholastic Achievement." Diss. Loyola University of Chicago, 1975.

4. What We Know About the Jewish Day Schools (in 1990).

Adams, L.J., Frankel, J. & Newbauers, N. "Parental Attitudes Toward the Jewish All day School." *Jewish Education*, 42(1).

Aron, I. and Phillips, B. Findings of the Los Angeles Teacher Census, Paper presented at the Fourth Annual Conference of the Network for Research in Jewish Education, New York, NY, June 1990.

Bloom, B. *Developing Talent in Young People*. New York: Ballantine Books, 1985.

Bock, G. "The Jewish Schooling of American Jews: A Study of Non-Cognitive Effects." Unpublished Diss. Harvard University, Cambridge, MA, 1976.

Cohen, D. "Why Curriculum Doesn't Matter." *The New Leader*, November 1971.

Cohen, S.M. "The Impact of Jewish Education on Religious Identification and Practice." *Jewish Social Studies*, July-October 1974, p. 36.

Coleman, J.S. and E.Q. Campbell. *Equality of Educational Opportunity*. U.S. Department of Health, Education and Welfare, Washington DC, 1966.

Dinin, S. "The All Day School." *The Reconstructionist*, October 5, 1945.

Dubb, A.E. and S. DellaPergola. "First Census of Jewish Schools in the Diaspora,

1981/82, 1982/83: United States of America." Research Report No. 4, Project for Education Statistics, The Hebrew University, Jerusalem, and Jewish Educational Service of North America, New York, 1986.

Flatto, Z. "Role Congruency and Job Satisfaction of Principals in Jewish Day Schools." Unpublished Diss. Yeshiva University, New York, 1978.

Feuerman, H. "A Study of the Views of Principal Role in Elementary Orthodox Hebrew Day Schools in New York City Area: Expectations Held by Principals and their Lay Board Chairmen." Unpublished Diss. St. John's University, New York, 1977.

Gans, M.Z. "Parent and Educator Ratings of Goals of Jewish Day Schools." Unpublished Diss. University of Colorado, Denver, 1986.

Greeley, A.M. and P.M. Rossi. *The Education of Catholic Americans*. Aldine Publishing Co., Chicago, 1966.

Hartman, E. "A Follow-up Study of Selected Hebrew Elementary Education Institutions." Unpublished Diss. Memphis State University, Memphis, TN, 1976.

Heimowitz, J. "A Study of the Graduates of Flatbush Yeshiva High School." Unpublished Diss. Yeshiva University, New York, 1979.

Helmreich, W.B. *The World of the Yeshiva: An Intimate Portrait of Orthodox Jewry*. New York: Free Press, 1982.

Himmelfarb, H.S. "The Non-Linear Impact of Schooling: Comparing Different Types and Amounts of Jewish Education." *Sociology of Education*, April 1977, p. 50.

Himmelstein, S. "A Comparative Study of Teacher Satisfactions and Dissatisfactions Between Teachers in Selected Jewish Day Schools and Teachers in New York." Unpublished Diss. Columbia University, New York, 1975.

Jencks, C., Smith, M., Acland, H., Bane, M.J., Cohen, D., Gintis, H., Heyna, B. & Michelson, S. *Inequality: A Reassessment of the Effect of Family and Schooling in America*. New York:Basic Books, 1972.

JESNA, *Trends*, Winter 1985, No. 9.

Jordan, C.B. "Perception of Role Conflict Problems Reported by Heads of Selected Private Schools: The Solomon Schechter Schools in North America," Unpublished Diss. University of Houston, 1983.

Kapel, D. "Parental Views of a Jewish Day School," *Jewish Education*, Spring 1972, Vol. 41, p. 3.

Kelman, S.L. "Motivation and Goals: Why Parents Send Their Children to Non-Orthodox Day Schools." *Jewish Education*, Spring 1979, Vol. 47 (1).

Kramer, D. "History and Impact of Torah Umesorah and Hebrew Day Schools in America," Unpublished Diss. Yeshiva University, New York, 1977.

Lasker, A.A. "Parents as Partners: Report of a Research Project." *Impact*, (35) Winter 1976–77.

Lazar, M. "Religious Academic Achievement of Boys and Girls of Hebrew Orthodox Day Schools as related to Selected Variables." Unpublished Diss. St. Louis University, St. Louis, 1969.

Lebovitz, G. "Satisfaction and Dissatisfaction Among Judaic Studies Teachers in Midwestern Jewish Day Schools." Unpublished Diss. University of Cincinnati, 1981.

Lewisohn, L. "The American Jew, Character and Destiny," Farrar Strauss and Company, New York, 1950.

Liebman, N. "Federation Allocations to Jewish Education 1985–1989." Council of Jewish Federations, Research Department, December 1990.

McMillan, M.M. and E. Gerald. "Characteristics of Private Schools: 1987–88." *E.D. Tabs*, National Center for Education Statistics, Washington DC, April 1990.

Nulman, L. "The Reaction of Parents to a Jewish All day School." Unpublished Diss. University of Pittsburgh, 1955.

Parsons, S., "The Role of Faivel Mendelovitz in the Founding and Development of Hebrew Day Schools in the United States." Unpublished Diss. New York University, New York.

Pollak, C. & Lang, C. "Budgetary and Financing in Jewish Day Schools – Does it Exist?" *Jewish Education*, 1984, 52(2).

Ravin, N. "The Effect of Individual and Job Characteristics on Job Satisfaction of Supplementary and Hebrew Day Schools' Hebrew Teachers." Diss. The American University, Washington, DC, 1981.

Rosenthal, S. "An Analysis of Factors Affecting the Mobility of Private Non-Orthodox Jewish Day School Directors." Unpublished Diss. University of San Francisco, San Francisco, 1987.

Schiff, A.I. *The Jewish Day School in America*. New York: Jewish Educational Committee Press, 1966.

Schiff, A.I. "Jewish Day Schools in the United States." *Encyclopedia Judaica Year Book*,. Keter Publishing House, Jerusalem, 1974.

Schiff, A.I. "Jewish Education at the Crossroads: The State of Jewish Education." The Joint Program for Jewish Education, in Conjunction with CJF, JWB, and JESNA, New York and Jerusalem, March 1983.

Schiff, A.I. "On the Status of Jewish All day Education." *Jewish Education*. Spring 1983, 51.

Schiff, A.I. "The American Jewish Day School – Retrospect and Prospect." *Pedagogic Report*, 1987, 38(3).

Schiff, A.I. *Jewish Supplementary Schooling in Greater New York: An Educational System in Need of Change*. New York: Board of Jewish Education, 1988.

Schiff, A.I. and Kessel, B. *Jewish Education in Greater New York: Comparative Demographic Report 1970–1990*. New York: Board of Jewish Education, 1991.

Shapiro, Z. "From Generation to Generation: Does Jewish Schooling Affect Jewish Identification?" Unpublished Diss. New York University, New York, 1988.

Solomon, B. "Curricula Integration in the Jewish All Day School in the United States," Unpublished Diss. Harvard University, Cambridge, MA, 1979.

Well, H.A. "Finances and the Jewish Day School: An Analysis of the Relationship of Teacher Instructional and per Pupil Costs to Scholastic Achievement." Unpublished Diss. Loyola University, Chicago, 1975.

Zeldin, M. "In Yesterday's Shadow: Case Study of the Development of a Jewish Day School," presented at the Fourth Annual Conference of the Network for Research in Jewish Education, New York, NY.

Note:

Nationally, the majority of Orthodox day schools and yeshivot have a relationship with Torah Umesorah (The National Society for Hebrew Day Schools). Most modern/centrist Orthodox day schools and yeshivot are affiliated with Yeshiva University's Max Stern Division of Communal Service via the Association of Modern Orthodox Day Schools (AMODS). Conservative day schools are affiliated with the Solomon Schechter School movement of the United Synagogue of America. The Reform day schools are organized as PARDES – the Progressive Association of Reform Day Schools – an affiliate of the Union of American Hebrew Congregations. In 1986, the transideological, pluralistic day schools, which significantly grew in numbers during the 1960s and 1970s were organized into the Jewish Community Day School Network, RAVSAK.

5. The Jewish Day School (in 1987) Looks to the Next Half Century.

Boch, Geoffrey, in his study, "Does Jewish Education Matter, Jewish Education and Jewish Identity New York," American Jewish Committee, 1977, has indicated that the threshold for Jewish school impact is 1,000 hours.

Himmelfarb, Harold S. "The Impact of Religious Schooling: The Effects of Jewish Education Upon Adult Religious Involvement." Unpublished Diss. University of Chicago, 1974.

6. On the Need for Moral Education in the Jewish Day School.

Cohen, David. "Why Curriculum Doesn't Matter." *The New Leader.* Nov. 15, 1971.

Coleman, James. "Equality of Educational Opportunity," Office of Education, U.S. Department of Health, Education and Welfare, Washington, DC 1966.

Combs, Arthur. *Myths of Education.* Boston: Allyn and Bacon, 1979.

Jencks, Christopher. *Inequality, A Reassessment of the Effect of Family and Schooling in America.* New York: Basic Books, 1972.

Lawrence, Jacob. Statement made at the New York State Board of Regents and State Education Department Bicentennial Convocation, 1986.

7. The Jewishness Quotient of Day School Graduates: The Effect of Jewish Education on Adult Behavior.

Bock, Geoffrey B. "The Jewish Schooling of American Jews: A Study of Non-Cognitive Educational Effects." Diss. Harvard University, 1976.

Cohen, Steven M. "The Impact of Jewish Education on Religious Identification and Practice." *Jewish Social Studies.* July-October 1974.

Dushkin, Alexander M. and Uriah Z. Engelman. *Jewish Education in the United States.* American Association for Jewish Education, New York, 1959.

Fishman, Sylvia B. and Alice Goldstein. *When They Are Grown They Will Not Depart: Jewish Education and the Jewish Behavior of American Adults.* Cohen Center for Modern Jewish Studies, Brandeis University, Waltham, MA, 1993.

Friedman, Natalie. "The Graduates of Ramaz: Fifty Years of Jewish Day School Education." in Jeffrey S. Gurock, editor, *Ramaz: School, Community, Scholarship and Orthodoxy.* Ktav Publishing House, 1989.

Gordon, Milton. *Assimilation in American Life.* New York: Oxford University Press, 1964.

Hartman, Emanuel. "A Follow-up Study of Graduates of Selected Hebrew Elementary Schools." Diss. Memphis State University, 1976.

Heimowitz, Joseph. "A Study of the Graduates of Flatbush Yeshiva High School." Diss. Yeshiva University, 1979.

Himmelfarb, Harold. "The Impact of Religious Schooling: The Effect of Jewish Education Upon Adult Religious Involvement." Diss. University of Chicago, 1974.

Himmelfarb, Harold. "The Non-Linear Impact of Schooling: Comparing Different

Types and Amounts of Jewish Education," *Sociology of Education*, April 1977, Volume 50.

Lipset, Seymour. "Education Findings from the Jewish Population Study." Council of Initiatives in Jewish Education, n.d.

Lookstein, Joseph. "True Integration." *Jewish Education*, Winter 1978.

Mayer, Egon. Letter to the Editor, *Jewish Week*, November 13–19, 1992.

McMillan and E. Gerald. "Characteristics of Private Schools: 1987–88." E.D. Tabs National Center for Educational Statistics, Washington, DC, April 1990.

National Jewish Population Survey, Council of Jewish Federations, 1990.

Pinsky, Irving. "A Follow-up Study of Graduates of one of the Oldest Existing American Jewish Day Schools: The Rabbi Jacob Joseph School," Diss. Yeshiva University, 1961.

Pollak, George. "The Graduates of The Jewish Day Schools: A Follow-up Study." Diss. Case Western University, 1961.

Ribner, Sol. *Study of the Effects of Intensive Jewish Secondary Education on Adult Lifestyles*. New York: American Association for Jewish Education, 1977.

Rimor, Mordechai and Elihu Katz. *Jewish Involvement in the Baby Boom Generation*. Jerusalem: The Louis Guttman Israel Institute of Applied Social Research, November 1993.

Schiff, Alvin I. *The Jewish Day School in America*. New York: Jewish Education Committee Press, 1966.

Schiff, Alvin I. "Jewish Education at the Crossroads: The State of Jewish Education." New York, Jerusalem, The Joint Program for Jewish Education in Conjunction with CJF, JWB and JESNA, 1983.

Schiff, Alvin I. "Jewish Supplementary Schooling: A System in Need of Change." BJE of Greater New York, 1988.

Schoem, David. "Ethnic Survival in America: Ethnography of a Jewish Afternoon School" Diss. University of California, Berkley, 1979.

Shapiro, Zvi. "From Generation to Generation: Does Jewish Schooling Affect Jewish Identification," Diss. New York University, 1988.

The Jewish Week, Advertisement, "1,000,000 Jews Can Now Be Rescued Right Here in North America," November 6–12, 1992.

Trends, Jewish Service of North America, Fall 1992.

8. The Case of the Jewish Day School (in 1997) in Light of the Debate on School Choice.

Fishman, Sylvia B. and Alice Goldstein. *When They Are Grown They Will Not Depart: Jewish Education and the Jewish Behavior of American Adults*. Cohen Center for Modern Jewish Studies, Brandeis University, Waltham, MA, 1993.

Fox, Marvin. "Day Schools and the American Educational Pattern." *The Jewish Parent*, 1953.

Lookstein, Joseph. "The Jewish Day School." *Jewish Schools in America*, American Association for Jewish Education, New York, 1946.

Rimor, Mordechai and Elihu Katz. *Jewish Involvement in the Baby Boom Generation*. Jerusalem: The Louis Guttman Israel Institute of Applied Social Research, November 1993.

Schiff, Alvin I. and MareleyneSchneider. *The Jewishness Quotient of Day School Gradu-*

ates: *The Effect of Day School Education on Adult Behavior.* New York: Yeshiva University, 1944.

10. Post-Yeshiva Jewish Day High School Programs for American Students in Israel.

Berger, Shalom. "A Year of Study in Israeli Yeshiva Programs: Before and After." Diss. Azrieli Graduate School, Yeshiva University 1997.

Bernstein, D., "Perspectives from Abroad: Continuing the Dialogue." *Ten Da'at* 6:24–25, 1992.

Blau, Yosef, "Torah Study for Men in Israel." *Ten Da'at* 2:30, 1988.

Goldmintz, J. "The Post-High School Yeshiva Experience: Goals and Benefits." *Ten Da'at* 5:32–34, 1991.

Kupchick, Abraham, "Focus on Study in Israel." *Ten Da'at*, 5, 32–33, 1987.

Martila and Kiley, Inc. Highlights from a Survey of Yeshiva College Undergraduates about

College Recruitment, New York, 1993.

Tobin, Dodi F. "Parent-Child Relationships in the Context of a Year of Study in a Post-High

School Yeshiva Program in Israel," Fellows 1999–2000.

Waxman, Chaim I. "In the End Is It Ideology? – Religio-cultural and Structural Factors in American *Aliya*." *Contemporary Judaism*, 16: 50–67, 1995.

PART IV – ON JEWISH SUPPLEMENTARY SCHOOLING AND JEWISH FAMILY EDUCATION

1. The Synagogue and Jewish Education in Historical Perspective

Morris, Nathan. *The Jewish School.* New York: The Jewish Education Committee Press, 1964.

Asaf, Simhah. "*Mekorot Letoldot Hahinukh*," Dvir, Tel Aviv, Volume 1.

4. The Jewish Supplementary School – A System in Need of Change.

Cohen, David. "Why Curriculum Doesn't Matter." *The New Leader*, November 15, 1971.

Coleman, James S. *Equality of Educational Opportunity.* Washington, DC: US Government Printing Office, 1966.

Glatzer, Shoshana. "Coming of Age as a Jew." Board of Jewish Education of Greater New York, 1989.

Greeley, Andrew M. and Peter H. Rossi. *The Education of Catholic Americans.* Chicago: Aldine Publishing Co., 1966.

Jencks, Christopher. *Inequality: A Reassessment of the Effect of Family and Schooling in America.* New York: Basic Books, 1972.

Segal, Abraham. "The Road to Learning in Celebration of the Founding of the Union of American Hebrew Congregations," *Jewish Book Annual*, UAHC, New York, 1972–73, Vol. 30.

Schiff, Alvin I. "The Jewish Family in Socio-Educational Perspective," *Jewish Education*, Summer-Winter 1989, 57 (2–4).

Schiff, Alvin I. & Botwinik, Chaim Y. "Jewish Supplementary Schooling: An Educational System in Need of Change." Board of Jewish Education of Greater New York, 1988.

Winter, Nathan H. "Jewish Education in a Pluralist society." New York: New York University Press, 1966.

PART V – INSTRUCTION AND LEADERSHIP

4. Teachers and Principals – The Crucial Link to Bureaus

A Nation Prepared: Teachers for the 21st Century, the Report of the Task Force on Teaching as a Profession, Carnegie Forum on Education and the Economy, 1986.

Boyer, Ernest. *The Condition of Teaching – A State-by-State Analysis*. The Carnegie Foundation for the Advancement of Teaching, 1988.

Brandt, Ron, "On Assessment of Teaching: A Conversation with Lee Shulman." *Education Leadership*, 46:3, November 1988.

Calder, Frederick C. *Bulletin M. 134*, New York State Association of Independent Schools, December 1988.

Darling-Hammond, Linda. "Beyond the Commission Reports – The Coming Crisis in Teaching." The Rand Corporation, July 1984.

Langlois, Donald E. and Colarusso, Mary Rita. "Improving Teacher Evaluation." *Executive Educator*, May 1988.

Lanier, Judith E. and Featherstone, Joseph. "A New Commitment to Teacher Education." *Education Leadership*, 46:3, November 1988.

McKibbin, Michael D. "Alternative Teacher Certification Programs." *Education Leadership*, 46:3, November 1988.

McMurrin, Sterling. "Introduction." James D. Koerner, *The Miseducation of American Teachers*. Boston: Houghton-Mifflin, 1963.

Reisman, Bernard. Lecture to National Jewish Executives Group, at UJA-Federation, New York, November 3, 1988.

Report of the Joint Federation/Planning Commission on Jewish Continuity. Jewish Community Federation of Cleveland, October 1988.

Schiff, Alvin I. "Career Choice and the Students of the Hebrew Colleges" in Oscar Janowsky, ed., *The Education of American Jewish Teachers*. Boston: Pilgrim Press, 1967.

———, et.al. *Jewish Supplementary Schooling: An Educational System in Need of Change*. Board of Jewish Education of Greater New York, June 1987.

———. "On the Making of the Jewish Teaching Profession." *Jewish Education*, 53:3, Fall, 1985.

Supplementary Education Action Plan, Board of Jewish Education of Greater New York, September 1987.

6. Leadership in Judaic Sources – A Comparative View.

Toffler, Alvin. *The Third Wave*. New York: William Morrow and Co. 1980, p. 416.

Brewer, J.H. "Essentials of Effective School Leadership," mimeo. n.d.

Brewer, J.H. Lecture on Leadership Styles at Special Conference of Bureau Directors Fellowship, New York, February 1985.

Brewer, H. "Leadership Training or Training Leaders?" *The Elementary School Journal*, April 1984.

Burns, James MacGregor. *Leadership*. New York: Harper & Rowe, 1978.
Heller, Robert W. "Characteristics of Successful School Executives." *The Executive Educator*, June 1985. *Prophets*. Jewish Publication Society, 1959.
Spain, Charles, *et al.*, *Educational Leadership and the Elementary School Principal*. New York: Rinehart and Co., Inc., 1956.
Teitelbaum, Deena and Lee James. "Development of Selection Criteria for Elementary School Principals – Final Report." New York City Board of Education, Board of Examiners, March 1972.

PART VI – ON ISRAEL, ZIONISM AND JEWISH EDUCATION

1. One Hundred Years of Zionism: Vision and Reality, Reality and Vision.

Ahad Ha'am. "Lo zeh Haderekh," in *Kol Kitvei Ahad Ha'am*, Dvir, Tel Aviv, 1949.
Carmen, Arye Z. The Political Center, in *Israeli and American Jews: Understanding and Misunderstanding*, New York: Hadassah, 1992.
Chinitz, Jacob. "The Original Sin of Ben-Gurion." *Midstream*, May 1996, p. 3.
Eisen, Arnold. *The Spiritual Center in Israeli and American Jews: Understanding and Misunderstanding*, New York: Hadassah, 1992.
Federbush, Simon. *Ha-Lashon Havrit be Yisrael U-va-Ami*, Mosad Huravikosh, Jerusalem, 1967.
Katz, Jacob. *The Jewish National Movement. A Sociological Perspective in Jewish Emancipation and Self-Emancipation*. Philadelphia: Jewish Publication Society, 1986.
Laqueur, Walter. *A History of Zionism*. New York: Holt, Rinehart and Wiston, 1972.
Parzen, Herbert A. *Short History of Zionism*, New York: Herzl Press, 1962.
Rosenak, Michael. "The Land of Israel: Its Contemporary Meaning, In Steven T. Katz (editor), *The Frontiers of Jewish Thought*, Washington DC: B'nai Brith Books, 1992.
Schiff, Alvin I. *The Mystique of Hebrew*. New York: Shengold Publishers, 1995.
Shimon, Gideon. *The Zionist Ideology*. Hanover, NH: Brandeis University Press, 1996.
Sokolow, Nahum. *History of Zionism 1600–1918*. New York: Ktav, 1969.
Wertheimer, Jack. *Israeli and American Jews: Understanding and Misunderstanding*. New York: Hadassah.
Yosef, Dan. *Al Post-tzionut, Al Ivrit Shel Ozen. v'al Mesichiut shel Shav* in Ha'Aretz, March 25, 1994.

2. Zionism and Jewish Statehood: Challenge to the American Jewish Community.

Ahad Ha'am. "Lo Zeh Haderekh" in Kol Kitvei Ahad Ha'am, Dvir, Tel-Aviv, 1949.
Carmen, Arye Z. "The Political Center in Israeli and American Jews: Understanding and Misunderstanding." New York, 1992.
Eisen, Arnold. *The Spiritual Center in Israeli and American Jews: Understanding and Misunderstanding*. New York: Hadassah, 1992.
Laquer, Walter. *A History of Zionism*. Holt, Rinehart and Winston, New York, 1972.
Parzen, Herbert. *A Short History of Zionism*. New York: Herzl Press, 1962.
Schiff, Alvin I. *The Mystique of Hebrew*. New York: Shengold Publishers, Inc., 1996.
Shenhar Report. *Understanding and Misunderstanding*. Hadassah, New York, 1992.
Shimon, Gideon. *The Zionist Ideology*. Hanover, NH: Brandeis University Press, 1996.
Sokolow, Nahum. "History of Zionism 1600–1918," New York: Ktav, 1969.

**PART VII – THE HEBREW LANGUAGE
AND THE JEWISH COMMMUNITY**

1. Linguistics and Longevity: The Interdependence of Language, Heritage and Nationalism.

Ahad Ha'am. *Hikkui Ve'hitbol'lut*. In *Kol Kitvei Ahad Ha'am*, Jerusalem: The Jerusalem Publishing House, 1893.

Berlitz, Charles. *Native Tongues*. New York: Grosset and Dunlop, 1982.

Federbush, Simon. *Halashon Ha'Ivrit B'Yisrael u'Va-amim*. Jerusalem: Mosad Harav Kook, 1967.

Ganzfreid, Shlomo. *Kitzur Shulhan Arukh*.

Glinert, Lewis. "The 'Back to the Future' Syndrome in Language Planning: The Case of Modern Hebrew." In *Language Planning*, David Marshall (editor), Amsterdam: John Benjamin, 1991.

Goldman, Shalom. *Hebrew and Bible in America – The First Two Centuries*. Hanover, NH: Brandeis University Press, 1993.

Harshav, Binyamin. "Language in Time of Revolution." Berkley: University of California Press, 1993.

Haramati, Shlomo. *Reishit Hahinukh Ha'Ivri a'Aretz U'trumato L'Hahayat Halashon*. Massada, Jerusalem, 1980.

Nissenbaum, Yitzhak *Imrei Drush*. Warsaw: Weiser, 1926.

Orman, Uzi. Hebrew Grammar. In *Encyclopedia Judaica*. C. Roth and G. Wigoder, eds., Keter Publishing House, Jerusalem, 1972, Volume 8.

Simpson, J.W. *A First Course in Linguistics*. Edinburgh: Edinburgh University Press, 1979.

Spiegel, Shalom. *Hebrew Reborn*. New York: Books and Jewish Publication Society, 1962.

Spolsky, Bernard and Cooper, Robert. *The Languages of Jerusalem*. Oxford: Oxford University Press, 1991.

St. John, Robert. *Tongue of the Prophets*. North Hollywood, CA: Wilshire Book Company, 1972.

2. Hebrew in New York

Alcosser, Edward. Interview with Executive Vice President of the American Sephardi Federation, April 1, 1994.

Band, Arnold J. "Jewish Studies in American Liberal Arts Colleges and Universities," in O. Janowsky (ed.) *The Education of America Jewish Teachers*. Boston: Beacon Press, pp. 255–264.

Bickerton, Derek. *Language and Species*. Chicago: University of Chicago Press, 1990.

Bloch, Sam. Interview with director of publications, World Zionist Organization, March 15, 1994.

Caspi, Ben. Communication from New York Bureau Chief of *Ma'ariv*, April 13, 1994. Deuteronomy 6: 7.

Dushkin Alexander M. *Comparative Study of the Jewish Teacher Training Schools in the Diaspora*. Jerusalem: The Hebrew University, 1970.

Fromer, Seymour. "The Colonial Period," in: *A History of Jewish Education in the United States*, The American Association for Jewish Education, New York, 1969.

Galanter, Harold. Communication from Histadruth Ivrith official, March 24, 1994.
Gates of Prayer – The New Union Prayer Book. The Central Conference of American Rabbis, New York, 1975.
Glin Halkinert, Lewis. "The 'Back to the Future' Syndrome in Language Planning: The Case of Modern Hebrew," David Marshall (ed.) *Language Planning*, John Benjamins, Amsterdam, pp. 215–243.
Goldman, Shalom. "Biblical Hebrew in Colonial America," in: Shalom Goldman (ed.), *Hebrew and the Bible in America – the First Two Centuries*, Brandeis University Press and Dartmouth College, Hanover, New Hampshire and London.
Grinstein, Hyman B. "The Rise of the Jewish Community of New York, 1654 – 1860." Jewish Publication Society, Philadelphia.
Grinstein, Hyman B. "In the course of the Nineteenth Century," in J. Pilch (ed.) *A History of Jewish Education in the United States*, American Association of Jewish Education, New York, pp. 25–50.
Halkin, Abraham S. "Hebrew in Jewish Culture," in O. Janovsky (ed.) *The American Jew: A composite Portrait*, Harper and Brothers, New York, pp. 122–132.
Harel, Yehezkel. Interview with Director of Student and Youth Leadership Response.

4. Ivrit in the Day Schools – An Endangered Species?

The references are listed in the body of the article. They can be found in Alvin I. Schiff, *The Mystique of Hebrew*, Shengold Publishing Co., 1996.

6. The Mystique of Hebrew.

Emden, Jacob. *Em la-Binah.*
Epstein, Baruch. *Safah La-Ne-emanim.*
Federbush, Simon. *Ha-Lashon Ha-Ivrit Be-Yisrael u'V-va-Amim*, Mossad, Jerusalem, 1967.
Haramati, Shlomo. *Ha Ivrit K'Leshon Ha Drashot v'Ha Hora'ah Ba-Yeshivot B'Mrutzat Ha Dorot,"* in *Am Va Sefer*, Jerusalem 1993.
———. *Ivrit Hayah Bim'rutzat Ha-Dorot*, Massada, Jerusalem, 1992.
Horowitz, Zvi Hirsh. *Lochammei Torah.*
Landau,Yehezkel. *Ahavat Zion*; chapter 18.
Paradise, Jonathan. "Hebrew – Who Needs It?" *www.ivrit.org*, The National Center for the Hebrew Language.
Robins, Frida D. "Monolingualism Can be Cured." Deuteronomy 30:11–13.

SOURCES

PART I – INSIGHTS ON JEWISH LIFE

1. Challenges for Jewish Living

"Tikun Olam." Parashat Breishit. *Torah Newsletter*, Young Israel of Oceanside, September 1992.
"Unity in Diversity." *Parashat Nitzavim*, www.torah aura.com, September 2000.
"Balancing the Two Sides of the *Luhot*." *Torah Newsletter*, Young Israel of Oceanside, June 1966.
"Jewish Leadership Then and Now." *Torah Newsletter*, Young Israel of Oceanside, August 1993.

2. Values of Jewish Tradition

"Heroine of *Matan Torah*." *Torah Newsletter*, Young Israel of Oceanside, June 1995.
"*Simhah* in Jewish Tradition." *Chadashot*, Young Israel of Oceanside, December 2002.
"The Purpose of Remembrance." Memorial Day, Veterans of Foreign Wars, Oceanside, New York, May 31, 1999.
"Post 9/11 Miracle." *Chadashot*, Young Israel of Oceanside, Rosh Hashanah 5703. (2003)

3. Transmitting the Jewish Heritage

"Teaching and Learning." *Parashat Bo*, *Torah Newsletter*, Young Israel of Oceanside, February 1993.
"The Essence of Leadership." *Parashat Naso*. Board Meeting, Board of Jewish Education of Greater New York, June 2000.
"Agnon and Zionist Education." Meeting of the American Advisory Council, The Joint Authority of Jewish Zionist Education, November 1995.

4. Eretz Yisrael – Dream and Reality

"Beyond the Peace Process – Parashat Lekh L'kha." *Torah Newsletter,* Young Israel of Oceanside, October 1993.

"*Shevat* and Israel's Jubilee." United Israel Appeal Board Meeting, January 28, 1997.

"Sounding the *Shofar* at the Israel Parade." The Salute to Israel Parade, New York, May 9, 1993.

"Centennial of Zionism." Salute to Israel Parade, New York, June 1, 1997.

"Pesach 5756 and Jerusalem 3000." *Torah Newsletter,* Young Israel of Oceanside, April 1996.

"Long Live Jerusalem." Salute to Israel Parade, New York, May 1996.

"A Special *Yovel* Tribute." Salute to Israel Parade, New York, May 1998.

"*Yovel* Plus One." Salute to Israel Parade, New York, May 1999.

5. Visit to Auschwitz

"The Shoah Message of the Shofar." March of the Living, Yom Hashoah, Entrance to Auschwitz, 1992.

"March of Silence." March of the Living, Yom Hashoah, Auschwitz, 1994.

"Remembering Must be Personal." March of the Living, Birkenau, 1990. Published in *Holocaust – A Guide for Observance,* The Board of Jewish Education of Greater New York. n.d.

6. Thoughts About Hebrew Words

Distributed at the General Assembly of the Council of Jewish Welfare Funds in Jerusalem, 1998.

PART II – THE JEWISH COMMUNITY AND JEWISH EDUCATION

1. "Changing Priorities in Education." Commencement Address, Boston Hebrew College, June 3, 1984.
2. "Marketing, Evaluating and Funding Jewish Education." Jewish Federation Council of Greater Los Angeles, October 28, 1988.
3. "Toward the Year 2000 – Condition of Jewish Life: Implications for Jewish Education." Conference of the Council for Jewish Education, Philadelphia, PA, 1990.
4. "The Central Agency for Jewish Education Looks in the Mirror." *Journal of Jewish Education,* Fall 1990.
5. "Jewish Continuity Through Whom? A Message to American Jewish Communal Leadership." *Journal of Jewish Education,* Spring 1994.
6. "Jewish Life and Jewish Education in Contemporary Society: Challenge and Response." Jewish Federation of Montreal, Fall 1995.
7. "Creating the Jewish Future: Insuring Effective Jewish Education." York University, Toronto, Spring 1998.
8. "A New Blueprint for Community: A Jewish Renaissance Perspective." New York: American Jewish Committee, February 2000.

9. "Thoughts About Holocaust Research, Documentation and Jewish Education." Presentation at Claims Conference Meeting, Jerusalem, November 2002.
10. "Educational Issues in Jewish Identity." Tel Aviv University, 1995.

PART III – ON JEWISH ALL DAY EDUCATION

1. "The REITS Centennial: An Educational Milestone." Yeshiva University Journal, 1997.
2. "The Non-Public School (in 1988) – Real and Ideal." Convention of the American Association of School Administrators, Las Vegas, February 1988.
3. "What Research Says about the Jewish Day School – Doctoral Dissertations 1970–1990." *Porat Yosef*, Ktav Publishing House, 1992
4. "What We Know About the Jewish Day School (in 1992)." *What We Know about Jewish Education*, Stuart Kelman, Editor, Torah Aura Publications, 1992.
5. "The Jewish Day School (in 1987) Looks to the Next Half-Century." *Judaism – A Quarterly Journal*, Volume 36, Number 2, Spring 1987.
6. "On the Need for Moral Education in the Jewish Day School. School of Education." Harvard University, Cambridge, MA, February 1986.
7. "The Jewishness Quotient of Jewish Day School Graduates: The Effect of Jewish Education on Adult Behavior." Yeshiva University, 1994.
8. "The Case of the Jewish Day School (in 1997) in Light of the Debate on School Choice." *Vouchers for School Choice: Challenge and Opportunity*. Wilstein Institute for Jewish Policy Studies and Catholic University, 1997.
9. "Jewish Day School Success: Jewish Communal Challenge (in 1997)." Community Dinner for the Solomon Schechter School, St. Louis, MO 1997.
10. "Post-Yeshiva Jewish Day High School Programs for American Students in Israel." Meeting of the Education Committee of the Board of Governors of the Jewish Agency for Israel, June 2002.

PART IV – ON JEWISH SUPPLEMENTARY SCHOOLING AND JEWISH FAMILY EDUCATION

1. "The Synagogue and Jewish Education in Historical Perspective." *Jewish Supplementary Schooling: An Educational System in Need of Change*, Board of Jewish Education of Greater New York, 1988.
2. "On the Status of the Jewish Supplementary School – 1982." *Journal of Jewish Education*, Fall 1982.
3. "Looking Towards the 21st Century: Who Needs Hebrew Teachers in our Supplementary Schools?" Colloquium, Benjamin S. Hornstein Program, Brandeis University, December 1983.
4. "The Jewish Supplementary School – A System in Need of Change." General Assembly, Council of Jewish Federations, Miami, FL, November 1987.
5. "The Jewish Family and the Jewish School." Amit Women, January 1987.
6. "Setting the Stage: The Jewish Family in Socio-Educational Perspective." BJE Principals' Center Conference, Columbia University, June 1989.
7. "Trends and Challenges in Jewish Family Education." *Journal of Jewish Communal Service*, Spring 1990.
8. "On Initiating a Process for Jewish Family Educator Training." Israel and Ida Berman Colloquium, Board of Jewish Education of Greater New York, June 1990.

9. "Spotlight on Adult Jewish Education in the United States." *Jewish Education News*, Conference on the Advancement of Jewish Education, New York 1999.
10. "Adult Jewish Education in the Modern Orthodox Synagogue." Presented at the First International Conference on Adult Jewish Education, Jerusalem, 1998.

PART V – INSTRUCTION AND LEADERSHIP IN JEWISH EDUCATION

1. "The *Melamed* at the Mid-Century." Jewish Education Committee Press, New York, Spring 1960.
2. "On the Making of the Jewish Teaching Profession." *Journal of Jewish Education*, Fall 1985.
3. "The Jewish School Teacher Today and Tomorrow." *Journal of Jewish Education*, Spring 1987.
4. "Teachers and Principals – The Crucial Link to Bureaus." Conference of Bureau Directors' Fellowship, New Orleans, LA, November 1988.
5. "Imperatives of School Effectiveness." Orientation Seminar at Combined Assembly of the faculties of the Five Schools of the Hebrew Academy of Nassau County, September 2000.
6. "Leadership in Judaic Sources – A Comparative View." *Journal of Jewish Communal Service*, Spring 1987.
7. "Shared Identity of Jewish Communal Workers: The Jewish Dimension. Scholar-in-Residence Address." Conference of Jewish Communal Service, Philadelphia, PA, June 3, 1990.

PART VI – ON ISRAEL, ZIONISM AND JEWISH EDUCATION

1. "One Hundred Years of Zionism: Vision and Reality – Reality and Vision." Lecture at Conference of American Jewish Educational Organizations, Fall 1997, *Journal of Jewish Communal Service*, Spring 1998.
2. "Zionism and Statehood: Challenge to the American Jewish Community." Leadership Conference, Center for Jewish Education, Baltimore, MD, Fall 1995.
3. "Building Zionist Commitment Through Education." American Zionist Congress, New York, February 1993.
4. "Towards a Mission Statement on Jewish Zionist Education." *Journal of Jewish Education*, Fall 1994.
5. "The Tomorrows of Jewish Education." General Assembly of the Jewish Agency for Israel, Jerusalem, June 1988.

PART VII – THE HEBREW LANGUAGE AND THE JEWISH COMMUNITY

1. "Linguistics and Longevity: The Interdependence of Language, Heritage and Nationalism." *Journal of Jewish Communal Services*, Fall 1999.
2. "Hebrew in New York in the Multi-Lingual Apple: Languages in New York City." Berlin, New York: Mouton de Gruyter, 1997.
3. "Twenty-first Century Renaissance of the Hebrew Language." Proposal to Avner Gilad re the establishing of the Ben Yehudah Center of Hebrew Language in Jeru-

salem of which the National Center of the Hebrew Language in New York would be a partner, Fall 2000.
4. "Ivrit in the Day Schools – An Endangered Species." Edah National Conference, Hyatt Hotel, February 20, 2003.
5. "How Critical is Hebrew for Jewish Continuity and the Effectiveness of Jewish Education?" Fourth Biennial Conference on Jewish Education, Association of Principals of Jewish Schools of Australasia, Sydney, Australia, July 14, 1996.
6. "The Mystique of Hebrew." Interview by *The Jewish Book News*, Fall, 1997

PART VIII – JEWISH EDUCATIONAL PERSONA, OF BLESSED MEMORY

"Samuel Belkin." *Journal of Jewish Education*, Fall 1976.
"Zvi Herbert Berger." Eulogy, Spring 2000.
"Yosef Burg." Letter to Avrum Burg, October 26, 1999.
"Gershon Churgin." Eulogy, 1978.
"Azriel Eisenberg." *Journal of Jewish Education*, 1980.
"Abraham Gannes." Private notes, 1997.
"Jacob I. Hartstein." *Journal of Jewish Education*, 1991.
"Sidney B. Hoenig." *Journal of Jewish Education*, 1980.
"Leo Jung." Eulogy, 1988.
"Asher (Arthur) Kahn." Eulogy, 2002.
"Abraham Katsh." CAJE *Journal*, August 2002.
"Joseph Hyman Lookstein." *Journal of Jewish Education*, 1980.
"Israel Miller." CAJE *Journal*, August 2002.
"S. Maurice Plotnick." Eulogy, 1992.
"Leonard Rosenfeld." Eulogy, 2000.
"Akiva Schiff." Eulogy, 1998.
"Joseph B. Soloveitchik." *Observer*, Stern College for Women, 1993.
"Nathan H. Winter." CAJE *Journal*, 2004.

ABOUT THE AUTHOR

Dr. Alvin I. Schiff is Distinguished Professor of Education Emeritus at the Azrieli Graduate School, Yeshiva University, which he founded in 1959 as the Graduate Program of Jewish Education, and directed for eleven years, and Executive Vice-President Emeritus, Board of Jewish Education of Greater New York, which he headed for twenty-one years. He is the author of fourteen books including *The Jewish Day School in America* (1966), *Issachar American Style* (1988), *The Mystique of Hebrew* (1996), and over 300 articles and monographs, and served as editor of the *Journal of Jewish Education* for thirty years. Dr. Schiff has taught and lectured in major universities in North America and Israel. He served as scholar-in-residence in Jewish communities on five continents and chaired numerous local, national and international academic, communal and educational committees and programs and was a founder of many major institutions of Jewish life. Among them are the Post High School Program in Israel (1958), the Salute to Israel Parade (New York 1964), the March of the Living U.S.A. (1987), and the Gruss Monument Fund/Program Development Fund for Jewish Education (UJA Federation of NY). In 2005, he received the Israel "President's Award for Jewish Education in the Diaspora." At the ceremony in Bet Hanassi in Jerusalem he was characterized as the "Dean of Jewish Education."

To Bunni + Susie
W/ Best wishes
Fondly
Marie + Odom

RAYMOND H. FOGLER LIBRARY
DATE DUE